Richard
Nixon

FAWN M. BRODIE

Richard Nixon

The Shaping of
His Character

HARVARD UNIVERSITY PRESS

CAMBRIDGE, MASSACHUSETTS
LONDON, ENGLAND
1983

Copyright © 1981 by W. W. Norton & Company
All rights reserved
Printed in the United States of America

10 9 8 7 6 5 4 3 2 1

This Harvard University Press paperback is published by arrangement with W. W. Norton & Company. It contains the complete text of the original hardcover edition.

Library of Congress Cataloging in Publication Data

Brodie, Fawn McKay, 1915–1981
  Richard Nixon, the shaping of his character.

  Bibliography: p. 555
  Includes index.
  1. Nixon, Richard M. (Richard Milhous), 1913–
2. Presidents—United States—Biography.   I. Title.
E856.B74   1983   973.924′092′4 [B]   83–10646
ISBN 0–674–76880–9 (pbk.)

To Richard, Bruce, Pamela, and Janet,
my children and daughter-in-law—
expert editors all.

Contents

• *Illustrations appear following page 258* •

Foreword

THE SUBTITLE OF THIS BOOK refers to the shaping of
Richard Nixon's character. There are many who believe he was
a man of no character. But that there was a "Nixon character" of
great complexity cannot be denied. Although this volume ends
technically with the assassination of John Kennedy, which had a
prodigious impact on Nixon, there are countless forays into the
presidential years. Some themes, such as the impact of the Kennedy killing and the nature of Nixon "the private man," are carried forward into the presidency in detail.

There are several chapters devoted to Nixon's childhood,
where the material proved unexpectedly illuminating. The Hiss
case, so crucial in Nixon's career, is examined in especial detail. As
the narrative unfolds, one can read here for the first time a carefully documented record of the evolution of Nixon's lying. The
volume also traces other basic themes which thread through
Nixon's life: the impact of death, the delight in punishment, the
failure to love, as well as the theme of fratricide.

There can be no certain evaluation of the Nixon impact on
America and the world without an exhaustive treatment of the
presidential years, although the negative judgments already pronounced are likely to be sustained by further research. My own
assessment, based on a carefully documented examination of
Nixon's first fifty years, has been put in the last chapter.

A similarly detailed study covering the presidential years cannot properly be written until the eight hundred presidential tapes
presently being transcribed at the National Archives are cleared
for security purposes and made available to scholars. Anything
published in advance of the release of that material is likely to be
made instantly obsolete. Nixon's character, full panoplied, will
remain just out of reach until those tapes let us see if there was a

responsible decision-maker as president, as many have insisted, to
be evaluated along with the shabby, pathetic felon of the White
House transcripts.

Nixon's lawyers are still fighting to regain total control of the
eight hundred tapes. This material the American people deserve
to have in its entirety, if for nothing else than as a corrective to be
read, on the one hand, alongside the presidential transcripts, and
on the other, alongside the presidential papers and the Nixon
memoirs. Only then can we know, among many other things, the
truth of Henry Kissinger's statement made before newsmen in
1974, "Al Haig is keeping the country together, and I am keeping
the world together."*

* Mel Elfin to FB, April 16, 1975.

Acknowledgments

MANY AMERICANS have pronounced judgment on Richard Nixon. From the explosion of indignation in the writings of editors, journalists, jurists, lawyers, educators, and novelists, I have learned much about the Promethean quality of American democracy. There has never been anything like this explosion in the history of the American presidency. About Nixon himself I have learned from many sources, from an extraordinary outpouring of excellent books and monographs, from congressional hearings, from the presidential papers and Nixon's other speeches and writings, from the presidential tapes, all of which are listed in the bibliography. I have conducted over one hundred fifty interviews, some with Nixon's former friends and admirers, some with relatives and old neighbors in Yorba Linda and Whittier, California, and in Prescott, Arizona. The interviews did not include Richard Nixon, who ignored my request for even a brief discussion of his childhood.

I greatly benefited from a four-hundred-interview oral-history Nixon archive collected at California State University at Fullerton, and must thank Shirley Stevenson and Renée Schulte for their aid in early access to this collection, and Dr. Arthur A. Hansen for permission to quote from it. My sister, Flora Crawford, greatly aided my research trip to Prescott, as did Rick Cook of the *Prescott Courier,* assisting with data on the tubercular years of Nixon's eldest brother.

Irving Wallace made it possible for me to meet Leonard Kaufman, Los Angeles lawyer, who together with Francis Schwartz supplied invaluable documentation on Nixon's first law case. Vice-Chancellor Harold Horowitz of the University of California at Los Angeles read and advised me on this chapter. Before his death, James Bassett, former Nixon press secretary and aide, gave me the full use of his private diary, which has been of great value, as well as his own rich recollections. Enrique Zeleri, editor of *Caretas,* in Lima, Peru, helped me reconstruct the Nixon experience in Latin America.

I wish to thank Admiral Stansfield Turner for making it possible for me to see declassified material on the Nixon planning for the invasion of Cuba, this with the aid of CIA historian Jack B. Pfeiffer. Stephen D. Tilley of the National Archives and Records Service supplied a copy of the valuable Paul R. Michel closing memorandum of the Hughes-Rebozo Investigation, October 16, 1975, released in *Fund for Constitutional Government v. Nars.* I am grateful to staff members of the Whittier College Library, the Harry Truman Library, the Manuscript Division of the Library of Congress, and the vice-presidential archive at the Los Angeles Federal Archives and Records Center, Laguna Nigel, California, as well as to Alfred Bush of the Princeton University Library, William E. King of Duke University Library, and Enid Douglass of the Claremont Graduate School Oral History Project. Joseph Coghlan, of the Norton staff, was invaluable in helping to select pictures.

A complete listing of those I have interviewed appears at the end of the volume. I wish to thank in particular Nixon's former friends and aides, Tom Dixon, Ralph de Toledano, John Dean, John Ehrlichman, Robert Finch, Stephen Hess, Herbert Klein, Richard Bissell, Gen. Robert E. Cushman, and the late Leonard Hall. Jessamyn West, Thomas Bewley, and Ola Welch Jobe were all generous with information. McGeorge Bundy, Sen. Alan Cranston, John Doar, Jerry Voorhis, and former California governor Pat Brown gave me informative interviews. Mrs. Stewart Alsop was generous with recollections and hospitality. To Peter Loewenberg and Lloyd Shearer go my special thanks for continuing support. Jeff Banchero, Wayland Hand, Sidney Troxell, William Fitzgerald, Jean Scott, Chad Flake, Joseph Ilick, Michael Rogin, Robert Kelley, Mort R. Lewis, Philip Blew, and Richard Romney all supplied Nixon data. The late Ladislas Farago, old and dear friend, was a continuing spur.

My debt to journalists is great. James D. P. Bishop, Jr., formerly of *Newsweek,* arranged for interviews with Anthony Marro, Laura Mulligan, John Lindsay, and Mel Elfin. All were generous with information. I wish to thank also Anthony Lewis, George

Reedy, James Reston, Jr., Jack Anderson, Adela Rogers St. Johns, Gladwyn Hill, Lou Cannon, Murray Framsen, Tom Braden, Leo Katcher, Robert Greene, Scott Armstrong, Bob Woodward, Dan Rather, and historian Alan Weinstein. Richard Bergholz, Jeff Bailey, and James Vowell of the *Los Angeles Times* supplied access to the *Times* clipping archive.

My late husband, Bernard Brodie, read and edited early chapters. My three children, Richard, Bruce, and Pamela, and my daughter-in-law, Janet, have all read the manuscript with care, each contributing expert editorial help and perceptive criticism. Dr. Nathan Leites read the manuscript, as did psychoanalysts Dr. Maimon Leavitt and Dr. Gerald Aronson. I greatly value their suggestions. Conversations with Konrad Kellen over a five-year period never failed to provide original and challenging insights.

I can never sufficiently thank my editor and publisher, George P. Brockway, whose support and advice has always had a special quality, but whose aid in this volume fulfilled a special need the nature of which I think only he can fully understand.

A portion of the material in the first and last chapters of this volume appeared in a speech at the Smithsonian Institution, read by March Pachter in my absence, October 30, 1980. I wish to thank the Smithsonian Institution for permission to use the material here.

Richard Nixon

I

Man of Paradox

WHEN RICHARD NIXON RESIGNED, the *London Spectator* observed that in the United States the presidency had come full circle, from George Washington, who could not tell a lie, to Richard Nixon, who could not tell the truth. The sense of national humiliation and betrayal affected everyone; those who voted for him felt shame, and those who had not were ashamed for their country. In his fall he was pelted with epithets, described as shabby, foul-mouthed, conspiratorial, manipulative, synthetic, vindictive, power-hungry, and morally bankrupt. George V. Higgins called him "a virtuoso of deception." John Kenneth Galbraith said he had "a deeply bogus streak." Arthur Miller wrote that he "marched instinctively down the crooked path."

Henry Steele Commager called Nixon "the first dangerous and wicked president," and Arthur Schlesinger, Jr., said his resignation had saved the presidency "from the man who did more to discredit and endanger it than any other President in our history." Even Fr. John J. McLaughlin, former stout defender of Nixon in the White House, said, "The incubus has been lifted from our backs."[1] President Ford said in his inaugural, "The long nightmare of the nation is over." And when he pardoned Nixon he continued the theme, saying, "I cannot prolong the bad dreams."

Moreover, unlike any other president save Woodrow Wilson, who suffered a paralytic stroke, Nixon went out of office suspected of suffering from severe mental illness. John Osborne, one of the most perceptive and the fairest of all the Nixon watchers, wrote of the president's relations with reporters in the last months that "there was a feeling that he might go bats in front of them at any time."[2] The aura of paranoia, "the bunker mentality," clung to the White House. Nixon's own doctor said he had "a death wish." David Eisenhower feared he would commit suicide.[3] Secretary of State Henry Kissinger said later that Nixon did not govern in his last eighteen months in office.

Since the resignation there has been a recovery few would have predicted on August 9, 1974. Nixon's memoir, *RN*, a masterful study in omission and half-truth, became a bestseller, as did his second book, *The Real War*. Victor Lasky's *It Didn't Start with Watergate* echoed the Nixon defense, and was also a bestseller. It takes a detailed knowledge of the history of the presidency to demonstrate the fallacy of the basic arguments: that what Nixon did was no worse and in fact not as bad as what other presidents have done—that they simply have not been caught—and that Nixon was brought down by a vindictive press. It may well be that the worst of the Nixon legacy, aside from his unnecessary prolongation of the Vietnam War, is that he has convinced so many Americans that what he did was normal for the presidency.[4]

In 1801, Thomas Jefferson, generally a cheerful optimist about the presidency, had predicted grimly, "Bad men will sometimes get in, and with such an immense patronage, make great progress in corrupting the public mind and principles."[5] The prophecy, it would seem, had finally come true.

Galbraith at the time of the resignation predicted that sooner or later some journalist would say, "There's a little bit of Richard Nixon in all of us," adding, "I say the hell there is!" Some journalists did say it, and psychoanalyst Leo Rangell wrote a whole book with this as the thesis. In *The Mind of Watergate* he argues that many Americans entered and continue to enter into a kind of mutuality with Nixon. There is a universal wish, Dr. Rangell writes, to triumph over one's conscience, to compromise one's integrity, to be cheered for doing the wrong thing, to flaunt the superego. "It is an intrapsychic dream come true." He describes a *New Yorker* cartoon showing two men at a bar, one saying to the other, "Look, Nixon's no dope; if the people really wanted moral leadership, he'd give them moral leadership." The Nixon sins brought, too, a sense of absolution; "if the president does it, I am no longer guilty."

David Eisenhower put the defensive argument succinctly in September 1974: "Fifteen years hence the offense is going to look pretty small." Nixon "simply acquiesced in the non-prosecution of aides who covered up a little operation into the opposition's political headquarters, which is a practice that was fairly established in Washington for a long time and that no one took that seriously."[6] The "pretty small" offenses, as itemized by the House Judiciary Committee, included lying, burglary, forgery, illegal wiretapping, obstruction of justice, destruction of evidence, tampering with witnesses, misprision of felony, bribery, and conspiracy to involve government agencies in illegal actions. These charges have not been forgotten by leaders of the Republican party. They do not invite him to the political conventions. Nixon remains a political pariah.

One finds, nevertheless, a palpable sense of mutuality with Nixon when conducting interviews among his friends. In his hometown of Whittier, California, Dr. Roy Newsom, who was president of Whittier College when Nixon resigned, said to me in 1975, "I feel that Nixon is as honest as I am." Thomas Bewley, the old lawyer who had given Nixon his first job in Whittier, was ambivalent. He began the interview by frankly deploring what had happened: "Nixon forgot the first thing you learn in law school, that you don't tamper with the evidence." But he insisted Nixon was "a man of destiny," and at the close of the interview he said, "Nixon made only two mistakes. First, he should have burned the tapes. Second, he used Julie. He should have taken her aside and said to her, 'Julie, we have a problem. It is better that you keep quiet for a while.' "[7] (In the last months Julie had made one hundred fifty speeches on her father's behalf.)

Many Republicans freely admit that despite Watergate they would still vote for Nixon over George McGovern, frankly preferring, they say, the knave to the fool. Two of Nixon's closest friends at Duke University speak lightly of the Nixon offenses. William Perdue said, "Nixon did not lie as much as FDR; it's just that we look differently upon his purposes." The second, Frederick Albrink, said, "Watergate was like fixing a traffic ticket."[8]

On the other extreme is Republican Sen. Barry Goldwater, who said on March 9, 1980, on the CBS television show "60 Minutes," "I don't think he should ever be forgiven. He came as close to destroying America as any man in that office has ever done. . . . we were teetering on the edge of disaster. . . . He did damage to all of us." He called Nixon a "basically dishonest" person, and implied that he had been dishonest all his life.[9] Even in the Whittier area there was March Butz, official historian of Yorba Linda,

Nixon's birthplace, who described how she sat before the television watching the president defend himself in the Watergate crisis. She recalled saying to him, in sorrow, "Oh, Dick, why don't you stop lying even if it brings you down!"[10]

People who voted for Nixon are divided, either defensive and forgiving, or still outraged and betrayed. Many are overcome with a kind of leaden malaise when his name is mentioned; they cannot bear to be reminded of him. Their common defense: "It's all been overstated. Too much has been made of a little thing."

Another reaction, common to both Republicans and Democrats, is an interest in "the psychiatric look." People ask, "What was wrong with Nixon?" They want a brief answer, in a paragraph, something to reassure them of how separate they are from him. One of the reasons for the anxiety Nixon continues to arouse is that he reminds us of our own lies. We need reassurance that his lying is pathological whereas ours is simply "white" lying, lying out of kindliness or unwillingness to give offense. We want to be told that our small evasions, if any, in reporting our income tax do not compare with his fraudulently backdating a deed to win a tax break of half a million dollars. In his memoirs Nixon is still proclaiming his innocence of fraud in this matter, and blaming his tax lawyers.[11]

Norman Mailer wrote in *St. George and the Godfather* that Freud is obsolete, that for Nixon nothing less than a new theory of personality will suffice. Many feel that if we could just put a psychiatric label on him—paranoid, sociopath—then we could dissociate ourselves from him; we could stand clean and pure and aloof and sweet-smelling, confident in our own integrity, far from his sordid history, and forget about him, forget especially that we voted for him two-to-one in 1972. Those who voted for him would then be absolved; they could say, "He was mentally ill but we did not know it," and those who voted against him would also be absolved, saying, "He was sick but we could not prevent his election because his illness was largely hidden."

Billy Graham, Nixon's "spiritual adviser," who had led the prayer breakfasts at the White House and had given the funeral sermon when Nixon's mother died, described to his own biographer, Marshall Frady, how he vomited after reading the Nixon tape transcripts. He said, "I thought like John Wesley when he said, 'When I look into my heart it looks like hell.' " He did not say "when I look into Nixon's heart," but "when I look into my own." Still, Billy Graham soon found his own escape from responsibility:

I think it was sleeping pills. Sleeping pills and demons. I think there was definitely demon power involved. He took all those sleeping pills that would give him a low in the morning and a high in the evening, you know. All through history drugs and demons have gone together.[12]

Psychiatrists will dismiss the demons, but they will pay attention to the sleeping pills. Actually clinical diagnoses have been accumulating for some years, several of them written when Nixon was still in office. Dr. Eli Chesen, in *President Nixon's Psychiatric Profile*, warned us that he was "a compulsive obsessive." Dr. David Abrahamsen, in *Nixon vs. Nixon,* called him a psychopathic personality, orally fixated and anally fixated, suffering from a severe character disorder. Biographer Bruce Mazlish as early as 1972 had written perceptively about Nixon's excessive fear of being unloved, his absorption in himself, his mammoth capacity for denial, and his fondness for acting, this in a brief study *In Search of Nixon, a Psychological Inquiry.* James Barber, whose examination of Nixon's childhood in *The Presidential Character* (1972) was the most complete of any publication up to that date, called him an "active-negative" character, indirect, devious, secretive, and ambivalent, with a core need for power, and a tendency to "fly off in the face of overwhelming odds." Dr. Arnold Hutschnecker, an internist with a special interest in psychosomatic illness, who treated Nixon for "stress" when he was vice-president, wrote a fascinating little volume in 1974, *The Drive for Power,* in which every third paragraph would seem to refer to his former patient. But it is written with such discretion and in such general terms— as indeed it had to be—that it cannot easily be used as a diagnostic aid.

A fascinating diagnostic model drawing in part on the writings of psychoanalyst Heinz Kohut appeared in *Political Psychology* in the spring of 1979 in an article by Prof. Lloyd Etheredge titled "Hard-ball Politics: A Model." Although Etheredge seldom mentions him by name, one has the impression that he has built the model largely by studying Nixon, whom he describes as suffering from a narcissistic personality disorder. The character Etheredge depicts is a divided man, nurtured by dreams of omnipotence on the one hand and on the other depleted by an incurable sense of insecurity. He suffers from inability to love, but cherishes fantasies of being universally loved, as measured by the vote. He is split into two selves, one empty and insecure, the other aggressive and power-hungry. He loves secrecy; he cannot enjoy recreation, and he has a defective sense of humor. He has episodes of hypomanic excitement. At his worst he is persecuting, delusional, and unable to distinguish reality from fantasy.

It is a wonderfully constructed model, but is descriptive only. There are many themes the biographer might pursue in writing about Nixon, and always in the background is an insistent "Why?" Why the insecurity? Why the divided man? Why the ineffable loneliness? Why the failure to establish an identity? Why, above all, the lying? One must go through the Nixon life—his childhood, adolescence, marriage, and early career—before one can reconstruct the beginning of the warping of his character and describe the evolution of his psyche. And disturbing the biographer incessantly is a kind of cautionary signal that lights up repeatedly to stifle speculation and snarl the writing. This is the role of accident in Nixon's life.

The accident of assassination obviously played a more dramatic role in the life of Andrew Johnson—who would surely have died in obscurity, like Lincoln's first vice-president, Hannibal Hamlin, had it not been for the bullet of John Wilkes Booth—and of Theodore Roosevelt, who became president also as a result of assassination, and who took an assassin's bullet in his own chest when president. But Nixon, too, would never have become president had it not been for the assassinations first of John F. Kennedy and then his brother Robert. These were the first decisive accidents in Nixon's political life. A later and equally decisive accident was the tape on the door in the Watergate compound that led to Frank Wills's discovery of the burglary of the Democratic National Headquarters. And finally there was the largely accidental question asked of Butterfield that led to the disclosure of the White House taping system. Erase these last two accidents in Nixon's life and ask, "Without them would we today be pondering the problems of Nixon's pathology and tendency to self-destruction?" Look at the distressing dilemma of Theodore White, who in *The Making of the President, 1972* had described Nixon as one of the great presidents of the twentieth century. In his follow-up volume, *Breach of Faith,* he conceded that biographers of Nixon would be working with the problem of psychiatric imbalance.

The man of paradox has been with us since the first campaign against Jerry Voorhis in 1948. But the presidency enormously magnified and dramatized the paradoxes that were implicit in Nixon's character from the earliest political years. They stand out starkly now. There is the paradox of the candidate who in Miami Beach in 1968 promised to bring us truth in government, and instead brought us massive untruth. There is the paradox of the Quaker president who ordered more bombs dropped than any man in history. There is the president with the feeling of omnipotence—who in his last speech in the White House could say to his staff, "I would love to have talked with you and found out how to run the world"—but who nevertheless suffered, as Henry Kissinger tells us, from "a fatalistic instinct that nothing he touched would ever be crowned with ultimate success."[13] He had the ambition to win more electoral votes than any president save Washington—the only president to win them all—but could still say to John Dean early in 1973, "Nobody is a friend of ours; let's face it."[14]

He is the supreme anti-Communist, who nevertheless establishes friendly relations with the largest bloc of Communists on the globe, and this at a moment in history when Chinese weapons are being used to kill Americans in Vietnam. He is a president who promises to return power to the people, but who secretly threatens the Constitution with his usurpations of power. He professes to have no interest in wealth, but shows an exaggerated fondness for the trappings and pageantry of royalty, including fancy-dress uniforms for White House guards and plans for the most palatial of presidential yachts.[15] He is a man of extraordinary fastidiousness in dress whose language in private is foul.

He is uptight with people—Ehrlichman said, "he worked off a piece of paper better than face to face"—and has severe problems with intimacy and loving, yet is capable of pouring out his feelings in print, and in public ramblings such as his farewell to his staff, which he insisted be televised, revealing an astonishing preoccupation with self-analysis. He can say on the one hand, "Without enemies my life would be dull as hell,"[16] yet complain shrilly of abuse by his political opponents and the press. He promises to restore law and order, but is capable of saying, as he did to David Frost, "If the President does it, that makes it legal."

He is catapulted to power through the microfilm of an informer, Whittaker Chambers, and is brought down in the end by his own tapes, emerging as the greatest informer of all time. Finally, there is the paradox of the man who manifests tendencies toward self-destruction, yet becomes the symbol of the supreme survivor.

All of these paradoxes suggest a man divided, a man at cross purposes with himself. These paradoxes cannot be explained without some understanding of the evolution of Nixon's fantasy life. In the absence of a sense of morality and self-worth, this fantasy of himself as a living symbol of the American dream served as a supportive force, buoying him up in times of depression and stiffening his capacity for attack and for survival.

Hatred, too, was a sustaining force. Where there is little love, fantasies of punishment can be energizing, almost pleasureable. William Safire wrote of the "deep dark rage" in Nixon, and John Ehrlichman described it as like "the flat dark side of the moon." Haldeman described Nixon as a multifaceted quartz crystal, with some sides dark and impenetrable. Nixon, he wrote, had a terrible temper which he "almost always succeeded in keeping under control in public. In private, with one of us who worked closely with him, he would really blow."[17]

In the 1960 campaign, in what Haldeman described as an unnecessarily long drive between cities, Nixon became angry at the bad planning of his staff. Sitting behind his aide, air force Maj. Don Hughes, he suddenly, "incredibly" began to kick the back of Hughes's seat with both feet. "And he wouldn't stop! Thump! Thump! The seat and the hapless Hughes jolted forward jaggedly as Nixon vented his rage. When the car stopped at a small town in the middle of nowhere, Hughes, white-faced, silently got out of the car and started walking straight ahead, down the road and out of town." "I believe he would have walked clear across the state," Haldeman said, "if I hadn't set out after him and apologized for Nixon and finally talked him into rejoining us."[18]

There was rage in Nixon as a child. At age seven, when he wanted a jar of pollywogs a six-year-old friend had captured in the irrigation canal, and the boy would not give them up, Richard hit him in the head with a hatchet. The victim bore the scar all his life.[19]

The warping in his capacity for love, and the influence of death in his life, are examined in this volume in detail, as is the evolution of Nixon's lying. All three themes are interwoven with his identity failure and with the grandiose fantasy life. The evolution of Nixon's lying has never before been documented. The press did not do it; in fact the press was never as hostile to Nixon as he complained. On the contrary, it gave him every advantage. Nixon could well have said, as Fidel Castro said in 1959, "The Yanquis have one good quality; they always believe I will change."[20] Even the most cynical of editors and journalists hoped that in the presidency Nixon would be purified and exalted, that the office would transform the man. George Reedy, almost alone among president watchers, noted that "the office neither elevates nor degrades a man. What it does is to provide a stage upon which all of his personality traits are magnified and accentuated."[21]

Nixon lied to gain love, to shore up his grandiose fantasies, to bolster his ever-wavering sense of identity. He lied in attack, hoping to win. Long before Watergate, Nixon counseled a friend: "You don't know how to lie. If you can't lie, you'll never go anywhere."[22] And always he lied, and this most aggressively, to deny that he lied. His denials were widely believed, and massive denial eventually became for him a way of life. Inevitably he pointed the finger of blame at someone else, saying, "He is guilty, not I." In the end, in the case of Watergate, it was "She is guilty," specifying Martha Mitchell. In his memoirs he wrote, "Without Martha, I am sure that the Watergate thing would never have happened."[23]

Finally, he enjoyed lying. Reminiscing at San Clemente with his former White House aide Kenneth Clawson shortly after his retirement, he was explicit about his pleasure in what he called, euphemistically, skirting "on the edges of the precipice":

What starts the process, really, are laughs and slights and snubs when you are a kid. But if you are reasonably intelligent and if your anger is deep enough and strong enough, you learn that you can change those attitudes by excellence, personal gut performance while those who have everything are sitting on their fat butts. . . . It's a piece of cake until you get to the top. You find you can't stop playing the game the way you've always played it because it is part of you and you need it as much as an arm or leg. So you are lean and mean and resourceful and you continue to walk on the edge of the precipice because over the years you have become fascinated by how close to the edge you can walk without losing your balance.[24]

Clawson interrupted to say, "Only this time there is a difference."

" 'Yes this time there was a difference,' Nixon said softly. 'This time we had something to lose.' "

Lean, mean, resourceful! Walking along the edge of the law. Some Americans always saw this in Nixon, but many more saw sincerity, piety, small-town virtue, and a disarming naïveté. Nixon's extraordinary success in hiding his dishonesty over the years has to do in part with the nature of his lying. He was given to exaggeration—"This is the greatest day since the Creation" when the United States put a man on the moon—but he rarely lied to embellish a story. He was never a teller of tall tales like Lyndon Johnson, who knew that many of his escalations from the truth would be properly taken as drama, Texas style. Oscar Wilde, in his essay "The Decay of Lying," wrote that "the aim of the liar is simply to charm, to delight, to give pleasure. He is the very basis of civilised society, and without him a dinner party, even at the mansions of the great, is as dull as a lecture at the Royal Society." "Lying, the telling of beautiful untrue things," he concluded, "is the proper aim of Art."[25]

Nixon never lied to delight, although there is evidence that he delighted in lying. He lied earnestly, intent above all on being believed. And with the lies went a stream of homilies about honesty and virtue. In Moscow, when vice-president, he said, "All irresponsible reporters should never forget that in the end the truth always catches up with a lie."[26] In March 1971, to the women members of the Washington press corps he said, "We must never permit even a little lie."[27] In his acceptance speech in Miami Beach at the Republican National Convention in 1968 he made an extraordinary promise to the American people:

Let us begin by committing ourselves to the truth—to see it like it is, and to tell it like it is—to find the truth, to speak the truth and to live the truth.[28]

Perhaps what Nixon was hoping was that were he elected president he would no longer have to lie. He would have made it. He could then be honest. But of course he had to win again in 1972—

"You can't stop playing the game the way you've always played it," he said[29]—and by then he had a new fantasy, the fantasy of getting all the votes in the electoral college. He wanted to match George Washington. That would have been proof, finally, that he was really loved. He almost made it.

One of the surprises of my research has been uncovering the extraordinary number of *unnecessary* lies Nixon told in his life. Their sheer quantity would suggest a pathological origin, for Nixon was caught in many of them, and they would seem to have done him no useful service, which is one of the indications of pathology in lying. In the "Checkers" speech, when he was desperately intent on restoring his credibility before the country, he made two lies which were essential to establish his political virtue: (1) he said the slush fund had not been kept secret, which it had; and (2) he said he had paid his donors no special favors, which was not true. But he also said, and at least one reporter was quick to spot the unnecessary untruth: "Pat's not a quitter; her name was Patricia Ryan and she was born on St. Patrick's Day." Actually she had been christened Thelma Catherine and called Thelma or "Buddy" by everyone save her father, who sometimes called her Pat. She changed her name to Pat when he died. And she was born not on the seventeenth of March but the sixteenth. An embarrassed Pat shortly thereafter told the truth.[30]

A similar story comes at the end of his presidency. On his last trip to France as president, Nixon spoke briefly at Orly airport; he said:

Forty years ago, I majored in French, had 4 years of French. After 4 years I could speak it, I could write it. I read all the classics. And today, I just understand a little.[31]

He did not major in French. He majored in history. It was another small bid for affection.

In 1972, when Nixon was courting the support of the movie industry, he was persuaded to give a medal to Samuel Goldwyn. The veteran movie maker was aged, ill, and could not talk above a whisper. He seemed almost comatose as Nixon made a little speech in the Goldwyn home, a speech which Samuel Goldwyn, Jr., said sounded as if it had been written for Walt Disney. The elder Goldwyn, hearing about the marvelous wholesomeness of

his films, the special cleanliness, began to listen. Finally he raised
his head and tugged at Nixon's coat. The president bent low to
hear him say in a whisper that only Nixon and Goldwyn's son
caught, "You'll have to do better than that if you want to carry
California."

Nixon abruptly stopped talking, cut the ceremony short, and
stalked out. Samuel Goldwyn, Jr., greatly embarrassed, walked
with him. As they neared the entrance Nixon asked in a whisper,
"Did you hear what your father said?" In an effort to lessen the
humiliation for the president, Samuel Goldwyn, Jr., said, "No, I
didn't." Whereupon Nixon relaxed and confided, "He said, 'I
want you to go out there and beat those bastards!' "[32] Thus the
president of the United States would lie to erase even a single
small shame.

To understand what caused the splitting between word and
deed in Nixon's life we must go back to his childhood, adolescence, and early career. These years give us clues, too, to the evolution of other major aspects of Nixon's life, his loneliness, his
sense of being an outsider, his distrustfulness, his lack of a real
sense of identity, his delight in acting, his inclination always to be
on the attack, and his narcissism. But along with the darker
aspects of Nixon's psyche we will see also the evolution of the
image so many found attractive: the earnest young moralizer, the
ardent patriot, the enunciator of virtue, the defender of clean living and sanitized language. The maintenance of this image was
one of the necessities of Nixon's life.

The impact of death was of compelling significance for Nixon,
beginning with the tragic deaths of his two brothers: Arthur, the
fourth son, who died after a brief and somewhat mysterious illness at age seven, and Harold, the eldest and favorite son, who
died at thirty after a five-year battle with tuberculosis. The death
of the eldest brother brought Nixon some advantages, and the
inevitable survivor's guilt. The fact that it took the deaths of the
two Kennedy brothers—a terrible reactivation of the early tragedies—to ensure his own victory in the presidency plagued him,
compounding his sense of melancholy in victory. A still more som-
ber theme, running as a counterpoint to the impact of death, is
the theme of fratricide. "For Nixon," one of his White House
aides said, "the shortest distance between two points is over four

corpses."[33] This theme, too, began long before Watergate. And overriding all others is the theme of survival, survival without love. This remains the most consistent, the most remarkable, of all the aspects of Nixon's life.

The Oil in the Lemon Grove

No lie is small when spoken by a President.
— RICHARD HARRIS, 1974[1]

WHEN RICHARD NIXON at the moment of his political dying bade farewell to his staff in the White House, he was haunted by deaths past. He spoke of the deaths of his two brothers, and of the four tuberculosis-ridden youths his mother had cared for in Arizona, all of whom had died.[2] He read a passage describing the death of Theodore Roosevelt's joyous young first wife. He mentioned his "saintly" mother, who had died shortly before he became president, and his father, who had died during his vice-presidency. Unlike his resignation speech the night before, in which he admitted no guilt for the conduct that had made his impeachment certain and his conviction likely, this one was unrehearsed.

Years before, as vice-president, Nixon had admitted to Stewart Alsop, "a major public figure is a lonely man. . . . I can't confide absolutely in anyone, even in Pat. . . . It's something like wearing clothing—if you let down your hair you feel too naked."[3] There were many on this morning who saw Nixon naked for the first time, naked not only before his friends but before a television audience of many millions. In the middle of the speech he said, "This country needs good farmers, good businessmen, good plumbers [here, at the surfacing of a word he no doubt wanted most of all to forget, he winced slightly and rushed on], good carpenters." The word "carpenters" apparently reminded him of his father:

I remember my old man. I think that they would have called him a sort of a little man, common man. He didn't consider himself that way. You know what he was? He was a streetcar motorman first, and then he was a farmer, and then he had a lemon ranch. It was the poorest lemon ranch in California. I can assure you. He sold it before they found oil on it. And then he was a grocer. But he was a great man, because he did his job, and every job counts up to the hilt, regardless of what happens.[4]

Almost every word in this cathartic speech represented layers of memories. When he spoke of his father, he permitted us to see only the outer layer like the lava outcropping of an old volcano. One must go beneath this layer to tap the smoldering hatreds of his childhood. The accent is on praise for his father; there is also the hint of foolishness and failure. The lemon ranch was sold, he said, before they found oil on it.

Old Yorba Linda residents, when interviewed in the weeks following the president's resignation, found the passage troubling. Oil had been found in the surrounding areas, they said. But on the Frank Nixon property no one had even drilled for oil. By 1974 the lemon trees planted by the president's father had been uprooted, and in their place stood the Richard Nixon Elementary School. George Kellog, then eighty-seven, who had worked with Frank Nixon in the Union Oil field, precisely located the presidential error. "Oil was found this side of Placentia," he said, "but at least a mile from the Nixon property."[5] March Butz, official historian of Yorba Linda, who had considered buying what had been the Nixon property in 1945 and who knew its history, explained the error as arising from the president's "terrible problems."[6]

But this untruth did not spring out of the gravest of Richard Nixon's crises. He had told the story to biographer Ralph de Toledano, who published it early in 1956. His mother had said to a journalist in 1960, "After we moved [from Yorba Linda], oil was found under the lemon grove—oil that would have made us millionaires if we had remained—but while we were there the lemon grove only kept us poor."[7]

What had actually happened was that Frank Nixon had been offered a price of $45,000 for his property by an oil speculator and had turned it down. "If there's oil on it, I'll hang on to it," he said. Later, when the lemon grove proved unproductive and he was forced to sell, the oil pools had been charted and no one wanted the property. Nixon's father then moved to Whittier, where he bought a lot and built a gas station. He had rejected his wife's urging to buy property instead in Santa Fe Springs, and it was there, in 1922, that a gusher came in and the area became, according to Edwin P. Hoyt, "the hottest field in the West."[8]

The oil in the lemon grove story, another of Nixon's "unnecessary" lies, takes on added significance because his mother had also told it. But is it fair to call it lying? Stories of almost striking it rich are endemic in America and nowhere more so than in California, where real estate and oil have made many millionaires and left countless thousands envious. The unlucky ones can embellish their tales without guilt. But a president is permitted no such license. Richard Harris wrote in 1974, "No lie is small when spoken by a President." Or, one might add, by a president's mother. Nixon himself complained about this at a National Prayer Breakfast early in 1974: "You know the difficulty with a President when he makes a statement is that everybody checks it to see whether it is true."[9]

Checking the truth of Richard Nixon's stories, even about his childhood, is time-consuming. At times he distorts deliberately. Often he is simply opaque. The truth about the oil in the lemon grove had appeared in several publications. Richard Nixon had returned to Yorba Linda many times since his childhood and knew the facts. On January 9, 1959, he had participated in a ceremony where a bronze plaque was placed in front of his birthplace with the inscription "We are proud of our native son, a man who has spared nothing of himself to make a great nation." But instead of correcting the family myth, or ignoring it, he perpetuated it by retelling it in that tearful farewell on the morning of August 9, 1974.

There are other maternal errors in the several friendly biographies written by men who talked with Hannah Nixon before her death in 1967. She is described as a sweet, generous, self-effacing, and religious woman who sacrificed for her sons. Without her encouragement, Nixon indicated many times, he would never have become president. But she was also a mythmaker and eager, after her son became vice-president, to document the workings of Providence in his rise. When Richard survived a nasty accident at age three, in which he fell out of a buggy and received a gash in his scalp from the wheel, Hannah described the event as "a miracle," a word she used also to describe his surviving pneumonia at age four and undulant fever during his adolescence.[10]

The use of the word "miracle" by mothers is so common that

its significance should not be overstated. But there are other examples of the innocent mythmaker at work, accumulating evidence of the hand of Fate. Biographer Earl Mazo, who had interviewed Hannah Nixon, began his second chapter: "Nixon has managed to stand out in one way or another for a good part of his life. He was the first child born in Yorba Linda, a farming village thirty miles inland from Los Angeles. (Next day there was a partial eclipse of the sun.)"[11] Actually the first birth on the real estate tract set aside as Yorba Linda was not that of Richard Nixon but Carl Albert Morris, born on December 5, 1911.[12] And there was no eclipse of the sun, partial or total, on January 10, 1913.

Hannah could theoretically have seen two eclipses, but neither occurred "the day after" the birth of any of her children. Arthur was born May 6, 1918; there was a partial eclipse on June 8. Edward was born on May 3, 1930; there had been a partial eclipse five days earlier, April 28. Both eclipses had been written about, with photographs, in the *Los Angeles Times*.[13] Richard could have seen the 1918 eclipse at age five and the 1930 eclipse at seventeen. No one seems to have bothered to correct the error for Mazo's second edition, and by the time James Barber repeated the story in *The Presidential Character* in 1972 the partial eclipse of the sun on the day following Richard Nixon's birth had become a part of the presidential myth.[14]

Why should these errors trouble the biographer? Hannah Nixon was a profoundly religious Quaker, intent always that her sons be honest men. When she caught Harold and Richard as small children eating grapes taken from a neighbor's vines, she made them take their saved-up pennies to pay Mrs. Trueblood, who hadn't really minded. "From that day on," Richard Gardner wrote in 1952, "nobody can remember the Nixon boys ever did a dishonest thing."[15]

Every adult distorts the truth about his past, or his family's past, and not always because of a lapse of memory. The conscious reasons for lying are varied, and may not be too disimilar from those which deceive the deceiver himself. One lies to glorify others or oneself; one lies for purposes of attack, or as a response to shame, or as a coverup of one's shortcomings or the shortcomings of one's parents or one's children.

Children lie in imitation of their parents or because they have never learned to tell the truth, and they continue to seek refuge from pain or punishment or anxiety in what seems to be the easiest hiding place. Small children have difficulty learning to distinguish between fantasy and lying—between thought, wish, and event—and the ability to make these distinctions is an important sign of maturity. Many never achieve it. But mostly children lie out of insecurity and fear. If they feel they are likely to suffer unjust punishment, they may lie with little or no shame or guilt.

Dr. Arnold Hutschnecker, who treated Nixon when he was vice-president, and who became profoundly disturbed at the president's behavior during Watergate, wrote about lying in *The Drive for Power*, published in 1974:

most people are brought up to speak the truth, but as judges know and all physicians know, not every patient who comes for help is *able* to speak the truth. Everyone knows that not all people are truthful. And there are people who do not know the difference between the truth and a lie. While most people as children are taught a code of ethics, they also learn early in life how to tell a lie to avoid the pain of punishment, or to imitate a parent who lies. . . . It has always puzzled me why grown people will lie about a misdeed they have committed, and I find it particularly disturbing in men in position of great political power. . . . By the time that we, the people the world over, discover the untruth, the damage has been done, a crime has already been committed.[16]

As we shall see in a later chapter, there is evidence that as vice-president Nixon had convinced Dr. Hutschnecker of his honesty as he had convinced millions of other Americans. It took the revelations of Watergate to strip from Nixon the mask of honesty he had worn successfully for so long. Few were like the president's lawyer, Fred Buzhardt, who found Nixon "the most transparent liar he had ever met. Almost invariably when the President lied, he would repeat himself, sometimes as often as three times—as if he were trying to convince himself."[17] For many Americans only the White House tapes convinced them, tapes which documented not only Nixon lying but also Nixon lying about his taping. One tape has him saying flippantly to a group of milk producers, when asked if the session was off the record, "Matter of fact the room is not taped. Forgot to do that."[18]

A major problem for any Nixon biographer is to explain not why he lied so much but why he did not learn to tell the truth, and to discover if there was some misdirection, conscious or unconscious, from either parent. What were the sources of

Nixon's special talent for distortion, for his ability to skirt so adroitly the edges of the truth? Who was responsible for his failure to learn to tell the truth (a failure shared by both his younger brothers) and his incapacity to live by the code of moral strictures he was so gifted at enunciating? Was it the gentle, mythmaking mother who, as we shall see, constantly denied and in the most innocent fashion covered up the ugliness in her own life? Or was it the father, of whom Richard Nixon the child was so deeply afraid?

The Punishing Father

*I did some of the big things rather well. I screwed up terribly on
what was a little thing that became a big thing, but I will have
to admit I wasn't a good butcher.*

— RICHARD NIXON, ON FIRING HALDEMAN AND EHRLICHMAN[1]

RICHARD NIXON BEGAN HIS MEMOIRS, "I was born in a
house my father built." He described Frank Nixon as "a man of
ambition, intelligence, and lively imagination." That he was also
punishing and often brutal we do not learn from this son. The
worst Nixon would admit was that his father had a hot temper
and was "sometimes impatient and—well—rather grouchy with
most people," that he had "temptestuous arguments" with his
brothers Harold and Don, and that "their shouting would be
heard all through the neighborhood."[2] In a film made to promote
the 1968 election campaign he said somewhat ambiguously,
"There were times when I suppose we were tempted to run away
and all that sort of thing. None of us ever did, but on the other
hand, it was a happy home." He remembered that his father
"didn't use very good grammar, but he was a self-educated man
and a very intelligent man," adding defensively if illogically, "He
was intelligent because he worked so hard."[3]

Frank Nixon, as we have seen, had been a streetcar motorman,
farmer, carpenter, and grocer. He had also, in the Nixon Market,
been a butcher.[4] One niece, who worked for him, remembered
with distaste his refusal to change his shirts, bloodstained from
cutting up the slabs of meat, oftener than once a week. "What's
the use," he would say, "Jes' get mess all over them." Thomas
Bewley, long a friend of the family, said, "I think Nixon felt sometimes he should apologize for his father."[5] The son, however,
became adept not so much at apology as at covering up. Although

he defended his father's imperfect grammar, he also muted his failures, denied his cruelties, exaggerated his virtues, and, in his farewell speech in the White House, slipped into total fantasy— my father, the great man.

The early Nixon biographers were gentle in writing about Frank Nixon, the "Black Irishman" born in Vinton County, Ohio, on December 3, 1878. Hannah told Kornitzer that her husband was descended from John Nixon, "a Philadelphian who gave the Declaration of Independence its first reading."[6] Edwin P. Hoyt delicately put the record straight. Frank Nixon, he noted, was actually descended from James Nixon, who came to America in 1731 and settled in Delaware.

It would be nice to think of the Nixons as deep in the councils of the colony. . . . But in 1774, when the Congress was held, James Nixon had died, and his sons (George and James) were barely men.

They took no part in the Continental Congress, but did fight in the Revolution.[7]

Frank, the son of Samuel Brady Nixon, had a harsh child-hood. His mother died of tuberculosis when he was seven, and he was sent to live with relatives. At eleven he returned home to a stepmother he hated and who beat him. "He became," his brother Ernest said, "aggressive . . . slow to anger but a wild bull if things went too far."[8] Frank fled from his stepmother at fourteen and became a drifter. When working as a streetcar motorman in Columbus, Ohio, he suffered frostbitten feet standing in the unheated cab. After trying to organize a movement to enclose the cabs, he decided to abandon Ohio winters and set out for Califor-nia. He was tough, resilient, and handy with tools. Everywhere he went, he carried one claim to fame: William McKinley, campaign-ing for president in Ohio in 1896, had shaken his hand, had urged him to vote Republican, and had admired his horse, which he rode in the Republican parade.

Making his way to the land of orange groves and perpetual summer, he got a job as a motorman for the Pacific Electric Com-pany, driving a suburban electric train that ran from Los Angeles east to Whittier and Yorba Linda. But after a year his train hit an automobile as it was crossing the tracks and he was fired. Bitter to have to return to work as a day laborer at age thirty, he sought work in the Whittier citrus groves, and he was befriended by a

well-to-do Whittier Quaker, Frank Milhous. Soon he met the six
Milhous daughters, and started a "whirlwind courtship" of the
second daughter, Hannah, a shy girl of twenty-three, who
although she had had two years at Whittier College and had gone
to many Quaker socials, had never had a date.[9] "I immediately
stopped going with the five girls I was going with," Frank said,
"and I saw Hannah every night."[10]

The Milhous family looked askance at the marriage. Frank
Milhous was a quiet, kindly man who played the guitar and sang.
The family members were all soft-spoken, reticient, and prim.
"There was not much hugging or kissing or daughters sitting on
their fathers' knees in Quaker families," Nixon's novelist cousin,
Jessamyn West, has said. Stewart Alsop, interviewing old Whittier
residents in 1959, said it was whispered about even then that Hannah had made "an unfortunate marriage." The youngest Milhous
sister, Olive, remembers climbing into the pepper tree in the
backyard and writing in her tablet, "Hannah is a bad girl."[11]

"Every Milhous daughter was convinced that she had married
beneath her," Jessamyn West reports. But Frank Nixon especially
sensed it. One sister, Jane Milhous Beeson, describing how Frank
refused to join in the family gatherings, retreating instead into an
angry isolation, said, "We all felt close to each other. . . . Maybe he
didn't want to share Hannah with the rest of us." Although he
formally joined the Quaker church and eventually taught a popular Sunday School class, he would never eat at church suppers.
Perhaps by way of retaliation for what he felt as snobbery, he
called his wife Mildred. "Hannah," he said, "sounded like the
backwoods."[12]

There is now a considerable archive of material on Nixon's
father. We know that he was often full of fun, irrepressibly proud
of his sexuality, responsible, and honest, but also gruff, bad-tem-
pered, and tight-fisted—a yelling man, a hollering man. He was a
great hater, and he seems to have felt pride rather than guilt
about his hates. He was untroubled by the fact that men of power
hated his son. When Richard Nixon was nominated for the vice-
presidency in 1952, Frank Nixon said to reporters of the *Los
Angeles Times* with obvious satisfaction, "Truman hates Dick like a
rattlesnake."[13]

Richard Nixon, as vice-president and as president, tried to
depict his shouting father as a battling father, transforming the

tight-fisted hater of "bums" into a responsible foe of welfare cheaters. To British journalist Kennedy Harris, in 1968, he described his father as "effervescent . . . mostly good natured."[14] But Frank Nixon was a chronically angry man, ulcer-ridden from the early years of his marriage, crude, and brittle, who invited hatred in his own family. He had, indeed, a talent for survival, but it was for survival without love. This talent Richard would learn from him.

Mostly, however, the son consciously tried to be as unlike his father as possible. Where Frank shouted, Richard prided himself on being "the coolest man in the room." Frank was untidy—"a slop-Jake at times," his niece said—content with a single suit to wear to church, and a scoffer at tuxedos, which he called monkey suits. Richard from his earliest years was fastidiously clean. As an adolescent he was fussy about how his shirts were ironed and at Whittier College he had two tuxedos.[15] Where Frank Nixon was adept with tools, comfortable handling farm machinery or oil-drilling equipment, the son refused to do any handyman's work about his own house. Ola Welch Jobe remembered that although he worked at his father's gas station, Richard had to go for help on one of their dates simply to change a tire.[16] "If a nail has to be driven," Pat Nixon told reporters in 1952, "I'm the one who has to swing the hammer."[17]

Frank Nixon was genial and teasing with women—"a hot man," said Edwin Hoyt, a pincher and squeezer of his nieces, according to Jessamyn West; in Thomas Bewley's phrase, "a horny old bastard."[18] He boasted that he gave up dancing, Jessamyn West remembers, not because the Quakers disapproved but because "when his arms went around a woman his amorous propensities were instantly aroused."

He never saw my mother, a plain woman, without exclaiming "Grace, I swear you get prettier every time I see you. How do you do it? I want your recipe. Come here and let me give you a hug." Mamma always protested afterward. "What does Frank want to embarrass me that way for?" She may have been embarrassed, but she was always secretly pleased.[19]

Richard Nixon did not easily embrace any woman in public, including his wife.

The father punished his sons savagely, in the heat of ill temper. The son when grown, punished too, but coldly, calculatingly, often secretly, and always, if he could manage it, through the agency of someone else. Sometimes he waited years after the action that had sparked his grudge.

Jessamyn West has made famous one story of Frank Nixon's punishment. As a child she lived next door to the Nixons in Yorba Linda. Between the houses ran the Anaheim Ditch, an irrigation canal that brought water through the town to citrus ranches south and west. Since the water was used for drinking as well as irrigation, a "zanjero," a patrol officer, regularly walked along the canal looking for "such foreign bodies as marooned cats, drowned ground squirrels and swimming kids." The big ditch was dangerous for two- and three-year-olds, but the water was seldom more than two feet deep and everybody older swam in it. But Frank Nixon forbade his sons to swim in the canal even when it was so hot, in his own words, "you could throw a bucket of water in the air and none of it would land on the ground." "I still remember Uncle Frank pulling Harold out by the scruff of the neck," Merle West remembers, and "beating him so hard his hollering could be heard all up and down the ditch." Jessamyn West and her Aunt Elizabeth were watching once when Frank caught Richard and one of his brothers in the canal. He hauled them out and then flung them back in again, shouting, "Do you like water? Have some more of it!" The aunt, fearing that he was drowning the boys, began screaming, "You'll kill them, Frank! You'll kill them!"[20]

"I've heard Dick tell that story," Thomas Bewley remembers. "The boys were raising hell and the old man was short-tempered and he threw them in the irrigation ditch. Dick laughed about it."[21] But at age six or seven, when this happened, Richard Nixon might well have felt that his father was trying to drown him like an unwanted puppy.

Hannah Nixon did her best to give the impression that Richard did not need punishment. Her husband, she said, "would not hesitate using the strap or rod on the boys when they did wrong, although I don't remember that he ever spanked Richard."[22] But Nixon told Bewley, "I got the strap," and to Kenneth Harris he said, "My father would spank us sometimes, my mother never."[23] That he was punished less than his brothers, however, Nixon made clear:

Dad played no favorites with us. However, when you got into mischief, you had to be pretty convincing to avoid punishment. I used to tell my brothers not to argue with him. . . . Dad was very strict and expected to be obeyed under all circumstances. He had a hot temper, and I learned very early that the only way to deal with him was to abide by the rules he laid down. Otherwise I would probably have felt the touch of the ruler or the strap as my brothers did.[24]

In learning how to be *pretty convincing to avoid punishment* young Richard got his first taste of power over his father. But he also learned that a boy who is cleverer than others in deceiving to avoid punishment may be despised by them for his very success. We get some hint of this in a story told by Nixon's mother. When Richard, age twelve, was living with his relatives in Lindsay, his uncle caught him throwing corn about with his two cousins instead of cutting it and storing it in the crib. Beeson took the stick to his own sons but did not touch Richard, who protested, "But Uncle Harold, I was throwing that corn too."[25]

Punishment, so long as it is not brutal, is acceptable for children if they know the parental rules, and if there is consistency in application. The threat of punishment can arouse extraordinary fantasies in children, not all of them unpleasant. Small sons, fantasizing being beaten by their fathers, especially when the fathers are beating siblings, can sometimes confuse punishment with love.[26] That Nixon was ambivalent about the punishment he received as a child is suggested by a comment he once made to Stewart Alsop. In discussing motivation in politics, he said, "It's always good to have the whip on your back."

Punishment is a key to the value system of the parent. Frank Nixon wanted not understanding but "instant obedience" from his sons. But even as he exacted it, he bewildered them by being an arguer and a teaser. Don Nixon said of his father, "There was nothing he liked better than to argue. He'd take either side." Nothing could have served better to confuse the boys about right and wrong, truth and untruth, especially when they were very young. Teasers of small children are crueller than they mean to be. Frank Nixon told his son Arthur, when he lost his front teeth, that it was because he'd eaten too much candy. There is a punishing edge to this. Richard Nixon reported the anecdote, without comment, in a school essay written at seventeen.[27]

Frank Nixon also punished with money. Penurious and an

obsessive hater of debt, he often withheld money he had, and made his wife and sons accountable for every penny. The men who came begging for food during the depression years should be made to work for every handout, he insisted, and ranted at Hannah for her frequent charities. "There's enough on the plate," he would say to his sons at dinner. "Don't add to it."[28]

When Nixon was vice-president, he complained indirectly of his father's stinginess to Stewart Alsop:

Once in a while we'd go to a movie, but that was a luxury. We never had any vacations—well, once in a long while we'd have a week at the beach maybe. But I never went hunting or fishing, or anything like that—there wasn't time. We never ate out—never.[29]

Although there was snow in the surrounding mountains every winter, he was never in snow "to feel it," he said, until he was fifteen. Still he said to reporters in 1971, "I remember as a young boy what a great thrill it was for me to go to Yosemite, the Big Trees, the Grand Canyon, and the other great parks in the West." There had been vacation trips after all.[30]

One deprivation was peculiarly symbolic. Lucile Parsons, who worked in the Nixon Market, said Frank "had everything paid and it was paid on time, whether the rest of the family had anything or not. . . . Uncle Frank was almost too tight with money. He didn't have to be. . . . He wouldn't spend a nickel for a firecracker. That was a waste of money."[31] Nixon made the unbought firecrackers famous in his election film of 1968:

I recall, for example, the Fourth of July we were the only ones in the neighborhood who didn't have any—we didn't have the money frankly—for firecrackers. In those days you could get them. But my mother wanted to do something. I remember some way she got some bunting and fixed the table with red, white and blue bunting. My father went out and got some ice cream and what a feast we had! I remember that Fourth of July more than all the ones that I've been through in my whole life when I've made speeches before huge audiences because it was such a rather wonderful thing for them to do.[32]

There was enough money to provide bunting and ice cream, but not enough for firecrackers, which in those days cost very little. Every child managed to scrounge enough money. "The prevailing rate for picking potato bugs," Herbert Hoover wrote in his memoirs, "was one cent a hundred, and if you wanted firecrackers on the Fourth of July you took it or left it."[33] Characteristically, Nixon let the world know his father was too stingy to buy firecrackers, but denied the anger that had contined to smoulder in him for many years, describing the occasion as "wonderful."

A more poignant story of deprivation, which Nixon told at least twice, involved his tubercular brother Harold, who desperately wanted a pony:

My father could have bought it for about seventy-five dollars. And my brother, who died when I was quite young, kept saying, "Oh, I want this pony more than anything in the world." Now, being the oldest son, he was kind of a favorite as you can imagine, with my father and mother, and they wanted more than anything else to give him what he wanted.

But his parents decided that if the pony were purchased there would be no money to pay the grocery bill, the clothing bill, or "shoes for the younger brother."[34]

Throughout his life Richard Nixon would be in deep conflict over gift-buying. He shared his father's contempt for "bums," and welfare cheaters. He gave many presents to his mother, and as an adult gave small gifts quietly and unexpectedly, often to dying children. He complained openly of the costliness of his wife's affection for porcelain birds, and his most celebrated gift to her, $5000 diamond earrings, was paid for with laundered campaign money. The penuriousness of his presidential tax listings for charity, exposed in 1974, troubled the nation almost as much as the fraudulent backdating of his tax statement made to ensure a tax credit of half a million dollars.[35]

Frank Nixon's reluctance to give was open; his son's was hidden. As president, Nixon would have the White House waiter hide a thirty-dollar bottle of wine in a napkin to be served only to him, while the other guests were given wine worth six dollars a bottle.[36] Even in his last speech in the White House the ambivalence about gift-giving surfaced. He said to his staff, "I only wish that I were a wealthy man—at the present time I have got to find a way to pay my taxes—[*laughter*]—and if I were I would like to recompense you for the sacrifices that all of you have made to serve in government."[37]

Frank Nixon, volatile, unpredictable, and explosive in his early days of poverty, did not become less surly and disagreeable

when he was no longer poor. "He made enemies," said one of
Hannah's friends, Mildred Jackson Johns. "You weren't right. He
was right." "People were kind of afraid of him," said Mildred Sullivan Mendenhall, who worked in the Nixon Market. "I can still
hear him yelling at Don in the store, and embarrassing him almost
to tears over nothing." Niece Wilma Funk said, "I was always
afraid of Uncle Frank. . . . He seemed to think the world of us.
But he just had that nasty loud way. . . . the Quaker way is not to
get in a big mad yell. . . . He laughed loud and he yelled loud . . .
he yelled more than he needed to at his boys. . . . They were good
boys." Don Nixon said bitterly of his father, "He worked us kids
to death." Edward Nixon described his mother as "the judge in
most cases," and his father as "the executioner."[38]

"My father the executioner" may be harsher than Edward
Nixon intended. Eisenhower called his father "the breadwinner,
Supreme Court, and Lord High Executioner."[39] And he
described an occasion when his father thrashed his brother so
brutally—for skipping school to earn money—that he had flung
himself on the pair trying to pull his father off. "I don't think
anyone ought to be whipped like that," he had protested, "not
even a dog."[40] But this seems to have been a single occasion.
Frank Nixon was often brutal and frightening, especially in a rage
when he was wielding his butcher's knives and cleavers. He kept
a gun under the cash register. Hadley Marshburn, a nephew,
reports Hannah as saying, "Now it's all right to use that to scare
somebody with, but don't fire it at anybody." But Frank said, "If
anybody tries to rob me, I'll shoot to kill him."[41] In any case, the
imagery of butchering came back to Nixon in the Watergate crisis,
when he had to fire his favorite aides, Robert Haldeman and John
Ehrlichman. As he described it later to David Frost:

I cut off one arm and then cut off the other. . . . I didn't want to be in a
position just sawing them off in that way. . . . I will have to admit I wasn't
a good butcher.[42]

Did Frank Nixon kick his sons? The theme of kicking, and of
being kicked, appears early in Nixon's life, and surfaces repeatedly. As we shall see, in a letter to his mother written at age ten
he complains about being kicked.[43] In Peru, when he was spat
upon, he kicked the hostile demonstrator in the shin, and
reported his satisfaction in *Six Crises*. His statement to the press in

1962, after the defeat by Pat Brown, become famous: "You won't have Dick Nixon to kick around any more." Less well known were private comments such as "We'll kick their toes off in 1968," and "Kick the weirdos and beardos on the college campuses." In preparing for his inaugural speech he told Raymond Price he had read earlier presidential inaugural addresses—Wilson's, FDR's, Teddy Roosevelt's, Kennedy's—and "the theme of each," he said, "was to kick hell out of someone else and tell the American people they're great."[44] Presidential tapes reveal him saying to John Dean, March 13, 1973, "Have you kicked a few butts around?" And of his enemies, "they got the hell kicked out of them in the election." When Dean turned against him in Watergate, Nixon said to Mitchell, "Kick him straight." In retirement he confessed to David Frost,

People blow off steam in different ways. Some of them kick the cat. I don't like cats, but my daughters do. I should not have said that. But nevertheless, if there were one around I would probably kick the cat.[45]

Whether Frank Nixon kicked his son or not is not as certain as that Nixon felt himself to be kicked around by his father. That the idea of kicking came easily to Frank Nixon his son made clear in *Six Crises*. After listening to his "Checkers" speech, Nixon wrote that Frank Nixon had observed, "It looks to me as if the Democrats have given themselves a good kick in the seat of the pants," and when Pat learned of this she remarked, "it sounded just like him."[46]

Nixon embraced two of his father's passions, football and political argument. Although he was small for football and seriously uncoordinated, his father, fearful lest his second son be thought effeminate, urged him to take up football and spent many an afternoon watching him practice. At Whittier College Nixon took a vast amount of brutal punishment for four years, but never made the team. His coach, Wallace Newman, worried about him: "When he scrimmaged he was the cannon fodder. I used to get concerned at how we worked him over."[47] His father insisted, too, on coaching him in his earliest school debates, in which he was patently more successful. It was from his father first, rather than Vince Lombardi, whom he often quoted, that Nixon learned, "To win is not the most important thing; it's the only thing."

Eventually politics became a bond with his father, a certain path to approval that had been chronically wanting. Don Nixon said that his father "would argue politics with anybody who came in . . . and he couldn't stand Democrats. So when he was giving it to a Democrat, I would butt in and say I was a Democrat and disagreed with my father. That would calm the customer. My mother used to cringe during some of these arguments."[48] For Richard Nixon, always the Republican, political argument became a way of life. He distinguished, however, between the political man and the shouting man. As an adolescent he found his father's shouting humiliating, particularly when Frank Nixon yelled at his wife. As Lucile Parsons described it,

Something went wrong and you could hear him bellowing clear up town. "Hannah up there." She couldn't be gone five minutes out of his sight without him yelling, because he didn't like to be left in that store alone. . . . And he didn't like a lot of the customers that came in. It was the same with them—they didn't like him either.[49]

Frank knew that customers wanted her to serve them, and that in telephoning in orders they would specifically ask for Hannah. It could not have soothed him to see his gentle wife so conspicuously preferred.

Hannah Nixon told biographer Kornitzer in 1958, "Father and mother never talked loud—never yelled orders. And I tried not to yell at my children. It does something to a child." As she explained it, "Some people like to blow off steam, and then some burn down inside."[50] To her sons and nieces she would whisper, "Frank's bark is worse than his bite. . . . Just let it go in one ear and out the other." "He used to yell at her too," Mildred Sullivan Mendenhall reports, "but he loved her dearly. I can remember one time when she was quite seriously ill, and he was so worried about her. Tears came to his eyes when he talked about her."[51]

Each son responded to his father in his own fashion. Eldo West, visiting the market when the Nixon sons were grown, wrote to his daughter Jessamyn his sense of shock at finding Donald and Eddie "so cruel, so loud-mouthed, so outspoken—so critical of their father in the store before everyone else. . . . They got it when they were young, and are now paying their father back." Merle

West says that Frank and Don "bellowed like two bulls," and Richard yelled at his father too.[52] But mostly, like his mother, Richard burned down inside. Like her, he covered up and denied his father's brutality. Unlike her, he became eventually a prodigious punisher in his own right.

As an adolescent, however, we see him not punishing but rather protesting against unjust punishment. This began seriously at age sixteen, when he found in the excitement of a high school speech contest an outlet for his accumulated grievances. Nixon's speech, "Our Privileges Under the Constitution," which won first place at Whittier High and also in the larger school district, a victory over fifty contestants, was published in the school annual, *Cardinal and White,* in 1929. It is a notable speech on many counts, with themes that one sees surfacing and resurfacing to the end of his political life—lying, coverup, and moral pollution. He began with the theme of unjust punishment:

For countless centuries man has aspired to freedom. . . . The chief desire of man is that his life and personal freedom may be well protected. While our forefathers were struggling for freedom, one of their grievances was that a man, accused of a crime, was not always given a fair chance to prove himself innocent, and was thus often unjustly punished.

With the writing of the Constitution, he said, all this disappeared: "Gone are the days of inequality and servitude." Then he described, out of the bookish knowledge of the adolescent, the constitutional process that threatened to engulf him forty-five years later:

No citizen of the United States can be tried for a capital crime without first being indicted by a grand jury. If he is indicted, he is given a public trial by an impartial jury. He may obtain counsel and witnesses. He is not compelled to testify against himself as in times past, nor is any evidence obtained by compulsion.

He condemned those who would use freedom of the press and speech "as a cloak for covering libelous, indecent, and injurious statements against their fellowmen." "Should the morals of this nation be offended and polluted in the name of freedom of the press?" he asked. In denouncing those who "have incited riots," and "assailed our patriotism," he did come down solidly in favor of punishment:

laws have been provided for punishing those who abuse our Constitutional privileges. . . . We must obey these laws for they have been passed for our own welfare.[53]

Implicit in the speech was the theme of his own adolescent conflict: I am abused by my father, but I must not have the right to libel him. And this he never did. Instead he came to transmute his rebellion into politics. When he became the father of his country, he acted, in effect, as if he had come to believe that "I can abuse in the name of the Constitution, but you must not abuse me."

Nixon did lash out at his father once in public, when electioneering in Whittier. His first-grade schoolteacher from Yorba Linda, Mary George Skidmore, was sitting in an automobile with Nixon's parents.

Mr. Nixon sat in the front seat at the time, and was very, very ill. I don't think he even knew where he was. I'll never forget that day. . . . Richard was on the truck talking. He told about his father, how hard his father was on them, how stubborn he was and hard to get along with sometimes. I was so surprised to hear him say that.[54]

After his father's death in September 1956, the son, increasingly intent on winning the presidency, was eager to rebuild Frank Nixon's image as well as his own. "I have often thought," he wrote in *Six Crises*, "that with his fierce competitive drive and his intense interest in political issues he might have been more successful than I in political life, had he had the opportunity to continue his education."[55]

The stingy father became sacrificing. He "sacrificed everything," Nixon told the millions listening to his acceptance speech for the Republican presidential nomination in Miami Beach in 1968, "so that his sons could go to college." Actually tuition for the Nixon boys at Whittier College had been paid for out of a sum set aside by their Grandfather Milhous. And Richard had to pay back all the money his father advanced to him for his three years at Duke University Law School.

The shouting man, however, Nixon never defended. To Robert Coughlan he said in 1953, "I've got a temper. I expect I got it from my father—but the only time to lose your temper in politics is when it is deliberate. The greatest error you can make in politics is to get mad."[56] His own coolness in a crisis became the basic theme of *Six Crises.* In his debates with John F. Kennedy he referred often to Khrushchev—a notorious shouter, who also, it might be noted, bore a certain resemblance in face and figure to Frank Nixon—and said repeatedly that he would be better than Kennedy in controlling the Soviet leader's rashness. In his 1968 acceptance speech he appealed to "the forgotten Americans, the non-shouters." And in his first inaugural, he said:

To lower our voices would be a simple thing. In these difficult years, America has suffered from a fever of words: from inflated rhetoric that postures instead of persuading. We cannot learn from one another until we stop shouting at one another.[57]

To students in a White House gathering in 1969 he said he had learned in talking with heads of state that "usually the man who talked the loudest had the least to say," that "whoever is talking the loudest is pretty sure to be bluffing," and that "those who talk quietly with firmness, yes, but with some quietness, have an enormous effect compared with the others who bluster and shout and repeat without reasoning."[58] His fondness for the statement "The first right of every American is to be free from domestic violence," while obviously referring to crime problems in the nation, may well have been reinforced by the fact that as a child he had heard, seen, and felt so much violence in his own home. So, too, his repeated appeals to "the silent majority" remind one that, as a child at any rate, he had been a member of the silent majority in his own family.[59]

Did Frank Nixon have early fantasies about his son's becoming president? Hannah told a reporter in 1960 she remembered looking at a picture of the graduating class of Whittier College in 1934 and saying to her husband, "Our boy is the only one who looks like he could be president." Frank answered, "It's true, and it's all right to say it because no one else can hear it."[60] Did the idea, then, seem preposterous? Probably. Hannah Nixon herself said candidly in September 1960, at the height of the presidential campaign, "I can truthfully say that while I felt he would be successful in his studies, I couldn't possibly imagine that he would attain the position he is in now." Ernest Nixon, Frank's brother, told Bela Kornitzer when Nixon was vice-president, "I noticed during my last visit with Frank he could never quite get it into his head that he was the father of that boy."[61]

Nixon himself, in a relaxed reception for movie stars at San Clemente in 1972, told a disarming story of how Congressman Rangel from Harlem had said to him in a telephone conversation, "You know, Mr. President, when I was growing up in Harlem, if I had told my old man that someday I would be talking to the President of the United States, he would have told me I was crazy." To which Nixon had replied, "Well, Mr. Congressman, if when I was growing up in Yorba Linda, had I told my old man that someday I would be talking to a Congressman on the phone, he would have thought I was crazy."[62]

Still, one must note that Frank Nixon was brash enough to think that Franklin Roosevelt in 1934 might be willing to talk to him if he sought him out. Edward Rubin, then a law student at Duke University, rode from Los Angeles to Durham, North Carolina, with Nixon's father when he drove Richard east to matriculate. Rubin recollects that he thanked the older man for the ride and then asked where he was going next. "I'm going to Washington," Frank Nixon replied, in all seriousness. "I'm going to see the President. I want to tell him about the Townsend Plan. I don't think he understands it."

The Townsend Plan, then a simmering issue in California, was a scheme to end the depression by systematic infusions of money into the elderly poor. It called for the government to give everyone over age sixty a pension of $150 per month. Frank Nixon was enthusiastic about the plan. In 1936 he even voted for Roosevelt, the only time in his life he abandoned the Republican party. But what happened when he got to the White House in 1934 remains a family secret.[63]

Perhaps the most important legacy of Frank Nixon was his contribution to Richard Nixon's conviction that power came through fear. "You know very well," the son once said to reporters, "being on page one or thirty depends on whether or not they fear you." To William Safire he said, "People react to fear, not love—they don't teach that in Sunday School, but it's true."[64]

Nixon feared and disliked his father as loud, brutal, and sometimes dirty. But Frank was also preeminently masculine. For Richard to be cool, fastidious, and quiet was to be like his mother. He would put his mother's manners into the service of his father's objectives. The need both to feel proud of his father and to show that he was unlike him—to redeem him by being successful and by the same token to surpass him, showing his lack of worth—stayed with him well into the presidency.[65] That a sense of shame stayed with him, too, we see in a happening at the AFL–CIO convention in Bal Harbour, Florida, in 1971. Nixon had gone there to speak, against the advice of his friends, who knew the labor leaders and the audience would be hostile. George Meany, in a conspicuous gesture of contempt, forbade the orchestra to play "Hail to the Chief." Nixon, angered, threw away the advance copy of his speech. Sweating, ill at ease, he spoke spontaneously, and in the course of the speech made two slips of the tongue.

First, he called Vice-President Agnew "President Agnew." The second slip came when he talked about his father. He described seeing a working man and his son, "a graduate of one of our better Eastern colleges," coming through the White House receiving line:

The father was a working man, a hard-working man. I could tell as he spoke briefly with me that he had not had the benefit of a college education. But he spoke from his heart, if his grammar may not have been the most perfect. And as I spoke to him, I saw the boy standing there embarrassed, ill at ease. Then it came over me. The boy was ashamed of his father. . . .

I will tell you how I felt. I was ashamed of the son. My father grew up in a very poor family. He quit school in the sixth grade because his mother died three years earlier. He worked, when we were growing up, as a carpenter, and as an oilfield worker, as a streetcar motorman, as a grocer, and as a service station operator. He raised five boys, and every one of them got a better education than he did, because of how hard he worked. He was very proud when I was elected Congressman, Senator, and Vice President.

Nixon meant to say, in conclusion, "And I was proud of him to the day he died." Instead he said, "I was proud of him to the day *I* died."[66]

Frank Nixon suffered from ulcers all his adult life. He nearly died of hemorrhaging on a transcontinental plane on December 22, 1953.[67] The arthritis in his feet became so painful that he had to wear pads between his toes, and a fractured hip in December

1954 left him practically bedridden. But he survived to be seventy-eight, dying finally in 1956 of a ruptured abdominal artery. The rupture came on August 22, during the San Francisco convention, where it was by no means certain that Eisenhower would support Nixon for renomination as vice-president.

The *Los Angeles Times* described the drama being played on the convention floor as coinciding with the drama of life and death in Whittier. "Almost as if by miracle," the paper reported, "a sudden improvement in the elder Nixon's critical condition was reported only a few minutes before the vice president's nomination reached the family by television."[68] Nixon left the convention to fly to Whittier. "He's always been a scrapper," he said of his father. "He's a hard man to down." He had earlier given his father a tape recorder, urging him to record the tribulations of his youth, but the old man had put nothing on tape. Eisenhower asked for prayers for his recovery, and the press reported that "the former Whittier grocer's will to live and his regenerative stamina defied his physician's belief." Kept alive by transfusions, Frank Nixon joked about whether he was getting Republican or Democratic blood. He died, after twelve days of bleeding, on September 4, 1956. The Rev. George Jenkins pronounced a judgment in his funeral sermon:

His sons were all stalwart men, and he taught them that honesty and charity are the great virtues, and lying and deceit the great sins.[69]

Nixon quickly resumed campaigning, flying first to Buffalo, New York. There he began his speech with the words, "My father"—then paused, as if to contain his emotions, gripping the podium, and went on—"I remember my father telling me a long time ago, 'Dick, Dick,' he said, 'Buffalo is a beautiful town.' It may have been his *favorite* town." Nixon flew on to Rochester, where he began his speech in exactly the same fashion, changing only the name of the city. He repeated the performance in Ithaca. One efficient reporter kept notes.[70] Nixon seems to have had no fear that his father, so newly laid to rest, or his father's ghost, would not have approved.

The Saintly Mother

She made you want to do what she wanted you to do.

— MARSHALL CLOUGH, JR., REMEMBERING HANNAH NIXON[1]

HANNAH NIXON DIED IN 1967, a year before her son was elected president. At her funeral she was likened to "Hannah of the Old Testament, who dedicated her son to God before he was conceived."[2] Nixon, in his last speech as president, said, "Nobody will ever write a book, probably, about my mother. Well, I guess all of you would say this about your mother—my mother was a saint."[3] In 1964, when she was ill and feared to be dying, he visited her in the hospital. She was under heavy sedation, he said, but alert enough to hear him say, "Now, Mother, don't you give up." "Her eyes flashed, she sort of leaned up in the bed, and she said, 'Don't you give up.' " When telling this story, as president, Nixon concluded, "I didn't give up. If my mother hadn't said that, I might have given up. She didn't live to see what her advice did."[4]

He emphasized her inner peace and determination never to despair, and credited his mother for what he described in himself as "peace at the center." It involved perspective and poise, he said. "Whatever storms are that may be roaring up or down," the "peace within" will see one "through all adversity." In his memoirs, in describing her death he wrote that she was "not pretty but she was beautiful, and she looked as beautiful in death as she had in life."[5]

To his biographers Nixon emphasized Hannah Nixon's ineffable tenderness. "I have never known anyone," he said to Henry Spalding, "as patient or completely dedicated to the needs of others as my mother."[6] Jessamyn West describes her as "not a saint in the sense that she had had a great spiritual experience," but as "enormously thoughtful and loving." She recalls her winsome manner, luminous brown eyes, and the "organ-like" voice that remained unchanged into her last years. She describes Hannah's ironing party dresses for her and warning her to use a mouthwash to keep her breath sweet. Evlyn Dorn, Nixon's secretary in Whittier, said she had a way of turning a conversation around so that you would talk about yourself. Bela Kornitzer found her, in her seventies, fiercely energetic: "She didn't walk, she ran." Stewart Alsop found her "a woman of genuine charm" who "looks like Whistler's mother with a ski-jump nose."[7]

Others were more critical. Oscar Marshburn, Hannah's brother-in-law, thought her too gentle, too soft-willed. We called her, he said, "the angel unaware." Adela Rogers St. Johns called her "a colorless little thing." Pat Nixon's best friend, Helene Drown, said, "she was no goody-goody saint. She could get very angry." Verna Hough who lived near her in Prescott, Arizona, described her as "cranky and Puritanical." One friend of the family, who conducted a good many oral history interviews, said, "she was a hard character in that you got the impression that inside this frail, skinny woman, who on the outside might be depicted as a typical Anglo-Saxon cold person, inside was pure steel, pure steel. . . . People said that they wouldn't give two cents for Frank Nixon. They hated Frank and they hated Richard. But Hannah was the exception."[8]

Hannah Nixon never made any public speeches on behalf of her son. When asked in 1960 if she would campaign for him, she replied, "It's been a campaign ever since he was born. All his life, I've been his campaigner."[9] She gave the impression that from the beginning theirs had been a special relationship. As a child, she said, "Richard always seemed to need me more than the four other sons did. He doesn't pour out his heart, but he confides in me. . . . he used to like to have me sit with him when he studied. My sisters, Rose Olive Marshburn, and Mattie Gibbons, would pass our house, see the light, and say, 'Richard is studying and Hannah is with him.' " Although he was "engulfed by public life," she said, "I have not lost him. He belongs to the world but he is also still very much mine."[10]

At her funeral Nixon handed the Rev. Billy Graham a note she had given him on his inauguration as vice-president and asked him to read it: "We know you have gone far but you must remember that your relationship with your Creator is the most important thing in your life."[11] It is one of the major paradoxes in Nixon's life that a man reared by this gentle Quaker "creator" should have so repudiated the Quaker legacy. And it is a still-greater mystery that a son reared by a woman he insisted was so loving should, in the end, have been so consumed by hate.

David Abrahamsen finds the image of "the saintly mother" false, and calls Hannah Nixon "a domineering (castrating) woman." The boy was "cheated out of love," he wrote. "Rejection by her was a direct threat to his good image of himself." He sees the young Nixon as "a tense frustrated, isolated angry child who felt abandoned by his mother and his father."[12] Abrahamsen reproduces early photographs of Hannah and sees in her grim face evidences of repressed anger and depression. The face is, indeed, strikingly glum. So, too, were most of the photographs of Richard in the high school and college annuals. Abrahamsen describes the Nixon family as one "without joy." But if this is true, why should the joylessness have been caught only in the unsmiling faces of the mother and second son and not in those of his more genial brothers? Evlyn Dorn, a friend and adviser to Hannah, said she was "undemonstrative, and her son Richard was just like her." Don, on the other hand, she said, "would love you and kiss you."[13]

Bruce Mazlish described Hannah Nixon as an abandoning mother. The "betrayal" and "desertion" he said came when Nixon was "around age twelve or thirteen," when young Richard "would have been moving into the swift currents of feelings that we call the reawakened Oedipus."[14] That Hannah Nixon in her later years was something of a mythmaker we have seen. But was she also a dominating and abandoning mother? And if so, was this legacy, along with that of her punishing husband, responsible for at least the beginning of the rage, the desire to punish, and the apparent need for being punished, that characterized Nixon as an adult?

The tendency of the clinician is to look only for the pathology, in both the son and the parents. Where there is catastrophe, as with this president, an entire portrait may be constructed by describing nothing but the step-by-step march along an inexorable route to doom. But it was never inexorable. No president has been more affected by chance than Richard Nixon. Rage and hatred did play their part, but also affection, respect, pride, ambition, and drive. Let us remember that Hannah Nixon rec-

ognized early that Richard was a gifted child, and she took pains
to teach him how to read before he entered kindergarten.[15]

A case can be made, however, for the depressed, or abandoning, or domineering mother, as hidden aspects of the saintly and
caring mother. Nixon himself once spoke publicly of "a deep
depression and other tragedies" in his mother's life, this in addition to the deaths of two of her five sons.[16] She did send Richard
away for five months when he was twelve. Believing that he had
musical talent, she sent him to live with his aunt Jane Beeson, a
music teacher. That he felt abandoned, pushed out of the family,
is likely. Hannah's real abandonment of her family in favor of
Harold did not come, as we shall see, until he had contracted
tuberculosis and she took him to a tubercular community in Arizona, leaving her husband with Richard and Don to fend for
themselves. This separation continued, with intervals of visiting,
for three years. It began when Richard was already fifteen.

It is the nature of Hannah's love during Richard's childhood
that is so difficult to reconstruct from the evidence, as well as
Richard's own feelings about it. Did he believe that she loved him
only for his obedience, his deference, his quickness at learning,
his cleanliness (about which she was fanatical), and his skill at
appeasing his father? When she said that he of all her sons
seemed to "need" her most, this suggests that she gave him less
than his brothers, although the deprivation may have been real
only to him. If so, this may be a clue to the mystery of how, in
Bryce Harlow's words, he was "badly, badly hurt" as a child. Harlow, Nixon's presidential aide, speculated that as a result of this
he never learned how to trust, and thus people never really
trusted him. "Richard Nixon went up the walls of life with his
claws."[17]

As president, Richard Nixon said repeatedly that women were
stronger than men, although he almost always qualified this by
emphasizing stronger "in character," which subtly changes the
assertion. He quoted on more than one occasion the old Jewish
proverb "Man was made out of the soft earth, but woman was
made out of a hard rib," but this he used first in a toast to Golda
Meir and never in reference to his mother.[18] To be stronger *in
character* does not mean to be more powerful, but to be more
upright. Garry Wills, writing about Hannah Nixon, said, "It is

hard to be married to a saint, even a real one." But what is it like to be the son of a saint? Marshall Clough, Jr., of Prescott, Arizona, a friend of Harold Nixon's, described Hannah as "the most wonderful woman I ever met in my life," but he added, "She made you want to do what she wanted you to do."[19] To live daily with this kind of mother can put an intolerable burden on a child.

Hannah's control was indirect. Edith Brannon described her as "very strong, quiet, quietly strong. She would have had to be to balance Frank—quick-tempered but soft-hearted. . . . while he may have demanded, she commanded respect." William H. Barton remembered her as "a really strong hand . . . the kind who would balance the wheel of the whole family." Hannah's sister Olive said, "It was Frank who made the decisions. . . . if she made them she made them quietly and didn't talk about it." Still, family friend Ralph Shook insists, "Nobody could dominate Frank Nixon. . . . Two sledge hammers and a crowbar couldn't move him."

Ola Welch Jobe, Nixon's girlfriend for four years, said Hannah was "a lovely lady, wonderful to me, but an iron fist in a velvet glove. She had to collect the bills." But she admitted that Frank "overpowered her."[20]

To be strong and live daily with this man required secretiveness and manipulation. Here one of Hannah's nephews was explicit. Frank, he said, "would just make a point-blank statement that this was the way it was going to be. . . . She would say, 'That's right, Frank.' . . . But all the time you knew that she was sort of scheming as to how she could kind of smooth this over and go around and do it some other way." Dick Nixon, he said, was like his mother in this: "He would not disagree with you."[21]

"Richard had his father's fire and my tact," Hannah Nixon said.[22] But tact often involves pretense, and a child sees through this even before he learns to imitate it. From his mother Nixon learned not only manipulation but also the art and necessity of denial. In describing the poverty of the early years of her marriage, Hannah told reporters, "Many days I had nothing to serve but cornmeal. I'd bring it to the table and exclaim, 'See what we have tonight—wonderful cornmeal.' And they would gobble it up as if it were the most delectable of dishes." So, too, the son, in his election film of 1968, would describe having to wear hand-me-down shoes as if it had never troubled him. Our childhood, he

said, was like that of Eisenhower, "who did not know that he was
poor." Every child who has a single well-off relative knows
whether or not he is poor. The hand-me-down shoes Abrahamsen
sees as a special humiliation.[23]

Nixon also learned from his mother how to give the appearance of stoicism in defeat. On the night he lost to John F. Kennedy, all the women surrounding Hannah Nixon were weeping.
But she bowed her head in prayer instead, murmuring, "It must
be God's will."[24] Something of this stoicism, subtly transformed,
became the "fatalism" that Nixon often described in himself. But
the fatalism masked great rage. And where the rage in his
mother, consistently buried, led to depression, in the son it led to
a hunger for power and a penchant for punishment.

Hannah Nixon was extremely fastidious in dress and person
and here the impact on her son was permanent. "Every day," his
first-grade schoolteacher reported, "he wore a freshly starched
white shirt with a big black bow tie and knee pants. He always
looked like his mother had scrubbed him from head to toe. The
funny thing is, I never remember him ever getting dirty." Each
morning, his mother tells us, "He would take great pains in brush-
ing his teeth, was careful to gargle, and asked me to smell his
breath to make sure he would not offend anyone on the bus." He
once said "he didn't like to ride the school bus," one cousin
remembered, "because the other children didn't smell good."
When it was the fashion for high school boys to wear corduroy
trousers as dirty as possible, his were clean.[25]

The habit of fastidiousness stayed with him into the presidency. Stewart Alsop described how an aide found him once in
his "hideaway office . . . his legs stretched out on a big silk-covered
footstool and underneath the feet a bath towel." "What other
president," the aide said to Alsop, "would have bothered to get
that towel? Certainly not Johnson, or Kennedy, or Eisenhower."
Alsop thought the towel to be a symbol of Nixon's "instinctive
cautiousness," his "relentless middle-classness." The towel, he
wrote, is a symbol of the president's squareness: "He is not just
square—he is totally square."[26]

Was it squareness or a fear of dirtying, drilled into him by his
mother and reinforced by his wife, who, Nixon tells us, always
kept the White House "shipshape" and who hated to let the dogs
inside.[27] Several times as president he expressed obliquely some

resentment against total cleanliness, which he called "the sanitized life." In his famous encounter with students at 4 A.M. in the Lincoln Memorial during the Kent State crisis, he promised that he would clean up "the dirty streets and the dirty air and the dirty water." Then he added, "But you can clean all that up and have sanitized, clean cities, but no color, no warmth, no human qualities. The real problem is finding some meaning to life. . . ." In his own summary of this occasion he wrote, "I just wanted to be sure that all of them realized that ending the war, and cleaning up the streets and the air and the water was not going to solve spiritual hunger—which all of us have and which of course has been the mystery of life from the beginning of time."[28]

Three weeks after this episode, in a Billy Graham religious rally in East Tennessee, he returned to the theme: "we can have what can be described as complete cleanliness and yet have a sterile life."[29]

He remained, however, throughout his presidency what Garry Wills has described as "the most *doggedly* dressed man imaginable," a man who stays "creased and encased" where others are rumpled and wrinkly. He would never permit himself to be photographed barefoot, even on the beach, and it was rare that cameras caught him without a tie. "His rigid wall of decorum, in dress and manner," Wills speculated, "is one of the means he uses to fend off the world. . . . He speaks across the palings of stiff custom and a tie. . . . Clothes structure a situation, make things predictable, reduce their menace."[30] As a child, Nixon feared being caught either undressed or unclean. His mother's love was conditional, tentative, geared to washing, neatness, and obedience. The "spiritual hunger" thus began early.

Nixon spoke critically of his mother only once in public, shortly after her death, when he described with distaste her method of punishment. This was in his 1968 campaign film, which was intended for maximum publicity, and this portion of the film greatly distressed Hannah Nixon's sisters. When questioned about spanking, Hannah had said to one reporter, "I may have paddled him a little when he was very small," and to another, "We never paddled him." She said she believed in "silent punishment—in making a child sit quietly while he thinks through what he has done. That makes it punishment enough. It gets better results."[31] However, one Yorba Linda neighbor remembered looking through the Nixon screen door and seeing Hannah sitting on the piano bench next to her small son Richard, holding a switch in her hand.[32] In his 1968 film Nixon said:

My mother used to say later on that she never gave us a spanking. I'm not so sure. She might have. But I do know that we dreaded far more than my father's hand her tongue. It was never sharp, but she would just sit you down and she would talk very quietly and then when you got through you had been through an emotional experience.

These were the times when Hannah insisted on making her sons want to do what she wanted them to do. She did not absolve them but only reinforced their resentment. Nixon put it bluntly in the film: "We would always, in our family, prefer spanking."

He described an occasion when his small brother Arthur had "smoked some cornsilk" and a neighbor had informed his mother. Arthur had pleaded with him, "Tell her to give me a spanking. Don't let her talk to me. I just can't stand it, to have her talk to me." Actually little Arthur had been smoking cigarettes; Richard had told the story more accurately in a school paper at the age of seventeen:

When he was about five years old, he showed the world that he was a man by getting some cigarettes out of our store and secretly smoking them back of the house. Unfortunately for him, one of our gossipy neighbors happened to see him, and she promptly informed my mother. I have disliked that neighbor from that time.[33]

One can see the hatred of the woman informer, bitter when Nixon was seventeen, surfacing again when he was fifty-five, for in the film he said again of the neighbor, "I have never liked her since." In the school essay he tells us also, "My parents had wanted him to be a girl in the first place, consequently they attempted to make him one as much as possible." Arthur had to beg for a boy's haircut. And then, at five, he had been caught by a prying woman and punished by his mother "for showing the world that he was a man."

Nixon's fear of his mother's displeasure remained a constant in his life. He defied her admonitions in countless ways, but not openly, or even honestly, in her presence. The night he was elected to Congress in 1946 he was invited to the home of Norman Chandler, publisher of the *Los Angeles Times*. With him came

Pat, his parents, and his brother Donald and his wife. As Mrs. Chandler, "Buff," tells the story, she asked them all what they would like to drink:

Mrs. Nixon and Pat said they'd just love some milk. And Pappa Nixon wanted some milk and the brother and his wife wanted some milk. So I went around to go into the kitchen to tell the cook everybody wanted milk . . . when Nixon came out in the hall and said, "Buff, could you get me a double bourbon? I don't want Mother and Father to see me take a drink."

It was "a very small thing," Buff Chandler told Lally Weymouth in 1977. But for "a man that age, who'd just won an election . . . it showed a funny cheating quality that never changed through the years."[34]

We know how Hannah Nixon punished Richard, but we know little of how much she valued him. As we shall see in a subsequent chapter, Nixon felt himself to be the least favored of the sons. Bela Kornitzer, who interviewed Hannah Nixon at length in 1958 and who dedicated his biography of Nixon to her, was troubled by her failure to praise him. A recent Hungarian refugee who hated the Soviets, Kornitzer looked on Nixon's trip to Moscow and his debate with Khrushchev as a triumph. But Hannah, he wrote, "refused to admit that he had done a remarkable job in Russia. The most she would say was, 'I just didn't think it could be a flop.' " When she noted on the television screen "someone futilely trying to poke a couple of sticks into his hands, she said, "People seldom dictate to Richard." "He was no child prodigy," she said. "It is true, however, that at grammar school and later in high school he showed remarkable progress in his studies."

Later, during the election campaign of 1960, Kornitzer interviewed both Hannah Nixon and Rose Kennedy, asking them the same questions. The difference between the measured answers of the Quaker mother and the enthusiastic outpourings of Rose Kennedy are striking. When Mrs. Kennedy was asked if she thought her son would make a good president, she answered, "I think he would make a wonderful president." Hannah Nixon answered by saying that he would make a good president "if God is on his side."[35]

By then, however, Hannah Nixon had lived through the

"Checkers" crisis and the far more worrisome and dubious negotiations involving a loan of $205,000 to Donald Nixon from How-
ard Hughes—concerning which both Richard and Donald had
lied to the press—and Donald's subsequent bankruptcy. She had
been burned. One party worker, who campaigned with Hannah
Nixon in the Whittier area in 1962, remembered, "The only thing
she ever seemed concerned about was his honesty. That was the
oddest thing about her."[36]

Still, "being on God's side" was an old Quaker theme. Nixon
as president quoted his Grandmother Milhous, "What thee must
understand, Richard, is that the purpose of prayer is to listen to
God, not to talk to God. The purpose of prayer is not to tell God
what thee wants but to find out from God what He wants from
thee." In accepting the presidential nomination for the second
time, on August 23, 1972, Nixon paraphrased Lincoln:

During the tragic War Between the States, Abraham Lincoln was asked
whether God was on his side. He replied, "My concern is not whether
God is on our side, but whether we are on God's side."[37]

Hannah Nixon's requirements for being on God's side were
not dismayingly difficult, yet Nixon was impelled to violate them.
His repudiation of her requirements, and indeed of the whole of
the Quaker heritage she embodied, came slowly, with persisting
denials that there had been any defection at all. Shortly before his
election in 1968 he said, "I recall my mother and my grandmother
saying, 'I have a concern for peace.' "[38] Some Americans were
misled into thinking that Nixon was certain to bring an immediate
end to the Vietnam War. In his first inaugural he reflected what
seemed to be a commitment to the Quaker way, to the private
whisperings of what is called in the sect "the inner light":

To a crisis of the spirit, we need an answer of the spirit. And to find that
answer, we need only look within ourselves. When we listen to "the better angels of our nature," we find that they celebrate the simple things,
the basic things—such as goodness, decency, love, kindness. . . . We can
build a great cathedral of the spirit.

In August 1972 he was still bombing in Vietnam and indignantly
denying that he was "the number one war maker of the world."[39]
And although he was still calling himself a Quaker when he left
office, the Quakers—save for the loyal church in East Whittier—
had almost all repudiated him.

Nixon confessed to David Frost in 1977, "I never cry except in public." When his mother died on September 30, 1967, he learned the news from his brother Don. "I did not cry," he said in his memoirs, "nor when I talked with Pat and the girls in the apartment, nor on the plane to California for the funeral." She had not lived to see him president and in her last years had drifted into senility and had been kept in a Whittier rest home. Richard and his family visited her several times a year; she had apparently become distant from Don.[40]

"Billy Graham had flown West to deliver the funeral sermon," Nixon wrote. "As I shook hands with Billy, our eyes met. I could no longer control my pent-up emotions. I broke into tears. He threw his arms around me and said, 'Let it all out.' "[41]

In his later years Nixon complained of hay fever. "It hits me in the eyes," he told newsmen. His presidential physician, Dr. Walter Tkach, denied it. "I'm not going to argue with him any more. In all the years I've known him he's never been known to have hay fever." Nixon said the affliction struck him annually on September 5 and persisted until the first of October.[42] It may not be entirely coincidental that September 4 marked the anniversary of the death of his father, and September 30 the death of his mother.

The Unsmiling Child

*What starts the process, really, are laughs and slights and snubs
when you are a kid.*
— NIXON, TO KENNETH W. CLAWSON, 1974[1]

MARY GEORGE SKIDMORE, Nixon's first-grade teacher, remembers him as "a very solemn child" who "rarely ever smiled or laughed." Hannah Nixon said he never went through a mischievous period: "He was thoughtful and serious. 'He always carried such a weight.' That's an expression we Quakers use for a person who doesn't take his responsibilities lightly." One elementary school classmate, Allen Gaines, said, "I don't recall ever hearing him really laugh." And this continued. A friend in the Whittier Little Theater group, Hortense Behrens, said, "I have never heard him *really*, honest-to-goodness laugh out loud. I don't think he does." Tom Dixon, who managed his radio campaigning in his early elections, was struck by his inability to laugh, except on cue.[2]

Whence came the "weight," the burden of control? Jessamyn West described Harold Nixon, who was three and a half years older, as "dashing and bold," but said that Richard as a child was "not a cuddly sort of thing you'd want to pick up. He didn't want to be picked up, didn't want to be cuddled. He had a fastidiousness about him."[3] Elizabeth Guptill Rez, the Nixon "hired girl" in the Yorba Linda years, confirms that Richard was always "clinging" to his mother and was very unlike Don, eighteen months younger, whom she described as affectionate and "so easy to love."[4] Arthur, born in 1918 when Richard was five, was also a shy child, but indulged as the baby. Edward was not born until 1930. Nixon has told us that Harold was the favorite of both parents, and his aunt Olive Marshburn states that Harold was also the favorite in the larger Milhous family.[5] There is considerable evidence that of the first four sons Richard felt himself to be the least loved, and the most difficult to love.

When in 1968 Nixon accepted the Republican nomination in Miami Beach, he described two children:

Tonight I see the face of a child. He lives in a great city. He is black. He is white. He is Mexican, Italian, Polish. None of this matters. What does matter is that he is an American child. . . . He sleeps the sleep of childhood and dreams its dreams. Yet when he awakens, he awakens to a living nightmare of poverty, neglect and despair. . . . For him the American system is one that feeds his stomach and starves his soul. It breaks his heart. . . .

I see another child. He hears the train go by at night and dreams of faraway places he would like to go. It seems an impossible dream. But he is helped on his journey through life. A father who had to go to work before he finished the sixth grade, sacrificed everything so that his sons could go to college. A gentle Quaker mother. . . . Tonight he stands before you—nominated for President of the United States.[6]

As we have seen, Nixon often described what was ugly in his past only to deny it. Did he, in this moment of triumph, remember himself as both the pampered child and the deprived child, brought up by parents who had indeed sacrificed for him, who had nourished his body and encouraged his ambition but who had also starved his soul? The evidence is in the whole life.

Frank and Hannah Nixon, after their marriage in 1908, were embarrassingly dependent on Frank Milhous. After Harold's birth in the big Milhous home on June 1, 1909, they moved north to Lindsay for a time where Frank Nixon planted orange trees on property owned by his father-in-law. Milhous, who had been a nurseryman in Indiana before coming to California in 1896, had a way with trees. He understood about fertilizing, pollination, watering, and insects. But Frank Nixon had a way only with tools.

He failed to make a living in Lindsay and returned to Whittier where Milhous, still hopeful of his son-in-law, helped him settle on ten acres in Yorba Linda, a beautiful hilly area to the east, where Frank dutifully set out a lemon grove. For someone with capital there was good money in citrus crops. Land cost about one hundred fifty dollars an acre, and could be expected to triple in value in five years. The Janss Investment Company advertised Yorba Linda land as *absolutely frost free* (which it was not), and promised 777,000 gallons of water every thirty days on every ten-acre plot, the water pumped from wells in the dry riverbeds, to be delivered at cost.

To the visitor Yorba Linda seemed like a languid paradise. Groves of gnarled live oaks accented the undulating hills, which were covered with grass that was a cool green in the rainy season and a glowing gold in the summer. The air was sweet-smelling from thousands of acres of young trees; it was clean and clear, save during the few nights of the year when frost threatened and smudge pots were lighted. Fog occasionally rolled in from the Pacific, smothering the area in a cool, moist blanket of gray. Picture postcards showing the fertile, evergreen valleys, rimmed by the stark, snow-covered mountains of the larger Los Angeles basin, advertised the Promised Land.

Children walked barefoot to school save on the coldest days. They picked armloads of California holly in December; poppies, lupin, Mariposa lilies, and yellow violets in February. They hunted rabbits or rattlesnakes in the summer and chased tumbleweeds in the fall. Jessamyn West, remembering the church parties, hayrides, and fragrant orchids, called it "the Midas-time" of her life. Although the roads were largely unpaved and most people drove wagons and buggies, the Pacific Electric cars ran nine times a day into Los Angeles, bringing lumber, machinery, and other supplies, and taking back oranges, lemons, vegetables, and avocados, as well as transporting passengers. Ben Foss, motorman and owner of one of the citrus ranches, would call out cheerily as the cars approached his hometown, "Yorba Linda! Capital of the World!"[7]

The area was largely Quaker. Smoking, drinking, and dancing were frowned on. Nixon's first-grade teacher recalls that she was threatened with the loss of her job for talking for an hour with a young man on the street, and school trustees tried to get an agreement forbidding the teachers to dance.[8] Blacks were forbidden by town ordinance to buy houses, and the few who worked there left each night. Although Nixon has told us that blacks and Mexican laborers ate at the same table with the Milhous family and in his own home, it is evident that Nixon's father, at any rate, hired mostly relatives, who were numerous, to help in the citrus groves and later in the Nixon Market. Chicano children were sent to a segregated school in Whittier. In Anaheim the town swimming pool was drained on Friday night and new water was added on Saturday—Friday was Mexican day. The little group of Mexicans in Whittier for a time had their own Catholic church, but finally built one in the less puritanical area of Pico Rivera. Black families did not move into Whittier until 1957.[9]

Frank and Hannah Nixon fitted easily into the nearby Yorba Linda community, where Frank built an unpretentious frame house and then helped others, either as a carpenter or in setting out new citrus groves. They raised chickens and rabbits and for a time had a cow. Water was sometimes scarce and during the dreaded desert winds—what the Indians had called "the Devil's breath"—the Quaker pastor would beg his congregation to organize bucket brigades to carry water to save the young trees.[10] Although her husband worked hard, five years of marriage brought for Hannah Nixon only poverty, shabbiness, and constant comparison of her husband with the respectable, gentle Quaker father she had left.

On the day of Richard Nixon's birth the *Los Angeles Times* printed a headline which will intrigue those who delight in historical coincidences. It said:

HOLMES DENIES HE WILL RESIGN
SUPREME COURT JUSTICE SAYS HE WILL NOT QUIT

Hannah Nixon said that Richard was born "on a windy, dusty day." There had indeed been a damaging wind, the worst since 1887 according to the *Times,* but on the fifth of January rather than the ninth, the actual date of his birth. Freezing weather had followed, with damage to the citrus trees. But on January 8 the cold wave had broken, and it had begun to rain.[11]

Frank Nixon, who had set up extra stoves for the expected birth, left home early in the morning and asked a young schoolteacher, Ella Eidson, to look after his wife. Although she had borne two daughters herself, she was unprepared for Hannah's day-long labor and excruciating pain. The doctor, H. P. Wilson, and his nurse, Henrietta Shockney, failed to come until half an hour before the birth at 9:35 P.M. "They just got there in time," Mrs. Eidson said. "I was very glad to see them." She was so upset that on leaving the house in the dark she stumbled into the irrigation ditch and had to be pulled out by Frank Nixon.[12] The nurse weighed the baby at eleven pounds, describing him later as "unusually big" with "a crop of black hair and a powerful ringing voice." Hoyt Corbit reports that the next morning Frank Nixon "threw his hands in the air and danced around the yard" saying, "I've got another boy." He was named Richard, his mother tells us, after Richard the Lion-Hearted.[13]

Dr. Abrahamsen has made much of the fact that Nixon's kin remember him as "a screamer" and suspected a seriously troubled infancy. It was indeed a bad year. "The labor was so difficult," Hannah Nixon said, "that I was ill for many weeks afterwards."[14] Whether her sickness was physical or whether she suffered a post-partum depression is not clear. Hannah's sister Olive, when questioned about this, remembered only that with Harold's birth Hannah had had an even harder recovery period.

When Richard was six months old another of Hannah's sisters, Elizabeth Harrison, bore a son whom she was too ill to nurse. Hannah took the baby to her own breast.[15] For sisters to share their milk was not uncommon, especially in those years when bottle feeding was still treacherous. How many weeks Hannah nursed her nephew along with her son we do not know. Richard could not have understood the coming of his rival at the breast nor his disappearance, but it is possible even in one so young that he was enraged at his cousin's arrival and rejoiced in his going, especially if his mother was failing in her basic nurturing.

Before Richard was a year old Hannah went to the hospital for a mastoid operation. She brought her young son to stay with her mother, who later reported his screaming.[16] By the time Richard was fourteen months old his mother was again pregnant. The new, and this time permanent rival, Donald, was born November 23, 1914, when Richard was not quite two. By then, or perhaps earlier, he had stopped screaming and had become "a very good kid, very quiet, never a cry-baby at least around his father." This, at any rate, is the description given by Ollie Burdg, a kin to Hannah Nixon, who came to work with Frank when Richard was less than a year old, and who for two years helped as a carpenter and laborer in the citrus groves.

Burdg, who regularly ate with the family, said Hannah was "the quietest woman." She "would hardly ever sit down and eat with us," and was "generally cooking and bringing stuff to the table . . . and then she'd feed herself." Richard, he said, "got along with his dad; he always sat with his dad at the table, and his dad always fed him. Then Donald came along and he had two of them." Frank would care for his sons when Hannah went to church.[17] This scene at the table implies much tenderness on the part of Nixon's father, this being all the more remarkable because of the absence of tenderness in the reminiscences of almost everyone else. It is Frank, not Hannah, who is feeding the child. It is the mother who refuses to share in this family intimacy.

Hannah Nixon tells us that Richard's first word was "Bird," the name of one of his father's horses. He seems to have been fascinated by them and quite fearless around them. Ralph Shook described how Frank Nixon once brought Richard along with him when he came to work on a drainage project, although he was not yet two. Shook noted in horror that the child had crawled behind the team: "When Frank backed up, I grabbed him just in time before the animals passed over him. They backed up and their hoofs tramped the spot where the little boy had been crawling only seconds before."[18] This was the first in a series of happenings which spelled survival—lucky survival, even miraculous survival.

The more famous "miracle" of his childhood came when he was three, and here it was his mother who was responsible for the accident. The story has many different versions. Hannah told Earl Mazo in 1959,

We had taken my aunt to the train at Placentia. . . . I held Donald, the baby, on my lap and drove the buggy. I couldn't handle both boys because Richard, then three, was too lively. So a little neighbor girl came along to hold him.[19]

Edwin Hoyt said the girl in the buggy was Mary Elizabeth Guptill, which Mary denied. Olive Marshburn insisted there could have been no aunt to be taken to the station at Placentia.[20] All accounts agree that the horse became ungovernable as they rounded a bend, that Richard was thrown out, and that the buggy wheel struck him in the head. Three men have claimed the honor of rushing the child to a hospital in the "only" automobile in Yorba Linda, usually described as a Ford. Whether it was twenty-five miles to a hospital in Los Angeles or to a doctor in Fullerton or Anaheim is still disputed.

According to Earl Mazo, the doctor told Hannah Nixon they reached the hospital emergency room "just in time to save his life." Mazo said a neighbor named Quigley was the driver of the Ford; Kornitzer said that E. H. Herbert, in Hannah's presence, identified himself as the driver and described how the doctor had administered anaesthesia and sutured the wound. "The deep scar is covered by his thick hair," Hannah told Kornitzer. "It really was a miracle."[21] Austin Marshburn was the third to claim he had driven the child to the hospital and said that he had a letter from Nixon himself authenticating the story.[22]

The girl in the buggy was Elizabeth Eidson, then eleven years old. Hannah Nixon had asked her to help with Richard and Donald when she went to a friend's house to get some promised grapes. Richard refused to sit down, she said, and when the horse "didn't slow down to make a short corner, Richard toppled over and out of the buggy, the wheel running over his head, cutting his scalp wide open." Elizabeth ran back to pick him up:

His scalp was hanging down and bleeding so. I held the scalp edges together while walking him back to the buggy—and oh the blood over my hands, to one so young it was awful, and my thoughts, that I had failed Mrs. Nixon in my duty to her. So for a good many years after, I blocked out a lot of that happening. . . . I don't think he was taken to a hospital, as there wasn't one in Yorba Linda, but to Dr. Marshburn who, if I remember right, was the only doctor there at that time.[23]

Did Hannah Nixon describe the story as a "miracle" from the beginning? We do not know. Her sister Edith could not remember in later years which son fell out of the buggy. Jessamyn West, living across the canal, never heard of the accident.[24] The confusion and mythologizing came later, when Nixon was running for president, and the variety of stories which then mushroomed serve to underline the hazards of the presidential biographer. In any case, one can be sure that the accident and suturing were traumatic. That they served to make the three-year-old feel for a time vulnerable and wary is possible.

Ollie Burdg came back to visit the Nixon family when Richard was three. He tells us how he brought his fiancée and how Richard sat in her lap. "He was quite a talker. He was telling her about how, when he got big, he was going to kill wild animals, and elephants, and lions and tigers."[25] The fantasy is commonplace among small boys, and would seem to indicate not a frightened but an aggressive child. Whether this was before or after the accident we do not know.

Nixon himself mostly ignored the childhood "miracle." But in his first published article as a Duke University law student, which dealt with liability in automobile accident litigation, he wrote with some care about the old horse and buggy laws, where "the driver of the horse and buggy owed to his guest the common law duty of ordinary care."[26] Years later, as president, he said in an interview: "I don't go overboard when we win and I don't get terribly depressed when we lose. . . . The Midwesterners have a term. They say, 'Steady in the buggy.' "[27]

Nixon did not have another accident, despite all the football scrimmaging, until February 1948, when he slipped on the ice when holding his daughter Tricia and broke his elbow and right wrist.[28] In 1952 he injured his foot, and in 1960, during the campaign against Kennedy, he damaged his leg against a car door. In addition to the usual childhood diseases he did have pneumonia at age four and undulant fever in high school. But according to friends and neighbors it was Harold, suffering from chronic colds and bronchitis, who was the sickly child. His bout with measles was so severe, and his mother so exhausted from nursing him, that the Quaker pastor, the Rev. Clifford Jones, persuaded Frank Nixon, despite his poverty, to hire Elizabeth Guptill to help in the house and to free her for an occasional vacation with her mother in Whittier.

Elizabeth confirmed the reports of the Nixons' poverty in Yorba Linda and their "tight budget." She also recalled a special paternal unkindness: Frank would not allow any other children to come and play. He was enraged once, Elizabeth said, when she allowed Harold to "con her" into playing with neighbor children without his permission.

They weren't allowed to run around the country very much. The only time there were extra children there was when Harold invited them to a birthday party and didn't tell his mother. Someone happened to call her and ask what kind of a present she should bring for Harold and she didn't know anything about a birthday party. So she promptly said, "No presents, please." We made a birthday cake and had a birthday party.[29]

Although later someone gave them an electric train, there were then no pets, and apparently few toys, certainly no dolls. Mildred Jackson Johns, who at age eleven had acted as babysitter

when Hannah brought Richard from Yorba Linda to visit in
Whittier, remembers that "the first thing that little tyke would do
was to hightail it upstairs and play with my dolls. He liked to play
with them more than I did."[30]

Elizabeth Guptill said that Richard was the quietest of the
three boys: "He lived more within himself." She remembers him
best at prayer, a "bright-faced boy, eyes closed and hands
clasped," saying:

> Jesus Holy Savior, Hear me while I pray,
> Look upon thy little child, help me all the day.
> Forgive me when I'm naughty, Take all my sins away.
> Help me to love Thee better, Dear Jesus, every day.[31]

When the fourth son was born in 1918, his parents had prepared the five-year-old Richard for his arrival only with deceptions. His mother had been so ill during the pregnancy that
Elizabeth Guptill had stayed for several months. He could hardly
have missed talk about the forthcoming birth, but when his
mother went to the hospital he was told only that she was away
"on a visit." Then Frank came to the Milhous home, where the
boys were staying, and told them there was "a real live doll" at the
hospital. Nixon in a school paper at age seventeen wrote:

Naturally we then began to quarrel over whose doll it would be,
although each of us wished to have it merely to keep one of the others
from getting it. . . . After learning that it was not a "girl doll," we finally
decided that its name should be Arthur.

Harold, Nixon continued, "who had reached the all knowing age
of nine," told them "secretly that it wasn't a doll but a baby. He
warned us, though not to let on he'd told us so."[32]

Deception about procreation and pregnancy is the commonest
of all parental lying, and we note here that Richard recorded his
father's deceptions, and that his mother preserved the school
paper, although it would seem likely that both of them looked on
such deception as normal and for the children's good. The school
paper was written when Nixon's mother was once again—and
unexpectedly—pregnant. She was then forty-five.

Arthur was born in May 1918, and Richard went to kindergarten that October. Virginia Shaw, a neighbor child then in the
third grade, remembers how Richard astonished others by his

ability to memorize. His teacher brought him into her class one day to recite a long poem. "It was amazing that a kindergartener could learn that vast amount of poetry. . . . I remember all of us were very, very envious."[33] Since his mother had already taught him how to read, he had an obvious advantage over his classmates. His first-grade teacher said, "He absorbed knowledge of every kind like a blotter. In that year I think he read no less than thirty or forty books, maybe more, besides doing all of his other work." She recommended that he be moved ahead into the third grade. The taste of approval was sweet, and Nixon became very competitive. Later he said, "I never in my life wanted to be left behind."[34]

Virginia Shaw remembers the Friends church offering prizes for "recitations" in the year Richard Nixon was six. "Harold and I were confident we were going to win," she said. "Richard won it, and we were so jealous."[35] This was his first recorded victory over his eldest brother.

Harold, like his father, was a teaser and practical joker. "He was always kidding somebody, playing jokes on them," Paul Ryan remembered. "Richard was always trying to keep up with Harold; sometimes he was shoved aside, but he always tried." When the older boys abused him, he cried bitterly. When Ryan reminded Nixon of this in later years, Nixon joked, "I was the biggest crybaby in Yorba Linda. My dad could hear me even with the tractor running."[36]

The uneven competition with Harold became very nearly intolerable when Richard was seven; two older cousins, Merrill and Floyd Wildermuth, moved in along with their widowed mother, Frank Nixon's sister. They stayed for over a year. There were now six boys in the small crowded house, three older than himself. Merrill, age fifteen, seems to have been gentle enough, but Floyd at eleven teamed up with Harold against Richard. Floyd remembers how he and Harold tricked the younger boy into running errands for them: "We would bet him that he couldn't get up to the house and bring cookies back to us before we could count to a hundred. He'd take off on the run."[37] But Richard learned very quickly that he was being used.

It was in the year the Wildermuths were living with them that Nixon took the hatchet to Gerald Shaw. Gerald, then six, remembers filling a jar with pollywogs from under the Nixon bridge:

"He didn't like that and he wanted them himself. . . . So he had
this hatchet in his hand. . . . he hit me on the head with the blunt
end of it! I have a scar on my head today to show for it."[38]

In competing with his younger as well as his older brother,
Richard generally used words rather than violence. He developed
a long memory. Donald Nixon related:

He wouldn't argue much with me, for instance, but once, when he had
just about as much of me as he could take, he cut loose and kept at it for
a half to three quarters of an hour. He went back a year or two listing
things I had done. He didn't leave out a thing. I was only 8 and he was
10, but I've had a lot of respect ever since for the way he can keep things
in his mind.[39]

In *Six Crises* Nixon wrote of his childhood yearning to be a
railroad engineer, and he called the whistle of the Santa Fe train,
which ran a mile south of Yorba Linda, "the sweetest music I ever
heard." In the fifth grade geography became his passion and he
listened avidly to the stories of one of his father's friends, who
had been an engineer. "From that early time," Nixon said in 1968,
"I seemed to have some wanderlust."

Later as vice-president and president he repeatedly told audiences how many countries he had visited—thirty, then forty, and
on up to more than eighty. The upward counting is in scores of
of his speeches. He listed the ever-growing number as some men
would their sexual contests. Always his theme was "I've been
there, and therefore I know."

The hunger to be rich he generally denied. But as we have
seen, the whole family was consumed by the fantasy of immediate
riches when oil was discovered near Yorba Linda. Frank worked
as a roustabout in the Union Oil Company field in nearby Placentia for two years, absorbing the lore of the instant millionaires.
But he did not sell the lemon grove for a profit when he might
have, and was forced to sell when the speculators had lost interest.
Then, against his wife's urging he bought the wrong lot, the Whittier corner instead of the lot that produced the gusher, in Santa
Fe Springs. So to the memories of poverty in Yorba Linda was
added the accumulated family bitterness over just missing out on
being rich.

The Nixons left the house and sweet-smelling grove when
Nixon was nine. Although they moved only a few miles to a larger

town, for Hannah it was a move back home. For Richard the move to Whittier destroyed the rhythm of family living that he had known for nine years. His father settled them in a small house in East Whittier, and built a gas station nearby on a Whittier Boulevard corner. Henceforth, six days a week, the family would be at the command of the customer—one usually driving a Model-T Ford—demanding at first only gasoline and oil, later fruit, groceries, meat, and Hannah Nixon's freshly baked fruit pies. Gone were the silences and privacy of Richard's childhood. A longing for privacy, rooted in the early years and compounded, as we shall see, by a yearning to invade the privacy of others, became one of the major conflicts of his adolescence, and would affect his whole life.

Splitting and Entitlement

My Dear Master: Nov. 12, 1923
    The two dogs that you left with me are very bad to me. Their dog,
Jim, is very old and he will never talk or play with me. One Saturday the
boys went hunting. Jim and myself went with them. While going
through the woods one of the boys triped and fell on me. I lost my
temper and bit him. He kiked me in the side and we started on. While
we were walking I saw a black round thing in a tree. I hit it with my paw.
A swarm of black thing came out of it. I felt a pain all over. I started to
run and as both of my eyes were swelled shut I fell into a pond. When I
got home I was very sore. I wish you would come home right now.
                                                          Your good dog
                                                              Richard[1]

MANY MOTHERS PRESERVE LETTERS written to them by
their sons when they are very small, including mothers of presidents. Abigail Adams kept a letter that her John Quincy had written at age eleven, having just arrived in Paris with his father. He
wrote with the affection and sturdy piety that illuminated their
whole relationship:

I must not let Slip one opportunity in writing To So kind and Tender a
Mamma as you have been To me for Which I believe I Shall never be
able to Repay you.
    I hope I Shall never forget the goodness of God in Preserving us
Through all The Dangers That We have been exposed to in Crossing
The Seas, and that by his almighty Power we have arrived Safe in france
after a Troublesome voyage.[2]

Franklin Roosevelt, at age ten, writing to his mother, was already
mischievously teasing and exuberant, and ended the letter by
signing his name backward:

I am flourishing & have only fallen 3 times from the top story window.
With bales of love to everybody
  Your devoted baby NILKNARF.

There are other such letters in the presidential archives. But the "good dog" letter written by Richard Nixon at age ten is likely to be the most celebrated. Barber sees it as a fantasy full of symbols, "a tale of hurt, panic, and depression."[3] Abrahamsen sees in the imagery "a high level of confusion and despair."[4] Both Barber and Abrahamsen suggest that the "very old" dog, Jim, may be Richard Nixon's father.

The letter raises many questions, not the least of them being what kind of mother would permit its publication. Kornitzer tells us that Hannah had kept it as evidence of Richard's "intelligence."[5] If she was proud of it, then she surely looked on it as a literary fantasy, one calculated to wrench a distant mother's heart. There were times when Hannah went home briefly to her mother "tired to death with her boys," as Jessamyn West has said. This may have been one of the times.[6]

One can see a notable reversal from the fantasy of Richard at age three. The child who was then dreaming of killing elephants and tigers now imagines himself kicked, stung in many places, blinded, and threatened with drowning, although he is also biting and striking out at "a black round thing." If nothing else the letter demonstrates how early he had begun to exaggerate the wrongs inflicted on him by others—a compulsion that affected his whole life.

But let there be a cautionary note in speculation about "the good dog" letter. Hannah Nixon kept two letters from this period, and had she kept only the second, written two months later, a different picture of Nixon as adolescent might have emerged in the clinical biographies:

Times, Office K, Box 240
Dear Sir: January 24, 1924
  Please consider me for the position of office boy mentioned in the Times paper. I am eleven years of age and I am in the Sixth grade of the East Whittier grammar school.
  I am very willing to work and would like the money for a vacation trip. I am willing to come to your office at any time and I will accept any pay offered. My address is Whittier boulavard and Leffingwell road.

The phone number is 5274. For reference you can see, Miss Flowers princaple of the East Whittier School. Hoping that you will accept me for service, I am,

Yours truly,
Richard M. Nixon[7]*

Norman Chandler, publisher of the *Los Angeles Times,* later an ardent supporter of Nixon, when shown this letter said, "This is just like him. It's a blueprint of his ambition, drive, and determination to meet a challenge. If he had gotten the job, it could have changed American history."[8] Hannah, who preserved memorabilia from all her sons, kept both letters, one showing Richard to be studious, ambitious, respected by the school principal, anxious to leave home if only on vacation, the other showing a boy full of rage and self-pity. But these are the two children Nixon described in Miami Beach in 1968: one who "hears the train go by at night and dreams of faraway places he would like to go," and the other who awakens "to a living nightmare of poverty, neglect, and despair." The divided child will grow into a divided man.

In *Six Crises* Nixon looked back fleetingly at his childhood and gave us not the facts about how he became interested in politics but a riddle. "When does a presidential campaign really begin?" he asked. "I suppose this would make a better story if I could fit the facts of my life into the Great American Legend as to how presidential candidates are born and made." What "would make a better story" he told as follows:

The legend goes something like this. A mother takes a child on her knees. She senses by looking into his eyes that there is something truly extraordinary about him. She says to herself and perhaps even to him, "You, son, are going to be President some day." From that time on, he is tapped for greatness. He talks before he walks. He reads a thousand words a minute. He is bored by school because he is so much smarter than his teachers. He prepares himself for leadership by taking courses in public speaking and political science. He drives ever upward, calculating every step of the way until he reaches his and—less importantly—the nation's destiny by becoming President of the United States.
So goes the legend. The truth in my case is not stranger than fiction—but it may be more believable.
The last thing my mother, a devout Quaker, wanted me to do was to

*The spelling is the original.

go into the warfare of politics. I recall she once expressed the hope that I might become a missionary to our Quaker mission fields in Central America. But true to her Quaker tradition, she never tried to force me in the direction she herself might have preferred.[9]

What he described as legend was partly true and what he called truth was something of a distortion. Hannah Nixon has told us that she and her husband saw "from the first, that Richard was a gifted child," and insists it was his grandmother who wanted him to be a preacher. Hannah had her heart set on his becoming a musician like her brother. At seven she had him taking piano and violin lessons from Griffith Milhous, who taught music in a local boys' school.[10] When Richard was twelve, Hannah, dissatisfied with his progress, persuaded her sister Jane, who was also a music teacher, to let him live with her for five months. Jane Beeson, less impressed with his talent than his mother, and hoping perhaps to lessen her sister's burdens, took him to Lindsay. There he learned to play Chopin's "Rustle of Spring," and won a prize in the family for practicing longer hours than her son Alden. When Nixon was president, he took his aunt Jane to hear pianist André Watts. She said tartly, "If thee had practiced more on the piano, thee could be down there now on the stage instead of up here."[11]

Although Nixon practiced well into high school, it is clear that the choice of his profession, and indeed the whole direction of his life, was decisively set by his father and not his mother. At age seven, when he trudged off to his music lesson, he was also astonishing his cousin Merle West by telling him why Warren Harding should be elected president.[12] Later, when Frank Nixon was enraged by the Teapot Dome scandal, which blackened the reputation of Harding and his aides, young Richard echoed his father's indignation. His mother remembered what he said and told it to reporters in 1952 and again in 1960:

One day in the house at Yorba Linda, when Richard was nine and the newspapers were full of stories about the infamous Teapot Dome lawyer-bribery scandals, Richard stood up against the door between the living room and kitchen and told me, "Mother when I get big, I'm going to be a lawyer they can't bribe."[13]

Actually the Teapot Dome scandal was not exposed until early 1924, when Richard was eleven, not nine, and when he was living in Whittier, not Yorba Linda. If the mother's memory was fragile, the story was sturdy, and found its way into all the Nixon biographies.

In grammar school, Nixon, like many shy boys, relied on memorizing in order to shine. He learned the whole of the episode in *Tom Sawyer* where Tom slyly beguiles Ben Rogers into painting his fence, and never forgot it. When Cyril Clemens, a Mark Twain kin, visited him as president, Nixon took pleasure in reciting it all, without error. Afterward, he said to Clemens, "Any boy who has read *Tom Sawyer* with enjoyment and appreciation . . . will not ever become a juvenile delinquent."[14]

He graduated as valedictorian from the East Whittier grammar school, another important "first" in his life. He had picked up a taste for debating—"Cows are better than horses"; "Insects are more beneficial than harmful"—and when he went on to high school he continued to debate, as well as entering speech contests that won him prize money. As a senior he took a part in Virgil's *Aeneid*, which won him his first girlfriend. As Ola Florence Welch, a pretty and popular senior, described it later,

Aeneas is a wanderer who comes to Carthage and falls in love with Queen Dido. At the end she throws herself on a bier. It was very romantic. We all wore white gowns. After that we started going together.

But it was an uneasy courtship. "He'd be harsh and I'd cry and then we'd make up," she said. Another classmate remembered, "He did not know how to be personable or sexy with girls. He didn't seem to have a sense of fun." "He was smart and set apart," Ola Welch, later Mrs. Gail Jobe, told a *Life* reporter. "I think he felt unsure of himself deep down."[15]

The failure to be "sexy" may well have been the most anguishing in his adolescence. But the only high school failure that he mentioned publicly as rankling him was his losing the election for student-body president.[16] All his school triumphs up to that point had come when he spoke from memory, or argued from a carefully prepared text, or acted in a play—when he was, in effect, someone other than himself. When it came to the test of group affection he failed.

Some former students remember him as prickly and aloof, others as aggressive and argumentative. Mildred Jackson Johns remembers that some of the high school students "hated him." "He didn't care whose feet he trampled on," she said, and "to get his point across he wouldn't hesitate to twist the truth. Kids in school would tell me how he would elbow his way right through to anything he wanted."[17] His debate coach, Mrs. Clifford Vincent, was disturbed by his ability "to slide round an argument, instead of meeting it head-on."[18] Nixon noted with chagrin that the winning student-body president had been "an athlete and personality boy."[19] This may have been one more reason why, despite his small size, he took up football.

Every aspect of Nixon's adolescence and youth was complicated by the Nixon Market. The gas station built in 1922 had flourished, and Frank Nixon had expanded it by buying an abandoned Quaker church across the street and transforming it into a large country grocery store. Richard, in charge of the fruit and vegetable counter, drove twelve miles every morning at 4 A.M. into the big Los Angeles market. He learned to be a sharp trader, but hated the washing and sorting. "I never drive by a vegetable stand," he said later, "without feeling sorry for the guy who picks out the rotten apples."[20]

Had it not been for the presence of oil derricks in the area, stimulating fantasies of riches, the Nixon family might have found more contentment on the corner of Whittier Boulevard and Leffingwell Road. But profits in the Nixon Market were all measured in pennies. Compared with the sometimes-barren cupboard of the Yorba Linda house, the store was a treasure house of canned food, candy, meat, fruit, clothes, and toys. But every item was marked to be sold for profit. The unsold and overripe fruit was carried to the kitchen where the thrifty Hannah, and later Frank, rose at dawn to bake it into pies.

To give out food no longer represented an act of affection or charity; food was something to be exchanged for cash or credit. It became difficult for Richard to think of food except in these terms. His mother remembered that at church picnics, to which the Nixon family contributed generously, "he used to say people took home, from left overs, more food than they had brought with them in the first place."[21] Moreover, since one or two in the family had to serve in the store at all times, the Nixons almost never sat down together to eat except on Sunday. The family dinner, which can be an occasion for communication, humor, and benediction, consisted often of a pot of stew on the kitchen stove. To eat on the run became a family virtue. Nixon accepted the discipline and carried it into his presidency with some pride. "Unless I have a guest," he said in 1971, "I eat breakfast alone in 5 minutes, never have guests for lunch—I do that in 5 minutes too. I perhaps put more time in, in a day, than any President."[22]

The market became a prison from which young Nixon escaped only by going to school or by delivering groceries or by playing football. The customer had to be cultivated, ingratiated, treated with courtesy even if despised. Richard refused to wear an apron in the store and learned to escape by retiring to the mezzanine to keep the books.[23] Sometimes he simply fled. His cousin Floyd Wildermuth said that Dick would hide out: "I remember one time, when they had a pumphouse back there with a bed . . . and we caught him under the bed with a book."

There were lighter moments, the cousin said. Harold, the practical joker, was fascinated by radio, and once rigged up a microphone system so that Dick could speak or play the piano in the living room and the voice and music would carry into the store as if coming from a radio station. "We made a little radio program all our own and fooled the customers."

Wildermuth tells us that Frank Nixon "was very much against foul words. Whenever one of the boys would get caught saying a bad word . . . they'd say . . . 'that's what Floyd says,' and I'd get the blame." Years later the cousin visited Nixon in Washington.

He sat there in the Vice-President's office, at a big desk. . . . He just let himself go. I'm telling you! All those foul words that I taught him when he was young. . . . I think he let them all out there.[24]

In the Nixon Market Richard felt the envy that every small-town grocer feels when he serves people in want. "I know what unemployment does to somebody," he said as president. "I have seen an unemployed man come into my father's store. I have seen the look in his children's eyes when he can't pay that bill."[25] By the coming of the depression the Nixons had a grocery store, two cars, and were sending their sons to college. As Jessamyn West has noted, "by some they were considered rich." Merle West remembers being with Richard when he bought his first car, in 1930 or 1931: "It was a Ford Model A Cabriolet, used, which cost $350 or $400."[26]

A yearly list of purchases can be a key to family weaknesses and even secrets. Frank would joke about the men who bought great quantities of fruit extract, known to be rich in alcohol. He grumbled about the men who gave significant sums in charity to the Quaker church but who left their grocery bills unpaid. Richard, poring over the books, found a whole new private world into which he could peer without having to ask anyone's permission.

Many who bought at the Nixon Market describe Hannah as a charitable and giving woman. She would slip extra food into the sacks of families where she felt the children were going hungry. But Frank, one niece said, was known to be a man whom "nobody got the best of."[27] The family doctor, I. N. Kraushaar, described how "when a siege of rain meant the Mexicans on Leffingwell Ranch would run out of food," Frank would "put on his big boots, shoulder a sack of beans and walk down the road and on to the grove where they had their houses, and see that they had some food." But "this was just the normal way of doing business; it wasn't charity."[28] Like many compulsive workers, Frank blamed the unemployed for their idleness and not the malfunctions of society. Still, as the depression deepened and massive unemployment crept into the area, he kept many families from real want simply by continuing to extend them credit. Old Whittier residents remember this with gratitude.

Richard graduated from Whittier High School with good grades, and won the Harvard Club prize as the best all-around student. But there was insufficient money to send him to Harvard, and in any case his grandfather had left a scholarship for the education of his grandchildren at Whittier College. Plans for freedom, for taking the Santa Fe Railroad on that fantasy journey of his childhood, continued to be aborted. No one better than he knew that much of his family's money was going to the unemployed, and resentment over this stayed with him, reflected in his railings against "welfare cheaters" in countless political speeches. It is true that as president he said he remembered "the look in the eyes" of those who could not pay their bills in the Nixon Market and talked as one who truly cared. But he could be betrayed by a slip of the tongue, saying "well-fed children" when he meant to say "welfare children" in his State of the Union message in 1971.[29]

Nixon told Bela Kornitzer in 1958, "The problems you have during the time you are growing up as a member of a working family are the ones that stay with you all of your life."[30] The grocery store brought him the secret envy and hatred of the poor, but it did not give him the status of his grandfather Milhous as a member of the "landed gentry," or the wild affluence of the oil millionaires. Nixon, like Andrew Johnson, who suffered humiliation all his public life over the fact that he had once been a "plebeian tailor," could never be proud of being the son of a grocer. He ran into the worldwide prejudice against "the man who keeps his thumb on the scales" in Moscow, in the kitchen debate with Nikita Khrushchev. The Soviet leader, Nixon said, "kept making references to me as a smart lawyer with the innuendo that I was a slick and dishonest manipulator of words in contrast with his own 'honest' background as a miner and worker." When he defended himself by describing how he had worked in his father's store, Khrushchev, "with a wave of his arms snorted, 'Oh, all shopkeepers are thieves.' "[31]

In the Nixon Market Hannah had been intent that every sack of potatoes or other vegetables have a few more ounces than the weight listed on the label. Of the scores of old Whittier residents who have been interviewed, none accuses the Nixons of cheating. But there were subtle problems all the same. The store shelves, piled with fruit, candy, and cigarettes in particular, represented temptation to the customers as well as to the Nixon sons. Merle West still remembers his annoyance at seeing little Eddie Nixon, greatly spoiled he thought, "stuffing himself" with cookies in the store.[32]

Once Hannah discovered that one of their best customers was putting high-priced items under her coat. "She was a respected woman, a family woman," Don Nixon said. "We had grown up with her two children." Hannah consulted a policeman, who promised to arrest her if she were caught, but he would not promise to suppress any publicity. In a family conference Richard argued, "Let's drop the whole thing. You can't let them arrest her. You know what it will do to those boys to learn that their mother is a thief. Work it out some other way."

Don said the policeman was in the store when his mother confronted the shoplifter, but Hannah stated that she followed her to her car, told her "to look under her coat, and then ran back into the store." The next morning, she said, the woman came by, weeping, and offered to pay a little each month, begging that it all be kept secret from her husband. "It took months and months, but eventually she paid us every cent. Richard *was* right."[33]

Preoccupation with shoplifting stayed with Nixon, and it infected an astonishing number of his jokes as president. To the visiting members of the League of Women Voters in the White House in 1969 he said, "You can stay and look around—and coffee—but don't take anything else, please." When the Daughters of the American Revolution were being shown through the family quarters as a special favor in 1974, he said lightly, "I wish that we could give each of you a little memento . . . but there are a few too many, I think, scheduled for the tour. Just don't take anything that is nailed down."[34] On his visit to Peking, when he was leaving the great museum, he joked with the guide, "You ought to search everybody now to make sure they don't have anything in their pockets."[35]

When he was showing some French newspapermen around the Oval Office, he pointed to the flags, saying, "These are the flags of the services. Incidentally, that is all the President takes with him, unless he steals something, but that he doesn't do."[36] Later, in showing a group of state legislators the State Dining Room, he singled out an inscription on the fireplace. "It's about John Adams," he said, "and it might be interesting to read it because most of you who are here perhaps don't get on the guided tours, and when you are . . . they usually keep people away from anything they can pick up and carry away." After the expected laughter, Nixon read the inscription, John Adams's famous prayer: "May none but honest and wise men ever rule under this roof."[37]

Lincoln, too, had had experience with a small-town grocery store. He went bankrupt in New Salem where he had spent a good deal of his time studying law. His humor became celebrated for its richness and variety, and for the skill with which he translated ancient jokes into political parables. But he did not tell jokes about petty thievery. Honest Abe seldom talked about honesty, certainly not to proclaim his own.

Nixon's preoccupation with thievery, surfacing as it did even in the presidency in jokes that were embarrassingly unfunny, suggests that all through these adolescent years he never resolved the problem of what was rightfully his in the store. Was all of it his, or none of it? Was he entitled to eat what he wanted, without permission, as a reward for all his washing and sorting? For all the petty humiliations inflicted on him by disgruntled customers, for the necessity of being nice to everyone, especially those whom he knew bought foolishly and could not pay, and for being yelled at by his father, no matter how hard he worked? In any case, when Nixon finally became president, he found it impossible to distinguish between what was "mine and thine" in the presidential store. His problem with entitlement—"My father owns it, therefore I am entitled to it," translated into "I have been elected president, therefore I am entitled to it"—had never properly been resolved when he was very young.

Death and Two Brothers

If we were to accuse X of having killed his mother, his two broth-
ers, and five friends, X and his allies would shout back, "That's
a lie! X never hurt a hair of his old mother's head and he only
wounded one *brother. Foul and unfair!" The counterattack*
would be on, with attention diverted from the five friends and
the other brother whom X had, indeed, actually killed.[1]

WHEN RICHARD NIXON WROTE *Six Crises,* he did not
include the deaths of his two brothers among the great crises of
his life. The only reference to brothers dying is the extraordinary
fantasy, quoted above, which he wrote in discussing Communist
tactics. Arthur died somewhat mysteriously when Richard was
twelve, and Harold died after a five-year fight against tuberculosis
in 1933 when Richard was twenty. Although he mentioned the
deaths of small boys, or older brothers of small boys, in a surprising number of speeches—including his defense of the death penalty—he has told us almost nothing about the compelling
tragedies of his youth. Except for a poignant high school essay,
"My Brother, Arthur M. Nixon,"[2] we have only memory fragments.

When David Abrahamsen said that Richard Nixon had "a
basic inability to express and give love and to receive it,"[3] he
missed seeing Nixon's love for the small boy who died in 1925. At
seventeen Richard wrote:

We have a picture in our home which money could not buy. It is
not a picture for which great art collectors would offer thousands of
dollars. . . .

The first thing we notice, perhaps, is that this particular boy has
unusually beautiful eyes, black eyes which seem to sparkle with hidden
fire and to beckon us to come on some secret journey which will carry us

to the land of make-believe . . . money could not buy that picture, for it
was the last one ever taken of my brother Arthur.[4]

In his final speech in the White House on August 9, 1974—
one day before the forty-ninth anniversary of Arthur's death—
Nixon returned to the theme of pictures that money cannot buy:

This isn't the finest house. Many in Europe, particularly and in China,
Asia, have paintings of great, great value. . . .

And he went on to talk about death and the many failures of his
mother to prevent it: "I think of her, two boys dying of tuberculosis, nursing four others in order that she could take care of my
older brother for 3 years in Arizona, and seeing each of them die,
and when they died, it was like one of her own."[5]

But did Arthur die of tuberculosis? Richard Gardner, the first
to interview Nixon for a major biography, wrote in 1952:

Little Arthur was playing in the school yard when another boy threw a
rock and hit him in the head. He was taken home with a fatal concussion.
As the child lay dying, he called his mother to his bedside and asked her
to pray for him. Dick remembered this tragic occasion vividly, and later
declared that he was glad he had a mother who taught him how to pray.[6]

When Nixon at age seventeen wrote of his brother's death he
said nothing of the rock throwing. He described his return from
Lindsay and remembered Arthur's solemnly kissing him on the
cheek. Then he said, "After our return home nothing eventful
happened until mid-summer."

Arthur then became slightly ill; just a case of indigestion, we thought.
But a week went by and his condition became worse instead of better.
He began to become sleepy; he did not want to eat; he wanted to rest
and sleep. Several doctors came to see him but none could see what his
trouble was. Finally, my father sent me with my younger brother to the
home of an aunt who lived nearby, fearing that we too would become ill.
One night my aunt awakened us and told us to get dressed. Arthur was
a little worse, she had said. We were bundled into the car, it happened
to be a Ford again, and were carried home. My father met us with tears
in his eyes. He did not need to tell us what we knew had happened. . . .

Two days before my brother's death, he called my mother into the
room. He put his arms around her and said that he wanted to pray
before he went to sleep. Then, with closed eyes, he repeated that age-
old child's prayer which ends with those simple yet beautiful words:

'If I should die before I awake, I pray Thee, Lord, my soul to take. . . ."

And so when I am tired and worried, and am almost ready to quit trying to live as I should, I look up and see the picture of a little boy with sparkling eyes and curly hair; I remember the childlike prayer; I pray that it may prove true for me as it did for my brother Arthur.[7]

The official death notice, signed by Dr. H. P. Wilson on August 11, 1925, listed the cause as "encephalitis or tubercular meningitis," which suggests an uncertain diagnosis. It stated further that Arthur had been ill for one month, that there had been a blood and spinal test, but no autopsy.[8] "Encephalitis" at this time for many Americans meant "sleeping sickness"—*encephalitis lethargica*—a mysterious illness which reached epidemic proportions in Europe and America between the end of World War I and 1926, after which it virtually disappeared. The cause is now believed to have been related to the wartime influenza virus.

Hannah Nixon told Kornitzer her son died of "sleeping sickness." Edith Gibbons Nunes, daughter of Nixon's aunt Mattie Gibbons, a professional nurse who helped care for the dying boy, insisted that "nobody will ever know how Arthur really died." "It was noised about at the time," she said, "that the blow from the rock brought on meningitis." Nixon's aunt Olive remembered the rock throwing, noted that "the family always said it was meningitis," and believed there may have been a connection. Floyd Wildermuth, a cousin, has said that the family "would never say exactly what it was he died of." Jessamyn West never heard of the rock throwing at all. Family friends Edith Brannon and Harry Schuyler thought the cause of death was a "brain tumor," and Virginia Shaw Critchfield remembered it as leukemia.[9]

Nixon at seventeen wrote that the doctors did not know the cause; in 1951 he told Richard Gardner death came from the rock; in 1968 he said the cause was "tubercular meningitis," in 1974 "tuberculosis," and in 1978 "tubercular encephalitis."[10] When Nixon's historian, Frank Gannon, helping with the writing of the memoirs in San Clemente, was asked to clarify this confusion by consulting the former president, he replied ambiguously, taking care not to quote Nixon directly:

I had not heard about the rock-throwing incident you describe. As you know, there is a lot of apocrypha about concerning the early years of

President Nixon's life. I am confident that if the rock-throwing story is in fact true, it did not produce a fatal concussion and it had nothing to do with Arthur's death which was from tubercular meningitis, following a period of sickliness and headaches. The story of Arthur's dying prayer is, however, true.[11]

Since the symptoms of a severe brain concussion, "sleeping sickness," and tubercular meningitis are not dissimilar, the confusion on the part of the doctors and Arthur's kin is not surprising, especially since the results of the spinal test in 1925 had made the diagnosis uncertain. There was tuberculosis on both sides of the Nixon family; his grandmother Nixon and two aunts had died of it. And it was known that an "ambulatory lunger," one with an unknown but arrested case, could infect others.[12] Tuberculosis in 1925 was one of the ten great killers, and the dry desert and mountainous area east of Los Angeles was dotted with sanatoria. If Richard at twelve pondered the question "Who killed my little brother?" he had no easy answers.

In his memoirs Nixon wrote that he cried every day for weeks after Arthur's death.[13] It must have been in secret, for his mother said that he "sat staring into space, silent and dry-eyed in the undemonstrative way in which, because of his choked deep feeling, he was always to face tragedy. I think it was Arthur's passing that first stirred within Richard a determination to help make up for our loss by making us very proud of him. Now his need to succeed became even stronger."[14]

Dr. Rita Rogers, studying children's reactions to the death of brothers and sisters, has written that often the surviving child believes his parents want him to substitute for the dead child, and this results in an acute identity problem, especially if the parents subtly convey that he can never be as good as the child who has died. Another "will try to adapt, to become extra successful and develop a more marked identity of his own." Occasionally a child who unconsciously feels himself to blame will reconstruct the circumstances in altered form in later life.[15] It is of more than passing interest to note that Nixon faced stone throwing as vice-president and president, and would appall his Secret Service men either by failing to take cover or by seeming to invite the abuse.[16]

Hannah sought solace in the Quaker church, which had held a prayer meeting for the dying child. "It is difficult at times to understand the ways of our Lord," she told one neighbor, "but we know that there is a plan and the best happens for each individual." Death is a testing, she said.[17]

Nixon tells us his father thought Arthur's death was a sign of God's displeasure and that he thereafter closed his service station on Sundays. Neighbors report that he now became extremely religious, to the point of being a fanatic. One Whittier Quaker remembers him in church "waving his arms and saying, 'We must have a reawakening! We've got to have a revival! We've got to get the people back to God!' "[18]

California Quakers were already unorthodox and evangelistic. They did not have regular silent services and often hired pastors. There had been occasional revivals with conversion experiences in Hannah Nixon's childhood.[19] But Frank Nixon had always found the Quaker church too restrained and had taken his sons into Los Angeles to hear evangelists Paul Rader, Aimee Semple McPherson, and Bob Shuler, who brought their congregations to the prayer bench in joyous and noisy displays of confession and rebirth.[20]

Nixon remembered Paul Rader especially, and described the occasion in a Billy Graham rally in 1962. "We joined hundreds of others that night in making our personal commitments to Christ and to Christian service."[21] Although he professed to be a Quaker, and even a pacifist, all through his presidency he was captured by the techniques of evangelism, if not also by the spirit, and seems to have embraced the old religion of his father with greater satisfaction than the quiet Quaker "inner light." He found a special comradeship with Billy Graham. Each admired the professionalism of the other, Nixon in bringing voters to the polling booth, and Graham in bringing souls to God.[22]

Harold Nixon, although the sickliest of the four sons, had grown up into a happy, ebullient, popular youth. He wrote poetry, and preferred the bull sessions in the clubhouse he fashioned in his father's barn, or playing tennis on the dirt court scraped out nearby, to the demanding work in the Nixon Market and hours of studying. Nixon tells us that his "biggest thrill" in these years was to see the light in his father's eyes when he brought home a good report card. When Harold brought home "C" grades, Frank was enraged, but he blamed the school rather than his son. After Arthur's death Frank became increasingly convinced that Harold's school friends were corrupting him, and complained that the high school principal was "a secret smoker."[23] To Hannah's consternation he sent Richard to Fullerton High, in the adjoining district, and he sent Harold across the continent.

For his favorite son Frank Nixon selected the Mount Herman School for Boys, a "Bible School" in Massachusetts founded by the evangelist Dwight Moody. There was much scripture reading and instruction in how to prepare for the Second Coming of Christ, as well as conventional high school learning. There were also cold showers every morning at 5:30 A.M., and students sometimes arrived in the dining hall for breakfast with icicles in their hair. Harold came home in the spring of 1927 with a raging case of tuberculosis.[24]

Hannah, remembering that Arthur had said to her before his death, "I wish you had another baby, so you would be home and wouldn't stay in the store," now fled from the store, and from her home, taking Harold to live with her in a guest house at the home of H. W. Smith, who lived in Hacienda Heights, which was more elevated than Whittier and presumably had more sunshine.[25] Later Harold went alone, briefly, to the Hillcrest Sanitarium in the nearby mountains. It was expensive and it did not cure him. Meanwhile, anxiety about infection and the terrifying fear that Harold might die quickly clouded every aspect of the Nixon family life. When Richard contracted undulant fever, probably from drinking unpasteurized milk, he was not in danger of dying. But Hannah, seeing his temperature reach 104 degrees every day for a week before subsiding, said, "My prayers were answered; it was a miracle."[26]

It was Harold, however, and not Richard, to whom Hannah now dedicated herself. She learned of a tubercular colony in Prescott, Arizona, with an extremely dry, sunny climate. There was a veterans' hospital at nearby Fort Whipple, full of men who had been gassed in World War I and who had afterward contracted tuberculosis. Dr. John Flynn ran a famous clinic there. In 1928 Frank Nixon drove his wife and ailing son across the four-hundred-mile-wide desert, only to learn that Flynn's was a "fatcat lunger clinic" with fees he found prohibitive. But Hannah, insistent, rented a small cabin for twenty-five dollars a month and took in three other tubercular patients, youths like her son, certain that she could manage the expenses by herself. Flynn prescribed bed rest on screened outdoor sleeping porches, a nourishing diet, and freedom from anxiety. Hannah believed that only she could keep Harold content and on his back. Frank had to manage the store with Richard and Don, now fifteen and thirteen, aided by Milhous relatives.

Did Hannah have no fears about infection for herself? Did she blame her husband for sending Harold into the New England winter? Had she come to find life with Frank intolerable? None of these questions can be answered, perhaps not even by Richard Nixon himself. He has said little save that his mother stayed in Prescott three years, and that while survival without her was not easy it brought a certain independence.

. . . My father in effect took care of all of us. He did the cooking, we all helped out and then in the summertime we would go over to Prescott, Arizona, to visit my mother and oldest brother. It was a rather difficult time actually from the standpoint of the family being pulled apart. But looking back I don't think that we were any the worse off for it. You shared the diversity and you grew stronger and took care of yourself. Not having your mother to lean on we all grew up rather fast in those years, those of us who remained home.

Now our store and service station, in which we all worked six days a week . . . was doing rather well. . . . But then this illness really ate into the income.[27]

Later he said, "It was, from a financial standpoint, a disaster." In the five years before Harold died, he remembered, "my mother never bought a new dress."[28]

For two school years—1928/29 and 1929/30—Richard rode the school bus into Fullerton save for brief periods when he lived with his father's relatives, Walter Nixon and the Wildermuths, who felt pity for the stricken family. School acquaintances said that he did not socialize or date, although he did play in the school orchestra and take part in school debates. His grades, which had been excellent in grammar school, now declined.

Periodically Frank loaded his car with food and made the eight-hundred-mile round trip on a weekend. "In our old car it took us 15 or 16 hours to get there," Nixon remembered. "It was no joyride."[29] In the summertime, when the Mohave Desert was 120 degrees in the sun, nobody in his senses tried to drive save at night. Even at midnight the bleak hills and flayed canyon walls radiated the accumulated heat of the day like a blast furnace. In the winter and spring one could see occasional scarlet and yellow cactus flowers glowing in the lower desert, and in the upper Arizona desert the apple green grass stretched in limitless expanses toward the wilder blue mountains. Clumps of cottonwood poplars surrounded the small ranch houses; long metal troughs filled with water in the corrals served the Texas Longhorn and Hereford cattle which came in from the open range to drink. This was not Quaker California but the authentic Old West. The road from Indio to Prescott climbed up to five thousand feet, arriving finally in an expanse of real forest—drought-resistant cedars—stretching out to the north and east.

Prescott, set aside by Abraham Lincoln as capital of the Arizona Territory, was now in a decline. Miners were working the last of the gold tailings and the cattle ranchers were in trouble from overgrazing the fragile desert. Cowboys still gathered in the Palace Bar, what had been one of the biggest saloons in the West, with a mirrored backdrop that had been brought in the nineties around Cape Horn. Although these were prohibition days, bootleg whiskey—made in the surrounding hills—was always available behind closed doors, and poker parlors, also outlawed, were open to the initiated twenty-four hours a day. "The best cat house was the Rex Arms," Budge Ruffner, Prescott resident and historian of the Southwest, remembers. "It's now a bank," he jokes, "and the interest rates are higher."[30]

For one week every summer Prescott had a big rodeo and festival variously called Pioneer Days or Frontier Days, with a concession area labeled "The Slippery Gulch Carnival," organized by professional gambler Ralph Stolough. At Slippery Gulch most of the accumulated sinning that went on behind closed doors came out into the open—bingo, poker tables, slot machines, wheels of fortune, roulette. "Strictly speaking it was all illegal," Ruffner says. "But it was a community effort. No imported B-girls were brought in."[31]

Spending the summer in Prescott for Richard Nixon meant moving into a small cabin with his mother and three young men who were coughing blood. But it also meant escape from the store, escape from his father, who had become increasingly despondent and tyrannical, and escape from the Quaker community with its four meetings at church every Sunday. Since there was no Quaker church in Prescott, he would for the first time in his life have his Sundays free. But where *old* Prescott spelled freedom and sin and the true West, Pinecrest, the lunger community on the edge of town, segregated from old Prescott by invisible barriers of caste and fear, spelled death. The Prescott Chamber of Commerce, anxious to capitalize on the perfect climate for tubercular patients, but afraid also of contamination, had offered free building lots in a carefully defined area where centuries before a volcano had spewed out black lava among the pink boulders. It was scenic and private with a generous scattering of cedar trees. But it had become a kind of leper colony. "I hate to say it," Verna Hough describes it today, "but TB was sort of like leprosy. You had to learn to live with it. It was infectious, not contagious."[32]

"I would never read a continued story," recalls Jessie Lynch Brandt, who lived across the street from Hannah and Harold Nixon, and who at eighteen had coughed and hemorrhaged and had had one lung collapse and still survived. "I saved all the stories to the end and then read them all. I could not bear to read a story thinking I might die before finding out how it all came out."[33]

Hannah Nixon's cabin had running water and a woodburning stove but at first no washing machine.[34] Harold and the three other tubercular youths slept outside on the sleeping porch even in winter, although an occasional snowstorm in January covered their bedspreads with a fine film of white. Those who could not afford consultations with Dr. Flynn taught each other. Hannah learned how to sterilize dishes and how to boil the sheets daily in water heated on the old wood stove. She emptied bedpans and disposed of the sputum cups. Bob Haldeman wrote of Nixon, "He never let us forget his mother had to scrub bedpans."[35]

The lungers lived on streets named after Indians—Apache, Cochise, Mojave, and Yavapai. More men than women were victims of TB and their wives and mothers carried groceries on their hips a full mile from the local store. Many scrubbed sheets on a board and used outdoor toilets. "We were too tired every night to think about recreation," one woman remembers. The radio was the only solace.

Sometimes whole families came to Pinecrest, but usually only mothers and children. All supported each other with stories of survival and lived daily with the denial of death. "There was a spirit of kindliness and unity then," Verna Hough remembers. "I think we had a goodness about our lives that we don't have now." Husbands slept with infected wives and wives with infected husbands. But greater care was taken with the children. "Mother never hugged us and got close, never kissed us," Virginia Green Williams remembers. And death was not inevitable. Patients in the Veteran's Hospital lived into their eighties.

The young tuberculars lived in pajamas and bathrobes, but nevertheless sought each other out and signaled at night with flashlights. Sometimes they fell in love. Jessie Lynch, bedridden at eighteen, remembers, "Harold Nixon had a crush on me and I had a crush on Larry Easton, who lived with them. There was a lot of jealousy." She describes Hannah as "austere, cranky, and straitlaced." "Harold was always writing notes to me and she didn't approve. She scared me to death." Jessie's younger sister Rose recollected, "She looked at me askance, thought I was a little devil." Virginia Green Williams described Harold as "rather plump, very jolly and lots of fun to know. He adored teasing us. He would tease his mother by putting his thermometer in hot water and pretending the temperature was his own."[36]

Harold was in love with the special intensity of the tubercular victim. Furiously jealous as he listened to Larry Easton talking daily to Jessie Lynch on the telephone, he crawled into the attic and, knowing something about electricity, wiretapped the phone. He listened to the young couple confess their affection and repeated the conversation to Jessie the next day. The story got out in Pinecrest and was not forgotten. "Harold was clever with tools and knew how to tap phones," Marshall Clough, Jr., said in 1976. "He'd have been good for the Watergate boys."[37]

Jessie and Larry were married and had a baby daughter, which was taken away at birth and not returned until she was three months old. Even then Jessie's father would not permit his daughter to live with her husband, and the youth died later in a sanatorium.

Richard came into this close-knit community of the dying an outsider, only to find himself, as at home, in his older brother's shadow. "Harold was flip and full of fun," Helen Rose Lynch remembered. "But Richard had no wit. He didn't dance. He would hang from the tree and talk about history and things that bored me to death." Verna Hough remembered him as self-centered and aloof, and said he seemed to want to keep his distance not only from his infected brother but from everyone.[38]

But when he went into old Prescott Richard found independence and excitement. He worked for a time doing "stoop labor" in the fields at twenty-five cents an hour; hating it, he got a job doing janitorial work in the local country club. Prescott, even then, was a summer spa for the Phoenix rich, who came north to the cedar forest to escape the debilitating heat. Richard saw firsthand how the very rich lived, but he saw it as the swimming pool boy swabbing out the locker rooms.

The best of Prescott, if we are to believe the attention paid it by the early biographers, was Slippery Gulch, where Richard was a barker for three successive summers. The pay varied from fifty cents to one dollar an hour, and Dick's "Wheel of Fortune," according to Richard Gardner, who interviewed Nixon, made more money in one week than any other concession.[39] Marshall Clough, Jr., who was in the carnival one summer himself, insists that Dick never gambled, but Budge Ruffner, who remembers Nixon as "a hustler" at many different concession booths, holds that Nixon "got his elementary education in gambling and poker at Slippery Gulch." His poker playing in the navy, he said, was Nixon's "postgraduate course."[40] How much he hid from his mother can only be guessed at. Henry Spalding wrote somewhat obliquely, "It was a strange and mystical game they played, Hannah and her son. She must have known how Richard was earning his wages, but she said nothing. When he brought her his pay, she lovingly patted his cheek—and they both thought of Harold, who was visibly sinking."[41]

Marshall Clough, Jr., is also certain that Nixon did not drink in Prescott, which is likely since these were prohibition years and he was underage.[42] But he picked up the bootlegging lore of the day and years later compared notes with Budge Ruffner at an election dinner. Bootlegging jokes found their way into his repertoire of humor. To his pharmacist cousin, Lyall Sutton, he said in 1956 in Whittier, "How can you make a living in a small business without bootlegging or running a bookie?"[43] As president he joked about the bootlegger who had been caught storing his whiskey in the White House bushes. "I've been looking in those bushes ever since," he said, "and there is nothing there."[44]

After two years of separation Frank Nixon brought his wife home in an unexpected and decisive fashion. Her sister Olive has described Hannah's chagrin at being caught pregnant with "a trailer" at forty-five, and remembers Frank blustering, "The doctor doesn't know what he's talking about." A new baby could not be exposed in a lunger cabin and Hannah came home to give birth to Edward in May 1930 in the Whittier Hospital. How Richard Nixon felt about the pregnancy, providing evidence as it did of the continuing sexual vitality of his parents, we do not know. Abrahamsen guessed that the essay Richard wrote about Arthur for school may well have been stimulated by the coming of the new baby, and that his resentment at how his parents had tried to bring Arthur up as a girl reflected Richard's own concern at the time "with how to be a man."[45]

When Edward was born his father was "really disappointed," Nixon tells us, because he was "hoping so much that he would be a girl." But he has said little of his youngest brother otherwise in public save that his mother thought he was "the smartest of us all."[46]

After Edward's birth Harold came home for brief periods and when his condition worsened he would return to Prescott. His father built him a cabin, and he was nursed and fed by Marshall Clough's wife for sixty dollars a month. Hannah Nixon went back to Prescott in 1931 and tried unsuccessfully to buy the lunger cabin she had rented on Apache Street. In 1932 she returned with Edward and once again took in two tubercular youths to help with expenses. For a time Don was in bed in Prescott, threatened with tuberculosis.

Edith Brannon remembered that when Hannah Nixon was away in Prescott, "the family couldn't get along without her here, and when she was here Harold thought he just couldn't stand to have her away. I don't know how she survived being torn like that." When Richard developed a sinus infection that would not disappear, his mother insisted on his coming to Prescott for a third summer with orders to rest. By this time, according to his girlfriend, Ola Welch, he had become fatalistic about contracting TB himself. "He thought he might get it too," she said.[47]

By now Frank was in such financial straits that he had to sell an acre of ground adjoining his store. Harold felt guilty about not paying his way. "He hated being idle," Marshall Clough, Jr., remembered, and described how he insisted on helping roll heavy foundation stones into place for the chicken houses they built. Merle West remembers his struggling up the slight incline to the service station in Whittier, coughing into his sputum cup. Despite his illness, Jessamyn West said, Harold "got himself engaged to a girl. He told Merle that if he was going to die he might as well have a fling. He was much more of a swinger with the girls than Richard. He was taller, more outgoing, more of a man."

Some of Harold's friends and kin insist that the youth invited death. "He was a headstrong, devil-may-care Irishman," one said, "who at every turn did the opposite of what his doctor and parents told him to do." He would haunt the local airport, indifferent to the deadly exhaust fumes, and in 1933 he took a job fumigating citrus groves. "Very dangerous work. People died."[48]

Seeing him much worse, his alarmed parents prepared the car for a return to Prescott, but he would not go. Floyd Wildermuth remembers begging him to make the trip: "He just flatly refused." Frank rented a house trailer and took him to the Mojave Desert, but after three days he had a hemorrhage and had to return. "I can still remember his voice," Nixon wrote, "when he described the beauty of the wild flowers in the foothills and the striking sight of snow in the mountains."[49]

On March 5, the day before his mother's birthday, he and his brothers pooled their savings to buy her an electric mixer. Harold insisted on driving into Los Angeles with Richard to help select it. When they returned, he said, "I think I'll lie down for a while before I tell Mom about her present." He died the next morning at 9 A.M. "That night," Nixon said, "I got the cake mixer out and gave it to my mother and said it was Harold's gift to her."[50]

Jessamyn West, who had herself been hospitalized with severe hemorrhaging from tuberculosis, tells of Frank Nixon's coming with her father to visit her. "Why is it," Frank said, "that only the best and finest of the flock has to be taken?" Jessamyn was expected to die too.[51] Years later Frank Nixon wrote a letter to the *Ohio State Journal* asking support for his son for the vice-presidency, composing it as if all his sons were still alive: "This boy is one of the five that I raised, and they are the finest in the United States."[52]

At Harold's death, his mother said, Richard "sank into a deep, impenetrable silence. From that time on, it seemed that he was trying to be *three* sons in one, striving even harder than before to make up to his father and me for our loss."[53]

Harold's death had come after five years of alternating expectations for his recovery and preparation for his dying. Periodically the family had been buoyed up by hope of "bringing Harold home," cured and robust. Abrahamsen has suggested that the deaths of Harold and Arthur made Richard's unconscious fear of death "uncommonly strong."[54] One may point out, however, that Richard had invited infection by going to Prescott for three summers, living first with four tubercular patients and later with three. He had not run away from death, but had in a sense invited it. And death had not touched him. Could he not, then, after Harold's death, point to his own record—the near accident at age two, the battered skull at three, pneumonia at four, undulant fever at eleven, and intermittent exposure to tuberculosis for five years at least—and conclude with some exhilaration that survival, not death, was his destiny? But if this happened, was there not an accompanying dread, however buried, that he must inevitably pay a terrible price for not having died? Or for having wished his older brother dead? Such death wishes are always present, especially where the illness is prolonged.

Robert J. Lifton, who has done much research on survival guilt, finds that many survivors suffer from "a psychic numbing," a diminished capacity for experience, whether of joy or grief. They fear they have survived *"because* someone else died, or that they have 'killed' the other person in some symbolic way by failing to sustain the other's life with needed support, help, and nurturance."[55] This may have been a factor in numbing Nixon's already warped capacity for elation, especially seen in his election victories. In a more profound fashion it may have deadened his general sensitivity and self-understanding, and contributed to the sense of meaninglessness and unfulfillment in his own life.

The hint that Harold had willed his own death could only have added to Richard's confusion and guilt. Albert C. Cain, in his study of survivors of suicide, has noted that the survivors can suffer from "a pervasive sense of complicity," and sees "massive insistent use of denial and repression, tangled webs of evasions . . . deliberate lies," and "concealment and anxiety-clouded confusion of memory."[56] Moreover, if Richard felt that with Harold's death he must become "all *three* sons in one," then the confusion in identity, the necessity of adopting a multiplicity of roles, was a further burden. It was impossible for this lonely youth, clumsy with his body, to transform himself into an outgoing, genial, joke-cracking darling of the girls, nimble with tools and a writer of poetry.

In any family constellation disturbed by death there are forbidden questions. We have seen that Don Nixon said of his father, "He worked us kids to death."[57] Why then should not a just God have taken the tyrannical father and spared the favorite son? Why should the old, the tough, the punishing, survive? Why also should the least loved of the sons survive?

A further complication in the pattern of guilt was that all the money being spent to save Harold's life could now be spent on Richard and Donald's education. Richard was doing well at Whittier College. But Donald was doing badly at Whittier High and his parents, certain that private eastern schools were superior to public schools in the West, talked of sending him to a Quaker preparatory school in North Carolina. When Richard won a tuition fellowship to Duke University Law School, his parents managed to find enough money to send both sons "back East," the land of promise.[58] Thus the brightest, the most studious, the most hardworking of the sons was rewarded by no greater financial favors than Donald, who cheerfully called himself "The dumbbell in the family."[59] And both were expected to repay their father.

Still, since it was Harold's death that made escape from Whittier possible, one wonders if Richard Nixon came to believe death to be his ally. If so, this would be reinforced when death struck down his greatest rival, Jack Kennedy, by psychopath Lee Harvey Oswald. Death cut down Robert Kennedy in 1968 and later eliminated Edward Kennedy as a rival with the tragic drowning at Chappaquiddick. Over and again Nixon would see the young, the heroic, and the innocent die, and the unheroic, the unloved, and the sometimes villainous survive. When Jules Witcover questioned him about his feelings when John Kennedy was killed, Nixon replied, "I think it would not have happened to me."[60]

Death also made Richard the first instead of the second son. And after his winning the fellowship to Duke—which his mother said pleased her more than any of his later victories—the family hopes finally centered on "the gifted child." Donald would never be a rival and Eddie, the menopause baby, was for years a family pet.

We know that delight in being "first" instead of "second" got into many of Nixon's speeches, although this might well have happened without any deaths in his family. But items about deaths of brothers also found their way into his speeches. During his vicepresidency, he had just returned from a tour of the Far East and was writing a speech to be delivered the next night to the nation, when he was informed that his father had nearly died of a gastric hemorrhage on an airplane going to California. In making his speech, which was mostly about the evils of Communism in China, he told a story having to do with the death of a brother:

I talked to a farmer . . . who told me how he, his wife and two small children had walked for a hundred miles through the mainland of China until they arrived at the border. . . . The reason was that his only brother was blind. . . . He couldn't produce as much as the Communists required. . . . The Communists took him away and shot him.[61]

As president he made many speeches demanding stiff mandatory sentences for drug pushers, often quoting from letters he had received. In 1972 he said:

I received a heart-rending letter from a teenage boy in the Midwest. He told me in his letter how his brother, a college student of exceptional promise, after slipping deeper and deeper into drug experimentation, had gone off into the woods with a gun one day, completely without warning, and had taken his own life.[62]

He told Golda Meir he had been taught as a child to oppose capital punishment.[63] Yet he became a staunch defender, and when the Supreme Court seemed to strike it down in 1973 he went before the nation to urge its restoration by Congress. Again he quoted from letters he had received about ill and dying sons. There was a five-year-old boy hospitalized with poisoning by LSD; there was an eighteen-year-old drug addict writing for help because his fourteen-year-old brother had begun to use drugs; there was a California youth—actually his cousin's son—"who could not end his drug habit, and so ended his life."[64]

In March 1974 he described telephoning an eight-year-old Florida boy who was dying of leukemia.[65] Later that summer, visiting the Khatyn Memorial outside Minsk, in the Soviet Union—built to commemorate the destruction of a Russian village by the Nazis—he stood for a very long time looking at the huge bronze statue of the village blacksmith carrying his fifteen-year-old dead

son in his arms. In his address to the Soviet people he described
it as "one of the most moving memorials I have ever seen." "As I
laid the wreath," he said, "I thought of the people of Khatyn, and
I thought especially of the children. . . ."[66]

The story that had moved him most, however, was about a
girl, and it had to do specifically with survival. When in 1972 he
visited the Leningrad cemetery where the three hundred thousand who died during the great siege in World War II are buried,
he was shown a picture of a twelve-year-old girl and pages from
her diary. He quoted from this diary in a speech in Leningrad
and again in Moscow. He quoted it a third time in the United
States, on August 24, 1972, in accepting the presidential nomination for a second term:

In the simple words of a child she wrote of the deaths of members of
her family. Zhena in December. Grannie in January. Then Leka. Then
Uncle Vasya. Then Uncle Lyosha. Then Mamma in May. And finally—
these were the last words in her diary: "All are dead. Only Tanya is left."

In his memoirs he repeated the story, adding, "Tanya died
too."[67]*

*As Jonathan Schell has noted, when Nixon was speaking in Moscow in 1972, pleading
that "all the children of the world can live their full lives together in friendship and peace,"
the heaviest bombing campaign in the history of warfare was being carried out in Vietnam
by American planes (Schell, *The Time of Illusion*, p. 251).

VIII

Presidential Fever

If I can paraphrase the Biblical injunction: the second shall be first.

— RICHARD NIXON, JUNE 16, 1969[1]

THE SAME YEARS that saw Harold Nixon sinking into death saw his brother transformed from a lonely, self-pitying adolescent into a competitive college student, seemingly self-possessed, confident, popular. By March 1933 when Harold died, Richard had been elected president of the freshman class, president of his fraternity, president of the History Club, and was campaigning against what he called "political dictators" to become president of the student body.[2] Much of this transformation had come from internal discipline and not from Dale Carnegie's *How to Win Friends and Influence People*, which he read later and to which he paid some homage. As president, remembering these years, he counselled Spiro Agnew: "You have got to make love to the people. It's always been a very difficult thing for me to do."[3]

The youth who disliked dancing presented as a major plank in his campaign for student-body president the right of students to dance on campus. The boy who would not wear a shirt to school unless it was freshly starched now helped to organize a new fraternity where the badge of membership was an open shirt without a tie. The fastidious child who could not stand the smell of the unwashed students on the high school bus had become a scrimmager on the football field, and had won fame by being the first in the college's history to add to the annual bonfire an outdoor privy with four rather than two holes. The brother who had isolated himself at family and church picnics was now an aggressive campaigner seeking evidence of public affection by soliciting votes.

One can see the yearning for contact, the hunger for abandon, a delight in the freedom finally to be dirty. Paul Smith, Nixon's history teacher and mentor, saw a frenetic quality in his involvements. "He was always in a hurry to get to the next whatever-it-was. There was a sense of motion about him. . . . always checking in and checking out."[4]

Despite rising daily at 4 A.M. to buy and prepare the fruit and vegetables for the family store while carrying a full academic load at Whittier College, he entered debate and speech contests as well as student elections. He was a member of the Student Council and the glee club, and an actor in five school plays. He remained "a punching bag" on the football squad for four years. Everywhere, as Paul Smith said, "He was out to win."

Was there a link between his brother Harold's hopeless contest with death and his own seeking out antagonist after antagonist in the competitive play of the college? Erik Erikson has written that the ritualization of play makes it possible for people to experience "alternations of symbolic doom and triumph," which if accepted in real life could mean absolute dominance or absolute defeat. In games, he says, the winning side enjoys "unambiguous victory without usurpation and clear-cut defeat without annihilation."[5] One thing Richard Nixon could not do after his elder brother contracted tuberculosis was to challenge him, since the threat of death had removed him as the natural antagonist. But he did challenge scores of other brothers, seeking in games to defeat his opponents "without annihilation." It was a way of saying, "I will be first and you will be second, but you will not be dead." His brother died shortly before his election as student-body president.

This special fraternal involvement, ending in death, may have been, as we have already suggested, one reason why Richard Nixon never found victory to bring the joy he had expected. In *Six Crises* he wrote:

A man will look forward to the end of the battle. He thinks, "Just as soon as this is over, I'll feel great." But except for a brief period of exhilaration if the fight ended in victory, he will then begin to feel the full effects of what he has been through. He may even be physically sore and mentally depressed.[6]

Jessamyn West sees similarities between the lives of Kennedy and Nixon, since both moved ahead when death claimed a handsome older brother who had been the parental favorite. But John

Kennedy never tried to step into his brother's shoes till after his death in World War II, and then only with reluctance. "I never would have run for office if he had lived," Kennedy said.[7] Nixon, however, was trying to be "all three sons in one" even before Harold died. His need to be first, so obsessive a preoccupation at Whittier College, diminished when Nixon was at Duke University after Harold did die. Later he would embrace a more dangerous object than winning—the *irreparable* destruction of an opponent.

At Whittier College along with his pattern of running to win there was also, as is common on campuses, an accompanying pattern of affectionate involvement with brothers—in the fraternity and on the football field—where obedience and not dominance was paramount. Something of what he learned in the politics of team playing would carry over into the gaming of his politics. Episodes involving trickery, in debate and in football rallies, were kept secret from the faculty, and some did not surface until after his resignation from the presidency.

Nixon was not a "straight A" student, but grading was tough at Whittier and he graduated second in his class, with Regina Kemp nosing him out as valedictorian.[8] His lowest grades were "C"s in journalism and news writing, which may have given him his first dislike for newspapers.

Nixon's reputation of being champion college debater, which has been much exaggerated, was established by his early biographers, who took his word without checking the facts that were readily available in the Whittier College *Acropolis*. Kornitzer said that he won all his sophomore debates on a trip to the Pacific Northwest. Actually he won seven and lost three. Mazo said that as a sophomore he participated in fifty debates, winning "the bulk of them." Neither mentions the debate tour of his junior year which was a disaster. He and his colleague won only one debate, this with Arizona State Teachers College, and lost to Nevada University, Brigham Young University, and Phoenix College. A misunderstanding caused cancellation of their debate with Stanford and a blizzard prevented their going to three other colleges.[9] Weldon Taylor, who debated against Nixon at Brigham Young University, remembers him as "very smooth and polished," but not as well prepared as his own team on the subject of the cancellation of inter-Allied war debts.[10]

Some Whittier students observed, but did not talk openly until later, of his ruthlessness and trickery. To his debate colleagues he would offer advice: "Pour it on at this point," or "Save your ammunition," or "Play to the judges; they're the ones who decide."[11] Yet he would "beat us down," his colleague William Hornaday remembered, when they were competing on the home campus. "He would always come up with something. . . . Always using the ace in the hole."[12] "A few times when I debated with him," Ken-

FRESHMAN YEAR	Eng. Comp. and Lit.	B	Journalism	C
	European History	B	Mathematics	B
	Elementary French	A	French	B
	College Algebra	B	Physical Ed.	B
	Public Speaking and			
	Debate	B		
SOPHOMORE YEAR	Economics	B	Am. Constitution	B
	News writing	C	Int'l. Relations	
	English and Am.		and Int'l. Law	A
	Civ.	A	Physical Ed.	A
	Interm. French	C		
JUNIOR YEAR	French	B	Philosophy of	
	French review	B	English Lit.	A
	Am. History	A	Shakespeare	A
	Greek and Roman		Dramatics	A
	History	A	Football	A
			Track	C
SENIOR YEAR	Hist. of Lit.	B	Glee Club	A
	Government	A	Track (withdrew)	
	French Survey	B	Football	A

These grades were first published by William Flynn in the *Boston Globe*, later in the *Kansas City Star*, November 2, 1955, p. 43.

neth Ball said, "he would come out suddenly, extemporaneously with some ideas I had not heard of before when we were going over the material for the debate."[13] Lois Elliott caught him pretending to be reading figures from a paper that had nothing on it at all. "I was editor on the school paper covering the debate . . . in the spring of 1933," she said. "I sat in the gallery and I saw when Nixon spoke in his rebuttal that he quoted from a blank paper. I told it later to my roommate; it was against all regulations, and very cunning. I remember it well."[14] But she did not report him.

His professors failed to see evidence of either ruthlessness or trickery. "Richard was a high-minded boy," his drama coach, Albert Upton, said in 1959. "Nixon was not a goody-goody. . . . he just didn't do bad things. He apparently didn't even want to."[15]

Although Nixon, like all debaters, did his research to win rather than to seek out truth, he did become a convinced partisan on some of the issues. In his memoirs he wrote that he became a thorough believer in free trade and also in the ending of reparations as essential to European recovery.[16] Although he debated on increasing the powers of the president, and in the process gathered considerable data on the current depression and the New Deal, he remained an inflexible Republican. "I thought Roosevelt was wonderful," his girlfriend, Ola Welch, remembered, "and he detested him."

Nixon's delight was not in solutions but in a place on the platform. "Nixon is a rather quiet chap about campus," the *Quaker Campus* reported, "but get him on a platform with a pitcher of water and a table to pound on and he will orate for hours."[17] This would not change. William Rogers, one of his few good friends during his early years in Washington, noted that while Nixon was "likely to maintain a serous, almost brooding countenance in a company of three or four persons, he lights up like a Christmas tree when confronted with a crowd."[18]

In Whittier College he sought applause as though it were a substitute for love, and the student vote fed this special hunger. Students cheerfully voted for him to be president of everything in sight; he worked, spoke with confidence, and seemed a natural leader. His obsessive busyness fooled almost everyone into thinking he had multitudes of friends. Ola Welch, his girlfriend, realized only in retrospect that he had almost none.[19]

But the successful debates, the speaking contests, and above all the votes fueled the lonely young Nixon's fantasies. Chance comments that he would one day be president of the United States he took more seriously than anyone realized. Ola Welch recalled, "Never in my wildest dreams did I ever picture him then as President of the United States." But she added, "I knew he'd be famous, but I thought he'd be Chief Justice of the Supreme Court."[20] Nixon said that his mother never took him on her knee to say, "You son, are going to be President someday."[21] But his uncle, Jessamyn West's father, told several people in those early years that of all the youths he knew Dick Nixon had the greatest potential to lead the nation. And the Quaker pastor, Harley Moore, echoed it.[22] This was heady stuff for a youth who had yet to be tested in the big leagues.

Only three out of fifteen presidents thus far elected in the twentieth century—Theodore Roosevelt, William Taft, and John Kennedy—have come from big cities. Nixon's multiple successes at Whittier College, unlikely had he attended Harvard, gave him the confidence to work at making these fantasies come true. In *Six Crises*, writing of the Great American Legend—how a boy becomes president—he described the youth who is "tapped for greatness," who "reads a thousand words a minute," who is "bored by school because he is so much smarter than his teachers." He prepares himself for leadership, Nixon wrote, "by taking courses in public speaking and political science. He drives ever upward, calculating every step of the way until he reaches his and—less importantly—the nation's destiny [surely an odd wording] by becoming President of the United States." But Nixon denied that he was this youth. "I won my share of scholarships, and of speaking and debating prizes in school," he continued, "not because I was smarter but because I worked longer and harder than some of my more gifted colleagues."[23]

Here, as so often with Nixon, the denial is a clue to the truth about himself. He knew he was brighter than his brothers and his parents. He may well have thought himself brighter than his professors since he had been encouraged to measure himself by winning in verbal jousting rather than by enlarging his intellectual horizon or deepening his understanding of man or the universe. It was not until he went to law school that he found himself surrounded by men his own age as gifted and clever as himself.

At Whittier, as later, he had an ear for grievances and learned how to inflate a small grievance into a major campaign issue while ignoring more demanding problems. Nixon campaigned for more student-body "spirit," greater publicity for football games, better relations with the alumni, and the right of students to dance on campus. The last plank won him the election.

Nixon himself, despite his musical training, was an awkward dancer. Abrahamsen may be correct in his speculation that he was especially maladroit because he could not escape his mother's conviction that dancing was sin. He had no talent for innocent abandon.[24] His argument for the right to dance was wholesomely moral: it was better to dance in the clean and chaperoned environment of the campus than in the dives of Los Angeles. The trustees agreed with him and relaxed the old Quaker proscription. But Nixon was never comfortable on the dance floor, and as president danced only at his daughter Tricia's wedding.

His real abandonment came in playing football at Whittier College. His passion for the sport endeared him to many Americans, and his failure to make the team became his most repeated joke on himself. Football language crept into his political metaphors and football tactics affected his politics. Stewart Alsop called his "a football obsession." Over and again he would quote football coach Vince Lombardi, "Winning isn't everything; it's the *only* thing." Speaking to the Baseball All-Stars in 1969 as newly elected president of the United States he said, "I am always awed in the presence of those who made the team and are champions."[25]

Since he weighed only a hundred fifty to a hundred sixty pounds at Whittier College—"all bones and hair" one student said[26]—and was matched against some men over two hundred pounds, students were mystified that he stayed with football for four years. Clint Harris, tackle, said, "Why he went out for four years is beyond me. I'd play opposite him in scrimmages, and we couldn't let up or the coach would be on us. So I'd have to knock the little guy for a loop. Oh, my gosh, did he take it."[27] He was never seriously injured; it was basketball, not football that cost him two front teeth.[28]

Nixon's father, eager to make a man out of his poorly coordinated, unathletic second son, frequently came to watch and instruct him in football practice.[29] The coach, "Chief" Wallace

Newman, was no less determined. Newman, an American Indian who had been All-American on the University of Southern California team, became the second most important man in Nixon's youth. He had no children of his own and treated many of his athletes like surrogate sons. Nixon saw him as a man very like his own father:

He was a hard driver. He was a great disciplinarian. There was no permissiveness. . . . no excuses for failure. . . . He said, "You know who a good loser is? It's somebody who hates to lose and who gets up and comes back and fights again." I think, perhaps, as I look back at those who shaped my own life—and there are a great deal of similarities between the game of football and the game of politics—that I learned a great deal from a football coach who not only taught his players how to win but who also taught them that when you lose you don't quit, that when you lose you fight harder the next time.[30]

"Chief" Newman, he said, taught him more about life than he did about football. "You must get angry," the coach told him, "terribly angry about losing. But the mark of the good loser is that he takes his anger out on himself and not on his victorious opponents or on his teammates."[31]

Newman gave Dick Nixon the license to be dirty, sweaty, and bloody, the license to get angry, to smash at bodies and be smashed at by other bodies, which had been denied him by his mother and by his own resentment against his yelling father. At football games he had at last the license to yell. At Duke University Dick's yelling at the games became a matter of comment among his friends: "He would be too hoarse to talk until the next day," Lyman Brownfield said.[32]

"Chief" Newman at Whittier took Nixon into that special world so intimately involved in the rites of manhood in America and taught him the rules. When after three years Nixon had still failed to "make the team," Newman coaxed him back for a fourth try. "You ought to come out," he said. "Really what is wrong is not losing. What is wrong is not making the team."[33] Thus Nixon remembered it in 1971. In 1972 he added further to the dual portrait of himself and the "Chief":

He was a great, great builder of men. He could take men who were not too talented in football and make stars out of them, except he couldn't do it with me. I never made the team. . . . I got into a few games after

they were hopelessly won or hopelessly lost, you know, when they put
the substitutes in, and finally the water boy, and then me.[34]

This melancholy reflection, calculated to bring a laugh, he made
at the dedication of a high school named after Dwight Eisenhower, the third paternal figure in his life.

Actually the occasions when he had been permitted to enter
the varsity games in the last minutes of play had not been humiliations. "I shall never forget the tremendous roar which went up
from the rooting section when Dick got into the lineup for the last
few minutes of a few games," one teammate remembered.[35] The
cheers were for the guts and tenacity of a Walter Mitty bench
warmer who wanted terribly to make a touchdown. The role was
not wholly comic; the applause was sweet.

Nixon comforted the injured on his team, and gave pep talks
to the discouraged. Once he gave a dinner party at his home for
his athlete friends, promising that for once they would have all
they wanted to eat. There were platters heaped with chicken, and
Hannah's pies. "Dick played the piano and we all sang," Wood
Glover remembered.[36]

Although Whittier College had strict rules for student conduct
concerning smoking, drinking, and profanity, there were pranks,
especially involving the main competitive event of the year, the
annual football game with nearby Occidental College. Nixon,
whether member of the Student Council or as president of the
student body, could be counted on to defend the prankster.
There was an uproar when Joe Gaudio and William Soeberg
painted "To Hell with OXY!" on the pillars and steps of the
chapel at Occidental. The paint penetrated the concrete and was
almost impossible to remove. The youths were threatened with
expulsion, and Whittier was almost tossed out of the football conference. "One of the most understanding people," Gaudio said,
"was Dick Nixon. He had appealed for the kind of thing we were
trying to do, albeit it cost a lot of money to rectify what he did.
. . . He was at the forefront of helping to mediate that thing."[37]

Nixon not only defended the pranksters, but devised and carried out a whole scenario of deception on his own. George Chisler
has described how Nixon "painted or had painted on the Whittier
College building the Occidental letters 'OXY' about three days
before the football game."

When the students came to school the next day they saw "Oxy" there, and they became indignant and got all emotional. And he organized a big bonfire rally, the team was there and Chief Newman gave a talk, and people were fired up for the game.[38]

He was not caught.

Nixon was once almost taken in by the police when he was caught rifling empty crates for one of the Whittier bonfires. Sandy Triggs described it:

Dick Nixon got this truck someplace and he and half a dozen of us were going down to Whittier after a second load of crates. The market's first load was already on the bonfire, and the police stopped us and had orders from the merchants or somebody to "Get those crates back! . . . or we're going to throw you in" and so we headed back with the crates.[39]

Later, however, participating with the football team in one of the irregular liberties which the members had come to take for granted—marching en masse into the local movie theater, the Roxy, without paying—he found himself in jail. Robert Halliday said:

We had gone several times. But this particular night . . . they had a new manager. . . . We just walked in, assuming everything was all right, and in a couple of minutes the lights came on, and the police came and got us and took us to jail for crashing the gate. It was very funny. Here was the student body president and most of the football team. . . .

"Nixon got the boys out of hock," Wood Glover said. Halliday reported that a telephone call to Judge Swain, "our benefactor . . . got us out about ten o'clock, so we really didn't spend much time there."[40]

Most of the members of the football team belonged to Nixon's own fraternity, the Orthogonians, which he had helped to found as a freshman. National fraternities were forbidden at Whittier, but a social club, the Franklins, founded originally as a literary society, had come to dominate the campus. "They were the haves and we were the have-nots," Nixon said. Generally the Franklins kept out the poor, the unwashed, and the physically strong. Dean Twiggs and Nixon organized the rival group, composed largely of athletes, which began as an underdog organization and even took into membership, in a conspicuous gesture of sportsman-

ship, athlete William Brock, who was black. Brock, who lived in
the dormitory, understood the courage of the gesture and later
defended Nixon against charges of racism.[41]

The name Orthogonian technically means right-angled or
upright, but the youths said it meant square or square-shooter,
and delighted in the label. As president, Nixon continued to take
pride in it, saying exultantly near the end of the 1972 campaign,
"Square America is coming back."[42] The Orthogonian creed
emphasized fair play, forthrightness, and honesty. Nixon wrote
in Marjorie Hildreth's college annual in 1934: "We honest Orthogonians is sure the best bunch of fellows in all the world, don't
you agree? Well, I appreciate your honesty anyway."[43]

The Orthogonian symbols were conspicuously masculine—an
open-neck shirt instead of the tuxedo (in which the Franklins
insisted on being photographed), and the "four Bs," a club motto
standing for "Beans, Brains, Brawn, and Bowels." The choice of
mascot of the wild boar led to the members' being derided as "the
big pigs."[44]* The Orthogonian battle cry was "Écrasons l'infame!"
Few besides Nixon and his French teacher knew that "Let us
crush the infamous!" had been Voltaire's cry against the Catholic
church. Nixon translated it as "Stamp out evil," and included it in
the Orthogonian song, for which he wrote the words:

> All hail the mighty boar
> Our patron beast is he
> Our aims forevermore
> In all our deeds must be
> To emulate his might
> His bravery and his fight. . . .
>
> Écrasons l'infame
> Our battle cry will be
> We'll fight for the right
> And win victory. . . .
>
> We'll fight our battles fair
> And always on the square
> Brothers together we'll travel on and on
> Worthy the name of Orthogonian.[45]

Nixon helped devise the secret initiation ceremonies. Although the Franklins made their initiations public—"marching

---

*"Beans have a double entendre related to Bowels," Bruce Mazlish has noted, in discussing
Nixon's "strong quality of anality" (Mazlish, *In Search of Nixon*, p. 101).

their pledges around in dresses," Dean Twiggs remembered—the Orthogonians went through "a very tough thing. Anybody who went through it was basically ready for World War II, or Vietnam, or Korea." In addition to the usual paddling, Herman Fink said, "They took us out and fed us a lot of spoiled meat, and stripped us off, and we ran around that way for awhile. They took us out blindfolded around midnight and dumped us off up in the hills, and we were to find our way home as best we could."[46]

The emphasis was definitely on exposure, and since Nixon was a charter member he did not have to suffer it but instead helped in the exposing. Joe Gaudio remembered "the man-to-man situation": "You would see in those closed affairs where Dick Nixon's attributes really had an opportunity to manifest themselves." Nixon, he thought "had a colossal sense of humor."[47]

As a freshman Nixon collaborated with a friend to write a skit which the Orthogonians put on before the student body. The scene opened in the men's dormitory with a youth pretending to be "Chief" Newman tucking the students into bed. Nixon impersonated his most formidable rival, Joe Sweeney, the school's best debater. The skit ended with one youth taking his clothes off behind an unsteady screen. As each article was flung over it, the students screamed louder. Finally it fell, and the youth was exposed—covered up—wearing a raincoat and carrying an opened umbrella.[48] This was Richard Nixon's first and so far as is known his last attempt at playwriting, save for what Pat Nixon called "the funny shows" he would improvise at parties during their courtship. "I will never forget one night when we did 'Beauty and the Beast,'" she said. "Dick was the Beast, and one of the other men was dressed up like Beauty. . . . It was all good clean fun, and we had loads of laughs."[49]

As a freshman Nixon was in Booth Tarkington's *The Trysting Place;* as a junior he appeared in John Drinkwater's *Bird in Hand* and in a one-act play; and as a senior he acted in *Philip Goes Forth.* The drama coach, Albert Upton, said, "He really loved the stage. . . . I could not think of him as a genius or as a boy destined for greatness . . . but I would not have been surprised if, after college, he had gone on to New York or Hollywood looking for a job as an actor." It was in *Bird in Hand,* where Nixon took the part of an old man whose daughter eloped with a scoundrel, that he relearned what had been largely destroyed in him as a child, the ability to cry. Upton did his best to teach him how to summon up a lump in his throat, but did not believe he could ever shed real tears until he watched the opening-night performance: "I saw his eyes brimming and then his cheeks were wet."

Thirteen years later, when Upton saw a picture of Nixon weeping on Sen. William Knowland's shoulder after Eisenhower had forgiven him in the "Checkers" crisis, Upton exclaimed, "That's my boy! That's my actor!"[50] Nixon had learned to cry, but only as an actor. As we have noted, he confessed to David Frost in 1977 that he could never cry except in public before an audience. When Frost asked him what he did when he was alone and sad, he replied, "I cry inside."

Many shy youngsters turn to acting, seeking for any identity other than the undesirable one they want to escape. Nixon in a play could easily give in to what he could not express offstage: love, or hate, or simple foolishness. The make-believe in these years was satisfying, even cathartic. But once he carried over into politics the techniques of the actor he ran the risk, as do all politicians, of playing false with reality, of substituting technique for truth. As Erik Erikson has said, "the delineation of prank from criminal deed, and of playacting from political act, is often difficult."[51]

In his public career Nixon hid his interest in acting. He did admit privately to Buff Chandler in 1960 that the reason he would run against Kennedy despite her opposition was that he'd "never been in the center stage, in the leading role. . . . And I'll never be satisfied until I'm in that role. No matter what anybody asks me to do."[52] He masked his preoccupation with television techniques, insisting that he never watched himself on TV. To Garry Wills he said, "Isn't that a hell of a thing—that the fate of a great country can depend on camera angles? I get so impatient with the whole process that I refuse to take coaching."[53] But Joe McGinnis in *The Selling of the President* unsparingly documented Nixon's professional interest in camera angles. And Nixon as president freely admitted to William Safire his dependence on the rules of make-believe:

You always have to make an entrance. You have to walk right in and take charge. A lot of politicians never learn that, they mosey in or kind of poke their heads in first—that's all wrong. You have to make sure the door is open, that they're ready for you, and you start striding out a few steps before you get to the doorway—then you sweep in like a leader, and they know you're there.

In discussing with Safire his 1968 acceptance speech he said:

They call me "intelligent, cool, with no sincerity"—and it kills them when I show 'em I know how people feel. I'd like to see Rocky or Romney or Lindsay do a moving thing like that "impossible dream" part, where I changed my voice. Reagan's an actor, but I'd like to see him do that.[54]

By 1972 the "pretension to honesty," the "disavowal of acting," as Richard Poirier pointed out, "had become his act."[55]

In 1934 Nixon graduated with a B.A. in history. What had he learned to prepare him for the presidency? Paul Smith, who had taught Nixon in a class on the Constitution, which consisted of an intensive analysis of the document itself, had given him a "B." In his formal history classes Smith did little icon-smashing.* His students read Samuel Eliot Morison and Henry Steele Commager's popular *Growth of the American Republic*. Smith introduced Darwin and Malthus in a filtered fashion by having students read Frederick J. Teggert's somewhat fusty *Theory and Processes of History*. The devout Quakers were certain to be shaken by Teggart's argument that human advancement throughout history had "to a marked degree been dependent upon war," and Nixon admitted that he lost most of his orthodoxy as a Quaker at Whittier College. Still he included in his memoirs what he wrote in a school essay in 1933, "I still believe that God is the creator, the first cause of all that exists. . . . that He lives today, in some form, directing the destinies of the cosmos."[56]

Hannah Nixon told one journalist that her son had read Voltaire, Rousseau, and other political philosophers of the French Revolution "mostly in the original French."[57] Nixon tells us that he spent all of one summer reading Tolstoy and that *Resurrection* was his favorite.[58] But he seems to have read only to forget. No

---

*Smith attributed Nixon's downfall in Watergate to "mental overload." He also said, "if he had just thrown all of the tapes out on the table, everything, no abridgment, and said to the American people that 'this was what we had said and this was what we had done—we shouldn't have done it, but we did' . . . the American people would have forgiven because that's an awful lot like the rest of us, you see" (interview with Janet Cramer, in *The Young Nixon: An Oral Inquiry* [California State University, Fullerton, Oral History Program, 1978], pp. 177, 181).

quotations from or references to Voltaire or Tolstoy found their way into his presidential papers. Rousseau he mentioned once, ridiculing his desire to "return to nature." "As we all know," he added, "man in his natural state is not a particularly admirable object."[59] As vice-president he did quote Tolstoy, and one wonders why this particular passage stuck in his memory as a youth. He used it in a speech criticizing governmental control:

Tolstoy had said, as I recall it, "I sit on a man's back choking him and making him carry me, and yet assure myself and others that I am very sorry for him and wish to ease his lot by all possible means—except by getting off his back."[60]

Like all presidents he would quote from other presidents, but he did not often mine the presidential archives for support for his own legislation. As Arthur Schlesinger, Jr., wrote wryly, "few presidents seem to have had such a limited acquaintance with the history of the Republic."[61] Still, Nixon was fascinated by the subject of the hero as president and had his own favorites. Anyone's hierarchy of heroes can be revealing. As Eric McKitrick has written, "the way you think about Thomas Jefferson largely determines how you will think about any number of other things." Nixon largely bypassed Jefferson. On entering the Oval Office he took what he thought was Woodrow Wilson's desk from the vice-president's office—it turned out later to be the desk of Henry Wilson, Grant's vice-president—and when asked about what Agnew would get for a replacement he said, "I think he has the Jefferson desk."[62] He did quote Jefferson numerous times in six years as president, but mostly used cliché fragments—"All men are created equal," "life, liberty, and the pursuit of happiness"—or garbled versions of other familiar statements. His favorite "Jefferson" quotation, which he repeated publicly many times, "We act not for ourselves alone but for all mankind," was not Jefferson's but a paraphrase of Thomas Paine's: "The cause of America is in a great measure the cause of all mankind."[63]

His quotations from Lincoln on the other hand were extremely personal. As a child Nixon had been given by his grandmother a picture of Lincoln which hung over his bed.

She virtually worshipped Lincoln. On my thirteenth birthday she gave me, in addition to a very welcome five-dollar bill, a picture of her idol.

Underneath written in her own hand, was the last part of Longfellow's
Psalm of Life. . . .

> Lives of great men oft remind us,
> We can make our lives sublime,
> And departing, leave behind us,
> Footprints on the sands of time.[64]

At Whittier College he read through the entire ten volumes of
Nicolay and Hay's monumental biography.

In his speeches as president he noted that Lincoln prayed in
silence, like himself, that he argued to win, also like himself, and
that he dismissed generals who would not follow up battle victories to win the war. In 1974, when he was reeling under the
impeachment threat, he said that no president had been more
vilified than Lincoln—implying, as many reporters noted—except
himself.[65] But Lincoln's compassion escaped Nixon, and the concept of forgiveness, implicit in Lincoln's whole life as well as in his
statements about Reconstruction near the end of the war, Nixon
rejected.

His approach to the presidents he admired most—Lincoln,
Theodore Roosevelt, and Woodrow Wilson—was not to ask "How
can I become like them?" but to say "How much like them I am
already!" Thus when Garry Wills asked him in 1960 about his
affinity with Theodore Roosevelt, he replied, "Not much in ideas,
I guess. I'm like him in one way only: I like to be in the arena."[66]
He admired Roosevelt's rise from an asthmatic child to boxer, big-
game hunter, and gladiator-president. He had a special feeling
for Roosevelt the soldier, for whom war had been the ultimate
test of masculinity. He would quote him occasionally as a conser-
vationist on specific measures he favored. But most of all he
admired a single Roosevelt quotation. After his defeat in 1960 he
gave copies of this passage to his staff and he quoted from it again
in his resignation speech in 1974:

It is not the critic who counts, not the one who points out how the strong
man stumbled. . . . The credit belongs to the man who is actually in the
arena, whose face is marred with sweat and dust and blood; who strives
valiantly . . . who, if he wins, knows the triumph of high achievement;
and who, if he fails, at least fails while daring greatly.[67]

It was Woodrow Wilson who became the major presidential
model in his life. "You ask if Teddy Roosevelt is my hero," he said

to Garry Wills in 1968. "Not in the sense that Wilson is. I think he was our greatest president of this century."[68] This interest had begun far back in his childhood. In the election of 1916 Hannah Nixon had defied her husband to vote for Wilson instead of Hughes. "When I told Mr. Nixon afterward," she said, "he just went pale and white."[69] Nixon, recalling this in a public speech in 1971, softened the parental discord:

The election was the background for my own interest in Woodrow Wilson. . . . My father and mother were both Republicans. California was the State, as you recall, that decided the election of 1916. The reason was that a number of Republicans voted for Wilson. My mother was one of them. She was a devout Quaker and a deeply dedicated pacifist.

I was only 3 years old in 1916, but for years afterward, in a friendly way, my mother and father sometimes spoke of that election of 1916 in which my father had voted for Hughes. But my mother, despite the fact that America did get into war after 1916, always had her faith in Woodrow Wilson. She used to say to me, 'He was a good man. He was a man who deeply believed in peace. . . .' He inspired her with his idealism, and she in turn passed on that idealism to me. . . . He died a broken man. . . . convinced he was a failure.[70]

Nixon told Jules Witcover that he admired Theodore Roosevelt as a man of action who could think, and Woodrow Wilson as a man of thought who could act. He told Garry Wills that Wilson "had the greatest vision of America's world role," but failed because he was not "practical enough." He hoped to combine Theodore Roosevelt's pragmatism with the idealism of Woodrow Wilson and bring lasting peace to a troubled world. Wills in *Nixon Agonistes* described in depth how Nixon went to Wilson for a theoretical justification for continuing the war in Vietnam, and how he transformed Wilson's concept, "We have no selfish ends to serve. . . . we desire no conquest or dominion," into a "doctrine of national selflessness," "a war of generosity."[71]

But more than anything else, it was to the mythical Wilson, the man without hate, that Nixon paid homage. He admired and quoted Wilson's statement "When we know one another we cannot hate one another."[72] He seems not to have learned, in college or later, that Wilson had been capable of great hatred, and that this quality had corroded his statesmanship and had contributed to the failure of the United States to join his League of Nations.[73] Nixon would always see Wilson through his mother's eyes, the idealist doomed by the hatred of others, the war leader "who in his heart was also a pacifist," and who died "a broken man."[74]

Nixon's own problems with hatred from others, of which we see only shadows at Whittier College, took a quantum leap once he entered politics. Hatred even spoiled something of his relationship with the college and eroded his pleasantest memories. In June 1954, when Whittier College honored him with a doctoral degree, two lines formed at the reception. As his mother noted with pain, in the second line stood those who did not want to shake her son's hand.[75]

The Monastic Years

He always kept himself in check.

— OLA FLORENCE WELCH JOBE, ON RICHARD NIXON[1]

WHEN RICHARD NIXON RECEIVED WORD of his fellowship at Duke University Law School, he drove to see Ola Florence Welch and beeped his horn outside her house, although—as she remembered—"mother was death against it." "Oh, we had fun that night. He was not only fun, he was joyous, abandoned—the only time I ever remember him that way."[2] The fellowship spelled escape from his parents, from the store, from all that was parochial and stultifying in Whittier. It meant, however, the end of a relationship with the only girl he had ever dated seriously, but which had become precarious.

Nixon had been going with Ola Welch for over four years, and assumed, as did their friends, that they would one day marry. But in their senior year at Whittier College both had started dating others. "He'd go out with other girls but would not tell me," she remembered, "and I'd find out about it. I'd go out, but he always knew."[3] It was in this year, 1933, that she began dating Gail Jobe, whom she married in 1936. But the breakup with Richard Nixon was slow and tortuous, not really final until the middle of his second year at Duke University. He wrote her lonely, sometimes desperate letters. "He sounded like he was close to quitting two or three times," she said.[4]

Ola was a small, brown-eyed girl with a turned-up nose who looked something like Nixon's mother as a young woman, although more beautiful and far more joyous. "I'm sure he would not have made it [to be president] if I had married him," she said. "I loved fun too much." They had met at a scholarship party in Whittier High School, and later were in the same Latin class. The enthusiastic teacher, in an ill-fated gesture to commemorate the

2000th anniversary of Virgil's birth, decided to put on a performance of *Aeneid,* and selected them to play the leading roles.

"We had absolutely no coaching," Ola remembered, "and the students had little idea of what was going on. At one point there was supposed to be a dramatic embrace. We had never practiced it. When we came to do it, it was very awkward, and the kids went to pieces. I just about died."[5]

Nixon in his memoirs said the embrace of Aeneas and Dido evoked "catcalls, whistles, and uproarious laughter." "It was my first experience in dramatics, and it is amazing that it was not my last."[6] Afterward, Ola said, neither of them could ever mention it to each other.

Once Nixon became famous, Ola Jobe was often interviewed, but remained reticent, determined to retain the privacy of her memories. To Lloyd Shearer she did say, "I don't know why in retrospect I found Richard Nixon so fascinating. I am not counting out sex appeal, which as a subject, believe me, we didn't discuss in those days. . . . I considered myself provincial and him worldly." Of his letters she would say only, "There was nothing mushy. He always held himself in check."[7] "We were very puritanical," she said to me. "There was no hanky-panky."[8]

To Dr. David Abrahamsen she admitted that she considered him "a shy boyfriend." Abrahamsen speculated in his *Nixon vs. Nixon* that the youth "was afraid of both men and women and had a great deal of passivity in him," writing that "he only wanted to *play the role* of dating. He *acted* as if he loved her but he was never emotionally involved. He did not really understand what feelings were all about. It is possible that he loved her as much as he was capable of loving anyone."[9] When asked about her response to Abrahamsen's book, Ola Welch Jobe said that his theories were "exaggerated," but conceded that Nixon "may have been playacting." Although she has insisted that that they did have "good times" together, she has also admitted, "I think I never really knew him."[10]

"We'd have marvelous arguments and talks," she told Lael Morgan. "We used to argue politics constantly."[11] But political argument by itself is poor nourishment for passion. Argument is a testing of each other and can be a barrier. It was what Dick Nixon had seen at home and what he seemed to think was masculine behavior.

Still, she recognized that beneath all the intellectual aggressiveness he was "lonely and solemn." "He didn't know how to mix," she said. "He would never double date. He had no real boy friends. And he didn't like my girl friends. He would stalk out of the room where they were, his head high."[12]

They never discussed each other's parents. Frank and Hannah Nixon were friendly to Ola, whose cheerful charm made her a favorite everywhere. But Ola's parents were dismayed by Dick Nixon. "My mother disliked him from the beginning," she said. "I don't quite know why." The Welchs were good Democrats, which made politics a barrier. "But what really made my mother mad," she said, "was the night he took me to a prom and we had a fight. He went home and I had to call my folks to come and get me."

When Ola, not surprisingly, chose to go to the Senior Prom with Gail Jobe, Nixon was shaken. He asked Marjorie Hildreth to go instead, and later wrote in her college annual, "Forgive all my nervous fits, and thank you for your soothing words."[13]

Nixon's favorite cousin, Edith Gibbons Nunes, who was extremely fond of him, said later, "I don't know why they broke up. I know what he told me was the reason, but I didn't believe it. It just burned out. Ola was a damn strong woman."[14]

Of the "burning out" Ola Jobe has said little save that after Nixon became student-body president at Whittier College she felt that he wanted to be "free and swinging." "For the first time," she said, "I began to feel that I wasn't good enough for him."[15] Their friends saw it differently. "Gail Jobe took her right away," Jewell Twiggs said. "I think Dick was not a ladies' man in that day. He wasn't the type that was queening all the girls. . . . He wasn't sexy." Thus the description that had been pinned on him in high school followed him, to be echoed by others, even his aunt Olive, who said, "he never was a ladies' man at all."[16]

Nevertheless, when he was at Duke University Nixon continued to consider Ola "his girl," and on his first visit home was enraged when he called her to find out that she was with Gail Jobe. "If I never see you again it will be too soon," he said. Still, when he went back to Duke, he kept on writing.

Looking at the six-year relationship one must agree with Dr. Abrahamsen, who saw Nixon as sexually passive and lacking in a strong masculine identity. Although most young men fear revealing their tenderest feelings, and many, including men who became president, like Jefferson, have been abandoned by a first love only to move on to a passionate and rewarding marriage, there was conspicuous failure here. At no time in her many interviews did Ola Welch Jobe intimate that Dick Nixon was either sexually aggressive or understanding and tender, although it may be that evidence to that effect can be seen in his letters, which she still keeps private. Although reluctant to talk about Nixon as president, she has stated that she and her husband turned against him in the Voorhis campaign, and followed his career from then on with dismay. "You can't blame Watergate on his early poverty," she said. "We were all poor."[17]

At Duke University Nixon chose to lead a monastic life of great austerity. According to his roommates he did not date any girl for the entire three years. There are divergent stories, and Nixon's own accounts differ, about where and how he lived, but all suggest a fanatical frugality. Mr. R. Blackman, a maintenance man for Duke University, told reporter William Flynn that Nixon first moved into an abandoned toolshed in a heavily wooded area near the campus. He discovered him there, studying, in the eight-by twelve-foot shed, lined with corrugated cardboard for warmth. There was a bed but no stove. "He told me his name was Nixon," Blackman said.

"You mean you're going to school and can't afford a room?" Blackman asked. "You'll freeze to death."

"I'll manage all right if you don't run me out," Nixon replied. Blackman thought, "This boy must want an education real bad." And he decided not to report him. Later he heard that "he eventually went to a farmhouse and got a room."[18]

In his memoirs Nixon wrote that in his first two years at Duke he lived "in a $5-a-month rented room."

. . . for my third year I joined three friends and moved into a small house in Duke Forest . . . a one-room clapboard shack without heat or inside plumbing, in which the four of us shared two large brass beds. . . . We called the place Whippoorwill Manor, and we had a great time there.[19]

In 1970 Nixon had told Edwin Hoyt that in his second year at Duke "he roomed with Carl W. Haley and two other divinity students who had taken a house." In 1972, however, he said publicly that he had roomed "for two years" with Bill Perdue, a law student.[20] Perdue, who shared Nixon's bed in Whippoorwill Manor, has said that in the final semester at law school he and Nixon moved into an apartment together.[21]

Whippoorwill Manor was cold in winter and the stove could not be stoked. Nixon, who rose two hours earlier than his friends to get to his library job, often dressed in the dark, his teeth chattering. In some ways it was like sharing a cabin at a boys' camp. The four youths closeted their clothes on campus where they also shaved and showered. All were able students. Lyman Brownfield was called "Brownie," Perdue was "Boop-Poop," and Nixon was "Nix" or "Gloomy Gus." The fourth, Frederick Albrink, has been described by Ethel Farley Hunter, one of the three women law students in the class, as "chunky in face and body, chunky also in personality."[22] Perdue, austere and reticent, when interviewed in 1976 described Nixon at Duke as "somewhat limited in humor," and "a very private person, in a one-to-one relationship as much as in a larger group."[23]*

Perdue was a Georgian and took some pains to educate Nixon about blacks and the Civil War. As president, when campaigning in Atlanta, Nixon acknowledged the impact:

I must admit, more than many recent American Presidents, I perhaps have a closer affinity to the South because of my education. I took my law at Duke University. . . . I learned some of the things I had thought were right when I got there might not be right. . . .

I was utterly convinced that Ulysses S. Grant was the best general produced on either side in the Civil War. After rooming for 2 years with Bill Perdue of Macon, Georgia, I found, and was almost convinced by Bill Perdue's constant hammering on it, that Ulysses S. Grant would be lucky to be about fourth behind Robert E. Lee, Joseph Johnson, and Stonewall Jackson.

It was Perdue who taught him to call the Civil War "The War Between the States."[24]

Perdue and Albrink both visited Nixon in California after his marriage, but saw little of him thereafter. All three roommates

*Perdue said to me in 1976, "I voted for Nixon both times. I'm not a strongly political person." On Watergate he said, "It's no worse than what other presidents have done . . . but it sure shocked the country. . . . In terms of violation of constitutional duties and concealment, I think Roosevelt did about as many bad things as Mr. Nixon did. . . . He did it concerning something we in retrospect have concluded was good."

remained his political supporters. Brownfield, interviewed by Stewart Alsop in 1959, was eager to dispel the image of Nixon as a "superficial, cardboard, calculating" character. He described their daily ride to lunch in his 1926 Packard, which he had bought for forty dollars and had christened "Corpus Juris":

Every day nine of us went to lunch at a boarding house run by a Mrs. Pierce, where she served all a person could eat for 25 cents. . . . Every time we collected in the car the group climbed on someone's back and din't let up until we reached the boarding house. Sometimes it was Nixon, sometimes it was someone else. In any event, Nixon was thoroughly at home in the horseplay and joined in both as subject and tormentor just like anybody else.[25]

In his first weeks at Duke, Nixon counted thirty-two Phi Beta Kappa keys, and confided his fears about the competition to an upperclassman. "Don't worry," William Adelson said, "You don't mind working hard. You've got an iron butt, and that's the secret of becoming a lawyer."[26] Stewart Alsop interviewed a dozen of Nixon's old classmates in 1958. Although many spoke of his prodigious capacity for work, and some mentioned his friendliness and general popularity, others used phrases that would continue to follow Nixon all his life: "He did not encourage comradeship"; "He kept pretty well to himself"; "He did not mix particularly"; "He was basically aloof, very sure of himself, and very careful to keep people from getting too close to him." One said, "I do not think he was popular in the class," and when asked about his winning the election as president of the Duke Bar Association, said, "It was a 'lonesome' kind of popularity." Bradley Morrah told Abrahamsen, "I always saw him as slightly paranoid for some reason. . . . Something of an oddball."[27]

Ethel Farley Hunter found him "dour and aloof, not given to fellowship." He never joined in the class's monthly beer party, as did Perdue and Albrink, and avoided even the coffee gatherings.

I found his value system unattractive. We disliked his "holier than thou" attitude. He was not unmoral, just amoral. He had no particular ethical system, no strong convictions. . . . He was there to learn skills and advance himself personally.

Once when she was playing Ping-Pong in the Bar Association room, Nixon was working nearby for Prof. Lon Fuller, mimeographing in his office. It was a hot day and all the doors were open. At one point Nixon stormed in and demanded that they close the door to block the game's noise. One of the students snapped, "Why don't you shut your own door?" "It would be too hot," he said.[28] They seem not to have seen, and Nixon could not communicate, his ineffable loneliness. But they could feel his rage.

Later, when Nixon was president, a *Washington Post* reporter noted that he frequently recalled how he earned his way through Duke, "working in a hot office, mimeographing." Did he remember the Ping-Pong episode when, in 1972, he welcomed the Chinese Ping-Pong team to Washington, D.C., to the cheering applause of press and TV commentators? The exchange of the Chinese and American teams presaged a diplomatic breakthrough, and led the way to Nixon's trip to China.[29]

Many of the law students were too poor to do much dating—over a third of the forty-five in the class were on fellowships—but Nixon seems to have wanted a moratorium on any kind of relationship with women. Not Perdue nor Albrink nor Edward Rubin remembered his writing to Ola Welch or even mentioning her name. When other youths were relaxing on weekends, he was studying in the library or working to earn extra money on a grant from Roosevelt's National Youth Administration. "I can't remember that he ever had a date," Perdue said. Richard Kiefer said he was "stiff and stilted when talking to girls, informal and relaxed with male students." Nixon himself said to Henry Spalding, "There were a few girls I liked and would have enjoyed dating, but I didn't have the money."[30]

He did find the money, however, for a trip to New York at Christmas in 1934. He went with friends in an old Chevrolet, and with his brother Donald, who had come from Greensboro, North Carolina, where he was going to school. They drove in heavy sleet through the night to save hotel expenses. In New York they purchased a gift for their mother. "They had saved a long time," Hannah said, "for a fur piece for me. It was my first."[31] Nixon also managed to save enough money to go home each summer, the first time by car, the second by train. These were his priorities.

Edward Rubin drove with him in the summer of 1935. On one of the endless expanses in the West they saw a woman hitchhiker. "I think if we had taken a vote Bill Branch and I would have been loath to pick her up," Rubin said. "We didn't know what the devil she was doing out there. But Richard was really pushing to help her. So we took her to where she was going." He remembered, too, having coffee at a small Mexican restaurant, where Nixon expressed compassion for the plight of the waitresses who worked only for tips. "These episodes stuck in my mind," Rubin said. After Nixon resigned from the presidency, Rubin wrote him a sympathetic letter. Nixon replied from San Clemente, saying that his years at Duke were the fondest memories of his life.[32]

Prof. Lon Fuller remembered Nixon at Duke as competent but "not terribly imaginative or profound. And he was what today we'd call uptight—there was the suggestion of an intellectual inferiority complex." David F. Cavers, Harvard Professor of Law, then teaching at Duke, said that he singled out Nixon along with two or three others because they were "active and able and wrote well."[33] With his help Nixon published two professional articles on campus in 1936. Both had echoes of accidents and tragedies in his own family. His "Changing Rules of Liability in Automobile Accident Litigation," as we have noted, paid attention to the old horse and buggy accident laws. Nixon did research, too, on the kind of accident his father had been involved in as motorman when his train hit an automobile at a crossing. He cited laws holding that the driver of the automobile must stop, not just look and listen, thus indirectly exonerating his father of the old accident.[34]

His second article, "Application of the Inherent Danger Doctrine to Servants of Negligent Independent Contractors,"[35] had to do with suits against contractors whose negligence had caused injury or death. None of the cases he cited involved fumigation of citrus groves. But the choice of subject suggests that he was still seeking an answer to the question "Who was really responsible for the death of my eldest brother?" He seems also to have been researching the question "Could we have sued to collect damages for his dying?"

Classmates at Whittier College had called Nixon "progressive." At Duke his friends described him as "a liberal" who admired Brandeis, Cardozo, and Stone on the Supreme Court. But Nixon did not agree with the ardent New Deal sentiments of Douglas Maggs, who had worked in Franklin Roosevelt's Department of Labor. "Nixon was among the first to stand up to Maggs,"

Lyman Brownfield said. "This was not easy, and for the first couple of months I think all who did so felt a little like Christian
martyrs facing the lions."[36]

Certainly at Duke some of the ruthlessness and arrogance that
students had complained about at Whittier vanished. Nixon had
one friend, Jack Anderson reported, "a crippled, dwarf-like student whom he met every day and carried up the stairs he could
not manage in his wheelchair."[37] "He was shot full of rectitude,"
Fred Albrink said. "Some of us might fudge on the hours we
worked at the library. Nixon never would. . . . He was industrious,
reverent, all of that. . . . None of us were overly obscene. The
worst we ever said was 'Get the lead out of your butt,' things like
that." Richard Kiefer said if Nixon used "damn" or "hell" it surprised them, and that he never drank. He did, however, drink at
the Senior Beer Bust, enough to improve his coordination and
loosen his tongue. His friends were astonished to see him catch a
baseball in one hand while holding a mug of beer in the other.
Lyman Brownfield watched him mount a table and deliver a
speech on "insecurity" that convulsed the onlookers. "He managed to get everything about Social Security so tangled up back-
wards that he sounded like Red Skelton." But he could never be
persuaded to be "the funny man" again.[38]

If Nixon had fantasies at Duke about going into politics he
kept them from his friends. "It just never entered our minds,"
Albrink said, "that he would make a career in politics." His winning the presidency of the Duke Bar Association over Hale
McGowan—later a Supreme Court Justice in Nebraska—they
thought to be a matter of establishing a reputation for scholarship, not popularity. One classmate told Stewart Alsop he would
have described Nixon "as the man least likely to succeed in politics."[39]

All his ambition seemed to be directed at being first in his class
rather than second, as at Whittier, where he had been denied the
valedictory spot by a woman. Perdue and Brownfield had nosed
him out for the first and second place in the first year. No one
knew who was first in the class till the dean released the grades,
and when the posting of grades at the end of the second year was
late, the competitive classmates became restless. As Nixon told it
to Kornitzer, he, together with Perdue and Albrink, "decided on
action":

Since Richard was the thinnest of the three, he was given the precarious assignment of entering the Dean's office through the transom for an informal look at the grades. The mission was accomplished with such finesse that years passed before the exploit became known on the campus.

Nixon told Edwin P. Hoyt much the same story. "The others," Hoyt wrote, "hoisted the skinny Nixon through the transom of the locked office, he moved with the finesse of a cat burglar, got what they wanted—a good look—and got out, and were never captured."[40]

In 1970 Albrink said that it was Perdue who was "boosted through a transom, found a key and located the records." After Watergate, when the episode was revived and described widely as Nixon's "first breaking and entering," Albrink held to his story about the transom, but included Nixon in "the entering":

We were working one night in the summer, and going past the Dean's office in June, 1936, someone said, "Well, the grades must be there now." We tried the door, noticed that the transom was open. Nixon and I boosted Perdue through the transom. He then opened the door. We found the files with the grades and looked at them. . . . didn't take any. . . . didn't change any. This was night; there was nobody in the building. What the heck!

Perdue did not remember the incident at all. He said in 1976:

I don't know. I'm not uncooperative. I know what the story says. I have no reason to deny the story. . . . I simply don't remember the incident. I'm sure I was there. . . . Albrink has a memory of this.[41]

Would there have been automatic expulsion had they been caught? Prof. David Cavers, questioned on this, said, "No, we would not have thought it a horrendous thing."[42] But they were not caught. One is reminded of this incident in reading Bob Haldeman's *The Ends of Power.* He reported how the young presidential lawyer John Dean was explaining to Nixon the difficulties of getting to the tax files of certain Democrats. The president responded, "There are ways to do it. Goddamit, sneak in in the middle of the night."[43]

Class standing was crucial in getting a job in a good New York law firm. Nixon, in the break-in, learned that he had dropped below third place, from an 81.6—an "A" rating—to 74.22. By graduation time he had made it back to third in the class of twenty-six, entitling him to membership in the honorary society, Order of the Coif. Bill Perdue won first place; Brownfield was second, Albrink sixth. Later, when president, Nixon said of Perdue, "He was the first man in our class. In fact, he made the best record at Duke of any man who has ever gone to Duke." Campaigning in 1960 he called Perdue "a real success; he's the Vice-President of Ethyl Corporation in New York, making a lot more money than I am."[44] A first in the 1936 listing at Duke would have helped Nixon in New York. Duke was then a new law school and its graduates were treated with some contempt by the city's best law firms. Nixon made the dreary round at Christmastime, several months before graduation. Perdue got a job; he did not.

Discouraged, Nixon went to the dean, Claude Horack, and asked him to write a letter of recommendation to the FBI. Horack, surprised, told him he was "too good a man for that," to which Nixon replied by saying that "he didn't know why, but he was attracted to it."[45] Fascination with "cloak and dagger life"— already evidenced in Slippery Gulch, in Orthogonian initiation ceremonies, in debate and football rally trickery, and in the transom prank—resurfaced many times in Nixon's life. A job with the FBI would have meant total anonymity with freedom to engage in extralegal actions with the secret sanction of the government. An opportunity to indulge in impersonation, spying, entrapment of others, all in the service of the law, could be a part of an FBI officer's life. This could have appealed to Nixon the actor, to Nixon the man intent on finding out the secrets of others, to Nixon who liked to walk "on the edge of the precipice," but not to Nixon the young man with the continuing fantasy of someday being "a president."

The FBI did receive his application and acted on it favorably, but a budget cut prevented his appointment and Nixon never learned until he was vice-president why he never received an answer to his application.[46] In June 1937 he had to suffer the humiliation of telling his parents and grandmother Milhous— who at eighty-eight had ridden back to celebrate his graduation— that he had failed to get a job either with a New York firm or with the FBI. It is not surprising that his resentment against the East— against Ivy League colleges and New York City in particular— would fester for many years.

X

The First Law Case: Failure

I don't remember that he ever lost a case.

— THOMAS BEWLEY, ON RICHARD NIXON[1]

THOMAS BEWLEY, who gave Nixon his first job as a lawyer, was a Quaker friend of Frank and Hannah Nixon and city attorney for Whittier. He taught Nixon the lore of the small-town lawyer, the intricacies of tax law and oil company contracts, and the involuted problems of death and property. He encouraged his going into politics and supported him over the years like a proud godfather. When interviewed in 1976, the tight-lipped old lawyer looked back on the Nixon decline with manifest pain: "He had an aura about him. I think he was one of the chosen. He was put here for a purpose." Troubled by the record of untruth, and particularly by the gaps in the presidential tapes, he said, "One thing we learned as attorneys, you don't destroy the evidence." Still he remained defensive about his protégé: "You don't have to apologize for what you don't say. . . . Sometimes you're pushed into a corner and have to speak with a forked tongue, as the Indians say."[2]

Nixon in 1937 had not wanted to join Bewley's firm. He had been so confident of a job in New York or with the FBI, and so reluctant to return to Whittier, that he had not even applied for permission to take the California Bar examination. At the last moment, with no job at hand, he asked Duke University's Dean Horack to intercede on his behalf, begging that he be granted special permission to take the examination in the summer. This was granted.[3] He reestablished his California residency, which had lapsed because he had for three years failed to vote by absentee ballot. His mother, meanwhile, had asked Bewley about giving her son a job. Evlyn Dorn, Bewley's secretary, said later, "I don't think Richard Nixon wanted to practice law in Whittier."[4]

He passed the bar exam—the hardest test in his life before entering politics, he said—and was sworn in before the State Supreme Court at Sacramento on November 9, 1937. Six days later he was acting for Bewley in Case No. 457600 in the Los Angeles Municipal Court on behalf of a young married woman named Marie Schee. His later bungling of her case led to a negligence suit that cost his firm $4800.[5]

But Thomas Bewley nevertheless kept him in the firm, denied his incompetence, and supported him with money and ungrudging praise through the years right up to his presidential resignation. Bewley was not simply a prototype of the Orange County Republicans who fell in at Nixon's heels by droves once he was on his way in politics. He was as much a surrogate father as "Chief" Newman, although he served different purposes in Nixon's life. He counselled him through bad times as well as good, and like many fathers permitted himself to be blinded by affection.

In an early interview with Bela Kornitzer, Bewley said:

> When I interviewed Dick I was impressed with his mature good looks, actions and thinking. . . . It took us no more than fifteen or twenty minutes to discuss our partnership. . . . When he tried a lawsuit, he had the right stance, and he used the right voice, which was low, but which he built up gradually with dramatic force. I don't remember that he ever lost a case. . . .

To William Costello he said, "Nixon could take hold of a cantankerous witness and shake him like a dog."[6] Kornitzer wrote incorrectly that "Nixon had already received offers from New York law firms but preferred to establish himself in his home town," and that "by the time he was twenty-seven, he had made a name for himself in the courts."[7]

The disastrous first law case remained buried until November 1973, when scanty details appeared in Tristram Coffin's *Washington Watch*.[8]

Bewley admitted in 1976 that his firm had settled the negligence suit out of court and he took the total blame for error upon himself: "Any mistake in that case was made by me, not him. . . . We made a mistake in that case and I gave it to Dick to straighten out."[9] Although not all the original records are available, those which remain make clear that while Bewley at one point did give bad advice to Marie Schee, it was Nixon who made the initial blunder.[10]

It began in a nasty family dispute over money. Marie Schee, who had loaned $2000 to an uncle, Otto A. Steuer, was forced to sue to get it back. Through Bewley's efforts, aided by Nixon, she was awarded a judgment by the court with the right to call for an execution sale of the Steuer house, said to be worth $6500. Nixon, who had never met Marie Schee but may have consulted with her father, Charles Force, went to the execution sale on June 29, 1938, instead of Bewley, who was ill. He was alone, and the only bidder. Instead of bidding as small a sum as possible, making possible a deficiency judgment should there prove to be liens on the house, he bid the whole sum due her, which by then was $2245.[11] This was the kind of error a green young lawyer could make who knew little about property and who had not taken the trouble to consult his superiors. He had instead naïvely consulted Steuer's lawyer, David Schwartz, asking him, "Could you be of a little assistance to me when this comes up for sale?" And Schwartz had told him to bid the entire sum due his client.[12]

As it turned out, there were liens on the house. A local minister, C. T. Scholz and his wife held two trust deeds worth $2700 and $725, and Alma J. Chapman held one worth $500. When Pastor Scholz started foreclosure proceedings based on the smaller of his trust deeds, Marie Schee stood to lose the value of her judgment.[13] Marie's mother, Emilie Force, had some money of her own, and Bewley recommended that she move swiftly to buy up the trust deeds to save her daughter's $2000, which she did. Legally the Steuers had the right to stay in the house a year and repay the loan to Marie Schee, providing that they paid rent. They stayed, but paid nothing. Bewley recommended that Marie's mother proceed with the foreclosure sale to force the Steuers out. Unfortunately he compounded Nixon's original error by suggesting that Emilie Force bid a nominal sum, the amount of her smaller trust deed, only to see the house unexpectedly sold to an outsider for under three thousand dollars. Although Emilie Force still held the first trust deed, Marie Schee's $2000 judgment was altogether lost.

The enraged women instituted a malpractice suit against Bewley's firm in March 1939, and Nixon, who was just establishing a career in Whittier, found his firm attacked in the court as incompetent, unskillful, and negligent. Bewley hastily settled out of court, and paid the women $4800.[14] The case was dismissed on March 7, 1939, and this could very well have ended the matter. But, as Bewley put it, "Dick Nixon is a person that people really like and admire, or they hate his guts."[15] Marie Schee, apparently angry, sought now through a legal tactic to undo the original execution sale where Nixon had blundered by getting the court to declare it invalid. Had this tactic been successful, it would have restored the Steuers to their home, but with Emilie Force in command of the mortgages, and with the execution sale weapon back in Marie Schee's hands.

When the Steuers on October 31, 1939, filed a motion in the original action against them to record "satisfaction of judgment"—in effect to have the record legally clarified so that Marie Schee's judgments could no longer be held against them—Schee moved in to block it. In the resulting hearing Nixon was a witness, not a lawyer, and was accused of having acted without any authority to bind his client Schee at the original execution sale. Marie Schee, who had been his first legal client, was now an enemy, and David Schwartz, the Steuer lawyer whom he had earlier opposed, was now helping him to defend his actions and trying to minimize his blunder.

Schee's new lawyer, David Knapp, called Nixon a mere "volunteer," an "outside man," insisting that Marie Schee had never been advised of Nixon's actions until it was too late and that she could not be bound by what he had done. He had never sent her a certificate of sale, Knapp said, and had mailed her no deed.[16] Nixon had to admit on the witness stand that he had never met Marie Schee before the execution sale:

I believe that on June 28, 1938, Mr. Bewley was ill at home. While I had no particular instructions from Mr. Bewley on the date of sale, it was a part of my duty to attend to such sale and it was always my understanding that we were to press . . . such sale and not to grant any further continuances. Mrs. Schee was not present at the time of the sale and I do not believe I ever talked to her myself.[17]

Nevertheless, the court ruled for the Steuers and declared the judgment against them satisfied.

The bungling of a first law case, taken on only six days after swearing-in before the State Supreme Court, cannot be that rare an experience. Even the greatest of trial lawyers must have many cases they would prefer to forget. The Marie Schee case cost his firm some money but clearly did not cost Nixon the respect or affection of his boss, Thomas Bewley. Yet there are hints in this case of an uncanny foreshadowing of the handling of the case that years later would bring Nixon plummeting from the presidency. These include suggestions of denial, a "questionable" affidavit, coverup, and, ultimately, Nixon facing the wrath of an indignant judge.

Unlike Watergate, however, where the tapes were preserved, the original court transcripts are no longer extant and thus no conclusive "smoking gun" will ever emerge. Evidence of questionable behavior comes from a painstaking reconstruction of the case from existing court records and lawyers' briefs submitted in the subsequent appeal, and from the memories of two prominent Los Angeles attorneys who claim to have seen the original transcripts.

Court records show that on December 10, 1937, Otto A. Steuer and Jennieve Steuer filed an affidavit before Judge Alfred Paonessa, presiding judge in the municipal court case. This affidavit is referred to in the respondents' brief in the subsequent appeals case as indicating that the Steuers vacated the house shortly after the sale. However, in the appellant's reply brief the original transcripts are quoted to belie this claim. Mr. Steuer is being questioned by attorney Daniel Knapp:

Q. by Mr. Knapp: You remember the foreclosure of the trust deed, don't you?
A. Yes, I do. . . .
Q. You were there on the premises?
A. I was.
Q. Still at the premises at the time of the foreclosure?
A. That's right.
Q. And moved at that time?
A. Yes.[18]

The foreclosure referred to occurred nearly six months after the original sale.

There is no direct evidence that Nixon himself had anything to do with the misrepresentation in this affidavit. But there is evidence that for some reason Nixon provoked harsh words from

Judge Paonessa. This evidence was originally gathered by Irving Wallace, who quotes Leonard Kaufman, one of the two attorneys who saw the transcripts:

One day in 1959, after lunch, we dropped by David Schwartz's office. Nixon was in the news, and David Schwartz said he had something interesting to show us. He had the transcripts of the case where he had opposed Nixon, and where Nixon had been bawled out and threatened with disbarment by the judge. He handed it to us. I remember it was a typewritten court reporter's transcript. I remember it vividly. . . . I was shocked. I never forgot it.

The words of Judge Paonessa that so shocked Kaufman were:

Mr. Nixon, I have serious doubts whether you have the ethical qualifications to practice law in the state of California. I am seriously thinking of turning this matter over to the Bar Association.[19]

David Schwartz has since died and his copy of the transcript has been lost or destroyed. His son, Merton L. Schwartz, who practices law in Beverly Hills, remembers seeing the transcript but recalls clearly only Nixon's "inept handling of the case."[20] Wallace reports that Kaufman's recollection was substantiated by his partner, a relative of Schwartz.[21] Thomas Bewley remembers that mistakes were made in the case but does not recall any rebuke from Judge Paonessa.[22] As for Judge Paonessa himself, he was deluged with inquiries when Wallace's allegations first appeared in print in Tristram Coffin's *Washington Watch*. Very old by then, he could remember nothing of the young Richard Nixon in his court. "I wish I could," he said.[23]

If Judge Paonessa did make such a threat it was never carried out and Richard Nixon never appeared before the California Bar Association. Still, one can only guess at how frightening these events were to the ambitious young Whittier lawyer, who by now was involved in Republican politics and hoping to run for the California legislature. He was also hoping to get married. Nixon at this time seriously thought of abandoning the United States and setting up a law practice in Havana. In early 1940, as nearly as can be determined, he took a vacation from his job and went to Cuba, where, according to Earl Mazo, he "spent a bit of his vacation time exploring the possibilities of establishing law or business connections in Havana."[24]

After his return, the case was settled in the Steuers' favor on

July 27, 1940, when it was affirmed on appeal,[25] and Nixon had every reason to believe that it would not haunt him further. He did not mention the trip in his memoirs. The first Caribbean trip he described in *RN* was a cruise he and Pat took on the United Fruit Company steamer *Ulua* in June 1941, a year after his marriage. He wrote, "Except for the fact that I was seasick for almost the entire trip, we enjoyed what turned out to be our last vacation for several years."[26] His first law case he mentioned not at all.

The case, astonishingly, continued even after Nixon joined the U.S. Navy in 1942. The tenacious Marie Schee in that year brought still another lawsuit. She might have been content to forget, since she had, after all, recovered her original loan to her uncle of $2000 through the settlement with Nixon's firm. In 1942, however, her lawyers used a new tactic, that of suing the Steuers and the marshall of the City of Los Angeles, Frank L. Holt, whose deputy had conducted the original execution sale. Once more Nixon was accused of having acted without authority. Schee lost, appealed, and lost again. The appellate court ruled on December 23, 1942, that Nixon's alleged misconduct at the original execution sale was irrelevant insofar as the validity of the sale was concerned.[27]

When Nixon finally learned the good news at the Naval Reserve Aviation Base in Ottuma, Iowa, it must have come as a pleasant Christmas present. He had every reason to believe that the case of Marie Schee and her mother had at last been laid to rest. So ended the five-and-a-half-year problem, to be largely forgotten until its revival in 1973.[28] Nixon had learned, meanwhile, that he could count on Tom Bewley, who had remained loyal throughout. The most Bewley would admit, when interviewed in 1976, was that "Dick Nixon was terribly upset about this case."[29]

A Problem with Touching

There was a look of happiness that she always had.

— MARY GARDINER, ON PAT NIXON IN HER YOUTH[1]

PAT NIXON, "Bride of Failure," and "the Mona Lisa of American politics,"[2] remains essentially unknown, and the nature of her marriage to Richard Nixon the subject of contradictory reports the reliability of which are difficult to assess. Her political role presents few problems. First Ladies by tradition have been expected to be circumspect and uninvolved in political decision-making, Eleanor Roosevelt being the most conspicuous exception. Mrs. Warren Harding was known to be a private termagant and Nellie Taft a husband-driver. The second Mrs. Woodrow Wilson acted as a kind of secret president after her husband's paralytic stroke. Several First Ladies were in varying degrees ill. Mrs. Franklin Pierce suffered from delusions over the death of her small son in a railroad accident en route to her husband's inaugural. Mary Lincoln was severely disturbed when maliciously accused of being a Confederate sympathizer because two of her brothers were fighting for the South, and she went into a depression after her son Willie Lincoln died. Mrs. Andrew Johnson, who had tuberculosis, was an almost total recluse, as to a lesser degree was Mrs. William McKinley, who had epilepsy.

Most of the presidential wives are remembered simply as gracious hostesses, supportive but unoriginal. Mamie Eisenhower confessed that she had been in the Oval office only five times in her eight years as First Lady.[3] Jackie Kennedy, it is true, had a special queenly glitter, and restored many of the rooms in the White House with elegance and taste. And Ladybird Johnson carved out a name for herself in her own right, in her programs for beautification and parks. But Pat Nixon, who told women's rights activist Gloria Steinem she admired Mamie Eisenhower above all other women,[4] could go down in history as the most baffling of all the presidential wives.

In 1960 Stewart Alsop called her "a major political asset to Nixon . . . a sort of extra backbone for a man whose backbone already had great tensile strength."[5] Paul Smith, former Whittier College president, said,

Pat is a far stronger man than Dick. She's much the stronger of the two, a real Hercules. I don't know of anyone who has so disciplined herself to endure a life she does not like. She wouldn't wish a political life for anybody. She's the hero in the whole lot, highly disciplined, instinctively moral.[6]

But these comments were made by men who did not know her well, and reflect the public image Nixon was eager for others to see.

"I have talked to many world leaders," he said at a dinner honoring Pat in 1973, "and I have found that whenever you find a strong world leader, you find usually by his side a very strong woman. I have been fortunate in that respect." And he went on to liken his wife to his mother.[7] When asked by a woman reporter in 1971 "What do you think is the greatest quality of Mrs. Nixon?" he said, "You always ask tough questions." Then he went on to speak of her "great strength of character and stamina." The wife, he said, "has to be the stronger partner of the two."[8] Through Watergate, Nixon wrote in his memoirs, "Pat was, as always, the strongest of all," and he described her strength of character as "unmatched, I believe, in the history of American politics."[9]

Earlier, in *Six Crises,* he had somewhat carelessly lauded her for her skill in deceiving the press. In describing how reporters swarmed about their house after Eisenhower's heart attack, he wrote, "Pat, with perfect poise developed over many years of handling similar situations, told them I was not at home."[10] That he valued this talent in a wife as vital to a man in politics he made clear in a governor's conference in 1969, when he repeated publicly a conversation he had just had with the wife of Gov. John A. Love of Colorado:

I tried to get in on some of her secrets. I said: "What do you do when somebody calls—and the man is sitting right there—and says, 'Is he in?' " She is a very smart wife. . . . because she said, "I begin by saying, 'He is not in. Who is calling?' " Now if it is a dumb wife, she would say, "Who is calling?" and then say, "He is not in."[11]

To be praised publicly for such deception, however innocently, could be difficult for the wife of any man in public life, especially for one who was, in Paul Smith's phrase, "inflexibly moral." The inner struggle of Pat Nixon with her husband's record of untruth may never be told, unless it is one day revealed in the publication of the diary she is said to have kept while in the White House. "I know the truth, and the truth sustains me," she said repeatedly to questioners during her last terrible year.[12]

Pat was indeed "upright," like Hannah Nixon, and like her, also, capable of infinite denial of the ugly. There is much evidence, however, that she was malleable and timid, and that she was easily intimidated. Where Hannah, confronted with overpowering difficulties, resorted to manipulation or outright escape, Pat Nixon found her major refuge finally in silence. "If I have a problem," she said in 1960, "I keep it to myself."[13] Although she spoke repeatedly of her husband as "a man of destiny," she dodged questions about the marriage, saying little save that her husband was "easy to live with." "We never have big fights," she said in 1969. "We just move away from each other."[14] Jessamyn West, who wrote a sensitive article about her in 1971, found her reticent beyond all expectation. It seemed impossible to probe this woman, who told reporters, "I just want to go down in history as the wife of the President of the United States."[15] Gloria Steinem, who interviewed her in 1968, found her altogether unapproachable.[16]

When Nixon discussed his wife with women reporters in 1971, he said, "Generally speaking, she shares my views, but I don't believe that on any issue you can have the wife talking one way and the husband talking another." When asked if he consulted her on public issues, he replied, "We will have discussions about problems . . . but in terms of the issues themselves . . . I don't even poll the cabinet, let alone the family."[17]

She lashed out at him occasionally in the presence of others in the early campaigns. Father Cronin reported that in 1956 when Nixon delivered a speech he did not like, written by Cronin, and did it badly, that Pat "chewed the hell out of him in front of his staff."[18] But this seems to have stopped by 1960. Henry Kissinger's story—that Pat early in 1969 replied to his effusive praise of her husband with a blunt "Haven't you seen through him yet?"— may have been banter.[19] Although Stewart Alsop reported in 1960 that "like Nixon, she is said to have a rare and furious temper," she denied this, telling *Time* journalists, "I never have tantrums. If anything makes me mad, I'm silent."[20]

Over the years Nixon praised her as a campaigner, often noting with envy how much more popular she was than he. Shortly before his resignation he called her "the best ambassador the United States has."[21] But he could slight her outrageously on public platforms, and in private, in the presence of friends, he could on occasion be caustic and boorish. Pat Nixon's White House aide, Helen McCain Smith, who told several stories of Nixon's public humiliations of his wife, was especially angered when on the night before the resignation he said to a group of congressmen, "I have a wonderful family and a pretty good wife." In his last tearful speech in the White House, the morning of his departure, he mentioned his cabinet, his staff, his parents, and his dead brothers, but he spoke of his wife not at all. "Who knows why?" Helen Smith said. "I suspect it was because he knew that there is a limit to what Pat can endure—and still keep her head high."[22]

Nixon did, however, in this final speech, quote from a brief memoir Theodore Roosevelt had written shortly after the death of his first wife, in childbirth, which may have in some fashion echoed his feelings about his own wife:

She was beautiful in face and form and lovelier still in spirit. As a flower she grew and as a fair young flower she died. . . . None ever knew her who did not love and revere her for her bright and sunny temper and her saintly unselfishness. . . . then by strange and terrible fate death came to her. And when my heart's dearest died, the light went from my life forever.[23]

The inclusion of this poignant description puzzled those who heard it, including Roosevelt's daughter, Alice Longworth, who had survived when her mother died. It is possible that Nixon saw in the glowing portrait of Alice Lee something of his own wife in her youth. Scores of Pat Nixon's old friends have described her as once warm and fun-loving, unselfish, and tender. One friend, staring at a newspaper picture of Pat in 1970, said, "It's the first time I've seen a look that reminded me of her years ago. . . .

There was a look of happiness that she always had. . . . She's so controlled now."[24]

That the sunniness had gone out of Pat Nixon's face had long been apparent to journalists as well as the Nixon friends. That the happy young wife of 1940 had died almost as certainly as had Theodore Roosevelt's "fair young flower" few who had known Pat Nixon in her youth would deny. Rumors of a possible divorce had been whispered about in the 1960s.[25] Nixon almost never referred either to his wife or to himself as a loving partner, and it is possible that in his final moments as president, when he was remembering the many deaths in his life, he chose to read the seemingly irrelevant passage about the death of Alice Lee Roosevelt because he felt compelled to say something—however disguised—about the death of love in his own marriage. That there was a kind of love on both sides in the beginning seems real enough, but the evidence of decline of love extends in an ever-darkening thread.

Many observers over the years have been struck by Nixon's failure to touch his wife. Tom Dixon, his radio coordinator in 1948 and 1950, said, "I never saw him touch Pat's hand. . . . She was farther away from him than I was . . . I never have seen quite as cold an arrangement."[26] Evlyn Dorn, Nixon's secretary in the Whittier law firm, and a longtime family friend, said that in all her years of knowing the Nixons she never saw him reach out to touch his wife save once, when they were standing together in the back of a car in an election rally, and he put out his hand to steady her.[27] Bela Kornitzer apologized for Nixon's reluctance to touch his wife in public in his friendly biography in 1959: "He hides his love for his wife as if it might wither when exposed to the light of publicity."[28]

Quakers are known for kissing each other freely in public, especially on the cheek.[29] But when Nixon, in accepting the vice-presidential nomination in 1952, greeted his wife as she came up on the platform and she leaned toward him for an embrace, he turned his face away. She had to reach up deliberately to kiss him twice, on the cheek.[30] Later, in his memoirs, he documented his own passivity: "Pat joined me on the convention floor and kissed me twice."[31]

On Pat's sixty-first birthday Nixon was helping to celebrate the opening of the Grand Old Opry in Nashville, Tennessee. She joined him on her way home from a Latin American trip. "There was a huge celebration," Helen McCain Smith remembered:

Pat, seated at the back of the stage, was surprised and delighted when an upright piano was wheeled out and the President played *Happy Birthday* for her with everyone joining in the singing. At the last chord, her face glowing, Pat rose from her chair and moved toward her husband. He apparently wanted to get on with the program. He turned, stepped brusquely to the center stage—and ignored Pat's outstretched arms. I shall never forget the expression on her face.[32]

The memoirs reflect Nixon's sensitivity about the fact that his failure to display physical affection had become a matter for public attention. He was careful to record how in Lima in 1958, when he was threatened by an angry crowd outside the hotel and finally reached the safety of his room, Pat "rushed over and embraced me." He described, too, his going to the hotel suite on election morning in 1968, where Pat had been waiting through the night alone. "I sat alone with Pat, and she told me it had been a terribly difficult night for her." He reassured her that the election had indeed been won. "I held her," he wrote, "and she burst into tears of relief and joy."

The memoirs reproduce also a remarkable diary entry he made describing his inaugural in 1973:

Mrs. Agnew kissed Agnew—Pat did not kiss me. I am rather glad she didn't. I sometimes think these displays of affection are very much in place, as was the case election night. Other times, I don't think they quite fit and on this occasion I didn't really think it quite fit.[33]

To Washington women journalists, Nixon in 1971 described Pat as "a sundowner." Recognizing belatedly that this was disparaging—in U.S. Navy parlance a sundowner is a strict captain who compels his men to return to the ship before sunset—he acknowledged that it was old navy talk and begged them not to repeat the word. Then he went on to say that the First Lady had come to prefer taking trips separate from his own—where "she is doing it rather than my doing it." And he added with unwitting cruelty, "She could go with me, and simply go along as excess baggage."[34] The phrase echoed throughout Washington, and Vice-President Agnew may well have been referring to the gaffe when, in welcoming Mrs. Nixon home from Africa some months later, he said, "who knows . . . women seem to be doing more things and perhaps you may visit these countries taking along the President as simply ancillary baggage."[35]

We shall look in later chapters at the silencing of Pat Nixon in the marriage and her subsequent struggles to become finally—in her husband's words—both "an independent woman and a supportive wife."[36] The graver questions of "touching" in the intimacies of marriage remain a tangle of conjecture and rumor. Helen McCain Smith, although reporting many examples of Nixon's publicly slighting his wife, nevertheless was certain that she continued to love him as she said she did. Others thought her protestations of affection were pure facade. A former friend, who saw a great deal of the Nixons before her estrangement from them during the presidential years, said to Chancellor Charles E. Young of UCLA, at the time of Nixon's resignation, "Can you imagine anything worse than for two people to be imprisoned together in San Clemente who hate each other so much!"[37]

Richard Nixon told his biographer Bela Kornitzer in 1959 that he first met Pat at the Whittier Community Playhouse:

A friend told me about the beautiful new teacher who was trying out for a part at the little theater. It was suggested that I go down and take a look. I used to be something of an actor in my college days; so I did, and I liked what I saw. Though, as a young lawyer just getting started, I was busy, I tried out for the part opposite her and got it.[38]

Later, as president, he said that he first met Pat at a football game. This was in a speech before the National Football Foundation where he astonished the athletes by the exactness of his memory of plays and passes seen fifty-one years earlier in a Rose Bowl game between Duke University and the University of Southern California. Of his meeting with Pat he said little, and it is possible that his mistakenly including her at all was one of his frequent inventions of the moment. The nuances, it may be noted, had to do with disappointment:

I remember that Duke came there undefeated, untied, unscored upon. The score was 3 to 0 in the last few minutes of the game. So out came a fourth-string quarterback, not a third-string, Doyle Nave, and he threw passes as they throw them today, one after another, to Al Kreuger, an end from Antelope Valley, California. And finally Southern California scored. It was 7 to 3. . . .

I must say that I was terribly disappointed, of course, but the woman who was to be my future wife went to Southern Cal and that is how it all worked out. We met at that game.[39]

In his memoirs Nixon returned to his original story, describing how in trying out for *The Dark Tower* he had seen "a beautiful and vivacious young woman with titian hair . . . whom I had never seen before. . . . For me it was a case of love at first sight." He offered her and a friend a ride home.

On the way I asked Pat if she would like a date with me. She said, "I'm very busy." I said, "You shouldn't say that, because someday I am going to marry you![40]

Pat had described the same incident earlier to Earl Mazo:

I thought he was nuts or something. I guess I just looked at him. I couldn't imagine anyone ever saying anything like that so suddenly. Now that I know Dick much better I can't imagine that he would ever say that, because he is very much the opposite, he's more reserved.[41]

Nixon's impulsive proposal of marriage was surely to a fantasy woman. They had spent the evening with other amateur actors reading parts from Alexander Woollcott and George S. Kaufman's comedy. Both tried out for secondary roles, Nixon that of a playwright Barry Jones, Pat that of Daphne Martin, a successful actress. Daphne's role was defined by the playwrights as that of "a tall dark, sullen beauty of twenty, wearing a dress of great chic and an air of permanent resentment." She is the jilted mistress of the leading man. Barry plays the piano while Daphne sings "Stormy Weather," and the two apparently become lovers, although this is not spelled out to the audience. Pat's part was that of a talented, beautiful, but also disagreeable woman who sings badly and who calls men pansies and sons of bitches.[42] Nixon was captivated.

Pat Ryan at twenty-five was not the sullen, sultry brunette prescribed by the authors of *The Dark Tower*, but a smiling woman with flashing eyes, a mass of red-gold hair, and cheeks—as one friend remembered—like apricots. Weighing then a generous hundred thirty pounds, she had nothing of the sunken look in her face that showed in her later pictures when her weight dropped to a hundred pounds and her doctors worried about her dismaying indifference to food. Evlyn Dorn, secretary in Nixon's law firm, said, "When I first saw Pat, I thought I had never seen a more beautiful woman."[43]

Pat took the role reluctantly. "He decided to take the part. I did too—not because of him, but because I was sort of pressured into it."[44] She was at the moment independent, free, enjoying her new salary, and looking forward to spending it traveling in the summer. Like Nixon she had taken part in debating and dramatics in high school, and she had been elected secretary of the student body. A graduate of the University of Southern California, she had also had two years in New York City, which added a veneer of sophistication. What was important for Richard Nixon—who would joke even as president about how he "adored celebrities"—she radiated the fragrance of Hollywood. At Fullerton Junior College she had been a member of the Nightwalkers Club, a group of girls with ambitions to be movie stars,[45] and had been an extra in many films. Later she denied having any ambition to be a star:

I never thought of movies as a career because it seemed so very boring. It was those retakes and retakes, and you would see those stars going over and over about three words until you almost went mad. I did the extra bits playing only for the money.[46]

But she had taken screen tests and had twice been given bit parts, one in *Becky Sharp,* where the single line she said ended up on the cutting room floor, and one in *Small Town Girl.* The pay was good, twenty-five dollars a day. Kornitzer would write of her movie career that she "actually rose to the level of a featured player,"[47] and Nixon would write in his memoirs, "Offers of bigger parts and even a career in the movies could not distract her from her education."[48]

She seemed poised and serene, with an aloofness that had frightened away the timorous in Fullerton Junior College and that would persist when she went to Washington. Richard Kiefer, a friend of Nixon's at Duke, later described how when one Republican party worker boasted that he would give Pat Nixon "a big bear hug," he received that "Down, boy!" look. "She had an ability to hold people off. There was a line you could not cross." Merle West, Nixon's cousin, joked, "No one ever got to know Pat well. I don't think Dick ever got very well acquainted with her."[49]

Richard Nixon pursued Pat Ryan for almost two and a half

years before she accepted his engagement ring, buried in a basket of flowers. Shortly afterward they agreed to pool their savings for a wedding trip to Mexico. She had treated him cavalierly, even shabbily at first. When she had a date in Los Angeles, she permitted him to drive her there, leave her with the other man, and then wait around to take her home. And she had persuaded him to date her roommate.[50] He had been patient and tenacious.

"I admired Dick from the very beginning," Pat told Mazo. "I was having a very good time and wasn't anxious to settle down."[51] Eventually she came to love him, to believe in his potentiality for greatness, and to defend him against vitriolic attack. One of her favorite phrases, "I say he's a wonderful guy," became the title of an article under her name in 1952. There she wrote, "I married a crusader."[52] Her first gift to him upon their marriage was a foot-high ceramic knight astride a plunging black horse. "It reminds me of him," she said.[53]

Nixon quickly learned that Pat Ryan was not a glamorous, sexually sophisticated actress with a potential Hollywood career but—in his words—"a shy and modest person."[54] She was also a hardworking typing teacher of limited interests, who had a capacity very much like Nixon's mother for selfless dedication and sacrifice. The fact that in New York Pat had nursed "lungers" like his brother Harold must certainly have been a bond between them. That he was willing to pursue her for so long before their marriage suggests that it was the "shy and modest" woman he really hungered for. Still, the fantasy of the glamorous movie queen died hard. He did his best to keep hidden the fact that she had been christened Thelma Catherine, not Patricia, and had been called Thelma or "Buddy" by everyone save her father until his death, when she formally adopted "Pat." And he misstated the date and the year of her birth, making her younger rather than older than himself.

When he did this in the "Checkers" speech, India Edwards, vice-president of the Democratic National Committee, pointed out that Nixon in this crucial speech defending his honesty "had told two unimportant lies, but lies nonetheless"—Pat was born Thelma Catherine, and on the sixteenth not the seventeenth of March—Nixon responded by saying, "How silly can the opposition get. From infancy she was called Patricia, and has used that name ever since. . . . to the best of her knowledge she was born on

St. Patrick's Day."[55] And he continued for years to say she was born in 1913.[56] In his memoirs he finally recorded the demographic facts accurately; Pat had corrected them years before.[57]

Thelma Catherine Ryan was born in Ely, Nevada, a desolate mining town. It is possible, she has said, that she was born in a tent. Her father, William Ryan, was a tall "Irish-looking" man, somewhat deaf, with a gift for storytelling. He had been an adventurer in his youth, a sailor, a surveyor in Alaska and the Philippines. Gold fever brought him to South Dakota, then Nevada. He did not marry until forty-one, when he courted a widow, Kate Halberstadt Bender. She had emigrated to America from Germany at age ten and had grown up in the Dakotas, where she married a miner and bore him two children, Matthew and Neva. After her husband's death in a mining accident, she married Ryan. They had two sons, William and Thomas. Thelma Catherine was her last child.

When Ryan began to suffer silicosis, his wife persuaded him to move to California. They settled on an eleven-acre hardscrabble farm in Artesia (now Cerritos), not far from Whittier, in a tiny house with neither electricity nor plumbing. One of Pat's earliest memories at age four was riding with her father in a buggy into town to buy weekly supplies. "I would never, never ask for anything," she said, "but how I hoped! I'd watch the corner to see if he came back carrying a strawberry cone. That was the big treat."[58]

Pat's father was "very stern and reserved," Julie Nixon has reported, "but once in a while he'd let his affection show through and it meant so much to her."[59] Pat grew up with fantasies of travel to far countries, like her father. He told her she was "all Irish," which pleased her. Despite the poverty her memories of the earliest years were happy:

It was a good kind of life when you look back on it. I worked right along with my brothers in the field, really, which was lots of fun. We picked potatoes; we picked tomatoes; we picked peppers and cauliflower. When I was real tiny I just tagged along. But when I got older I drove the team of horses. . . . And of course all my friends lived on little ranches, as they are called there, too. My mother baked a lot. She was very good. She baked bread and cinnamon rolls. . . . We walked a mile each day to and from school.[60]

Artesia was poorer and less snobbish than Whittier. Mexican and Japanese students were permitted to attend the grammar school and there was little religious bigotry. Pat's father was a non-practicing Catholic and her mother a Christian Scientist. In time they improved the house with electricity and plumbing, and added an old grand piano. The truck farm gave way to orange trees; her half brother and sister moved away. She played in the snow in the mountains in the winter, and occasionally went to the beach in the summer. She joined the Girl Scouts, and put on plays in her father's pump house, using sheets as curtains on an improvised stage.[61]

When Pat was fourteen, her mother, age forty-six, died of cancer on June 18, 1926. The long illness and loss changed her life irrevocably. "As a youngster life was sort of sad," she remembered, "so I had to cheer everybody up. I learned to be that kind of person." She faced death as most American children are taught to face it, by secret mourning and public denial. "Wasn't mother beautiful," she said at the funeral, and her schoolmates supported her in the denial of death. "Thelma returned to school and looked very sad around the eyes," one friend wrote in her diary. "We asked her to play tennis with us the next day."[62]

Pat now became the housekeeper for her father and brothers. A young neighbor, Myrtle Raine, remembered, "Both of us lost our mothers within a year's time, so we both did housework at each other's place, back and forth." Each of them, she said, became very close to her father. Myrtle Raine Borden remembered him chiding his daughter affectionately when he could not hear her well, saying, "Thelma, what are you plotting now?"[63]

William Ryan died of tuberculosis on May 5, 1930. Pat was eighteen. "I don't like to think back to that time," she told Jessamyn West. She had been a child nurse since twelve, a housekeeper since thirteen. In later years she prided herself on being never tired, never ill. As Jessamyn West put it,

in those days when, motherless, her father was ill, she was a student, housekeeper, and breadwinner all in one, and no doubt told herself, "You cannot be tired. You dare not be tired. Everything depends on you. You are *not* tired."[64]

When Gloria Steinem questioned her about her childhood, she said Pat became angry:

She had started to say that she hadn't had time for dreams and had always had to work too hard—this whole kind of stream of anger and resentment came out. . . . "I don't have to worry about whom I identify with. I've never had it easy. I'm not like all you . . . all the people who had it easy."[65]

Still, scores of her old schoolmates, interviewed in 1970, remembered her as happy and outgoing. Leona Stine kept her high school yearbook with Pat's inscription, "You have been one of my dearest, kindest and sweetest friends, and I love you. Thelma Buddy Ryan."[66] Her high school class elected her to office and applauded her as the lead in the senior play, *The Rise of Silas Lapham.* They admired her ambition and described it without malice.

But the death of her father was devastating. Outwardly tough and resilient like her brothers, she found odd jobs to support herself at Fullerton Junior College, where she joined the dramatic society and played the leading role in *Broken Dishes.* Through Ryan relatives in Connecticut she was promised help in studying radiology. Her ambition was to work with lung patients like her father. It would be reliving, as an adult, all the old pain, but it would also mean helping patients with the advantages of medical science her father had not had. To finance her trip east in 1931 she drove an older couple, friends of her family, across the continent. She worked at Seton Hospital in the Bronx, run by the Sisters of Charity, first as a stenographer and then, after a summer course at Columbia, as an x-ray technician. In her last six months she worked directly with tubercular patients. She described this experience to Jessamyn West as "the most haunting of my life":

They were so young, most of them, so eager to live. And most of them were doomed to die young. . . .

They weren't supposed to do it, but some of the young patients would sneak away to go bobsledding, and I went with them. It gave them a lift to have someone who was well with them, not looking after them, not avoiding them. It almost seemed that they believed they might contract health from me. My being with them made them feel less separate from the real world. And that is what gives me the deepest pleasure in the world. Helping someone.[67]

Still, she seems finally to have become surfeited with death and dying, and she left New York in 1933 to finish her education at the University of Southern California. There she turned away from the healing arts and graduated in business. And in this period came renewed fantasies about Hollywood and the life of a star. It was during her two years at the university that she helped finance her schooling by working in the movies. She also graded papers for her professors, and worked on weekends in department stores, and as a dental assistant. Frank Baxter, her Shakespeare teacher, remembered her as "a quiet girl, and pretty." "It always used to disturb me how tired her face was in repose. . . . She was a good student, alert and interested. She stood out from the empty-headed, over-dressed little sorority girls of that era like a good piece of literature on a shelf of cheap paperbacks."[68]

After graduating cum laude in 1937 she hoped to make a career in merchandising, but when offered $190 a month by Whittier High School to teach typing and shorthand, she accepted. "I had great visions of those free summers," she said. "I could have found other jobs in other places," she told Jessamyn West. "But I went to Whittier and I taught. And there I met Dick. It was Fate."[69]

Who, except Pat Nixon herself, can say if the attentive young lawyer promised her a kind of stardom, and at what point she came to believe that if she married him she might well become the wife of "a man of destiny."

No one has explained why the courtship lasted two and a half years. Nixon was tenacious, but also timid in matters relating to sex. Even eighteen years after his marriage he confessed to Stewart Alsop:

I remember when I'd just started law practice, I had a divorce case to handle, and this good-looking girl, beautiful really, began talking to me about her intimate marriage problems. . . . I turned fifteen colors of the rainbow. I suppose I came from a family too unmodern, really.

And he went on to confess, "I can have fun playing poker, being with friends. But any letting down my hair, I find that embarrassing, even with Pat."[70]

In the beginning of their courtship it was she who took the initiative in choosing friends. "We had a young crowd, mostly my friends from college," she said. "We liked to do active things. . . . The artificial ice rinks had just opened up and it was the gay thing to do. But it was awful for Dick. He almost broke his head two or three times, but he still kept on going."[71]

Neither of the Nixons ever discussed in detail what may have been the most significant reason for delaying getting married, Dick's disastrous venture in the frozen orange juice business. Shortly after they began going together, hoping to make a fortune, he borrowed $10,000 from friends in Whittier and started the Citra-Frost company. For over a year and a half he spent all his spare time squeezing oranges and trying out various kinds of packages—glass, cardboard, and cellophane. "He worked like a dog," Thomas Bewley remembered. "He was out there cutting oranges and squeezing oranges day and night after he'd do the work here, and he just couldn't realize that they couldn't make a success of it." He got a contract with the Owl Drug Company, but the first shipment spoiled in a refrigerated car and the venture collapsed. He had made the mistake other businessmen would later avoid, that of freezing the whole juice instead of first concentrating it. He also used inferior containers. "He lost all the money he had saved," Bewley said. "We're still carrying on the books some of the costs we extended in that venture. . . . You'll find people here who hate his guts because of that, people who put money in."[72]

To earn extra money Nixon opened a part-time office in La Habra, but spent most of his time waiting vainly for clients. He taught a course in practical law at Whittier College and was soon made a member of the college board of trustees. Mrs. Herbert Hoover was also a trustee, and Nixon never forgot his excitement, at age twenty-five, at this, his first contact with the White House. "She was a good Quaker," he said, "and devoted to that small college. She had all the ability to communicate, to be warm, that Mr. Hoover had in his heart, but found it so difficult to express."[73]

Everything, it would seem, appealed to Nixon more than practicing law. When he learned that the local state assemblyman was to be made a judge, he decided to run for the office, but he needed a nod from the party leaders. He began giving talks attacking Roosevelt and applauding Wendell Willkie. He went from one service club to another attacking in particular FDR's plans to pack the Supreme Court.[74] The Republican leaders "talked about running me for the Assembly," he told Stewart Alsop, but in the end they turned to someone else.

Later, after the war, when he ran for Congress, Nixon was intent on having people believe that he never thought of entering politics until the local Republican leaders wired him in 1945 asking if he would like to be their candidate. He told Kornitzer, "the idea that I might myself play even a minor part in practical politics never occurred to me." Pat echoed this, telling Mazo that in their courtship days, "there was no talk of politics."[75]

When the couple finally did decide to get married there was remarkable haste in the planning, and it came as a surprise both to Nixon's office staff and to his parents. Evlyn Dorn said, "Dick never came in and said, 'I'm going to marry this girl.' "[76] Nixon's aunt, Edith Timberlake, said Frank and Hannah Nixon just dropped by her house in Riverside, pulled into the driveway, and said, "You're going to Richard's wedding." Frank had a big square wedding cake in the car which he had hastily baked. There was no time even to notify her husband, who was at the university. "I think they had just patched it up, maybe the night before," Mrs. Timberlake said, although Hannah had confided to her earlier that "she felt pretty sure he was going to ask Pat to marry him," but had to talk to her about it first.[77]

Actually they had been engaged since May first, but this was apparently kept secret from the larger Nixon family and may well have been kept secret from his parents. The marriage took place on June 21, 1940, in the romantic old Spanish-style Riverside Inn. Richard arranged for the ceremony to take place in the presidential suite, which had housed William McKinley, Theodore Roosevelt, William Howard Taft, and Herbert Hoover. There were no relatives present save "Aunt Edith," the parents, and two cousins. The remainder of the two dozen guests were friends. The refreshments were simple: cake, coffee, and orange juice. Pat wore a simple, light-blue dress. No one seems to have had a camera; apparently there are no wedding pictures.[78]

Pat told Mazo nineteen years later, "We just took off in our car . . . heading, generally, for Mexico City, but without any particular destination. We didn't have any trip outlined. We just went. We felt really splurgy."[79] They took canned food along to save money, only to discover that their friends, as a joke, had changed all the labels. Nixon described his getting married, somewhat inaccurately as to time, reminiscing in New Orleans on the campaign trail of 1968. Theodore White took notes:

When Pat and I first got married . . . we went to Mexico. That was just after I graduated from Duke and I went from Duke to Lansing. I still remember that bus ride and I bought a car with her money—she had the money—a 1939 Oldsmobile, and I drove it back all the way across the country, and then we split the cost of our honeymoon, and went to Mexico for two weeks. Sometimes we drove all night to save the cost of a hotel, and I think we saw every temple, every church in old Mexico, and it all cost us only $178.[80]

Fighting Quaker

*My service record was not a particularly unusual one. I went to
the South Pacific. I guess I'm entitled to a couple of battle stars.
I got a couple of letters of commendation, but I was just there
when the bombs were falling.*

— NIXON, IN THE "CHECKERS" SPEECH, 1952

SIR RICHARD BURTON once said that it was his fate
never to be believed when he was telling the truth and always to
be believed when he was lying. The history of Nixon's credibility
cannot be compressed into any such epigram, but it is true that
there were times when he told that which was specifically the
truth, but which nevertheless, in the end, came to be widely disbe-
lieved. When in November 1945 he was being interviewed by
Republicans seeking a congressional candidate and said he had
talked to many veterans "in the foxholes," no one doubted him.[1]
Nor did they doubt his campaign leaflets, which described him as
a "clean, forthright young American who fought in defense of his
country in the stinking mud and jungles of the Solomons."[2] Lynn
Bowers and Dorothy Blair, interviewing Nixon for a *Saturday Evening Post* article in 1949, came away with the impression that he
had been "under fire frequently" on Bougainville, Vella Lavella,
and Green Islands, and "earned two battle stars."[3]

But by 1952 newsmen who researched the Nixon war record
were openly skeptical about the foxholes and the falling bombs.
Even friendly biographer Henry Spalding admitted in 1972 that
"Nixon has often been criticized as one attempting to pass himself
off as a veteran who had seen actual combat."[4] In 1976 Dr. David
Abrahamsen wrote flatly that Nixon's claim to have been in the
foxholes was "a fabrication."[5]

Nixon was not guilty of inventing a record as blatant as that of
Sen. Joseph McCarthy, who totally fabricated an extensive combat

history, claiming first to have been on fourteen bombing missions, then twenty, then thirty, and who managed to wangle for himself a Distinguished Flying Cross after he became senator.[6] Nixon blurred and embroidered and failed to correct exaggerations he encouraged among friendly biographers and journalists. He did not correct Ralph de Toledano, who wrote that Nixon had been "under bombardment twenty-eight nights out of thirty on Bougainville,"[7] although the figure was correct for American troops fighting Japanese on one end of the island and not for Nixon himself. Chastened, apparently, by the accumulating accusations of inaccuracy and invention, Nixon in his memoirs did describe what seems to have been one experience of real danger, and claimed nothing beyond it, although he did not clarify or deny the inaccuracies of others in the past.

"Shortly after I arrived," he wrote, "the Japanese staged an assault. When it was over, we counted thirty-five shell holes within a hundred feet of the air raid bunker six of us shared. Our tent had been completely destroyed."[8] To his anxious mother he wrote from Bougainville, "The only thing that really bothered me was lack of sleep and centipedes."[9] In 1970 he told Donald Jackson of *Life*, "I didn't get hit, or hit anyone. All I got was a case of fungus."[10]

Shortly after he became president, Nixon had his official war record made public.[11] The Office of Naval Operations stated that he had helped support air action in the Treasury-Bougainville operations, October 2 to December 15, 1943, and had supported consolidation of the northern Solomons (Bougainville and Green Islands) as officer in command of SCAT, the South Pacific Combat Air Transport Command, from January 1 to July 22, 1944.

The confusion over accuracy was in part semantic. Nixon was an operations, not a combat officer. He went to the South Pacific in the spring of 1943, and was stationed first in New Caledonia and then Vella Lavella, neither of which was menaced at the time by Japanese air assault. Abrahamsen mistakenly accepted as accurate the memory of a fellow officer, who remains anonymous, who insisted that Nixon was with him on Vella Lavella "until February or March, 1944," which, if true, would have meant that Nixon missed out altogether on the final Japanese battle on Bougainville in January 1944.[12] That Nixon was transferred to Bougainville on January first is, however, established beyond doubt by the official navy record, and by a citation with the relevant dates signed by Vice-Admiral J. H. Newton shortly after the war's end, praising Nixon's role. The citation had been preserved by Nixon's mother, and was published by Bela Kornitzer in 1960.[13]

In late 1943 an American beachhead at Empress Augusta Bay had been established; the airstrip known as "Piva Uncle," permitting the operation of C-46s as well as bombers, had been completed and the island had then fallen largely into American hands, all this by the time Nixon arrived on or shortly before New Year's Day of 1944. The bombers were being used primarily to reduce to impotence the powerful Japanese base at Rabaul, 115 miles away on the island of New Britain. But fighting continued at one end of Bougainville for about a month, until the Japanese lost the last of what had been a six-thousand-man garrison.[14]

Nixon's job on Bougainville as officer-in-charge of SCAT was to see that supplies brought in on the C-46s were unloaded quickly, that bombers for Rabaul were loaded with ammunition, and that battle casualties from the end of the island were placed aboard planes for evacuation to rear hospitals. Vice-Admiral Newton's letter commended him "for sound judgment and initiative . . . able leadership, tireless efforts, and devotion to duty."[15] Although Nixon specifically mentioned only one bombardment where bombs fell close to the airstrip, he did see mutilated and bloodied American soldiers brought back from the battle area to the strip, where they were transferred to larger planes to be taken to the hospital at Guadalcanal. Once he watched in horror as an army B-29 bomber damaged over Rabaul landed on its belly only to crash into a bulldozer and explode. "The carnage," he said, "was terrible. . . . I can still see the wedding ring on the charred hand of one of the crewmen when I carried his body from the twisted wreckage."[16] It may have been this episode he was remembering when he said in a speech in Moscow in 1959, "I saw boys as close to me as brothers die on barren islands four thousand miles from home in World War II."[17]

Nixon said nothing of his experiences in the Pacific War in *Six Crises*. The idea that he had been in active combat he communicated by scattered references to friends and reporters about "foxholes" and "bombardments." De Toledano he had misled, as well as Kornitzer, to whom he said, "During the lull in bombardments, when we didn't have anything else to do, men from various neighboring islands would get together in the evenings for games, and it wasn't always poker."[18] He told Wallace Black, a Whittier lawyer friend, in 1946 that he had met Harold Stassen, "in a foxhole in the Solomon Islands during a Japanese air raid," a statement Stassen strenuously denied.[19] Stassen had been in the South Pacific at the same time as Nixon as an aide to Admiral Halsey. He may have shaken hands with Lieutenant Nixon in February of 1943, in Bougainville, as Nixon told Mazo,[20] and quite forgotten the incident. It is unlikely that he would have forgotten sharing a foxhole with him in an air raid. Black remembered Nixon's saying that Stassen had told him that if he ever ran for Congress he'd come out to California and help him campaign. But Nixon, in writing to Stassen to solicit his endorsement in the 1946 congressional campaign, said only: "As you may recall, I met you on Bougainville in February of 1943. I was the Officer-in-charge of the SCAT department there, and you arrived on one of our airplanes on an inspection tour."[21]

There happens to be more data available on Nixon's poker playing in the Pacific than on any other single aspect of his war experience. The poker was not unimportant; it became his passion, his defense against ennui. It opened a door to the comradeship he cherished but against which he normally raised barriers. It also brought him a great deal of money.

Although his later intense involvement in the tactical and technological as well as the strategic aspects of the Vietnam War would suggest a bridge stretching back in time to his participation in the war against Japan, if there was such a bridge he has kept the evidence hidden. He never wrote about the role of SCAT in the larger war picture. At the same, "breaking the Bismarcks barrier" (i.e., clearing the Bismarck Archipelago of Japanese) may have seemed to him of small consequence compared with the mighty assaults in Africa and Europe of late 1943 to mid-1944. He had, it is true, missed out on the great actions in both oceans.

The sight of the casualties on Bougainville may have served, moreover, to heighten his sense of shame that he was still— although an officer in uniform—truly a noncombatant, an observer, with no real opportunity for heroism. He would never have an experience like Lt. John F. Kennedy, also in the South Pacific, who had his PT-109 sliced in two by the Japanese destroyer *Amagiri* in August 1943. Swimming hard to escape an area of burning gasoline, Kennedy had also managed to tow a badly burned engineer out of danger of death by holding the ties of his lifejacket between his teeth. Befriended by natives on the Japanese-held island he had reached, Kennedy later made his way to safety at Wana Wana, hidden under ferns in a war canoe, and returned in another PT boat to rescue those of his men who had survived. In 1950 when Kennedy and Nixon were both freshmen congressmen, Samuel Eliot Morison published his graphic history of the naval war in the South Pacific and described Kennedy's heroism.[22]

Nixon had to be content with the modest sobriquet "Fighting Quaker," which he came to cherish. *Time* magazine chose the phrase as the caption for its cover story on him in 1952, and Richard Gardner, Nixon's first biographer, decided to use it for the title of his volume, which was never published.

Even as president, Nixon could not resist delicately exaggerating the time he spent in the war zone. Addressing an Air Lift Command force in 1970, he said,

the outfit I was with in World War II was an outfit called SCAT. . . . they flew DC-3s up through the Solomons, Guadalcanal, Bougainville, Vella Lavella, Green Island and the rest. . . . I really feel close to you in a way, because I was in that kind of command during the period of 3½ years that I was in the armed services.[23]

His words were exact, but the impression conveyed was of much greater service in the war zone than had taken place. Of his forty-five months in the navy, Nixon spent thirty-one in the United States, fourteen in the South Pacific, and only six in "that kind of command."

The Nixon war record required no apology. He had worked conscientiously at every post and had received two citations for merit and three medals, everything but the "battle stars" he coveted. The exaggerated nuance was a necessity for a man who, unlike Lincoln, could never joke about missing out on being a hero. In Congress, in 1848, Lincoln had described his own battle history:

By the way, Mr. Speaker, did you know I am a military hero? Yes, sir, in the days of the Black Hawk war, I fought, bled, and came away. If General Cass went in advance of me picking huckleberries, I guess I surpassed him in charges upon the wild onions. If he saw any live, fighting

Indians, it was more than I did; but I had a good many bloody struggles
with the mosquitoes. . . .[24]

Nixon left the navy in 1946 with an indestructible awe for the
might of the United States and a respect for U.S. military leadership untempered by the usual junior officer cynicism. Admirals
and generals had become models whom he admired and whose
judgment he would defer to through his years as president.
Shortly after his inaugural he said to top officials of the Pentagon,
"I always feel a little embarrassed when an admiral comes up to
me and says, 'sir.' I think it should be the other way around."[25]
And he decorated the Oval Office with 307 battle streamers commemorating the military engagements of the United States from
Ticonderoga to Vietnam.

His favorite movie was *Patton,* which he saw several times in
the White House, and he kept at his bedside the Ladislas Farago
biography on which the movie was based. Another favorite film
was *Fort Apache,* which, like *Patton,* glorified a general who defied
orders and became a hero. In *Fort Apache* Henry Fonda plays the
role of an American officer who yearns to become a hero fighting
Indians, and who provokes an attack among the peaceful
Apaches, only to lose his own life along with those of all his men.
Still, like General Custer, he becomes a hero. Henry Kissinger
sensed the importance of the hero-general in Nixon's life when
he described in his memoirs how Nixon "reminded" him and
Haig of "the unconventional brilliance of Patton and MacArthur,"
and "lamented that the military, abused for years by civilian leadership, proved unable to respond imaginatively when given a
freer hand."[26]

Traces of his Quakerism remained, however, when as president he said in an interview in 1971 with Sulzburger of the *New
York Times,* "I can assure you that my words are those of a devoted
pacifist"[27]—but this affected his rhetoric, not his decision-making.

Nixon's repudiation of Quakerism was decisive if unspoken,
and the rejection seems to have crystallized early with his decision
to enter the navy. About 50 percent of those Quakers eligible for
war service enlisted in World War II, or permitted themselves to
be drafted, because they held Hitler in horror and because both
Japan and Germany had declared war against the United States.

Quakers in the West were known to be less doctrinaire pacifists than those on the eastern seaboard. Herbert Hoover fondly remembered his Quaker uncle in Seattle saying, "Turn your other cheek once, but if he smites it, then punch him!"[28]

Before Pearl Harbor, Nixon had been an ardent isolationist. "In 1939 I thought Neville Chamberlain was the greatest living man and Winston Churchill a madman," he said. "It was not until years later that I realized Neville Chamberlain was a good man, but Winston Churchill was right."[29] Of his private problem about whether or not to be a conscientious objector Nixon again made contradictory statements. To Donald Jackson he said in 1970, "The idea of being a conscientious objector never crossed my mind." But in his election film of 1968 he said:

When the war began, I enlisted in the navy. I could have been a conscientious objector of course very easily. I say easily because I was a Quaker, a birthright Quaker, and I would have had no legal problems whatsoever.[30]

Even this was inaccurate. He did not enlist "when the war began," but took a job in Washington with the Office of Price Administration. De Toledano wrote of his "waiving his military exemption" when he finally enlisted, and Henry Spalding said the decision came "after many months of agonized soul-searching."[31] The soul-searching was not a confrontation with George Fox and the Quaker martyrs but rather a personal one in his own family. In his 1968 election film he said:

I could have engaged in other activities during the war such as my uncles and others had during World War I. Red Cross and other activities. But I just had a different attitude . . . from my mother, grandmother, my father, their ideas, and I was convinced with this threat of worldwide aggression that was sweeping across the globe that no one could stand aside.

When asked by the film commentator if joining the navy had meant "a kind of wrench . . . an entering into another world different from his parents," he replied, "I think the war was probably the break point."[32]

Nixon's aunt, Olive Marshburn, doubted if Frank Nixon "instilled very much Quaker pacifism in Richard," and Nixon in 1971 explicitly indicated that it was his mother and grandmother who had "strongly disapproved" of his entering World War II.[33] In any case, it was when Nixon was three thousand miles away from his mother, and after five and a half months in a war-related job that he detested, that he formally joined the U.S. Navy.

Thomas Emerson, the professor of law at Yale who gave Nixon his job in the OPA, believed Nixon decided to join the navy as soon as his sensitive political antenna had picked up "the accepted dogma" that any young man who wanted to go into politics after the war must have a record of war service.[34] Had he remained a conscientious objector he would never have won a seat in Congress in the California Twelfth District. But one must remember that Nixon joined the navy, like many other Quakers, when Hitler was triumphant in Europe, when American and British naval losses in the Pacific were catastrophic, when Japan had control of the Pacific and was moving southward to menace Australia. There is no reason to doubt Nixon's statement that opposing "worldwide aggression" was a cause from which "no one could stand aside."

Pat said later, "I would have felt mighty uncomfortable if Dick hadn't done his part. Sure I was unhappy, but so were thousands of other young wives. Because of Richard's upbringing he did much soul searching before he made his decision. But once it was made, I knew it was all for the best."[35]

Emerson hired Nixon on his twenty-ninth birthday, January 9, 1942. "We desperately needed lawyers," he said. "We had to ration sugar, rubber, gasoline, butter and meat. I thought him articulate and intelligent and hired him on the spot."[36]

Although his starting salary was only $3200, a drop from the $6000 a year he was said to be making in Whittier, it was quickly raised to $5000. His immediate superior, Jacob Beuscher, later a professor of law at the University of Wisconsin, found him "a warm and likeable person" and a man who was "impatient with bureaucratic red tape and incompetence." Still, Nixon found his specific job—devising codes for tire rationing—stifling, and he disliked his New Deal colleagues. Nixon's father had made a good deal of money selling tires and the son did not share the indignation of many OPA lawyers against war profiteers. J. Paull Marshall, the only other conservative Republican on the staff, said later, "We both believed in the capitalistic system, but the other lawyers were using rationing and price control as a means of controlling profits." Nixon deplored what he saw as hostility to businessmen:

I saw the terrible paper work. . . . I also saw that there were people in government . . . who actually had a passion to GET business and used their government jobs to that end. These were of course some of the remnants of the old violent New Deal crowd.[37]

Thomas E. Harris, also in OPA, said he felt "Nixon was uncomfortable among the liberals, the Eastern law-school graduates, the Jews he rubbed shoulders with on the job. No one thought of him as a right-winger in those days, but in style if not in politics he was thought of as a conservative. Because he lacked sophistication and the big-city graces, he never quite fit in."[38] Once, as president, when urged by economic advisers in 1969 to adopt wage and price controls to combat a ruinous inflation rate, Nixon burst out, "Controls, O my God, no! I was a lawyer for the OPA during the war and I know all about controls. They mean rationing, black markets, inequitable administration. We'll never go for controls."[39] Later he reversed himself.

Much as he disliked the OPA, Nixon was even less happy, at first, with navy life. He entered the Naval Training School at Quonset Point, Rhode Island, on June 15, 1942. Returning there twenty-nine years later as president, he confessed his old distaste to reporters and students at the Naval Officer Candidate School at Newport. He admitted that he had found the navigation courses difficult and said, "I did not graduate with distinction from Quonset."

I was a Lieutenant Junior Grade, and that incidentally was a very low form of life in the Navy in those days. . . . the chiefs run the Navy. They did then, and I think they do now. . . . Believe me, those Navy chiefs— they put you in your place and that is good for anybody. . . . Humility is one thing you learn when you go into the service.[40]

Although he had desk jobs as "executive officer" for thirty-nine of his forty-five months in the navy, he did taste the sweetness of command during his six months in the South Pacific. By the time he left the navy, which was not until March 1946, he had been promoted to lieutenant-commander and had become very fond of his uniform. He had a large quantity of pictures made of himself wearing it when he began campaigning for Congress, and discarded them with reluctance when he was told by campaign aides to throw them out in favor of a more relaxed "Dick Nixon civilian" image.[41] As vice-president he was happy to accept a promotion to "commander" in the naval reserve. There is no evidence that Nixon ever did wide reading in military history or even in the naval campaigns of World War II. His defense of Mac-Arthur against Truman came with the Korean War, to which Nixon was deeply committed. By that time he had begun to pay serious attention to military strategy, not before. His affection for the navy seems to have been a gut feeling, based on personal happenings and affections, which are deserving of some scrutiny but not easy to assess because they are fragmentary and because here, as in every other period of his life, Nixon played different roles with different friends.

Whittier acquaintances report that Nixon returned from the navy a different man: smiling, open, friendly, and confident. High school friend Richard Heffren, who had known him as solemn and aloof, found him "completely changed."[42] "I grew up in the Navy," Nixon once said to reporters. Here he learned for the first time even how to drink coffee—he said, "because I had to."[43] And it was here, his early biographers have written, that he also learned how to drink, smoke, swear, and play poker. Lt. James Stewart, Nixon's aide on Green Island, told Kornitzer, "Nixon didn't drink. He didn't smoke. When I first knew him he didn't swear, and he read the Bible regularly."[44] Henry Spalding wrote that "prior to his enlistment he would inveigh against the evils of alcohol with all the fervor of a fundamentalist preacher," and that as deputy district attorney in Whittier he had discouraged the wine drinking permitted in a few of the town's restaurants by posting policemen at the exits to arrest the drunks. Nixon himself told Mazo, "I never knew what poker was till I joined the Navy."[45]

Most of this is Nixon mythology. He had learned to swear at age seven from his cousin Floyd Wildermuth, if not earlier from his father. He had learned to play poker as an adolescent in Arizona at Slippery Gulch. He admits in his memoirs drinking gin in a San Francisco bar on his first Whittier College debate trip. Members of the Whittier "20–30 Club" remember Nixon as a young lawyer drinking at their parties. Wallace Black helped Nixon carry champagne and brandy to one of the meetings, ignoring the protests of the hotel manager, who wanted him to use the freight instead of the main elevator. Philip Blew, also a "20–30" member, once invited several members to his room after a meeting, including Nixon. "After a few rounds of drinks the affair turned into a spree," he said. "Our problem was forgotten and we, in effect, had to pour Dick into bed."[46]

In the navy as in Whittier, Nixon continued to wear different masks with different men. Lt. James Stewart naïvely believed that it was he who first taught him how to play poker:

One day I noticed Nick lost in his thoughts. . . . Finally he asked: "Is there any sure way to win at poker?" I had a theory for playing draw poker. It was that one must never stay in unless he knows he has everyone at the table beaten at the time of the draw. Nick liked what I said. I gave him his first lessons. We played two-handed poker without money for four or five days, until he learned the various plays. Soon his playing became tops. He never raised unless he was convinced he had the best hand.[47]

Actually by the time Nixon met Stewart on Green Island in late February or early March 1944 he had been winning pots from naval officers for many months. James Udall, who shipped out with Nixon to the Pacific in April 1943, and who played with him at least three nights a week with Edward McCaffrey and Nelson Coombs, said, "Nixon was as good a poker player as, if not better than, anyone we had ever seen. He played a quiet game, but was not afraid of taking chances. He wasn't afraid of running a bluff. Sometimes the stakes were pretty big, but Nick had daring and a flair for knowing what to do. . . . I once saw him bluff a lieutenant-commander out of $1500 with a pair of deuces."

Lester Wroble said, "Dick never lost, but he was never a big winner. He always played it cautious and close to the belt. . . . He seemed always to end up a game somewhere between $30 and $60 ahead. That didn't look like showy winnings, but when you multiplied it day after day, I'd say he did all right." "There are a hundred Navy officers," another friend said, "who will tell you that Nick never lost a cent at poker."[48]

When Kornitzer asked Nixon about his total winnings he was evasive, "unable to recall even an approximate figure."[49] Spalding estimated his winnings at thirty-five hundred dollars, Stewart Alsop at ten thousand. It is possible that Nixon kept the sum secret even from Pat; Evlyn Dorn remembers his writing to the

Bewley law firm about money matters when he was in the Pacific and specifically requesting that Pat not be told. Nixon did tell Earl Mazo that when he went to Washington in 1946 as congressman he had ten thousand dollars in war bonds, although some of this may have included the savings of his wife, who had worked at various jobs throughout the war.[50]

Nixon showed still another face in the navy besides the innocent Bible-reading boy from Whittier and the seasoned poker player. This was Nixon as "Mister Roberts," the kindly officer who ignores protocol and goes out of his way to look after the needs of his men. James Udall remembered Nixon bringing him crackers and soup every day on the S.S. *President Monroe,* when he was violently seasick. Edward J. McCaffrey, with Nixon on Bougainville, described how once when thirty planes arrived one after another each carrying 135,000 pounds of rockets for transference to combat planes, "Nick peeled off his shirt and sweated through the hard physical labor" along with the enlisted men.[51]

In 1944, in his months on Green Island, which completely escaped Japanese bombardment, Nixon had more leisure, and set up a class in business law. He also opened what was called "Nixon's Snack Shack" near the airstrip, where SCAT pilots and their crews were able to get free coffee, sandwiches, fruit juices, and occasional liquor. As McCaffery described it,

Nick was able to wheedle the supplies for his Snack Shack from other outfits that were better stocked. Some of the stuff was, shall we say "liberated"—but Nick would swap anything. Just a small trade would set in motion a series of bigger trades. . . . If you ever saw Henry Fonda in *Mr. Roberts,* you have a pretty good idea of what Nick was like. Some of the items on the menu were not on the government issue list; an occasional bottle of whiskey for example—a rare treat which he doled out among the men without regard to their rank.[52]

He fed them, as he fed the Whittier football team with food from the Nixon Market, with food that had cost him nothing. This scrounging was a test of his old talents learned in bargaining at the Los Angeles fruit and vegetable markets, the excitement heightened by the fact that it was all against regulations. He was "liberating," as he had liberated boxes for the Whittier football bonfires, although this time from a new and inexhaustible store.

The night before he left Green Island to return to the United

States in July 1944, his outfit rewarded him. As Lt. James Stewart remembered it,

As you know, liquor was prohibited to enlisted men. Luckily, however, there was always some to be found, if one knew where to look for it. The enlisted men in our outfit went on a search party, "borrowed" all the liquor they could find, and gave him a big party. All of them were strong for him, and hated to see him go.[53]

He had become loved—as he may never have been loved again in his life—not only because he had fed his men in an unexpected fashion, but especially because he had defied regulations to do it. He was never reprimanded. Green Island was then inhabited largely by friendly Melanesians and by twenty-five thousand New Zealand troops, who had liberated it in mid-February.[54] But as far as the American SCAT men were concerned, Nixon was "in command."

XIII

The Dragon Slayer

When I first came to Washington in 1946, I was a bit naïve about public service, I suppose, a kind of dragon slayer.

— NIXON, TO STEWART ALSOP, JULY 1958[1]

IN THE CONGRESSIONAL ELECTION OF 1946 Nixon was not asked to slay dragons but to defeat a saint. Jerry Voorhis, his New Deal liberal opponent, had been in office ten years and was still popular in a district that was predominantly conservative Republican. Nixon was one of many who believed, mistakenly, that Voorhis had inspired the film *Mr. Smith Goes to Washington,* a story of the triumph of innocence and integrity over evil forces in Congress.[2] The Republicans had been desperate enough even to advertise for a candidate. Walter Dexter, former president of Whittier College, had been offered the spot, but had refused because he felt he could not win and had suggested Nixon. Herman Perry, a Whittier banker and friend of Nixon's parents, had invited him to fly home to be looked over and had been authorized to pay his expenses.

Nixon met with the local party leaders and in a vigorous speech attacked the New Deal for stifling initiative by pernicious controls. The returning veterans, he said, wanted jobs, not government handouts, and he promised an aggressive campaign "on a platform of practical liberalism." When he finished, committee organizer Roy O. Day said with satisfaction, "That is saleable merchandise."[3]

When told that he was the committee choice, Nixon wrote exultantly to Day:

I am going to see Joe Martin and John Phillips and try to get what dope I can on Mr. Voorhis' record. His "conservative" reputation must be blasted. . . . I am really hopped up over this deal, and I believe we can win.[4]

Already he had chosen his line of attack and "blasting" would be his favorite technique.

Seasoned Republicans meeting Nixon after his discharge from the navy in March 1946 saw only a personable young conservative, a respectable enough candidate, but one certain to lose. Kyle Palmer, political editor of the *Los Angeles Times*, whose word to publisher Norman Chandler would make or break many a Republican, remembered Nixon's first visit to his office:

My first impression of Nixon was that there was a serious, determined, somewhat gawky young fellow who was on a sort of giant-killer operation. . . . a forlorn effort, particularly when it was being made by a youngster who seemed to have none of the attributes of a rabble rouser who can go out and project himself before a crowd.

Only later, Palmer said, did he realize "we had an extraordinary man on our hands." He introduced him finally to Chandler, who after a twenty-minute talk said, "He looks like a comer. He has a lot of fight and fire. Let's support him."[5]

Palmer in the first interview had picked up Nixon's image of himself—giant killer or dragon slayer. Between 1946 and 1951 Nixon would mount attacks on four widely varied opponents and slay them all. Jerry Voorhis, whom he smeared as a dangerous Socialist with ties to the Communist party, would never go back into politics. Gerhart Eisler, whom Nixon assailed as a Communist spy in his maiden speech in Congress, would flee the country. Helen Gahagan Douglas, her political career snuffed out in 1950, would spend her later life in comparative obscurity, daubed indelibly as "the pink lady." Alger Hiss would go to jail. Nixon succeeded in persuading Americans that all were linked in one fashion or another to the Communist party. Hiss and Eisler had been truly tied to the party in their pasts; Voorhis and Douglas certainly had not.

When Voorhis's aide, Stanley Long, later accused Nixon to his face of lying during the campaign, he replied, "Of course I knew Jerry Voorhis wasn't a Communist. . . . The important thing is to win. You're just being naïve."[6] To Stewart Alsop, Nixon said with similar frankness and contempt, "Voorhis was a Don Quixote, an idealist, a man of very high ideals, who never accomplished anything very much."[7]

Early in the campaign Laura Scudder—of peanut butter

fame—persuaded Voorhis to pay a courtesy visit to Nixon at his father's home. "It was the coldest reception I've ever had from anybody," Voorhis remembered. "I thought he hated me."[8]

Enemies were vital to Nixon. He made no apology in private when he avowed a commitment to winning at all cost, although he would always deny that he resorted to overkill. In politics in 1946 Nixon found his ideal calling. As a naval officer he had missed out on combat, and when he said, "I didn't get hit, or hit anyone, all I got was a case of fungus," he was expressing a deprivation of consequence in his life. Now he could annihilate without killing—and apparently without guilt.

The theater was also Nixon's métier and when he was on the offensive it is not easy to distinguish when Nixon was motivated by simple opportunism—putting on an act for political advantage—or by hatred rooted in ancient conflicts he had never exorcised. In his first campaign there was a lot of debating, which inevitably involved theater. But Voorhis left the contest more bloodied than anyone expected. Although Nixon himself was tarnished with a record of unfair tactics, it seemed not to trouble him and he repeated the tactics in his senatorial campaign of 1950. To be a dirty campaigner was also to be tough. Day counseled him in 1946, "Nice guys and sissies don't win elections."[9]

Jerry Voorhis had grown up in a wealthy family and had graduated from Yale Law School. In the twenties he had been a Socialist and with money from his family had founded an orphanage for destitute children. When he came to California from Illinois, he started the Voorhis School for Boys in San Dimas. In Congress he was widely respected, although considered something of a radical, with a quixotic preoccupation with monetary reform. In 1939 Washington newsmen had voted him the most honest congressman, and in 1946 the House had voted him its most hardworking member and the runner-up in putting the nation's welfare above politics.[10]

Deeply concerned with the rightness and wrongness in his voting, he had been one of the few in the House to protest the internment of the California Japanese in concentration camps during the hysteria that followed the attack on Pearl Harbor. Although he detested Harry Bridges, Communist head of the International Longshoremen's Union, he nevertheless opposed his deportation to his native Australia, which was to have been effected by a bill of attainder, because he recognized that the device was unconstitutional.[11] He had a reputation in the House for being nonpunishing and caring. Yet he had been tough enough to expose a monopoly contract Standard Oil had with the navy giving Standard Oil control of the Elk Hills oil reserves. This action guaranteed that the oil interests would support Nixon in the election.

Nixon at first assailed Voorhis for favoring continued government controls still in effect from World War II. Actually Voorhis had been flexible about controls, voting for a relaxation of some, but holding fast especially to a ceiling on housing for returning veterans—which Nixon himself would vote for when he got to Congress. But Voorhis had continued to vote for the Office of Price Administration, which he thought to be a useful brake on inflation. Nixon, remembering his own uncomfortable months there as a conservative among liberals in 1942, denounced the OPA as "shot through with extreme left-wingers . . . boring from within, striving to force private enterprise into bankruptcy, and thus bring about the socialization of America's basic institutions and industries."[12]

As the campaign developed, the young candidate who had begun with a promise of "practical liberalism" swung to the far right, vilifying the New Deal as a "foreign" ideology and equating it with socialism. He assailed Voorhis as "Communist-supported," and campaigned as a young embattled patriot standing almost alone against the floodtide of revolution threatening the quiet, middle-class towns nestled among the citrus groves of the California Twelfth District.[13]

Nixon later admitted that "Communism was not the issue at any time in the 1946 campaign. Few people knew about Communism then, and even fewer cared."[14] It was indeed a peripheral issue, although old and chronic, but Nixon made it a major issue, capitalizing on the ignorance of the electorate and preying on ancient fears. More significant problems in 1946 were the winding down of the war effort; the intransigence of big labor, intent on higher wages; the restiveness of both agriculture and the business community, intent on quick profits; a black community clamoring for long-denied civil and political rights; and the problem of control over the potentially world-annihilating atom bomb.

There had been a paralyzing rash of strikes. Harold Stassen counted 4985 strikes with a loss of 116,000,000 man-days, and publicly blamed Truman's "alternating whimpering pleas and senseless floggings."[15] Truman in a single year seized the coal mines twice and briefly took control of the railroads, meat-packing plants, tugboats, and twenty-six oil-producing and refining companies. He had also to deal with strikes against General Motors and U.S. Steel. Near the end of 1946 cattlemen forced him to lift controls on beef by refusing to slaughter their herds, and finally, in the face of the national Republican cry "Had enough?" Truman put an end to most government controls.[16]

Nixon dramatized his own hatred of controls by accumulating for sale in his election headquarters a good many electrical items in short supply. People flocked to buy electric irons and toasters, and left with Nixon literature which promised that all these items would be available with a Republican victory. But mostly he concentrated on the then-exotic issue of domestic Communism and by an orchestrated campaign of distortion managed to destroy a congressman who was actually hated by American Communists and who had been denounced in the California Communist paper *The People's World* as "a smart reactionary boring from within the liberal camp."[17]

Nixon's campaign was never adequately described until 1973, when Paul Bullock of UCLA published a comprehensive study of it in preparation for his life of Voorhis. Meanwhile, Nixon's early denials of deception—reinforced by biographers like de Tole-dano, who characterized as "invention" what he called the "horrendous" anti-Nixon accounts of the 1946 campaign—were widely believed even by the most skeptical of journalists.[18]

In California as elsewhere, the American middle class as well as the far right for years had feared Communism. The wartime alliance with Russia had brought only the briefest interlude, ending even before the war was over in protests against Roosevelt's controversial concessions to Stalin at Yalta. After the war's end, Stalin's defiance of the Yalta agreements and Soviet expansion into Poland and Bulgaria had alienated Churchill and Truman, as did Stalin's speech of February 1946 revising the dogma of the inevitability of war between East and West—in a world that now had atomic bombs.

Anxiety over Soviet expansion in Europe affected both parties, but the Republicans in 1946 did their best to capitalize on it as a specifically Republican issue, and their various headquarters

were piled with literature on "the Communist threat." Sen. Robert
A. Taft of Ohio, a major Republican party spokesman, warned
that the Democratic party was "divided between Communism and
Americanism." The United States Chamber of Commerce in 1946
distributed four hundred thousand copies of *Communist Infiltration in the United States*. In San Francisco on September 30, 1946,
J. Edgar Hoover warned the American Legion that "at least
100,000 Communists were at large in the country."[19] In exploiting the issue of domestic Communism, Nixon demonstrated a
sharp ear for electoral anxieties but he was hardly original. He
did bring to the issue a special vituperation and a concentrated,
highly organized campaign of press deception.

Many Nixon watchers have blamed the trickery of the 1946
campaign on the lawyer-politician Murray Chotiner, variously
described as the Machiavelli of California politics, master smear
artist, and Svengali to Nixon's Trilby. Voorhis wrote that he was
"the first victim of the Nixon-Chotiner formula for political success,"[20] implying an equality of responsibility, but he also
described the tactics as largely Chotiner's. He thus contributed to
the notion, reiterated as late as 1974 by Garry Wills, who wrote
that until Nixon took up politics and learned too well the lessons
of Murray Chotiner he was "a fundamentally decent man."[21]

Chotiner, sallow-skinned, overweight, self-effacing, and often
obsequious, was easy to misjudge. Actually he was an aggressive
and hostile man who seriously equated Communists with Democrats. He was also unabashed in his cynicism and defense of trickery. Politicians of both parties admired his organizational skill and
his canny instinct for political infighting. Tom Dixon, a radio
announcer who worked with Nixon in 1946 and 1950, said Chotiner "for all his evil twists and turns was nevertheless a warm
person, warmer than Nixon. He'd make jokes. I can't remember
Nixon laughing at anything."[22] Clark Mollenhoff, who knew Chotiner in the White House, found him "a likeable scoundrel,"
whereas Bob Haldeman said of him, "He has the guts of a burglar."[23] When Chotiner first met Nixon, he was a full-time public
relations man for Sen. William Knowland, but he agreed, for
$500, to help advise on publicity techniques. Nixon himself,
according to Paul Bullock, who interviewed other members of the
staff, "determined the campaign strategy."[24]

But Chotiner, Bullock notes, was responsible for press releases, a vital task. He taught the eager Nixon all the artifices of his profession, including the technique of the Communist smear based on a dredging-up of material from the remote past. Chotiner helped destroy Knowland's opponent, Will Rogers, Jr., in the same campaign by having a Democrat publicize the story that Rogers had long ago given money to the Communist *People's Daily World*.[25] Nixon shortly spread the word in ads that Voorhis had been a member of the Socialist party.

Nixon learned from Chotiner not as a Quaker innocent but as a sharp lawyer and a veteran of campus politics and countless poker games in the Pacific, and especially as a man with kindred tastes and kindred political morality. Earl Warren, too, had employed Chotiner, as had Knowland, but neither of these men chose to enter into a symbiotic relationship with him. Chotiner became Nixon's friend, crony, and adviser of influence for many years, save for an interlude beginning in 1956. Chotiner then was the subject of a congressional investigation, accused of having halted the deportation of a New Jersey gangster—Marco Reginelli, involved in white slave activities—and also to have used Nixon's name in setting up appointments.[26] In 1960, when Chotiner wanted to run for Congress, Nixon opposed it and supported the more respectable Alphonso Bell. It was then, according to Los Angeles Superior Court Judge Jerry Pacht, that Chotiner briefly took his big photograph of Nixon off the wall.[27] The quarrel was later patched up, and Chotiner became a behind-the-scenes advisor in the White House, where he remained until his death in an automobile accident in 1973.

In 1955 the Republican National Committee employed Chotiner to tour the country giving secret lectures to "GOP schools." When a copy of his fourteen-thousand-word syllabus of instructions fell into the hands of reporters, it established Chotiner nationwide as Nixon's Svengali, a title Nixon never repudiated since it relieved him in the most useful fashion of the burden of guilt for tactics that many thought included the use of fraud.

Many of Chotiner's methods would have seemed hackneyed to America's oldtime party bosses. But in California, where the cross-filing system permitting voting in either the Republican or the Democratic primary had served not only to destroy bossism but also to disintegrate party organizations, the Chotiner formula seemed original and clever, if also diabolical. He said, briefly: Discredit your opponent before your own candidate gets started—organize a separate group of Democrats or independents to support your candidate—associate your opponent with an unpopular idea or organization, with just a suggestion of treason—if your opponent objects to defamation, complain that he is using unfair political tactics by calling you a liar—above all, attack, attack, attack, never defend.[28] Garry Wills called the Chotiner formula "the denigrative method." "Find the opposition's weak point and then just lean on it all through the race." Eventually, as Wills said, Nixon became "a virtuoso manipulator of discontents."[29]

Nixon himself wrote almost nothing about the campaign against Voorhis, but Pat, normally the most reticent of woman, wrote a good deal about it in collaboration with Joe Alex Morris in a *Saturday Evening Post* article in 1952. Her warmly sentimental "I Say He's a Wonderful Guy" painted a picture of a young crusader contending against poverty—"so broke that I wept because at a critical moment there wasn't any money to buy stamps to mail campaign literature for which we had paid dearly"—badgered by bullhorn-carrying hecklers and plagued by Democrats pretending to be Republicans who carried off their leaflets only to destroy them.

They started with a brokendown desk and borrowed typewriter, she said, and risked their savings, "everything we had right after the war":

Dick couldn't even buy a suit that would fit him because of wartime shortages. He finally got a gray number, much too small, to replace his uniform, but it was weeks before a friend in Los Angeles could get him a blue suit that fitted. The day it arrived we sold the gray for enough to buy another batch of office stationery.

Contributions, she implied, came mostly from little people. "I've known an indescribable kind of emotion that comes when men and women obviously in poor circumstances stop to shake hands," she wrote, "and to press a hard-earned half dollar or perhaps a dollar into my palm for a campaign in which they believed just as sincerely as we do." When Nixon backer Roy Day was discouraged, she would say, "Don't worry about Dick. The tougher the going the better he gets."

Tricia had been born on February 21, 1946, but Pat left her each morning with Frank and Hannah Nixon, campaigning all day and returning exhausted, to hold her on her lap. "But I'm glad now that I resisted the temptation to prop up the bottle," she said, "and let her have it alone in her crib."[30]

The Nixons told many that they used their war savings for the campaign. Journalists Lynn Bowers and Dorothy Blair reported a sum of four thousand dollars "pretty well used up," and Whittier lawyer Wallace Black, who thought Nixon had ten thousand dollars in savings, said he spent it all.[31] Actually, after the *Los Angeles Times* endorsement, money flowed freely into the campaign coffers. Harrison McCall, the campaign manager and treasurer, estimated the sum at thirty-two to thirty-five thousand dollars, but admitted that all the records had been destroyed.[32] William F. Ackerman remembers being pressured by a leading California executive at a company conference in Ojai in 1946 to give a hundred dollars "in cash" to get rid of Jerry Voorhis. Nixon had complained of his need for money, and the executive explained the technique: "This three-day deal will give everybody a big enough expense account to hide it. Taxis, entertainment. This and That. We're all experts at it. Gotta get at least five thousand."[33] Nixon carelessly admitted later that when he went to Washington he took with him ten thousand dollars in government bonds and three thousand in savings, so it would seem that he had, after all, kept his poker winnings intact.[34]

Although Roy Day remembered Pat Nixon as "nervous, uptight and tense,"[35] it was in the 1946 campaign that Pat Nixon established her reputation as a great trouper. She took notes in shorthand of the speeches of her husband's opponents and watched Nixon—eagle-eyed, some said—to help him against error. Although she loyally insisted that she enjoyed every speech, Nixon described her critiques as "thoughtful, and sometimes quite persistent."[36] Very few heard her criticisms. Georgia Sherwood, former wife of Tom Dixon, who helped Nixon set up a network of radio addresses in 1946, often traveled with her husband and the Nixons. She reported that Pat "had only two interests, her daughter and her husband, and that she talked incessantly about what a great man her husband was."

Nixon, on the other hand, Mrs. Sherwood remembered, treated Pat with almost routine incivility. "He would always hold the door for me," she said, "but would walk through in front of Pat as if she wasn't there at all."

Once when the two women were sitting on uncomfortable chairs in a tiny anteroom and Pat got up and walked into the radio office, "Nixon flared at her like a prima donna." He ordered her out "with as little ceremony as he would have a dog, saying, 'You know I never want to be interrupted when I'm working!' " Dixon, who was nettled by the outburst, said, "It gave me an insight into the man. If he had been doing a brand new speech, I could have understood it, but this speech he knew by heart."[37]

Dixon, a Democrat, had joined the Nixon entourage reluctantly, persuaded because he was paid double the usual fee. Nixon liked the sound of "This is Tom Dixon introducing Dick Nixon," and came to look upon the pleasant young announcer as a kind of talisman. Dixon remembered Nixon's coaching him in the proper technique of introducing him at rallies—"Get them to the point where when I come out they stand and cheer," he said. Amused at first, Dixon came to respect Nixon's professionalism and voted for him in 1946. Later, revolted by his smearing of Helen Gahagan Douglas, he broke with Nixon altogether.[38]

Nixon worked mostly through the local newspapers, of which thirty out of thirty-two were Republican. Here, William Costello noted, he employed "the half-truth, the misleading quotation, the loose-joined logic, that were indispensable to the creation of the Big Doubt."[39] Paul Bullock later documented from the newspapers a detailed record of how Voorhis was smothered not by a single reiterated lie, nor by a "Big Doubt," but by a blizzard of lies constantly repeated. In the past Nixon had lied furtively; his lies had gone undetected because they had been sporadic and because he had been sufficiently gifted as an actor to cover them. But under Chotiner's tutelage Nixon absorbed the technique of repeated, consistent, and organized lying.

The most damaging single lie spread was that Voorhis had received the endorsement of the radical Political Action Committee of the CIO. In 1944 Voorhis had accepted this endorsement, but now he rejected it because of the infiltration of the CIO by Communists. There was, however, a separate, less radical organization with a similar name, the NCPAC (National Citizens Political Action Committee) consisting largely of literary, religious, academic, and entertainment figures, and also some labor leaders. The Los Angeles chapter of this group did endorse Voorhis, but so quietly he had not learned of it, and the members of his staff who had heard of it had not bothered to inform him. Nixon had learned of it, however, and counting on public confusion and ignorance over the initials, intended to use it as evidence that Voorhis was close to what he would describe as a Communist-dominated group.

This he did in the first "debate," actually a multiple-candidate meeting on September 13, 1946, organized by Voorhis's friends among the Independent Voters of South Pasadena. Nixon had agreed to speak only if he could appear last on the program. At a strategic moment he asked Voorhis if he had been endorsed by the CIO–PAC. When he denied it, Nixon produced a copy of the local mimeographed NCPAC bulletin. Voorhis, caught by surprise, stammered that the two organizations were different, whereupon Nixon read out the names of several men who served on the boards or committees of both groups. He was cheered and Voorhis booed. The local press disingenuously trumpeted that Voorhis had conceded the "PAC" endorsement, neglecting to point out that there were two organizations. The damage was serious.[40]

In 1978 Nixon, who had requested a copy of Bullock's data, conceded in his memoirs that "the leadership of both groups was non-Communist."[41] He made no such admission in 1946. Voorhis admitted later that he should have said simply, "Mr. Nixon keeps dubbing me with this name, which I don't deserve. I have no control over what an organization is going to do." And he failed to go on the offensive, and to remind his constituents that his own Voorhis Act of 1940, which had forced both Communist and Fascist organizations to register with the Justice Department, had made him anathema to the Communist party as well as the German-American Bund.[42]

Nixon now challenged Voorhis to four formal debates and Voorhis foolishly agreed. Long-winded and discursive, an intellectual by temperament, he was no match for Nixon's staccato style and stilleto tactics. The debates alone would have finished Voorhis, but Nixon continued on to destroy Voorhis totally with distortions of his record. His leading newspaper ad, appearing in thirty-two newspapers, blazoned in large type:

DON'T BE FOOLED AGAIN

Voorhis has the endorsement of the National Political Action Committee because he voted their viewpoint 43 times out of 46 opportunities during the past four years. . . . the CIO Political Action Committee looks after the interests of Russia . . . REMEMBER, Voorhis is a former registered Socialist and his voting record in Congress is more Socialistic and Communistic than Democratic.[43]

The statistics had come originally from the *New Republic Voters' Supplement,* but nineteen of the votes were duplicates and in three instances Voorhis had voted the opposite. The so-called Communist votes were for such measures as the Reciprocal Trade Agreements, a wartime loan to Britain, abolition of the poll tax, a school lunch program, and unemployment insurance for federal workers.[44]

Another ad said: A VOTE FOR NIXON IS A VOTE AGAINST THE COMMUNIST-DOMINATED PAC WITH ITS GIGANTIC SLUSH FUND. Nixon warned that the PAC would "flood the district with paid workers to spread their doctrines and defeat those who stand for the preservation of the American way of life." Voorhis had no CIO-paid workers, and ran the campaign in his traditional amateurish and badly organized fashion.[45] In only one newspaper did he have more ads than Nixon, who was spending money freely and who at one point was advertising to pay campaign workers at nine dollars per day.[46]

Nixon's workers distributed twenty-five thousand thimbles bearing the inscription "Elect Nixon: Put a Needle in the PAC." Organized claques cheered Nixon at speeches and booed Voorhis. Specially trained hecklers, taught the tactic of "diamonding," followed Voorhis, asking him about the NCPAC endorsement, even in small church gatherings. Voorhis's followers retaliated by using bullhorns against Nixon in his rallies and by tearing down what they thought to be dishonest signs saying VOTE FOR NIXON, YOUR CONGRESSMAN. They spread no lies about Nixon and felt increasingly helpless in combatting the falsehoods heaped on their own candidate, including statements that Voorhis had voted to raise the ceiling prices on Florida but not on California oranges, and that his School for Boys had been given to the state to save taxes.[47] The local papers reported that Buron Fitts, former lieutenant-governor of the state, had said that Moscow had had "the insolence" to tell Americans "to select PAC candidates, such as Mr. Voorhis."[48]

In the last days of the campaign anonymous telephone calls were made to registered Democrats. A voice would say, "Did you know that Jerry Voorhis is a Communist?" and then hang up.

Voorhis verified the nature of the calls from trusted Democrats, and learned the identity of at least one young woman who had been paid nine dollars a day for two days to perform the anonymous service. She said she worked "in a boiler room with the phones going all the time." Nixon's workers denied this as an "invention," and when Nixon was queried about it in his vice-presidential campaign in 1952 he said he had never heard of such calls.

In the end it was Nixon's denials that were believed.[49] No other single episode demonstrates how successfully he had learned that repeated, organized falsehood must be accompanied by denial of guilt. If the liar wins an election, his denials are likely to be accepted, for few want to believe evil of a man for whom they have voted.

The slyest of all Nixon's attacks on Voorhis concerned his failure to see his own bills through to successful passage. Voorhis had spread his workload wide and had spent much time on civilian control of atomic energy. Like many congressmen—including later Nixon himself—he had few bills passed under his own name and none during the wartime years. Nixon ridiculed the record adroitly in a newspaper ad:

Did you know that your present Congressman introduced 132 public bills in the last four years, and only one of them was passed? That the one bill adopted transferred activities concerning rabbits from one federal department to another?[50]

The image of the rabbit was thus indelibly associated with Voorhis. And most voters believed, in the end, that Nixon had slain a rabbit and not a dragon.

Nixon won with a majority of 65,586 to 49,994 in the district, and 5727 to 2678 in his hometown of Whittier. Looking back in 1968 he said, "There's nothing like winning the first time."[51] Still, he went to Congress in a Republican landslide, one out of seven California Republicans to push Democrats out of the House, and he joined a Congress which had a majority of Republicans in both houses for the first time since 1928. Had all the lying then been necessary? Could he have won with a conventional campaign and without all the deception?

Voorhis sent him a generous letter wishing him well, referring gently to the calumny only in his last sentence:

I have refrained for reasons which I am sure you will understand, from making any references in this letter to the circumstances of the campaign recently conducted in our District. It would only have spoiled the letter.

Nixon did not reply. When later he visited Voorhis in his office it was to request copies of his mailing lists. Voorhis, enraged at the effrontery, refused but kept his temper. He said to the press at the time that he hoped they parted "as personal friends."[52]

In his *Confessions of a Congressman* Voorhis wrote only a few details of Nixon's slander and then took a vow of silence: "I observed a self-imposed rule not to make any public references to Richard Nixon." This he adhered to until 1972 when he published a scathing indictment of Nixon's career, *The Strange Case of Richard Milhous Nixon*. Even this omitted the full details of the fabrications Nixon had made in the campaign, which were not put into print until Paul Bullock's searching study in 1973.[53] Nixon was saved, as he would be many times in his life, by depression, shock, and inertia on the part of his defeated opponent, and by a generally uncynical electorate and press.

But there were two small groups for whom the Voorhis campaign became a watershed in their relations with Richard Nixon. One was a block of citizens in Whittier, the two thousand or more who had voted against him in 1946 and who would vote against him in about the same numbers in 1950. As one of them put it to Earl Mazo, "There was never anything ruthless about Dick when we were growing up. It was a fair fight, anything went . . . but not anything dirty. That's why I could never understand the positions he took in the campaigns. . . . Dick knew that a lot of us who are liberal are not Communists, in fact we are anti-Communists." And another said, "Real Quakers look at men with a level eye. Dick Nixon doesn't."[54]

It was these citizens who blocked the Whittier City Council's plan to name a new street for Nixon when he became vice-president. Hubert Perry, son of the banker who helped launch him into politics, watched the evolution of his old high school friend with mixed feelings. He remembered him as a youth "who did not get into scrapes" and "who didn't do crazy things." But when Nixon was elected president, Perry said to the Whittier press, "I think as President he will be much admired, but I don't think he is ever going to be loved."[55]

The second group to be disturbed were men in the House of Representatives. Nixon has told us that when he first went to Congress he "had the same lost feeling as when he first entered the Navy."[56] But there was a palpable difference. In the navy he had been lost in anonymity. In Congress he was known instantly as the victorious young Republican who had accused Voorhis of being a Communist. No one better than the members of the House knew how preposterous was the charge, and a dozen years later there were still members who spoke bitterly of his defeat.[57] When Nixon entered the House he was gently reminded, by Republicans as well as by Democrats, of the widespread affection for "good old Jerry." This was the most that congressional etiquette permitted by way of censure.

It had an impact and may help to illuminate why Nixon, in searching out that most difficult of problems for a freshman congressman—the subject of his maiden speech in the House—chose to make a vituperative attack on a man who really was a Communist. He singled out Gerhart Eisler, who had been a spy for Russia, and with all the vitriol at his command pressed for a contempt citation and a jail sentence. Thus he would maintain his reputation for aggression and patriotism. But this time he was certain that he was helping to destroy not a rabbit, nor a good and decent man, but a real dragon.

XIV

The First Informer

THE TRUTHTELLER, by convention, is a person of character, but the informer, who also tells the truth, is not. An informer may be a courageous penitent or a despised stool pigeon rewarded by the police, but however motivated he is still under a cloud because his truthtelling results in the punishment of another. That the punishment of the guilty may be healthy for society does not necessarily absolve the informer, either in his own eyes or in the eyes of others, for except when one testifies against the most disreputable of criminals, there is an inevitable odor of treachery and betrayal. Even at best, the health of society is a fairly remote abstraction.

At critical moments in his career Richard Nixon would use informers eagerly; no other president has so benefited from this kind of testimony. In the end he was destroyed by informers on his presidental staff, and by releasing transcripts of the presidential tapes—in advance of the Supreme Court order—he became an extraordinary informer in his own right, an informer most of all against himself.

As a lawyer he had little to do with police informers since he specialized in tax and corporate law rather than criminal law. He did handle divorces, however, and must have seen how husbands and wives could become informers on each other. Informing is, whether we like it or not, a universal experience, rooted in childhood, and Richard Nixon, like every other child, would have experienced the often agonizing difficulty of distinguishing between truthtelling and tattling on friends. How his parents responded to his and his brothers' telling about each other's small sins we don't know, although the general failure of trust among the Nixon brothers as adults may suggest that as children they had seldom united in a phalanx of silence with each other and against their father and mother.

All children learn from their peers that tattling is despicable. Nixon, we remember, never forgave the neighbor who told his mother little Arthur was smoking cigarettes. In his debating tricks and football pranks at Whittier College, and in the over-the-transom episode at Duke University, he had been lucky that no one had informed on him. And he protected his fellow Orthogonians, when caught, against punishment. It was not until he became a congressman, however, that he used an informer to further his political career. The first was not Whittaker Chambers, as one might suppose, but a German scholar refugee intent on exposing and punishing her two brothers.

On February 6, 1947, little more than four weeks after being sworn in as congressman, Nixon sat as a new member of the House Un-American Activities Committee (HUAC) and watched Elfriede Eisler, formerly a leading figure in the German Communist party, denounce her brothers Gerhart and Hanns as Soviet agents. Gerhart was not only a spy but also "a dangerous terrorist," she said, responsible in China, between 1928 and 1930, for the execution of many Chinese Communists thought to be hostile to Moscow. As an informer for Stalin he had been guilty of the executions of anti-Nazi refugees in the Soviet Union during the brief alliance with Hitler, and he had persuaded Stalin to hand over many German women prisoners to Hitler. Since 1933, she said, Gerhart had been an active spy in the United States.

Her denunciation was a chilling spectacle even for the chief committee investigator, Robert Stripling, who had been preparing the case on the Eisler brothers for some months. Gerhart, who had asked permission to emigrate to East Germany, was then being detained on Ellis Island for passport fraud. He had entered the United States several times under false names, and the FBI had good evidence that his role as an anti-Fascist refugee masked Communist party activities. Ex-Communist party member Louis Budenz testified that Gerhart had molded the U.S. Communist party into a well-knit, functioning agency for conspiracy. The sister, however, portrayed her brother as no ordinary spy but a moral monster. He had informed even against men who had befriended him, she said, notably the German Communist leader Hugo Eberlein and the Russian Communist theoretician Nicolai

Bukharin, both of whom Stalin had had executed. "A man who serves Stalin is conditioned to hand over to the GPU his child, his sister, his closest friend," she said. "Since I learned that Eisler was in this country [she almost spat his name, Stripling said], I have been exposing him."[1]

Elfriede had been a founder of the German Communist party in Austria, a leader of the party in Germany, and once a member of the Presidium in Moscow. By 1926 she had developed differences with Moscow's line. Expelled from the party, she had been subjected to much abuse and even accused of plotting Stalin's assassination. At the time of Gerhart's trial she was writing a scholarly account, *Stalin and German Communism*, which was to be published under her political name Ruth Fischer, by Harvard University Press.

Her youngest brother Hanns, a musician of some reputation in Europe, had been permitted to enter the United States in 1941 partly through the intervention of Eleanor Roosevelt. Elfriede seems to have had no evidence that he was a spy, but let the committee know that he had been invited to Moscow to help set up the International Music Bureau, intended as a worldwide liaison between musicians and labor groups, and that as a young man in Austria he had written music for revolutionary songs.

Gerhart, who looked, it was said, as innocuous as "an underpaid bookkeeper," was subpoenaed to testify in the same session as his sister. He was contemptuous and hostile, refusing to answer questions unless he was allowed to make a statement before taking an oath. Denied this, he refused to speak at all, claiming he was being kept as "a political prisoner." Nixon was enraged at Eisler and galvanized by his sister's denunciation. Although he had told newsmen some weeks earlier, on his first day in the House, "I was elected to smash the labor bosses,"[2] and was expected in his maiden speech to lash out at unionists, he decided now to use instead this corrosive family tragedy.

Eisler was already in custody and would shortly be convicted for passport fraud and sentenced to one to three years in prison, but Nixon wanted him first found guilty of contempt of Congress, "put out of circulation for a sufficient period of time for the Department of Justice to proceed against him on more serious charges." In his maiden speech on February 24, 1947, he attacked Eisler, alias Berger, alias Brown, alias Gerhart, alias Edwards, alias Liptzin, alias Eisman, a seasoned agent of the Communist International, who has been shuttling back and forth between Moscow and the United States from as early as 1933, to direct and master mind the political and espionage activities of the Communist Party in the United States. . . . a man described by his own sister as an arch terrorist.[3]

Nixon accused him of lying and of forgery; both charges were true. But Nixon had lied extensively too in the Voorhis campaign, and he could not easily have forgotten the "dubious affidavit" of his first law case, which, had Judge Paonessa been more punishing, might have resulted in a hearing before the California Bar Association. It can be said that in denouncing Eisler he was doing a public service, although actually the prosecution of the case more properly belonged with the Immigration and Justice departments. But in this attack Nixon was also using a defensive mechanism which we shall see many times in his career, saying, in effect, "It is the Communist who lies, not I." He could never successfully bury the memory of his lying in the Voorhis campaign since he would be reminded of it periodically by unfriendly writers all his life. But he could deny it and reinforce the denial by attacking others for lying. The combination of denial with projection upon others of what one feels guilty of oneself, which almost everyone resorts to on occasion, would become with Nixon almost a reflex, a protective device that he employed all his life, and which failed him only in the deluge of falsehoods of Watergate.

In his maiden speech attacking Eisler, Nixon also went back to an argument he had used in his first prize-winning speech in high school:

It is essential as Members of this House that we defend vigilantly the fundamental rights of freedom of speech and freedom of the press. But we must bear in mind that the rights of free speech and free press do not carry with them the right to advocate the destruction of the very Government which protects the freedom of an individual to express his views.[4]

Despite all his classes in government and constitutional law he was still in fundamental disagreement with Thomas Jefferson, who had helped define the First Amendment in his first inaugural:

If there be any among us who would wish to dissolve this Union or to change its republican form, let them stand undisturbed as monuments of the safety with which error or opinion may be tolerated where reason is left free to combat it.

Newsweek praised Nixon's speech as "deeply impressive," with "a quality of steel behind the voice," a welcome change for him from the disparaging attitude of the *Washington Post,* which had earlier called him "the greenest Congressman in town."[5] The House voted to cite Eisler for contempt; he was sentenced to one year in jail and fined $1000. Later, out on bail, which had been fixed at $23,500, and waiting the appeal of this sentence and the subsequent one imposed for passport fraud, he stowed away on a Polish liner and made his way to East Germany. There he was warmly received and given a professorship at the University of Leipzig. He died in the Soviet Union in 1968, and the *New York Times* obituary described him as one who had "guided revolutions in four countries."[6]

His brother Hanns was permitted to leave for Czechoslovakia in February 1948. The committee had found no evidence of his Communist activities in the United States, although it had denounced him as "the Karl Marx of the musical field." Black-listed by the film industry for which he had been composing music, and harassed by the FBI, he chose to leave with his wife, even though deportation proceedings had been dropped.[7]

The exposure and punishment of the two Eisler brothers, and later the radical Leon Josephson,[8] beyond what was already being done quietly by the Justice Department, won Nixon fame, and he became an instant hero to the conservatives. Influential Helen Reid, inviting him to speak before the *New York Herald Tribune* Forum audience on October 19, 1948, wrote, "The *Herald Tribune* wants to have the honor of making you known to the country."[9] Fr. John F. Cronin, of St. Mary's Seminary in Baltimore, to whom J. Edgar Hoover had leaked data on American Communists for a report to Catholic bishops in 1945, now sought Nixon out and became for a time his speechwriter. He vastly expanded the young congressman's knowledge of anti-Communist propaganda.

There were several routes to prominence possible to Nixon in 1947, but he deliberately gambled on the riskiest when he chose to dominate HUAC, which even then, more than any other congressional committee, carried a stench of jingoism and paranoia. Nixon told one fellow congressman from California it might be "the kiss of death," but that he hoped to correct the injudicious procedures of the past and make the committee respectable. Washington reporter William Costello, one of the first to see Nixon's skill in manipulation of power, said, however, that actually he worked hard behind the scenes to get the committee assignment.[10]

Another shrewd political move was Nixon's organizing the fifteen Republican freshmen congressmen into the Chowder and Marching Club—Gerald Ford was a charter member—with a reputation for being underdogs and "square," not unlike the old Orthogonian Society. The members met every Wednesday to plan voting strategy. Republican party whip Joe Martin gave Nixon a committee plum, selecting him as the only freshman congressman to accompany Christian Herter's committee to Europe for a study that would result in House approval for the Marshall Plan. Nixon came back something of an internationalist, committed to massive financial and economic aid to the stricken states of Western Europe. In Trieste, on September 17, he had watched street rioting between Communists and non-Communists and had seen the body of a boy with his head blown off by a Communist grenade.[11] He needed no more traumatic evidence of the malevolence of the Communist expansion abroad. A stout defender of the Marshall Plan despite hostility to it in his own district, he argued for it from the beginning not on humanitarian or economic grounds but as the only way to block further Soviet expansion into Western Europe.

He came to favor, too, the Reciprocal Trade Agreements Act and the formation of NATO, positions which led many in Congress to believe him to be a liberal Republican. Actually in his voting he moved easily across the whole spectrum from left to right. He introduced a bill giving control of the tidelands oil to the states, thereby rewarding the oil companies of California which had assisted in his election. As a member of the House Education and Labor Committee he helped write the provisions for the Taft-Hartley bill, counting it an opportunity to "smash the labor bosses." The nation had lost six billion dollars in industrial strife since V-J Day, he argued on the floor of the House, and it was the laborer who suffered. The Taft-Hartley bill would be the workman's Magna Carta. When it passed, he joined with other Republicans in "exultant shouts" on the floor.[12]

He voted with the conservative Republicans against soil conservation payments, federal crop insurance, school lunch programs, and loans to tenant farmers. He voted to reduce the federal appropriations for aiding crowded schools in areas where there was defense industry, and voted to reduce all appropriations for public power, rural electrification, and public health. He voted for a resolution to cut 750,000 working people off Social Security rolls and for an override of a Truman veto of a bill that would have deprived even more people of old-age benefits.[13]

But it was HUAC which became Nixon's major forum and he moved into its activities with zest. Martin Dies, the original chairman, had made the committee notorious for harassment of witnesses and for xenophobia. J. Parnell Thomas of New Jersey, the succeeding chairman, was little better. Coarse, opinionated, and partisan, he used the committee hearings chiefly to discredit the New Deal. He hated Eleanor Roosevelt and left no opportunity unused to caricature her. Parnell Thomas shortly left Congress, imprisoned for taking kickbacks from his staff.

Karl Mundt (R., South Dakota), who replaced Thomas as chairman, was a cunning investigator, and a partisan intent on maximum publicity for himself. He taught Nixon much about winning headlines. John McDowell (R., Pennsylvania) was so ignorant and so inept he had difficulty following the committee hearings. John Rankin (D., Mississippi) hated Jews and blacks, and used the HUAC hearings to discredit both. He saw Communism not only as an international Jewish conspiracy, with headquarters in the Soviet Union, but also as a world movement going back in time:

Communism hounded and persecuted the Savior during his early ministry, inspired his crucifixion, derided him in his dying agony, and then gambled for his garments at the floor of the cross. . . .[14]

F. Edward Hébert (D., Louisiana), who had been a newspaperman, was intelligent, vigorous, and less bigoted. He derided Nixon and Mundt for their "hysteria for headlines," but fully shared in their hatred of Communism, which he likened to venereal disease. "I propose to do something about Communist ideas," he said. "That same argument—the spread of disease—all these signs around—particularly the drive against venereal disease—the more you say about it the more you make it popular."[15]

Voorhis before his defeat had resigned from HUAC in disgust, and other moderate congressmen who belonged simply avoided the hearings. The committee had been run entirely by those members who looked on Communism in apocalyptic terms as a conspiracy of absolute evil. Nixon, however, who succeeded in getting partial control of the committee, remained courteous and moderate in his questioning and refrained from adopting wholly what Richard Hofstadter has called "the paranoid style in American politics." He never looked on Communism as the Anti-Christ against which every resource of the nation should be pitted. He was flexible and opportunistic, using Communism as a bogeyman, with a plethora of conspiratorial rhetoric on the hustings, but ready to retreat when confronted by able men with arguments from constitutional history.

In one hearing he jousted with Arthur Garfield Hays, liberal lawyer for the American Civil Liberties Union, on the question of whether or not to outlaw the Communist party altogether. Hays warned that it was impossible to legislate against dangerous thoughts. He likened the anti-Communist furor of the moment to hysteria over the Jacobin Republicans during Jefferson's day, to Know-Nothing assaults on Catholics in the mid-nineteenth century, to the suppression of Anarchists in the 1880s, and to the Red Scare of the 1920s. He described William Z. Foster and Earl Browder, leaders of the American Communists, as "confused, futile men with wild ideas who have been able to get nowhere in all these years. Why we treat them as important people developing a big political movement is beyond my comprehension." He warned that suppression would promote, not halt, the growth of the party.

Nixon, retreating from his original position of total suppression of the party, replied that the committee was in favor not of suppression but only of exposure.[16] Exposure by HUAC in 1947 meant attack and punishment by others. Many Americans who had flirted with Communism in their youth, whether embittered by the depression or as a response to the rise of Fascism in Europe, now found themselves pilloried by the committee, their reputations as professors, actors, and writers besmirched, their livelihoods threatened or ruined.

There were no hearings on right-wingers, although in 1946 there had been an interrogation of the anti-Semitic, pro-Fascist

Gerald L. K. Smith. The whole thrust of the seven sets of hearings in 1947 was against either suspected individual Communists or the so-called Communist fronts, such as the American Youth for Democracy, Southern Conference for Human Welfare, and the Civil Rights Congress. There were hearings on Communist infiltration in labor unions and the film industry. Nixon was active in the former, but stayed somewhat aloof from the latter, although as a congressman from California he might have been expected to chair the sessions in Hollywood. He did not take the lead in accelerating blacklisting of many actors and screenwriters. But neither did he discourage it.

Committee attempts to discover what was "subversive" in movies like *Mission to Moscow, North Star, None But the Lonely Heart,* and *Song of Russia,* most of them made when the Soviet Union was America's ally and losing millions of soldiers and citizens in the war against Hitler, offended thoughtful citizens across the country. But the hearings were reported so irresponsibly in much of the nation's press that many were led to believe that Hollywood was a hotbed of Communism. As Alistair Cooke wrote in his *A Generation on Trial,* the press was worse than HUAC in "putting people into discreditable associations, and presuming guilt before innocence can be proved. . . . the worst indignities were done by the headline writers."[17]

The famous "Hollywood Ten," who resisted the inquisition as unconstitutional and refused to inform on their friends, went to jail on contempt charges. None was ever tried for the substantive offenses with which the committee in effect charged them—being card-carrying party members and introducing pro-Communist ideas into their films—activities which had never been written into American law as criminal. In the following year similar HUAC hearings on espionage of nuclear weapons development demonstrated that there were some scientists who were or had been Communists, but failed to demonstrate that any of them had done anything improper.[18] HUAC members abandoned traditional Anglo-American concepts of criminal justice, assumed guilt rather than innocence, and conducted most of their questioning with the assumption that to believe in Communism was a crime.

Although the Smith Act, an antisubversive bill passed in 1940, had sufficient teeth in it so that under its provisions eleven leaders of the American Communist party were tried and sentenced to prison in 1948, Nixon and Mundt wanted a still more punishing bill and spent a good deal of time in 1947 drawing up provisions for H.R. 5852. This, the Mundt-Nixon bill, called for registration with the Department of Justice of all Communist party officials and members; identification of the sources of all material printed and broadcast by "Communist front" groups (to be designated by the attorney-general); disclosure of all names and officers in such front groups; denial of federal employment to Communist party officials; discontinuance of tax-exemptions for Communist front organizations; disclosure of sources of money; deportation of aliens convicted of Communist party activity; denial of passport privileges to American-born Communists; increasing the penalty for peacetime espionage to a $10,000 fine and ten years in prison; and the creation of a subversive activities control board which upon application by the attorney-general would decide what was and what was not a "Communist front" group.

Thomas E. Dewey—in spite of his presidential ambitions— spoke out courageously against the bill in May: "Stripped to its naked essential, this is nothing but the method of Hitler and Stalin. It is thought-control borrowed from the Japanese. It is an attempt to beat down ideas with a club. It is a surrender of everything we believe in."[19] The leading newspapers supported Dewey and deplored the defense of the bill by Harold Stassen. Although the Mundt-Nixon bill passed the House by a vote of 319 to 56, it died in the Senate, at least for the moment. Later many of its provisions were incorporated in the even more blatantly unconstitutional McCarran Act which passed Congress in 1950.

The Mundt-Nixon bill was Nixon's first serious legislation under his own name and reflects his predilection for proscription and punishment. Although his own methods on HUAC were less offensive than those of Mundt, Rankin, and Thomas, he worked easily with these men, who were given to abusiveness and harassment. He did not separate himself from their methods or from their racial and religious bigotry. Instead he learned from them how to use the committee for maximum publicity for himself and how to turn anti-Communist publicity generated in the hearings to political advantage. By contrast, especially with Rankin and Thomas, he seemed a model of sobriety and reasonableness. Only when he was matched against genuinely moderate Republicans did the press get a true perspective on his deep conservatism and his secret pleasure in destructive attack.

President Truman was alarmed by the enormous publicity, so often favorable, which HUAC generated and the antidemocratic uses to which it was put. The growing climate of fear in the country was rendered possible by the advancing *Gleichschaltung* of Central Eastern Europe, by Soviet threats in Greece and Turkey, the spread of Communism across China, and the exposure of a sizeable Soviet espionage ring in Canada. Already in 1946 Truman had accepted the recommendations of a Justice Department committee studying the danger of domestic Communism and was committed to a new loyalty program. There had been an informal attorney-general's list of so-called subversive organizations, but it had been kept secret. Truman's new Loyalty Review Board published it late in 1947, thus opening the way, as Robert Donovan has written, "to doubt and calumny on all the organizations listed."[20] Thus the pressure of HUAC contributed to the spreading mischief. HUAC methods offended many Americans, who found it offensive to be asked to turn informer on the friends of one's past, even a misguided past. But the fear of loss of reputation and livelihood turned many a decent American into an informer despite his best intentions. Sen. Joseph McCarthy accelerated the trend after 1950.

Nixon was not tarred with the worst HUAC abuses of 1947. But his canny use of the committee can be seen in his reelection campaign of 1948. In his political advertisements he utilized the headlines won by HUAC hearings: NIXON LEARNS UNION MEN FEAR LEADERS; NIXON ASSAILS MUSIC CZAR (Caesar Petrillo); REDS AND PINKS IN FILMLAND. His new opponent, Stephen Zetterberg, a local lawyer-Democrat who ran against Nixon knowing he had little chance of winning, has described Nixon's use of HUAC and also the adroitness with which he exploited California's system of cross-filing in the primary. Advertising himself as "Your Congressman," disguising his party affiliation, and taking advantage of his national reputation as an anti-Communist battler, Nixon sent out postcards with his portrait to Democrats. The inscription began, "Fellow Democrat." Only in one corner in small print could one read, "Democrats for Richard Nixon." Many newcomers to the state, not understanding cross-filing, thought Nixon to be a Democrat. And Zetterberg, somewhat naïvely, as a matter of principle, had refused to cross-file in the Republican primary.

Zetterberg had little money; he reported that he spent exactly $1123.21 in the campaign. Although of Swedish descent, his name suggested to many a Jewish origin, and this cost him votes among the numerous anti-Semites in this strongly conservative WASP district.[21] Nixon won easily in both primaries. This early victory in June, which meant he did not have to campaign at all in November, brought a special bonus. For Nixon could now spend the several crucial months beginning with August 1948 in Washington rather than in California. And it was on August 3 that Whittaker Chambers turned public informer against Alger Hiss, and set in motion the forces that would catapult Nixon into the vice-presidency.

The Impact of
Whittaker Chambers

On the road of the informer it is always night.
— WHITTAKER CHAMBERS[1]

THE HISS CASE reads like a Henry James novel with extra Gothic overtones. One wanders in a labyrinth of lying, intrigue, and perjury. There is still some argument about the truthfulness of the leading characters, and in the subplots there are unsolved murders and unexplained suicides. Controversy over Hiss's trial, one of the most divisive in the century, has refused to die. At the time Hiss was called a Benedict Arnold and Chambers was denounced as a sadist and moral leper. A small but influential core of Americans continued over the years to believe Hiss to be the American Dreyfus; the larger number who read seriously about the case thought him to be simply a resilient liar.

In 1978 historian Allen Weinstein's brilliant volume of historical detection, *Perjury: The Hiss-Chambers Case,* concluded that Hiss had been guilty of perjury and espionage. Weinstein, who had first thought Hiss might well be innocent, found himself finally tracking down one lie after another. His book, definitive in its accumulation and analysis of the evidence, did not quite end the controversy—the author had predicted it would not—partly because he stayed with the facts and was chary about divining motives or character. Hiss in particular remained a well of mystery. The case lived on, troubling those who believed that to find Hiss guilty would be to sustain Nixon, which some could not do even if he was in the right.

Whittaker Chambers, who published an agonized confession, *Witness,* in 1952, and who died of a heart attack in 1961, had during his exposé suffered the penalties of the informer, as he had said he would. In death he was remembered by many as an effervescent editor for *Time*, by others as a disturbed, even unsavory man who had surprisingly become a hero in a national morality play. Those who knew him best believed him when he said that he exposed Hiss reluctantly and that he did it for the nation's safety. Arthur Schlesinger, Jr., called him "a figure out of Dostoievsky."[2] Others called him savagely destructive.

Hiss steadfastly resisted telling the truth about his Communist past, which, had he done so early as many others did, would have kept him from going to jail. After forty-four months in federal prison he continued to profess his innocence and to attack Chambers as a psychopath and "rejected homosexual."[3] His own book, *In the Court of Public Opinion*, which he admitted was written "as a legal brief,"[4] won few converts to his cause. Instead of a passionate defense of his innocence, he evolved conspiracy theories involving forged typewriters, writing with an odd calm that dismayed his friends, and concluding with remarkable ambivalence,

the name of Alger Hiss has become synonymous with treachery and betrayal in high office. If he was guilty this is perhaps as it should be. But if he was not, it is tragic that the fear and hysteria of the times should be allowed to impede so gravely the efforts of his defenders to unearth and present the evidence which would clear his name.[5]

Efforts to clear his name had in fact been prodigious.

Watergate brought Hiss a belated fame on college campuses, where students who were ignorant of the massive evidence against him were happy to parade him as Nixon's first victim. He regained his pension and his right to practice law in Massachusetts, although the court took some pains to say that it continued to believe him guilty but thought he had earned the right to restitution. He continued to press for a *coram nobis*, asking the court to review the old decision because of errors of fact, his insistence on his innocence thus stretching into three decades.

In *Six Crises*, Hiss and Chambers are black against white, evil against good, the Communist traitor against the reformed Communist who has become the Quaker man of God. Nixon described the case as "the first major crisis of my political life. My name, my reputation, and my career were ever to be linked with the decisions I made and the actions I took in that case, as a thirty-five-year old freshman Congressman in 1948."[6] Here Nixon wrote truer than he knew. He could never escape the meshing of his life with that of Hiss, and in the crisis of Watergate his references to the case would confound friend and foe alike.

Chambers died while Nixon was writing *Six Crises*, which may explain why his descriptions are wholly respectful; he called Chambers "thoughtful and introspective," a man with "inner strength and depth" and "extraordinary intellectual gifts."[7] Earlier, in reviewing *Witness* in 1952 for the *Saturday Review of Literature*, he had betrayed some distaste for the man himself. Although calling *Witness* a great book, he also predicted that

epithets will be directed against it in the drawing rooms, around dinner tables, and during the cocktail hours among the "better" people—"too emotional," "long and repetitious," "one of those anti-Communist things." After all, "how could any good come from that fat, repulsive little creature who said those terrible things about a 100 percent certified gentleman, Alger Hiss."[8]

The book gave the lie, he said, to those who hold that "anyone who becomes a Communist must have been queer and unstable to begin with."

A second review of *Witness* in the same journal, written by a young law professor, Charles Alan Wright, titled "A Long Work of Fiction," said, "I think Hiss is innocent. And I am sure that if the verdict was right and he *is* guilty, it is the purest chance that the jury guessed the correct answer."[9] Years later, during Watergate, Nixon—oddly, it would seem at first glance—turned to Wright to aid in his own defense. He was then urging his staff to read *Six Crises* for clues in handling his multiplying problems, an urging that was mystifying, since Nixon had always held Hiss to be a liar. Perhaps he felt in hiring Wright that if so gifted a lawyer could be persuaded that Hiss had not been lying, he might be exactly the right man to turn to, and persuade that he himself had not been not lying either.

Although Nixon over the years lauded Chambers as a man of truth, he had no illusions about his fate. To John Dean he said on February 28, 1973:

These guys you know—the informers. Look what it did to Chambers . . . the greatest single guy in the *Time* of 25 or 30 years ago, probably *Time*'s best writer of the century. They finished him. Either way, the informer is not one in our society. Either way, that is the one thing people can't survive.

And to Haldeman he said on March 27, 1973, "Hiss was destroyed because he lied—perjury. Chambers was destroyed because he was an informer, but Chambers knew he was going to be destroyed."[10] And although he detested Hiss from their first meeting for his arrogance and "100 per cent certified gentleman" manners, it was not Chambers but Hiss—"twisting and turning and squirming . . . evading and avoiding"[11]—whom Nixon would imitate in Watergate. This would be one of the most arresting ironies in Richard Nixon's life.

If one looks beyond the three major participants of the case and their families and involved friends, one cannot but be struck with how many Quakers there were, how many suicides or suspected suicides, how ubiquitous the rumors of homosexuality, and how murderous the family ruin. Chambers and his wife and children in 1948 were all Quakers, as was Nixon. So, too, was Hiss's wife Priscilla. Noel Field and his wife, friends of Hiss who fled to Hungary when exposed as Communist agents, were also Quakers. Rumors of homosexuality circulated about both Chambers and Hiss, also about Chambers's father and Hiss's stepson.

Priscilla Hiss's father and Alger Hiss's father, as well as Hiss's older sister, had all committed suicide. Russian defector and former Soviet intelligence official Gen. Walter Krivitsky, a friend of Chambers, had been found dead of a bullet wound in a Washington hotel in 1941. Although police called it a suicide, Chambers was certain he had been murdered, like Trotsky, by Soviet agents.[12] Two men peripherally involved with Hiss—Lawrence Duggan and W. Marvin Smith—apparently committed suicide during the crisis of exposure: some thought they had been murdered. Another Hiss friend, Harry Dexter White, died of a heart attack when Hiss was first being questioned; there were those who suspected he had taken his own life. When Chambers died of a heart attack and was buried without an autopsy, and his wife was hospitalized in collapse at the same time, rumors spread of a double suicide pact.

Hiss had a special family constellation very like that of Nixon's. Each had a younger brother named Donald, and each had seen an older and more attractive brother die in his youth after a prolonged illness. Alger Hiss's small, seemingly fragile wife professed to be a practicing Quaker and used "the plain language" in the privacy of her home, as had Nixon's mother. All of this may have contributed to Nixon's concentration on Hiss more than on other suspected Communists in government. Robert Stripling, chief HUAC investigator for the case, told Allen Weinstein, "Nixon had set his hat for Hiss. It was a personal thing. He was no more concerned whether Hiss was [a Communist] than a billy goat!"[13] Certainly Nixon seemed more concerned in pinioning Hiss as a liar than as a Communist. "Through that case," he wrote, "a guilty man was sent to prison who otherwise would have remained free; a truthful man was vindicated who otherwise would have been condemned as a liar."[14]

In his memoirs Nixon would quote with satisfaction what Eisenhower said to him on their second meeting, "You not only got Hiss, but you got him fairly." He would also write, underlining his own multiple motivations, "I recognized the worth of the nationwide publicity that the Hiss Case had given me—publicity on a scale that most congressmen only dream of achieving."[15]

The Hiss Case "began for me personally," Nixon wrote, "on a hot, sultry Washington morning—Tuesday, August 3, 1948." Three days earlier ex-Communist Elizabeth Bentley had made headlines when she named thirty-two government officials who she said had once provided information for a Soviet spy ring. She had not mentioned Hiss. Whittaker Chambers was also subpoenaed by HUAC. Nixon described him as short and pudgy, with unpressed clothes, who spoke in a bored monotone, "an indifferent if not reluctant witness." "None of us thought his testimony was going to be especially important." Chambers named eight government officials, among them the Hiss brothers, who had in the thirties been Communists intent on infiltrating the highest offices of government. "This was the first time," Nixon wrote in *Six Crises*, "I had ever heard of either Donald or Alger Hiss."[16]

It was not the first time. Nixon had been briefed extensively on Alger Hiss in February 1947 by Father Cronin, to whom FBI agent Ed Hummer had leaked from FBI files Whittaker Chambers's secret denunications of Hiss. But Nixon chose to keep this fact a secret even from his HUAC colleagues. Later he would mention the Cronin briefing to Earl Mazo and Bela Kornitzer, both of whom published the fact,[17] but apparently he forgot the admissions when he wrote *Six Crises* and there renewed the fiction that August 3, 1948, was the first time he had heard of Hiss.

Nixon wrote also that he had thought of skipping the public hearing altogether, but he had been delayed by an "extraordinary quality" in Chambers "which raised him far above the run of witness." It was especially when he said "I know that I am leaving the winning side for the losing side, but it is better to die on the losing side than to live under Communism" that Nixon was captured by what "sounded like the ring of truth."[18]

He now moved decisively into Chambers's life, questioning him in executive sessions, visiting him for long hours at his Maryland farm, the first time alone and later with newspaperman Bert Andrews and HUAC investigator Robert Stripling. "The old farmhouse smelled of another generation," Stripling said. "A stuffed raven stared at us from a wall. An old German Bible lay opened on a table."[19]

Chambers's son and daughter liked Nixon. "To them he is always Nixie," Chambers later wrote, "the kind and the good, about whom they will tolerate no nonsense." Nixon even invited his parents to the Chambers farm. Frank and Hannah Nixon had turned the Whittier store over to Donald and had bought a farm in Pennsylvania, and when Nixon realized that they were worried over the newspaper furor concerning the case, as well as about his own anxiety and insomnia, he arranged a meeting with Chambers to quiet their fears. When his mother had urged him to drop the case, he had said to her, "Mother, I think Hiss is lying. Until I know the truth, I've got to stick it out."[20] Their visits to Chambers put the seal of "family" on the relationship.

Very early Nixon saw his chance to turn the case into an embarrassment for Truman, and was at least as intent on finding out why Hiss had been left untouched by the Justice Department as he was in exposing him. Chambers told him much about his friendship with Hiss, but kept secret the fact that both had been involved in espionage. He admitted that he had been "in the underground," that he had collected party dues from Hiss and others in the secret Harold Ware cell, but held that they had all acted as "functionaries" intent on influencing policy. Hiss, Chambers said, as an aide to Roosevelt at Yalta, had been in an ideal position to urge pro-Soviet diplomacy.

Chambers broke with the party in 1938. In 1938, after the

Stalin-Hitler pact, he turned informer, fearful lest the whole Communist underground apparatus in the United States be put at the service of Hitler's Gestapo. Isaac Don Levine, anti-Communist journalist and Soviet expert, who had found him living penniless and in terror of assassination by a revengeful GPU, had taken him to Adolf Berle, then undersecretary of state. Chambers had wanted to see Roosevelt and ask for immunity, but he could get no closer than Berle, who listened with some consternation and took notes. He said he would speak to FDR and he did, but Roosevelt—not surprisingly, since Chambers presented no documentary evidence—had turned the story aside with an epithet.[21]

When nothing happened to Hiss, Chambers remained silent. He found work writing book reviews for *Time*. Henry Luce liked him and eventually made him an editor. "*Time* gave me back my life," Chambers said. "It gave me my voice. It gave me sanctuary, professional respect, peace, and time in which to mature my changed view of the world and men's destiny, and mine in it."[22] Meanwhile he watched with increasing anxiety the rise of Alger Hiss in government, as an important aide to Roosevelt, then as chief organizer of the San Francisco Conference that set up the United Nations. Chambers told FBI men, who had sought him out in 1945, that if Hiss were made secretary-general of the United Nations (as had actually been secretly urged by Andrei Gromyko to Secretary of State Stettinius in London, September 7, 1945) that he would expose him publicly.[23]

Still, Hiss had remained seemingly untouched and the apparent inaction on the part of the FBI and the Justice Department smacked of treason to Richard Nixon. Chambers described him standing by the barn on his farm shaking with anger, saying, "If the American people understood the real character of Alger Hiss they would boil him in oil."[24] Actually Secretary of State James F. Byrnes and others had become suspicious of Hiss as evidence of his Soviet sympathies and possible espionage dribbled in from sources other than Chambers, including Canadian and French intelligence. France's premier, Edouard Daladier, had warned American Ambassador William C. Bullitt that "two brothers named Hiss" in the State Department were "Soviet agents." And a defecting Russian code clerk at the Soviet embassy in Ottowa, Igor Gouzenko, had implicated "an aide" to Stettinius.[25] Hiss had worked for Stettinius in 1945.

Hiss had been questioned by the FBI on February 4, 1942, and later warned by Secretary of State Byrnes, Dean Acheson, and John Foster Dulles that he was suspected.[26] To one and all he denied that he had ever been a Communist and that he had ever known a man named Whittaker Chambers. He made the same denials under oath to a New York grand jury investigating Soviet espionage in the United States. Nevertheless, J. Edgar Hoover had put Hiss under surveillance for a year beginning in November 1945, and the State Department had quietly eased him out of government into the nonsensitive, wholly academic Carnegie Endowment post in February 1947, in such a fashion that his reputation and livelihood had not been destroyed. None of this was known to Nixon, or Chambers, or apparently even to Harry Truman.

Although the long sessions in the battered rocking chairs on his farmhouse porch deepened the trust Whittaker Chambers felt for Nixon, the latter was troubled by persisting rumors—later stated openly by Hiss—that Chambers was an alcoholic, that he had been in a mental institution, and that he was a homosexual. Every aspect of his story that could be checked by committee investigators was researched. Nixon as a canny lawyer probed Chambers's memory looking for weakness and dissimulation. He found no evidence of alcoholism and became satisfied that the rumors of hospitalization for mental illness came from Chambers's two serious heart attacks, one of which meant months of rest in bed.

He could hardly have escaped learning about Chambers's ferociously damaged childhood, which was later described in the apocalyptic *Witness*. There Chambers told almost everything about his childhood and youth save that his father had been a homosexual. An unwanted baby, given a name he detested, Vivian, he had grown up in genteel poverty in Lynbrook, Long Island. His mother, a frustrated actress, was intent chiefly on seeing that he grew up into a man of "breeding." His father, a talented but chronically depressed artist, ignored both his sons, played for hours at a time with a miniature theater, dolls, and toys to which they were forbidden, and finally ran off with a male lover when Chambers was nine. His mother put her two sons in her bedroom, kept an axe in the closet for protection, and vowed she would live "entirely for her children." "A woman with an axe is a match for any man," she said. Chambers never quite escaped the cot in his mother's bedroom. Even as senior editor of *Time* he would spend five nights a week with his mother in the old Lynbrook home and the remainder of the week with his wife and two children on the Maryland farm.[27]

Whittaker's father, Jay Chambers, had returned after two years, but had lived in continued estrangement from his family in an upstairs bedroom. Jay's own mother, Grandmother Chambers, who had become psychotic, also moved into an upstairs bedroom. When she emerged at all it was to tell gentle memories of her peaceful Quaker childhood or to scream that she was being poisoned with kitchen gas and to threaten her son and grandsons with scissors and kitchen knives. Young Chambers's hands were scarred, he said, "where the scissors missed my father and caught me." For years, he said, "this dark, demonaic presence sat at the heart of our home."[28]

As an adolescent Chambers had been fat, effeminate, and friendless. He ran away from home and lived for a time under a new name as a day laborer. It was the first of many identities. When he returned, he entered Columbia University. Lionel Trilling, who put him in a novel, said he moved in a group of young men "of intimidating brilliance" despite a physical presence "calculated to negate youth and all its graces," especially his mouth, which was "a devastation of empty sockets and blackened stumps."[29]

Chambers's formidable talents as a linguist and fledgling writer were recognized by his adviser, Mark Van Doren. His one-act drama *A Play for Puppets,* published under a pseudonym in the Columbia *Morningside,* betrayed the death fantasies that would always plague him. It showed Jesus in the tomb protesting when the angels came to wake Him, "Who is breaking my sleep? Heaven? . . . Let me sleep. . . . Roll back the stone and go thy way." It also showed Roman centurians idly discussing the recently crucified Christ. One says casually, "They say he never lay with a woman."[30]

When Dean Herbert Hawkes found the play blasphemous and ordered Chambers to confiscate all copies and make a public apology, he refused and left college. Shortly afterward, he joined the Communist party, finding among the tough labor organizers and disciplined party men and women, most of them immigrants, what seemed to be a dedicated brotherhood. They gave him orders, told him never to drink and to forget about the pursuit of wealth. And they promised to save the world.

The childhoods of Nixon and Chambers were similar in that each had felt himself to be the least loved by his parents. Each too, as with Hiss, had seen a more favored brother die after a harrowing period of illness. Richard Chambers, the younger son, handsome as Whittaker was not, and a natural athlete, had returned from college drinking heavily and depressed, and had begged his brother to join him in death. For two years the family had faced the relentlessly aggressive and numbing behavior of the alcoholic and would-be suicide. Twice Whittaker had resuscitated Richard when he found him in a coma from inhaling kitchen gas, and he never recovered from guilt over not having been present to save him from the gas on the final night of death.

Chambers wrote that his brother's suicide made him an "irreconcilable" Communist. Communism, he said, "speaks insistently to the human mind at the point where desperation lurks," and the choice seemed to him at the time as one "between a world that is dying and one that is coming to birth." Eleven years later he had come to believe the party to be "the malevolent god that failed," and he had begun "like Lazarus," the impossible return. This led him through a religious conversion, first to Episcopalianism, and finally to the Quaker church of his grandmother's childhood. He described it as "a transit that must be made upon the knees or not at all. For it is not only to the graves of dead brothers that we find ourselves powerless at last to bring anything but prayer. We are equally powerless at the graves of ourselves, once we know that we live in shrouds."

In 1948 Nixon united with Chambers in planning the destruction of a man whom Chambers had sought out in affection, like the brother he had lost. Nixon organized the details with the eagerness of a hunter stalking a kill. But Chambers was tormented, as he wrote later, by the question God asked of Cain, "Where is Abel, thy brother?" He remained for months "a man constantly wavering."[31] Although he described his own life freely as a writer for *The Daily Worker* and *The New Masses,* and some of the activities of the Communist cell where he had met Hiss, he kept secret the details of Hiss's espionage, hoping to bring him "back to life" in the free world—as he had hoped, vainly, to save his own brother—but also acting aggressively to ruin him.

In their many sessions together Chambers educated Nixon about Soviet espionage, with particular attention to passport racketeering, and he also provided the intellectual underpinnings for Nixon's anti-Communism. He taught him his own concept of the Stalinist mind as "instantly manipulable, pragmatic, motivated by the instinctive knowledge that political position . . . is indispensable to political power." Perhaps the most damaging of Chambers's concepts was that the New Dealers would do anything to hide the Communists among them in order to stay in power. This Nixon came to believe, and it formed the major thrust of his attacks on Acheson and Truman.

Chambers also gave Nixon a sense of the vigor of what he called the Communist call: "Have you the moral strength to take upon yourself the crimes of history so that many at last may close this chronicle of age-old senseless suffering, and replace it with a purpose and a plan?" The Communist vision Chambers saw as "the vision of Man without God," the "vision of man's displacing God as the creative intelligence of the world." He polarized the world into two great contending forces and thus transmuted his personal struggle against Hiss into world terms. In *Witness* he wrote that "the two irreconcilable faiths of our time—Communism and Freedom—come to grips in the persons of two conscious and resolute men. . . . For, with dark certitude, both knew, almost from the beginning, that the Great Case could end only in the destruction of one or both of the contending figures."

Nixon would himself preach the doctrine of the divided and polarized world, but he never came to believe, like Chambers, that "the problem of evil was the central problem of human life," nor could he ever have described himself, as Chambers did, as "an involuntary witness to God's grace and to the fortifying power of faith."[32] He used Chambers's ideas about the concept and uses of crisis, and he referred repeatedly in his speeches to truth and character, but he would never become messianic. He would remain instead relentlessly political, very like Chambers's own description of the Stalinist.

At the Maryland farmhouse Nixon also came to know Chambers's wife of seventeen years, the dark, soft-spoken, apprehensive Esther, who feared no less than her husband that his turning

informer would wreck their lives. Hardworking as any pioneer
woman—milking eighteen cows a day—she was also endlessly supportive. At the Hiss trial, when her husband was under venomous
attack, she cried out, "My husband is a great man and a decent
citizen."[33]

Chambers always wrote about his wife with tenderness—"all
selfless love and forgiveness," he said—and in describing their
friendship with Alger and Priscilla Hiss he said that "the fact that
both couples were firmly and happily married drew us
together."[34] Yet he confessed secretly to the FBI in February 1949
that during his years in the Communist underground he had
been an active and at times an obsessive secret homosexual.
Whether Nixon learned this from Chambers himself, or only
from the FBI, we do not know. Fearing that his homosexuality
would become public at the Hiss trial and used to discredit him as
a witness, Chambers had admitted to the FBI in advance what he
said was the entire history of his indiscretions. He had sought out
only men whom he did not know and men who did not know him,
and the rendezvous was inevitably in a "flea-bag" hotel.

It had all begun, he said, when he was alone in New York in
in 1933 or 1934—two or three years after his marriage—when a
young miner's son had begged him for a meal and a night's lodg-
ing.

I was footloose, so I took him to a hotel. . . . He taught me an experience
I did not know existed. . . . At the same time he revealed to me, and
unleashed, the . . . tendency of which I was still unaware. It was a revelation to me. . . . it set off a chain reaction in me which was almost impossible to control.

His homosexual life ended, he said, "with God's help," when he
left the party in 1938, and when for the first time he embraced
religion. He denied that Hiss was ever his lover: "At no time did
I have such relations, or even thought of such relations with Hiss
or with anybody else in the Communist Party."

He described Hiss as "a man of great simplicity and a great
gentleness and sweetness of character," and said that he and his
wife were friends "as close as a man ever makes in life." Gossip
that Chambers had been attracted to Hiss sexually was common
during the years of the case, and eventually Hiss said publicly that
Chambers was persecuting him as "a spurned homosexual who
testified . . . out of jealousy and resentment."[35] Although only a

handful of men knew about Chambers's confession to the FBI (which was not published until the Freedom of Information Act made the material available to Weinstein in 1977), the gossip did not die. Psychoanalyst Meyer Zeligs, in *Friendship and Fratricide*, developed an elaborate speculation based on Chambers's damaged childhood, writing in 1967 that he was both a homosexual and a pathological liar.[36]

Richard Nixon's reaction in 1949 to the truth of what most people knew only as a rumor, that Chambers had a bisexual past, remains a mystery. When Chambers's own lawyer learned the fact from the FBI, he was full of consternation, fearing that if the knowledge became public Chambers would have no credibility. Hiss's lawyers, who did not have the FBI data, spent a good deal of money investigating this aspect of Chambers's past, and apparently found enough evidence to consider using the homosexual smear, finding one man who was willing to testify in this regard. One of the lawyers argued at one point, "I have no objection to such smearing and hope that it will be very thoroughly and effectively done." He came to fear, however, that the tactic would backfire, writing that "it will smear Alger because it will be believed by some jurors that he is a homosexual."[37]

Nixon scrupulously avoided mentioning any of this gossip in *Six Crises*. He insisted, with some exaggeration, that he maintained a warm friendship with Chambers until his death in 1961. The news of his death, he wrote in his memoirs, "hit me hard."[38] Actually the two men had drifted apart. When Nixon visited him in 1960 to describe his presidential aspirations, Chambers wrote to William F. Buckley, Jr., "I came away with a most unhappy feeling. . . . I suppose the sum of it was: we have really nothing to say to each other." Nixon, Chambers felt, "with dismay and a gnawing pity," was inadequate for the "awful burden he was inviting."

Still, Chambers wrote to Nixon after his defeat by John F. Kennedy, urging him to run for the governorship of California:

Almost from the first day we met, (think, it is already 12 years ago), I sensed in you some quality very deep going, difficult to identify in the world's glib way, but good, and meaningful for you and multitudes of others. . . . Service is your life.[39]

This was his last letter to Nixon. After his death, a few months later, Nixon wrote to his widow that Chambers was "a very great and a very good man." He also sent her a copy of his telegram to the press at the time, saying that *Witness* was "the most penetrating analysis of the true nature and deadly appeal of Communism produced in this generation."[40]

As president, Nixon told several persons privately that Hiss and Chambers had been lovers, apparently forgetting that he had once described such gossip as "a typical Commie tactic." Hiss's son Tony published this fact in a memoir of his father, *Laughing Last,* and denied the truth of it.[41] Allen Weinstein wrote delicately in *Perjury:*

at the height of the impeachment crisis a Congressman who spent an evening sailing down the Potomac with Nixon on the presidential yacht said later that Nixon had told him "the true story of the Hiss case." The Congressman was highly amused: "I didn't know those two guys were queers." Others close to Nixon had confirmed his current use of this analysis: that a homosexual relationship between Hiss and Chambers caused Hiss to steal the documents. Thus Nixon, in his adversity, turned to "explaining" the complex Hiss Case with an unproved rumor, a persistent one during the 1948 HUAC hearings, revealing far more about himself under pressure than about the Case.[42]

One special aspect of the legacy of Whittaker Chambers remains to be noted. In *Six Crises* Nixon wrote that Chambers "had systematically collected documents which had been given him by Hiss, White, and other members of the espionage group so that he would have some physical evidence of their activities to hold over their heads in the event of threatened reprisals. . . ." which appeared on the rolls of microfilm.[43] So Nixon, too, would systematically collect on tape during his presidency the spoken words of everyone who came into three presidential offices. The reasons for the taping are many. Whether one of them was to hold over the heads of aides "in event of threatened reprisals" was suggested by Nixon in his memoirs when he wrote that the tapes were his "best insurance against the unforeseeable future, some protection in case people close to me would turn against me."[44]

The Destruction of Alger Hiss

That son-of-a bitch Hiss would be free today if he had not lied.
... But the son-of-a bitch lied, and he goes to jail for the lie
rather than the crime.

— NIXON, TO JOHN DEAN, APRIL 16, 1973[1]

WHITTAKER CHAMBERS BY HIMSELF could not have brought about the downfall of Alger Hiss. As he wrote in *Witness,* "Richard Nixon made the Hiss Case possible."[2] There are extraordinary similarities between Hiss under fire from Nixon and Nixon as a target in Watergate. Both men in crucial moments of decision chose what seems to have been the self-destructive path. Neither reacted under fire like a seasoned lawyer, and each denied his guilt when the evidence was ruinous. Nixon said Hiss "made the fatal mistake no client should ever make—he had not told his own lawyer the full truth about the facts at issue."[3] He would do the same.

Allen Weinstein wrote that Nixon's behavior in the case "could be best characterized not as cool, confident and decisive but as cautious, calculating, indecisive and at one point, at least, hysterical—foreshadowing in many respects the President of the White House Watergate tapes during the last, end-game crisis."[4] Hiss stonewalled, built elaborate fantasies about forged typewriters, and never acknowledged his guilt even long after he was out of prison. During his own long exile at San Clemente, Nixon admitted only to having made "mistakes" and toyed with Haldeman's conspiratorial fantasies about the Democrats in the National Committee headquarters bugging themselves.[5]

Neither Hiss nor Nixon had an intimate understanding of criminal law. Hiss had never before his own trial been inside a courtroom with a jury. Unprepared for cross-examination, he reacted to Nixon's first questions in the HUAC hearings in a fashion almost certain to hurt his chances of success. "He was rather insolent toward me," Nixon wrote in his notes at the time, and "his manner and tone were insulting in the extreme."[6]

Hiss represented many things Nixon had coveted in life. A graduate of Harvard Law school, former law clerk for Supreme Court Justice Oliver Wendell Holmes, an aide to Roosevelt, one of the builders of the United Nations, and now president of the Carnegie Endowment for International Peace, he was also, in Nixon's words, "Tall, elegant, handsome, and perfectly poised."[7] Preoccupied with clothes, as was Nixon, he had, according to his son Tony, "an astonishing number of suits and shoes and shoe trees and ties, and he always wore a white handkerchief in the breast pocket of his jacket."

That Hiss, who had charmed a great many influential men over a long period, fully expected to charm Richard Nixon he indicated to his son Tony when he was a bitter, old man, long out of prison:

Of course I didn't realize then what shits they were. And then I just couldn't believe that anyone wouldn't love me, once I was there. And in fact, the hearings at first seemed to bear that out and go my way. Right up until the Pumpkin Papers, I was in clover.

His saying "I just couldn't believe that anyone wouldn't love me" reflected affection he had won from three Supreme Court justices—Stanley M. Reed and Felix Frankfurter, as well as Holmes—and from educators, secretaries of state, and Roosevelt himself. It reflected, too, his incapacity for sensing dislike of himself, a defect in his antennae for danger. As he admitted to his son, "Dr. Rubenfine, my analyst, says I have a phobia against fear and don't get afraid even when I should get afraid."[8]

Chambers in 1939 had blown Hiss's cover as an espionage agent by going to Adolf Berle with his story. Hiss knew that this would be a possibility as soon as the friend he knew as "Carl" or "David Breen" came to him in 1938 with a recitation of Stalin's evils, begged him to abandon the party, and threatened to expose him if he did not. Priscilla Hiss had reacted disdainfully, Chambers said, calling his arguments "mental masturbation." But Hiss, who said he could not follow him out of the party, had wept.[9]

By late 1939, thanks to the Stalin-Hitler pact, the Communist espionage system in the United States was in shambles. Chambers himself had been exposed by a former Communist, and only the most naïve or doctrinaire of men would have continued, as Hiss apparently did as late as February 1945, to try to funnel information secretly to the Soviet Union.[10] Despite the wartime alliance, suspicion of Stalin remained endemic, and the Yalta pact, negotiated to a small extent with Hiss's assistance, had caused cries of outrage. From 1942 on, as we have seen, Hiss had warnings from Secretary of State Byrnes, the FBI, Dean Acheson, and John Foster Dulles that he was suspect. Still he trusted to simple denial.

Denial had been a way of life in the Hiss family. Alger was not yet three years old when his father, a Baltimore businessman, had cut his throat with a razor. Although there must have been a lot of blood and hysteria in the home at the time, Hiss insisted that only his two older sisters knew and that he and his two brothers grew up in ignorance of the suicide. The conspiracy of deception on the part of mother, sisters, relatives, and friends remained unshattered until he was an adolescent, when a neighbor told him the truth. Bosley, the eldest brother, then sought out the Baltimore newspaper obituary and brought home the grisly details.

Although some have described Hiss's childhood as happy, the family record suggests that his father's suicide had a terrible impact on the whole family. Events suggest, too, that his mother was in many ways deficient as a parent. Bosley Hiss, whom Alger called "a near genius," ran away from home several times, drifted into dissipation, and died at twenty-six of a kidney ailment said to have been "alcohol induced." Alger admitted eventually that Bosley had too many women, too much alcohol, and a disposition to shock, to "épater les bourgeois." These traits he said he never admired.[11] Still, no one was to shock his mother and her bourgeois friends more than Alger, who destroyed himself no less certainly than his father and older brother.

Two years after Bosley's death, an older sister, Mary, who had been in and out of sanatoria, killed herself after a midnight quarrel with her husband. The manner of her death, like Bosley's alcoholism, was buried in still another conspiracy of Hiss family denial.[12] Later Alger Hiss out of a sense of propriety would also cover up the fact that Priscilla Fansler Hobson, whom he wanted to marry, had had an abortion. Still later he would try to hide the fact that his stepson had been discharged from the navy for emotional problems relating to homosexuality.[13] All these coverups, however dictated by the mores of his time or by the exigencies of common decency, confirm the presence of a climate of denial in his life and help to explain his naïve and steadfast habit of lying when questioned about himself.

Hiss, who counted himself the least loved of five children, described his childhood as "female dominated." His son wrote with some cruelty, "It's a wonder Al didn't turn out gay. . . . He became a prig instead." He reported that his father described his mother, Minnie Hiss, as an "unloving" woman who never lost an argument. "All we got from Minnie was preaching," Hiss said. Although he told his defender, Dr. Meyer Zeligs, that from the earliest time he could remember "he knew it was necessary to resist his mother's will," and that he was contemptuous of her insistence that he be "especially pleasant to important people,"[14] he did develop a special skill at cooperating with dominating people—his mother, older siblings, teachers, bureaucrats, and finally presidents.

Hiss married a woman who, like his mother, had conspicuously preferred others to himself. Priscilla Fansler rejected him first to marry Thayer Hobson. After Hobson abandoned her for another woman, she had an affair with a New York newspaperman, who, when she became pregnant, refused to marry her. Hiss comforted her through the abortion and finally won her for his wife.[15]

Priscilla Hiss was one of the new women of the twenties, demanding respect for her own intellect and career, dabbling in Marxism and psychoanalysis, and also, somewhat incongruously, converting to Quakerism. Donald Hiss in 1939 described her privately to Maynard Toll as "a red hot Communist," but later testified that neither she nor his brother had been party members any more than himself. Some of Hiss's defenders, like Eleanor Roosevelt, and for a time his lawyers, thought he was lying to protect his wife. But there is abundant evidence that by the early 1930s both Hiss brothers and Priscilla were united in their secret dedication to the party. They numbered among their friends Noel Field and his wife, both of whom later fled to Hungary, Henry Collins, Lee Pressman, John Abt, Victor Perlo, Nathan Witt, and Julian Wadleigh, all of whom save Wadleigh, who broke with the party in 1940, "took the Fifth Amendment" rather than testify against themselves in the HUAC hearings.[16]

According to Chambers, Hiss's commitment to the party was total. Unlike most of the young idealists flirting with the party who thought joining a secret Communist cell no more sinister than becoming a Freemason, Hiss turned early to espionage. When Chambers first met him, he was an aide to Francis B. Sayre, assistant secretary of state. For a period of about two years he copied or summarized cables that came across Sayre's desk and turned them over to Chambers for transmission to Soviet agents for photographing. Priscilla, a better typist than her husband, copied Hiss's summaries and occasionally whole cables, which were sometimes in code, on her Woodstock typewriter.

How much material Hiss turned over to Chambers can only be guessed at. When Chambers left the party in 1939, he kept, by way of what he called insurance against assassination, documents Hiss had given to him from January 5 to April 1, 1938. These included four memos in Hiss's hand, sixty-five pages of State Department documents, consisting mostly of cables marked "Secret" or "Confidential," sixty-four pages of which had been copied by Priscilla Hiss. Chambers also kept five rolls of film, three undeveloped (one of which happened to be blank); two consisted of Navy Department material. The developed film, which had come from Hiss, included three cables from Sayre's office bearing Hiss's initials. An eight-page memo in the hand of Harry Dexter White completed the fateful package. Chambers put everything in a big envelope and gave it to a nephew in Brooklyn, Nathan Levine, with instructions to make it public only if he should meet a violent death. Levine hid it on the shelf of an unused dumbwaiter in his mother's home, where it gathered cobwebs for almost ten years.[17]

For Adolf Berle there was something ineffably juvenile in the spectacle of Hiss, the impeccable bureaucrat, stealing state secrets and passing them on furtively to the enemy. In testifying before HUAC, Berle indicated that at first he refused to get excited about Hiss. "The idea that the two Hiss boys and Nate Witt were going to take over the United States government didn't strike me as being much of an immediate danger. . . . Frankly, I still don't know whether this is a boy that got in deep and then pulled clear, or what goes on here."[18] Even after Hiss left prison, editor Hiram

Haydn of Random House, from whom he sought a job, found him "gaminlike, elusive, answering my questions with the manner of a shrewd, precocious little boy who was playing games and admiring his skill at them. . . . Mask succeeded mask, role role, personality personality."[19]

As a boy Hiss and his brothers had sold plucked pigeons for pocket money, advertising themselves as THE BAD HISS BOYS PIGEON COMPANY (BAD for Bosley, Alger, and Donald).[20] By the 1930s Alger was truly "the bad boy." Hiss's friends found the very idea of espionage from this gentle and attractive man incredible, although it is likely that Hiss had no conscious moral qualms about it, given his faith in the Soviet Union. Weinstein has speculated that Hiss compartmentalized like British physicist Klaus Fuchs, whose arrest in 1950 and confession that he had delivered atomic secrets to the Soviet Union between 1943 and 1947 rocked the free world.[21]

Hiss described to his son Tony his satisfaction in "the band of brothers" he found among the lawyers of the New Deal, although he would never admit that the more intimate friends among this brotherhood had all been Communists.

However Hiss may have justified his espionage as constructive activity for a better world, his betrayal suggests great hatred, whether acknowledged or repressed. Hiss's stepson said in later years that until Hiss went to prison he had "no sense of evil."[22] Chambers, who was enamored of Hiss's gentleness, saw in him also "a streak of wholly incongruous cruelty." He was shocked to hear him brutally ridicule Franklin Roosevelt's crippled body and compare it to the crippled American middle class. He reported, too, Hiss's speaking venomously of "the horrible old women of Baltimore,"[23] among whom he may well have been numbering his own mother.

Lee Pressman said of Hiss, "He gave you a sense of absolute command and absolute grace."[24] Hiss had moved with grace among giants, but he had never been in command of anything until he became head of the Carnegie Endowment in February 1947. Even after Chambers threatened to betray him in 1938, he had continued to prefer the brutal Stalin to the crippled Roosevelt.

As the HUAC hearings unfolded, however, under Nixon's prodding, Hiss's life underwent great upheaval. All of the lying, evasion, and acting that had gone into preserving intact his two separate lives were now united in preserving the new man in command at Carnegie. Hiss the actor never disappeared. Chambers, watching him, sensed what was happening and learned belatedly that Hiss would destroy him, if necessary, to preserve not the old "secret compartment" but the now-valued open life. Nixon, himself an inveterate actor, also sensed from the beginning that Hiss was acting out a role and that he was less than adept at it:

From considerable experience in observing witnesses on the stand, I had learned that those who are lying or trying to cover up something generally make a common mistake—they tend to overact, to overstate their case.[25]

In his first encounter with Nixon, Hiss came to the hearings without a lawyer, thus communicating a strong impression of innocence. As Dean Acheson said later, "he has conducted himself with calm and dignity and not at all in the way of a person who has been caught in a really terrible crime."[26] When Hiss denied knowing a man *named* Whittaker Chambers, Nixon was the only one to note the precision of language with suspicion. Hiss described his career with appropriate modesty and insisted that he had never been a Communist and had no Communist friends. Shown a picture of Chambers, he stared at it with what Nixon described as "an elaborate air of concentration" and said, "If this is a picture of Mr. Chambers, he is not particularly unusual looking." Turning to Karl Mundt, he added, "He looks like a lot of people. I might even mistake him for the Chairman of this Committee."

What was lost in the laughter Nixon alone caught. Mundt was round and pudgy like Chambers; more important, his first name was Karl, and "Carl" had been the pseudonym Chambers had used with the Hiss family. This was one of many unconscious evidences of guilt, the first of numerous small and inadvertent blunders.

"I didn't mean to be facetious," Hiss went on, "but very seriously I would not want to take an oath that I had never seen that man. I would like to see him and then I would be better able to tell whether I had ever seen him. Is he here today?" And he looked about him.

"Not to my knowledge," Mundt replied.

"I hoped he would be," Hiss said, with an air of regret. Nixon said later, "It was a virtuoso performance."[27]

Every committee member but Nixon was convinced of Hiss's innocence and eager, in Edward Hébert's words, to "wash our hands of the whole mess." But Nixon won the right to question Chambers further and to arrange for a meeting between the two men. Still, it was a sobering experience for him to emerge from the hearing and learn that President Truman, in a news conference that morning, had called the HUAC hearings "a red herring" and had insisted that "no information has been revealed that has not long since been presented to a federal grand jury." All but two of the employees involved, Truman said, had left the government and the remaining two were on voluntary leave. As Nixon described it,

I had put myself, a freshman Congressman . . . opposing the President of the United States and the majority of press corps opinion . . . against one of the brightest, most respected young men following a public career. Yet I could not go against my own conscience and my conscience told me that in this case, the rather unsavory-looking Chambers was telling the truth, and the honest-looking Hiss was lying.[28]

With considerable sagacity Nixon now enlisted some powerful men on his side. Bert Andrews was a Pulitzer Prize-winning New York *Herald Tribune* journalist who had been critical of unfair firings of State Department employees and who was expected to support Hiss. Nixon gave him a copy of Chambers's second testimony with its recollections of the Hiss households. They included descriptions of interior rooms and small but graphic details, like the fact that the Hiss cocker spaniel had been boarded in a Wisconsin Avenue kennel and that the Ford car had a windshield wiper that worked only by hand. Of the Hiss passion for birdwatching Chambers had testified, "They used to get up early in the morning and go out to Glen Echo out the canal, to observe birds. I recall once they saw, to their excitement, a prothonotary warbler." After reading the testimony, Andrews said, "I wouldn't have believed it after hearing Hiss the other day. But there's no doubt about it. Chambers knew Hiss."[29]

Second, Nixon won over William P. Rogers, counsel for the Senate Internal Security Subcommittee investigating the Elizabeth Bentley charges. This was the beginning of a crucial friendship. Nixon made Rogers a confidant, and later his secretary of state. Finally, Nixon took the Chambers testimony to John Foster Dulles, expected to become secretary of state if Thomas E. Dewey won the November election. With Dulles was his brother Allen, who had been with the Office of Strategic Services in Europe during the war. Nixon did not know that John Foster Dulles was already suspicious of Hiss. As he described the meeting,

Dulles paced the floor, his hands crossed behind him. It was a characteristic I was to see many times in the years ahead when we discussed important issues. He stopped finally and said, "There's no question about it. It's almost impossible to believe, but Chambers knew Hiss." Allen Dulles reached the same conclusion.[30]

This was the first meeting of three men who would be linked in many national decisions, Foster Dulles as secretary of state under Eisenhower, and Allen Dulles as head of the CIA.

HUAC members who heard or read Chambers's second testimony were also impressed and agreed to call Hiss for more questioning on August 16. Hiss had learned, meanwhile, that Nixon had spent time with Chambers at his farm, and that he had learned innumerable details from him. Had he been a cleverer actor, arguing that everything Chambers had learned about his houses and himself came from others, including members of HUAC, and had he never sued Chambers for libel, Hiss might have survived. Instead he came forward with an elaborate fantasy.

He admitted that in 1934 and 1935 he had known a man who might well have been Chambers, one George Crosley, an impecunious freelance writer who had sought him out for material concerning the Nye Committee hearings, for which Hiss had then been serving as legal counsel. He had befriended Crosley and his wife and child, Hiss said, subletting his apartment and loaning him small sums, although not the actual sum of $400 Chambers said Hiss had given to him in 1938 to buy a car.

Chambers had used a score of pseudonyms. Hiss had known him as "Carl" and as "David Breen," but chose to identify him as George Crosley. This was a blunder, revealing that Hiss knew a great deal about Chambers, for George Crosley was the name Chambers had used as a young man in 1926 when he sent several poems with a strong homosexual flavor to a publisher of erotica named Samuel Roth.[31]

Hiss's unexpected admission that he might indeed have known Chambers as Crosley gave Nixon an opportunity to question him deftly about those details of his life that Chambers had recalled most vividly. Hiss fell into what became a famous trap. When Nixon asked him to list his hobbies, he replied, "Tennis and amateur ornithology." Then Congressman McDowell, himself a birdwatcher, asked delicately, "Did you ever see a prothonotary warbler?"

"I have, right here on the Potomac," Hiss said, his face lighting up. "Do you know that place? . . . They come back and nest in these swamps. Beautiful yellow head. A gorgeous bird."

The committee fell silent. Hiss could not have suspected that his prothonotary warbler would shortly become, in the nation's press, the most famous warbler in America.

During the session Hiss made two unnecessary and serious blunders. He mentioned that Chambers, unable to pay his rent, had given him a rug that "some wealthy patron gave him." "I have still got the damned thing," he said. He also said,

I sold him an automobile. I had an old Ford that I threw in with the apartment, that I had been trying to trade in and get rid of. A slightly collegiate model. It wasn't very fancy, but it had a sassy little trunk on the back.

The Bokhara rug was one of four that Col. Boris Bykov, chief of the Soviet intelligence in the United States, had ordered Chambers to buy and distribute to four Americans as an expression of Soviet gratitude. A second one had gone to Harry Dexter White.[32] The Ford car, as it turned out, had never been given or sold to Chambers. When investigators traced the sale they would prove, as Chambers had predicted, that in a most unusual transaction Hiss had turned the car over without payment to the Cherner Motor Company. The Ford transaction would take on ominous proportions when W. Marvin Smith, a Justice Department lawyer and old friend of Hiss—who admitted that he had notarized Hiss's signature on the transfer of title—fell, or as some said, jumped, or was pushed, to his death down an office stairwell some weeks later.[33]

Hiss was shaken when Hébert said bluntly, "Either you or Mr. Chambers is lying, and whichever one of you is lying is the greatest actor that America has ever seen. . . . What motive would he have to pitch a $25,000 a year position as Senior Editor of *Time* out of the window?" When Hiss protested that Chambers was "a self-confessed traitor," Hébert, who knew New Orleans police courts, replied, "Some of the greatest saints in history were pretty bad before they were saints. . . . I don't care who gives the facts to me, whether a confessed liar, thief, or murderer—if it's the facts." Thereafter, as Nixon described it, Hiss was "twisting, turning, evading, and changing his story to fit the evidence he knew we had."[34]

Nixon had arranged a confrontation between Hiss and Chambers for August 25. On August 16 Harry Dexter White died of a heart attack. Although he had been described by both Elizabeth Bentley and Whittaker Chambers as "a fellow traveler" and not a party member, he had been questioned at length in HUAC meetings only a few days earlier. He seemed to have acquitted himself brilliantly, with a ringing defense of democracy.[35]

The death of White, the former assistant secretary of the treasury and chief architect of the World Bank, coming as it did when HUAC had never been lower in public esteem, appalled Nixon. Rumors that White's own doctor had not been in attendance, and that his body had been cremated hastily without an autopsy, later fed the appetites of those who fantasized that he had been slain by the Soviet secret police.[36] Nixon called Robert Stripling at 2 A.M. on the morning of the seventeenth and insisted that the confrontation between Hiss and Chambers be held that very day. Chambers was rushed to New York, and Hiss, also disturbed by the news of White's death, was ushered hastily to the Commodore Hotel.[37] Chambers was at first kept in an anteroom while Hiss was questioned.

When finally he was ushered in, everyone stared at him save Hiss, who looked resolutely out the window. Nixon had to ask him to stand and face the man "he had been so anxious to see 'in the flesh.'" When asked if he had ever known Chambers, Hiss replied, "May I ask him to speak? Will you ask him to say something?"

Chambers, requested to give his name, said, "My name is Whittaker Chambers." Hiss then walked forward and looked down into his mouth.

"Would you mind," he said, "opening your mouth wider?"[38] Chambers was then asked to read from a magazine as Hiss contin-

ued to peer into his mouth. The bizarre behavior Hiss explained
later:

None of the photographs of Chambers that I saw showed poor teeth.
. . . Crosley's teeth were decayed and one of them was split, the forward
half having come away, leaving the gleaming steel of a pivot against the
darkened rear of the broken tooth. . . . I wanted to hear his voice and
see if he had Crosley's bad teeth before expressing my feeling that this
was George Crosley.[39]

When Chambers stated that he had had some extractions and
bridgework, Hiss asked the name of the dentist.

"Dr. Hitchcock, Westminster, Maryland," Chambers said.
Then Hiss went on, "I would like to find out from Dr. Hitchcock
if what he has just said is true."

At this point, after the mocking laughter in the audience qui-
eted, Nixon interposed sardonically, "Mr. Hiss, do you feel that
you would have to have the dentist tell you just what he did to the
teeth before you could tell anything about this man?" Only then,
Nixon said, did Hiss realize that he had overplayed his hand. "All
his poise was gone. . . . With a look of cold hatred in his eyes, he
fought like a caged animal."

When the two men were permitted a direct interchange,
Chambers said, "Alger, I was a Communist and you were a Communist." Hiss shortly after challenged him to say it outside the
protective limits of the committee so that he could sue him for
libel. Striding close to him he shouted, "I challenge you to do it,
and I hope you will do it damned quickly." One of the staff, thinking Hiss was about to strike his enemy, took him by the arm. Hiss
recoiled, Nixon said, "as if he had been pricked with a hot
needle," and continued shrilly, "I am not touching him. You are
touching me." Before the confrontation was over, Hiss had abandoned all caution. "The ass under the lion's skin is Crosley," he
said contemptuously. "If he had lost both eyes and taken his nose
off, I would be sure."

When Nixon adroitly introduced a question to Chambers that
many had been wondering about, "Is there a grudge that you
have against Mr. Hiss?" Chambers replied,

I do not hate Mr. Hiss. We were close friends but we are caught in a
tragedy of history. Mr. Hiss represents the concealed enemy against
which we are all fighting, and I am fighting. I have testified against him

with remorse and pity, but in a moment of history in which this nation now stands, so help me God, I could not do otherwise.[40]

Hiss's friends, who had found his problem with identification troubling and his behavior in the confrontation inexplicable, were even more shaken when they saw photographs of Chambers taken in the mid-thirties, which were not noticeably different from the man in the hearing room. They could not know it, but already Hiss was sliding into a morass of deception from which he could never extricate himself. In later years, after leaving prison, Hiss described the meeting with Chambers as having brought on "a sense of fantasy or dream."[41] Chambers himself wrote of it:

I was swept by a sense of pity for all the trapped men of which the pathos of this man was the center. . . . Under the calculated malice of his behavior toward me, which I could not fail to resent, under his impudence and bravado to the congressmen, he was a trapped man—and I am a killer only by extreme necessity. . . . I prayed that he would not be trapped. . . . So I was rent.[42]

Nixon recollected his own feelings of the moment when writing *Six Crises:*

I should have been elated. The case was broken. The Committee would be vindicated, and I personally would receive credit for the part I had played. We had succeeded in preventing injustice being done to a truthful man and were now on the way to bringing an untruthful man to justice. Politically, we would now be able to give the lie to Truman's contemptuous dismissal of our hearings as a "red herring." . . .

However, I experienced a sense of letdown. . . . There was a sense of shock and sadness that a man like Hiss could have fallen so low. I imagined myself in his place. . . . It is not a pleasant picture to see a whole brilliant career destroyed before your eyes. I realized that Hiss stood before us completely unmasked—our hearing had saved one life, but had ruined another.[43]

But his compassion was momentary. The next day, he said, he learned that "the point of greatest danger is not in preparing to meet the crisis or fighting the battle; it occurs after the crisis of battle is over," when one is "spent, physically, emotionally, and mentally." His error, Nixon explained, happened the next morning when Hiss brought his wife Priscilla to coroborate his story about Crosley. Nixon was the only committee member present.

Priscilla Hiss was a small, fragile-looking woman, primly dressed, with great liquid hazel eyes, and a turned-up nose not unlike that of Nixon's mother.

I subconsciously reacted to the fact that she was a woman. . . . She played her part with superb skill. When I asked her to take the oath to tell the truth, she inquired demurely if she could "affirm" rather than "swear." Subtly, she was reminding me of our common Quaker background. . . . She succeeded completely in convincing me that she was nervous and frightened, and I did not press her further. I should have remembered that Chambers had described her as, if anything, a more fanatical Communist than Hiss. I could have made a devastating record had I also remembered that even a woman who happens to be a Quaker and then turns to Communism must be a Communist first and a Quaker second. But I dropped the ball and was responsible for not exploiting what could have been a second breakthrough in the case.[44]

Priscilla Hiss was never indicted, although it was generally agreed by experts hired by both the government and Hiss's lawyers that it was indeed she who had typed most of the State Department material later called "the Pumpkin Papers." Donald Hiss also escaped indictment, although there is considerable evidence of lying in his case also.[45] But before the case was over, at least four deaths and one near-death were publicly linked to the Hiss-Chambers probe. We have already noted Harry Dexter White's fatal heart attack and Marvin Smith's apparent suicide. Lawrence Duggan, a former State Department official and friend to Hiss, jumped or fell—or as some thought, was pushed—to his death on December 20, 1948, from the sixteenth floor of a Manhattan office building. He was wearing one galosh at the time; the other remained on the office floor.

Nixon and Mundt at once released HUAC testimony by Isaac Don Levine accusing Duggan of having been a Communist agent, and Mundt boasted callously that the committee would reveal the names of others in the probe "when they jumped out of the window." Assistant Secretary of State Sumner Welles, a good friend of Duggan, wired New York Mayor William O'Dwyer saying it was "impossible to believe" Duggan's death a suicide and urging an investigation. Four days later, Welles was found almost frozen to death from exposure after an apparent heart attack on his Virginia estate.[46]

A final death, wholly accidental, came when Esther Chambers, driving on December 17, 1948, from Westminster to the Baltimore train station to meet her husband, who had been testifying before a new grand jury, hit and killed a seventy-year-old deaf woman who had stepped out in front of her car. She was acquitted of a charge of reckless driving and manslaughter.[47]

That Nixon was to some degree shaken by all these deaths, and that he continued to be troubled by the destruction of Hiss long afterward, is apparent when he wrote in *Six Crises* of his feeling of "letdown." There was also, he said, "a sense of shock and sadness that a man like Hiss could have fallen so low. I imagined myself in his place."

But his compassion for Hiss was short-lived. In the end he had only one real regret—that he had not destroyed Hiss's wife as well. "I could have made a devastating record," he wrote, "but I dropped the ball."[48]

The case was by no means finished with the crucial unmasking of Hiss in the HUAC hearing in the Commodore Hotel, for Hiss did not go to prison until March 22, 1951. In the intervening period we see Nixon not only as the diligent sleuth and master of detail of *Six Crises* but also as a man giving way to panic, belaboring his staff and abandoning a friend who had done him conspicuous service.

Chambers formally called Hiss a Communist on "Meet the Press" on August 27, 1948, and three weeks later Hiss launched a libel suit for $50,000, later raised to $75,000. Although it was soon apparent that Hiss intended to wage a savage fight, Nixon left Washington and traveled about the country giving hundreds of "nonpolitical" speeches describing the case. Since he had won both Republican and Democratic primaries in June, he did not have to campaign formally on his own behalf. By election time he had been heard by thousands of people and had become one of the most visible congressmen in the country. Lynn Bowers and Dorothy Blair, in an admiring article in the *Saturday Evening Post,* described the tour, quoting him as saying, "Anyone who thinks communism in this country is just an idea is crazy."[49]

Chambers, who had resigned from *Time,* watched Nixon's political exploitation of his life with dismay. When he realized, belatedly, that he could very well lose the libel suit without documentation of his charges against Hiss, he made a trip to the home of his Brooklyn nephew and retrieved from the shelf of the unused dumbwaiter the envelope hidden there almost ten years earlier. On November 17 Chambers went to the pretrial deposition hearing with his lawyer, Richard F. Cleveland, and turned over to Hiss's lawyers, William Marbury and Edward McLean, the four memos in Hiss's hand, the sixty-five pages of cables and cable summaries typed by Priscilla Hiss, and the eight-page summary in the hand of Harry Dexter White. He kept in secret reserve the five rolls of microfilm. After an hour of "stunning itemization," Marbury and McLean were aghast.[50]

Watching the scene was a young lawyer, Nicholas Vazzana, hired by *Time* to assist Chambers. When almost a fortnight passed and the Justice Department, to which copies had also been delivered, still had not yet contacted Chambers, Vazzana feared a coverup and decided to leak the story to Nixon. He found the young congressman preparing to leave the following day on a vacation cruise with his wife to Panama. Stripling, who also heard the story, was bursting with excitement and urged that they drive immediately to interview Chambers at his Maryland farm. But to the astonishment of both Vazzana and Stripling, Nixon broke into a rage. "He cussed me out real good," Stripling told Weinstein, shouting "I am so God-damned sick and tired of this case, I don't want to hear any more about it, and I'm going to Panama. And the hell with it and you and the whole damned business."[51]

Furious because Chambers was no longer confiding in him, and because he had lost the chance to exploit the new and sensational evidence that Hiss had been not only a Communist but also a spy, Nixon now refused to see Chambers at all. Stripling persuaded him to make the drive hours later only with the greatest difficulty. When they arrived at the farm, Chambers was cool and evasive, admitting only that he had turned over "a bombshell" to Hiss's lawyers and the Justice Department, and that he held a second one in reserve. Nixon could do little but beg him to turn his secret bombshell over to HUAC.

When they got into the car, Nixon said to Stripling, "What do you think he's got?"

"I don't know what he has, but whatever he has, it'll blow the dome off the Capitol. Certainly you're not going to Panama now?"

"I don't think he's got a damned thing," Nixon said. "I'm going right ahead with my plans."

He did take the time to issue a subpoena on Chambers for all the relevant documents and, mindful of keeping on good terms with J. Edgar Hoover, reported the story to the FBI, promising the agent that he would reopen the Hiss Case for HUAC on his return on December 15.[52] Vazanna and Stripling, who were angered by Nixon's description of himself in this episode in *Six Crises* as the ever-confident detective hero, saw him at the time as "cautious, irascible and fearful," fleeing Washington on his "cruise-ship vacation" in order to miss out on any embarrassment should the Chambers papers prove to be of no consequence or fraudulent, but keeping open the option to return instantly should he be summoned. Thus he could "steal the headlines and claim credit for the coup." "*Six Crises* is pure bullshit," Stripling told Weinstein. "Mr. Nixon did not break the Hiss case."[53]

When HUAC investigators Donald Appell and William Wheeler arrived at the Maryland farm with the subpoena, Chambers, with a flair for melodrama, mystified them by walking into his pumpkin patch, where he fumbled about for a moment and then took five rolls of film wrapped in wax paper out of a hollowed-out pumpkin shell. He had hidden them there that morning, he said, because of prowlers on his farm. Back in Washington Stripling examined the two already-developed films, with their confidential State Department cables, and instantly wired Nixon on the S.S. *Panama*, "CASE CLINCHED. INFORMATION AMAZING. . . . CAN YOU POSSIBLY GET BACK." Nixon transferred from the boat to a Coast Guard amphibious plane and flew to Miami. When newsmen beseiged him with questions about papers Chambers had found in a pumpkin, he thought for a time, "we might really have a crazy man on our hands."[54]

After returning to Washington, where he was briefed by Stripling, Nixon welcomed in the press, and the photograph taken of him looking at the microfilm with a magnifying glass, presumably at the spot where it said "Department of State, Strictly Confidential," was published all over the nation. He did not correct Stripling when he told newsmen that the developed films had made a stack of letter-sized documents three or four feet high. Actually they barely reached an inch.[55]

The Nixon euphoria suffered a catastrophic if brief setback when Stripling, on a routine check with the Eastman Kodak Company concerning the age of the film, which Chambers dated early

1939, was told that it had not been manufactured before 1945. The news, said Nixon, "jolted us into almost complete shock."

We sat looking at each other without saying a word. This meant that Chambers was, after all, a liar. . . . We had been taken in by a diabolically clever maniac who had finally made a fatal mistake.

Vazzana, who was in the office at the time, remembered Nixon shouting, "Oh, my God, this is the end of my political career!" Turning abusive, he hurled the blame on the young lawyer who had leaked the story of the espionage documents to him in the first place. "Well, you got us into this. This is all your fault." Vazzana, who thought he had done Nixon a great favor, protested helplessly, "I didn't know there was any microfilm there."

When Nixon finally located Chambers in New York and demanded an explanation, there was a long silence. Then Chambers said, "in a voice full of despair and resignation, 'I can't understand it. God must be against me.' "

"You'd better have a better answer than that," Nixon said. "The Sub-Committee's coming to New York tonight and we want to see you at the Commodore Hotel at 9:00 and you'd better be there!" And he slammed down the receiver without waiting for an answer.

Stripling said later that it was he who now insisted on calling in the press to admit that they had been "sold a bill of goods," but that Nixon would have none of it. Nixon in *Six Crises* said it was he who called the press conference. "This would be the biggest crow-eating performance in the history of Capitol Hill, but I was ready to go through with it."[56] As it turned out, the Eastman Kodak representative saved Nixon's reputation by telephoning just in time to say that he had been in error, that films with the same emulsion figure had been produced through 1938, discontinued because of the war, and then manufactured again in 1945.

Chambers, meanwhile, wandered about the streets of New York in a state of deep shock. When he finally learned of the Eastman Kodak error he felt not so much relief as rage. "An error so burlesque, a comedy so gross in the midst of such catastrophe was a degradation of the spirit," he said. A "pointless pain continued to roll under me like a drowning wave." Once again he walked the streets, finally going into a seed store, where he bought some insecticide that contained cyanide. This he stored in a locker in the Grand Central Station and then went on to the Commodore Hotel.

There he found what seemed to him idiocy and paranoia. Nixon had been met by enraged Justice Department agents who forbade him to question Chambers because he had just begun testifying again before the grand jury. They threatened Nixon with a contempt citation if he would not turn over the microfilm. After a shouting match, with charges of meddling on the one hand and coverup on the other, Nixon won the right to question Chambers, provided that he would turn over enlargements of all the film. Chambers described the committee as being "in the preposterous position of having the microfilm in its possession, but of not knowing what it was all about." A seige mentality convulsed the HUAC congressmen:

The Committee was convinced that the Justice Department had it surrounded, that the hotel was wired or that the session could be overheard by wireless devices. . . . Certain comments were not spoken at all. They were scribbled on a scrap of paper and passed around the room. None of them was important. . . . members of the Committee's staff stood guard at the doors to challenge intruders and keep off the press.

After testifying, Chambers went back to Grand Central Station, retrieved his insecticide, and rode to his mother's home, experiencing what he called "a drought of the soul, a sense of estrangement and of being discarded." Late at night, after writing letters to his wife and children, and one to the general public, he moistened the chemical in the tin and breathed in the fumes.[57]

Perhaps because he had read the instructions improperly—or possibly because he had not really wanted to die—he awakened later suffering only from a terrible nausea. When Nixon learned of the suicide attempt, he felt himself to blame. "I had been the one public official who had stood by him and on whom he thought he could count. And now I was deserting him."[58]

Thereafter Nixon aided Chambers as best he could through the protracted agony of the two Hiss perjury trials. When it looked as if the Justice Department might indict both Chambers and Hiss for perjury, as J. Edgar Hoover was urging, Nixon made a powerful public plea that Chambers be left alone. In the previous September, in a moment of folly and without benefit of counsel, Chambers had testified before the New York grand jury that he had no evidence of Hiss's espionage, thus laying himself open to the perjury charge. Nixon, aided by the testimony of Isaac Don Levine, explained it as the act of a man who could not bring himself to destroy a friend. Should Chambers be indicted, he said, his effectiveness as a witness in any trial of Alger Hiss would be forever destroyed.[59]

The gesture helped. Hiss was indicted for perjury on December 15, 1948, and Chambers was left free to testify against him without being under a cloud. Since the statute of limitations on espionage in peacetime was only three years, neither man could be indicted for spying. Nixon followed the two trials with care, secretly submitting questions to the government prosecutor, Thomas Murphy, through his newspaper reporter friend, Victor Lasky.[60]

When the first trial resulted in a hung jury, eight to four for conviction, an enraged Nixon called for an investigation of Judge Samuel H. Kaufman's "fitness to serve on the bench." Several of the jurors who had voted guilty said they thought the judge had been partial to Hiss. Kaufman blocked the crucial testimony of Hede Massing, who was the one witness prepared to testify that she had known Hiss as a Communist agent. And there was some evidence that the judge had been informed quite early that the foreman of the jury had from the beginning been determined on an acquittal.[61] In the second trial, conducted by Judge Henry W. Goddard, Hede Massing did testify.

Hiss's main defense in both trials, aside from a parade of character witnesses, not all of whom did him service, was that Chambers was mentally unstable. In the second trial Dr. Carl Binger, a psychiatrist friend of Hiss, who testified that Chambers was a psychopathic personality, withered under Thomas Murphy's cross-examination and left the court looking something of a fool. The jury decided the case primarily on the evidence in the pile of documents collectively if inaccurately called "the Pumpkin Papers." A great deal of argument centered about Priscilla Hiss's Woodstock N230099, which Hiss said he had given to their maid, Claudia Catlett, before the dates typed on the crucial pages. The prosecution established that the Catlett sons had received it in the same month that Chambers had defected from the Communist party and had threatened to expose Hiss. Switching his story, Hiss then said that Chambers had somehow gotten into his house to type the papers. The fact that experts testified that the typing of the papers matched that of the "Hiss standards"—letters typed by Priscilla Hiss earlier than 1938—convinced all twelve members of the second jury that Hiss was indeed guilty of passing on documents to Chambers, and he was sentenced on the charge of perjury to five years in prison.[62]

After his conviction, Hiss developed six elaborate conspiracy theories to explain his innocence. The best publicized one held that Chambers had constructed a phony machine using samples of Priscilla Hiss's typing from the 1930s, and typed the papers in imitation. Loyal Hiss followers raised $10,000 to construct a typewriter matching the Woodstock N230099, but it failed to be an exact reproduction. The other conspiracy theories proved to be just as improbable.

Priscilla Hiss, who had separated from Alger some years after he left prison, continued to defend his innocence, although there is some evidence that she once struck consternation at a family dinner with her sister-in-law by announcing that "she was sick of all the lies and coverups." Tony Hiss reported that his father had described his mother as being "hysterical" and "into a near paranoid state" at the time of his indictment. "She believed the walls of our apartment were bugged."[63] This is a very different description from the calm, innocent woman described in Hiss's own book.

Whether Hiss managed to convince his son Tony of his own innocence is uncertain. As Jeff Greenfield said in his review of Tony's *Laughing Last,* "if this is the best case that his own flesh and blood can make for him, then Alger Hiss's last laugh is hollow indeed."[64] Tony's memoir of his father, far from being a ringing defense, was flip and oblique. That Alger Hiss, too, could be oblique in talking to his son we learn from *Laughing Last.* When Tony asked his father why, if Noel Field was "a good guy," he didn't "take better care of himself," Hiss replied:

I think a lot of good people get crushed. A lot of shits survive. And a lot of them get crushed too.[65]

On Women and Power:
Pat and the Pink Lady

*I am confronted with an unusual situation. My opponent is a
woman. . . . There will be no name-calling, no smears, no misrepresentation in this campaign.*

— RICHARD NIXON, 1950[1]

WHEN NIXON RAN FOR THE SENATE in 1950 against Congresswoman Helen Gahagan Douglas, it became apparent shortly
after the primary that he would not treat her gently, as he had
Priscilla Hiss. Although he promised a clean campaign, especially
because his opponent was a woman, and insisted even in his memoirs "I knew that I must not appear ungallant in my criticism of
Mrs. Douglas,"[2] this was the most vicious campaign of his political
life. Even the friendly Earl Mazo called it "the most hateful" California had experienced in many years.[3]

The Hiss case had put Nixon securely on the ladder to the top
in politics, and had hardened his conviction that destructive attack
was the certain way to victory. "Throughout the campaign I kept
her pinned to her extremist record," he said,[4] and indeed he
treated Helen Douglas as if she were an exotic red butterfly.
Actually her record was that of a left-wing Democrat, hewing for
the most part close to the party line laid down by Harry Truman.
This record Nixon distorted into a pro-Communist stance even
more than he had that of Voorhis. His speeches, moreover, were
laced with contempt not for "the woman" but for the idea of the
actress as senator. And at the end of the campaign, as his radio
director Tom Dixon described it, "in almost every statement he
made it was Helen Gahagan Douglas and Alger Hiss. . . . He got
the two together somehow, ingeniously. He never beat her. Alger
Hiss beat her."[5]

Although in 1958 Nixon said to British publisher David Astor, who questioned him about the campaign, "I'm sorry about that episode, I was a very young man,"[6] there were no apologies in his memoirs of 1978. Recollecting anew that she had called him "a pipsqueak" and "a peewee who is trying to scare people into voting for him," Nixon wrote that her campaign "for stridency, ineptness, or self-righteousness" would not be equalled "until George McGovern's presidential campaign twenty-two years later." "She may have been at some political disadvantage because she was a woman," he said, "but her fatal disadvantage lay in her record and her views." And of his famous "pink sheet," long described as a classic of distortion, he insisted still that it consisted of facts, and that "no one was ever able to challenge their accuracy."[7]

That she was a woman running for the Senate already meant a near-fatal vulnerability. No club in America has been, and has remained, harder for women to penetrate. Whether Nixon's campaign would have been less deceptive had his opponent been a man is problematical, but the zest and cunning he brought to the attack is worth a close look, especially when set against the background of Nixon's general attitude toward women in politics, including his wife.

As a young Quaker Nixon had seen women speaking in church, and there was a tradition of women serving as Quaker ministers in his mother's Milhous background. Nixon's grandmother and great-grandmother Milhous were vocal women, in church and out. Only his mother was quiet, and it was her model that he came to praise and to encourage his wife to imitate. That he disliked even women who wore pants he made obvious to the women in the press corps when he was president. His daughter Julie, it is said, was the only student at Smith to wear skirts during her entire four years in college. In the early 1950s he encouraged Murray Chotiner to incorporate a prohibition against women in slacks in a manual Chotiner wrote for Republican party women workers. With this went advice to the wives of politicians to avoid controversy—"Never embarrass your husband"—"Always look at your husband when he is talking"—and be content with the image of a supportive subordinate.[8] James Bassett, a key aide in the campaigns of 1952, 1956, and 1960, said Nixon looked on women as "an extra appendage, a different species." To aide Richard Whelan, Nixon said privately in the 1968 campaign, "You will have to put out a folder saying what you're for and against, where you stand on the issues. Woman particularly like it. They don't have the slightest idea what it means, but the voter's been taught to expect it."[9]

Not only was Nixon contemptuous of women's intellect generally, but he was also oblivious to women as individuals. As Pat Nixon once admitted, "I can hardly recall his paying a woman a compliment, except to remark on her hat." Pat learned early that she must wear only conventional clothes. "I never buy anything because I like it," she said. "I think, 'Will it pack?' 'Is it conservative?'" Although her husband insisted on her campaigning with him, it was understood that she would never speak, but simply greet the crowds pleasantly, smile even at hecklers, and hand out campaign literature. Her biographer, Lester David, said, "she developed to a high art the knack of giving non answers to questions." "A wife's first duty," she said, "is to help and encourage her husband in the career he has chosen."[10]

Nixon as president paid tribute to this discipline. "Any wife who can do as my wife has, listen to my speeches through campaigns, at home and abroad in over 60 countries for 23 years, and sit there transfixed, as if she is hearing it for the first time, believe me, that is service far beyond the call of duty."[11] But there were friends who remembered a less supportive wife. Adela Rogers St. Johns, a Hearst newspaperwoman whom Nixon liked and trusted, has said of Pat, "God, she made it rough for him. She would say, 'That was certainly a disaster,' or 'Well, I've heard you make lousy speeches, but that was the worst.'"[12]

What Pat continued to say in private we cannot know, but there is evidence that it was in the 1950 campaign that she learned to keep silent before his staff. In this campaign, too, she was decisively shut out of decision-making. Kenneth Chotiner, the son of the first of Murray Chotiner's four wives, said it was then that Pat came to share with Kenneth's mother a sense of abandonment, of being excluded totally from the smoke-filled rooms.[13] She continued to be used, but only as an ornament, a theatrical prop. By 1960 she was describing her role somewhat ambiguously: "I've always been a part of what's done, but a silent partner." Nixon put it differently in his memoirs: "Pat is one of those rare individuals whose ego does not depend on public attention."[14]

Even when Pat became First Lady, Nixon made all the decisions, including running the White House during the first two years. By then she was so used to being seen and not heard that television crews found it painful to interview her. Nancy Dickerson, trying futilely to get her to talk freely on one Asian trip, sensed the fear in her. "She seemed to have no thoughts or opinions of her own, or else she was scared to voice them." After much difficulty she persuaded Pat to comment briefly on the beautiful places they had visited, and superimposed these on the superb photographs taken on the trip. The show pleased Nixon. Pat later told Nancy Dickerson he kept "pounding the table in front of the TV saying, 'That's right! That's right! That's the way you are, and that's the way they should see you."[15]

After 1970, according to Marlene Cimons, Pat Nixon was finally permitted to make trips on her own, well briefed and accompanied by experts. Reporters were charmed to discover that away from her husband she dropped her mask and came alive, a shy but nevertheless independent woman. But "in the man's world of politics," as Henry Kissinger was reported to have put it—with an ungracious slip of the tongue—"she was a silent patriot . . . a loyal and uninterfering female . . . speaking only when spoken to and not sullying the cigar smoke with her personal opinions."[16]

Tom Dixon, who saw the Nixons almost every day through the 1950 campaign, when questioned about Pat's always remaining silent, said,

I think he would have made it very miserable for her if she hadn't. I liked her so much. I felt sorry for her. She was gracious and honorable, but weak with him. His ego had to be toadied to. Why did she take it unless she wanted to see her man scale the ladder? She had a little of the martyr complex in her to take that with so little grumbling.[17]

James Bassett, who was witness to some painful scenes of Nixon humiliating his wife, said he had "a total scorn for female mentality. He would rant and rage when he had to speak before the National Federation of Republican Women, rank and file workers, 'I will not go to talk to those shitty ass old ladies!' "[18]

When vice president, he was so enraged at one California party worker, Democrat Vita Remley, that he risked scandal in the national press by slapping her in public. Mrs. Remley, who knew Nixon and had been an active organizer in the Voorhis campaign, had helped expose his trick of organizing an anonymous telephone campaign where women made calls to Democrats saying "Jerry Voorhis is a Communist." She had become a deputy assessor of Los Angeles County with the job of checking the veterans' exemptions. In 1952, just after the election, Nixon sent a notorized letter to her Los Angeles office requesting a veteran's tax exemption, which was granted only to veterans who, if single, had less than $5000 worth of property in California or elsewhere, and if married, $10,000. Knowing from the newspapers that Nixon had just purchased an expensive home in Washington, she denied the request. Drew Pearson learned the story indirectly and obtained a written statement from Mrs. Remley, which he published in his column and read over the air.

Shortly afterward, when Nixon was speaking in the Long Beach auditorium, Mrs. Remley went to hear him. Arriving late, she listened from near the open door. As he emerged he recognized her. In a sudden fit of rage, he walked over and slapped her. His friends, horrified, hustled him away in the dark. There were no cameras or newsmen to catch the happening, and Mrs. Remley, fearful of losing her job, told only a few friends.[19]

Generally Nixon hid his dislike and fear of political women with skill. He had the good sense not to attack Eleanor Roosevelt publicly, even when she continued to state her belief in the innocence of Alger Hiss. It is true that when president he made little effort to hide his difficulties with Indira Gandhi. His affection for Golda Meir—an exception of importance—seems to have been warm and genuine. But his general bias against women in politics was implicitly stated when, in thanking the members of the Seventeenth Annual Republican Women's Conference in 1969, he said his most heartfelt approbation went not to the women holding office but to those "who hold the hands of the husbands who do hold office."[20]

The Washington press corps women resented the fact that when he was president and spoke to them as a group, he kept the discussion rooted in trivial or feminine concerns, "kitchen matters," as Newsweek's Norma Mulligan said.[21] When they interviewed him about Pat's birthday celebration in 1971, they did manage to get some revealing preferences he felt concerning presidential wives. He recalled his surprise at seeing Eleanor Roosevelt visiting the troops in New Caledonia during the war. "It made an enormous impression on me. Not negative. An enormous impression." In discussing Ladybird Johnson's beautification program he said most people would dismiss it as " planting a few pansies on the freeways," but conceded that "it helped." His warmest words were for the nonpolitical First Ladies, Grace Coolidge, Mamie Eisenhower, and Bess Truman. When Harry Truman was in trouble, he speculated, "I'm sure Bess stood there like a rock." What really mattered to him, he said, was to have around him, when faced with a tough decision,

people who are standing with him, people that are strong, people who aren't panicking, people who aren't throwing up their hands about what they heard on television that night, the lousy column or the terrible cartoon or this or that or the other thing; somebody who brings serenity, calmness and strength into the room. That makes a great difference. That is why, for example—did you meet Mrs. de Gaulle, a marvelous woman. . . .

Thus he left some of the women reporters wondering if it was Pat who brought serenity, calmness, and strength, like Mrs. de Gaulle, or Pat who threw up her hands about the lousy column or the terrible cartoon. In any case Nixon firmly defined the ideal helpmate: "A wife complements her husband by shoring him up."[22]

Although when Pat was given the Homemakers Forum award in 1957 as the Nation's Ideal Wife she said frankly, "I must admit I don't deserve it," she took great pains to give an impression of solidarity in her marriage. To repeated questions about disagreements with her husband she replied, "We don't permit any dissension in the home. We are too busy. We just can't afford it."[23]

But the discipline took its toll. The *London Spectator* caught something of the heavy penalty she was paying in a chilling little portrait, published December 5, 1958, when the Nixons were visiting London:

She chatters, answers questions, smiles and smiles. . . . Only her eyes, dark, darting, and strained, signal that inside the black suit and pearls there is a human being, probably perfectly content not to get out.[24]

Nixon was uncomfortable with women generally, not just political or intellectual women. Adela Rogers St. Johns remembered him in one Republican rally being put "in the ring" of an arena with a galaxy of movie stars. "You never saw such beautiful flesh," she said. "And he acted like a man utterly unsexed. It was as if he didn't know they were there."[25]

The women Nixon openly resented were those gifted at attack. And in Helen Gahagan Douglas he found a beautiful and intelligent woman with a fine political presence who could hold her own with any man in spitting out the sharp and cutting epithet. It was she who first publicized the phrase "Tricky Dick." Congressman Vito Marcantonio, whose name Nixon paired with that of Mrs. Douglas in an effort to prove that she had Communist sympathies, privately called her a bitch. Nixon, who could be disarmed by the seeming gentleness of Quaker Priscilla Hiss, even though she was lying, found the open political attacks of the political woman matched against him intolerable. Murray Chotiner, his campaign manager, shared in the same hatred. His son Kenneth said that as a boy he was led to believe that Mrs. Douglas was wholly evil. Later he met her and found her to be "a truly gracious woman."[26]

Helen Gahagan Douglas was a former operatic singer and a Broadway star who in 1951 married the popular movie actor Melvyn Douglas. An active New Deal supporter, inspired by Eleanor Roosevelt, who became her friend, Mrs. Douglas had first caught the interest of politicians when she testified about the plight of California's migrant workers. She had been elected to Congress in 1944. Left-wing in sympathy and an ardent supporter of Henry Wallace for vice-president in 1944, she had nevertheless abandoned him when he started his Progressive party and had shifted to a more moderate position, stoutly supporting Harry Truman. As anti-Communist as Voorhis, she had worked hard for the passage of bills providing military aid to the free nations of Europe, this through the House Committee on Foreign Relations. "The Soviet Union," she wrote in *The New Republic* of August 29, 1949, "has done its utmost to prevent European recovery . . . has deliberately created an atmosphere of fear and danger." And she warned that it could overrun other European states as it had Czechoslovakia. She opposed recognition of Communist China and its admission to the U.N. She had, however, also opposed Truman's unilateral United States aid to Greece and Turkey, which she felt should have been linked to a larger United Nations collective security system. Her failure to vote for this, the linchpin in Truman's anti-Soviet program, cost her dearly in the election.

She had, moreover, incurred Nixon's enmity by attacking HUAC. "I do not believe in trial by headline," she said. "I do not believe we can make a committee of Congress into a court and maintain justice."[27]

When the popular Democratic incumbent, Sen. Sheridan Downey, withdrew from the senatorial race because of ill health, Nixon was elated. He was even more pleased when Mrs. Douglas defeated in the primary the wildly swinging conservative Democrat Manchester Boddy, publisher of the *Los Angeles Daily News,* who called the congresswoman one of "a small subversive clique of red-hots" who were out "to capture through stealth and cunning the nerve center of our Democratic Party." Senator Downey, whom Mrs. Douglas had alienated by calling him a tool of big business, especially the oil business, damaged her severely by supporting Boddy and calling her inadequate for the post. Mrs. Douglas, like Harry Truman, wanted to keep the tidelands oil under federal rather than state control. Downey had favored state control, and oil, it was said, controlled the California Democratic party.

Helen Douglas won the primary despite lack of party support because of her extraordinary personal popularity. (One of her champions at the time was Ronald Reagan, then a Democrat.)[28]

When the Korean War broke out in late June 1950 and President Truman reacted as a gutsy, anti-Communist fighter and rallied the nation around him, it seemed for a time as if Communism would cease being a partisan issue in the United States. Nixon was warned by his staff to leave all talk of Communism out of his campaign. Instead he talked about little else. He managed adroitly to ride two horses at once, supporting the war enthusiastically, urging the all-out mobilization and a tax increase, but also blaming the invasion of South Korea by the Communist North Koreans on the former appeasement policies of the U.S. Democrats, particularly those in the State Department. "The fall of China was due, certainly in part," he said, "to the fact that our State Department accepted the advice of a clique who assumed that Chinese Communists were . . . 'agrarian reformers,' and 'liberals.' . . . China having fallen, the Korean war became inevitable."[29] Specifically he charged that Helen Douglas had "consistently supported the State Department's policy of appeasing Communism in Asia, which finally resulted in the Korean War," and that she "follows the Communist Party line."[30]

Truman and his secretary of state, Dean Acheson, had meanwhile gratuitously handed Nixon two weapons. The president, instead of conceding publicly that Alger Hiss was probably guilty, when questioned by the press simply repeated his charge that the HUAC hearings were "a red herring." Nixon learned, however, that Truman had said privately to a Justice Department aide, after reading through the Hiss papers, "Why that son-of-a-bitch, he betrayed his country!" And this story Nixon told and retold, including it in his memoirs.[31]

Dean Acheson, on the day of Hiss's sentencing, January 25, 1950, when questioned by reporters on his feelings about Hiss's going to prison, had said, "I will not turn my back on Alger Hiss," and referred reporters, without actual quotation, to a New Testament verse, Matthew 25:35–37. Those reporters who took the trouble to open their Bibles found the words:

> For I was hungered and ye gave me meat. . . .
> I was in prison, and ye came unto me.

Acheson's statement was meant to be an expression of compassion rather than defense and was not inappropriate. Nixon called it "disgusting" and demanded Acheson's resignation. Sen. Joseph McCarthy, who had recently joined Nixon's anti-Communism crusade and who was already outdoing him in vitriol and misrepresentation, trumpeted in a Nixon rally in California, "Acheson must go!" and called the Truman government "the administration Commicrat Party of Betrayal." Nixon applauded the speech, saying of McCarthy, "God give him courage to carry on!"[32] He himself hinted at a possible Soviet attack on Alaska, accusing Truman of hiding the weakness of West Coast defenses. And he warned that American Communists "have orders from Moscow to start 'a reign of terror if we ever cross swords with Russia.' " Their blueprint for revolution, he said, included the sabotage of defense and power plants, contamination of food supplies, and the seizing of American arsenals.[33]

In attacking Mrs. Douglas, Nixon was not content with linking her to the State Department's supposed appeasement of the Soviet Union, but moved on, as he had with Voorhis, to overkill. On August 20 he issued a broadside:

During five years in Congress, Helen Douglas has voted 353 times exactly as has Vito Marcantonio, the notorious Communist party-line Congressman from New York. . . . How can Helen Douglas, capable actress that she is, take up so strange a role as a foe of communism? And why does she when she has so deservedly earned the title of "the pink lady?" . . . To the Communist newspaper the *New York Daily Worker,* Helen Douglas and Vito Marcantonio are heroes.

This was the "pink sheet," printed on pink paper and distributed in over half a million copies, which became a celebrated model of "guilt by association." The pink sheet said Helen Douglas and Marcantonio had voted alike 354 times, whereas Nixon had voted "exactly opposite to the Douglas-Marcantonio axis."

The attack was simple and devastating, and Helen Douglas had no response that was not intellectual and complicated. The "axis" was imaginary. Nixon himself had voted with Marcantonio 112 times. Of the 354 votes, most were noncontroversial and minor; only 76 were key "roll-call" votes. Of these, Douglas had voted with Marcantonio 66 times, 53 times with a majority of the Democratic party. Of the 13 in which she did not vote with the party, 11 dealt with housing, rent, and price controls. Two dealt with internal security, the Mundt-Nixon bill, which she opposed and which the Senate refused to pass, and the McCarran internal security bill, where she voted to sustain Truman's veto. On all foreign policy issues she had voted with the bipartisan "containment of Russia" majority save on the Greek-Turkish aid bill. On ten crucial roll-call votes she had voted against Marcantonio.[34]

She had voted for many contempt citations for HUAC witnesses—who refused to be subpoenaed or who "took the Fifth"—but not all, choosing with discrimination. As William Costello later pointed out, more than half of the HUAC witnesses whose cases resulted in indictments by grand juries were finally acquitted in jury trials. "Any member voting in the negative, far from being pro-Communist, had a better than fifty-fifty chance of being in the right."[35]

But none of this could really be communicated to the electorate, especially—as President Truman noted—since Mrs. Douglas was faced with an almost total newspaper blackout. The *Los Angeles Times* printed only Nixon's attacks on her, and his replies when she attempted to defend herself. When she finally resorted to a full-page ad, titled "Thou shalt Not Bear False Witness," he called it "sacrilegious." In an effort to get coverage she turned to intemperate attack, calling Nixon and his supporters "a backwash of men in dark shirts," an unfortunate allusion to Hitler's and Mussolini's Fascists, and issued a broadside called THE BIG LIE, which said, "Hitler invented it—Stalin perfected it—Nixon uses it."[36]

She carelessly distorted Nixon's own record, especially on two votes in which he was able to prove triumphantly that she was in the wrong. She charged that he had voted against aid to Korea; actually he had refused to support the bill until aid to Formosa was included. And she said he had helped the Communists by voting with Marcantonio in an effort to cut European aid in half. Nixon had voted for a one-year rather than a two-year bill, with a renewal provision. As Chotiner said, "She made the fatal mistake of attacking our strength instead of sticking to attacking our weaknesses."[37]

Nixon plastered the state with billboards carrying his picture with the caption underneath: ON GUARD FOR AMERICA. He toured with his usual prodigious energy, making, it was said, a thousand speeches. He sent out misleading literature, AS ONE DEMOCRAT TO ANOTHER, suggesting to unsuspecting or uninvolved Democratic newcomers to the state that he was one of them. Each candidate encouraged hecklers to harass his opponent; Nixon supporters once spattered red ink on Mrs. Douglas's face and dress as she was about to give a speech. At one whistlestop Nixon said Helen Douglas was "pink right down to her underwear."[38]

Gerald L. K. Smith, an anti-Semitic right-winger, directed his Christian Nationalist Crusade to support Nixon. "Help Richard Nixon get rid of the Jew-Communists," he urged, and in an undercover campaign directed at Melvyn Douglas, urged his following, "Do not send to the Senate the wife of a Jew." Nixon after some delay issued a statement saying he did not want Smith's support: "I denounce anti-Semitism in whatever form it appears." And the Anti-Defamation League of B'nai B'rith, which had been publicly concerned, issued a statement exonerating him.[39]

Mrs. Douglas was not helped when Democrat George Creel—administrator under Woodrow Wilson in the "Red Scare" of the twenties, which had seen gross violations of the civil rights of thousands of Americans of Russian origin[40]—led a group of sixty-three prominent Democrats to Nixon's support. *Los Angeles Times* editorials echoed the specifics of his campaign, attacking Mrs. Douglas as "a glamorous actress, who, though not a Communist, voted the Communist party line in Congress innumerable times . . . the darling of the Hollywood parlor pinks and Reds."[41]

Much of the normally Democratic Catholic vote now turned to Nixon. In his memoirs he underlined this fact when he revealed with satisfaction that $1000 for his campaign had come from Joseph Kennedy by way of his son Jack. "I obviously can't endorse you," he reported Congressman Kennedy as saying, "but it isn't going to break my heart if you can turn the Senate's loss into Hollywood's gain."[42] Finally, in the last week of the campaign the Chinese Communists began pouring across the border into North Korea, and this finished Mrs. Douglas. As Harry W. Flannery put it in *Commonweal,* she "had a broom trying to sweep back the sea."[43]

Nixon, it was estimated at the time, spent between $1,000,000 and $1,750,000 on the campaign, although the only figures made available showed that organizations supporting him had spent $62,899. The total of those reporting support for Mrs. Douglas was $156,172.[44] When letters surfaced indicating that Union Oil had given Nixon $52,000, he denied it and insisted on a full investigation by a Senate committee. The letters attesting to the fact turned out to be forgeries.[45] No demands were made upon Nixon, however, to describe the sources of his campaign funds other than the $62,899 already made public, and given the lax laws of the time concerning campaign contributions, there was no way of forcing disclosure.

Later a minor scandal erupted when Sen. Owen Brewster of Maine, chairman of the Republican Senatorial Committee, admitted that he had illegally loaned Nixon $5000 for his primary campaign, although committee rules provided that money be made available only for the final campaign. "Beseiged," Brewster said, by Nixon and Philip Young of North Dakota for money for their primaries, he borrowed $10,000 from a Washington bank, turned it over to Harry ("the Dutchman") Grunewald, who sent half to Nixon's manager and half to Young's. Later, when both men had won the primaries and money began pouring in, the loans were repaid to Grunewald and then to Brewster.[46]

A Mervin Freed poll on October 30 showed that Nixon had a ten to two lead. Still, Pat Nixon said that her husband was in an agony of apprehension. He won by 2,183,454 to 1,502,507, a 680,000-vote margin, 7 percent ahead of the Republican congressional slate. "We hopped from one victory celebration to another far into the night," Pat said. "Dick was so exuberant. Wherever he found a piano he played 'Happy Days Are Here Again.' "[47]

Nixon had silenced Helen Douglas permanently. She went out of politics and, save for a brief return to the stage, out of public life. But she had left an epithet, "Tricky Dick," that would be a small but permanent albatross about his neck.[48] The campaign left with Democrats a distaste for Nixon that would never be dissipated. He, with his wife, got a taste of this in the most cruelly personal fashion shortly after returning to Washington as senator. Joseph Alsop, popular Washington columnist whose Sunday-night suppers were famous, invited Nixon and his wife, along with other celebrities. Nixon had been courting Alsop, sending him appreciative letters on his columns, and once giving him copies of his own interviews with ambassadors from Iron Curtain countries.[49] Mrs. Stewart Alsop, also at the party, remembered Nixon as being ill at ease. "He sank quickly into a big wing chair," she said. Shortly afterward Averell Harriman, former ambassador to Russia and special assistant to Harry Truman, who had been sent to California to try to rescue Helen Douglas's campaign, arrived at the party. Since he was slightly deaf, Harriman's voice was louder than normal and carried across the room. When he saw Nixon he said, "I will not break bread with that man!" He turned off his hearing aid, refused to eat anything, and shortly left the party.[50]

The effect of the 1950 campaign on Pat Nixon, as she watched her husband destroy the actress-politician—a role not altogether unrelated to her own—can only be guessed at. Some years later when Eleanor Roosevelt was questioned about Nixon on "Meet the Press," the former First Lady said:

I have no respect for the way in which he accused Helen Gahagan Douglas of being a Communist because he knew that was how he would be elected, and I have no respect for the kind of character that takes advantage and does something they know is not true. He knew that she might be a Liberal, but he knew quite well, having known her and worked with her, that she was not a Communist. I have always felt that anyone who wanted an election so much that they would use those means did not have the character that I really admire in public life.

Pat, who had been a Democrat and an admirer of the Roosevelts when she was married, "was upset" by the remarks. So wrote her biographer Lester David, who added, "but Nixon told her to pay no attention, because it was just politics."[51]

Nixon among the Giants

*Dwight Eisenhower was that rarest of men, an authentic hero
. . . one of the giants of our time.*
— RICHARD NIXON, 1969[1]

RICHARD NIXON first saw Dwight Eisenhower in a tick-
ertape parade in New York City shortly before V-E Day in 1945.
"Maybe I just think it was that way," he told Robert Coughlan
eight years later. "I was about 30 stories up—but I have this picture that there he came, with his arms outstretched and his face
up to the sky, and that even from where I was I could feel the
impact of his personality." In his memoirs he recalled that Eisenhower's arms were raised high over his head in the gesture that
soon became his trademark.[2] Nixon adopted the gesture for his
own, and as president employed it in parades. But he used it as a
weapon as well and it became for many in the nation a detested
gesture, a salute that had somehow become defiled. At San Jose,
California, on October 29, 1970, facing a hostile antiwar crowd,
he stood upright in his limousine with his arms outstretched and
his fingers moving in the Eisenhower salute, and said to an aide,
"That's what they hate to see." Students hurled rocks and bottles
at him.[3]

When Eisenhower died in 1969, Nixon called him a giant and
a hero, "probably more loved by more people in more parts of the
world than any president America has ever had . . . truly the first
citizen of the world . . . a moral authority without parallel in
America and the world."[4] "This patently good man," Robert Donovan wrote, "made the phrase 'father image' fashionable," and
"that image in the election made him impregnable."[5]

Nixon had fantasies of being counted among the giants of history. He used the word "giant" frequently—to describe Chiang
Kai-shek, Charles de Gaulle, personal friends like J. Edgar Hoo-

ver and Sen. Everett Dirkson, and, somewhat surprisingly, an enemy, John L. Lewis.[6] He was fond of quoting Sir Isaac Newton, who had said, "If we can see further than the ancients it is because we stand on the shoulders of the giants who have gone before us."[7] His affection for the quotation suggested not only his indebtedness to Eisenhower, the giant on whose shoulders he rode to political stardom, but also his hope for a heroic image of his own.

Nixon courted Eisenhower like a humble supplicant, hoping to be accepted as his legitimate political heir, as John Adams had been to Gen. George Washington and as Martin Van Buren had been to Gen. Andrew Jackson. In his memoirs Nixon quoted from many Eisenhower letters, which would indicate affection and esteem. Actually their relationship was corroded by suspicion and mistrust almost from the beginning. To the many evidences of distrust and repudiation by Eisenhower, Nixon remained dumb. Like Nixon's father, Eisenhower was a preeminently masculine figure, and like Frank Nixon he also had a capacity for towering rage. But Eisenhower's rage rarely exploded. He was controlled and often conciliatory. He also had the habit of command, all the more awesome to his subordinates because the full limits of his rage remained largely unknown.

With President Harry Truman, the other major political giant in his life, Nixon could be brash, arrogant, and sometimes libelously freespoken. In 1950 he had even been capable of implying, slyly, in civic clubs in California that "there was something sexual going on between Mrs. Douglas and Harry Truman." "There was not, of course," wrote David Halberstam, who was the first to publish this, and to note that the *Los Angeles Times* was careful not to put it in print.[8] In the 1952 campaign Nixon denounced Truman along with Dean Acheson and Adlai Stevenson as "traitors to the high principles in which many of the nation's Democrats believe," and he accused Truman in particular of "covering up for political reasons an internal Communist conspiracy in the United States."[9]

Truman, who always insisted Nixon had called him "a traitor to his country," accused him of using the Fascist "big lie." As years passed the vendetta became ever more bitter, with Nixon accusing Truman of coddling Communists eight years after he left office. In a taped interview with Merle Miller in 1961 Truman called Nixon "a shifty-eyed, goddamn liar." "All the time I've been in politics," he said, "there's only two people I hate and he's one. He not only doesn't give a damn about the people; he doesn't know the difference between telling the truth and lying."[10]

Nixon made an effort to mend matters when he became president, making Truman a gift of the piano he had played on in the White House. He did not see the Merle Miller interview until after Truman's death. Had he done so, he might have been less inclined to praise him in an obituary speech, calling him a man of enormous courage, exceptional vision, and guts.[11]

Truman was never the giant in the eyes of the world that Churchill or Roosevelt had been, and never had the widespread affection and respect during his lifetime of an Eisenhower. But he never agonized over this. Tough, resiliant, with astonishing inner fortitude, he had moved into the decision-making of the postwar years confident in his judgment, willing to exercise power and sustained by an extensive knowledge of history in which he was largely self-taught. Enraged by Stalin's repudiations of the Yalta agreements, he had provided for unilateral aid to Greece and Turkey, and had helped set up NATO in 1949 as a coalition of Western nations against Soviet aggression. When the Soviets shut off supplies to West Berlin, Truman organized, with the aid of the British, a 327-day airlift which saw 2,343,000 tons of supplies flown into the beleaguered city. The Russians on September 20, 1949, finally backed down and opened traffic by land into the city.

Truman blamed Russia for the invasion of South Korea by Communists from the north and in his war message to Congress had denounced the Soviets for conducting "an evil war by proxy." He called it a move by "the Russian Communist dictatorship to take over the world step by step."

Today, when revisionist historians are denouncing Truman for having been too truculent, too aggressively anti-Communist, too much architect of the Cold War, one looks back with ever-greater incredulity at Richard Nixon's success, aided by Sen. Joseph McCarthy, in convincing so many Americans that Truman was a secret protector of a "Communist conspiracy" in the United States.

Nixon in attacking Truman was not content merely to accuse him of obstructing the investigation of Alger Hiss. He also accepted and publicized the propaganda of the "China Lobby,"

among them old China hands, who held that American withdrawal of material support from Chiang Kai-shek ten months
after the ending of World War II had added six hundred million
Communists to the enemies of the United States. Echoing this in
the Senate in 1951, Nixon said, "As a direct result, I may say, of
that action on the part of our State Department and our Government, China did go Communist." And he went on to define world
power in arithmetical terms:

When we consider the lineup of the people of the world, what do we
find? We find that today there are only 590,000,000 people on our side;
there are 800,000,000 people on the Communist side, and there are
600,000,000 people who have to be classified as neutral.

The odds today, he said, "are 5 to 3 against us."[12]

Nixon applauded the decision to go to war in Korea, but later,
seeing the war's unpopularity, blamed Truman for the American
casualties, saying that without the loss of China there need have
been no Korean War at all. But when MacArthur wanted to
extend the war into China, bombing beyond the Yalu River, and
Truman, determined to keep the war limited, brought him home
on charges of insubordination, Nixon called the decision
"appeasement." He sponsored a resolution in Congress calling for
MacArthur's return to Korea, saying that Americans were
"shocked, disheartened, endangered," and that "the happiest
group in the country will be the Communists and their stooges."
Nixon called for the destruction of the Chinese bases. "Our broad
objective, of course, is peace with honor. . . . Communist aggression, unchecked at this time, can lead only to a war which the
United States could lose in a week."[13]

Nixon was careful never to include Eisenhower in his
denunciations of the men who had "lost" China to the Communists, even though as chief of staff the general had concurred in
the Truman-Acheson decisions, including the specific Acheson
declaration of January 12, 1950, concerning the "defense perimeter" of the United States, the distortion of which many thought
had led to the North Korean invasion of the south. And Eisenhower deplored MacArthur's plans to carry the war into China.

As late as the fall of 1958 Nixon was still insisting that Acheson
had announced in January 1950 that the United States "would
not defend Korea." Acheson had actually stated that the "defen-

sive perimeter runs along the Aleutians to Japan and then goes to
the Ryukyus . . . from the Ryukyus to the Philippine Islands. . . .
In the north, we have direct responsibility in Japan and we have
direct opportunity to act. The same thing to a lesser degree is true
in Korea." When reporters corrected Nixon, he changed his statement to the still-incorrect one that Acheson had announced that
"Korea was outside the defense zone of the United States."[14]

It was Herbert Hoover who introduced Nixon to Eisenhower.
Both Republicans and Democrats had been wooing Eisenhower
since his political affiliation was obscure. Truman as early as 1945
had told him in Berlin that he would help him get the presidency
in 1948 if he wanted it, and renewed his pledge quietly in 1952.
Eisenhower at first dodged all the importunities, believing—like
Andrew Jackson—that he was not fit to be president but changing
his mind when he looked at the quality of his rivals, especially
General MacArthur, who made no secret of his conviction that
the presidency was properly his. Voters in the Minnesota primary,
where MacArthur's name was on the ballot alongside that of Harold Stassen, gave him only one half of 1 percent, a demonstration
that the public could come down solidly against megalomania.
Stassen got 44.4 percent; the remaining 37.2 percent was an
unprecedented write-in vote for Eisenhower.

Hoover as early as the summer of 1950 had invited Eisenhower to a meeting of major California party contributors at the
posh Bohemian Grove and had asked Nixon also to be present.
Sensitive to ranking, Nixon remembered that Ike sat on Hoover's
right, and that he himself was "two places from the bottom." His
introduction to Ike was fleeting. "I doubted then if he would
remember me," he said.[15] But this he was determined to remedy.
Already he had rejected the idea of campaigning for Sen. Robert
Taft, with whom he had tangled on details of the Taft-Hartley
bill, and whom he had found "honest in a way that could be painfully blunt."[16] Gov. Earl Warren he could never forgive because
of his refusal to endorse him against Jerry Voorhis, and his last-
minute, lukewarm support against Helen Douglas.

Warren, a genial, handsome bear of a man who had run with
Dewey on the national ticket in 1948, and who had won the governorship on both Republican and Democratic tickets, recoiled
from the rigors and corruptions of a presidential campaign. "I

haven't the money and I can't go out and make the deals necessary to raise the money to stage a real campaign," he told Drew Pearson. "You have to check your soul in order to do it."[17] He had decided, however, to go to the convention as a favorite son, hoping to win the nomination if a deadlock loomed between Taft and Eisenhower.

Nixon, like many others, was impressed by Ike's physical presence and manly bearing. Later, when he sought him out at SHAPE headquarters outside Paris in May 1951 on a trip to Geneva as Senate observer for a World Health Organization conference, he found him "erect and vital and impeccably tailored." Eisenhower had read *Seeds of Treason,* Ralph de Toledano and Victor Lasky's glowing account of Nixon's work on the Hiss Case, and praised him for it.[18] Later Ike would recall that he found Nixon "young, vigorous, ready to learn, of good reputation." He especially liked the fact that "he did not persecute or defame." This impression was enough, as it turned out, to carry Nixon into the vice-presidency. Ike seems to have known nothing of his reputation in California for slander; he was even misinformed about his age—thirty-nine—which he thought to be forty-two.[19]

Elated to find himself valued, Nixon wrote of the interview, "It was clear that he had done his homework. . . . I felt that I was in the presence of a genuine statesmen, and I came away convinced that he should be the next president."[20]

Although Nixon did not advertise his preference, it was soon known to party professionals. He attended a secret strategy session in New Jersey with Harold Stassen, who agreed to pull out of the race should Eisenhower run—a promise he did not keep—and he proceeded to make himself the most visible and efficient fundraiser among the nation's Republican senators. Nixon gave a dozen speeches a month, Earl Mazo said, blossoming into "a Republican meld of Paul Revere and Billy Sunday." It was a single speech with variations. He urged " a fighting, rocking, socking campaign," deploring the "whining, whimpering, groveling attitude of our diplomatic representatives who talk of America's weaknesses and of America's fear rather than of America's strength and courage." He castigated Truman for failing to oust the "fifth column" which he claimed was infiltrating "the very highest councils of his administration."[21] The speech brought thunderous applause when he delivered it for a New York fundraiser chaired by Gov. Thomas E. Dewey. Afterward Dewey leaned over to Nixon and whispered, "Make me a promise: don't get fat, don't lose your zeal, and you can be President someday." Late that night Dewey asked him if he could propose his name as vice-president on the Eisenhower ticket.[22]

Nixon was only thirty-nine, and was the youngest vice-president save for John C. Breckinridge, who in 1856 went into office at age thirty-eight, with James Buchanan. He had rocketed into company with political giants, but he was not yet one of them—and knew it. Press speculation that he might be on the ticket he disavowed as unlikely or ridiculous. But that he believed his chances to be good we learn from his memoirs, in which he recalled an evening with Alice Roosevelt Longworth. The daughter of Theodore Roosevelt had befriended the Nixons, intrigued by his admiration for her father and perhaps enjoying a Republican as gifted at attack as herself. Nixon asked her if he should take the nomination if offered. Her father, he remembered, had said becoming vice-president was like "taking the veil." "Would it not be," he asked her "a stepping stone to political oblivion?" "Father used to tell me that being Vice-President was the most boring job in the world," Mrs. Longworth said. "By some act of God you might become President too, but you shouldn't plan on it."[23]

The "act of God," as Nixon well knew, was statistically significant. Although only two vice-presidents, John Adams and Martin Van Buren, had managed to be elected to the presidency, six vice-presidents had moved into the Oval Office because of the death or assassination of Presidents William Henry Harrison, Zachary Taylor, Abraham Lincoln, James Garfield, William McKinley, and Warren Harding. Alice Longworth may not have been the first to talk to Nixon of the possibility of the sixty-two-year-old Eisenhower's dying in office, but she was not the last.

"Until this conversation," Nixon wrote in one of the more disingenuous paragraphs in his memoirs,

I had never taken the possibility of the nomination seriously enough to consider that I might not want the job. . . . It was one thing for me to believe that Eisenhower was the best man for the job and it was quite another to renounce my own political career just as it had reached a national stage in the Senate. If I had had presidential ambitions—which I did not at that point—I probably would not have considered becoming Vice President.[24]

Actually in late 1951 and early 1952 he largely abandoned his senatorial work to make himself as visible in the party as possible, and indispensable to Eisenhower.

Although California delegates had taken an oath to support Warren on the first ballot, Nixon did his best to erode the guarantee. He used his franking privilege, illegally, to mail a questionaire to twenty-three thousand Californians asking their favorite choice for the Republican nomination. Warren, angered when he learned that the consensus was for Eisenhower, prevented Nixon from publishing the results, but they became known. When the train carrying California delegates to the convention left California, Nixon did not board it until Denver, where he paid Warren his respects, saying, "if any of my friends get out of line let me know." Then he spent the night in caucuses with delegates, spreading the word through Murray Chotiner that Eisenhower could win in the first ballot. To avoid being photographed with Warren, Nixon dropped off the train in a Chicago suburb. And when Warren went to pay his respects to Eisenhower in Chicago, he was startled to see Murray Chotiner open the door to him in the general's suite.[25]

Although Eisenhower was ahead of Taft in the polls and expected the nomination to be handed to him on a platter, Taft waged a dogged battle. He had at first more delegates than Ike, 727 as against 427. But there were 75 disputed delegates from the South, where grass-roots organizations preferring Ike had sent rival delegates to the convention. Nixon and other Eisenhower supporters argued for a "Fair Play amendment" which would make it impossible for any contested delegate to vote on the seating save those who had been approved by more than 80 percent of the 106-member National Committee.[26] In the preliminary skirmishing Taft forces won the contested seats in Geoegia, and it looked as if the Texas votes would follow suit. At this point Nixon seized the microphone to denounce "the Texas grab." If the party approved it, he argued, "we will be announcing to the country that we believe ruthless machine politics is wrong only when the Democrats use it." Later, in the floor fight broadcast over national TV, the Eisenhower forces won the Fair Play amendment 658 to 548 and picked up 32 delegates. Warren united with Nixon and Knowland to support it, although he knew it was likely to cost him his dark-horse chances. Once it passed, there was no stopping the general.[27]

Nixon had been considered an ideal keynote speaker, but he had made an enemy of Republican National Committee Chairman Guy Gabrielson, who had been investigated by a Senate committee on a conflict-of-interest charge involving the Reconstruction Finance Corporation. Although he had been acquitted, Nixon, with self-righteous zeal that helped to spread his reputation for political purity, had nevertheless demanded Gabrielson's resignation for the good of the party. Gabrielson in retaliation vetoed Nixon's name as speaker and gave the keynote address to General MacArthur. Nixon quietly ordered the California delegation not to applaud the general, presumably because the clapping might do Eisenhower harm, and many obeyed.

Sen. Joseph McCarthy, chosen to speak for the right wing, gave Nixon indirect but unmistakable publicity. In his peroration, which brought roars from the convention, he chanted themes Nixon had been the first in Congress to carry to the nation:

> I say, one Communist in a defense plant is one Communist too many.
> One Communist on the faculty of one university is one Communist too many.
> One Communist among American advisers at Yalta was one Communist too many.
> And even if there were only one Communist in the State Department, that would be one Communist too many.[28]

The first ballot showed Ike only six votes short of victory. Stassen's Minnesota delegates, led by Warren Burger (later appointed by Nixon Chief Justice of the Supreme Court), rushed to end the contest.

California delegates had stayed true to Warren on the first ballot, but all knew the special services Nixon had rendered the victor. Buff Chandler, powerful wife of the publisher of the *Los Angeles Times,* busy lobbying for an "Ike and Dick" ticket, persuaded John S. Knight of the Knight newspaper chain to predict it, and he ran the appropriate headline in the *Chicago Daily News.* "I was the one," she said to Bela Kornitzer, "who threw Nixon's name in the ring." Years later she told William Halberstam that she had always thought Nixon a little tacky.[29]

Mamie Eisenhower, the *New York Times* reported, was "ill all day" when her husband was nominated to the presidency. Pat

Nixon's reaction to the choice of her husband for the vice-presidential nomination was pure act. She told reporters she was "amazed, flabbergasted, weak, and speechless." "We heard rumors," she said, "but we heard rumors about a lot of people. I wasn't prepared for this."[30] Nixon, too, maintained the fiction of being surprised. He insisted at the time, and even in his memoirs, that he considered the possibility "so unlikely" that he sent out for extra copies of the *Chicago Daily News,* saying, "That will probably be the last time we'll see that headline, and I want to be able to show it to my grandchildren," even though the *New York Times* said he had been the obvious frontrunner three days before his nomination.[31]

What the newspapers did not report was that Pat, for reasons still somewhat mysterious, was deeply chagrined. We know now that on the night of July 10, when the victory over the Fair Play amendment virtually ensured an Eisenhower victory, an elated Nixon returned to his hotel about midnight. As he described it in his memoirs:

Pat was waiting up for me. Although campaigning did not come easily to her because of her deep-rooted sense of privacy she did it superbly. But now that we actually had to consider the possibility of a long and grueling nationwide campaign, she was having second thoughts about what accepting the nomination could mean to us and to our young daughters.

Nixon admitted that they talked "nearly all night." Chotiner later told Earl Mazo that Nixon woke him up at 4 A.M. and asked him to join them. "I could tell that Pat had been talking against it," he said. Nixon in his memoirs relates that Pat acquiesced: "I guess I can make it through another campaign." Lester David, Mrs. Nixon's biographer, insists, however, that "Pat was sure she had won and that he would refuse an offered bid."[32]

Pat Nixon has never explained publicly why she argued with her husband for five hours trying to persuade him to refuse so distinguished a post, and one he had fought so tirelessly and adroitly to win. Concerned as she was about her daughters, she had the choice of campaigning less, as did Bess Truman and Mamie Eisenhower, and later Jacqueline Kennedy. Moreover, even if Ike lost it would not have meant the loss of her husband's Senate seat.

When Abigail Adams, during her husband's term as vice-president, learned that George Washington was dangerously ill and might well die, she wrote to her sister in dismay:

I dreaded his death from a cause that few persons, and only those who knew me best, would believe . . . neither our Finances are arranged nor our Government sufficiently cemented to produce duration. His death would I fear have had most disasterous consequences. Most assurredly I do not wish for the highest post. . . . thanks to Providence he is again restored.[33]

We do not know if Pat also suspected that her husband was not equal to "the highest post" and feared that the possible death of Eisenhower, with her husband succeeding to the presidency, would have "most disasterous consequences." In any case, Nixon at this point, with the prize almost in his outstretched hand, could have been only stung and angered by his wife's failure to share in his exhilaration.

This may explain why on the following afternoon when, several hours after Ike's nomination, it was announced over the nation's television networks that he had chosen Richard Nixon as his running mate, Pat did not learn it from her husband but from a TV set in a restaurant where she was lunching on a sandwich with her friend Helene Drown. As Pat described it, "The bite fell out of my mouth and we rushed back to the convention hall. I guess I was one of the last to learn that he had accepted."[34]

Nixon at first told reporters he was lunching near the Convention Hall when he learned that he was Eisenhower's choice. Later he corrected the story. Desperate for sleep because he had been up all night arguing with his wife, he had returned at noon after Ike's nomination to the Stockyard Inn with Murray Chotiner and Bernard Brennan. Stripping to his shorts in the hot room, he lay on the bed, "trying to think cool thoughts." Chotiner had the good news that Ike had turned the choice over to his advisers and that he had submitted a list with Nixon's name on it. Herbert Brownell shortly telephoned to say, "We picked you," and told him Eisenhower wanted to see him as soon as possible.[35]

Nixon flung on his clothes and sped to Eisenhower's hotel in a limousine with a motorcycle escort. Chotiner remembered that Nixon, "calm and pensive," asked him to call his parents. "Tell them it looks as if I'm going to be nominated for vice-president." No effort had been made, apparently, to find Pat.[36]

Eisenhower greeted him warmly, introduced him to his wife, and after some informal words describing all the reasons he had not wanted to run, he explained that he did not want a vice-president who would be a figurehead. Nixon shortly went on to the convention hall where he arranged for Senator Knowland to nominate him and Gov. Alfred Driscoll of New Jersey to make the seconding speech. It was not until after these speeches had been made and Nixon's name had been accepted by acclamation that Pat Nixon was maneuvered into view by Jack Drown and Alan Pattee and brought to her husband's side. As the *New York Times* described it,

Mr. Nixon, standing with a tremendous grin among his colleagues of the California delegation, flung his arms around those nearest him—one of whom was Mr. Fine [Gov. John S. Fine of Pennsylvania] and looked all about for Mrs. Nixon. Soon she made her way forward through the crowd and kissed the Senator twice on the cheek. They walked together to the convention platform. . . . Mrs. Nixon, a pretty blond . . . kissed the Senator again.[37]

Nixon did not kiss his wife. But there was no reticence in the crowd. "Endless waves of cyclonic cheers," the *Times* reporter said, from "11,000 taut throats" shook the hall as the band played the GOP theme song, "There's Gonna Be a Great Day." Nixon said in his memoirs he felt "exhilarated—almost heady." And Pat, he reported, "said later that for those few minutes it actually made her forget the long campaign we would have to endure."[38]

When Pat was interviewed, she said she liked campaigning and meeting people. "We work as a team," she said, and described herself as doing the secretarial work, taking care of the mail and the news releases, and occasionally attending women's meetings and speaking informally, although not about politics.[39] There was something wistful and a little pathetic in all this. It was if she had gone back in time to the Whittier days, before her husband had a $70,000-a-year expense account for mail clerks and secretaries, before Chotiner had taken over the news releases, before the invasion of ambitious men had pushed her out of the decision-making altogether. A few weeks later she told a *Saturday Evening Post* writer that she had seen everything in politics "except a smoke filled room." "We haven't been in any and don't intend to be. . . . I married a crusader."[40]

Eisenhower in his acceptance speech called for a crusade against a wasteful, arrogant, corrupt administration too long in power. Nixon spoke briefly, beginning with a gesture in the direction of the general: "Haven't we got a wonderful candidate for the President of the United States!" He applauded Joe Martin and other party regulars and made the expected gesture of conciliation toward Senator Taft. There was no scene stealing from Eisenhower. The most frequently published photograph of the convention showed Eisenhower and Nixon with their wives, acknowledging the cheers of the crowd. The two men's hands are raised high together, but not held tight in a firm clasp of friendship as one might expect. Instead, Eisenhower has his hand outstretched. Nixon's hand is behind, grasping the general's wrist, and hanging on. The uncertain quality of the gesture proved to be symbolic.

Nixon was finally riding with the giants. But he was uneasy in the saddle. As he remembered, years later:

In 1953, Senator Knowland—who had been appointed to the Senate by the Chief Justice when he was Governor of California—at my request, swore me in. He proceeded, in swearing me in, to read the entire oath, and then I had to repeat it from memory. Even though I had been a Member of the Senate, I did forget a line. Some people were even wondering whether I was really the Vice President or not.

The memory came back to him the day after he was inaugurated president of the United States.[41]

At the Whittier College Commencement, June 1965

Frank and Hannah Nixon with Harold, Donald, and Richard, 1917

Harold at Prescott, Arizona, 1929

Nixon's Service Station, 1931

Nixon's Grocery, 1945

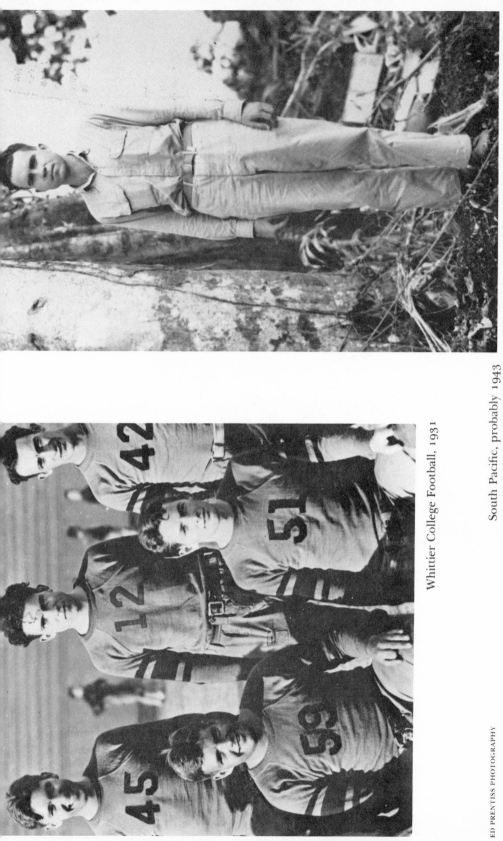

Whittier College Football, 1931

South Pacific, probably 1943

Thelma Catherine Patricia Ryan, about 1937

ELECT

RICHARD M. NIXON

WORLD WAR II VETERAN

YOUR CONGRESSMAN

MR. AND MRS. RICHARD M. NIXON AND PATRICIA

"I pledge myself to serve you faithfully;
To act in the best interests of all of you;

To work for the re-dedication of the United States
of America to a kind of opportunity for your children and mine;

To assist with all my powers the encroachments of foreign isms
upon the American way of life;

To preserve our sacred heritages, in the name of my buddies and
your loved ones, who died that these might endure;

To devote my full energies to service for you while opposing
regimentation of you;

To remain always humble in the knowledge of your trust in me."

Richard M. Nixon

Dick Nixon is a serious, energetic individual with a high purpose in life—to serve his fellow man. He is a trained scholar, a natural leader and a combat war veteran. He has acquired the "human touch" the hard way—by working his way through college and law school; by sleeping in fox-holes, sweating out air raids; by returning from war confronted with the necessity of "starting all over again."

There is in Richard Nixon's background much that is typical of the young western American. There are the parents from the mid-west, the father who has been street car motorman, oil field worker, citrus rancher, grocer. There is the solid heritage of the Quaker faith; the family tradition of Work—and Service.

The effects of this background show in Richard Nixon. He has worked in a fruit packing house, in stores, as a gas station attendant. He has made an outstanding success of his law practice. He played college football ("not too successfully," he says); maintains an intensive interest in sports.

Of course, the No. 1 Nixon-for-Congress enthusiasts are Mrs. Richard Nixon, born Patricia Ryan on St. Patrick's Day, and six-months-old baby daughter Pat. Mrs. Nixon is a public servant in her own right, having worked for the government as an economist while her husband was fighting for his country in the South Pacific. Like so many other young "war couples," the Nixons resumed civilian life on a financial foundation comprised solely of War Bonds purchased from the savings of the working wife and sailor husband.

Mr. and Mrs. Richard Nixon have been very busy this year. Individually or jointly, they have (1) been looking for a place to live; (2) practiced law; (3) been taking care of their little girl; (4) been active in veterans' affairs, particularly those relating to housing for Whittier College veteran-students and their families; (5) been looking for a place to live again; and (6) they have been campaigning to ELECT RICHARD NIXON TO CONGRESS.

r *New, Progressive, Representation
in Congress*

VOTE FOR

RICHARD M. NIXON

ON NOVEMBER 5

Jerry Voorhis, 1939   Helen Gahagan Douglas, 1950

Murray M. Chotiner, 1956   Earl Warren, 1942

CALIFORNIA POLITICIANS

"NAUGHTY NAUGHTY"

October 29, 1952

"HERE HE COMES NOW"

October 29, 1954

'S SEE—WHAT'LL I WEAR TODAY?"

February 15, 1956

"NOW YOU KIDS BEAT IT"

October 26, 1956

A SAMPLING OF HERBLOCK COMMENTS

FROM *Herblock Special Report*, 1974: W. W. NORTON & COMPANY, INC.

The vice-president with Secretary of State Dulles and Konrad Adenauer

*To general Dwight D. Eisenhower,
with grateful appreciation for his wise counsel,
and loyal friendship through the years*
Dick Nixon
February 2, 1969

With former President Eisenhower, 1969

With Bebe Rebozo and Robert Abplanalp at Key Biscayne

X I X

Checkers

I knew I had done nothing wrong and had nothing to hide.
— RICHARD NIXON

You don't have to be phony if you're honest.
— PAT NIXON, ON "THE FUND CRISIS" [1]

THE FUND CRISIS was the most scarifying episode in Nixon's life until Watergate, an ordeal that saw him triumph over near political ruin, but which left him cynical, soured, and obsessively suspicious of political friendships. He learned his lesson, he said, that "in politics most people are your friends only as long as you can do something for them or something to them." [2] The fund crisis was also, in James Barber's phrase, "an agony of self-definition." [3] To resist the clamors for his resignation coming from the men he had thought to be his best friends in the party, he was forced to ask himself, "Am I taking money illegally?" "Am I cheating on my income tax?" "Am I a liar?" Had he done what Earl Warren refused to do—had he hocked his soul?

It was not until years later that he admitted that he had felt "like a little boy caught with jam on his face." [4] His instinct for survival and his skill at denial were not seen again in so dramatic a fashion until Watergate. The very success of 1952 made his denials of twenty years later predictable, although the differences between the crises were many, chief among them being that the problem in the "fund crisis" was ethical and not legal.

Nixon's "Checkers speech" of September 23, 1952, watched by fifty-eight million people on television, the largest audience up to that time, convinced most Americans, including many cynical journalists, that he was a man wronged. It did not quite convince Eisenhower, who likened Nixon to Gen. George Patton, who, he said, had made a mistake and been forgiven. [5] Democrats who were jubilant over the fund disclosure subsided into embarrassed silence when Adlai Stevenson was forced to admit publicly that he had a fund of his own, although actually it was drawn from campaign contributions, not "a slush fund," and was used to supplement the salaries of some of his aides, not his own. Still, despite his conspicuous victory, Nixon showed palpable anxiety about attacks on his speech, and we see the beginning of a pattern of public confession, an intermittent open agonizing over the nature of his own character without real insight into it. He was accused of being a crook and a tax dodger, and successfully cleared his name on both charges. What he had done was declared legal by a Los Angeles law firm and this was never challenged. But Nixon also insisted that the fund could have been "immoral" or "unethical" if it had been kept secret, which in fact it had, but which he denied was the case, and if he had granted favors to his donors, which he also denied. This denial was also untrue. He had spent money only for "political expenses," he said, which was accurate.

Nixon was not accused of being a liar in the fund crisis, although he had certainly lied to reporters of the *Kansas City Star* when he declared that he had no income other than his senatorial salary.[6] But the journalists were so caught up in the debate over the legality and ethics of the fund that they overlooked this, a transgression of some significance, and few Americans were told that he had even said it.

Nixon began the 1952 campaign with a friendly press. The *New York Times* called him an intelligent conservative, alert, vigorous, and serious-minded, and this was generally echoed in the newspapers supporting Eisenhower. Robert J. Donovan saw him as "a hard, narrow, ambitious aggressive man, cheerless and partisan to the point of repugnance," but he noted that most journalists admitted that he had been "on to Soviet espionage sooner than they were," although they agreed that he had "a singularly one-track mind that never ran very far beyond Red hunting and Red baiting." Ernest Brashear wrote in *The New Republic* just before the crisis, "Nixon's public personality and his private personality shake hands as strangers when they meet."[7] But such criticisms were rare.

His public image had not really changed from the slugger of the Voorhis and Douglas campaigns; only the victim was more generalized. Nixon was now the orator who was scourging the crooks and Communists out of the temple of Washington and Jefferson, and who, if necessary, would use more deadly weapons than a whip. In Bangor, Maine, he said on September 2, "If the dry rot of corruption and communism, which has eaten deep into our body politic during the past seven years, can only be chopped out with a hatchet, then let's call for a hatchet!"[8] Eisenhower was content to let him take the low road in the campaign, while he stayed on the high road, but Nixon, no less than Eisenhower, was intent on an image of public virtue.

In early September Nixon was described as riding a meteor, with the presidency across his horoscope. No journalist was responsible for "discovering" the fund, and none seems to have made an effort to research Nixon's finances. The reporter for the *Kansas City Star* who wrote, "The Californian said he and his wife, *with no other sources of income except his salary as Senator,* are as familiar as most Americans are with the household budget crimp resulting from 'the twin pincers of high taxes and high prices,'" had not troubled to check on Nixon's income from speechmaking, an obvious extra source. In 1951 it had come to $6611.45.[9]

It was not a reporter, or a Democrat, but two influential California delegates to the Republican Convention, bitter at Nixon's betrayal of Warren and weary of being importuned for money for Nixon, who leaked the fund story. Dan Green, pro-Democratic publisher of the *Independent Review,* one of the first to be told, alerted Ernest Brashear of the *Los Angeles Daily News,* Leo Katcher of the *New York Post,* and Richard Donovan of *The Reporter* who traced the fund through cancelled checks and told the nation that Nixon was receiving a secret subsidy of about a thousand dollars a month. Katcher interviewed one of the contributors who had begun to sour on Nixon, who said, "We've been paying his expenses for some time now. I give a hundred and my wife gives a hundred. I don't like the idea of this man being a heart beat away from the presidency."[10]

Nixon, called by columnist Peter Edson, denied nothing and suggested that reporters call Dana Smith, the fund's "trustee." At first he said the fund had been set up by his supporters "at Smith's suggestion"; later he admitted that the idea had come from Murray Chotiner and himself.[11] With a senatorial salary of only $15,000, he said, he could ill afford expenses for travel, printing, and mailing of speeches, extra trips to California, only one of which could be charged to his expense account. The four thousand dollars a year he spent on Christmas cards to his campaign workers particularly galled him. With an old fundraiser friend, Dana Smith, a small organization had been set up to raise money for what was called euphemistically a "permanent campaign fund."

Stewart Alsop wondered later why the canny Chotiner did not "smell the terrible danger in the fund."[12] Nixon did have in addition to his salary, as it was soon pointed out, an expense account of $70,000, free office space, free medical care, and access to the services of a congressional research staff that cost the American taxpayers $866,000 a year.[13] Had the money been solicited openly in a public subscription from all his well-wishers there would have been no outcry. Instead requests were made quietly, mostly by telephone at first, to a few hundred wealthy contributors, men in real estate, manufacturing, distribution, and oil, and it was these solicitations that were kept secret. Later, on September 25, 1951, a letter went out to several thousand, asking for contributions to Nixon for "preparation of political material, radio and TV publicity," and "Christmas cards to 20,000 campaign workers."[14] By July 1952 seventy-two men had contributed $18,168.97. Later it was admitted that $11,000 more had been deposited to the fund after Nixon's nomination for the vice-presidency. There were consistent rumors of a second fund, still secret, but this was not substantiated.[15]

Trustee Dana Smith, questioned by reporters on September 15, explained affably, "We realized his salary was pitifully inadequate for a salesman of free enterprise. . . . the best salesman against socialization available." When asked if Governor Warren did not also qualify as a salesman of free enterprise, Smith replied, with a candor that did Nixon some damage, "Frankly, Warren has too much of the social [socialist?] point of view, and he never has gone out selling the free enterprise system. But Dick did just what we wanted him to do."[16] Despite Nixon's insistence that the fund was not secret, it had indeed been kept so, certainly from the press.

The *New York Post* headlined Leo Katcher's findings NIXON SECRET FUND: SECRET RICH MEN'S TRUST KEEPS NIXON IN STYLE FAR BEYOND HIS SALARY. The article described the fund contributors as "a millionaire's club" devoted exclusively to Senator Nixon's financial comfort. Katcher described what happened to him as a result of his article:

I was Nixon's first enemy. He sic'd the FBI on me afterward. The agents came to me, investigated my bank account, interviewed my friends. One of the agents, who was a good Democrat, told me frankly that Nixon had initiated the search, hoping to prove me a Communist.

Katcher found the experience ugly and frightening. A Ph.D. in psychology from Columbia University, with what he describes as "a perennial fascination with swindlers," he now became a dedicated Nixon enemy. Years later he said:

God, for twenty-five years that man has to some extent possessed me. He stands in the same relationship to morality as a color-blind man stands to color. This is a man with an id and an ego but no superego. He has no ideology. I once described him as a man who followed the Gallup poll by fifteen minutes. He always believed he could keep the complete truth hidden.[17]

The national press, mostly Republican and ardent for Eisenhower, did not leap eagerly to spread the "fund" story. As William Costello noted, five of the seventy-five leading dailies suppressed it altogether; most buried it on inside pages, and some, like the *Los Angeles Times,* waited three days and then published a denial, NIXON ANSWERS CRITICS, before printing the original account. Except for the Katcher piece in the *New York Post* and one in the *Sacramento Bee,* which called Nixon a subsidized front man for the California rich, newspapers did not give front-page coverage to the story until it had been widely discussed on radio and TV.[18]

News of the fund nevertheless appalled Eisenhower, who had been calling for an end to "shady and shoddy government" and "cancerous conditions of dishonesty," and who had been promising to drive out of office the "crooks and cronies," and the "sticky-fingered crew now contaminating the national capitol." Herbert Brownell, Harold Stassen, eventually even Thomas E. Dewey, scrambled to dissociate themselves from Nixon. Stassen sent him a hostile wire, with a suggested model resignation letter, and urged that Earl Warren be his replacement.[19] Nixon was not surprised when the unfriendly *Washington Post* called for his withdrawal, but was devastated when his most influential newspaper advocate, the *New York Herald Tribune,* suggested that he make a formal offer of resignation, to be accepted or not by Eisenhower as he saw fit. Leading Democrats happily denounced him, save Adlai Stevenson, who said he would reserve judgment until Nixon explained how he used the money, causing the suspicious Murray Chotiner to guess correctly that Stevenson must have some kind of fund of his own.

Sherman Adams, Arthur Summerfield, Herbert Hoover, Karl Mundt, Gerald Ford, and Warren Burger all stayed with Nixon, as did Senator Taft, who surprised everyone by his spirited defense. Taft's father had benefited greatly from his brother's financial aid in climbing to the presidency. He said,

I see no reason why a Senator or Representative should not accept gifts from members of his family or friends or his constituents to help pay even personal expenses which are not paid by the government. The only possible criticism would arise if these donors asked for or received legislative or other favors. I know that no such motives inspired the expense payments in the case of Dick Nixon.[20]

But Congress had never devised an instrument for probing motives of its own members, nor had it passed a law guaranteeing their integrity. Prosecutions under the Corrupt Practices Act, meant to be a step in that direction, had been nonexistent since its passage in 1926.[21]

Still, the practice was common enough. After Nixon weathered the crisis, several California congressmen sheepishly admitted that they had such funds too. Sen. Paul Douglas of Illinois was alone among senators publicly refusing to accept any gift worth more than $2.50.

Earl Mazo believed that the Nixon fund would have gone unnoticed if he and Eisenhower had not "sold their Crusade for Political Purity so well."[22] Nixon had been caught like the lust-abhoring pastor found petting in the choir loft. Even though Gibson, Dunn & Crutcher, a law firm hired to give an opinion on the legality of the fund, stated that Nixon had violated no law and would not have to pay taxes on the money, and although a second firm audited the record and found nothing irregular, the ethical problem remained. And the smell of scandal raised questions about the past. A citizens committee in Whittier began asking who paid the cost of his $1,600,000 campaign in 1950.[23]

Nixon denied repeatedly that he had done any favors for any of the contributors, insisting in the "Checkers" speech that he had never made so much as a single telephone call to a federal agency on their behalf. The law firm which cleared Nixon interviewed "a number of contributors"—how many was not stated—and found two requests for aid, which seem to have been discounted as innocuous. Accounts of special favors immediately surfaced in Washington, however, and proved intriguing. Drew Pearson and Jack Anderson discovered that two oilmen contributors, who had been refused government permission to explore for oil on a military reservation, were now beneficiaries of a Nixon bill to open up that reservation for exploration. And they found evidence that Nixon's office had interceded on behalf of another contributor in a tax refund claim of $100,000. William Rogers—later attorney-general under Eisenhower and Nixon's secretary of state—wired Drew Pearson from Nixon's campaign that if he printed anything about the Nixon fund he would be blasted as a "Communist operative." Pearson published the data anyway.[24]

The *St. Louis Post Dispatch* on October 20 alleged that Nixon had been in Havana with Dana Smith in April 1952 when Smith had lost $4200 gambling at the San Souci casino. Smith had paid by check, then stopped payment on it, and Norman Rothman, operator of the casino, had brought court action in Los Angeles to recover the sum. Nixon, it was said, had written a letter to the American embassy in Havana asking them to help his friend. Drew Pearson on his weekly broadcast demanded a State Department investigation.

Nixon, who was skilled at denying only those portions of a damaging story that were untrue and ignoring the reminder, called the story "a blatant lie," and introduced travel documents to prove that he had been in Hawaii when Dana Smith was gambling in Cuba. But the problem of the letter to the embassy in Cuba remained. Drew Pearson noted in his diary that "apparently there are some Republican spies in the State Department since the Dana Smith letter has been filched from their files." But the State Department sent to Havana to get the original. It had been sent from Nixon's office and signed with Nixon's name, but Nixon insisted that "he did not know the letter had been written or anything about it." A secretary, it was said, had written it and signed it "on the instruction of a superior." Even when the story was aired in detail in *Look,* it did little damage to Nixon. The article was written by Richard Wilson, who dismissed the whole matter of the letter as "bad office practice" and denied that it was "an effort by Nixon to help the man who had raised his political funds."[25] He smelled neither corruption nor coverup.

How many of these stories found their way to Eisenhower during the 1952 campaign is not clear. Certainly the first published stories about the fund enraged him. Although in his earliest public statement on the fund he said, "I believe Dick Nixon to be an honest man," and added that he would "talk with him at the earliest time we can reach each other by telephone," he did not call.[26] Nixon waited in increasing agony for four days. Although the men who had pressed Nixon on Eisenhower only a few weeks earlier were now urging him to drop him from the ticket, the general was fair-minded. Whether he was more astute politically than some of his advisers is debatable. He sensed that a peremptory repudiation might damage an innocent man, and would in any case be an admission of his own bad judgment. "If Nixon has to go," he confided to Sherman Adams, "we cannot win,"[27] which may not have been true.

Ike was campaigning from his "Look Ahead Neighbor" train in the East and Midwest; Nixon was on his own train in California and Oregon. Calls from Eisenhower's aides to Murray Chotiner and William Rogers kept Nixon precisely informed. Nixon would talk with no one except the general, and he remained silent.

Reporters on the Eisenhower train took an informal poll and voted forty to two in favor of scuttling Nixon. When the general learned of this, he called them together and said, off the record:

I don't care if you fellows are 40 to 2. I am taking my time on this. Nothing's decided, contrary to your idea that this is a setup for a whitewash of Nixon. Of what avail is it for us to carry on this crusade against this business of what has been going on in Washington if we, ourselves, aren't clean as a hound's tooth.[28]

The remark was instantly leaked, and the phrase "clean as a hound's tooth," was remembered when almost every other aspect of the campaign was forgotten.

Hannah Nixon, caring for Tricia and Julie in Washington, was angry and frightened at the charges against her son. Nixon tells us that Pat was "constantly on the phone to my mother." Whether he talked to her himself he did not say, but she felt the necessity, finally, of putting her thoughts into a telegram to him. It arrived when Nixon was in a hotel in Oregon, and was brought to him by California Rep. Pat Hillings, a close Nixon friend. Hillings watched with some embarrassment as the vice-presidental candidate began to weep. The wire said: "Girls are okay. This is to tell you we are thinking of you and know everything will be fine. Love always, Mother."

"In our family," Nixon explained, "the phrase 'we are thinking of you' meant 'we are praying for you.' "[29] Later he learned that his father had given way to bouts of weeping as the charges against his son mounted.

Composing himself after the wire from his mother, Nixon went to a dinner speech. "For all we knew," Chotiner said later, "it was going to be the last speech of the campaign for him." Another aide said, "Dick was ready to chuck the whole thing, and frankly it took the toughest arguments of some of us to hold him in check."[30] As the expected call from Eisenhower still did not come, Nixon talked to Pat of resignation. Thinking always of her daughters, she reacted with a steeliness of resolution that could only have astonished him, remembering as he must have her all-night pleas during the convention to turn down the nomination in the first place:

You can't think of resigning. If you do Eisenhower will lose. He can put you off the ticket if he wants to but if you, in the face of attack, do not fight back but simply crawl away, you will destroy yourself. Your life will be marred for ever and the same will be true of your family, particularly your daughters.[31]

The crowds assembling at the whistlestops on the campaign trail never saw evidence of Nixon's weakness and anguish. From the first he was pugnacious and defiant. In Marysville, California, just as the train was pulling out after a speech he heard a heckler shout, "What about the $16,000?" Nixon yelled, "Hold the train!" Then as the crowd gathered a hundred yards down the track he launched into what was essentially a rehearsal for the national television speech he gave four days later:

After I received the nomination for the vice-presidency, I was warned that if I continued to attack the Communists and crooks in this administration, they would smear me. . . . They started it yesterday. They said I had taken money—$16,000. What they did not point out was this: what I was doing was saving you money. The expenses of my office were in excess of the amounts allowed under the law. . . . What I did was to have those expenses paid by people back home who were interested in seeing that the information about what was going on in Washington was spread among the people of their state.[32]

Nixon was saying, actually, "I am saving you money by having someone else pay for certain of my expenses, which it would have been illegal to charge you with in the first place." Stewart Alsop would be one among many to point out the basic deception; he called it "a sleazy debater's trick."[33] No one looking seriously at the flow of funds, however kept separate from Nixon's bank account, could deny that the thousand dollars a month increased his standard of living. Nixon himself indiscreetly admitted to columnist Peter Edson that had it not been for the fund he could not have purchased his new home in Washington.[34] But simplicity is strength in politics, and Nixon had found a simple formula which would convince many Americans that he was wholly innocent, and which would capture the secret admiration of others who envy the skill of a man who can profit successfully on the fringes of political graft.

Nixon also publicly deplored the fact that the Democratic vice-presidential candiate, Sen. John Sparkman, had put his wife on his payroll. "Pat Nixon," he said, "has worked in my office night after night, and I can say it proudly, she has never been on a government payroll." Sparkman later replied tartly that there had been nothing "sub rosa" about the job his wife had, and that she had given "excellent service." Nixon took credit also for taking no legal fees as senator, as did some of his colleagues—which was not true as he admitted later. "I could legally but not ethically have done so. And I am never going to do so. . . ."[35]

At subsequent whistlestops hecklers appeared with canes and dark glasses, shaking cups and crying, "Nickels for poor Nixon." Signs were painted: NO MINK COATS FOR NIXON, JUST COLD CASH, and PAT WHAT ARE YOU GOING TO DO WITH THE BRIBE? Nixon supporters turned ugly. One University of Oregon student carrying a sign reading SHH! ANYONE WHO MENTIONS $16,000 IS A COMMUNIST was publicly derided as a Communist and homosexual. When Nixon left the rally, the crowd surged over him, fists flying. "People kept calling him 'Dirty Communist,'" said Charles O. Porter, later a Democratic member of Congress, who was appalled by the episode.[36]

When Eisenhower at 10:05 P.M. on the fourth day finally telephoned Nixon, he began sympathetically, "You've been taking a lot of heat in the last couple of days." Nixon replied drily, "The last four days haven't been easy." Eisenhower did not apologize for his delay in calling. He said:

I have come to the conclusion that you are the one who has to decide what to do. After all, you've got a big following in this country, and if the impression got around that you got off the ticket because I forced you off, it is going to be very bad. On the other hand, if I issue a statement now backing you up, in effect the people will accuse me of condoning wrong doing. . . . I don't want to be in the position of condemning an innocent man.

And he urged him to go on national television, as planned, and tell everything.

"General," Nixon then asked, "do you think after the television program that an announcement could be made one way or the other?" Eisenhower hedged, suggesting that they wait three or four days to see "the effect of the program." The prospect of four more days of indecision Nixon found unendurable, and he replied to Eisenhower with a vulgarism out of his childhood that shocked his listening friends:

If my staying on the ticket would be harmful I will get off and take the heat. But there comes a time to stop dawdling; once I have done this television program you ought to decide. There comes a time in matters like this when you've either got to shit or get off the pot.[37]

Whether Eisenhower thought him insolent or simply exasperated we do not know. The conversation trailed off, Nixon said, with Eisenhower's last words, "Keep your chin up." Later events suggest that the confrontation had increased Ike's testiness.

On Monday, September 21, the day before the broadcast, Nixon was handed three weapons that left him jubilant. A Chicago business executive, Kent Chandler, publicly charged that Adlai Stevenson also had a special fund. The lawyers of Gibson, Dunn & Crutcher issued their statement clearing him of any violation of the Corrupt Practices Act, and Price, Waterhouse, and Co. reported a clean audit of the fund. Stevenson immediately admitted having leftover campaign funds, which he said had never been secret. That some of the money had been used to supplement the salaries of men who left better paying jobs to assist the state was unusual, however, and the admission damaged him as much as it seemed to exonerate Nixon. Later, incorrect reports of a second fund of "upwards of $100,000" where the money was spent by Stevenson himself, without a trustee, effectively silenced the Democrats on the fund issue.[38]

Dewey telephoned Nixon with a hostile message just before he left for the TV studio. Ike's advisers, he said, recommended that he submit his resignation at the conclusion of the broadcast. He further suggested on his own that Nixon resign as senator and call for a new election, vindicating himself "by winning the biggest plurality in history."

Nixon exploded in bitterness, "Tell them that I haven't the slightest idea what I am going to do, and if they want to find out they'd better listen to the broadcast. And tell them that I know something about politics too." And he slammed the receiver on the hook. For all his seeming truculence, Pat Hillings said, "Dick looked like someone had smashed him."[39]

Nixon had ordered that there be no audience in the El Capitan Theater, and faced only cameramen, electricians, and his wife, who he instructed should sit on the stage with him. "I want to feel she is here," he said.

As he sat alone with Pat in the dressing room before the broadcast he confessed to being "suddenly overwhelmed with despair."

"I just don't think I can go through with this one."

"Of course you can," she said.

It was the firmness and confidence he "desperately needed," Nixon later wrote. "She took my hand and we walked back onto the stage together."[40]

Nixon, as we have seen, in talking of his father once said, "when you got into mischief you had to be pretty convincing to avoid punishment."[41] The "Checkers" speech was not an isolated act of defense, but a cumulative response based on many earlier confrontations in his life, more than his new political friends could have dreamed possible. All were surprised at his skill in parrying accusations, and also at his stagecraft. Murray Chotiner shouted with delight as he watched the television performance in a room nearby.

"The best and only answer to a smear or an honest misunderstanding of the facts is to tell the truth," Nixon said. He avowed that the fund was legal, and quoted the Gibson, Dunn & Crutcher opinion absolving him of breaking the law. Still, he admitted, the fund would be immoral if, first, it had been kept secret; second, if any of the $18,000 had been spent for personal use; and third, if any of the contributors had received personal favors. All three he denied—although the first and the third were certainly true and the second partly so—even though the $18,000 was spent for political purposes, Christmas cards, mailings, and special trips to California, it certainly permitted him freer use of his personal salary, as in buying a house. His denials, made with the imprecision that had become his trademark, served as a counterfeiting of truth that was sufficiently close to it to capture the unwary. These he enunciated with authority and an air of injured innocence.

He went on to add that he had not "feathered his nest" by taking money in cash in secret, although he had not been accused of this. As proof he listed everything he owned—and the holdings were indeed modest, a mirror of middle America—a 1950 Oldsmobile, a $3000 equity in a California house where his parents lived,[42] a $20,000 equity in his Washington house, $4000 on his life insurance policy. He admitted for the first time getting money from lectures (an average of $1500 annually for six years), and $1600 from his law practice, based on estates he had settled earlier, and $4500 in inheritances. He owed $10,000 on his California house, $20,000 on the Washington house, $4500 to a Washington bank, $3500 to his parents, and $500 on his life insurance.

And that's what we owe. It isn't very much. But Pat and I have the satisfaction that every dime that we've got is honestly ours. I should say this, that Pat doesn't have a mink coat. But she does have a respectable Republican cloth coat, and I always tell her that she would look good in anything.

One gift he said he would not return, a little black and white cocker spaniel named Checkers, given to him by a Texan:

And you know the kids, all the kids, loved the dog, and I just want to say this, right now, that regardless of what they say about it, we are going to keep it.[43]

Stevenson, he pointed out, had inherited a fortune from his father. "But I also feel that it is essential in this country of ours that a man of modest means can also run for President because, you know—remember Abraham Lincoln. . . . he said, 'God must have loved the common people he made so many of them.' " He slipped in a mention of his war experience—"I was there when the bombs were falling"—he slapped at Truman for losing China, and reminded his audience of Alger Hiss, blaming the smears as coming from the same commentators who had attacked him "in the dark days of the Hiss Case."

"I am not a quitter," he said, "And Pat's not a quitter. After all"—and again, as we have noted, he slurred around the edges of accuracy—"her name was Patricia Ryan, and she was born on St. Patrick's Day, and you know the Irish never quit."[44] The decision to resign, he said in conclusion, was not his; it rightly belonged to the Republican National Committee, and he urged the audience of fifty-eight million to send wires and letters to "help them decide." Thus he tried to take the decision out of the hands of Eisenhower, whom he had come to distrust.[45]

His timing, usually faultless, was a little off. Learning that he had been cut off the air before giving the address of the Republican National Committee temporarily shook him. As he left the stage he gave way to tears of mingled exasperation and anxiety. He thought he had done badly. But almost two million Americans sent in wires expressing confidence in him, and three million more sent letters. Mamie Eisenhower watched the broadcast with her mother; both wept. Women in California sent almost twice as many wires as men, and twice as many letters. The *Los Angeles Times* said that of the first four thousand telegrams counted only twenty-one were negative. A later study showed only thirty-nine negative out of eight thousand. A random selection of letters showed a favorable ratio of seventy-four to one.[46] While a few called the speech childish and evasive, "a shoddy soap opera," most were favorable to ecstatic—"America loves a good fighter"; "Keep Nixon, a big man"; "A Great Man"; "A Modern Day Lincoln."[47]

Nixon insisted that the press used him ill in the fund crisis, and treated Stevenson "with kid gloves." But a careful study by Arthur Edward Rowse had demonstrated the reverse to be true. He noted characteristic headlines slanted in Nixon's favor: PUBLIC BACKS NIXON: ADLAI WON'T AIR LIST in the *New York Journal;* CORRUPTION IN STATE NOTHING NEW TO ADLAI in the *Des Moines Register.* The *Chicago Tribune* had a front-page cartoon showing

Truman as king and Stevenson as "the clown prince." The Luce publications, as usual, were friendly to Nixon. *Life,* in a glowing article, "Nixon Fights, Wins and Weeps," noted that Marshall Field had given Adlai Stevenson a campaign contribution of $7100.[48] *Time* reflected a common editorial judgment:

His fund was probably a mistake in political judgment (as was Stevenson's) but by the time Nixon had finished speaking, the snowballing charges against him had melted down to a tactical error, and no more.

The presidential campaign is more than a debate, *Time* said; it is an ordeal, a trial of character. Nixon had indeed "established himself as a man of integrity and courage." Even Philip Graham of the *Washington Post* said Nixon had answered "eloquently and movingly," and that he had simply made an error in judgment. Hostility like that of *Commonweal*'s editor was rare; he called it "a cheap attempt to exploit decent human motives."[49]

But it was the instant and positive reaction of one man that Nixon wanted, and he did not get it. Ike, angered when Nixon tried to rob him of the right of decision and turn it over to the Republican National Committee, and annoyed at the embarrassment of the whole episode, refused to contratulate him by telephone.[50] He sent him a wire instead; it was for a time lost among the two million. Eisenhower's and Nixon's aides were in communication by phone, but Nixon would speak only to Ike, and Ike would not call. In a speech to a crowd in Cleveland chanting "We want Nixon!" he praised the vice-presidential candidate as courageous and honest, but he did not commit himself to keeping him on the ticket, a fact instantly recognized by newsmen when he read aloud the wire he had sent:

Your presentation was magnificent. While technically no decision rests with me, you and I know the realities of the situation require a pronouncement which the public considers decisive. My personal decision is going to be based on personal conclusions. I would most appreciate it if you can fly to see me at once. Tomorrow I will be at Wheeling, W. Va. Whatever personal affection and admiration I had for you—and they are very great—are undiminished.[51]

For Nixon, reading a somewhat garbled wire-service announcement of the telegram, Eisenhower was still "on the pot." Furious, he dictated a telegram of resignation to Rose Mary Woods. She showed it to Chotiner, who tore it up. "What more can he possibly want from me?" Nixon raged. Chotiner soothed him by agreeing that he must not allow himself "to be put in the position of going to Eisenhower like a little boy to be taken to the woodshed, properly punished, and then restored to a place of dignity." Even when the full text of Eisenhower's wire was read to him, with its warm praise and words of personal affection, Nixon still refused to go to Wheeling. Instead, in an action he reported neither in *Six Crises* nor in his memoirs, he sent a wire to Eisenhower saying that he intended to resume his campaign tour, which would end on Saturday, September 27. "Will be in Washington Sunday," he concluded, "and will be delighted to confer with you at your convenience any time thereafter."[52] And he began preparations to take off for Missoula, Montana.

To Ike's aides the wire seemed an act of incredible insolence, and had it been published the acrimonious private duel would have been publicized, damaging both leaders and party. Arthur Summerfield called Chotiner, and was told that "Dick is not going to be placed in the position of a little boy coming somewhere to beg forgiveness." Bert Andrews, a *Herald Tribune* reporter friend from the days of the Hiss Case, caught Nixon by phone just as he was about to leave for Montana and talked to him, Nixon said, "like a Dutch uncle." Andrews reminded him that Eisenhower had led the Allied armies to victory, that he was the "boss of the outfit," and that he had a right to make the decision in his own way. It was a useful scolding. Nixon agreed to fly to Wheeling from Montana on the following day. Eisenhower himself tried to reach Nixon by phone, but he had already left, and it was Summerfield who roused Nixon the following morning in Missoula with the promise that "everything would be all right."[53]

Among the blizzard of telegrams and news items that the Nixon staff singled out to show him was a crow-eating telegram from Harold Stassen, congratulating him on "a superb presentation," and a news report saying Dewey had called him "a man of shining integrity." The flight to Wheeling was a "victory ride," Nixon said, with reporters and staff "in rollicking spirits, singing songs with familiar tunes and somewhat pungent words." "Within twenty four hours," Mazo wrote wryly, "the entire Republican hierarchy was singing hosannas, including the leaders who felt the program's emotional pitch to be revolting."[54]

After the plane landed, Nixon, somewhat delayed in leaving

it, was flabbergasted to see Eisenhower coming down the aisle, his hand outstretched.

"General, you didn't need to come out to the airport," he said. "Why not," came the reply. "You're my boy."

Instead of being "taken to the woodshed," he was off to a rally in the Wheeling stadium. There Eisenhower read a wire from Nixon's mother:

Dear General: I am trusting that the absolute truth may come out concerning this attack on Richard, and when it does I am sure you will be guided right in your decision to place implicit faith in his integrity and honesty. Best wishes from one who has known Richard longer than anyone else. His Mother.

He then read a wire reporting that all 107 of the 138 members of the Republican National Committee who had been contacted had voted for his staying on the ticket. Arthur Summerfield, in concluding the telegram, called Nixon "a truly great American who walked unafraid through the valley of despair and emerged unscathed and unbowed. Let there be no doubt about it—America has taken Dick Nixon to its heart."[55]

Nixon, in reply to thunderous cheering, said, "I want you to know that this is probably the greatest moment of my life." Afterward the stiff and somewhat pompous Knowland, who had flown back from his Hawaii vacation in the hope that he would be chosen to replace the erring Nixon, warmly congratulated him on his speech. "All the pent-up emotion of the whole week burst out and tears filled my eyes," Nixon said. "Knowland put his arms around me and I hid my face on his shoulder."

When Nixon's old drama teacher, Albert Upton, who had taught him how to cry, saw him weeping in the broadcast, he said, "Here goes my actor."[56]

The ordeal seemed over, but there was an unexpected and souring aftermath which the memory of five million favorable telegrams and letters never really erased. Eisenhower invited Nixon and his wife to see his private car on the campaign train. What had seemed the friendliest of gestures turned out to be an excuse, they discovered, for Ike to question them about rumors of "several other scandals involving my personal finances." Nixon described only one, that he "had spent $10,000 with an interior decorator in furnishing our home in Washington." Nixon wrote that "there was not a shred of truth to the charge and a very routine inquiry could have knocked it down before it was passed on to him."

Actually, public relations director Robert Humphreys had already emphatically assured Eisenhower that the rumor was a canard. He had seen the "decorations" in the Nixon home, he said; they consisted of draperies and a circular couch from Nixon's home in Whittier. Eisenhower had nevertheless elected to ask the Nixons about the rumor in its full ugliness—which Mazo would report but Nixon would not—that Mrs. Nixon had paid the ten thousand dollars *in cash*. Pat, the most frugal of women, who had made her own draperies and slipcovers for years, was devastated.

"This is just like a war, General," Nixon said hotly. "Our opponents are losing. They mounted a massive attack against me and have taken a bad beating. It will take them a little time to regroup, but when they start fighting back, they will be desperate. . . . The minute they start one of these rumors, we have to knock it down just as quickly as we can."

Later, in the car on the way to the hotel, Nixon said, Pat reached out to hold his hand and said nothing. "But I knew from that time on, although she would do everything she could to help me and help my career, she would hate politics and dream of the day when I would leave it behind."[57]

The day after this confrontation Nixon's staff, knowing nothing of the final humiliation, organized "The Order of the Hound's Tooth," with Nixon as president. Nixon himself designed the membership card, with a picture of Checkers. The charter members were given a key ring with a sliver of bone, "the hound's tooth," attached.

Pat later let reporters know she loathed being questioned about the fund. When Helen Erskine mentioned it in an interview in 1954, she watched her face "drained of its color," as she replied:

We have gone into this thing so often, do I have to explain it again? Dick is so scrupulously honest. I knew he hadn't done wrong. I didn't say anything except to let him feel I loved him and believed in him. . . . We had over a million responses. After all, you don't have to be phony, if you're honest.

Earl Mazo felt that "in retrospect the affair was bad for Nixon. The people who remembered it most vividly thought it was horrible." No one, Democrat or Republican, he said, came out of it "clean as a hound's tooth."[58]

The "Checkers" speech did give Nixon a sense of the power of television, and of his special talent in using it, and with this came an important liberation from the press. Ted Rogers, Nixon's television adviser for ten years, believed that this crisis made Nixon an electronic candidate. He ceased being solicitous about reporters. "If the bus was ready to roll and they weren't there, he'd simply say, 'Fuck 'em, we don't need them.' "[59]

There were times when Nixon took an actor's satisfaction in the "Checkers" speech, in 1955 telling one group of TV executives with a certain pride, "I want you to be the first to know, I staged it." He confided to Stewart Alsop, "Daryl Zanuck had wired me that it was wonderful, and I had a lot of confidence in his judgment."[60] But he was uneasy with the speech all the same. He made no effort to preserve the film for history, and may indeed have gone to some trouble to see that it was not preserved. When Emile de Antonio tried to find a copy for revival in his anti-Nixon film *Millhous: A White Comedy* in 1971, he had great difficulty. Neither the Republican National Committee, nor the White House, nor the networks, had the film. When he finally found one, and featured the "Checkers" speech along with other shorter clips, his film opening in a small art theater in New York in September 1971 caused consternation in the White House. John Dean reported that Haldeman "sent us frequent questions" about it. "Would it hurt us with the youth vote? Could we stop it?" Jack Caulfield recommended an IRS audit of de Antonio and the distributor, Daniel Talbot. An FBI dossier on de Antonio was sent to the White House, apparently showing some left-wing sympathies. "We planned to leak it," Dean said, "if the movie became a hit or if the Democratic Party sponsored showings. Neither occurred."[61]

Nixon recalled the "Checkers" crisis in discussing the Watergate burglary with John Mitchell on March 22, 1973. He remembered Eisenhower's insistence:

That's what Eisenhower—that's all he cared about. He only cared about—Christ, "Be sure he was clean."[62]

X X

McCarthy

*I think McCarthyism has been created by Truman. I believe it is
the creature of Truman.*
— RICHARD NIXON, AUGUST 29, 1952[1]

SEN. JOSEPH McCARTHY and Richard Nixon both went
into political oblivion condemned for multiple untruth. McCarthy
in 1954 was censured by his peers, the sixth such censure in Senate history.* Nixon, who watched the spectacle from the Speaker's
chair just after the election of 1954, chose to resign twenty years
later when it came his turn to face the Senate as a court. He had
seen one man's ordeal. McCarthy had been Nixon's political,
although not his personal protégé, and they were for many
months, in Roy Cohn's words, "quite cordial."[2] They went hand
in hand in 1952, competing for the invention of the most slanderous epithet, the most degrading metaphor, in their efforts to
defeat Adlai Stevenson. Where Nixon called Stevenson a
weakling, a waster, a small-caliber Truman, an appeaser who "got
his Ph.D. from Dean Acheson's College of Cowardly Communist
Containment," McCarthy said, "If you will get me a slippery-elm
club and put me aboard Stevenson's campaign train, I will use it
on his advisers and perhaps I can make a good American out of
him."[3]

They urged each other's election and Nixon gave McCarthy
the use of his files. But by 1954 Nixon was mortified to see
McCarthy attacking Eisenhower—extending "twenty years of
treason," his epithet for the Democratic party, to twenty-one

*Timothy Pickering of Massachusetts was censured in 1811 for violating secrecy; Benja-
min Tappan in 1844 for furnishing confidential documents to a newspaper; John
McLauren and Benjamin Tillman in 1902 for fighting on the Senate floor; Hiram
Bingham in 1929 for employing a manufacturing representative in writing a tariff bill.
McCarthy received a "censure" vote, but this was changed to "condemnation" afterward
because the word "censure" had not appeared in the original resolution.

years—and he moved openly to disengage him from the party. Secretly he moved to discredit him altogether, but with such skill that he did not antagonize McCarthy's supporters. His March 13 speech against McCarthy, ordered by Eisenhower, was an exercise in ambiguity but still a signal that the administration had turned against the senator. What is not generally known is that Nixon also quietly arranged for the release of evidence resulting in the Army-McCarthy hearings, the damaging "chronology" on McCarthy, Roy Cohn, and David Schine—what Cohn called "the final stiletto."[4]

McCarthy was Nixon in caricature, Nixon out of control, Nixon turned nihilist. In three tempestuous years his name became an eponym, what one of his biographers, Richard Rovere, called a synonym for "the hatefulness of baseless defamation," for "whatever is illiberal, repressive, reactionary, obscurantist, anti-intellectual, totalitarian, or merely swinish."[5] He had become a master of obfuscation and the nonfact. He left a swath of destruction among innocent men and women. By 1954 McCarthy had intimidated two presidents and had transformed the politics of civility in America into the politics of conspiracy and fear.[6]

For a time his excesses helped Nixon, who was made to seem a moderate by contrast. But the growing detestation of McCarthy spilled over on Nixon when he refused to disavow him. Stevenson called Nixon "the white collar McCarthy." As early as 1952 Nixon tried to blame McCarthyism on Truman, arguing that without Truman's supposed sell-out of China there would have been no war with Korea and no Communism at home. Eisenhower said privately to Bryce Harlow, "That damn fool Truman *created* that monster. He didn't exist until Truman went eyeball to eyeball with him."[7] But for Nixon the problem of McCarthy was acutely personal. Could he destroy a man who had become "a brother" in the cause, but who had also by his excesses come to dramatize Nixon's own failures in political morality? In undermining McCarthy he must inevitably strike out at that which was most hostile in himself.

Eisenhower in his memoirs condemned McCarthy absolutely: "No one was safe from charges recklessly made inside the walls of congressional immunity. . . . The cost was often tragic."[8] But Nixon in his memoirs skipped over McCarthyism. He made no mention whatever of McCarthy's lying and fabrications of evidence, saying only that he "exaggerated his facts." He had himself acted as "a buffer," he said, between McCarthy and the administration. When it came to problems between McCarthy and the army, he was "the only person with enough credibility in both camps to suggest a compromise." He omitted all reference to McCarthy's financial peculations, save only to note that when Winston Churchill asked him in June 1954 why the Senate had not investigated McCarthy's finances and other irregularities getting elected, he had replied that "Senators did not want to set the precedent of investigating a colleague for fear that it might someday react in a case against themselves."[9]

In 1959 Nixon told Earl Mazo he thought McCarthy's downfall "a tragedy," calling him "a casualty in the great struggle of our times, as Hiss was a casualty on the other side. Both deeply believed in the cause they represented." He came to modify this somewhat, writing in his memoirs,

I never shared the disdain with which fashionable Washington treated him because of his lack of polished manners. In fact, I found him personally likable, if irresponsibly impulsive. At the end, I felt sorry for him as a man whose zeal and thirst for publicity were leading him and others to destruction. But it is despicable to make a racket of anticommunism or any other cause—to stir people up and then give them no positive leadership or direction.[10]

When writing his memoirs Nixon could hardly have escaped seeing in McCarthy's ruin a rehearsal of his own, a warning to which he had paid no heed. But the parallel could be acknowledged only in denial. Nixon never wrote about McCarthy, as he had about Hiss, "I imagined myself in his place."

The crusade of which McCarthy assumed leadership had been years in the making, and there can be little doubt that he had his eye on Richard Nixon as a model. In the speech that made him famous, in Wheeling, West Virginia, on February 9, 1950, McCarthy plagiarized from Nixon without embarrassment. Nixon had said in the House on January 26:

The great lesson which should be learned from the Alger Hiss case is that we are not just dealing with espionage agents who get 30 pieces of silver to obtain the blueprints of a new weapon—the Communists do that too—but this is a far more sinister type of activity, because it permits the enemy to guide and shape our policy.

McCarthy said:

We are not dealing with spies who get thirty pieces of silver to steal the blueprints of a new weapon. We are dealing with a far more sinister type of activity because it permits the enemy to guide and shape our policy.[11]

McCarthy embraced the Hiss Case as if it had been his own, and so successfully that Eisenhower twitted Nixon in 1954, saying "there are great numbers of people who think McCarthy got Hiss."[12] After 1950 Nixon largely abandoned investigations, content to hint darkly that there was "a host of government officials" corrupting the sources of power in Washington.[13] McCarthy, however, as chairman of a subcommittee of the Committee on Government Operations, expanded investigations with an irresponsibility that made Nixon look like a moderate. And he invented a deadly numbers game, which despite its gross inaccuracy, served to inspire imitation on the part of Nixon, Truman, Eisenhower, Dewey, and scores of others. The game began in Wheeling when McCarthy, waving aloft a paper, said, "I have in my hand 205 cases of individuals who would appear to be either card carrying members or certainly loyal to the Communist Party, but nevertheless are still helping to shape our foreign policy."[14]

McCarthy carried a bulging briefcase everywhere; as Rovere notes, the smell of the archives gave him credibility. The few reporters permitted to examine some of the documents were mystified at their irrelevance, but afraid to doubt their significance lest they be proved wrong as they had been in the Hiss Case. Unused to such audacious mendacity, eager for a hot story, they reported "McCarthy says," but did not run a parallel column, "McCarthy offers no evidence."

Anti-Communism was increasingly popular, fueled by casualties in the Korean War and by the hysteria that followed the announcement that the Russians had an atomic bomb, the secrets of which, many believed, had been provided by Julius and Ethel Rosenberg, whose execution came during the Eisenhower administration.

During this period Nixon and McCarthy maintained a guarded comaraderie. When Sen. Margaret Chase Smith, with four other senators, issued a Declaration of Conscience against the "Four Horse-men of Calumny—Fear, Ignorance, Bigotry, and Smear," and charged that the Senate had been "debased to the level of a forum of hate and character assassination," McCarthy saw that she was ousted from his subcommittee and replaced by Richard Nixon.[15]

Both McCarthy and Nixon had been castigated by Drew Pearson, Washington gadfly columnist and radio commentator. Although Pearson had been called a liar by FDR, Truman, and a score of congressmen, he was nevertheless widely feared for the general accuracy of his exposures and his willingness to risk libel suits. Only long after his death was he recognized as one of the nation's most courageous investigative reporters. McCarthy was under Pearson's gun in December of 1950, particularly for his dealings with Lustron Corporation and his failure to pay income taxes. McCarthy, for his part, boasted that he kept a baseball bat in his apartment with the name "Drew Pearson" written across it.[16]

On the night of December 12 Nixon was dining at the Sulgrave Club when he overheard Pearson and McCarthy in a violent altercation. Later, on going to the cloakroom, Nixon saw the powerful McCarthy, who had been a boxer, with his big thick hands around Pearson's neck, and his knee thrusting at his groin. The older man was "struggling wildly to get some air."

"When McCarthy spotted me," Nixon said, "he drew his arm back and slapped Pearson so hard his head snapped back."

"That one was for you, Dick," he said.

"I stepped between the two men and pushed them apart. 'Let a good Quaker stop this fight,' I said. Pearson grabbed his overcoat and ran from the room. McCarthy said, 'You shouldn't have stopped me, Dick.'"

Later, McCarthy told a friend that he had heard from an old Indian that "if you kneed a guy hard enough blood would come out of his eyes." "I would have found out if that was true," he said, "if Dick hadn't come along when he did." And Nixon said, "I never saw a man slapped so hard. If I hadn't pulled McCarthy away, he might have killed Pearson."[17]

Eisenhower continued to remain aloof from the McCarthy problem, saying to his staff repeatedly, "I'm not going to get down in the gutter with that guy."[18] Nixon wrote in his memoirs that he tried to convince all parties, including Eisenhower that "until a break was unavoidable we should attack McCarthy only when his facts were wrong."[19] But his facts were almost always wrong. And Nixon never attacked him, not when he defamed Gen. George Marshall, or Charles E. Bohlen, or James B. Conant, or Philip Jessup, or Owen Lattimore, not when he demoralized the State Department, the Voice of America, or the scientists working on missile and radar development at Fort Monmouth. Arguing, as Emmet Hughes said, like an effective trial lawyer "with an oddly slack interest in the law," he had instead done everything within his power to encourage Eisenhower's passivity. Although he talked persuasively of bringing McCarthy "back on the team," what he wanted, it seemed, was to bring Eisenhower onto his own team, involving him in a cause which he had embraced long before McCarthy, and to which he was still committed.

True, Nixon had cautioned McCarthy against exaggeration. He had persuaded him, when McCarthy was about to attack the appointment of Bohlen as ambassador to Russia, to use a "rough" speech instead of one that was "real dirty." He had defended Conant, and had talked McCarthy out of investigating William Bundy, then with the CIA, who had given money for Hiss's defense. And he had invited McCarthy to Key Biscayne, where he had tried unsuccessfully to persuade him to seek out a new cause, investigating tax settlements made during the Truman years. This was Nixon playing buffer.

When Nixon moved secretly but decisively against McCarthy, he struck at him where he was most vulnerable, his choice of staff, but it was not until early in 1954, when Eisenhower made it clear to him that the burden of McCarthy in the party had become intolerable. Nixon makes no mention of either Roy Cohn or David Schine in his memoirs, although they were crucial in McCarthy's ruin. Roy Cohn, son of a distinguished New York judge, who had graduated from Columbia Law School two years before he was old enough to take the bar exam, was McCarthy's favorite. He had proved his anti-Communism by helping to prosecute Julius and Ethel Rosenberg and had gathered much of McCarthy's data. Cohn had brought to the staff David Schine, heir to a hotel fortune, former press agent for a jazz band, who had neither investigative talents nor any special knowledge of Communism. He had written a six-page denunciation of Communism which his father had printed and put in each of the hotel rooms in the Schine chain. An avid collector of cigars, David claimed that his private museum had the largest and most varied collection in the world.[20]

When McCarthy sent the two twenty-seven-year-old youths to Europe in the spring of 1953 to ferret out subversive literature in American libraries and possible subversives on embassy staffs, Cohn and Schine quickly made themselves the most hated young men in government. Rovere, who was in Europe, said that panicked bureaucrats began to "pulp, ignite, and donate to charity" books that might be considered offensive even before the pair arrived.[21] The junket embarrassed Eisenhower, who spoke out mildly against book-burning on June 14, 1953, at Dartmouth College.

Nixon, however, defended Cohn and Schine, saying of the book-burning in early September:

I think all of us will agree that the taxpayers of the United States should not have to pay for the dissemination of Communist propaganda in the special-purpose libraries set up abroad for the express purpose of presenting the American position in its best light.[22]

After their return from Europe, Schine was inducted into the U.S. Army despite anguished protests from McCarthy. He failed first to get him into the CIA, and second to get him an army commission. Once Schine was a private at Fort Dix, McCarthy made altogether forty-four demands for preferential treatment. Schine was given seventeen passes to leave the base when the ordinary private could expect but three; he was permitted to leave drill to answer 250 long-distance phone calls, and to spend about 50 percent of his nights in New York, "on subcommittee business." McCarthy tried to get him out of basic training altogether, with a job as an aide to Secretary of War Stevens; failing that, McCarthy asked that he be detailed to West Point to screen the textbooks for subversive literature.[23]

Drew Pearson leaked some of this in mid-December 1953, followed by reports in the *Baltimore Sun* and the *New York Post* in January 1954. But every effort by Democratic members of Congress to get accurate information from the army was repulsed. McCarthy was at the time investigating the army radar and missile center at Fort Monmouth, insisting—falsely—that he had found thirty-three "espionage agents" there.[24] Secretary of the Army Stevens was doing everything in his power to placate the now powerful and intimidating Wisconsin senator, and at the same time struggling to keep him from being a further embarrassment to Eisenhower. Nixon and Sherman Adams secretly ordered that the army prepare a chronology of the successive badgerings of McCarthy on behalf of Schine, hoping to use the threat of publication of the document to get McCarthy to abandon the Fort Monmouth hearings. Originally a seventy-five-page document, full of "disgusting obscenities," according to columnists Joseph and Stewart Alsop, it was "defanged" and stripped to thirty-four pages. McCarthy and Cohn knew it had been prepared, and that its publication would be extremely damaging.[25]

McCarthy's hatred of the U.S. Army, with its strong irrational component, had meanwhile led him into the most bizarre of all his investigations. Failing everywhere to find a verifiable Communist, he had finally settled on a hapless army dentist, Maj. Irving Peress, who had refused to fill out an army questionnaire about his political leanings—not in itself an illegal act—but one which for McCarthy was proof enough of Communist affiliation. When McCarthy learned that Peress had been eased out of the army with an honorable discharge, he saw it as a sinister clue "to the deliberate Communist infiltration of Army generals and the Secretary of the Army." Gen. Ralph Zwicker, who had been decorated thirteen times for gallantry in action in World War II, happened to be the officer called before the subcommittee to explain the Peress case. McCarthy said that he "had the brains of a five-year-old" and was "unfit" to wear the army uniform.

Secretary of the Army Robert T. Stevens, whose timidity made him a classic McCarthy victim, now was sufficiently enraged to tell the senator that he would testify in Zwicker's place, but would not tolerate the abuse of his officers, and that he would forbid any of them to testify further. McCarthy replied, "Just go ahead and try it, Robert. I am going to kick the brains out of anyone who protects Communists."[26]

At this point Nixon had to face Eisenhower's anger. Discussing the problem of McCarthy late at night with James Bassett, Nixon said after three drinks, "It's probably time we dumped him." Bassett noted the fact in his diary on February 24. But he still continued briefly in his role as "buffer," persuaded that he could defuse the crisis and bring McCarthy back "on the team." It is worth noting that even now he continued to side with McCarthy, and in his memoirs wrote that in the Peress case "the Army was on very weak ground." Urging compromise, he arranged for what became a famous "chicken luncheon" next door to his own office, with Secretary of War Stevens, McCarthy, and the other Republican members of the subcommittee, Dirksen, Potter, and Mundt. Stevens— "like a goldfish in a tank of barracuda," one reporter said—was persuaded to sign a statement that he would permit Zwicker and other officers to testify after all; McCarthy gave only an oral promise that he would stop being abusive. Later McCarthy told the press that the secretary of the army could not have surrendered "more abjectly if he had gotten down on his knees." A *London Times* correspondent cabled his editor, "Senator McCarthy this afternoon achieved what General Burgoyne and General Cornwallis never achieved—the surrender of the American Army."[27] Stevens telephoned Nixon, weeping with rage it was said, to inform him that he would resign the next day.

The humiliation of his own cabinet member before the world roused Eisenhower from his torpor. Part of the problem was ambivalence; the president feared the spread of Communism in America. He had even toyed with the idea of trying to persuade Britain and France to join with the United States in a compact outlawing the Communist party.[28] He had followed McCarthy in publicizing dubious figures about the numbers of Communists dismissed from government; he had not intervened when the Republican National Committee in February endorsed a nationwide tour by McCarthy—part of the Lincoln's Birthday observances—although the theme had been "Twenty Years of Treason."

By now he had come to believe what several on his staff—Harold Stassen and Emmet Hughes in particular—had been insisting for months, that McCarthy's methods were Communist methods, that the wild bull from Wisconsin had embraced what he most professed to hate. In quiet conversations about McCarthy with Sen. Charles Potter, the one Republican on the subcommittee who had turned against McCarthy, Eisenhower even used the word "psychopathic."[29] Still, he did not speak out against the senator but ordered Nixon to draft a statement for Secretary of the Army

Stevens to read, insisting that there be no more harassment of his officers. He did tell Nixon that he planned to make a frontal attack on McCarthy in his next press conference, but Nixon warned him that the polls now showed that 50 percent of Americans favored McCarthy, with only 29 percent against, and begged him to water down his attack.

This was a bad Nixon error. Eisenhower agreed, and on March 3, 1954, he made only a weak plea for justice and fair play. He thereby handed a weapon to Adlai Stevenson, who four days later made a speech defining the president's moral dilemma in a fashion that electrified the nation. One of the great speeches in Stevenson's life, it put steel back into the spines of many Democrats in Congress, who had been as supine as Eisenhower, and who had been hiding behind the pretense that McCarthy was only a Republican problem. Stevenson first defined the general problem:

When one party says that the other's is the party of traitors who have deliberately conspired to betray America, to fill our government services with Communists and spies, to send our young men to unnecessary death in Korea, they violate not only the limits of partisanship, they offend not only the credulity of the people, but they stain the vision of America and of democracy for us and for the world we seek to lead. . . . those who live by the sword of slander also may perish by it, for now it is also being used against distinguished Republicans.

Then he struck directly at the Nixon wing of the Republican party:

And why, do you ask, do the demagogues triumph so often? The answer is inescapable: because a group of political plungers has persuaded the President that McCarthyism is the best Republican formula for political success. . . . A political party divided against itself, half McCarthy and half Eisenhower, cannot produce national unity. . . . as Democrats we don't believe in political extermination of Republicans, nor do we believe in political fratricide. . . .

Attacking the numbers game, he quoted White House releases saying 2427 "spies and traitors" had been "kicked out of government," and then noted the contradictory release, also from the White House, with "the government's reluctant admission that out of more than two million federal employees only one alleged active Communist has been found." "It looks as though the Great

Crusade had practiced a Great Deception," he said. "They may consider this good politics. But it is vicious government."[30]

Eisenhower, stung more than he could admit, and acting perhaps with some malice against Nixon, the chief architect of the policy of appeasing McCarthy, delegated him to make the official party reply. When Leonard Hall told him to make the speech, he flatly refused. Then Eisenhower called Nixon in person. Realizing finally that he was in deep trouble with the president, Nixon agreed. It was the most difficult speech, he told Bassett, that he had ever had to write. Bassett, helping him, noted in his diary that Nixon had said "he'd love to slip a secret recording gadget in the President's office." He went on to explain that he'd use the recording "to capture some of those warm, offhand, greathearted things the Man says, play 'em back, then get them press-released."[31] But the fantasy of secretly tape-recording the president of the United States, an extraordinary admission in itself, surely betrayed Nixon's great anxiety.

Writing the speech took five days. During this period Edward R. Murrow's long-planned and much-delayed television attack on McCarthy, on his program "See It Now," was released for a national audience by CBS. For the first time Americans saw the snarling, bullying McCarthy, humiliating General Zwicker, harassing innocent witnesses, equating Stevenson with Hiss in a deliberate slip-of-the-tongue: "Alger, I mean Adlai. . . ."

Murrow had concluded:

> . . . the line between investigating and persecuting is a very fine one, and the junior Senator from Wisconsin has stepped over it repeatedly. . . . We must not confuse dissent with disloyalty. . . . This is not the time for men who oppose Senator McCarthy's methods to keep silent. . . . Cassius was right, "The fault, dear Brutus, is not in our stars, but in ourselves."

For Nixon, enamored of the television that had saved him in the "Checkers" crisis, this program should have been a portent.

In his speech of March 13, 1954, he was not unadroit. He defended the president's long silence on McCarthy and did it by slapping at Stevenson:

> It is true that President Eisenhower does not engage in personal vituperation and vulgar name-calling and promiscuous letter writing in asserting his leadership, and I say, "Thank God he doesn't!"

He never once mentioned McCarthy by name, but did strike at him obliquely: "Men who have in the past done effective work exposing Communists in this country have, by reckless talk and questionable methods, made themselves the issue rather than the cause they believe in so deeply." Slipping into cruder language, and quoting one of McCarthy's favorite phrases, he talked of "rat killing," tapping, as Edward Shils has said, the dormant anxieties of many who would otherwise not listen:[32]

I have heard people say, "After all, we are dealing with a bunch of rats. What we ought to do is to go out and shoot them. Well, I'll agree; they're a bunch of rats, but just remember this. When you go out to shoot rats, you have to shoot straight. . . . you might hit someone else who's trying to shoot rats too. And so we've got to be fair. . . . And when through carelessness, you lump the innocent and guilty together, what you do is to give the guilty a chance to pull the cloak of innocence around themselves.[33]

He went on to slash again at Truman, Hiss, and then at Acheson, saying, "Isn't it wonderful, finally, to have a Secretary of State who isn't taken in by the Communists, who stands up to them." And echoing McCarthy's quoting of numbers, he continued by saying that of more than 2400 employees separated from government under the risk program, there had been 422 subversives, 198 sexual perverts, 611 convictions for felonies and misdemeanors, and 1424 with records indicating "untrustworthiness, drunkenness, mental instability, and possible exposure to blackmail."[34]

Since at least half of the speech consisted of the extravagant praise for Eisenhower, it is not surprising that afterward he had a call from the president who said, "I think you did a magnificent job." Nixon, quoting this in his memoirs, recalled also that Ike had "seemed very pleased that I had smiled a couple of times during the speech and said that at one point he had turned to the others in the room with him and said, 'There's that smile I told Dick to use.' "[35]

The speech received much praise—*Time,* consistently pro-Nixon, said he had handled the problem "with dignity and dispatch,"[36] and the polls showed a drop in McCarthy's popularity.

Nixon, who was fond of quoting the admonition "When you strike at a king, kill him," had also moved in quietly in the same week with what Roy Cohn called "the final stiletto." It was all done covertly, and Nixon kept his own tracks covered. In what Cohn said was "a formal little ritual used to lend artistic verisimilitude," Sen. Charles Potter called Secretary of Defense Charles Wilson and said, "I hear there is a report about the existence of the activities of Senator McCarthy, Roy Cohn, and David Schine." Wilson called back to suggest that Potter make a formal request for the report from the army. It was brought to Potter's office in less than thirty minutes.[37]

Sen. Everett Dirksen, smelling the danger for McCarthy, urged that a subcommittee be set up to investigate only Roy Cohn. But Senators McClellan, Symington, Potter, and Jackson had had their fill of McCarthy. Symington told him frankly, "I'm going to come out against you, Joe."

McCarthy replied, "Then I will destroy you, Stu."[38]

Shortly thereafter McCarthy revived an old election canard—that Symington as a teenager had stolen a car and taken a joyride with several other boys—and would greet him in the committee hearings, putting his arm around his shoulder ostentatiously, and saying, "Stolen any cars recently, Stu?"[39]

The thirty-four-page report describing the forty-four efforts to get preferential treatment for Private David Schine was released by the army to the press on March 11, just two days before Nixon's muted public attack. It caused a national sensation. The *New York Times* printed it in full, and also a front-page picture of McCarthy looking fondly at Cohn. *Time,* on March 22, showed a picture of McCarthy, Cohn, and Schine, captioned, "After an idyllic gambol, the harsh note of an Army bugle."

McCarthy's own subcommittee now forced him to resign while they investigated him; he countered with a suit against the army. Thus began the Army-McCarthy hearings, which Senate minority leader Lyndon Johnson cheerfully permitted to be televised. A frantic McCarthy accused the army of trying to "blackmail" him into stopping his crusade against Communists by holding Schine as a "hostage." Senator Potter, meeting with Eisenhower in private, now reported McCarthy behavior in terms of "obsession" and "lunacy." Leonard Hall paid McCarthy a visit and was appalled to find him opening the door with a .45 automatic pistol in his hand and to be told that he carried it everywhere. Hall told Nixon he thought McCarthy ready to blow up. Senator Mundt called to tell the same thing, offering the opinion that McCarthy was in no condition to participate in any hearings.[40]

But McCarthy did appear, and for two months Americans sat riveted to their television sets, watching a fluid, unrehearsed drama of compelling fascination. McCarthy, although the defendant, won for himself the right to cross-examine. He interrupted constantly, with a cry that became a national byword, "Point of order, Mr. Chairman!" He was living out not the role he fantasied, the heroic fighter of the enemies of America, but his own real self, the juvenile bullyboy. Joseph Welch, the deceptively gentle Boston lawyer who was defense counsel for the army and whose skill served to exacerbate and expose the worst of McCarthy, became almost overnight a national hero to devout believers in the First Amendment.[41]

Nixon in his memoirs called the hearings "a grotesque melodrama," and reported Eisenhower's caustic judgment at the time, "a damn shameful spectacle." How Nixon really felt at the time, involved as he had become in McCarthy's destruction, remains something of a mystery. James Bassett and Nixon tried to cut the hearings short, as did Leonard Hall, but Bassett told Hall that the president "wants blood," and nothing was done.[42]

When Sen. Ralph Flanders introduced his formal resolution of condemnation of McCarthy on the Senate floor, the Wisconsin senator, enraged, told reporters, "I think they should get a man with a net and take him to a good quiet place." Flanders, normally a quiet, even reticent Republican senator, had come to believe that McCarthy should be "washed out as thoroughly as a Kansas flood washes out the stockyards."[43] He saw his resolution pass seventy-five to twelve.

Roy Cohn insists that it was Vice-President Nixon who now picked the Senate committee and stacked it against McCarthy. The press was told that Knowland picked the Republicans and Lyndon Johnson the Democrats. All the members were conservatives; none had taken a strong stand against McCarthy, but all had a deep sense of propriety, especially regarding the Senate. Arthur Watkins, a stern Mormon moralist, who wrote later in his book about the "dark and fetid" depths coming to public attention, was made chairman. The choice was crucial. He kept McCarthy's outbursts to a minimum with "the gavel crack heard round the world."[44]

McCarthy henceforth did himself nothing but harm, calling Watkins stupid and cowardly, styling the committee "a lynch bee," and "the unwitting handmaiden of the Communist party." Committee member Sam Ervin, later famous in the Senate Watergate hearings, demanded McCarthy's expulsion. Sen. John Stennis, also on the committee, said McCarthy had poured "slush and slime" on the Senate.[45]

During the debate McCarthy went to the hospital for what was called bursitis, but may have been the removal of broken glass from his elbow. Nixon permitted a ten-day delay. On December 2, 1954, when the final debate began, Nixon was again presiding. "A hush fell over the Chamber," he said, "as a lone figure came through the swinging doors at the back and walked slowly down the aisle. Joe McCarthy had arrived for the vote on his own censure. His arm was in a sling."[46]

The crippling was real in every sense, and Nixon never forgot the drama of it. Until this point McCarthy had never in his public career really been punished for his lying or his destructiveness. Now he was being punished for quite incidental folly having to do with affection. But if Nixon saw the irony of this, either at the time or in writing about it in San Clemente many years later, and if he saw any parallel with his own career, he kept all such reflections carefully buried. The condemnation vote came on a series of technicalities, mostly having to do with McCarthy's abuse of the Watkins committee, and his contemptuous refusal in earlier years to answer Senate inquiries about his finances. The vote was sixty-seven to twenty-two, with every Democrat voting against him, and the Republicans voting twenty-two for and twenty-two against. Senator Knowland, loyal to the last, voted for McCarthy.[47]

A few days later, McCarthy, in the grandiloquent gesture suggesting how far he had departed from reality, took an informal poll of the Republican leadership to see if he could become president of the United States with Knowland as his running mate. Cohn wrote that he was told only 3 percent would support him.[48] McCarthy now sent a series of insulting telegrams to the White House, and apologized to the American people for having urged them to vote for Ike. But the press was no longer listening. TV cameras deserted him. He had become the impostor exposed, and he crumpled no less certainly than if he had been cut down by a rifle bullet.

Columnist George Sokolsky said McCarthy felt particularly betrayed by Nixon, whom he had believed to be his friend. Cohn, echoing this when interviewed after Nixon's resignation, said,

"Nixon was perfectly willing to turn on his conservative friends and cut their throats—one, two, three. . . . He was a superb hatchet man."[49]

McCarthy, always a heavy, if secret, drinker, now became a severe alcoholic. Deeply depressed, he was in and out of the hospital for a variety of ailments related to his drinking. In what was effectively suicidal behavior he continued to drink even after a bout with hepatitis. McCarthy had long been cut off the White House guest list, but now became a true pariah. Bassett's diary for May 5, 1954, describes how Nixon and William Rogers came to agree, "after a vast evening of hair-letting down," that "the only method for dealing with McCarthy was ostracism of the man." McCarthy's loyal ally in defamation, Sen. William Jenner, explained it all to him, "You're the kid who came to the party and pee'd in the lemonade."[50]

Whittaker Chambers wrote to McCarthy's longtime supporter William Buckley, "McCarthy as a man, a man of pathos, maimed and forever crippled in spirit . . . that man I would gladly comfort—as a fellow man. Of McCarthy as a politician I want no part. He is a raven of disaster."[51]

Jack Anderson described how at one Republican rally in Wisconsin McCarthy "was asked to leave his place on the dais so as not to embarrass—of all people—Vice-President Richard Nixon. The old tiger left in a docile manner; the curious witness followed him outside the building and found him sitting on a curbstone weeping."[52]

McCarthy's depressions worsened. Not even the adoption of a baby daughter six months before his death served to stem the fatal decline. Roy Cohn, trying to rouse him, urged him one day to return to the old crusade. But McCarthy's reply inadvertently provides what is perhaps the best metaphor describing his own life: Continuing the battle, he said, would be as futile as "shoveling shit against the tide."[53]

Stevenson and Nixon

*This is a man of many masks, who can say they have seen his
real face?*

— ADLAI STEVENSON ON NIXON, 1956[1]

THERE WAS NEVER ANYONE quite like Adlai Stevenson in
Richard Nixon's life. A major foe in the elections of 1952, 1954,
and 1956, in his attacks on Nixon he etched a demonic image that
left the younger man permanently scarred. Voorhis and Helen
Douglas as opponents facing the Nixon onslaughts had been little
more than walking wounded. Although Eisenhower and not
Nixon was Stevenson's major opponent, he found the general difficult to assault. When hecklers shouted "I like Ike" in one Democratic rally, Stevenson replied, "Well, I like him too, but I would
ask you fellows to listen a minute."[2] Against Nixon, however, Stevenson was scathingly contemptuous, pertinaciously moral. He
was the first major candidate to define for the nation the nature
of Nixon's political ethics, to describe his corrupting influence on
Eisenhower, and to dare to speculate openly what would happen
to the nation if the general died in office. His 1952 slogan, "Better
to lose the election than to mislead the people," and his attacks on
"lies, half-truths, circuses and demagoguery," were directed
against Nixon and McCarthy, not against Dwight D. Disenhower.
Of McCarthy he said,

The pillorying of the innocent has caused the wise to stammer and the
timid to retreat. I would shudder for this country if I thought that we
too must surrender to the sinister figure of the Inquisition, of the great
accuser.[3]

Nixon he said was "the kind of politician who would cut down a
redwood tree, and then mount the stump and make a speech for
conservation."

Although Republicans derided Stevenson as an egghead, Nixon among others could not help but respect his intellect. A fine craftsman with words, a speechmaker with a gift for epigram and trenchant political definition, he raised electoral debate to a level it had not seen since the days of Franklin Roosevelt. Mary McGrory said, "For the first time in my life I read political speeches for pleasure. I did not realize until much later how bold they were."[4] Stevenson drew into his orbit some of the ablest minds in the nation; students flocked to him. Eric Sevareid wrote to a friend, "He has caught the imagination of the intellectuals, of all those who are really informed; he has excited the passions of the *mind*."[5]

He also attracted a galaxy of able and influential women—Eleanor Roosevelt, economist Barbara Ward, Agnes Meyer, Dorothy Fosdick, Alicia Patterson, Mary Lasker, Ruth Field, Marietta Tree—there has been nothing quite like this ever in American history. They gave him money, fed him ideas, and bolstered him when he felt degraded and exhausted. Agnes Meyer, wife of the publisher of the *Washington Post*, who said he had "an extraordinary gift for eliciting the best from people," described her involvement with him as "beautiful but incredible . . . harder than a love affair."[6]

Although Nixon mocked Stevenson as an egghead, he hungered to be counted an intellectual in his own right. That he had an abiding respect for Stevenson went unsuspected until 1968 when Brock Brower published a revealing interview in *Life*. When asked if as president he would behave like Eisenhower, Nixon said:

"I've more of a philosophical bent I suppose, in a way I'm probably much closer to the kind of politician that"—and the eyes widen again, full of surprise—surprise even to himself—"Adlai Stevenson was."[7]

The disclosure, although important, seems to have been inadvertent and temporary. In his memoirs he echoed his old attack. Toward Stevenson, he wrote, he felt "instinctively negative": "I considered him to be far more veneer than substance, and I felt that beneath his glibness and mocking wit he was shallow, flippant, and indecisive. He reminded me of Oscar Wilde's definition of a cynic as a man who knows the price of everything and the value of nothing."[8]

The epigram fit Stevenson less than any politician of his time. Perhaps Nixon by then had learned from his young historian aides in exile that Stevenson was on record as saying that Nixon was the only man in public life he ever "really loathed."[9] The allusion to Oscar Wilde, however, could hardly have been inadvertent. Early in the 1952 campaign Nixon had labeled Stevenson "Side-saddle Adlai," trying to ride "the Truman nag" and turn away from it at the same time. "Like all side-saddle riders," he said, "his feet hang well out to the left." The side-saddle, no one had to be told, was ridden only by women. And he used the same blend of innuendo—left-wing and effeminate—in saying, "I would rather have a khaki-clad president than one clothed in State Department pinks."[10]

Eisenhower in the beginning had difficulty attacking Stevenson, saying to friends on a fishing trip, "If I'd known two months before that a guy as decent as Stevenson was going to be the nominee, they might never have gotten me to take the nomination."[11] But the general proved to be far more thin-skinned under political attack than anyone expected, and he came to dislike Stevenson more than Nixon did. After his stroke, Nixon tells us, "the doctors ordered us to steer clear of discussion of Stevenson because it always caused the President's blood pressure to rise alarmingly."[12]

Ike did not like having Stevenson quote history against him, accurately and adroitly. When the general parroted Nixon, blaming Truman and Acheson for the loss of China and the outbreak of the Korean War, Stevenson reminded the nation that the initial "abandonment" of Korea as being outside "the defense perimeter" of the United States had been a military decision, and one in which Eisenhower as chief of staff had concurred. He quoted him as saying that South Korea was of little strategic interest to the United States, and recommending withdrawal of U.S. forces. Still, Stevenson was too honest about his own ambivalence over the unpopular war, too concerned with the stalemate and continuing casualties, to defend American involvement without reservations. And he said candidly to a group of Marines on September 20, 1952:

It is fighting undertaken in the name of the common collective security of the great majority of the nations of the world, against the brutal aggressiveness of one or more of them. It is fighting which might, conceivably, have been avoided on that particular battlefield had we acted otherwise than we did—though as to that, no man can surely say.[13]

Stevenson, as Eric Sevareid said, was a questioner, the nation's gadfly and conscience, "the intellectual proctor." Eisenhower, he said, "empty of ideas or certitude himself," was careful not to ask other people to think. He appealed to them as father or big brother, with "an illusion of Authority, or Competence," where Stevenson, "in his almost painful honesty . . . makes it clear that he does not know all the answers, that nobody really can or does."[14]

What the nation wanted, however, and has always wanted in its presidents, was not a conscience or a proctor, not one who would *define* the nation's problems but one who would *solve* them. Thus when Eisenhower said "I will go to Korea," an idea Stevenson had toyed with and rejected, he appeared the more active candidate. As Stevenson's biographer, John Bartlow Martin, has said, the phrase "turned victory into a landslide."[15]

As in his campaigns against Voorhis and Douglas, Nixon did not have to defame in order to win. He was campaigning on the coattails of an unbeatable candidate, a hero who seemed strong where Stevenson seemed weak, decisive where Stevenson seemed indecisive, and plain speaking where Stevenson was artful and diffuse. Although Stevenson was a man of irreproachable patriotism who detested Soviet tyranny, Nixon chose to excoriate him as a semitraitor. His proof—that Stevenson had written an affidavit attesting to the good character of Alger Hiss. "If Stevenson were to be taken in by Stalin as he was by Hiss," he said, "the Yalta sellout would look like a great American diplomatic triumph by comparison." And he accused him of "going down the line for the arch traitor of our generation."[16]

Stevenson, thrown on the defensive, said he never doubted the jury verdict finding Hiss guilty. He read letters from John Foster Dulles praising Hiss, and pointed out that Eisenhower along with Dulles had sanctioned Hiss's reappointment to the presidency of the Carnegie Endowment. Dulles, he said, had had secret warnings that Hiss was a Communist, "but no such report or warnings ever came to me."

I testified only as to his reputation at the time as I knew him. His reputation was good. If I had said it was bad, I would have been a liar. If I had refused to testify at all, I would have been a coward. But while the brash and patronizing young man who aspires to the Vice Presidency does not charge me with being a communist, he does say that I exercised bad judgment in stating honestly what I heard from others about Hiss's reputation. "Thou shalt not bear false witness" is one of the Ten Commandments, in case Senator Nixon has not read them lately. . . . He has criticized my judgment. I hope and pray that his standards of "judgment" may never prevail. . . .

He attacked Nixon for lies and half-truths, for corrupting by fear and falsehood, and for undermining "basic spiritual values." In the final accounting, he said, "What shall it profit a man if he shall gain the whole world, and lose his own soul."[17]

Nixon responded publicly by still more savage attack, linking Stevenson's name with that of Acheson and Truman in his famous Texarkana speech of October 27, calling them all "traitors to the high principles in which many of the nation's Democrats believe." And on October 30, 1952, he said in Los Angeles, "Stevenson holds a Ph.D. degree from Acheson's College of Cowardly Communist Containment."[18] Privately he seems to have been shaken by the confrontations with Stevenson. But his response was not regret, or introspection, or self-appraisal, or a change in tactics. Instead we see evidence, at least momentarily, of a brief descent into persecutory paranoia, a kind that foreshadowed his behavior in Watergate. At the height of the campaign he summoned to the Barclay Hotel in New York his old aide at HUAC, Robert Stripling, who had worried with him through the worst of the Hiss crisis. He seemed "highly agitated," Stripling remembered.

"Strip, those sons of bitches are out to get me," said the man who had been spending the past months denouncing Adlai Stevenson, Dean Acheson, and Felix Frankfurter because of their character depositions for Alger Hiss. "They got Mr. [J. Parnell] Thomas, and they tried to get me, and they'll try to get anybody that had anything to do with the Hiss case."

Thomas, it should be noted, the old HUAC chairman, had gone to jail for eighteen months and been fined $10,000 for taking kickbacks from members of his staff.[19]

In 1952 Eisenhower and Nixon had won by over six and one-half million votes, with 55.1 percent against and 44.4 percent for Stevenson and Sparkman. The Republicans gained twenty-two seats in the House, one in the Senate. Stevenson continued to be the titular head of his party, and a formidable Nixon antagonist. Defeat did not silence him. Never a presidential winner, he became a teacher of presidents, with enormous influence on Kennedy, and more influence on Nixon than Nixon ever admitted.

Stevenson, like Thomas Jefferson, was both fascinated and repelled by power, and embarrassed by his compulsion to seek it. His had been a long love-hate relationship with politics. A grandson of Adlai Stevenson, vice-president under Grover Cleveland, and a great-grandson of Jesse Fell, friend of Lincoln, Stevenson grew up with politics and history. An only son, with one sister, he also grew up with parental expectations for greatness. His early life had been clouded by a tragedy far worse than Nixon had seen in the loss of his two brothers; at age twelve at a party in his home he had accidentally killed a young girl by firing a .22 rifle he thought to be unloaded. The incident was never thereafter discussed—Stevenson did not even tell his wife about it—but that it haunted him is suggested in the pervasive melancholy and self-doubt barely hidden behind his good humor and wit. He told Barbara Ward, who wrote speeches for him, that he was distrusting and defensive, and "underneath it all, afraid."[20] When a woman wrote to him that her son had killed a friend accidentally, as he had done, he replied, "Tell him that he must live for two." To one friend he wrote complaining of the vicissitudes of the 1948 campaign for governor of Illinois, "and so on and on, to the end of time, or until my sins are expiated."[21]

Stevenson's parents were unhappily married, estranged for a time when he was six, when his father went to Europe for treatment for headaches and malaise. He returned home to become active in Illinois politics. Young Stevenson followed the proper route to national politics—Choate, Princeton, Harvard Law School. But he abandoned Harvard after failing in two classes, shifting to Northwestern. He married what his father called "the wrong girl." Ellen Boardman was beautiful, demanding, and jealous of people's love of him and of his preoccupation with politics. She was also a demanding and apparently unloving mother of their three sons. They were divorced during his gubernatorial campaign—"She takes all the fire and vim out of him," one friend said[22]—and later greatly embarrassed him by telling the press she thought him an indecisive Hamlet, unfit to be president. Stevenson never married again.

After his divorce he fell in love with Alicia Patterson, wife of Harry F. Guggenheim, and after her death, with Marietta Tree. His biographer reports that the rumor was spread by his political enemies that he might be a homosexual; he dismissed the rumors lightly. Some friends said he was in love with Dorothy Fosdick, one of the several attractive women who fed him political material and lavished upon him affection and domestic advice. But it was Alicia Patterson with whom he was deeply in love, and his letters to her, returned to Stevenson when she knew she was dying, reveal among many things that Stevenson had no anxiety about his own masculinity, but a great deal about the presence of evil in the world. To Alicia he wrote after the 1952 defeat, "I've no regrets; did the best I could, didn't trim, equivocate or clasp dirty hands." When Barbara Ward wrote to him, "I still think you can make a rational argument for the belief that goodness & love are the fundamental meaning of the universe," he put a question mark in the margin.[23]

Stevenson in the 1954 election continued to be, for Richard Nixon, a distant conscience, at times mocking and contemptuous, at times indignant and appalled, sometimes simply cautioning and judicious. Another Democrat, like Congressman Emanuel Cellers of New York, called Nixon "an inept, naïve, Piltdown statesman . . . a maladjusted purblind Throttlebottom, a hoax of a statesman,"[24] but Stevenson always attacked with point and elegance. Evidence of his luminous intelligence and moral fiber can be seen in his private letters as well as in his speeches; ghost writers contributed but did not enhance the best that Stevenson was constantly putting to paper. John F. Kennedy seems to have learned, at least in part from Stevenson, never to talk down to an audience. Nixon felt compelled to talk down, even to degrade the best that was in himself. Jim Bassett in his diary tells of listening to the increasing simplification and sloppiness in Nixon's major 1956 campaign speech as he repeated it on the whistlestops. Appalled, finally, at what the speech had become, he had it taped and played it back to show Nixon that it had become a caricature of the original.

Early in the 1954 congressional campaign Nixon shouldered the major speech-making, at Ike's request, and it seemed for a time as if he and Stevenson—neither running for office—were major opponents in a national debate. Nixon watchers who had admired his political sagacity up to this point were incredulous at the failure of imagination, the paucity of new themes. Although

Ike had declared an end to McCarthyism and the nation was patently weary of it, Nixon continued to speak, act, and smear like the man he had so recently helped to destroy.

He was trapped in the habits of attack and denial. And in the 1954 campaign he added a favorite McCarthy tactic, fabrication, which we had himself used in the past. In Van Nuys, California, on October 13, and in later speeches, he said that when the Eisenhower administration came to Washington,

we found in the files a blueprint for socializing America. This dangerous, well-oiled scheme contained plans for adding $40 billion to the national debt by 1956. It called for socialized medicine, socialized housing, socialized agriculture, socialized water and power, and perhaps the most disturbing of all, socialization of America's greatest source of power, atomic energy.

When reporters asked for documents, Nixon referred them to his press secretary, who said that Nixon was using "figurative language to describe the philosophy and proposals of President Truman."[25] The "numbers game" he played ever more carelessly. On October 4, in Pineville, Kentucky, he said "thousands of Commies and security risks have been thrown out of government. I have the facts and figures to back up the statement." Actually, Eisenhower's own Civil Service Commission chairman, Philip Young, testified toward the end of the campaign "that he knew of no single government employee who had been fired by the Eisenhower administration for being a Communist or fellow traveler."[26]

"Atomic spies" became the focus of many of his speeches, and he repeatedly attacked Stevenson for his deposition in favor of the character of Alger Hiss. Instead of McCarthy's "twenty years of treason," the party slogan became "twenty years of Double Deal, a record of communism and corruption."[27] When Stevenson urged greater expansion of the American economy, which he said was lagging behind that of the Soviets, Nixon said, "Mr. Stevenson has been guilty, probably without being aware that he was doing so, of spreading pro-Communist propaganda as he has attacked with violent fury the economic system of the United States and praised Soviet economy." The Russians, he said, were eager for a Democratic victory, and he claimed to have "a secret memorandum of the Communist party" showing "it is determined to conduct its program within the Democratic Party."[28]

As Cabell Phillips said in the *New York Times,* Mr. Nixon "is adept at planting the dark and ominous inference," and the *Times,* although favoring Eisenhower's reelection, editorially protested Nixon's "increasingly strident suggestions that the Democrats are somehow tied up with Communism."[29]

Nixon set the tone for Republicans generally, and Eisenhower applauded him in a public letter of appreciation on October 27: "No one could have done more effective work." Stevenson summed up the Republican campaign: "The President smiles while the Vice President smears," and said Nixon had turned the campaign into "a cheap, sordid, ugly slugfest of slogans, charges, and epithets." Nixon, thoroughly angered, called the Stevenson attack "vicious" and "scurrilous." He wired him on October 30:

You have been following your usual tactics of covering up the record and failing to answer the facts by screaming "smear, slur, and slander." Your principal target seems to be me. All I have done since September 15 is to cite the hard facts from the record. . . .

The following day he indicted "the Stevenson-Truman-anti-Eisenhower-ADA-leftwing campaign" for "the most despicable political tactic—that of the big lie."[30]

Early in October the polls showed that the Nixon tactics were leading to monumental Republican failure. Eisenhower was persuaded to campaign strenuously in the last weeks to stem the impending debacle. Despite the president's earnest pleas for Republican votes, the electorate moved decisively back into the Democratic party. Republicans lost sixteen seats in the House and two in the Senate, giving the president a Congress with Democrats in control of both houses. The national totals for the House of Representatives pointed up the Nixon failure:

	REPUBLICAN	DEMOCRAT
1952	28,399,286	28,336,127
1954	20,033,673	22,175,228

The results, Nixon said, "were about what I expected."

In his memoirs Nixon described how he cheered up a disconsolate Eisenhower and his cabinet at their first meeting after the election:

I took up a little wind-up toy drummer from my pocket, released the catch, and put it on the Cabinet table. Everyone watched, puzzled, as the little fellow picked out a zigzag course across the polished surface and the sharp sound of his drum filled the room. "Gentlemen," I said, "we should take a lesson from this: this is no time to be depressed, and we have got to keep beating the drum about our achievements." Eisenhower beamed.[31]

It was good enough theater for the moment. But Nixon was sick at heart. On Election Day, flying back to Washington with Murray Chotiner who had managed the campaign, he had taken out of his briefcase a folder with several pages of handwritten notes. "Here's my last campaign speech, Murray," he said, handing him the folder. "It's the last one, because after this I am through with politics."[32]

Prelude to Vietnam

Eisenhower had sent Nixon and his wife on a goodwill tour to the Far East in 1953. It was an exhilarating seventy-three-day adventure, with stops in New Zealand, Australia, Indonesia, Malaya, Cambodia, Laos, Vietnam, Formosa, Korea, Japan, the Philippines, Burma, India, Pakistan, and Iran. Until now, of the Far East Nixon had seen only the jungles of the Pacific atolls. Pat had never been farther from home than Canada and Mexico. They were entertained more extravagantly than he could ever have dreamed possible in his childhood fantasies of "faraway" places, and the trip gave him a taste for royalty he never thereafter relinquished.

He was well briefed, and he studied assiduously. His speeches were courteously received abroad, and decently publicized at home. *Look* had a display of pictures of the Nixons in the showplaces of Asia. One showed Pat, serene and beautiful, kneeling shoeless in the great Burmese Shwedagon Pagoda with a wishing stone in her hands. The temples, she said, were like a fairyland.[1]

Nixon met Ramón Magsaysay, Nehru, Chiang Kai-shek, Syngman Rhee, King Sihanouk, Prince Souvanna Phouma, and Ayub Khan, some of whom were to be of much consequence in his life as president. Pat's guide through the Burmese temples was U Thant, later secretary-general of the United Nations. Bao Dai, puppet monarch in Vietnam, whom the French had restored to power in Saigon in 1949, invited Nixon to his luxurious palace in Dalat. In Indonesia he was entertained by Sukarno.

In Iran the Nixons met the young shah, Mohammed Reza Pahlevi, recently restored to the throne after a military coup which overthrew Mohammed Mossadegh with the secret help of the American CIA. John Foster Dulles, who believed Mossadegh to be pro-Soviet because he had nationalized the British-owned

Anglo-Iranian oil company, although actually he had blocked Soviet attempts to win oil concessions in northern Iran, had sent Kermit Roosevelt to Iran "with a suitcase full of money" and some covert operators. The coup had been quick and Roosevelt was secretly awarded the National Security Medal by Eisenhower.[2]

The shah, who had narrowly missed an assassination attempt, "was only thirty-four," Nixon wrote in his memoirs. "I sensed the inner strength in him, and felt that in the years ahead he would become a strong leader."[3] This friendship became a political force of much consequence. The coup gave Nixon an exaggerated respect for the CIA, and a mistaken notion of its capacity to keep secret its covert actions, which would have evil consequences with the rise of Fidel Castro in Cuba in 1959.

Nixon's visit to India left him with a sour taste, and may well have begun the long history of hostility toward this state which colored his presidency. His interview with Nehru in New Delhi was not a success, and later, when he went on to Pakistan and intimated to the press that he would support that country's requests for military aid, Nehru called him "an unprincipled cad."[4]

The trip, Nixon wrote in his memoirs, "had a tremendously important effect on my thinking—and my career."[5] He moved easily into the role of visiting monarch, luxuriating in the formality, elegance, and sumptuous entertainment, some of which he would try to bring to the White House as president. But it was as an American monarch that he toured the Far East. There was a vast deal of handshaking, although one finds it difficult to believe that he shook a hundred thousand hands, as he said—including five thousand at a single 4-H Club exhibition in the Philippines—the timing and logistics problems are too staggering.[6] The press reported particularly his individual stops, when he ordered the motorcade to halt and reached out to greet a single unknown man or woman. One such contact, in Japan, he described twenty years later when the Japanese prime minister, Kakuei Tanaka, was visiting the White House:

We were riding along the road out toward a village, and as we rode along, I saw two workmen in the field. We stopped the car, we went out, we met them. I didn't understand their language; they didn't understand ours. But as I met them and as I felt in their hands the strength and determination that was there, I knew here were the representatives of a great people. And that is why Japan today is a great nation.[7]

The contact at the time was symbolic, never real, just as his public description of it two decades later was fantasy for the theater of the moment. As vice-president he remained a loner, and as president he became a lone monarch. When Gerald Ford moved into the White House, he and his wife found to their astonishment that Nixon had taught the members of the staff not to reply verbally to him or to his wife when greeted by them except under special circumstances. Ford wrote in his memoir, "We changed that, and almost overnight the atmosphere turned cheerful again."[8]

The Far Eastern trip was Nixon's first taste of international diplomacy. He was receptive, bold, unorthodox, especially in Japan, where he spoke out in favor of an increase in Japanese military strength, and deplored the demilitarization of the U.S. after World War II. In Vietnam he watched an artillery barrage by French troops against the Communist Vietminh near the Chinese border. "I was right there on the battlefield or close to it," he told reporters. He talked with French officers who told him with some bitterness that Ho Chi Minh had originally been aided by the American OSS, and came home eager to tell Eisenhower and the press that if Indochina fell Thailand would follow, then Malaya, "with its rubber and tin," then Indonesia, and probably Japan.[9] He fitted everything into his capacious and well-organized memory, absorbing with easy facility, and arrived in Washington bursting with impressions and policy proposals. He was met at the plane by all the ambassadors from the countries he had visited, seven Republican senators, and a delegation from the State Department, a royal welcome to match those he had been given abroad.

Eisenhower's welcome, in marked contrast, was at best perfunctory. When Nixon and his wife were driven from the airport to the White House, the president greeted him on the porch. As the New York Times reported it, Ike walked forward, grasped Mr. Nixon's hand, and snapped: "It looks like we have a little interest in you, Dick."[10] Explaining that Mamie had a cold, he invited them upstairs only for coffee. The meeting lasted but half an hour.

The next day Eisenhower sent him a handwritten letter saying he was glad to have him home, that he missed his "wise counsel," "energetic support," and "exemplary dedication," adding, "I look forward to some quiet opportunity when I can hear a real recital of your adventures and accomplishments." Nixon said he thought this to be "an extraordinarily warm and personal gesture" coming from "one who meted out praise in very small doses."[11] If Eisenhower ever called him back for that "real recital" of his adventures, Nixon did not mention it in his memoirs, and one has the impression in reading this account that his only reward from the president was a cup of coffee and a thank-you note. Actually Nixon did brief the National Security Council. But there was no dinner with Eisenhower and Mamie in the family quarters of the White House, and there never would be.

Six months later Churchill was at the White House. There were thirty guests. Pat, who sat on his right, marveled at Mamie's relaxed and folksy manner with the great British hero—when Churchill had difficulty cutting his meat with his gold knife, the First Lady explained smilingly that the knives weren't sharp, they came with the house.[12] When the men adjourned for cigars, Nixon talked with Anthony Eden, who told him courteously that his recent trip to Malaya had "made a great impression in Britain." Later Eisenhower, who had been chatting with Churchill, beckoned to him to join them. "This is one of the young men I have been telling you about and I want you to get acquainted with him," he said.

Nixon recorded it all in his diary that night, concluding, "This is perhaps the most enjoyable occasion we have ever had at the White House."[13] Still, it will be seen that Eisenhower had introduced him oddly. He seemed unaware that Nixon had formally met Churchill and Eden at the airport, and had escorted them to the White House. And he did not say, "This is my vice-president," but "This is one of the young men I have been telling you about." Thus Nixon was reminded, as he would be increasingly in the following months, that he was not necessarily the favorite son.

Shut out by Ike's coldness, chafing to be part of the decision-making on foreign matters, and bitter that the president had not made him a true working partner as he had promised, Nixon turned to John Foster Dulles, and this became an alliance of much significance in Nixon's life. The secretary of state gave the impression of being "severe, dour, almost ascetic . . . a cold fish, devoid of human emotions"—few came to his funeral because they loved him—Nixon said.[14] Dulles nevertheless permitted him inside his small circle of friends and became his confidant. Actually Dulles had been almost as shut out by Eisenhower as had Nixon. Biographer Leonard Mosley says "they had no intellectual or cultural rapport and no level of off-duty conversation. . . . the President admired Foster and was a little frightened of him, sometimes referring to him as an Old Testament prophet."[15]

Nixon had no problem emphathizing with a genuinely religious man. He could guard his tongue and slip easily into the accents of the devout, as with Billy Graham. "We shared a fascination with the world and had the same basic outlook on America's role in it," Nixon said. "Many nights I would have cocktails or dinner with him, and then we would sit for hours talking our way around the world. It was an incomparable opportunity for me to learn from one of the great diplomats of our time." Dulles was never Machiavellian, Nixon told Princeton's Richard Challener in 1966, "and being Machiavellian," he added, "was not necessarily bad. It could be very good."[16]

Dulles was not hostile to a working alliance with Eisenhower's young Machiavelli, and embraced the opportunity, as Nixon recognized, to use him "as his political eyes and ears to keep him abreast of what was going on in Washington."[17] Nixon for his part embraced the Dulles rhetoric, in all its self-righteousness. Dulles was like the evangelists Nixon had listened to in his youth; he believed in using God's sword to smite the ungodly, and he treated diplomacy, as Arthur Schlessinger has written "as a subbranch of theology."[18] Dulles wanted not compromise with Communists but Communist defeat. When, after Stalin's death in 1953, India had offered to assist in negotiating a peace settlement in Korea, Dulles had confided in Emmet Hughes, "I don't think we can get much out of a Korean settlement until we have shown—before all Asia—our clear superiority in giving the Chinese one hell of a licking."[19]

Eisenhower had succeeded in breaking the armistice stalemate in Korea by threatening to renew hostilities with the use of the atomic bomb, and had sent nuclear missiles to Okinawa to make good the threat, a fact he admitted in his memoirs but which had for a time been kept secret from the public.[20] Dulles, exhilarated by the successful use of the threat of nuclear war, now saw it as an easy way to conduct diplomacy. On January 12, 1954, he enunciated his new policy of "massive retaliation," which Nixon instantly supported and helped to make famous. On February 12, in New Haven, the vice-president defined it as the use of "massive retaliatory power rather than the maintenance of American ground forces in every potential trouble spot in the world." On March 13, in a national address, he said, "We have adopted a new principle. Rather than let the communists nibble us to death all over the world in little wars, we will rely in the future on massive, mobile retaliatory powers."[21]

That massive retaliation meant the use of nuclear bombs was implicit in the description. As Secretary of Defense Charles Wilson interpreted it, with a logic that remains baffling to this day, "We can only afford to fight a big war, and if there is one, that is the kind it will be."[22] Massive retaliation in Wilson's and Eisenhower's view meant essentially a doctrine of noninvolvement. But noninvolvement was the last thing Dulles and Nixon had in mind. As Eisenhower put it wryly to Cyrus Eaton in later years, "one of his problems as president had been to restrain Nixon and Dulles who were forever urging the dispatch of American troops to every continent to destroy Communism by force."[23]

The danger was that every minor international incident could become either a nuclear showdown, or, in Townsend Hoopes's words, "a glaringly transparent bluff that would (by proving wholly inapplicable to the task of guiding revolutionary change in the fringe areas) serve to weaken the credibility of American policy everywhere."[24]

The doctrine saw its first decisive test in Vietnam in the spring of 1954. The French had been burrowing in to save their colonial holdings in Indochina ever since their return to the area after the Japanese were forced out at the end of World War II. FDR had hoped to see the end of colonialism everywhere, but Truman had backed the French against the gifted insurgent leader Ho Chi Minh because he was a Communist. Indochina had been split into Cambodia, Laos, and Vietnam, with the French still entrenched in Vietnam, where for seven years they had been fighting a frustrating guerrilla war, a war as savagely divisive in France as the subsequent Vietnam War would be in the United States.

When Eisenhower assumed office, thirty thousand tons of

materiel were being shipped to Vietnam every month from the United States. By July 1954 the total U.S. aid would reach $2.6 billion. Agreeing with Nixon and Dulles that if Vietnam went Communist the whole of Southeast Asia would follow, Eisenhower expressed his certainty in a metaphor that became famous and caused much mischief: "You have a row of dominoes set up, you knock over the first one, and what will happen to the last one is that it will go over very quickly."[25]

In the spring of 1954 when the last major French stronghold, Dien Bien Phu, was about to collapse, Gen. Paul Ely, head of the French General Staff, flew to Washington to beg for American air strikes. Admiral Arthur Radford, feisty chairman of the American Joint Chiefs of Staff, without noticeable enthusiasm from the other chiefs, devised Operation Vulture, a plan calling for massive bombing with sixty B-29s, and the dropping of three small atomic bombs. Nixon and Dulles strongly supported it, as did Lewis Strauss, chairman of the Atomic Energy Commission, and Gen. Curtis LeMay, later to become notorious for advocating bombing North Vietnam "back to the stone age."[26]

Eisenhower, who did not believe in using "the bomb" unilaterally, asked Nixon on April 29, 1954, what he thought of the idea of telling American allies about plans to use atomic weapons to save Dien Bien Phu. In a revealing passage, surprisingly included in his memoirs, Nixon wrote, "I said that whatever was decided about using the bomb, I did not think it was necessary to mention it to our allies before we got them to agree on united action," adding that "a few conventional air strikes" might be all that was necessary.[27]

Nixon's and Dulles's acceptance of the plan to use A-bombs on Communist forces at Dien Bien Phu appalled men like Robert Bowie, director of policy planning in the State Department, who felt that the military had misled them in their assurances that the destructiveness of these tactical weapons was "moderate."[28] Nixon had been briefed on the power of the bomb by Robert Oppenheimer, leading American nuclear physicist, who had become a crusader against the use of nuclear weapons and who had even tried to discourage the making of the H-bomb. After the second meeting with Nixon, in which he had answered the vice-president's knowledgeable questions, Oppenheimer told a friend, "I have just come from a meeting with the most dangerous man I have ever met."[29]

On May 5, 1954, Jim Bassett noted in his diary:

RN thinks the temper of the country is for firmness and decision. . . . Formosan Chinese may be called in, though the British (if they join) would, of course object. Use of Chiang's 500,000 troops? Only, says RN, if the Red Chinese make overt threats. . . . "Then, by God, we'd have to employ the atom bomb. Mark my words. . . ."

A week later, May 11, after dinner at the Capitol Hill Club, Bassett described another conversation, "with RN letting his hair down on Indochina." The vice-president reiterated that

the British haven't got it anymore. . . . the Asian mess is significant of dire future events; i.e., eventual confrontation of white- vs. dark-skinned races, unless somehow we can align ourselves on the side of freedom for these downtrodden colonies.[30]

Here Nixon was echoing an ancient demonology, especially rife in the California of his youth, where there was a long history of chronic racist agitation concerning "The Yellow Peril."

Lyndon Johnson, taken into Ike's confidence along with other selected congressional leaders, discouraged Operation Vulture unless the British also agreed to become involved.[31] John F. Kennedy, who was not privy to the secret consultations but who had visited Southeast Asia in 1951, on April 6 warned that no amount of American military assistance in Indochina can conquer "an enemy . . . which has the sympathy and covert support of the people. Pouring money, materiel and men into the jungles," he said, "without at least a remote prospect of victory would be dangerously futile and self-destructive."[32]

Dulles, meanwhile, had devoted enormous energy and guile trying to get the British involved. To a degree Eisenhower went along with this. French Ambassador Henri Bonnet was informed through acting Secretary of State Walter Bedell Smith, that "a resolution authorizing the President to use air and naval forces in Indochina had already been prepared; it might be approved by Congress as early as April 28." Dulles, in Paris, indicated to Foreign Ministers Eden and Bidault on April 24 that even if Dien Bien Phu fell, the United States was prepared to move "armed forces" into Indochina to protect Southeast Asia as a whole. In a display of force, an American aircraft carrier with atomic weapons was sent toward the Indochina coast from Manila. But the British refused to be stampeded. Churchill said privately, "Dulles is the only case of a bull I know who carries his china closet with him."[33]

Nixon's public role in the Dulles effort consisted of an extraordinary war-oriented speech before the American Society of Newspaper Editors on April 16, 1954, the importance of which as a forewarning of his behavior as president in the Vietnam War has been underestimated because of his insistence that he was misunderstood and his quick retreat from the hawkish stance. The speech showed his deep aversion to "limiting" a war as against "winning" a war, and his willingness to employ atomic weapons. And it bared major contradictions between what Nixon was saying for campaign purposes and what he had been advocating in secret.

The speech was billed as an off-the-record address, and the transcript was never released by the White House. But the explosive extracts quickly leaked. They dismayed Nixon's friends, agitated Congress, and jolted the nation. The vice-president who only a month earlier had said he wanted no more small wars, wars which "nibble us to death," now said in response to a question about Indochina, ". . . if to avoid further Communist expansion in Asia and Indochina, we must take the risk now by putting our boys in, I think the Executive has to take the politically unpopular decision and do it, and I personally would support such a decision."[34]

And he who had been condemning Truman for getting into the Korean War, and praising Eisenhower for getting out of it,[35] who had been deploring the casualty lists and commiserating with the wives and mothers of the victims, now said it was unwise to have ended the Korean War without victory, and that thrusts to the north and bombing over the border in China would have meant a substantial defeat of the Chinese Communists. The ending of the war without victory, he said, "produced the present French crisis by permitting the Chinese Communists to increase their help to the Communist-led Vietminh."[36]

The nationwide reaction to the Nixon speech was instantly negative. Eisenhower, who had never favored MacArthur's plans to bomb Chinese bases beyond the Yalu in the Korean War, and who had no intention of going into Vietnam without the British, did his best to soothe congressional leaders and to quiet Dulles. Republican majority leader Charles Halleck had said Nixon's speech "really hurt."[37] When Dien Bien Phu fell with the Americans having done nothing, Ike said to James Bassett, "I want to talk to Dulles. I want to tell him the sun's still shining. . . . Dien Bien Phu isn't the end of the world; it's not that important."[38]

It was generally recognized, however, that Ho Chi Minh had called Dulles's massive retaliation bluff. Lyndon Johnson said, "American foreign policy has never in all its history suffered such a stunning reversal. . . . We have been caught bluffing by our enemies."[39]

Nixon denied that he had ever countenanced sending land troops to Vietnam, and insisted that his statement had not been a trial balloon for the administration. He continued, however, to echo Dulles, telling the Whittier College commencement audience in June:

there is only one threat to world peace, the one that is presented by the internationalist communist conspiracy. . . . Secretary Dulles said it last night, "Peace without surrender."[40]

Nixon was not invited to the nine-nation conference in Geneva in July 1954 which saw the official withdrawal of the French from Indochina and the formal division of Vietnam into a Communist north and a non-Communist south. Dulles—acting, Hoopes wrote, "with the pinched distaste of a puritan in a house of ill repute"[41]—attended for one week only, long enough to cause an international incident by refusing to shake the hand of the Chinese foreign minister, Chou En-lai.

When the conference settled on thirteen principles as a basic agreement for settlement, both Eisenhower and Dulles opposed them, and refused to participate in what was expected to be a multilateral guarantee of the integrity of Vietnam, Laos, and Cambodia, with the Soviet Union and China among the nine signatories. As a result none of the conference participants signed; each nation made its own unilateral declaration. The fact that there were *no contracting parties* and thus *no collective obligations*, Hoopes has written, "had tragic consequences." "Thereafter the United States guarantee stood in splendid isolation." Thus the way was paved for unilateral involvement by Eisenhower, Kennedy, Johnson, and Nixon.[42]

Nixon's role throughout was peripheral, but his conviction that the United States must act unilaterally to prevent the further spread of Communism in Southeast Asia was set in cement. Fearful that Eisenhower might now be charged with the loss of North Vietnam, as he himself had charged Truman with the loss of China, the vice-president now added a new line to what might be called his "Who Is To Blame?" chart. "To sum it up bluntly," he said in Milwaukee on June 26, 1954, "the Acheson policy was directly responsible for the loss of China. And if China had not been lost, there would have been no war in Korea, and there would be no war in Indochina today." Elmer Davis wrote drily in the *Washington Post* on June 29:

The Vice-President is holding out on us. . . . Why doesn't he add that this is the same Acheson who shot Lincoln?

The news that Nixon had favored dropping three atomic bombs to save the French garrison at Dien Bien Phu was not leaked to the press during either the 1954 or the 1956 elections, although there was much general criticism among Democrats about Dulles's having brought the nation to the brink of nuclear war. But had the news been leaked, it would have done him little damage in the party. The Russians had exploded an atomic bomb on September 22, 1949, and a hydrogen bomb in August 1953, and the frenetic race to keep ahead of the Soviets had few vocal critics in either party. Americans had watched with mingled pride, fascination, and horror the pictures of the "Mike" shot, November 1, 1952, the first American H-bomb, which had obliterated the small Pacific island of Elugelab and left an underwater crater one mile across and 175 feet deep, large enough "to hold fourteen buildings the size of the Pentagon."[43] Two subsequent and larger shots had demonstrated that a single H-bomb could destroy any city in the world.

It was not recognized for some time, however, that the tests resulted in unexpectedly large amounts of radioactive debris— ash falling on Japanese fishermen far from the blast had burned them severely—and that the "fallout" could be carried for many miles in the stratosphere spreading a new radioactive isotope called Strontium-90, a deadly poison—a bone-seeker—that could not be discharged from the body and that would create genetic defects, blood diseases, and cancer. Once alerted, many scientists organized and lobbied, imploring members of the Eisenhower administration to stop nuclear testing altogether.

The Federation of Atomic Scientists, with twenty-one hundred members, urged the immediate ending of the testing of large bombs, and were joined by Atomic Energy Commissioner Thomas E. Murray, a Democrat. Another commissioner, physicist Willard Libby, a Republican, argued that the dangers of Strotium-90 were greatly exaggerated. (Later he would reverse his stand.)[44] An alarmed Adlai Stevenson advanced his own proposal to suspend testing of the H-bomb, and urged that the issue be kept nonpolitical. It was not. Although members of Eisenhower's National Security Council, meeting in September 1954, voted *unanimously* for a proposal very like that of Stevenson's, the decision was kept secret and not acted on until months after the election.[45]

Meanwhile Stevenson was denounced by a whole galaxy of Republican leaders, including Eisenhower, who in the face of all the scientific evidence to the contrary denied the fallout danger, called Stevenson's proposal "a theoretical gesture," and implied incorrectly that it would reduce American defenses and bring an end to atomic weapons research. Thomas E. Dewey said the idea was "an invitation to national suicide."[46] Nixon in Philadelphia on October 3 called it "extraordinary . . . appalling . . . catastrophic nonsense . . . the height of irresponsibility . . . naïve . . . the most dangerous theme of the campaign." Ike issued a white paper saying that "continuance of the present rate of H-bomb testing—by the most sober and responsible scientific judgment—does not imperil the health of humanity."[47]

Stevenson, buttressed by an ever-increasing number of appalled scientists who were independent of government, kept up his own courageous campaign of education, although it cost him votes, insisting that continued testing of hydrogen bombs could "destroy the whole balance of life on earth." Russia and Britain, he said, had indicated a willingness to go along with a nuclear-test ban; inspection would be easy: "You can't hide the explosion any more than you can hide an earthquake." He warned of nuclear proliferation, and the possibility of an H-bomb's falling into the hands of a new Hitler.[48] Only after the campaign did he learn of the secret National Security Council vote of September 1956 for a test ban similar to his own. By then the issue had done him much damage. Most of the nation chose to trust the military man in the Oval Office.

Stevenson wrote despairingly to a friend in India on November 16, 1956:

I had hoped that my country might take some initiative in saving the human race from the incalculable risks of this weapon in war and peace. What I fear most is that they rejected my idea for political reasons more than on the merits . . . such wondrous things can now be done with propaganda and a docile press in this country . . . that it may be they will contrive ways of adopting my proposals without discredit. . . . The world is so much more dangerous and wicked even than it was barely four years ago when we talked, that I marvel and tremble at the rapidity of this deterioration.[49]

Eisenhower reversed his stand against testing once the election was over, but ignored Stevenson's useful suggestion that the ban begin with H-bomb testing. On August 21, 1957, he agreed to suspend the testing of all nuclear weapons if the Russians would agree to stop producing fissionable materials for military purposes. Not surprisingly, the Soviets rejected the proposal. In April 1959 he proposed a prohibition of nuclear tests above ground, and this marked the beginning of more fruitful negotiations.[50] The test-ban treaty was not achieved, however, until the administration of John F. Kennedy.

Nixon, like Eisenhower, was belatedly sobered by the fearsome fallout data, and retreated from his easy readiness to drop atomic bombs as in Operation Vulture. Eventually he followed Stevenson in advocating a test ban, as he would follow him many years later in opposing a national draft. But he held fast to his simplistic and unhistorical paradigm, which might be called "the Munich syndrome applied to Asia," and which could be read as follows:

America could have prevented the spread of Communism in China.
America could have prevented the war in Korea by preventing the spread of Communism in China.
America could have won the war in Korea by bombing the Chinese beyond the Yalu.
America could have destroyed Ho Chi Minh with small atomic bombs or massive conventional bombs in 1954.

All of this was predicated upon Nixon's belief in the myth of American omnipotence, a belief that would have deadly consequences in the Vietnam War.

XXIII

Hidden Problems:
The Early Surfacing

Thus the dilemma of a doctor who treats a national leader. To tell or not to tell is not the question. He cannot tell.

— DR. ARNOLD HUTSCHNECKER[1]

WHEN NIXON TOLD MURRAY CHOTINER on Election Day 1954 that he was through with politics, it was no spontaneous statement born of campaign fatigue. He had told many friends earlier that this was the worst year of his life and that he would leave politics in 1956. As proof of his seriousness he would take out of his wallet a small piece of paper with a promise to that effect addressed to his wife.[2] This was the year he had betrayed McCarthy, whose message he had shared and promulgated, and he had watched the slow process of chastisement of the Wisconsin senator by the Senate, climaxing in December. This was the year that the Duke University faculty, sixty-one to forty-two, voted against giving him an honorary degree.[3] Offended and bitter, Nixon cancelled plans to speak at the commencement exercises. He had spoken at Whittier College, which did give him an LL.D. On the platform, before an audience that included his parents and 125 relatives, he said, "To ask a college to choose which of its graduates to honor is like asking a mother to select a favorite among her children."[4] But what had been intended as a joyous and solacing event soured at the reception after the speech, when two lines formed, one made up of students and citizens who refused to shake Nixon's hand.[5]

Although he had been widely praised for his Asian trip the previous year, and lauded as "the busiest vice-president in history," even though *Time*, the *Saturday Evening Post*, the Republican press everywhere, and even the *New York Times* gave him largely steady support, reporters speculated constantly about his relations with Eisenhower. "Was Nixon being taken to the woodshed?" "Would he be dumped in 1956?" He feared inordinately what he called "the whispering campaigns" charging him with "bigamy, forgery, drunkenness, insanity, thievery, anti-Semitism, perjury, the whole gamut of misconduct in public office," all stimulated, he wrote, by the Hiss case. Who reported these rumors he did not say.[6]

The open dislike of some of his colleagues in Congress gnawed at him. Someone told him that Speaker of the House Sam Rayburn had said to a friend that of the five thousand people he had served with in the House Richard Nixon had "the most hateful face." Rayburn apologized.[7] On July 15, 1954, Nixon told Bassett that Thomas E. Dewey was "keeping a spot open for me." Patting the lush upholstery of his chauffeured Cadillac, he said, "This is the only thing about this goddam job I like. Except for this, they can have it."[8]

When facing the 1954 election campaign, Nixon remembered the 46,000 miles, 92 speeches, and 143 whistlestops of 1952, and said to a friend there was some consolation that it would be his last. "I'm tired, bone tired. My heart's not in it." In his memoirs he wrote:

I still resented being portrayed as a demagogue or a liar or as the sewer-dwelling denizen of Herblock cartoons in the Washington *Post.* As the attacks became more personal, I sometimes wondered where party loyalty left off and masochism began. The girls were reaching an impressionable age, and neither Pat nor I wanted their father to become the perennial bad guy of American politics.[9]

Herblock's pitiless cartoons were widely syndicated, and stamped a national image of Nixon as a mudslinging little man with an evil, unshaven face. Nixon would not let the *Washington Post* be delivered to his home lest his daughters see the cartoons. Halberstam reports that the vice-president tried to hide the scarring, joking with the *Post*'s Chalmers Roberts that he "really loved the cartoons," adding, "You know, a lot of people think I'm a prick but I'm really not." In the 1960 campaign, when Nixon worked strenuously to project an image of himself as statesman, Herblock published a cartoon showing him wearing a clean-shaven, pious-looking mask over the sinister and darker face.

Defending his own muted campaign attacks on Kennedy at a Republican policy meeting, Nixon said, "I have to erase the Herblock image first."[10]

During the vice-presidency, it was for a time kept a secret that Nixon was making frequent if irregular trips to New York to see a physician who was treating him for "the stresses of his office." Dr. Arnold A. Hutschnecker, later called—not altogether incorrectly—"the President's shrink," was not a psychiatrist but an internist specializing in psychosomatic problems, in what he called "the emotional conditions—the mystery, tension, the unhappiness," of his patients.[11] Later he called himself "a psychoanalytically oriented psychotherapist." Dr. Hutschnecker had written a popular little book, *The Will to Live*, a copy of which Sen. Sheridan Downey had given to Nixon shortly after its publication in 1951. "I liked it and looked the doctor up," Nixon told Helen Erskine in 1954, adding lightly what was essentially a half-truth, "I go to him once a year for a physical checkup. My heart is strong, lungs in fine condition, blood pressure 120 over 80."[12]

Actually Nixon made the trip to New York more often than once a year, as Dr. Hutschnecker has admitted. Nixon's invaluable press secretary, James Bassett, before his death in 1976 told a friend that Nixon sought out therapy because he was suffering from sexual impotence. His visits to Hutschnecker continued intermittently for four years. Then in 1955, when gossip columnist Walter Winchell raised eyebrows at the frequency of the vice-presidential visits to the doctor's Park Avenue office, they ceased abruptly. This termination, the doctor wrote, was at the urging of Nixon's political advisers, and the vice-president turned instead to a conservative "military doctor" in Washington.

In 1974 Hutschnecker wrote guardedly in his book *The Drive for Power:*

There had been no secrecy about the Vice-President's visits to me. His limousine and Secret Service men had been clearly in evidence in front of my door. At the time I was engaged in the practice of internal medicine, and Mr. Nixon came simply for occasional checkups and to discuss how to deal with the stresses of his office, including the many official dinners he had to attend—in short how to stay fit. There was no evidence of any illness.

But he went on to describe his sadness at the necessity of ending "a trusting doctor-patient relationship," and then expanded on the nature of his own help:

How strange, I thought, that a man in public life would be allowed, even encouraged, to visit a heart specialist, say, but would be criticized for trying to understand the emotional undercurrent of his unconscious drives, fears, and conflicts, or possible neurotic hangups.[13]

The doctor visited Nixon at least once in Washington, where they had lunch in his office. The vice-president, he wrote, "spoke of 'the General,' as he called President Eisenhower, hoping I could see him professionally, and then referring to the foundations of the Capitol building explained that that part of the basement facing the Washington Monument had originally been meant to serve as a fortress with gun emplacements."[14] Dr. Hutschnecker wrote more frankly of the relationship between Eisenhower and Nixon than of any other specific aspect of the vice-president's life. Nixon, he wrote, suffered "debilitating, painful and depressing rejection by an authoritative father figure." Their relationship was "in many ways reminiscent of the ancient conflict of father and son, the elder man watching critically the performance of his son, as if saying, 'show me.' "[15]

That Nixon should have voiced a wish that Eisenhower might also see Dr. Hutschnecker "professionally" suggests his enthusiasm for his doctor. Later Nixon persuaded Gerald Ford to seek him out. Ford did pay him one uneasy visit. Later, when Ford was being scrutinized by a Senate committee for his fitness to be vice-president, Hutschnecker testified that he had never treated him. He also briefly described his work with Nixon, saying that it had ended in 1955 and that he had never visited him in Florida or in California.[16]

Meanwhile Hutschnecker published several articles, one urging the psychological testing of children to sort out the potentially dangerous and to provide treatment for them, which brought him much criticism, and one urging the setting up of a Department of Peace. Harold Stassen, called to the Executive branch by Eisenhower to handle problems of arms control, was dubbed "Secretary for Peace" by the press. The doctor also urged, in the fifties, that "mental health certificates should be required for political leaders."[17]

There can be little doubt that Dr. Hutschnecker, on such a screening board, in 1968 would cheerfully have passed Richard Nixon. He wrote in Look, July 15, 1969:

During the entire period that I treated Mr. Nixon, I detected no sign of mental illness in him. As I came to know him over the years, we developed a trusting as well as amicable personal relationship. There was mutual respect and trust. He always impressed me as a man with superior intellect and keen perception. He was an intense listener and would ask questions aimed directly at the heart of the matter. We became friends, and, as such, we discussed many subjects in an open and relaxed manner. After his election as President, I felt confirmed in my belief, which I had expressed in a casual discussion back in 1955, that Richard Nixon had not only the strength but the imagination and clarity of goal that I thought were prerequisites for a successful leader.[18]

This statement is revealing on several counts. Nixon is *the intense listener,* guarded and questioning. It is the doctor who is talking, as a supportive friend, telling him that he has the intellect, perception, imagination, and strength to be president, and this in the very period when Nixon is threatening to abandon politics for good. We learn from Hutschnecker's *The Drive for Power* also that he gave Nixon useful diagnoses of McCarthy and Dulles, and that he deplored the Cold War. He may even have planted some seeds in Nixon's mind which germinated later, contributing to the relaxation of his intense anti-Communism, and to his eventual conversion to the idea of détente with the Soviet Union. We may assume that the doctor noted Nixon's "neurotic hangups," but these he cannot discuss. He seems not to have found anything frightening about Nixon's psyche in 1955.

Later, in the agony of Watergate, Dr. Hutschnecker wrote in the *New York Times* of July 4, 1973:

A deeply disturbed nation has been watching—in rapid progression— the unfolding of bizarre deeds and the painful spectacle of a group of men who had held powerful positions only yesterday, giving the image of frightened small men as they confessed their crimes and, worse, seemed to have difficulty in dealing with the first law of morality: Truth.

After Nixon's resignation, Dr. Hutschnecker in *The Drive for Power* struggled to explain Nixon, along with Presidents Wilson, Kennedy, and Lyndon Johnson, without violating the confidence of his own famous patient. He writes:

I have not analyzed President Nixon. I have only made my own observations. Some I must keep confidential and others can be shared because other people have reported on some of his attitudes.

Again he describes him as *an intense listener*, adding, "He never asked, and I never volunteered, how I would 'diagnose' him."[19]

We are told in general terms that a drive for power may result from "a painful or enormous sense of insignificance," "an unconscious fear of death," or "an unconscious wish to die and have others die as well." "A sexually inadequate man may seek power as a substitute for poor sexual performance," he writes, and "an excessive drive for power is born out of weakness. . . . it moves on wings of aggression to overcome inferiority." And he adds, "Those whose power to love, and consequently, to create, has been broken or never developed will choose war in order to experience an intoxicating sense of power or excitement.

The doctor is bold in diagnosing others rather than Nixon. MacArthur "clinically (as his own doctor told me) was not a stable personality." Dulles was "a basically angry and mentally disturbed man who kept the world in a state of jitters with his brinksmanship and who if he could have his way, would seek military confrontation with the Russians." John Kennedy, for all his charm and talent, was a tragic figure "not only because of the cruel fate that struck him down at the zenith of success, but because of his constant need to prove his masculinity and his courage."

One can guess that Hutschnecker might well be writing about Nixon when he complains of "man's compulsive need to fight, to live up to some chauvinistic slogan of national honor," but we can be more certain when he writes,

Who gave the orders to defoliate the Vietnam countryside? . . . who covered up and falsified reports on unauthorized bombings in neutral Cambodia, lying so they could continue playing the deadly game of murder? Shall we shrug our shoulders, sweep things under the rug and say, "That is war"? And give the generals a medal for bravery?

The doctor has some perceptive things to say about lying, writing that some patients do not know how to tell the truth even to a doctor, and that politicians, like other men, may not be aware that they lie. By the time the truth is discovered "the damage has been done, a crime has already been committed."[20] Dr. Hutschnecker, writing in 1974, represented the agonizing dilemma of many Americans who had voted for and supported Richard Nixon.

Dr. Hutschnecker, a Viennese refugee from Hitler described by one journalist as "a small leprechaun of a man,"[21] is an intense but gentle doctor who smiles rarely and wryly. He has sharply peaked brows and a corrugated look to his face, as if each of his patients had etched a line in it. His ambition, as stated in the preface of his *The Drive for Power*, is "to leave this world just a fraction less wicked" than when he entered it. A row of ivory elephants, a gift from Nixon, is one of the varied memorabilia that clutter the shelves of his book-filled office. "There's nothing political in it," Nixon had said when he gave the gift.[22]

One question among many that the doctor refuses to answer is what specific problem caused Nixon to seek him out in 1951. No one goes to a doctor who specializes in emotional problems unless he is driven by a special wretchedness. Hutschnecker's *The Will to Live,* the reading of which, Nixon said, had prompted his initial visit, had a great deal in it about the healing of patients suffering from "the will to die." He describes vividly one woman, dying of tuberculosis, whose disease was magically abated for a time by her falling in love. Nixon could hardly have read it without remembering how his brother Harold had died, whereas his cousin Jessamyn West, similarly stricken, had survived. Hutschnecker's chapter "Fight or Flight" is clearly echoed later in Nixon's *Six Crises.*

The Will to Live owed something to Freud, more to Franz Alexander's *Psychosomatic Medicine,* still more to Hutschnecker's own clinical experience. Dr. Carl Binger, who had testified for Alger Hiss at his trial, had read the book in manuscript. If Nixon saw the note to this effect in the "Acknowledgments," he did not thereby dismiss the book, even though Binger had been convinced that Hiss was a truthful man and had denounced Chambers as a pathological liar with a defective conscience, a history of deceiving, and "a disposition to smear, degrade, and destroy."

The volume had many appealing stories of cures for impotence, insomnia, ulcers, fear of death, and psychosomatic pain. Leonard Hall said that Nixon suffered from chronic insomnia.[23] If Nixon's major problem was sexual impotence, as James Bassett said, that surely was agony enough. But there were problems in addition to impotence, insomnia, and stress. Except for William Rogers, Nixon had found no real companionship among his political friends after five years in Washington. And even this friendship had become laced with tension and distrust. Kissinger, who described Rogers as "psychologically dominant" in these years, said Nixon described Rogers to him as "one of the toughest, most cold-eyed, self-centered, and ambitious men he had ever met."[24] Nixon made Rogers his secretary of state in 1969, only to engage in one of the most extraordinarily systematic humiliations of a cabinet member ever seen in the annals of the presidency.

Leonard Hall, who recognized that Nixon "ached for people to like him," described him as "not cold but offish." "No one would look forward to spending a week with Nixon fishing," he said.[25] Nixon admitted in 1954 that he found Washington social life "too much ice cream . . . unattractive and extremely boring. The difficult part is that you can't allow your boredom to show."[26] For Helen Erskine in 1954 he listed his best friends in Washington as William Rogers, Alice Roosevelt Longworth, and William C. Bullitt, former ambassador to France under Roosevelt, surely an odd assortment. Mrs. Longworth did indeed occasionally invite what she called "the darling Nixons." Bullitt, who had written a hostile book on Nixon's favorite president, Woodrow Wilson, with the sometime collaboration, he claimed, of Sigmund Freud, is not mentioned in any Nixon memoir.

Mazo described Nixon in the vice-presidential years as "shy and taciturn," a man who "broods, abhors backslapping and gives the appearance of being a friendless 'loner,' a top-smooth and humorless perfectionist."[27] Mrs. Stewart Alsop, Washington hostess whose parties were celebrated for sparkling talk and whose husband had often written kindly about Nixon, found both Nixons "wooden and stiff," and "terribly difficult to talk to." At one dancing party at their home, she said, "Nixon danced only one dance, with me. He's a terrible dancer. Pat didn't dance at all. They stayed only half an hour. It was as if the high school monitor had suddenly appeared. I couldn't wait for him to go."[28]

Even in game playing at parties that required intelligence and concentration Nixon was unrelaxed and fiercely competitive. W. T. Jones and his wife remember Nixon playing charades at a party in Pomona, California. "He was extraordinarily rigid in sending out or receiving signals in the game," Jones recalled, "and though the situation was entirely social, he broke out into a sweat in his anxiety." "In acting out a phrase he was absolutely riveted to one idea," Molly Mason Jones remembered, "and couldn't switch even if his team did not respond."[29]

Pat was disappointed in Washington, and complained increasingly how little she saw of her husband. To a California friend she said that Dick frequently worked so late in his Senate office he would simply go to sleep there on the couch and not come home at all:

He'll work over there until the small hours of the morning. Maybe if he gets through early enough he'll come back home, but many times he works until two or three o'clock in the morning. He'll curl up on the couch and get a few hours sleep. Then he'll get a little breakfast and shave, and go right down to the Senate chambers to work.[30]

Kornitzer said he came home for dinner only five or six times a month.[31]

Pat told Helen Erskine in 1954, "We don't have as many good times as we used to."[32] She was banned from the "post-mortems" Nixon held after every major speech. James Bassett, who attended many of these sessions, described one after Nixon's speech of March 13, 1954, in which he attacked McCarthy. Nixon took him in his "gold-plated Cadillac" to the Statler Hotel, Bassett wrote in his diary, where they met William Rogers, Ted Rogers, their technical assistant, and "a drab female" who had helped with the broadcast.

"Nixon was in that 'high' mood he always develops after a tough deal like this," Bassett noted. "Hardest speech I ever gave," he said. He took two scotches, "fast, heavy, and straight," and began what was an important ritual for him, calling his political friends and associates to learn their reaction. At three in the morning, Bassett wrote,

Nixon wanted to get Hildegard, the singer, up to the suite for conversation. Ted, our talent expert, drew *that* assignment. But Hildegard was packing for New York City and although polite, seemed rather skeptical, thanking Ted and opining that "this is the cutest gag I've ever heard."[33]

Bassett told another story of taking his wife to a small fashionable restaurant hidden in the Maryland countryside, where he found Nixon with William Rogers and six young Washington secretaries. "Nixon was very drunk," Bassett remembered. Rogers left early but Nixon didn't want to go home. Bassett, then publicity director for the Republican National Committee, was appalled. He paid the bill and urged Nixon into his car. The next day he called Rogers "to chew him out," and called Rose Woods to report the indiscretion. Rose was furious, he said. Rogers shortly sent

Bassett a check for $62.50 to cover his cost of the dinner. Bassett said he never cashed the check, keeping it as a souvenir of the evening.[34]

Pat's natural discretion helped her mask whatever difficulties were corroding the marriage. One journalist, in an article titled "No Trouble in Our House," wrote:

Mrs. Nixon has learned rapidly. She knows when to be the silent, demure partner of the great man who is only a heartbeat away from the White House. . . . She always has the right reply, the right greeting, the gracious smile.[35]

To Helen Erskine, Pat said, "We've never quarreled."[36] But Jessamyn West heard differently from her mother, Hannah Nixon's sister:

My mother told me that Aunt Hannah had a call from Dick to come back to Washington. Pat was not speaking to him. "What will you do?" my mother asked her, troubled at the idea of her sister being asked to referee a quarrel between the Vice-President and his wife. Aunt Hannah replied, "I will go back to Washington and say nothing. I will just help out Pat in every way I can." And she did.[37]

Most politicians are gregarious, requiring constant contact with people for nurture and sustenance as well as for business and pleasure. Many Nixon watchers have been puzzled at his desire to escape from people, save for the ritualistic handshaking which meant an important symbolic touching but no real contact. As vice-president he had three offices, the formal one adjacent to the Senate Chamber, which he almost never used, and the second a suite in the Senate Office Building. But he also sought out a remote single room on the Capitol mezzanine, which Bassett said, "only a birddog could find without a guide." Here he could escape from people. As Leonard Hall put it later, "Nixon loved power, but power to sit in that Oval Office and just issue orders, not to meet with people. He was a complete loner."[38]

In January 1955 when Nixon hired Robert L. King as an assistant, he told him that one of his prime duties would be to "protect" him so that he could have time to study, read, and think. "He needed protection," King said, "and I, as the only male member of his immediate staff in those days, was the chief buffer."

Nixon also told King that *he* needed protection, and must take care to keep himself aloof from others.[39]

For Nixon there was danger in real contact, but what it was exactly that he feared is not easy to define. This tense, taut, humorless man, who through his childhood and even young manhood had found it almost impossible to laugh out loud, and for whom total control extended to pleasure as well as anger, nevertheless could give way to both inexplicable rages and to uncontrolled laughter. James Bassett, who reported several of Nixon's quarrels with his staff, also reported his "laughing fits." Although he had found Nixon to be an inept joke-teller, he said he did enjoy the jokes of others in his special restrained fashion. But there were two jokes, Bassett said, that Nixon especially savored, and which he liked to have told and retold.

The first was about two farmers talking over a fence. One had heard about Alfred Kinsey's volume *Sexual Behavior in the Human Male,* and was regaling his neighbor with the darker discoveries of the celebrated American sexologist:

You know what they say about us farmers in that book—that we copulate with lambs—with calves—with dogs—(pausing each time for increasing emphasis, then, after a final, long pause)—with snakes!

This story, Bassett said, would make Nixon break into ungovernable laughter, and the word "snakes" quite by itself, in company where the joke was well known, would do the same.

The second joke Nixon enjoyed in repetition was about the oversexed man who makes love to his wife before breakfast, who comes home to make love at lunch, and at teatime, and before dinner, and who continues to make love through the night. When, in the morning, his exhausted wife protests, he calls her "Deadass!" Once, on the campaign train, Bassett remembered, Nixon emerged from his compartment for breakfast followed by Pat. Nixon turned to her, and in what apparently was meant to be a new variation of his favorite joke in an effort to get a laugh from members of his staff who were nearby he said, "Deadass." No one thought it funny.[40]

William Safire, Nixon speechwriter, in his memoirs recalled a bizarre Nixon joke. Late at night on the 1968 election eve telethon titled "Dial Dick Nixon," Safire had been appalled to hear Nixon say, on television, instead of "Let's get down to brass tacks,"

" 'Let's get down to nut-cutting' . . . the vernacular based on castration that was so often used in political backrooms." The next
day Pat Buchanan said, "That 'nut-cutting' remark of yours on
TV last night almost killed us all."

Nixon leaned back and smiled. "You fellows ever eat 'lamb fries'? I did,
twenty years ago. Helping some Congressman in Missouri. We all
ordered 'em—tasted like veal, breaded, you know? Then I asked what
they were. They told me we'd been eating sheep's nuts, that the farmers
'bite 'em off.' When this is over, we'll go out and have a mess of them."
Everybody looked suitably horrified and we were laughing as we left.[41]

Nixon's seeking out entertainment and relaxation without his
wife seems to have begun shortly after he was elected senator in
1950, when he began to take brief vacations in Florida. Congressman George Smathers, elected Florida's senator in 1950, was the
most celebrated host of stag parties in the nation's Congress, and
Nixon, although a Republican, was among those he invited to
Florida to the famous Cocolobo Club, on Adams Key. This was a
millionaire's hideout, which had seen parties for Presidents Harding and Hoover. The club was presently owned by Smathers and
three Miami businessmen.

One of the three was Charles G. (Bebe) Rebozo, a handsome,
unmarried Florida native of Cuban descent who had a reputation
for discretion. Since Rebozo became Richard Nixon's closest
friend, and since their relationship, in George Reedy's words,
"remains the most important unsolved mystery in Nixon's life,"[42]
we will look at the story of their early friendship in considerable
detail, and in a later chapter continue to explore the flowering of
this friendship into the presidential years. He was the only Nixon
friend who endured, who still endures in the years of exile, the
only one who was not tossed out, or betrayed, or who did not on
his own choose to flee.

Nixon first met Rebozo in 1950. Richard Danner, an ex-FBI
agent who had been Smathers's campaign manager, introduced
them.

He was tired, worn out, and wanted to relax. I was living in Vero Beach.
He stopped off there, visited with me. He was not dressed for Miami
weather. He bought some summer clothes. I then took him down to
Miami to go fishing. Bebe had a boat. We took him out on Bebe's boat
and that resulted in their friendship.

Eugene C. McGrath later reminded Danner of this occasion:

I remember all too well how you met "the Congressman" in Miami when he was dressed in a heavy winter suit in the middle of Miami heat. You took him to buy clothes, and held his hand during his most difficult days. I also know how fond you are to Bebe, and how much influence Bebe can have on the ex Congressman.[43]

Rebozo, when questioned in the Senate Watergate hearings, said only that on the first meeting Nixon said so little he thought he had offended him. "I doubt if I exchanged a dozen words with the guy." But Nixon sent him a warm letter of gratitude and returned in 1951. The friendship flowered swiftly. After what seems to have been only three visits with Rebozo in Florida, the last one with Pat and his daughters, Nixon wrote to him, on November 28, 1950:

You were wonderful to give us so much of your time, and, believe me, you were just what the doctor ordered. . . . we have put your name at the top of the list for the inaugural ceremonies.

Rebozo was not only at the top of the list; he was invited to share the Nixon inaugural box.[44]

Letters between Nixon and Rebozo preserved in the vice-presidential archive are brief, warm, and unpretentious. In 1955 Nixon sent Bebe for his birthday cocktail glasses with the vice-presidential seal. Bebe's gift to Nixon in January 1956 was a box of fruit and wine. Nixon, who had by then been vice-president four years, and was accustomed to lavish entertaining on his travels, replied warmly,

You know, if we were not already "Florida Californians" your continued kindness would convert us, I'm sure. Now that, thanks to you, our tastes are so cosmopolitan, we certainly are enjoying the generous sized crate of Florida fruit and other delicacies which you were so good as to send us.[45]

Rebozo took Nixon to football games in Miami, and introduced him to coaches and local athletes. Always the emphasis was on relaxation. During the campaign of 1956 Nixon wrote, "I have a feeling that I might be applying for one of the famous Rebozo 'rest cures' after the battle is over." Later he wrote, "One of the reasons why I enjoy myself so much and relax so completely is because everything goes so smoothly, and back of it all, I'm sure, is your guiding hand."[46]

Nixon invited Rebozo to be among the guests in 1957 having luncheon with Queen Elizabeth II. Rebozo wrote gratefully, "It was one of those rare occasions that would never ordinarily come to a poor country boy like me were it not for your thoughtfulness."[47] Shortly after he became president, Nixon invited both Rebozo and Richard Danner to a stag dinner for Prince Philip.[48]

Rebozo was Nixon's age, and they shared in common memories of childhood poverty. Charles Gregory, nicknamed "Bebe" by a sibling, was the youngest of nine children of a Cuban immigrant. He earned money from his earliest years, first as a paperboy, then plucking chickens, later working in a gas station and garage. Unlike Nixon, Rebozo had been a beautiful youth, called "the best looking boy" in his high school yearbook. Although in middle age his face coarsened, he remained handsome, and one woman in the White House said he had "the most beautiful eyes in Washington." Dan Rather said he was "one of the most sensual men he had ever seen."[49]

As a boy Rebozo suffered the usual Miami snobbery against children of Cuban descent.[50] In 1968 one Key Biscayne businessman said of him, when it finally became known that he was the best friend of the newly elected president, "Poor Bebe never had more than five friends, and now everybody on the island is his best friend."[51]

When Nixon first met him in 1950 it was generally known that Rebozo was the one who furnished entertainment for Smathers's parties at the Cocolobo Club, and he was frequently seen at Miami nightclubs squiring handsome women, to none of whom he was ever attached. As one neighbor put it to Clay Blair, Jr., "Everytime I saw him at a party he had a different girl."[52]

The sensitive Jules Witcover saw this as a facade, and thought of Rebozo as being "like Nixon, a loner and introvert."[53] Moreover, when Nixon first met Rebozo, he counted among his friends Florida's governor, Claude Kirk, as well as George Smathers. And Rebozo had been host to Lyndon and Ladybird Johnson, and Sens. Russell Long, Richard Russell, and Stuart Symington. Ladybird Johnson had given Bebe a watch in appreciation of his hospitality. Congressmen liked him because he picked up their checks and asked for no favors in Washington, although *Newsday* reported that George Smathers had interceded for Rebozo in getting a Small Business loan for which he did not really qualify.[54] At this time he made most of his money from two loan businesses and real estate.

Robert Greene, the *Newsday* editor who in 1971 led a team of six reporters to Miami to research the meshing of Rebozo's finances with those of the president, speculated in an interview, "My own particular thought was that he was one of those guys who has an extremely low sex drive. He had a tendency to keep the company of whiskey-drinking, fishing, rather masculine-type men, with the exception of Nixon. Nixon studied the part, but he really wasn't."[55] In 1970 Clay Blair, Jr., uncovered the story of a secret high school marriage, later annulled.

Rebozo, meanwhile, who was too poor to go to college, had worked as a mechanic, then as a steward on seaplanes linking Miami with the West Indies and Panama. He later spent time chauffeuring tourists to swank Miami hotels, restaurants, and on boat trips, and there was probably very little he did not know about the habits of men vacationing in Florida and the Bahamas who left their wives at home. Later he went into the gas station and tire-recapping business, began investing in real estate, and became the owner of a small loan company. He learned to fly, and during the war became a civilian navigator in a Miami-based unit of the Air Transport Command, helping transport empty planes to Africa from Miami via Puerto Rico, British Guiana, Brazil, and then on to Accra, Gold Coast.

When his former wife returned to Miami after the war Rebozo persuaded her to marry him again. He left her after only eight months, and came back briefly. They were divorced in 1950. She married for the fourth time in 1953, and died of cancer in 1957. Rebozo never remarried. Clay Blair, Jr., whose sensitive story, "Bebe's Search for Machismo," was published in the *Boston Globe* on October 4, 1970, underlined the man's loneliness.[56]

As we shall see, Rebozo came to fill two needs in Nixon's life, the need to be shored up by someone absolutely uncritical, supportive, and discreet, and the need to be rich. But the second need Rebozo did not begin to act on until 1962, when Nixon was out of public office. By that time the friendship had been flourishing twelve years.

Bebe Rebozo came into Nixon's life at about the same time he was seeking out Dr. Arnold Hutschnecker. The doctor was eased out in 1955. Although it is evident that Nixon's advisers felt that his seeing Hutschnecker was politically dangerous, it is also possible that Nixon abandoned the therapy because the probing had become too threatening. In any case, it was Rebozo who took over the role of confidant, the one friend who could be counted on to relieve Nixon's "stress." As we shall see, it was Rebozo to whom Nixon turned in many crises; it was he who also shared in the family's happiest times, birthday parties, weddings, victory celebrations. Nixon made every effort to keep his friendship with Rebozo out of the limelight of the press. The Miami friend was not mentioned by the *New York Times* until 1968.

Nixon was also careful to dispel the rumors that he had had psychiatric help, insisting that he had gone to Dr. Hutschnecker only "for checkups." In 1966 he said, "People go through that psychological bit nowadays. They think they should be reevaluating themselves. I fight the battles as they come along. That sort of juvenile self-analysis is something I've never done."[57]

XXIV

Death Wishes

When President Eisenhower suffered a heart attack . . . the heart of all America stopped for a moment, and for that matter, the heart of the world.

— RICHARD NIXON, 1971[1]

WHEN EISENHOWER WAS INAUGURATED PRESIDENT for the second time in 1956, a crass witticism began circulating in Washington: when Nixon heard "Taps" being played he said to his wife, "That's our song, dear."[2] Such graveyard jokes are as old as the vice-presidency. Nixon himself began his chapter on Eisenhower's heart attack in *Six Crises* quoting Vice-President Charles G. Dawes, who described the job of vice-president as "the easiest in the world." Dawes said, "he had only two responsibilities—to sit and listen to the United States Senators give speeches, and to check the morning newspapers as to the President's health."

Nixon apparently cherished the story, only to add that "During the three years I had been Vice President, I had not consciously thought of the possibility of his becoming ill or dying."[3]

No vice-president can wholly blot out fantasies of being an instant president, nor can members of his family. Alice Roosevelt Longworth described cheerfully how when news of President McKinley's assassination reached her as a girl, she "did a little dance of happiness."

I was never so pleased about anything. I didn't give a damn. Father wanted the White House. Father must have the White House.[4]

Lyndon Johnson admitted with grisly honesty that "Every time I came into John Kennedy's presence, I felt like a goddamn raven hovering over his shoulder."[5]

The president, too, is affected by what corrodes even an affectionate relationship. John Adams in 1801, suddenly uneasy in the giant presence of his friend Jefferson, now vice-president, urged him to go to Paris, and made no secret of the fact that his being close at hand made him uncomfortable. Jefferson drily declined. Eisenhower in his first meeting with Nixon after choosing him vice-president plucked on the theme of death. "I want you to be able to step into the presidency smoothly in case anything happens to me." And once, when he and Nixon rode in the same plane, Ike said, "I've made a bad error here," and never did it again.[6]

All vice-presidents try to bury their death wishes, and Harry Truman at least, who lived in an agony of apprehension as he saw Roosevelt's health decline in 1945, did not want to be president. Eisenhower was threatened with death three times during his eight years in office, first with a coronary attack, second with ileitis, requiring intestinal surgery, and finally with a stroke. On each occasion when Nixon seemed close to taking the presidential oath, he was blocked by the return of Eisenhower's stamina. Ike admired Nixon's tact in all these crises, and worked out a memorandum of agreement in case he should be totally incapacitated. But he did not die, and Nixon was left to fight for the presidency against John F. Kennedy without the inestimable advantage of being an incumbent.

Even before Ike's coronary, when Nixon in 1954 feared that he would be replaced by a less controversial vice-president and decided to abandon politics altogether, he betrayed his passion to be president in a candid interview with Helen Erskine. In discussing his unhappiness in Washington, he was reminded of Henry Clay:

You just don't sit down and say: "I'm going to be Vice President or President." Henry Clay was consumed with ambition to be President, but he never made it—though his every action, thought and deed were motivated by his burning desire. . . .

The big test of a man is not how well he does the things he likes, but how well he does things he doesn't like. The thing that destroys a person is to be constantly looking for something else—thinking how much happier you'd be in another job.[7]

Bryce Harlow, Nixon's speechwriter, said, "I think Nixon during that first term had the same dismal inner emptiness that Lyndon Johnson had with John Kennedy as long as Kennedy was alive."[8]

When Earl Mazo asked Nixon why he changed his mind about abandoning politics, the vice-president of course did not mention Ike's heart attack. Instead he said:

Once you get into this great stream of history you can't get out. You can drown. Or you can be pulled ashore by the tide. But it is awfully hard to get out when you are in the middle of the stream—if it is intended that you stay there.[9]

There is little evidence that Nixon, like many great leaders, had had from his earliest years an abiding sense of destiny, although he certainly had been sustained by a powerful fantasy life. But up to this point, as Bryce Harlow has said, he had "climbed up the walls of life with his claws."[10] Ike's heart attack came when he was ready to retreat backward into the law practice that he disliked. After the coronary he may well have come to believe that fate did indeed *intend* that he stay in the middle of the stream of history.

It was a Saturday afternoon, September 24, 1955, when Ike's press secretary, James Hagerty, telephoned with the news that the president, vacationing in Denver, was hospitalized.

"My God!" Nixon whispered.

He was silent so long Hagerty thought the phone had been disconnected. When he found his voice, Nixon spoke like a man who believed himself to be already in command not of the nation but of the crisis,

Are they sure? Doctors can make mistakes. I don't think we should announce it as a heart attack until we are absolutely sure.

Hagerty, who did not like Nixon, delicately kept the decision-making, for the moment, in his own hands.

We are absolutely sure. The press is to be informed in half an hour. Let me know where you can be reached at all times.

For fully ten minutes, Nixon said, he sat alone. "To this day I cannot remember the thoughts that flowed through my mind. . . . it was like a great physical weight holding me down in the chair." When he did move, it was to reach out for the telephone to call William Rogers, a friend, he said, "to whom I could speak with complete freedom." Only when he hung up did he realize that he had not spoken first to his wife. "I went upstairs," he said, "and told her the news."[11]

Dodging reporters, Nixon spent that night in the Rogers home. He could not sleep, nor could he breathe, save with great difficulty. "The pollen count must have been at an all-time high," he said, blaming the problem on hayfever, although his doctors would tell him repeatedly that he had no such allergy.[12] Rogers agreed with Nixon that he should hold no immediate press conference, and should not even permit himself to be photographed.

"Even a camera can misquote or misinterpret a man," Nixon explained in *Six Crises*. "An unconscious, unintentional upturning of the lips can appear in a picture as a smile at so grave a moment."[13] For whatever happened, he had been truly reprieved; he was certain to stay, at least for a time, in the mainstream of history. Should Eisenhower die, he would shortly be president. If he did not die, he would not run in 1956, and Nixon would. Of the latter the vice-president was certain. Describing a meeting the following night with Leonard Hall, Sherman Adams, William Rogers, Jerry Parsons, and Lou Guylay, he said, "I do not think any of us in that room believed Eisenhower would run again even if he recovered completely."[14]

In *Six Crises* Nixon spent fifty pages describing how he faced the possibility of Eisenhower's dying not once but three times. There is nothing like "The Heart Attack" in all the literature of the vice-presidents. He observed everything and forgot nothing. He gives us feeling, nuance, conversation, medical details, all so minutely that one has the odd feeling in reading these pages that Nixon, after September 24, 1955, was preoccupied with little else but Eisenhower's death. His own father died during this period—between Ike's ileitis operation and his stroke—but of Frank Nixon's agonizing and lingering death, coming at a most inopportune moment in his son's life, during the 1956 Republican Convention, he gives us not a single word. There is irony in this omission, but also much that is understandable, for surely, as far as the benefits for Richard Nixon's future were concerned, it would seem to have been the wrong father who died.

After Eisenhower's heart attack, Nixon moved easily and discreetly into the seat of power, chairing cabinet and Security Council meetings, and signing ceremonial documents. "There were no jealousies and no struggles for power among the members of the

Cabinet," he wrote. "Opinion was unanimous that 'the team' must carry on." "I continued to work out of my office at the Capitol rather than in the White House," he said, although had he moved there would have been an instant cry of usurpation. As it was, there was actually intense jockeying for power behind the scenes. Dulles acted as quarterback, maintaining, as Nixon admitted, "a strong guiding hand."[15] Sherman Adams—of whom Nixon said "A lot of us have ice in our veins but on him it shows"[16]—was dispatched to Denver. Sen. Styles Bridges from New Hampshire, a devoted Nixon man, wired him, "You are the constitutional second-in-command and you ought to assume the leadership. Don't let the White House clique take command." But at the moment Nixon's best instincts were in command. "I had no desire or intention to seize one iota of presidential power," he said. "The crisis was how to walk on eggs and not break them."[17]

Ike's speechwriter, Emmet Hughes, often critical of Nixon for his partisan excesses, clichés, and banalities, said that during this period he was "poised and restrained . . . a man close to great power *not* being presumptuously or prematurely assertive. This discreetly empty time was surely his finest official hour." He appeared vastly different, Hughes noted, from the Nixon speaking before worshipful crowds; he was "laconic and clinical, reflective and withdrawn, not confident, but—groping."

What Nixon had not foreseen was that Eisenhower, for whom the presidency had often seemed an intolerable burden, and who had talked about not running in 1956, now in convalescence began to equate the office with the gift of life itself. "It was then," Hughes wrote, "that he really faced the sheer, god-awful boredom of not being president,"[18] and in fighting that boredom he was encouraged by his doctors and friends. Gen. Lucius Clay said, "I don't care what happens to the Republican Party, but if he quits, it'll kill him."[19]

Once he was back in Washington, however, the president found it difficult to respond to the young man who had been acting so circumspectly in his name. Nixon had expected to receive the usual thank-you note (Ike was always more gracious and generous in his letters to Nixon than face to face), but for this, "the most difficult assignment of all—treading the tightrope during his convalescence from the heart attack—there was no personal thank you." Thus Nixon in *Six Crises* reported his sense of being wronged, adding characteristically a denial, "Nor was one needed or expected."[20]

But even this failure to be thanked did not prepare Nixon for the blow that Eisenhower delivered the day after Christmas. Although he had not yet announced that he would run again, and would delay the public statement until February 29, 1956, he suggested to Nixon that instead of running as vice-president he become a cabinet officer in the second term, perhaps secretary of defense, replacing Charles Wilson. Dulles, ill with cancer, would be replaced by Herbert Hoover, Jr. A cabinet post, Ike casually explained, would be better training for leadership.

Nixon was staggered. He knew instantly that this was an effort to dump him, as Henry Wallace had been dumped by FDR in 1944, when Harry Truman became the running mate and Wallace was reduced to secretary of commerce. Bryce Harlow later told John Osborne that Nixon now "went through a period of absolutely indescribable anguish."[21] But in writing *Six Crises* Nixon did his best to cover up the signal rejection. "I did not take the suggestion seriously," he wrote, saying that it was a mere trial balloon.

With people he knew and trusted, Eisenhower liked to think out loud. He would sometimes make what would seem to be completely outlandish and politically naïve remarks just to test them.

He did admit that Eisenhower had expressed disappointment in the polls, which showed that Nixon as a presidential candidate would lose to Adlai Stevenson, although Earl Warren, whom Eisenhower had appointed as Chief Justice, would not. It was a pity, Ike said, that Warren would not leave the Supreme Court to run. Ike indicated he would not "jettison" Nixon at this point. "He felt it would hurt the ticket." Besides, he said, "we could win as handily as we had before."[22]

What Nixon did not reveal, either in *Six Crises* or in his memoirs, was that Eisenhower, after a second suggestion in January that Nixon take a cabinet post, delegated Leonard Hall to tell him bluntly that he wanted him off the ticket. Ike often used such a "prat-boy" to take over unpleasant duties. Nixon's face darkened, Hall related. "He's never liked me," he said. "He's always been against me." What the president had said, among other things, was, "Nixon will never be President. People don't like him."[23] And he explained to Emmet Hughes later, "Well, the fact is, of course, I've watched Dick a long time, and he just hasn't grown. So I just haven't honestly been able to believe that he *is* presidential timber."[24]

For Nixon the president's social slights had become increasingly painful. Not only had he and Pat never been invited to share a dinner in the family quarters in the White House, but also at parties at the Gettysburg farm they had never even been invited inside. Republican party workers at a picnic at Gettysburg in September 1956, watching the president and vice-president talking together, were embarrassed to hear Eisenhower say cheerily, "Did you hear that? Dick says he's never seen the inside of the house here!"

"On that note," William Costello reported, "he seemed fully prepared to let the subject drop, and would have, save for Mrs. Eisenhower, who had simultaneously been reminded of the oversight by Mrs. Nixon. There was a whispered colloquy between the First Lady and her husband, after which the Eisenhowers whisked the Nixons into a jeep and whirled them away to the house for a quick circle of the first-floor living quarters." Not until Christmas 1958 did the Nixons entertain the Eisenhowers in their home in Washington.[25]

In his memoirs Nixon was more candid than in *Six Crises* about the "dump Nixon" movement, attributing it to palace intrigue and fear that he would be "a drag on the ticket." But he continued to write as if he believed the president was sincere in judging that the cabinet post would indeed bring him invaluable administrative experience. Eisenhower was too naïve politically, he said, to see that the media would represent the change as a repudiation. Thus he continued denying "one of the greatest hurts of his whole career."[26]

What made it worse was that Eisenhower at every opportunity praised the merits of Robert Anderson, his secretary of the navy. Anderson, a former manager of the vast King Ranch in Texas, with interests in oil, was a lean, scholarly looking man, deeply religious, who had caught Eisenhower's affection. In the second term he elevated him to be secretary of the treasury and architect of most of his domestic program. Although Anderson was nonpolitical and virtually unknown to voters, Eisenhower vastly preferred him to Nixon as a candidate in 1960. Emmet Hughes had learned this in 1957, in discussing possible candidates with Ike; the president also mentioned William Rogers and Sherman Adams, putting Nixon last.[27] Some of this Nixon knew as early as 1956; the full details he certainly learned with the publication of Hughes's *Ordeal of Power* in 1963. Once again, as in his childhood, he was the least loved among several sons.

It is not surprising, then, that Nixon described Eisenhower in *Six Crises* as a "far more complex and devious man than most people realized. . . ." If Nixon's account is to be credited in detail, Eisenhower was indeed devious with him, and there is good evidence from other sources that he was devious with the press concerning Nixon. Ike would always answer his questions about whether or not he should get off the ticket obliquely, Nixon said, replying "No, I think we've got to do what's best for you."[28] To the press Eisenhower said on February 29, 1956, that despite his "tremendous admiration for Mr. Nixon"—"I am very fond of him"—he would not choose a vice-president until after his own nomination. Seasoned reporters naturally took this as a "dump Nixon" euphemism.

Later, on March 7, when pressed further, Eisenhower said to reporters,

If anyone ever has the effrontery to come in and urge me to dump somebody that I respect as I do Vice President Nixon, there will be more commotion around my office than you have noticed yet.

But then he continued, with yet another body blow to the vice-president, to say that he must "chart his own course and tell me what he would like to do." He had also said to reporters, earlier, what Nixon knew to be quite untrue, "I have never talked to him under any circumstances as to what his future is to be."[29]

But actually Eisenhower was ambivalent. No one can read his letters to Nixon without seeing that there was indeed affection—as for all of Eisenhower's surrogate sons—along with a certain distaste, and real regret that he "hadn't grown." It is said that he treated his own son John in the same fashion.[30] Michael Rogin was probably right when he wrote, "Fathers like Eisenhower always withhold the unconditional love their sons seek. For eight years Nixon had to contain his rage while Eisenhower contained his love."[31]

By early 1956 the polls had made it clear to Nixon that if he was ever to be president he must continue to nestle under Eisenhower's wing. The Republicans had been losing voters consistently since 1946. Nixon had said to party workers in March 1955, "The Republican Party is not strong enough to elect a President. We have to have a presidential candidate strong enough to get the Republican Party elected."[32] If he was jettisoned as vice-president, there was no hope for him, and his best chance to be president lay in the possibility of Eisenhower's dying in office. The president understood this perfectly, saying coldly to Emmet Hughes:

The thing Dick may have figured was that 1960 didn't matter too much, and in the event of my—er—disablement, he'd take over and at least have the presidency for *that* long.[33]

As Walter Lippmann put it in February, "The central thing is that Eisenhower unites the country and heals its divisions. This is precisely what Nixon does not do. He is a politician who divides and embitters the people."[34]

Thus it is not surprising that Nixon dug in his heels, ignored the president's innuendoes and the Hall ultimatum, and chose to fight to stay on the ticket. What Eisenhower could not understand, and even Nixon's friends who were privy to his anguish did not recognize, was that repudiation could toughen Nixon instead of destroying him. Hatred and dislike could be a catalyst, fueling his psyche as much as love. Moreover, he knew that he was held in genuine affection by the Republican right. The conservative Leonard Hall, pained by the Eisenhower ultimatum, encouraged Nixon to battle, as did others on the Republican National Committee. The hostile Sherman Adams wrote later that it was the committee, not Eisenhower, who made the essential decision.

What undermined Eisenhower finally was an organized campaign of key men of the Republican right to improve the Nixon image. It was all done quietly and seemed spontaneous. Sen. Styles Bridges of New Hampshire made eighty-seven telephone calls in advance of the bellwether primary election in his state, scheduled for March 13, suggesting a "voluntary" write-in vote for Nixon as a gesture of support. Of the 56,464 voters who marked their ballots for Eisenhower, 22,936 added the name Nixon. In *Six Crises* Nixon described this as "a surprising, unsolicited write-in." Most reporters recognized it as a disciplined if unusual party maneuver.[35] The device was later repeated in Oregon.

Meanwhile a quiet but feverish in-party effort resulted in private pledges of support for Nixon from eight hundred of the delegates to the San Francisco convention.[36] Nixon's friends argued on his behalf at stag dinners Eisenhower held in the White House. Charles Jones, president of Richfield Oil, reproached the president, "Ike, what in hell does a man have to do to get your support? Dick Nixon has done everything you asked him to do."[37] Rep. Pat Hillings, Nixon's protégé in the House, succeeded in getting a petition for Nixon endorsed by 180 out of 203 Republicans in the House.

Eisenhower who, recognized that he had been outflanked by party professionals, remained aloof for a time, but when he was questioned by reporters about the New Hampshire primary, he showed that he was moving toward acquiescence in the inevitable. What he said was very personal:

apparently there are lots of people in New Hampshire that agree with what I have told you about Dick Nixon. . . . Anyone who attempts to drive a wedge of any kind between Dick Nixon and me has just as much chance as if he tried to drive it between my brother and me. . . .[38]

Still he made it clear that Nixon must himself declare his intention of running before he would endorse him—surely a backhanded indication of continuing reluctance and dislike. And it was Nixon on April 25[39] who had to swallow his pride and call the White House for an appointment with the president to tell him that he had indeed "charted his course," and that he would be honored to be on the ticket. There were striking similarities in this shadowboxing to what had happened in 1952, and it is not surprising that Nixon in his memoirs said, "I felt as if the clock had been turned back to the fund crisis."[40]

But in 1952, after the "Checkers" speech, Ike had boarded an airplane, called Nixon "my boy," and stood with him before a cheering audience in Cleveland to celebrate his forgiveness. This time it was all dismayingly perfunctory. Eisenhower simply picked up the telephone and asked for Jim Hagerty.

"Dick has just told me that he'll stay on the ticket," he said. "Why don't you take him out right now and let him tell the reporters himself." Then he added, "You can tell them that I'm delighted by the news."[41]

Eighteen months later, in October 1957, Emmet Hughes, who had been away from the White House for some months, spent an hour with Eisenhower in the White House. Hughes later wrote:

Our talk swung back to domestic politics, and he unqualifiedly stated his personal choice for Republican presidential nominee in 1960—his new Secretary of the Treasury, Robert Anderson. . . . "Boy, I'd like to fight for him in 1960!"[42]

A fortnight after Nixon's announcement that he would run on the ticket, Hagerty telephoned him with the news that Eisenhower was in the hospital under surgery for ileitis, an obstruction in the lower bowel. Although he seemed to recover quickly, he was in more pain during the convalescence than with his heart attack; he hobbled about, bent over, for some days. Nixon, ever the indefatigable observer, said in *Six Crises* that Eisenhower "became more aware that age was creeping up on him," and told friends that if illness struck again and he could not physically carry the burdens of his office, "he would resign."[43] For Nixon it was now imperative that the president not resign before being reelected.

Meanwhile the new illness stimulated a resurgence of the "dump Nixon" movement. It was obvious that Nixon was now paying heavy penalties for the hatreds incurred in his past, especially with Ike's own coterie. Fred Morrow, a black on the White House staff, wrote in his diary that the mere mention of Nixon's name "outside of one's own household is like throwing gasoline on a smoldering fire."[44] Harold Stassen, recently returned from a disarmament conference in London, who did not realize how solidly entrenched Nixon had become with the Republican National Committee in his absence, presented Eisenhower with a private poll which indicated that Nixon on the ticket would lose 6 percent of the vote. He suggested that Ike choose instead the popular Republican governor of Massachusetts, Christian Herter, and offered to lead a movement for his support at the convention. Eisenhower said he could not lend his name to the movement, but he did not discourage him. The fact that Eisenhower did not at once slap Stassen down appalled Nixon. Friends reported that he was "eating his heart out" with apprehension.[45] But the party regulars moved in, persuading Herter to nominate Nixon at the convention, and forbidding Stassen to see Eisenhower at the convention until he had promised to second Richard Nixon's nomination himself.

Still, Nixon was full of anxiety. It was at this point that he learned that his father had suffered a ruptured abdominal artery and was expected shortly to die. When he flew from San Francisco to Whittier, Frank Nixon urged him to return to the convention: "Don't let that Stassen pull any more last-minute funny business on you."[46] But Nixon stayed in Whittier, watching on TV as Herter put his name in nomination. He was renominated by a vote of 1323 to 1—the single dissenting vote cast for a nonexistent Joe Smith.

James Bassett, who was with Nixon in his father's home, was appalled by the sounds of Frank Nixon's strangled breathing upstairs. "It did not seem to bother Dick but it bothered me. He was busy planning his campaign and I was arguing against his plans to visit all fifty states—told him it was a gimmick to show how much superior he was to the ailing Ike."[47] The old man rallied with the news of his son's nomination, and Nixon flew back with Pat for his acceptance speech. "The skill of the fine doctors who are attending my father," he told the convention, "could not possibly have equalled the lift which you were responsible for yesterday." He went on to eulogize Eisenhower as "the man of the Century."[48]

Frank Nixon died a few days later. He had been in an oxygen tent, suffering from great pain. Massive transfusions had kept him alive eight days.

Talk of Ike's possible death permeated the 1956 campaign; there was no exorcising it. Not since the paralytic stroke of Woodrow Wilson paralyzed the process of governing the country had there been such national preoccupation with the health of a president. The Democrats rode the issue hard. Nixon was called "the vice-hatchet man," "traveler of the low road" who would become president if Eisenhower died in office. Stevenson skirted the issue at first, then said bluntly the vice-presidency was "the nation's life insurance policy," and with an Eisenhower-Nixon victory the nation would "go for four years uninsured," phrases Nixon reported with great bitterness in his memoirs.[49]

At first, at Ike's urging to "give 'em heaven" instead of hell, Nixon took the high road. And the major resources of the party were turned to magnify the new image—the new Nixon—the incumbent statesman, a worthy successor to the beloved Eisenhower. Stevenson mocked at the vice-president who "has put away his switchblade and now assumes the aspect of an Eagle Scout":

People prefer men who "don't have to be changed." . . . A lot of people just don't believe that Richard Nixon is really at home in this role as the Little Lord Fauntleroy of the Republican party. They wonder if he doesn't yearn for his old tar bucket and brush. . . .

This man has no standard of truth but convenience and no standard of morality except what will serve his interest in an election. . . . In one direction lies a land of slander and scare, the land of sly innuendo, the poison pen, the anonymous phone call, and hustling, pushing, shoving; the land of smash and grab and anything to win. This is Nixonland.[50]

Nixon, who had found his own audiences apathetic, became increasingly testy and decided to return (with a nod from Eisenhower) to his old tactics.

I felt as if a great weight had been lifted from me. I had not realized how frustrating it had been to suppress the normal partisan instincts and campaign with one arm tied behind my back while Stevenson bombarded us with malicious ridicule and wild charges.[51]

He attacked Stevenson's plan to end nuclear testing of hydrogen bombs as dangerous folly, and scorned as idiocy his suggestion of ending the draft. The Eisenhower administration had ended Truman's plans for socializing America, he said, and had restored an honest government.

Truman, who was not happy about the choice of Stevenson as the candidate, emerged from retirement to joust again with Nixon. "Why," he asked, "is the Republican Party offering us this over-ambitious, unscrupulous, reactionary boy orator as a possibility for the President? Why are they imposing this terrible choice on the people?"[52]

A Gallup poll just before the election dramatized the extraordinary gap in popularity between Eisenhower and Nixon:

	EISENHOWER	NIXON
Extremely favorable	58%	22%
Mildly favorable	18%	23%
Neutral	16%	27%
Mildly unfavorable	4%	9%
Extremely unfavorable	4%	19%

A fortnight before the election trouble broke out in two areas abroad which made Stevenson's election virtually impossible. Nasser had seized the Suez Canal; Israel had sent a force into the Sinai, defeating an Egyptian army, and Britain and France had joined Israel in an effort to recapture the canal. Eisenhower and Dulles, instead of backing old and respected allies, were putting enormous pressure on both the British and French to withdraw their forces. Meanwhile an uprising against Communist rule in Hungary was being smashed with great brutality by the Soviets. Facing the simultaneous crises, Americans trusted their military hero and scorned Stevenson, who seemed by comparison indecisive and soft. Nixon wrote later that he deplored the Eisenhower-Dulles failure to cooperate with the French and British at Suez, but at the moment he praised the policy as "a second declaration of independence" against Britain.[53]

Stevenson protested vainly against the failure of the Eisenhower leadership abroad. And many thought tasteless his last speech of the campaign when he warned bluntly that Eisenhower might die,

that every piece of scientific evidence we have, every lesson of history and experience, indicates that a Republican victory tomorrow would mean that Richard M. Nixon would probably be president of this country within the next four years.[54]

The election was a landslide for Eisenhower, 57 percent of the vote. He carried forty-one states to Stevenson's seven, and won a 35.6-million popular vote against 26 million. But the vote was a personal tribute only to the nation's continuing love affair with Eisenhower, not to the Republican party. For the first time in 108 years a president went into office without carrying with him either house of Congress. Eisenhower, watching the returns with the Nixons in the Sheraton-Park Hotel, became increasingly sober as the congressional tabulations came in.

"You know why this is happening, Dick," he said. "It's all those damned mossbacks and hardshell conservatives we've got in the party. I think that what we need is a new party." The president left him and went out to receive the plaudits of the crowd and to praise the virtues of his own "Modern Republicanism."[55]

It was Sherman Adams who called Nixon to report the third crisis in Eisenhower's health. "This is a terribly, terribly difficult thing to handle," he said. "You may be President in the next twenty-four hours."[56] Less than a year into his second term, on November 25, 1957, Ike had suffered a stroke. For a day or two it left him with so serious a speech impairment that his jumbling words made little sense. The first night of the illness he had been scheduled to appear at dinner with King Mohammed V of Morocco. Nixon took over as host, with Mamie Eisenhower gamely acting as if the illness was trivial, but confessing her despair privately to Nixon.

The doctors predicted that it would be at least sixty days before the president would be working again; Nixon, with no opposition apparently, made plans to go in his stead to a NATO conference scheduled for December 16. Newspaper editors who would have been the first to denounce Nixon for usurpation during the convalescence from the heart attack, fearful now of a repetition of the Woodrow Wilson experience, called upon the president in considerable numbers to resign. But on the fourth day after the stroke, with his speech returning to normal, Eisenhower took his wife to Thanksgiving Day services at church. Shortly afterward he insisted on assuming his old activities, "acting belligerently," Nixon said, "when anyone tried to shield him from an important issue," saying, "Either I run this damn show, or I'll resign." The very necessity of speaking, as it turned out, was good therapy. Although Eisenhower was extremely sensitive about the words coming out wrong, and embarrassed by minor "fluffs," he made impressive progress and began to talk about "dying with his boots on."

An administration plan was worked out allowing the vice-president to become an acting president during presidential disability, but Nixon said the Democrats in Congress "would not approve any plan which might put Richard Nixon in the White House before the 1960 election."[57] Democrats as well as Republicans prayed fervently for Ike's good health.

John Foster Dulles died of cancer in April 1959. Eisenhower, acting for the first time as his own secretary of state, proved to be superior to Dulles in directing the nation's foreign policy. Ike would have six more heart attacks, but none came in his second term as president. We know that in 1960 Eisenhower gave Nixon his blessing as the presidential candidate, although it did not come without indirect Nixon pressure. Lewis Strauss told Barry Goldwater that Nixon had asked his help in persuading Ike to endorse his candidacy. "Nixon said it was an urgent matter because he believed the President was in very poor health and he was afraid Ike might die before he got round to making a supportive statement." Strauss, who was close to the president, got a strong endorsement, and Nixon wrote a grateful letter, which Goldwater saw.[58]

When Nixon talked with Eisenhower about a schedule for campaign speeches, the president said he would arrange the timing on his own, and delayed to the end of the campaign. The word went out to the Nixon staff that the vice-president "would campaign as a man in his own right, not as Eisenhower's little boy." This was a mistake, Bryce Harlow thought. "They overdid that."[59]

Nixon had brought a roar from the Republican convention when in accepting the nomination he shouted, "Let's win this one for Ike!" But Ike was cool. As the campaign developed and Kennedy pulled ahead in the polls, it was evident even to the president that his own failure to campaign extensively for Nixon was hurting. By October 1960, stung by Kennedy's description of his administration as eight Rip Van Winkle years, he was eager to go on the hustings, and agreed to Leonard Hall's plan for an expanded program of speech-making in the final week. Hall's account of what happened to block this differs from Nixon's. "Nixon wanted to do everything," Hall said. "He wanted no other voice, no other partner." And when he finally arranged a meeting between the two men, with Nixon's promise that he would ask the president to add to his campaign schedule, Hall was astonished to hear Nixon say, almost at once, "Mr. President, I think you've done enough already." Ike turned red, Hall said, and the meeting broke up quickly. Later the president demanded an explanation from Hall. He was still in a rage, and mimicked the vice-president's hunched shoulders and bent head, saying, "Did you see that? When I had a front-line officer like that in World War II, I relieved him."[60]

Nixon's own explanation is in his memoirs. He had received telephone calls, he said, from a tearful Mamie Eisenhower and a worried physician begging him to limit the president's appearances lest he have another heart attack. Nixon felt he had no choice but to curtail the schedule, but he did not tell Eisenhower why. At first, he wrote, Ike was "hurt and angry." "His pride prevented him from saying anything." Had Eisenhower carried out the expanded schedule, Nixon continued, "he might have had a decisive impact on the outcome of the election."[61]

Years later, in his own memoirs, Eisenhower wrote that when Kennedy won he felt as if he had been "hit in the solar plexus with a ball bat." He was "haunted," he said, by the thought that he might have kept the Republicans in power "if I had withdrawn from politics in 1956 and thus allowed Dick Nixon, *or some other nominee,* to carry on the campaign of that year."[62]

By the time of the 1968 election Julie Nixon and David Eisenhower had married, inseparably bonding Richard Nixon and Dwight Eisenhower in a fashion neither could have predicted in their uneasy eight years together in office. Eisenhower went to the hospital in August 1968 with his seventh heart attack, and never returned home, dying on March 28, 1969. When David and Julie visited him during the campaign, he pushed back the coverings and showed them the electrodes attached to his chest. Each one had a circle saying NIXON. They were campaign decals he had pasted on by himself.[63]

On the Throwing of Rocks

The greatest cowardice of all is intellectual cowardice . . . those who have it are afraid to hear the facts, are afraid to listen to the truth.

— NIXON, IN LIMA, PERU, 1958[1]

To SPIT ON A MAN OR WOMAN is a special act of defilement. To hurl stones can be an act of murder. Stones were flung at Nixon by students at San Marcos University in Lima in 1958, one grazing his throat, and in Caracas, Venezuela, the vice-president and his wife were covered with spit when they walked out from under a balcony leaving the airport. En route to the city center, his motorcade was stopped by roadblocks, and the windows of the car in which he was riding were smashed by stones as big as grapefruit. Later Nixon said he had never been in such danger in his life.[2]

An alarmed Eisenhower ordered a thousand troops, an aircraft carrier, a missile cruiser, and six destroyers into the area for a rescue, if it became necessary. When Nixon returned to Washington, Ike met him at the airport, along with the entire cabinet and a cheering crowd of eight thousand.[3]

In *Six Crises* Nixon relates that he had not wanted to make the trip, and had agreed only at the insistence of Eisenhower, who wanted him to attend the inauguration of Arturo Frondizi, the newly elected president of Argentina. Nixon warned newspapermen that the trip, widened to include seven other countries, would be dull. Instead it turned into a trial of fortitude, a kind of medieval ordeal, from which he emerged for the first time in his life a hero, showered with bouquets and telegrams, cheered by throngs in the streets, embraced by the nation's father, and his bravery displayed in photographs in the press of the Western world.

Rock-throwing for Nixon had a deadly significance, ever since his seven-year-old brother Arthur had been hit in the head on a school playground and had died—some thought as a result—little more than a fortnight later. "I did not have any fear," he said afterward. "I am pretty much a fatalist as far as accidents are concerned."[4] However, it is evident that he had courted the confrontations despite many warnings. That he came to welcome and even invite being stoned, as happened in the election campaigns of 1970 and 1972, represents still another dimension in the phenomenon of Nixon as victim-survivor.

Anyone examining this fourth of Nixon's six crises must ask whether other United States officials, making the same tour of Latin America, would have encountered the same hostility. Uruguay, Colombia, Venezuela, and Argentina had all recently overthrown dictators, and there were clashes between the left and the military juntas that had thrown out the old regimes. Nixon's main purpose in helping celebrate the first free election in Argentina in twenty years was to help destroy the impression that the United States had consistently sympathized with the overthrown dictator Peron.

That Nixon himself had a record of embracing Latin American dictators was better known below the border than in the United States. He had been photographed with the murderous despot of the Dominican Republic, Trujillo, and the hated Somoza of Nicaragua, and had praised Batista, "the butcher of Cuba." And although he professed to dislike all dictators, Nixon openly praised Latin American military leaders in *Six Crises* as "a great and stabilizing force" against Communism.[5]

In Venezuela the Eisenhower administration was particularly disliked. Dulles in 1954 had attended an Inter-American Congress in Caracas called to ventilate the hemisphere's appalling economic problems, but had stayed only long enough to introduce a resolution against Communism. Eisenhower had earlier awarded the Legion of Merit to Pérez Jeménez, the recently overthrown Venezuelan dictator, and had granted asylum to him and to his hated chief of police. Jeménez was living in a four-hundred-thousand-dollar home in Miami. Peruvians were angered at U.S. tariffs on lead, zinc, and wool, and the dumping of American cotton on the world market. European nations since 1945 had been granted almost thirty billion dollars in foreign aid, with Latin

America getting but a tiny fraction as much. A three-billion-dollar aid bill passed Congress in May 1958 with only one hundred million dollars for the whole of Latin America.[6] When a gunman put twenty-five bullets into the American embassy in Port-au-Prince, Haiti, on the same day Nixon was mobbed in Lima,[7] the message seemed to be that the vice-president was not the only Yankee official in danger of assassination.

Although the State Department had warnings that Nixon would face hostile demonstrations, officials nevertheless expected that his coming would be deemed an honor by heads of state. Had he confined himself to wreath-laying and negotiations there might have been only five instead of six crises for his first book. What Eisenhower had not counted on was Nixon's appetite for publicity, and his delight in confrontation.

He continued his habit, developed on his Asian trips, of making the "unexpected" stop, usually chosen in advance, where he encouraged questions, bantered briefly with the audience, expounded on the dangers of Communism, meanwhile providing journalists with a lively story they could not count on as emerging from formal diplomatic meetings. One such stop was at the University of Montevideo Law School in Uruguay. "Events worked out as I hoped they would," Nixon relates. "Word that I was there spread like wildfire through the school. Students swarmed around, asking for autographs, shaking hands as I moved into one of the law school classrooms." There he answered questions about "alleged United States imperialism, unfair trade practices, economic exploitation, and support of dictatorships in South America." The few Communist hecklers, he said, were shouted down, and the press notices excellent.[8]

In Argentina Nixon was so intent on mingling with crowds, and engaging in impromptu debate that he got caught in a crush of onlookers and missed the inaugural ceremony of Frondizi, the major reason for his trip.[9] He insisted that the reason he sought out such confrontations was not to convince the adversary, "which I realized was impossible, but to convince those in the audience who might otherwise have been taken in by such persistent and shamefully false propaganda against the United States." He told the National Press Club later that from such student groups would come the new rulers of Latin America.[10]

In Lima, however, there were warnings of serious trouble.

Thousands of leaflets urged workers and students to gather at the gates of the University of San Marcos and bar Nixon's entrance: JOIN US—GATHER TO SHOUT WITH ALL YOUR FACES—DEATH TO YANKEE IMPERIALISM—AGENT OF GREAT NORTH AMERICAN MONOPOLIES AND PARTISAN OF ATOMIC WAR.[11] The university director and Lima's police chief privately recommended that Nixon cancel his visit, as did State Department aides Roy Rubottom and Maurice Bernbaum. But the American ambassador to Peru, Theodore Achilles, warned that not to go would mean a Communist victory. Lt.-Col. Vernon Walters, Nixon's translator, voicing one of his favorite apothegms, said that in France or Brazil the greatest virtue was intelligence, but wherever Spanish was spoken the supreme virtue was courage and the lowest vice cowardice. Ruminating on the problem, Nixon remembered how he had been accosted in Burma by a hostile group near a temple and had "swung the crowd to my side." And he decided, "While I might not be able to break through a mob at the gates of San Marcos, there was a chance that I could face them down and possibly still win the day."[12]

San Marcos Square was thronged with about two thousand demonstrators. As Nixon approached the university, a wooden and stucco building whose pleasant interior courts housed the oldest university in the hemisphere,[13] he saw only a massed throng blocking an iron gate and nence-like grill. There were signs: NIXON—MERCHANT OF WAR; NIXON GET OUT; NIXON PIRATE; NIXON DOG; and shouts of "Death to Nixon!" Following his plan, Nixon emerged from the car with only his translator and one Secret Service man. He approached the students, smiling, and asking the police not to push them back. With Walters shouting the translation in Spanish, Nixon began:

I would like to talk to you. If you have any complaints against the United States, tell me what they are and I shall try to answer them. This is the free way, the democratic way, to discuss the differences we have.

At first the students in front gave way, listening. Some shook hands with him. Walters said he heard one say, " 'El gringo tiene cojones' (the Yankee has balls), about as high a tribute as can be paid in Spanish."[14] But those in the rear began to hurl oranges, bottles, and an occasional rock.

"Pale with anger, but keeping a tight smile on his lips, Mr.

Nixon stood his ground for four minutes," Tad Szulc of the *New York Times* reported. "When one policeman tried to arrest a demonstrator, Nixon said, 'Let him go, I want to talk to him.' "[15] This was Nixon at his most courageous, acting not unlike the Quaker preacher his mother had once envisioned, and in that very Latin America where she had hoped to see him as a missionary.

Then one of the rocks grazed Nixon's neck, and landed in the face of his Secret Service aide, Jack Sherwood, breaking a tooth. His calm shattered, Nixon shook his fist at the crowd, shouting, "What's the matter? Are you afraid to talk to me? Are you afraid of the truth?" As Walters called out the translation, Nixon leaped up on the trunk of his car and held his hand high above his head in a prizefighter's gesture, shouting several times, "Cowards, you are cowards! You are afraid of the truth! You are the worst kind of cowards!"[16] Thus he hurled back upon the students what Walters had told him was the unforgiveable Spanish insult.

Although Nixon wrote in his memoirs that "a shower of rocks rained down on us," and "I realized that we had no choice but to leave," actually none but Sherwood was hit. The stories of what happened thereafter are contradictory. As the car moved slowly toward safety, Nixon said Tad Szulc ran alongside shouting, "Good going, Mr. Vice-President, good going," a story Szulc denies.[17] Nixon wrote that he ordered the motorcade to go on to Catholic University, although Walters said the decision to stop there was entirely spontaneous; when Nixon asked him what buildings they were passing and Walters informed him that it was the university, he said suddenly, "Stop the car!" got out, and hurried up the steps into a classroom.

"A lecture was under way and a startled professor and students looked up at us in evident surprise," Walters remembered. Nixon said to them:

I have just come from the University of San Marcos and I found there that they do not believe in the old university tradition of hearing all sides of a question discussed. . . . I just wanted to know whether this was also true at the Catholic University.

Once he had translated this, Walters said, the students rushed to Nixon, hoisted him on their shoulders with shouts of *"Viva Nixon!"* and carried him back to his car, roaring their approval when he thanked them for their answer to his question. Szulc, reporting for the next day's *New York Times,* had a quite different story. Nixon went unannounced into a literature class, he wrote, and received a mixed reception. Many of the questions, especially those having to do with American tariffs on lead and zinc, were hostile. But mostly the students crowded around him in a friendly fashion begging for autographs. Both he and Robert Hartmann of the *Los Angeles Times,* who was also present, agree that Nixon was not carried by the students on their shoulders back to his car.

Nixon in *Six Crises* said he walked unannounced into a student election:

When I entered the auditorium, bedlam broke loose. . . . I said, "Nothing must interfere with a free election," and sat on the stage with the student officers for about five minutes while they completed the counting of the ballots.

Afterward, he said, he answered questions until "Communist hecklers tried to regain the initiative . . . cut their own loudspeaker into the public address system and tried to drown me out. But the students were so overwhelmingly on my side that they tore out the wires of the loudspeaker, threw the hecklers out of the building and asked me to continue." When he left they were shouting *"Viva Nixon!"* Hartmann remembers some hecklers: one, he said, called Nixon a dictator; Szulc, whose Spanish was excellent, said the student election was a Nixon invention.[18]

There is no disagreement, however, in the several accounts of what happened when Nixon returned to the Gran Hotel Bolívar. The handsome old hotel fronts on San Martín Square, normally a relaxing and pleasant place for strolling, where children play among the sparse bushes of Spanish broom at the foot of the equestrian statue of the Peruvian hero, San Martín, who first threw off the Spanish yoke. But on this day the square was thronged with anti-Nixon demonstrators, many of them converging on the Bolívar Hotel entrance. The Secret Service men, together with Walters, formed a wedge to protect the vice-president, and eased him through the crowd. At the door, as Nixon described it, one of the militants

let fly a wad of spit which caught me full in the face. I went through in that instant a terrible test of temper control. One must experience the sensation to realize why spitting in a person's face is the most infuriating insult ever conceived by man. I felt an almost uncontrollable urge to tear the face in front of me to pieces. .... I at least had the satisfaction of planting a healthy kick on his shins. Nothing I did all day made me feel better.

When he entered his room, Pat, he said, who had been watching anxiously from her fourth-floor hotel room window, "rushed over and embraced me."[19]

In his Lima press conference that afternoon, Nixon described what happened: "One of the demonstrators spat in my face. He was spitting on the good name of Peri and on the memory of San Martín, on the thousands of men and women who died for the cause of freedom. This day will live in infamy in the history of San Marcos university." He went on once again to attack the demonstrators as cowards, not physical but intellectual cowards, "who are afraid to hear the facts, are afraid to listen to the truth."[20]

Everywhere he went afterward, Nixon said, "I was hailed as a hero in Peru." Cheering crowds tried to erase the memory of the jeering students. Bouquets filled his hotel room; telegrams of apology and admiration covered his table. Ike wired him: "Dear Dick, Your courage, patience, and calmness in the demonstration directed against you by radical agitators have brought you a new respect and admiration in our country." The Lima *El Commercio* showed a cartoon of Nixon astride a bucking horse labeled Communism, with the caption, as translated in the *Los Angeles Times*, "He's an ornery critter, but I'll ride him at home and abroad."[21]

The only jarring note came from his military aide, Robert Cushman, who reported that State Department officials Rubottom and Bernbaum were saying that "the episode had embarrassed the Peruvian Government and had compromised the good-will of the entire tour." Nixon in a rage ordered the two men to his room, although they were then dressing for a state dinner.

"The two men appeared half dressed before me," he said. "I ripped into them." He demanded their unqualified loyalty, and defended his own actions:

we are up against opponents who are out to beat us, not just hold their own. We, too, must play to win. Too often what we try to do is to play not to lose. What we must do is to act like Americans and not put our tails between our legs and run away every time some Communist bully tries to bluff us.

The metaphor surfaced once again in his account in *Six Crises,* when he wrote that the problem of facing the students at the San Marcos gate was not "simply a case of Nixon being bluffed out by a group of students, but of the United States putting its tail between its legs and running away from a bunch of Communist thugs."[22]

Nixon's intelligence sources predicted hostile demonstrations in Ecuador and Colombia, but they did not materialize. Still, when he learned of plans for a huge anti-American rally in Caracas, and rumors of plots to assassinate him, he was prudent enough to ask for assurances of protection from the Venezuelan government. Jeménez had been overthrown by a popular-front coalition which included Communists, and the party was no longer outlawed. Nixon was promised police protection, and his Secret Service unit was raised from four to twelve men.

Having made a point with his own aides of not "running away," Nixon would probably have risked the perils of Venezuela at all cost. But he had become cocksure. San Marcos, he said, had been "a graduate course in how to handle a mob":

A mob has lost its temper collectively. An individual dealing with a mob must never lose his . . . since those who make up a mob are basically cowards, one must never show fear. Since a mob is not intelligent, but stupid, it is important whenever possible to confront it with an unexpected maneuver.[23]

In a barbershop in Quito, Ecuador, Nixon told reporters that when a situation became tough he became "analytical and cold." "I did not lose my temper," he said. "When someone is trying to damage you—to tear you up—the way to hurt him is not to become angry, but handle him with detachment."[24]

But Nixon had lost his temper at San Marcos gate. He had called the students cowards, and later he had kicked the shin of the man who spat at him. News of this traveled, as did news of his fulminations against Communists, and Nixon would discover that what he was to meet in Caracas was not stupidity and loss of temper but organized deadliness. When he landed at Maiquetía airport, twelve miles from Caracas, he was met by the largest crowd on the tour. Walters, listening to the chanting, GO HOME NIXON: YANKEE IMPERIALIST, and numerous obscenities, whispered, "They aren't friendly, Mr. Vice President."

Walking out of the airport, Nixon and his wife were subjected to a rain of spittle. "I was almost beside myself with anger and a sense of helpless frustration," Walters said. "The police made no attempt to interfere." "Pat shared this trial at my side," Nixon said. "In one sense, I was horrified that she should be subjected to it. In another sense, I was proud that she was with me." As they walked to the limousine, her new red suit stained, Robert Hartmann of the *Los Angeles Times* said that Pat reached out between the bayonets to shake the hands of a girl demonstrator, and that "hate came off the girl's twisted face." Nixon said that she "turned her head and wept in shame."[25]

The Nixons were scheduled to go to Bolívar's tomb in the Panteon Nacional for a wreath-laying ceremony, but even before reaching the city limits in Caracas they ran into roadblocks. The first was a dump truck in the center of the street. When the motorcade stopped, men approached, ripped the flags off Nixon's car, and began kicking at the fenders and doors. As the Secret Service men pushed them away with their flat palms, the police moved the truck and the cars moved forward. The third blockade was a major traffic tieup, with buses, trucks, and automobiles blocking Nixon's way, worsened by the noon-hour traffic. Out of the side streets gathered what photographs showed to be about a hundred fifty men, some carrying rocks, sticks, and lengths of pipe. They beat the limousine shouting, *"Muera Nixon!"* Pictures taken by the press photographers in the truck ahead showed the motorcycle police escort staring stolidly and motionless.

Three windows were smashed in the Nixon car. The Venezuelan foreign minister, Oscar Garcia-Velutini, got a splinter of glass in his eye and became, Walters said, almost hysterical. Walters's own mouth was full of broken glass, his lips bleeding. "Spit the glass out," Nixon ordered. "You are going to have a lot more talking to do in Spanish for me today."

"My first thought was of Pat," Nixon later wrote. "I looked through the rear window and was relieved to see that the mob was concentrating on us and ignoring her car." When the mob began to rock the limousine, Secret Service men Jack Sherwood and Wade Rodham pulled their revolvers. "Let's get some of these sons-of-bitches," Sherwood said.

"Put that away," Nixon ordered. "You take it out when they open the door and grab for me and not before. You don't shoot unless I tell you to."

"Why I did this at the time," Nixon wrote, "I cannot say, except that I knew intuitively that the firing of a gun would be the excuse for the mob to get completely out of hand."[26]

After twelve excruciating minutes the police fired a tear gas bomb, and as the press truck pulled forward down the wrong side of the street Nixon's limousine followed, with Mrs. Nixon's car behind. Walters wrote later that the windows in her limousine were also shattered; actually only the flag was torn off her car. Windows were shattered in the third car.

Nearing the Panteon Nacional, they saw a great crowd assembled, and at this point Walters persuaded Nixon to abandon the assignment and drive to the safety of the American embassy. Once out of the danger zone, they stopped at a hospital where the foreign minister could get medical attention, and it was at this stop that Nixon first communicated with his wife. Here, again, memories vary. Nixon wrote, "I went back to the car and found that Pat was probably the coolest person in the whole party." Walters, however, wrote that Nixon directed him to go back to her car. He found her, he said, "in a very composed fashion, with her hands folded on her lap," and said formally: " 'Mrs. Nixon, the Vice-President wants to know how you are. He says he is all right and we are going to the American Embassy residence.' She looked at me quietly and said, 'Tell him I'm all right too, but it was quite a sight to watch him from back here.' " Robert Hartmann, who was in the press truck, wrote for the *Los Angeles Times,* "Pat was magnificent today . . . only when newsmen cheered her did her eyes fill with tears."[27]

At the embassy Nixon learned that the crowd in the central square had destroyed the American wreath, had manhandled members of the embassy staff, and had had to be dispersed by soldiers. Later, he said, a cache of homemade bombs intended for his assassination had been found. Meanwhile communications between Caracas and Washington had become fouled, and Ike received word that the Venezuelan security system had broken down completely. He ordered two companies of paratroopers and two companies of marines airlifted into the area as fast as possible. Fearful that the embassy itself might be under attack, military authorities planned to parachute the soldiers into Venezuela and secure the airfield. This would be followed by a sea landing with marines from the missile cruiser *Boston* and the carrier *Tarawa*. Helicopters were to rescue Nixon at the embassy and bring him to the airport. By the time the vice-president left Caracas, the carrier, cruiser, and six destroyers were only thirty miles off the coast.[28]

When word of these plans—officially called Operation Poor Richard—reached Nixon, he was aghast. Venezuelan troops were now in command of the city and the crisis was past. Nixon needed no rescue and wanted Eisenhower's aid even less. Moreover, he knew enough history to remember the resentment aroused by United States military incursions into Latin America in the past. Forty-four years earlier, in 1919, when a U.S. naval officer and seven seamen from the U.S.S. *Dolphin* had been arrested in Tampico, Mexico, and marched through the streets, President Wilson had demanded a formal apology and a twenty-one-gun salute to the American flag. When dictator Victoriano Huerta refused, Wilson sent naval forces which occupied the port of Vera Cruz for nearly seven months. Latin Americans had never forgiven the humiliation, and Nixon guessed correctly that the Eisenhower rescue gesture would be misread and exploited. Nixon did his best to mitigate the damage with public assurances that the Venezuelan government was in control, and blamed the problems on the former dictatorship. He said his government would not oppose the extradition of Jeménez and his police chief, and would send them back to Caracas for trial, but that the Venezuelan government had never requested it.

The damage, however, was irreparable, and counteracted whatever good Nixon had accomplished. The combination of his own provocations and Eisenhower's overreaction caused a rash of criticism at home. The *New York Times* called the sending of troops "publicly threatening and futile," Walter Lippmann called the tour "a diplomatic Pearl Harbor," and the *Boston Globe* said it was "one of the most ineptly handled episodes in this country's foreign relations." The *New York Post* said that Nixon "had established his valor in Peru. His insistence on a repeat performance in Venezuela indicates that he was utterly seduced by his press notices, and was incapable of recognizing his own limitations." Eleanor Roosevelt in her column said it was natural for a young man to want to "prove his courage" but called the trip unwise.

Many editorials demanded a new look at Latin American policy.[29]

Despite this, the Eisenhower administration turned the event into a party triumph. Nixon delayed his return home by one day so that "a welcoming reception" could be arranged. Government officials in Washington were told they could give a holiday to their employees, who were urged to take part in the city fete. Leaders of Congress were at the airport as well as the president and his cabinet, along with fifteen thousand cheering citizens. Lyndon Johnson, then Democratic majority leader, was among the first to embrace the vice-president. When a reporter, who had earlier heard Johnson privately call Nixon "chicken shit," asked him about the embrace, it is said that Johnson replied, "Son, in politics you've got to learn that overnight chicken shit can turn to chicken salad."[30]

One hundred thousand lined the streets to see the Nixon and Eisenhower motorcade approach the White House under a triumphal arch made by the extension ladders of fire trucks. Standing with his wife before the microphone at the White House entrance, Nixon said, "I don't think either of us has ever been so moved."[31]

For weeks afterward the Nixons met spontaneous applause wherever they went. Thousands of telegrams from a cross section of America poured into the vice-presidential office. The *New York Herald Tribune* editorialized:

The flag that was dragged in the dirt of Caracas was the flag of all of us. The spittle that struck Nixon and his wife was meant for all of us. And the perils which Nixon braved were braved for all of us.[32]

In June the polls for the first time showed Nixon leading Adlai Stevenson for president, and running even with John F. Kennedy. James Reston, who held that Nixon had been "sent south as a substitute for policy," described the phenomenon somewhat acidly:

As an exercise in national self-bamboozlement, the reaction here to the Vice President's trip is a classic. A national defeat has been parlayed into a personal political triumph, and even when the Nixons are decorated for good conduct under fire, the larger significance of this event cannot be overlooked.[33]

Many Democrats suspected that the trip had been designed from the beginning to build up Nixon as a candidate. Columnist Gerald W. Johnson wrote in *The New Republic* on May 26:

Protection of the honor and dignity of the United States is worth a war; but the nomination of Slippery Dick Nixon is not worth the life of the dumbest doughface in the United States Army.[34]

But it was Eisenhower who took the brunt of the criticism, after all the heroics faded, and the caustic editorials did not further endear the vice-president to his chief. In his memoirs Ike, who had himself been booed by Communist crowds in Europe in 1951—"When the fences are painted 'Go home, Ike!' you feel it," he had said—gave only a perfunctory single page to the whole of Nixon's tour.[35]

Ike's popularity, thanks to the most serious recession since 1946, had now shrunk to an all-time low, 49 percent, and he faced the 1958 elections with dread. Sherman Adams, his most trusted aide, found to have been involved in petty graft, had been forced to resign, and the Republican administration lost much of its reputation for purity.[36] Many blacks were deserting Eisenhower as it became increasingly clear that he was dismayed with the Supreme Court decision ordering desegregation of the schools. His delay in ordering troops to assist in the integration of schools in Little Rock, Arkansas, where black children had been subjected to shocking abuse—seen by Americans nationwide on TV—cost the Republicans dearly. Nixon had been taunted by shouts of "Little Rock" in Latin America.[37]

The Soviet launching of the first space satellite, Sputnik, had, in Nixon's words, "cast doubts upon the Administration's defense and science programs." A thoroughly dispirited vice-president campaigned doggedly, stumping twenty-five thousand miles in twenty-five states, but the Republicans lost twelve seats in the Senate and forty-eight in the House. "It was the worst defeat in history," he admitted, "ever suffered by a party having control of the White House."[38]

Thus Nixon learned how ephemeral is the life of the hero in politics. As he noted dryly in Six Crises, the same Nelson Rockefeller who had cabled him in Peru, "Your courage and determination have inspired democratic forces throughout the hemisphere," on November 9 replied in Spanish to reporters in Venezuela who asked him "What about Nixon?" " 'No tengo nada quever con Nixon,' I have nothing to do with Nixon."[39]

Later, with the publication of Six Crises Nixon recaptured

some of the public glory he had lost so quickly; his account of the Caracas episode was dramatic; the courage he and his wife demonstrated was not overstated. And he rewrote the experience more briefly for a still larger audience in his memoirs. Most important, Nixon and members of his staff learned from the Latin American violence the value of the thrown rock. On October 17, 1970, when Nixon was in Burlington, Vermont, giving support to the candidacy of Winston Prouty in his race for the Senate, two or perhaps three rocks were thrown from the crowd. One, a chip of cement, landed about one hundred fifty feet from the president's plane. Charles Colson said to a reporter, "Those rocks will mean ten thousand votes for Prouty." Nixon "mentioned the rock-throwing at every subsequent stop," John Osborne noted, "and would continue to mention them the following week." Nixon's men ordered the police to floodlight the hecklers each night, so that the president could make his set statement against obscenities and rock-throwing. Once, Osborne noted, the staging was unsynchronized; the audience failed to notice the hecklers, and the effect was ludicrous.[40]

At the height of the protest against the Vietnam War, five days before the election of 1970, when Nixon was leading a rally in San Jose, California, reporters received word in advance that there might be trouble that night. The president left the auditorium to face a crowd of about two thousand. What followed was a remarkable replay of the saga of San Marcos gate. As Nixon described it,

They were chanting their favorite slogans, including "One, two, three, four—we don't want your fucking war," and I could not resist showing them how little respect I had for their juvenile and mindless ranting. I stood on the hood of the car and gave them the V-sign that had become my political trademark.

Reporters heard him say to an aide, "That's what they hate to see!" "It had a predictable effect and a chorus of jeers and boos began," Nixon wrote, "Suddenly rocks and vegetables were flying everywhere. Within seconds I was inside the car and Secret Service agents were following emergency evacuation procedures."[41] Nixon aides, according to columnists Rowland Evans and Robert Novak, were "jubilant." The next day Nixon called the young rebels not "cowards" but "misfits," and said, "It is time to sweep that kind of garbage out of our society."[42]

On October 14, 1972, Nixon's closest adviser in the White House, Robert Haldeman, received from an election advance man a memo stating that in a forthcoming rally where Nixon was to appear with Billy Graham they "could expect demonstrations that were 'violent.' " Haldeman wrote "Good" in the margin.[43]

Nixon had learned in Latin America that to stand up against stoning was political good fortune. It was also proof to the populace that "the Yankee has balls." The opportunities for encouraging repetition he found irresistible.

XXVI

Khrushchev

There is no question but that Khrushchev wants to rule the world.

— KONRAD ADENAUER TO NIXON, 1959

I should love to have been by your office and shaken hands, and I would love to have talked to you and found out how to run the world.

— NIXON TO HIS WHITE HOUSE STAFF, THE LAST SPEECH, AUG. 9, 1974[1]

JAMES BASSETT was fond of telling a story of how Nixon, as vice-president in 1960, in a manic mood after a few drinks, told several of his staff who were Catholics how much he would like to be the pope. "He spent an altogether extraordinary but irrecoverable twenty minutes elaborating on how well he would run the Vatican," Bassett said. "I wish to God I'd had a tape recorder."[2] It was rare for Nixon to open any kind of window into the wilder aspects of his fantasy life, but there was no doubt among his friends and newsmen that from 1952 onward Nixon's determination to be president had been no mere fantasy but a controlled and consuming ambition which occupied the greater part of his waking life. The solid surge of popularity as a result of his "ordeal" in Latin America had taught him that he might even overcome the common vague distaste for his image and win the respect of a majority of Americans as a man of fortitude under fire. That his preoccupation was with power and not people, Leonard Hall sensed early. "He loved power, but power to sit in that Oval Office and just issue orders, not to meet with people. . . . He was a complete loner."[3]

After Dulles resigned as secretary of state on April 15, 1959, Eisenhower assumed full control of U.S. foreign policy, and set forth on a series of world tours to improve his country's image. Except in Latin America, where he was subjected to some harassment from students and Peronists, his trips were those of "the first man of the world." The memory of his victory over Hitler was still fresh. He was feted by the great and cheered by hundreds of thousands. Nixon could no longer tour as a hanger-on to the hero's coattails, but must establish his own heroic image, as he had begun to do in Lima and Caracas. Thus in 1959 he planned to seek out, in a special display of courage, his most obvious international enemy, the Soviet premier Nikita Khrushchev, who was one of the world's most aggressive verbal swordsmen.

When Stalin died in 1953, Khrushchev as first secretary of the party had become part of the oligarchy that assumed power. He did not rise to supreme power until 1956, when he elbowed out Premier Nicolai Bulganin after a sensational speech to the Soviet Communist party on February 5 denouncing Stalin for his murderous purges of the 1930s and his creation of a "cult of personality." In June 1957 Khrushchev expelled his remaining rivals, Molotov, Malenkov, Kaganovich, and Shepilov, from the Central Committee, but did not execute them, and it seemed to many that patterns set by the psychopathic Stalin were being replaced by some degree of reasonableness and sanity. As Mikoyan said to Nixon, "We sleep much better now since Comrade Khrushchev is our Premier."[4]

Khrushchev had freed many political prisoners, and was urging "peaceful coexistence" with the West and actively seeking accommodation with the United States. He had, however, brutally crushed the Hungarian uprising of October 1956, which had succeeded briefly in expelling Soviet troops. During the rebellion, which left twenty thousand people dead, two hundred thousand Hungarians had fled into Austria. Eisenhower had sent Nixon to Vienna on Operation Mercy to help supervise the admission to the United States of 21,500 of the refugees, and the vice-president had denounced Khrushchev as "the butcher of Budapest." The Soviet premier had recently caused consternation in the West by announcing that if American troops were not withdrawn from Berlin in six months he would turn the city over to East Germany.

For Nixon, the foremost anti-Communist in the United States, to confront the Soviet leader in his own capital seemed a dangerous adventure, a young David seeking out Goliath. Nixon himself told the story of how a twelve-year-old boy, caddying for him and

William Rogers shortly before he left for the Soviet Union, when told by Rogers that the vice-president would shortly be flying to Moscow, replied, full of concern, "Won't they shoot him down?"[5]

Khrushchev had already been an affable if volatile host to several Americans. Adlai Stevenson had talked with him for over two hours in August 1958. Stevenson found him "friendly, stubborn, shrewd—tired and old," asking repeatedly how to improve relations with the United States.[6] Only when Stevenson mentioned the Soviet "intervention" in Hungary did Khrushchev become angry, retaliating by denouncing Eisenhower for his recent military incursions in Lebanon, Jordan, and Guatemala. To Stevenson, as to all Western visitors, he distinguished between his personal admiration for Eisenhower and his abhorrence for American foreign policy. In expressing his rage at being encircled by troops in hostile bases in Europe, he blamed Dulles. In talking of Dulles's desire to roll back the Iron Curtain, he said curtly, "History will roll him back." Later, in his memoirs, Khrushchev described Dulles in Geneva in 1955 as "that vicious cur . . . always prowling around Eisenhower, snapping at him when he got out of line."[7]

Hubert Humphrey had also interviewed Khrushchev in 1958. The Soviet premier liked the brash, voluble young senator from Minnesota, called for an impromptu dinner to be sent in, and kept him talking for over eight hours. He jabbed and poked like a boxer, Humphrey said, shifting and feinting, leaping from sentimental reminiscences of his boyhood and the death of his son in World War II to a harsh denunciation of Dulles. In a boistrous confidence he called his comrades Bulganin and Voroshilov "fools," and then said slyly, "Now I've told you about my fools; you tell me about yours." At one point, after asking Humphrey to point out his hometown, Minneapolis, on a world map, he said jovially, "I promise you, we shall never bomb it." He was at his most acrimonious in talking about American troops in Berlin, which he called "a bone in my throat."

Humphrey's interview won him a cover picture on *Life*, and national discussion of his potential as a presidential candidate. The interview had been a testing of some severity, and Humphrey looked back on it with satisfaction. "I knew now," he wrote in his memoirs, "that I was able to deal effectively with heads of state."[8]

Nixon wanted to repeat and improve on the Humphrey experience. He found an excuse to visit Moscow in discussions with

Abbott Washburn, deputy director of USIA (U.S. Information Agency), who was arranging for the first American exhibition ever held in the Soviet Union. A scientific exhibition from Russia, including a model of Sputnik, had been shown in New York City in early 1959, and Nixon had spoken at the opening. He asked now to open the exhibition in Moscow.

Eisenhower was easily persuaded to let him go. Ever since Sputnik had underlined the mutual vulnerability of the Soviet Union and the United States, and even more since the Russians had demonstrated their superiority in rocketry by sending a probe to the moon, the president had been eager to better relations with the Soviets. Moreover, Eisenhower was bitter about the costs of maintaining American ground forces in Europe. "They bother the devil out of me," he told Emmet Hughes, "ground forces that *we* supply while Germany enjoys the great bonanza of not paying for its own defenses and France wastes all its forces trying to settle Algeria. . . . Airbases ought to be enough, with our nuclear power, to defend these places—*not* ground troops." And he toyed anew with an idea earlier vetoed by Dulles, of inviting ten thousand Russian students of college age to study in the United States.[9]

Freed increasingly from the influence of his secretary of state, who had been called by one European editor "the conscience and strait jacket of the Free World,"[10] he decided to invite Khrushchev to the United States. Fearful, however, lest his heavy-handed and volatile vice-president damage the negotiations, he kept the invitation, sent on July 11, secret from Nixon until the day before Nixon's departure on July 28. Then he cautioned him that he must not discuss the invitation with Khrushchev save in absolute privacy. On August 3, when Ike finally announced that Khrushchev was coming, he humiliated Nixon by making the whole matter public in a press conference. The president's syntax, as often, was garbled, but the lack of confidence in Nixon he made very clear:

I told him, and I said, "So that you will not be astonished or surprised and feel let down by your government, should they [references to Khrushchev's coming] be opened up by the other side, if you are not, yourself, and of course will not open this subject."[11]

The president sent along in Nixon's party his own brother, Milton, who disliked Nixon,[12] and Admiral Hyman Rickover, father of the atomic submarine, who was eager to see the atomic ice-breaker *Lenin,* recently finished by Soviet engineers. Also in the party was a tough critic of Soviet policy, Harvard's William Yandell Elliott, mentor of the still-unknown Henry Kissinger.

Nixon prepared for this ordeal as for none other in his life. He interviewed scores of experts, and was briefed to answer questions from Khrushchev on over a hundred topics. He sought out Humphrey, and journalists Bill Hearst and Bob Considine, who had interviewed Khrushchev, also Walter Lippmann and Turner Catledge, managing editor of the *New York Times*—everyone it would seem but Adlai Stevenson. He visited the dying Dulles, who was still lucid enough to warn him to tell Khrushchev that his protestations about peace, in the light of his actions, "had a false and hollow ring."[13]

Nixon got personal appraisals of Khrushchev from Britain's Prime Minister Harold Macmillan and Chancellor Konrad Adenauer of Germany. Macmillan, who had found the Soviet leader "expansive, irrepressible, eloquent . . . petulant," and occasionally "impossible but not unlovable," told Nixon he thought he "desperately wanted to be 'admitted to the club'—accepted and respected as a major world figure in his own right."[14] Adenauer said to Nixon, "There's no question but that Khrushchev wants to rule the world. But he does not want war. He does not want to rule a world of ruined cities and dead bodies." And he told Nixon of one exchange when the Soviet premier had burst out, "I will see you in Hell before I will agree with that," to which Adenauer, then past eighty, had replied, "If you see me in Hell, it will only be because you were there before I got there."[15] Thus Nixon was nerved for the expected verbal assault.

Insomnia always plagued Nixon in crises, and the coming confrontation with Khrushchev on July 25, 1959, kept him awake through most of his second night in Moscow. At 5:30 A.M. he arose and asked to be driven to the big Danilovsky produce market. The choice was not accidental:

As a boy, working in my father's store, I used to drive a pickup truck to the produce markets in Los Angeles in the early morning hours so that I could get the fresh fruits and vegetables back in the store ready for sale when we opened at 8:00. I thought it would be interesting to compare the Soviet market . . . with the one I had known as a boy.[16]

It was also a going back in time to the bickering, bartering, and testing of wits he had learned as a youth, and the inevitable inspection by his demanding father. Of all the heads of state Nixon would encounter, none was so much like his father as Nikita Khrushchev. A hot-headed, shouting man, loving argument for its own sake, quick to rage and quick to laughter, he was, in Nixon's words, "at times almost seductively charming; at other times he was boorish and obtuse." When Nixon first saw him, he found him shorter than expected, but a man of "great physical strength and vitality."

He kept looking me up and down from head to toe, as a tailor might estimate a customer's size for a suit of clothes, or perhaps more as an undertaker might view a prospective corpse with a coffin in mind.[17]

That there was a certain physical resemblance between Khrushchev and his father can be seen by comparing pictures of the two men. And when Nixon described him as "a crude bear of a man," whose "rough manners, bad grammar, and heavy drinking caused many diplomats to underestimate him," and who "despite his rough edges . . . had a keen mind and a ruthless grasp of power politics," he could well have been describing (save for the heavy drinking) Frank Nixon of Whittier.[18] The bad grammar, which gave Nixon so much embarrassment when his father spoke, he could never have learned on his own about Khrushchev, since he knew no Russian, but that he singled out this disability suggests the resemblance Nixon felt.

In the Nixon descriptions of his encounters with the Soviet leader we see also his envy of the man who can successfully use anger as a public weapon. In his arguments he wrote that he found himself handicapped by diplomatic niceties, subject to Marquis of Queensberry Rules, pitted like a man with one hand tied behind his back against a major-league baseball player, who uses "blinding speed, a wicked curve, plus knucklers, spitters, sliders, fork balls—all delivered with a deceptive change of pace." On only one occasion, when no members of the press were present, did he feel free to duel with Khrushchev as an equal. Then, he wrote, "it was cold steel between us all afternoon."[19]

In Six Crises, when Nixon was bent on maintaining the myth of his own innocence and the fastidiousness of his own language, he described how shocked he was to be met in the first interview with "a tirade of four-letter words which made his interpreter blush as he translated them into English."[20] The Soviet premier was angered because just a week before Nixon's arrival Congress had passed a "Captive Nations Resolution," urging a week of national prayer for the "enslaved peoples" behind the Iron Curtain. Nixon wrote that Khrushchev said "the resolution stinks." The rest was "beyond the pale of diplomacy." With the publication of his memoirs, however, since the whole world now knew about Nixon's own affection for four-letter words, he felt more relaxed about telling what was really said.

The Captive Nations Resolution, Nixon wrote, reminded Khrushchev of an old peasant saying, "People should not go to the toilet where they eat." "This resolution stinks," he said. "It stinks like fresh horse shit, and nothing smells worse than that!" Remembering from his briefings that Khrushchev had once been a herder of pigs, and recalling also from his own childhood the stench of pig manure on a neighbor's field, Nixon shot back: "I'm afraid the Chairman is mistaken. There is something that smells worse than horse shit—and that is pig shit."

"For a split second after the translator had finished, Khrushchev's face hovered on the borderline of rage," Nixon said. "Then suddenly he burst into a broad smile. 'You are right there,' he said. 'So perhaps you are right that we should talk about something else.' "[21]

Khrushchev returned to the attack on the Captive Nations Resolution when he was touring the American exhibition with Nixon in Sokolniki Park. When an RCA executive steered them into a model studio featuring color TV and asked them to try out the mechanism, Khrushchev put the blame for the resolution directly on the vice-president:

You have churned the waters yourself. Why was this necessary? God only knows. What happened? What black cat crossed your path and confused you?

Singling out one of the Soviet women laborers present, Khrushchev said, "Does this look like a slave?" Waving at other laborers above him in the still unfinished area, he shouted, "You know who this man is? He is the Vice President of the United States. He says you are slaves. Are you slaves?" When the embarrassed woman replied "Nyet," the premier embraced her in a bear hug.

Boasting that within seven years the Soviet Union would be on the same economic level with the United States, he said gaily, "When we catch up with you, in passing you by, we will wave to you!"

Seeing himself outmaneuvered by a master actor, Nixon tried to switch the subject to the technology of color TV, in which he said the Americans were superior. Urging freer exchange of ideas, he continued somewhat clumsily, "After all, you don't know everything. . . ."

When this was mistakenly translated as "You don't know anything. . . ." Khrushchev interrupted in a fury. "You don't know anything about Communism—except fear of it."[22]

As they watched the playback of their conversation on the studio television set, Nixon saw that Khrushchev, "aggressive, rude, and forceful," had easily bested him. Reporter Bob Considine, he wrote later, compared the episode to the first round in the Dempsey-Firpo fight; he had "started the encounter by knocking me out of the ring."[23]

Presidential speechwriter William Safire, then a press agent representing the homebuilder exhibiting the "typical American house," watched Nixon come out of the studio, "sweating profusely, knowing he had 'lost,' and anxious to find a way to make a comeback." Safire pushed down a fence blocking the area and yelled to Nixon's military aide, Don Hughes, "This way to the typical American house," and Hughes led Nixon and the Soviet authorities into the interior. Onlookers poured in from both sides, and for a few moments Nixon and Khrushchev were closeted for a second confrontation, in what became famous as "the kitchen debate." It was an important rescue, for which Nixon was not ungrateful to Safire. In the "second round" he held his own.[24]

Most of the kitchen debate consisted of good-natured banter about the relative merits of Soviet and American kitchens, with Khrushchev insisting disingenuously that the new Soviet kitchens already had the same gadgets and that Soviet workers had equivalent housing—the model American home had the latest in labor-saving gadgetry and was built to sell for $14,000—at the same time ridiculing the useless technology. "Don't you have a machine that puts food in the mouth and pushes it down?" he asked derisively. "These are merely gadgets. We have a saying if you have bedbugs you have to catch one and pour boiling water into the ear."

To which Nixon replied, "We have another saying, 'The best way to kill a fly is to make it drink whisky. But we have a better use for whisky.'"[25]

When talk shifted to weapons technology, Nixon conceded the superiority of Soviet rocketry, but warned that the United States was strong in other ways. Khrushchev began to shout, "We, too, are giants. You want to threaten—we will answer threats with threats." But Nixon turned the shouting aside with a soft word, as he had done in countless kitchen debates in his youth, and the confrontation ended amicably.*

James Reston described Khrushchev as "not a hopelessly rigid demagogue, but a tough, freewheeling politician who loves to talk big and provoke arguments." Nixon, he said, was "friendly, dogged, if not brilliant," arguing in "good frontier language." Later, watching the crowds cheering Nixon in the Russian hinterland, he said the vice-president had chosen "the perfect way to launch a campaign for the U.S. Presidency." All he had to do was to "say 'peace and friendship' in bad Russian." *Time* said Nixon "was the personification of a kind of disciplined vigor that belied tales of the decadent and limp-wristed West."[26]

Life put an elegant portrait of Nixon on the cover, with the Kremlin towers in the background, and newspapers generally treated Nixon handsomely. *Newsweek* was lyrical:

It was first a contest of men. Here was Dick Nixon, young (46), slender, eager—the son of a California grocer, an American man of success. Opposing him was Khrushchev, aging (65), short, bull-strong—the son of a peasant, ex-coalminer, successor to Stalin. It was, too, a contest of nations. . . . their secret deadly talks could change the course of history.[27]

Adlai Stevenson wrote privately that Nixon had "scored heavily" and would no doubt be "a formidable candidate." "All of which," he added, "fills me with a feeling that must be nausea and

---

*Despite his tension during the kitchen debate, Nixon carried out a promise he made to Donald M. Kendall, and managed to get Khrushchev to be photographed with a bottle of Pepsi-Cola in his hand. Later, when Nixon was looking for a job with a law firm, Kendall pledged the Pepsi-Cola account to anyone who would take Nixon in as a partner. Nixon went round the world as a Pepsi-Cola man during his years out of office, and when he became president he handsomely rewarded his friend Kendall; the soft-drink franchise for the Soviet Union went to the Pepsi-Cola company (interview with Anthony Marro, April 16, 1975).

wonder about the new image of the American hero to inspire our little boys."[28]

The kitchen debate caught the imagination of Americans, who paid little heed to the rest of Nixon's Russian experience. What was most remarkable was not the special debate, or Nixon's private talks, in which little was said that had not been said by Ambassador Llewyllen Thompson and numerous others, but that Nixon's speech opening the exhibit was printed in full in *Pravda* and *Izvestia,* and that later his uncensored half-hour speech was televised live to the Russian people. The first speech was a paean of praise for capitalist America, which had brought to forty-four million American families fifty-six million cars, fifty million TV sets, a hundred forty-three million radio sets, and thirty-one million owned homes. He called the American ideal "prosperity for all in a classless society." But he also spoke as an earnest young moralist, saying "Man does not live by bread alone."

In his televised speech he spoke with considerable courage of specific acts of Communist aggression, and the Soviet rejection of American proposals to alleviate tensions between the two peoples. He implied that the Soviet citizens had been systematically lied to, and prevented from learning the truth about the West by the suppression of Western magazines and newspapers, and the jamming of radio broadcasts. As a dramatic example of Soviet distortion of the truth he told what had happened to him on the first two days of his visit. At the Danilovsky Market, he said, he had been treated with great friendliness, and when ready to leave had been asked if he had tickets to the American exhibition. He had none, but his aide offered the questioner a hundred-ruble note to purchase some. When it was explained that the problem was not money but the unavailability of the tickets, Nixon promised to check into the matter and see what could be done. *Pravda,* Nixon said, had, however, twisted the story, saying that "I tried to give money to a poor Soviet citizen with the hope that the American press photographers might take pictures of the incident and send them around the world. There was not a shred of truth to the story."

"I can only add," he concluded, "that all irresponsible reporters should never forget that in the end the truth always catches up with a lie."[29] Thus he appeared as the wronged young moralist, and not—as Khrushchev had called him in the American exhibition—"a slick, dishonest manipulator of words."

In Nixon's private talks with Khrushchev, which were unprecedented in length and frankness, the themes of truth and lying, of enslavement and freedom, surfaced again and again. We have noted earlier that when Nixon said as a youth he had worked in his father's grocery store, Khrushchev said contemptuously, "All shopkeepers are thieves." To which Nixon replied by pointing out that in the Moscow market there were two sets of scales, one for the customer to make sure he was not being cheated by the state. When Nixon bluntly demanded why Khrushchev had permitted the Soviet radio to encourage violence against himself and Pat in Latin America the previous summer, the grizzled leader took the question seriously. "I never evade a tough question," he said, and quoted the Russian proverb, "You are my guest but truth is my mother." There had been nothing personal in the Venezuela attack, he said. The problem was not Nixon but United States imperialism. When Khrushchev called Nixon "a slick, dishonest manipulator of words," Nixon replied with tact, "Men like you and President Eisenhower are tough, reasonable men who are not soft or frightened."

When the Nixons were entertained at Khrushchev's elegant dacha on the Moscow River—the first statesman to be kept there overnight—the Soviet leader took him out in a motor launch. As they passed the bathers in the river, Khrushchev had the boat stopped and called out, "Are you captives?" Are you slaves?" They shouted back, *"Nyet! Nyet!"* He would nudge Nixon, saying, "See how our slaves live." After the eighth such stop, Nixon said, "I really must admire you; you never miss a chance to make propaganda."

"No, no," he retorted. "I don't make propaganda. I tell the truth."[30]

There can be little doubt, however, that Khrushchev was disturbed by the American charges of enslavement. No one better than he knew the truth about the murderous terrorism of the Stalin period, to which he had himself contributed. He looked upon himself, however, as a kind of hero who had led his people out of the nightmare of imprisonment. Konrad Kellen has noted that Khrushchev in 1957 had likened himself to the Jew in a famous Russian story by Vynnychenko, "little Pinya," who had been elected by fellow prisoners to a position of authority as a gesture of contempt but who had talked them into digging a tunnel and had himself led the way out, the first to brave the outside guard. "That little Pinya, that's me," Khrushchev said.[31] Later, on his visit to the United States, Khrushchev said in Los Angeles:

There are still some people in your country who keep harping that people in the Soviet Union are little short of slaves. . . . The reason why Roman civilization, as well as Greek civilization declined . . . was that it was a civilization built on slave labor, which shackled men's energy, will and freedom.[32]

Thus spoke "little Pinya," who would shortly be seen ordering the building of the Berlin Wall. And Nixon, who said on TV in Moscow "we do not and will not try to impose our system on anybody else," would shortly begin secret plans for the invasion of Cuba.

Nixon's trip was a triumph at home, but of no consequence for American foreign policy. He admitted even before his return that there had been "no substantial progress" as a result of his visit. He did, however, on his return encounter unexpected good fortune. Khrushchev had made the mistake of denying him the right to fly across Siberia, and he returned by way of Poland. Khrushchev had himself visited Warsaw a fortnight earlier, and had found the crowds ordered into the streets to cheer his coming passive and surly. The Poles remembered all too well that it was Khrushchev who had been in charge of partitioning Poland between Germany and Russia after Hitler's invasion in 1939. Hundreds of thousands of Poles had been imprisoned and most of the Polish officer corps slain, almost certainly at the order of Stalin, who had also presided over the liquidation of the leadership of the Polish Communist party.

Nixon in Warsaw was greeted with an astonishing display of spontaneous affection. Even the Polish Honor Guard broke tradition to cheer and applaud him as he passed. Two hundred fifty thousand—alerted by Radio Free Europe of his coming—lined the streets to shout "May you live a thousand years!" The limousine had to stop frequently to clear the windshield of bouquets flung at the car. "This time we brought our own flowers," several said. Admiral Rickover, born in Warsaw, was treated like a hometown hero.

There had never been anything like this in Nixon's life. "These people," he wrote later, "and millions like them in the other satellite countries, represent Khrushchev's greatest danger and the Free World's greatest hope."[33]

Nixon's impact on Khrushchev was minimal; Khrushchev's impact on Nixon was profound. The Soviet premier disliked the brash and hostile young American even before he came, and resented his public attack on the Soviet system on Moscow's television, and even more the cheering crowds that greeted him in Poland. When Khrushchev came to the United States in September—a visit that was widely and mistakenly heralded in the press as having been engineered by Nixon—he noted with anger that the vice-president had made a hostile speech against him "timed to coincide with his arrival." "He was addressing an association of dentists," Khrushchev said. "However, Mr. Nixon's speech was far from medicinal in content. He, so to speak, added a chill to the toothache."

On his first meeting with Eisenhower, Khrushchev asked him bluntly why the vice-president had made such a speech "on the eve of my visit." Ike told him he had not read it. "I told him," Khrushchev said, "that he need not bother to read it, since it was already past history."[34] Eisenhower in his memoirs said the Soviet leader "seemed to take particular delight in hurling barbs at the Vice President. Dick replied briskly and pointedly to each of the Chairman's sallies."[35] But seeing Khrushchev's obvious distaste for Nixon, Ike decided that he should be kept as far from him as possible, and a more subtle diplomat, Henry Cabot Lodge, was delegated to accompany the Soviet leader around the nation.

Khrushchev toured like a barnstorming candidate, alternately clowning and fist-shaking, his sallies of good humor interspersed with mockery and threats. His most misunderstood statement, "We will bury you," made in 1956, he explained meant only "We will outlive you" or "we will surpass you." Press treatment was friendly, especially in Los Angeles, where Khrushchev ogled Marilyn Monroe with obvious pleasure and complained in exaggerated dismay about being forbidden to visit Disneyland because his security there could not be guaranteed.

Like Nixon, he insisted on an unscheduled visit to an American supermarket, and was impressed. He mentioned Nixon publicly only once. In Washington, meeting with leaders of Congress, when Sen. Richard Russell, chairman of the Armed Services Committee, asked him, "We have setbacks in launching rockets; what about you?" he replied:

Why do you ask me? You had better ask Nixon—he answered your question when he said that the launching of our moon rocket had miscarried three times.

One rocket had indeed given them difficulty, he admitted, and then continued with a sally that brought great laughter and applause, "I can swear on the Bible that this is so. Let Nixon do likewise."[36]

Nixon described his confrontation with Khrushchev as one of the great personal crises of his life. It changed his attitude toward the Communist, whom he had heretofore looked at largely as a liar or a dupe. Now he saw "a steel-like quality, a cold determination, a tough amoral ruthlessness."[37] In Khrushchev, he wrote, he had seen "the Communist at his dangerous best." And in this dexterous and resourceful leader, protagonist of *Realpolitik* as well as Communism, he found much to admire. If one scrutinizes Nixon's portrait of Khrushchev in *Six Crises* with care, one will find a likeness—save for the aggressive sense of humor—to Nixon himself:

Intelligence, a quick-hitting sense of humor, always on the offensive, colorful in action and word, a tendency to be a show-off, particularly where he has any kind of gallery to play to, a steel-like determination coupled with an almost compulsive tendency to press an advantage—to take a mile where his opponent gives an inch—to run over anyone who shows any sign of timidity or weakness. . . . a man who does his homework, prides himself on knowing as much about his opponent's position as he does his own, particularly effective in debate because of his resourcefulness, his ability to twist and turn, to change the subject when he is forced into a corner or an untenable position.

Khrushchev's anger, Nixon noted, was always controlled and purposeful. In critical discussions he was "sober, cold, unemotional, and analytical." Khrushchev played chess not poker, but would have been "a superb poker player . . . like any good poker player he plans ahead so that he can win the big pots."[38]

In 1965, six years after his first visit to Moscow, twice defeated for office, Nixon returned to the Soviet capital. He went there largely unnoticed, as a lawyer for two oil companies, Macmillan Ring-Free Oil Company, and Golden Eagle Refining Company.[39]

Khrushchev, deposed in 1964 by younger men, notably Leonid Brezhnev, who had been a silent listener to the "kitchen debate," was said to be living in seclusion in Moscow. Nixon inquired about his whereabouts and was given his address by a Canadian newsman in a restaurant. As William Safire told the story:

Nixon rose from the dinner table where two Soviet Intourist guides had been assigned to stay with him, asked directions to the men's room, left the restaurant and took a cab to Khrushchev's apartment house, where he was met by two stony-faced burly women who insisted Khrushchev was not there.

Nixon, frustrated, left a handwritten note "expressing hope they could meet and talk again."[40] It would seem that there was some affection in the gesture, and it is a pity that history was deprived of what they might have said. As it is, we have only Khrushchev's brief comment in his memoirs, written secretly and smuggled out to be published in the West in 1970. He called Nixon "an unprincipled puppet" of Sen. Joe McCarthy and "a son-of-a-bitch."[41]

XXVII

The Assassination Track

Senator Matthias. *Let me draw an example from history.*
When Thomas Becket was proving to be an annoyance, as
Castro, the King said, who will rid me of this man. He
didn't say to somebody to go out and murder him. He said
who will rid me of this man, and let it go at that. . . .
Mr. Helms. *That is a warming reference to the problem.**
— CHURCH COMMITTEE HEARINGS, U.S. SENATE, 1975[1]

IN 1964 RICHARD NIXON DESCRIBED Fidel Castro as "the
most momentous figure in John F. Kennedy's life." It was Castro,
he said, who was a major factor in his winning the presidential
election; it was Castro "who brought him to the lowest point of his
career at the Bay of Pigs; it was Castro who supplied the opportunity for Kennedy's greatest act of leadership as President, during the blockade." And finally, Castro—"hero in the warped mind
of Lee Harvey Oswald"—was "an indirect cause of the tragic
snuffing out of John Kennedy's life. . . ."[2]

If this arresting scenario be true, then it must follow that Castro was almost as momentous a figure in his own life. Even if it be
in part inaccurate, the fact that Nixon in 1964 believed it to be
true is conceivably of much consequence in his inner life. For having become convinced that there was a line, however indirect,
linking Castro to Oswald's killing of John F. Kennedy, then he
could not escape the inevitable corollary, that his own active role
in the acceleration of Castro's hatred of the United States involved
himself.

A personal feeling of guilt for the death of an assassinated

*The reference to Henry II, concerning Thomas à Becket, archbishop of Canterbury, was
made by Sen. Charles Mathias, Jr., of Maryland. Richard Helms, former director of the
CIA, made the reply. Henry II is supposed to have said, "Who will rid me of this troublesome priest?"

leader can haunt even the innocent.[3] The accuracy of the Nixon
scenario, and his personal reaction to Kennedy's death—including attempts to have the assassination of Vietnam's Diem blamed
on Kennedy—we shall look at in a subsequent chapter. But they
cannot be assessed without an examination of Nixon's participation in the evolution of Castro's enmity, much of which was
exacerbated by the Cuban leader's realization that the U.S.
government and the CIA from an early date were bent not only
on his overthrow but also on his assassination.

In August 1975 Fidel Castro gave Sen. George McGovern a
list of twenty-four assassination attempts he blamed on the CIA;
the Church Committee found evidence that there had been at
least eight, some of them not overlapping.[4] Nixon denied any
knowledge of the assassination attempts,[5] but he was close to
Allen Dulles, who, although publicly abhorring the idea of assassination, nevertheless quietly countenanced several assassination
plots, and encouraged the killing of Castro the first time it was
suggested.[6] Richard Helms testified under oath before the House
Assassinations Committee in 1978 that the assassination plots
were known "to almost everybody in high positions in government."[7] And Dulles himself wrote before his death that the CIA
"never carried out any action of a political nature . . . without
appropriate approval at a high political level in our government
outside the CIA."[8]

Richard Bissell, chief coordinator of the covert attempts to
overthrow Castro, described to the Church Committee the many-
pronged plan to bring Castro down: the invasion of Cuba by CIA-
trained exiles, the simultaneous uprising of guerrilla units within
Cuba, and the assassination of Castro, and probably his brother
and Che Guevara as well. Initially everything was planned to take
place as early as September 1960, during Nixon's election campaign, and as a decisive factor in that campaign.[9]

But nothing worked out as expected. The guerrilla units in
Cuba did not materialize; the invasion force being trained in Guatemala was plagued by difficulties and was not kept secret from
Castro, who mobilized against it. The "troublesome priest,"
described in *Look* in September 1959 by William Attwood as "the
world's likeliest target for an assassin's bullet," survived to see
John F. Kennedy elected, the invasion fail, Kennedy assassinated,
and Nixon himself forced out of office in ignominy and disgrace.

Eisenhower was anti-Castro from the beginning but tried to preserve neutrality. In 1958 he stopped the sale of arms to Batista and confiscated cargoes of arms headed for Castro. Former American ambassadors to Cuba Arthur Gardner and Earl T. Smith were extremely hostile to Castro, as was William Pawley, former ambassador to Brazil and Peru, a wealthy Florida businessman and close friend of Richard Nixon. Pawley had lived in and out of Cuba for thirty years, and had organized the first Cuban aviation company. He had also built aircraft factories for Chiang Kai-shek, and had been one of the influential members of the "China Lobby."

Pawley had four or five meetings with Eisenhower, in which he did his best to persuade him that Castro was a Communist and must not be permitted to come to power.[10] Eisenhower was especially disturbed by rumors that Castro at one point in July 1958 had threatened to cut off the water supply for American forces stationed at the naval base at Guantanamo Bay. After checking with Batista, he had sent in a contingent of Marines.[11]

Meanwhile Batista's own troops were defecting in great numbers, and Castro won an easy victory, moving triumphantly into Havana on January 1, 1959. Batista fled to Miami with what was said to be "hundreds of millions" of dollars, and Castro set up as provisional president a moderate democrat, Carlos Manuel Urrutia Lleo, and promised eventual free elections. To the stories that he was a Communist Castro reacted with rage and vehement denial.

Like Batista before him, Castro legalized the Communist party upon coming to power, but the Cuban Communists were wary of his romanticism and wildly undisciplined political tactics. Although his brother Raul, and the Argentine revolutionary Che Guevara, were close to the party, the organized Cuban Communists kept aloof from Castro for some months. The Russians were as yet far from realizing that they had a brother and ally of formidable quality in the Western Hemisphere. Khrushchev in his memoirs said that Castro was "pursuing a very cautious policy toward us," and that his government had "nothing to go on but rumors." To illustrate Castro's own ambivalence, Khrushchev told the following story:

The leaders of the Cuban revolution had all gone to heaven, and Saint Peter, ordering them to line up, called out, "All Com-

munists, three steps forward." Raul Castro and Che Guevera
moved ahead; Fidel did not. Whereupon Saint Peter barked,
"Hey! you, the tall one with the beard! What's wrong. Did you not
hear what I said? All Communists three steps forward!"

The point of the story, Khrushchev explained, was "that while
Saint Peter and everyone else considered Fidel a Communist,
Fidel himself did not."[12]

New York Times correspondent Herbert Matthews, who had
interviewed Fidel in the Sierra Maestra, had stimulated a friendly
press in the United States. Most of the Latin American experts in
the State Department were pressing for friendship and recognition, despite chilling reports of Castro's summary executions of
Batista army officers and policemen. Nixon—like Saint Peter—
from the beginning considered Castro "an unwitting front man
for the Communists or perhaps even a Communist himself."[13]
When the American Society of Newspaper Editors invited Castro
to speak in Washington on April 17, 1959, Eisenhower, in a calculated gesture of evasion, went off to play golf in Georgia, and
Nixon agreed to talk to him only under certain humiliating conditions—"that the two of us would talk alone, without members of
his staff or mine present, and that there should be no photographs taken or other attempts made to exploit our conference
for publicity purposes."[14]

Castro, who could hardly have forgotten that Nixon had earlier publicly praised Batista's "competence and stability," said
politely afterward that it had not been an inquisition and that his
personal impressions of the vice-president were good.[15] He complained, however, that when he tried to tell Nixon about Cuba's
illiteracy, poverty, and unemployment, Nixon "simply listened."[16]
It is also apparent that when Nixon confronted Castro with lists
of suspected Communists in his movement, Castro also remained
deaf.[17]

To Eisenhower Nixon wrote an immediate four-page report,
published in part in his memoirs, in which he concluded that
"Castro is either incredibly naïve about communism or under
communist discipline—my guess is the former."[18] Later, in 1964,
when Castro had become a minion of the Soviet Union, Nixon
wrote a description of this interview in which Castro emerged as
uglier and more sinister. Here Nixon reported that he tried to
lecture Castro about the values of democracy and asked him,

"Why don't you have free elections?" To which Castro replied, "The people of Cuba don't want free elections; they produce bad government." When Nixon asked Castro why he was not giving fair trials to the opponents of the revolution—executions by April had reached 521[19]—Castro said, "The people of Cuba don't want them to have fair trials. They want them shot as quickly as possible."

Still, Nixon recognized the charismatic leader. "He had a compelling, intense voice, sparkling black eyes, and he radiated vitality. After 3½ hours of discussion I summed up my impressions in this way—he looked like a revolutionary, talked like an idealistic college professor, and reacted like a communist."[20]

In April 1959, save for the chilly interview with the vice-president, Castro managed an eleven-day triumph. The American Society of Newspaper Editors found him good copy, affable, and at times compelling, and cheered him when he said "a free press is the first enemy of dictatorship."[21] Nixon's gut reaction, from the moment he met Castro, was one of suspicion and hatred. He never deviated from his conviction that the pro-Castro men in the State Department were "gullible," and that "our choice was not between Batista and somebody better, but between Batista and somebody far worse."[22] Here he was reinforced by Allen Dulles, J. Edgar Hoover, Sen. George Smathers of Florida, and his friend Bebe Rebozo, who, Henry Kissinger tells us, "hated Castro with a fierce Latin passion."[23]

For Nixon the political advantages of an anti-Castro attack in the coming election of 1960 were obvious. His press secretary Bert Klein admitted later, "He was eager for the Republican administration to get credit for toppling Castro before the election."[24] Like a hound dog on the scent, veteran of many Communist "discoveries," Nixon would now add still another he had flushed out of hiding. But let us note the chronology with care. Nixon was already planning the Cuban leader's downfall before Castro's land-reform program, before his confiscation of American property, before there was the slightest hint of cooperation with the Soviet Union, and when the only exiles in the United States were the hated *Batistianos*. Nixon was nonetheless already convinced that Castro's protestations of affection for democracy were pure act, and here he was right. Castro was a hardcore narcissist, dedicated to supreme power for himself, with a prodigious capacity for lying and a grandiose dream of liberating all of Latin America from Yankee imperialism. Nixon instinctively sensed his delight in the execution of his enemies, and his contempt for the will of the people he professed to admire.

The delirious joy of the Cubans over the fall of Batista was shortlived. In May, Castro began his extensive "land-reform" program, but did not pay for the confiscated acreages as he had promised. The island's economy was shortly in a shambles, with unemployment increasing. In June, Castro secretly sent a guerrilla force to the Dominican Republic to overthrow the dictator Trujillo, and established training camps for invasions of Panama, Guatemala, and Haiti. Trujillo annihilated the Cuban force, and Castro kept the defeat a secret from his own people, as he did later setbacks in Nicaragua and Haiti. The CIA was now convinced that Castro intended to ignite leftist or Communist revolutions throughout the whole of Latin America.[25]

One fourth of the island's arable land was in sugar plantations, and the United States controlled 40 percent of the sugar-production facilities. Not surprisingly, Castro began thinking of confiscation, and as early as midsummer 1959 said to an aide, "they will howl with fury when they see what we are going to do with their sugar mills." Although the new U.S. ambassador, Philip Bonsal, was friendly, Castro refused to see him except socially for three months, and met with him officially only twice thereafter. Cuban Finance Minister Fresquet, despairing of ever bringing about a rapprochement with the United States, resigned in March 1959 and fled to Florida. To one aide Castro confided cynically in this period, "The Yanquis have *one* good quality. They always hope I will change."[26]

Angry Cuban exiles in Florida began hiring boats and raiding the Cuban mainland, committing sabotage and spreading disaffection. One Cuban, Castro's former private pilot, Maj. Diaz Lenz, in October rented a B-25 bomber which had been converted to a cargo plane and dropped leaflets over Havana describing Castro as a Communist. The resulting antiaircraft flak killed two Cubans and wounded fifty. Castro, "roaring defiance, foaming at the mouth," Ambassador Bonsal said, "comported himself in a manner reminiscent of Hitler at his most hysterical and odious," and described the leaflet dropping as Cuba's Pearl Harbor. Although

Eisenhower denied responsibility and said he was doing everything he could to stop the raids, the episode, Bonsal wrote, "spelled the end of my hope for rational relations between Cuba and the United States."[27]

Look editor William Attwood wrote from Havana in September 1959, "the armor is tarnished, the banners wilting. Former associates are calling him a Red or plotting his assassination. . . . You can smell a police state in the making."[28] In December Tad Szulc described with horror the continuing executions. "Some of the gentlest, friendliest, gayest creatures on earth," he wrote, were transformed into men of frenzied hate. When Castro shouted, "What shall we do with these traitors?" they would yell in an endless monotone, "The Wall! the Wall!" By the spring of 1961, two thousand had been killed. The *Batistianos* in Miami were now joined by a new wave of Cubans, as professional men and women fled in ever-increasing numbers. By 1975 the number would reach 560,000, the greatest mass migration in the history of the Western Hemisphere.[29]

In December 1959, observers like Szulc and Ambassador Bonsal thought Castro reminiscent of Hitler and too jealous of his personal power ever to become an international Communist puppet.[30] Nixon thought otherwise. Here he was reinforced by key men in the CIA. When Castro was given a hero's welcome in Caracas, Venezuela, in December, Jake Engler, the CIA chief of station in the city wrote to Washington in alarm and was called home, not only for consultation, but to be made head of a small paramilitary force to train Cuban exiles for a Castro overthrow. Col. J. C. King, CIA chief of the Western Hemisphere Division, in what seems to have been the first written memo suggesting the possibility of Castro's assassination, recommended on December 11, 1959, that "thorough consideration be given to the elimination of Fidel Castro," saying, "the disappearance of Fidel would greatly accelerate the fall of the present Government." Allen Dulles wrote a note in his own hand indicating approval, as did Richard Bissell.[31] This was the beginning of what came to be called Track II, "The Assassination Track."

Track I, the organization of a paramilitary force, officially came into existence on January 18, 1960, with the CIA meeting in Washington that saw Jake Engler put in charge. By that time Nixon had been secretly agitating for a CIA-backed invasion of

Cuba for at least eight months. He had been, he wrote in 1964, "the strongest and most persistent advocate for setting up such a program."[32] It was during this crucial period, too, that the Soviets, moving slowly, took their own measure of Castro. One month after the secret organization of Track I, Mikoyan was in Havana negotiating the purchase of Cuban sugar and arranging for a Soviet loan.

There is a fugue-like quality to U.S.–Cuban relations in 1959–60, with assertion, denial, and counterdenial surfacing and resurfacing simultaneously on different levels. Eisenhower and Nixon denounced Castro for trying to carry his revolution to other Latin American countries, publicly promised nonintervention in the affairs of Latin American states, meanwhile privately planning Castro's overthrow and sending arms to anti-Trujillo men in the Dominican Republic.[33] Castro blistered American policy as imperialistic and interventionist, but he did indeed plan to carry his own revolution into the Dominican Republic, Haiti, and Panama. American journalists predicted Castro's assassination by his own dissidents, unaware that their own CIA was planning it. Castro's own intellectuals denounced him as a Communist; Castro, angrily denying it, moved steadily into the Soviet orbit.

Nixon, who had promised on Moscow television on August 1, 1959, "we do not and will not try to impose our system on anybody else,"[34] was in the forefront of the secret movement to overthrow Castro. Eisenhower, who on a trip to Latin America in February 1960 had "assured every audience that my country would not intervene in their local offices," in a meeting of the National Security Council on March 10, 1960, formally authorized "A Program of Covert Action Against the Castro Regime."[35] "I was present," Nixon said, "at the meeting in which Eisenhower authorized the CIA to organize and train Cuban exiles for the eventual purpose of freeing their homeland from the Communists. . . . It was a policy I had been advocating for nine months."[36]

Even this March 10 meeting, which was to have momentous consequences, had innuendoes of assassination. Allen Dulles and Nixon had won Eisenhower's collaboration chiefly by raising his fears with CIA reports suggesting that Castro planned to capture the U.S. naval base at Guantanamo Bay. Discussing these reports at the meeting, the president speculated somberly that "we might have another Black Hole of Calcutta in Cuba."[37] Allen Dulles then reported that "a plan to effect the situation in Cuba was being worked out." And Admiral Arleigh Burke, who more than any other man in the military had been Nixon's ally, suggested *"that any plan for the removal of Cuban leaders should be a package deal, since many of the leaders around Castro were even worse than Castro."*[38] The word "removal" was ambiguous. So were other words and phrases like "eliminate," "get rid of," "disappear simultaneously," "straightforward action," "direct positive action," which CIA men considered mere euphemisms for assassination.[39]

Many of these men had gone into intelligence in the war against Hitler. There was a special fraternity of OSS men in the CIA. They were proud of their past, which included heroic exploits. Some saw the Cold War against the Soviets as a normal extension of the shooting war against the Fascists. Almost all had embraced a new and beguiling fantasy, that a little group of daring men could protect America and prevent the spread of Communism without war. Under Eisenhower and Nixon the CIA had burgeoned into an enormous clandestine power virtually without rein or oversight. It had already interfered successfully in Iran in 1953, restoring the young shah to the throne and cementing a pro-Western alliance that would last until 1979. It had interfered unsuccessfully in Indonesia in 1958, but had managed to keep the error secret, at least in the United States.[40]

The CIA had helped install a supposed pro-Western government in Egypt in 1954, and had masterminded a virtually bloodless coup that overthrew the left-wing Jacobo Arbenz in Guatemala in the same year. But however imaginative and talented the personnel, the secrecy itself, the lack of guidelines, the free use of unlimited funds without accountability, and the living in what Arthur Schlesinger has called "the ultimately hallucinatory world of clandestinity and deception,"[41] served to erode the morality and even the sense of reality of many able men. And in this unhealthy climate there developed also the noxious concept that the spread of communism could be controlled by preventive assassination. Even the Soviets, who used assassination regularly as a tool to control their own dissidents—Allen Dulles said the KGB had a special "Executive Action section. . . . Murder, Inc.—at this point did not extend it to foreign leaders.[42]

There was scarcely anyone who had lived through the Hitler

years who did not at one time indulge in the speculation that had Hitler been murdered early in life there would have been no World War II, and the fantasy of being the one who might have killed him was entertained by many people. The corollary notion that potential Hitlers ought somehow to be eliminated before they became dangerous sprang up after the war. A few men acted on it. One was Lee Harvey Oswald, who told his wife Marina, trying to dispel her horror when he admitted that he had tried to kill Gen. Edwin A. Walker in 1963, "If someone had killed Hitler in time, many lives would have been saved."[43]

Allen Dulles was another. This deceptively gentle, urbane, soft-voiced, and civilized man had been in the OSS in Switzerland during World War II, and had become peripherally involved in knowledge of the plot of a group of German generals to kill Hitler on July 20, 1944, which very nearly succeeded.[44] This may be one reason Dulles so easily fell in with Col. J. C. King's suggestion of December 11, 1959, that *"consideration be given to the elimination of Fidel Castro,"*[45] and later okayed the CIA attempts to poison Patrice Lumumba, the pro-Soviet leader of the Congo, whom he denounced in a National Security Council meeting on July 15, 1960 as "a Castro, or worse."[46]

Nixon had known Allen Dulles since the summer of 1947 when they worked together on the Herter Committee in Europe. Dulles had been one of the first men in government to agree with Nixon that Hiss was or had been a Communist, and he and Nixon had become friends.[47] They agreed from the beginning that Castro was an international menace, and worked together to persuade Eisenhower of the seriousness of his threat. When the Cuban invasion finally took place, ending disastrously as "The Bay of Pigs," it was Dulles who briefed Nixon—then out of office—about the failure in Washington on April 16, 1961, saying in despair, "This is the worst day of my life."[48] It was Dulles who covered up almost totally his own role in the planning for the Bay of Pigs, this in his *The Craft of Intelligence,* a masterful example of evasion and omission. And he covered up for Vice-President Nixon, the most ardent backer of the invasion plans, by omitting his name from the book altogether.[49]

Dulles died before he could be questioned by the Church Committee, and we have no direct evidence from him that Nixon and he consulted freely about "the assassination track." The evidence comes from Richard Helms, and is supported by Nixon's extraordinary attempts, shortly after his election as president, to wrest the whole Bay of Pigs file from the CIA and get it into the Oval Office. Haldeman, among others, as we shall see, eventually came to believe that Nixon's frantic efforts in this regard were an effort to cover up "the assassination track," particularly because of one of the indirect consequences—the assassination of President Kennedy.[50]

Richard Bissell, CIA coordinator of the combined anti-Castro operations of 1959, has said that he never discussed the possibility of assassinating Castro with Nixon, although he conceded that Dulles would have been the logical person to conduct such discussions, and no one at a lower level.[51] He has described the assassination efforts freely to numerous investigators as well as to members of the Church Committee. "The morality of the idea did not trouble him one bit," he told Peter Wyden. Assassinations were, after all, "as old as history." "It seemed to Bissell," Wyden wrote, "far more humane to take the life of one dangerous, charismatic leader than to start a military effort in which hundreds or thousands might die, not to apeak of the risk of civil war in Cuba." Bissell said he felt at the time that an assassination might be arranged "if we can't do anything else."[52] But it is evident that as the plans coalesced, Track II was meant to be meshed with Track I, and the assassination of Castro coordinated with the invasion. E. Howard Hunt was recommending this to Bissell in May 1960. "Assassinate Castro *before* or coincident with the invasion," he wrote, ". . . without Castro to inspire them the Rebel Army and *milicia* would collapse in leaderless confusion."[53]

The idea of assassination of foreign leaders, once accepted, became a contagion. Allen Dulles, after what seemed to some to be a nod from Eisenhower in a National Security Council meeting on August 18, 1960, arranged for some poison to be sent to Africa to kill Lumumba, the Congo leader who had declared independence from Belgium on June 30, 1960, and who was threatening to invite Soviet troops into the area. In addition to the poison, Dulles guaranteed the expenditure of up to $100,000.[54]

Although the Church Committee in 1975 concluded that there was "a reasonable inference that the plot to assassinate Lumumba was authorized by President Eisenhower," they had no such inference concerning Castro. Could "the green light,"

Arthur Schlesinger has asked, "have been flashed by the Vice President of the United States?"[55]

Eisenhower, Dulles, Gen. Charles P. Cabell, and Tracy Barnes of the CIA—all of whom could have answered this question—were all dead before the Church Committee hearings convened, and Col. J. C. King died during the hearings, before he could be queried on this subject. Nixon sent a statement to the committee, dated March 9, 1976, saying that "assassination of a foreign leader" was "an act I never had cause to consider and which under most circumstances would be abhorrent to any president." Here he echoed similar public pronouncements of Allen Dulles. But Nixon did admit that there were "circumstances in which presidents may lawfully authorize actions in the interests of the security of this country, which if undertaken by other persons, or even by the president himself under different circumstances, would be illegal."[56]

Helms maintained before the Church Committee that nothing was communicated directly. "Nobody wants to embarrass a President of the United States," he said, "by discussing the assassination of foreign leaders in his presence." A mechanism was set up, he said, "to use as a circuit breaker so that these things did not explode in the President's face and that he was not held responsible for them." This was called the "Special Group 5412," one of the most secret agencies in the government, composed of the deputy undersecretary of state, deputy secretary of defense, director of the CIA, and special assistant to the president for national security affairs. The CIA automatically acted, Helms implied, under the concept of "plausible denial." That is, it strove to implement covert actions in such a way as to conceal CIA involvement if the operations were exposed.[57]

Helms repeatedly testified before the Church Committee that "he felt explicit authorization was unnecessary for the assassination of Castro in the early 1960s." "We had been asked to get rid of Castro," he said, ". . . and there were no limitations put on the means." When reminded by Senator Mathias of the resemblance to the assassination of Thomas à Becket, Helms said, "That is a warming reference to the problem."[58]

Helms's testimony before the Church Committee in 1976 was a tissue of evasions, denials, and contradictions. He was eventually brought to trial and made to pay a moderate fine.[59] He consist-

ently protected Richard Nixon, who had given him an ambassa-
dorship to Iran, and who had—in Nixon's words on one of the
presidential tapes—"protected him from a hell of a lot of things."
But when Helms was called to testify in 1978 before the House
Assassinations Committee he was no longer so circumspect, and
as we have seen, he said the Castro plots were known "to almost
everybody in high positions in government." He said it was a mistake to have withheld the data from the Warren Commission. "If
I had it to do over again, I would've backed up a truck, taken all
the documents down and shoved them on the Warren Commission's desk."[60]

Although Nixon acted with extreme circumspection in regard
to the "Assassination Track," this was not true of Track I, plans
for the Cuban invasion. Both Nixon's aide, Gen. Robert E. Cushman, Jr., and Richard Bissell have described his intense preoccupation with the activities in what was called, in code, "the
Institute," an old World War II "temporary" building near the
Lincoln Memorial, which housed the CIA group.[61]

Nixon did not know that Bissell was an anarchic administrator,
and a fatal misjudger of men, locked into the in-group conviction
that Castro was "psychotic," and therefore vulnerable. Bissell had
no compunction about setting up plans to assassinate Castro. But
he recognized, with many others, that a dead Castro would be
replaced by his brother, or Che Guevara, and that plans must be
laid for a pro-U.S. government to replace the whole Castro leadership. The plan he presented in outline to the Special Group
5412 in the third week of March 1960 consisted of an invasion by
Cuban exiles trained in Guatemala, to be supported from an air
base to be built in Guatemala, to be coordinated with guerrilla
units set up within Cuba. A government-in-exile, set up in Miami,
was to be flown to Cuba to take command of the government.
September 1960 was the target date.[62]

This invasion, which Nixon helped plan, was based on the
model of the Guatemalan coup of 1954, which had overthrown
leftist President Jacobo Arbenz and had installed a CIA hand-
picked conservative colonel, Carolos Castillo-Armas, who had
been trained in the U.S. Army Command and General Staff
School. Arbenz had roused the fears of the Dulles brothers when
he legalized the Communist party and expropriated four
hundred thousand acres of idle banana plantation land belonging

to the U.S.-controlled United Fruit Company. Castillo-Armas was given CIA funds to train a rebel army of several hundred men in Honduras. A secret CIA radio station spread denunciations of Arbenz and misleading reports of a large invasion underway. The Castillo-Armas air force, comprising U.S. B-6s and P-47 fighters, dropped leaflets and a few token bombs. When two of the three P-47s were shot down, Eisenhower was persuaded hastily to "sell" more to the insurgents. CIA pilots flew a few more sorties, and on June 27, 1954, one week after "the invasion," Arbenz resigned. Castillo-Armas, having lost only one man, entered victorious in the embassy plane of U.S. Ambassador John Puerifoy. Eisenhower, after being secretly briefed on the coup by Allen Dulles, said to him, "Thanks Allen, and thanks to all of you. You've averted a Soviet beachhead in our hemisphere."[63]

The American press had accepted Eisenhower's denials of CIA interference, although to the citizens of Guatemala, as Powers has said, it was "so blatant it amounted to an insult." And Nixon's statement in one of the 1960 debates with Kennedy that the people of Guatemala had driven out a pro-Communist regime was greeted in that country with derision. Everyone in Guatemala knew, as historian Boris Goldenberg has noted, Arbenz "had been toppled by the intervention of a reactionary colonel backed by the United States."[64]

Bissell brought to the Castro overthrow the same ideas and many of the same men who had participated in the Guatemalan coup—David Atlee Phillips, Tracy Barnes, Gerry Droller, and E. Howard Hunt. Jake Engler, put in charge, had been the CIA chief in Caracas when Nixon barely escaped assassination. Crucial in the planning was Jack Hawkins, loaned to the CIA at Dulles's request by Marine Corps commandant Gen. David Shoup, as well as DOP (Directorate for Plans) official Jacob Esterline.[65]

It was easy enough to set up a radio station on Great Swan Island, where at the proper moment rumors of multiple landings of unknown proportions could be broadcast. But the training of five hundred to a thousand exiles in the Guatemalan mountains proved to be a nightmare of bad logistics and inept leadership. The airstrip, built presumably for commercial purposes, took ninety instead of thirty days to build, and news of the operation quickly spread to Castro. Allen Dulles managed to keep the news out of the U.S. press until after the election, save for one description in an obscure academic journal, the Stanford University *Hispanic-American Review*.[66] German-born Gerry Droller (alias Frank Bender), who could speak no Spanish, and E. Howard Hunt were disastrous choices for the task of setting up a government in exile. It never materialized. The guerrilla units in Cuba, which Bissell had envisaged as springing to the aide of the invading force like the Free French at the Normandy invasion in Europe, also did not materialize. Castro was still far more popular than the CIA was willing to concede—a poll conducted in 1960 by Lloyd Free showed 86 percent supporting him—and his militia seized the airdrops and imprisoned the CIA agents as quickly as they were dispatched to the island. Richard Helms, whom Bissell disliked and who remained aloof from the planning, came to believe the invasion was "harebrained," and Gen. Richard E. Cushman, Nixon's liaison man with the group—whom Nixon later made commandant of the Marine Corps and afterward deputy director of the CIA—seeing the escalation in the planning and knowing that U.S. involvement could not be kept secret, found it all "pretty hairy."[67]

Eisenhower, cool to the project from the beginning, could not be persuaded to authorize $13,000,000 for the project until August. He was especially disturbed at the failure to set up a government-in-exile. "I'm going along with you boys," he said, "but I want to be sure the damned thing works."[68]

Nixon, according to General Cushman, kept pressing the president for speedy action, and fretting over the delays. "How are the boys doing at the Institute?" he would ask. "Are they falling dead over there? What in the world are they doing that takes months?" "How the hell are they coming?" And he repeatedly asked how his own office could cooperate. At one point he sent Cushman to Palm Beach to discuss with Nixon's good friend William Pawley a scheme "to print up some Cuban bonds, presumably to jar the Castro economy." Wyden, to whom Cushman related this, said, "Nothing ever came of the project."[69] Nixon pushed for Mario Garcia to replace Castro, but this was vetoed by the CIA. He urged cutting off tourism and pulling out private business altogether.[70] He remained hopeful, confiding to his press secretary Bert Klein that he expected the overthrow of Castro by October. Klein said that "a successful Cuba operation would have been 'a major plus' indeed 'a real trump card' in the election."[71]

Meanwhile, no one was helping Nixon more than Castro himself. In June 1959, when British and American oil refineries, after checking with Eisenhower, refused to process Soviet crude oil, Castro confiscated the refineries, worth, it was said, seventy-five million dollars. On July 6 Eisenhower retaliated by reducing the quota of sugar to be imported from Cuba into the United States before March 31, 1961, by 700,000 short tons.[72] Khrushchev, who had finally recognized Castro's extraordinary potential value for the Soviet Union, made a truculent outburst on July 9, saying, "In a figurative sense, if it became necessary, the Soviet military can support the Cuban people with rocket weapons." Although he later temporarily retreated from this stance, the phrase was an electrifying signal that Cuba might well become a military as well as an economic satellite of the Soviet Union.[73]

Eisenhower replied that the U.S. would not tolerate a Cuban regime run by international Communism, and proclaimed an embargo on all deliveries of American goods to Cuba save medical supplies and foodstuffs. Castro retaliated by nationalizing all other American concerns, including the U.S. government–owned nickel mines, and the last of the sugar mills, a billion-dollar investment. By the end of October 1959 the Cuban government controlled tobacco, cement, iron, sugar, about 70 percent of the island's production. "In a matter of days," Theodore Draper wrote, "the entire Cuban bourgeoisie was wiped out." Claims against Castro, later formally put to paper, totalled a billion and a half dollars; the total value of the confiscated property was said to be over three billion.[74]

Freedom of the press disappeared. Castro, in response to the invasion threat, organized a people's militia, including both sexes, which became an island-wide military organization, and armed them with guns from Czechoslovakia and the Soviet Union. Executions mounted; by the spring of 1961 two thousand had been killed, and fifteen to twenty thousand imprisoned. Raul Castro was reported in *Life* on July 18, 1960, as saying, "My dream is to drop three atom bombs on New York."[75]

The embargo proved virtually meaningless as the Soviet Union moved in to fill Cuba's needs and cemented the alliance. Even nonreading Americans were made aware of the union when they saw on TV in July 1960 Khrushchev and Castro embrace publicly in a great bear hug on the steps of Castro's specially selected Theresa Hotel in Harlem, and heard Khrushchev say, "I'm proud of Castro; he's a heroic man!"[76] The Soviet leader had been invited to visit the United States by Eisenhower during the placid period before U.S. reconaissance pilot Francis Gary Powers had been shot down over the Soviet Union in his U-2 plane. Despite the worsened relations, Khrushchev came to speak at the United Nations, along with Tito, Castro, Eisenhower, and Macmillan, in what was perhaps the most remarkable session in United Nations history. The Soviet leader also traveled across America, alternately disarming and enraging his audiences, demonstrating his skill as a showman and debater, and genuinely delighting in seeing the United States. Eisenhower found him a responsive human being when playing with his grandchildren at Gettysburg, an insulting guest when he heckled Richard Nixon at a dinner in the White House, and a skillful international foe when he attacked the United States in the U.N.[77]

Castro, reduced to an obvious Khrushchev minion, now faced an almost universally hostile U.S. press. *Life* called his trip "A Boorish Odyssey." Eisenhower insulted him publicly by giving a luncheon for Latin American leaders and leaving him off the guest list; Castro responded by having luncheon with the black waiters of his Harlem hotel, and later delivering a four-and-a-half-hour anti-American harangue in the United Nations. Khrushchev was one of the few spectators who sat through it all, occasionally saluting by lifting his right arm; when Castro would not be gaveled into silence, his microphone was shut off.[78]

Meanwhile the secret plans for the assassination of Castro had ground but slowly.[79] In the summer of 1960 an air force liaison officer with the CIA, L. Fletcher Prouty, flew two Cuban exiles from Eglin Air Force Base, Florida, to the outskirts of Havana. They were equipped, he said, with a rifle with a telescopic lens, intended for the assassination of Castro. Nothing came of it.[80] In this same summer a pretty German girl who had been Castro's mistress in 1959 was persuaded with a promise of CIA money to poison the Cuban leader. The CIA contact was Frank Fiorini, an adventurer who had fought with Castro but had turned against him and had become a CIA informer. He had assumed the alias Frank Sturgis, by which he was later known when he became involved in Watergate. The girl secreted poison capsules in a jar of cold cream, and managed to secure a liaison with Castro in a hotel. When Castro went to sleep she went to the bathroom to retrieve the capsules and put them in his coffee, but found that they had melted. "It was like an omen," she said. "I thought, 'To hell with it. Let history take its course.' "[81]

The failures contributed to the CIA decision in the late summer of 1960 to recruit someone in the U.S. underworld to murder Castro. Col. J. C. King suggested this to Bissell, who thought it made good sense. There were many gangsters who hated Castro because he had cut off their lucrative drug and gambling traffic. When Batista fled, his presumed partner in this business, Meyer Lansky, fled at the same time, and it was said that he had joined in a pledge of a million dollars for Castro's head. Frank Sturgis claimed in 1975 that the underworld had offered him $100,000 to kill the Cuban leader. The CIA offered $150,000.[82]

CIA's Sheffield Edwards, at Bissell's urging, in August 1960 sought out for a contact with the underworld one Robert Maheu who later became the confidant of Howard Hughes, a friend of Richard Danner and Bebe Rebozo, and intermediary for the notorious $100,000 in cash intended as unreported pocket money for President Nixon in 1970.[83]

Maheu took on the assassination of Castro with reluctance, agreeing, he testified, only because it was described to him as "a necessary ingredient . . . of the overall invasion plan." He sought out a Las Vegas hood, John Rosselli, who had been tutored by Al Capone and who had extorted millions from the movie companies in the 1930s. Rosselli brought in two of the ten most wanted criminals in the FBI roster, Sam Giancana, a Chicago gangster, and Santos Trafficante, Jr., formerly involved in organized crime in Havana, who had mistakenly stayed on after the Castro revolution and had been imprisoned until September 1959, when he had been freed and had fled to Tampa, Florida.[84]

Happy at the chance to earn points against prosecution by the FBI, and promised $150,000, the gangsters proved to be choosy about the choice of weapons. They wanted nothing so crude as a shoot-out execution, and demanded a poison "that would disappear without a trace." A successful batch, treated on monkeys in CIA laboratories, could not be provided before February 1961. Apparently $10,000 was paid to a Cuban in advance funds. Rosselli said Maheu "opened up his briefcase and dumped a whole lot of money in his lap . . . and also came up with the capsules and he explained how they were going to be used," a story Maheu denied.[85]

The gangsters were sloppy and loose-mouthed. J. Edgar Hoover, whose agents were trailing the men independently, learned that Giancana in September had been overheard saying that Castro was to be assassinated in November 1960, that he "had already met with the assassin-to-be on three occasions," that the assassin "had arranged with a girl, not further described, to drop 'a pill' in some drink or food of Castro's." Hoover passed the information on to the CIA, with comments not recorded publicly by the Church Committee. The Cuban, it was said, unable to carry out the assignment, subsequently returned the cash and the pills.[86]

The 1960 election came and went; there was no assassination and no invasion. Fifteen years later on June 19, 1975, shortly before Giancana was to have appeared as a witness before the Church Committee investigating assassinations, he was murdered in his home in Oak Park, Illinois. Seven .22-caliber bullets were pumped into his neck. In August 1976 Rosselli's body, decomposing, was found by fishermen sealed in an oil drum and weighted by chains off North Miami Beach. Whether either murder was related to their being subpoened by the Church Committee, or were simply gang-related, is not known. The murderers have never been found.[87]

In the election campaign, as the invasion plans matured, Nixon praised Eisenhower for his restraint on the Cuban problem. In San Francisco he said on September 12, 1960, "We could have turned Cuba into a second Hungary. But we can be eternally grateful that we have a man in the White House who did none of these things."[88] Nixon was especially intent that John F. Kennedy not be told of the Cuban invasion plans. Eisenhower had done the routine courtesy of ordering CIA chief Allen Dulles to discuss with Kennedy more or less generally the secret aspects of American foreign policy, and the *New York Times* on July 24, 1960, had reported that Dulles, in Hyannis Port, had briefed the Democratic candidate on "hotspots Cuba and the Congo." Dulles, at the next meeting of the National Security Council, described briefing Kennedy on the training of guerrilla units within Cuba. Nixon was present, and according to Robert Amory "exploded." "Under no circumstances," he said, "should Kennedy be told about the invasion."[89]

Although invasion stories were circulating in Miami and details of the invasion force being trained in the Guatemalan mountains were known in Cuba, where feverish activity was underway to prepare against it, astonishingly Kennedy seems not to have known about the invasion effort, nor did the *New York Times,* which did not send a man to Guatemala to check out the rumors until early January 1961.[90]

Kennedy, who had been under fire for being "soft on Communism," was now coming out strongly against Castro, and in October attacked Eisenhower for having permitted Communism to flourish "eight jet minutes from the coast of Florida." He said also, "I wasn't the Vice President who presided over the Communization of Cuba."[91] Nixon, worried, in a speech on October 18 called Castro "a cancer" and demanded his eradication "in full association with our sister American republics."[92] On October 19 Kennedy's aides were writing a press statement which they hoped would counter the Nixon anti-Castro counteroffensive. It was late at night and Kennedy was asleep. Richard Goodwin wrote the release, in Kennedy's name:

We must attempt to strengthen the non-Batista democratic anti-Castro forces in exile, and in Cuba itself, who offer eventual hope of overthrowing Castro. Thus far, these fighters for freedom have had virtually no support from the government.

Without checking with Kennedy—something he had not done before—Goodwin showed the statement only to Pierre Salinger and Theodore Sorenson and then gave it to the Scripps-Howard newspaper chain. He said later he considered his words just "political rhetoric."

The next morning, when Nixon saw the headline KENNEDY ADVOCATES U.S. INTERVENTION IN CUBA. CALLS FOR AID TO REBEL FORCES IN CUBA, he was certain that Allen Dulles had briefed Kennedy about the invasion plans without consulting him, and was enraged. Kennedy, he was also certain, had violated Eisenhower's confidence by "publicly advocating what was already the covert policy of the American government."[93] Later Nixon wrote:

I was faced with what was probably the most difficult decision of the campaign. Kennedy had me at a terrible disadvantage. . . . By stating such a position publicly, he obviously stood to gain the support of all those who wanted a stronger policy against Castro but who, of course, did not know of our covert programs already under way. . . .

There was only one thing I could do. The covert operation had to be protected at all costs. I must not even suggest by implication that the United States was rendering aid to rebel forces in and out of Cuba. In fact, I must go to the other extreme; I must attack the Kennedy proposal to provide such aid as wrong and irresponsible because it would violate our treaty commitments.[94]

Thus Nixon justified what became the baldest lie of his vice-presidency, what he called in his memoirs "an uncomfortable and ironic duty."[95] In the fourth debate with Kennedy he denounced his opponent's recommendations as "the most dangerously irresponsible recommendations that he's made during the course of this campaign." To follow them would mean the loss of friends in Latin America and condemnation in the United Nations. "It would be an open invitation for Mr. Khrushchev . . . to come into Latin America and to engage in what would be a civil war and possibly even worse than that." He called instead for "a strict quarantine" of Cuba, economic, diplomatic, and political. On October 22 he said of Kennedy's Castro statement, "This mistake should convince many Americans that they could not rest well at night with a man with such a total lack of judgment as Commander in Chief of our Armed Forces."

Had a successful invasion of Cuba followed in the coming week, with Castro's assassination and a quick coup, with American CIA involvement kept to a minimum—as the ideal plan envisioned—Nixon would probably have won the election.

As it was, there was no invasion, and the election was razor thin. "The position that I had to take on Cuba hurt rather than helped me," Nixon wrote. "The general 'image' to the end of the campaign was to be one of Kennedy stronger and tougher than I against Castro and Communism."[96] "Most observers," he said, "agree that our positions on the Cuban issue could well have been the decisive factor." Thus, ironically, it was his own major lie, he believed, that did him in; it was, he said in 1964, "the most costly decision of my political career."[97] Still, his quick recourse to this special lie he always justified. As he saw it, it was not the lie that cost him the election but the image of being "soft."

There is a crucial precedent here. This lie is worth more than a casual look. It was full of virtue—to aid the Cuban freedom fighters would mean loss of friends in Latin America, condemnation in the United Nations, and an open invitation to Khrushchev to interfere in Latin America. The lie won him immediate praise from the *Washington Post*. After the failure of the Bay of Pigs under Kennedy, Nixon freely admitted his part in the planning of the invasion and denounced Kennedy for not having provided proper air cover. He even advised Kennedy in private to "find a proper legal cover" and invade Cuba, even though it might mean, as Kennedy feared, that Khrushchev would move on Berlin.[98] Had the initial invasion failed under Nixon as it did under Kennedy—as it was certain to do, for fifteen hundred exiles could hardly have seized control over seven million mostly pro-Castro Cubans aided by over a hundred thousand well-trained and well-armed Castro militia[99]—there can be no doubt that as Nixon said later he would have involved the U.S. Air Force. This would have meant—as he warned in his own speech—the loss of friends in Latin America, condemnation in the United Nations, and trouble with Khrushchev. All this he would have risked to rid the hemisphere of Castro. And whatever happened, he would have justified the election speech lie as "an uncomfortable and ironic duty." Had Castro been assassinated he would have denied knowledge or complicity, and he would have been largely believed.

XXVIII

Nixon and Kennedy

*I feel sorry for Nixon because he does not know who he is, and
at each stop he has to decide which Nixon he is at the moment,
which must be very exhausting.*
— KENNEDY, ON NIXON, 1960[1]

SHORTLY BEFORE NIXON DROVE to the television studio
for the first of his four debates with John F. Kennedy in the presidential election of 1960, his running mate, Henry Cabot Lodge,
telephoned him and in a long call urged him to "erase the assassin
image."[2] Nixon in any case was determined to modify his image
of a pugnacious destructive campaigner. There would be no more
cries of "We can win if we start slugging!" as he had said in 1958.
He would now be the enlightened statesman, superior in wisdom
and experience to the brash young senator from Massachusetts
with small knowledge of foreign affairs and none at all in administration.

Although cartoonists made merry with Old Nixon and New
Nixon masks, the press on the whole gave the vice-president
respectful treatment, especially after he successfully routed Nelson Rockefeller's weak bid for the presidency without publicly
saying a word in opposition to him. *Time* and *Life* were openly
partisan, praising his wisdom and compassion.[3] Stewart Alsop, in
an influential little book, *Nixon and Rockefeller,* predicted that
Nixon would make a good president, saying he had "the boldness
and decisiveness, the instinct for 'moving quickly to shape events,'
the sure feel for the realities of power, the strong intelligence, the
cool toughness and simple guts in time of crisis."[4]

But Nixon found himself running against a man of formidable natural gifts, who brought intellectuals swarming into his
camp as had Franklin Roosevelt, and who charmed even the most
cynical of reporters. Lean, athletic, handsome, a shock of boyish

hair falling over his forehead, his cool gray eyes crinkling at the corners when he grinned, he caused palpable excitement among the women in every gathering, and his appearance on motorcades sent girls into paroxysms of shrieking and jumping. "They don't want to listen to him," NBC's Sander Vanocur said, "They just want to touch him."

Kennedy had already won political visibility by running for vice-president in 1956, when Adlai Stevenson threw open the contest for the office in the convention, losing out finally to Estes Kefauver. He had published two successful books. His senior thesis at Harvard, *Why England Slept,* a study of European appeasement of Hitler, had sold eighty thousand copies, and *Profiles in Courage,* a series of brief biographies of distinguished American political dissenters, had won him the Pulitzer Prize. Although he had been plagued by illness, including two back operations which almost cost him his life, and was in frequent pain, he radiated vitality instead of crippling. He had only one major handicap, his Catholic religion, which very nearly cost him the election, but which Nixon could not attack lest he appear a bigot. There was no good answer to Kennedy's disarming statement, "I refuse to believe that I was denied the right to be president on the day I was baptized."[5]

According to Nixon, his relations with Kennedy in the House had been cordial. Kennedy had invited Nixon to his wedding. He had even congratulated him on his victory over Helen Gahagan Douglas, and his father had sent him money for that campaign.[6]

In a subtle sense the coming of Kennedy as a rival in Nixon's orbit was like having his brother Harold come to life again, handicapped by illness, but still the exuberant, fun-loving charmer. For the first time in an election campaign Nixon began to talk about Harold, whom he described as "a kind of favorite with my father and mother." In three different cities he told the story of how his brother had wanted a pony "more than anything in the world," but his practical parents denied him so that they could purchase food, and "shoes for the younger brother." "It was an awfully hard decision for them," he said, "but it was the right thing."[7]

Although he distorted many of Kennedy's statements, scoffed at his plans for a "peace corps," and emphasized his immaturity— "The White House should not be a training school for Presidents"—there was no real bludgeoning as in the past. He called

Kennedy a Pied Piper, surely with some envy. In denying Kennedy's accusation that Republicans had always opposed Social Security, he called it "a bare-faced lie." Kennedy responded with a witticism: "Having seen him four times close-up and made-up, I would not accuse Mr. Nixon of being bare-faced."[8]

The contrast between the Kennedy family and his own was painful to Nixon. Jack, Bobby, and Teddy—all handsome, talented, rich, and fanatically fraternal—formed a political flying wedge, with the Kennedy sisters and their mother an attractive supporting backfield, and the silent but expectant Joseph Kennedy on the bench, an inexhaustible source of financial strength. Robert, as Jack's campaign manager, was tough, resourceful, indefatigable, a genius at improvisation. Jack said of him, "He's the hardest worker. He's the greatest organizer. . . . Bobby's easily the best man I've ever seen."[9]

Nixon's two brothers, especially the obese Donald, were unattractive looking, political embarrassments, and bumbling financial failures. Hannah Nixon's enthusiasm for her son's candidacy for president was notably muted. When Bela Kornitzer told Nixon in the spring of 1960 that she hoped he would be elected president, Nixon said in surprise, "I never thought mother would express her feelings with regard to the presidency." Although Hannah had preserved a piece of the red carpet her son had stood on when sworn in as vice-president, which she showed off proudly to visitors, her failure to praise her candidate son was troubling. When journalists asked her if she saw "a new Nixon," she replied, "No, I never knew anyone to change so little."[10] As we have earlier noted, when Bela Kornitzer interviewed both Hannah Nixon and Rose Kennedy and asked each if she thought her son would make a good president, Rose Kennedy replied in lyrical praise, but Hannah said only, "I think he would make a good president if God is on his side."[11] Nixon told both his brothers he would never use his family the way Kennedy was doing.[12] Actually he could not.

To Nixon everything seemed to come easy to the Kennedys. Joseph Kennedy had built a fortune in the twenties, and had luckily taken all of his money out of the stock market a month before the crash of October 1929. He had given each of his sons a trust fund of a million dollars on his twenty-first birthday. His money had flowed freely into the crucial primary campaign of Jack Kennedy against Hubert Humphrey in West Virginia, where Jack demonstrated for the first time that a Catholic could win over a Protestant in a non-Catholic state. To the accusation that Old Joe had bought the election Jack made no heavy-handed denial, countering the charge with a light-hearted joke, pretending to read from a letter from his father which said, "I won't pay for a landslide."[13]

Nixon made repeated references to the Kennedy wealth, saying, "It's not Jack's money he wants to spend; it's yours," and told stories accentuating his own childhood poverty. But in the end the citizens forgave Jack Kennedy his wealth, as they had forgiven that of the patrician Roosevelt. The public knew that wealth had protected neither family from tragedy. The terrible polio crippling had effectively destroyed the early image of the callow aristocratic young FDR, and it had brought him compassion and maturity. Accidental death had already cut down three members of the Kennedy family. The eldest son, Joseph, had been killed in 1944 when his plane, crossing the Channel on a dangerous mission to try to destroy a German V-2 rocket site, exploded midway. Three weeks later the British husband of Kathleen Kennedy, William Cavendish, had been killed. Kathleen herself died in a plane crash in France in 1948.

Wealth had made the Kennedys members of Boston's Irish elite, but not Boston's elite. Although Rose Kennedy was the daughter of a Boston mayor, "Honey Fitz" Fitzgerald, the couple had been blackballed when Joseph Kennedy tried to join the fashionable Cohasset Country Club, and over the years they had tasted the snobbery of Boston's old guard. "Tell me," Rose Kennedy said to one of her son's friends at Harvard who had come from the upper Wasp Boston society, "when are the nice people of Boston going to accept us?"[14]

Joseph Kennedy, a friend of Franklin Roosevelt's, had been named by him ambassador to Britain. But he caused consternation after Britain entered the war against Hitler by urging American nonintervention and predicting a Communist takeover of the world. Roosevelt recalled him in dismay, and he remained thereafter largely isolated from the Democratic party.[15]

Everyone in Massachusetts knew that Old Joe, who had once had presidential ambitions of his own, had been grooming his eldest son to be the first Catholic president, and that after his death

he began pressuring Jack to go into politics. To Charles Colling-
wood Jack admitted, "I never wanted to be in politics until nearly
almost the time I ran. I was always interested in writing. . . . the
war changed my life." To others he said, "I'm just filling Joe's
shoes."[16] He described the elder Kennedy frankly to reporters as
good with money but not politics, and once said bluntly, "My disagreement with my father is total." His *Profiles in Courage*—a study
of seven American men in politics who had defied "the angry
power of the very constituents who controlled their future"—
included John Quincy Adams, "the irritating upstart" who defied
his father to side with Thomas Jefferson in supporting the
embargo against England, just as Kennedy had defied his own
father to support FDR.

Still, the elder Kennedy performed useful services during his
son's campaign, especially in financing the making of the documentary film *PT-109*, which glorified Jack Kennedy's heroism in
the Pacific in World War II.

Joseph Kennedy had been a womanizer, providing a model
followed by all three of his sons. Jack Kennedy, described later as
"compellingly polygamous,"[17] did not seem to fear the gossip
about his own favored women friends, which circulated by word
of mouth during the campaign, nor the damage to his marriage.
The rumors remained unpublished till after his assassination and
Jackie's remarriage, when several women took their stories to
newsmen.

Nixon by comparison had the reputation of being a model of
marital propriety. But he also appeared stodgy and unimagina-
tive. In describing his courtship of Pat, in Nevada on August 2,
1960, he joked somewhat clumsily that he had been advised by a
law teacher to marry for money and to practice law for love. "I
found a school teacher who was making more than I was, and I
married her and she helped buy the engagement ring. Of course
there was some love."[18] Jack Kennedy on the other hand,
although generally reticent about his marriage, could say lightly
of his first meeting with Jackie, "I leaned across the asparagus and
asked her for a date."[19]

Jackie, too, although extremely shy, conveyed a sense of tension and excitement. When asked about her life since her marriage she replied, "I married a whirlwind." When Pat Nixon was
queried about her married life she replied, "We both work hard;

we are both self-sufficient; we don't show temper or irritation. We are friendly and try to give off warmth. We think we succeed, for why else would so many people come up to us and want to talk to us and tell us they are for us."[20]

The secondary competition between Jackie Kennedy and Pat Nixon was conducted entirely by the media, for both women avoided speech-making and served chiefly as ornaments. Since Jackie was pregnant and had a history of loss—one miscarriage and a stillborn baby before the birth of Caroline in 1957—she stayed out of campaigning altogether, save in New York City, where she rode in one motorcade that roused enthusiasm described as orgiastic. Her youth, offbeat piquancy, immense haunting eyes, and atypical beauty made her overnight an international sensation. Thanks to her maiden name, Bouvier, the French counted her peculiarly their own.

When one reporter asked Jackie if the rumor was true that she spent thirty thousand dollars annually on her exquisite wearing apparel, she replied with a flash, "I couldn't spend that much unless I wore sable underwear."[21] Pat's clothes in contrast, although tasteful, made her look by comparison like a country girl. It was not until 1968 that Pat spent lavishly on clothes in a campaign; the *New York Times* would put the figure at nineteen thousand dollars.[22] Although *Time* in 1960 put Pat on the cover and called her "one of the United States' most remarkable women," with "formidable reserves of poise and aplomb, and a retentive mind," it also noted that she preferred to keep an image of "a housewife who presses her husband's pants, cooks the meals and scrubs the floors." *Time* underlined her defensiveness about her subordinate role, "I've always been a part of what's done . . . but a silent partner," she said, and hinted at a deeper disquiet, quoting her as saying, "I've given up everything I've ever loved."[23]

Nixon, sensitive to the cruelty of the competition between his wife, now forty-eight, and the thirty-one-year-old Jackie, took extra pains in introducing her, saying repeatedly that she was "the stronger one" of the two of them, that "she should be the one running rather than me" and "I can't say who ought to be President, but I'm for Pat for First Lady." Once when he had promised a crowd outside an auditorium to bring her out after the rally was over, he introduced her by saying, "Isn't she wonderful. Wasn't she worth waiting for!" TRB in *The New Republic* described her, however, as "drawn, almost wasted." She followed her husband everywhere, he said, "her quiet charm never ruffled.". She "bore his exertions with a stoic weariness and tired sweetness, that, to some who followed her, was close to tear-provoking."[24]

She continued her habit of never answering political questions. Asked about her marriage when talking to a group of Republican women, she said lightly, "Dick is still the gay young blade I knew when we were courting."[25] She did let reporters know he forgot their twentieth wedding anniversary: "Dick didn't give me a thing, but the jaycees gave me a spray of red roses, so I guess my flowers will have to do." Nixon made a public apology.[26]

Nixon was in better health than Kennedy. The latter had chronic back pain because of a football injury at Harvard which had been worsened by the sea accident in the Pacific in 1944, and had not really been improved by the two back operations. It was kept secret that he lived in almost constant pain unless medicated by Novocaine injections given by his physician, Dr. Janet Travell. He always wore a back brace in motorcades. John Connally said publicly that Kennedy's Addison's disease—an adrenal deficiency requiring cortisone treatments—made him unfit to be president.

But Kennedy continued nevertheless to walk, swim, and swing a golf club with more grace than Nixon, giving the impression that he was in robust health, and he celebrated Election Day by playing a violent game of touch football with his family. Like FDR, who was much more seriously crippled, he radiated a sense of urgency and power. It was as if each of them, after so much illness and pain and immobility, felt he must carry out important tasks while there was still time. Nixon, for all the passion in his speeches, by contrast still seemed defensive. Kennedy's special coolness and detachment, his contempt for applause lines, conveyed a sense of freshness and genuineness. Nixon had no hesitation in adopting Eisenhower's "V for Victory" symbol; Kennedy said he'd forego the presidency altogether if he had to win it by waving his two arms above his head.

Although both men had been born in the twentieth century, it seemed that it was only Kennedy who spoke for the young and who was disentangled from the past. Adlai Stevenson sensed this special quality when he acknowledged Kennedy's supremacy over himself in the Democratic National Convention in Los Angeles, saying generously in defeat, "Do you remember that in classical times when Cicero had finished speaking, the people said, 'How well he spoke,' but when Demosthenes had finished speaking, they said, 'Let us march!' "[27]

Nixon constantly emphasized his superiority over Kennedy in experience, expressing it in the form of statistics. He had had 173 meetings with Ike, he said, and 217 with the National Security Council, over which he had presided 26 times. He had attended 163 cabinet meetings, presiding over 19. He had visited 54 countries, with extended discussions with 35 presidents, 9 prime ministers, 2 emperors, and the shah of Iran.[28] Meg Greenfield derided this in *The Reporter* as "leadership by association."[29]

When Nixon boasted of the accomplishments of the Eisenhower administration, Kennedy replied with metaphor:

What Mr. Nixon does not understand is that the President of the United States, Mr. Eisenhower, is not the candidate. You've seen those elephants in the circus with the ivory in their heads—you know how they travel around the circus by grabbing the tail of the elephant in front of them. That was all right in 1952 and 1956. Mr. Nixon hung on tight. But now Mr. Nixon meets the people.[30]

Joseph Alsop, following Nixon on the campaign, wrote privately to Paul Miller of his personal disappointment and shock. "I have not only liked and admired Nixon, I have also helped considerably to build him up as a man who has grown great with experience." But his speeches, he said, are "a steady diet of pap and soothing syrup," with "the approximate content of a television commercial." Of Kennedy he wrote to David Barrett, "He is the first American politician I have ever known who seemed to me to have the promise of true greatness."[31]

For several weeks both candidates were upstaged by Nikita Khrushchev, who was visiting the United States, touring farms in Iowa, sampling supermarkets in major cities and a cancan show in Hollywood, embracing Castro in Harlem and thumping his fist in the United Nations. Nixon and Kennedy competed furiously, each trying to convince the nation that he could best handle the truculent, volatile Russian leader. Nixon, whose denunciations of Khrushchev very often led to stories of his own father, continually promised to be "the coolest man" in a confrontation with Khrushchev, and reminded his listeners of the Moscow kitchen debate. Kennedy responded, "Mr. Nixon may be very experienced in kitchen debates. So are a great many other married men I know." "This is no time," he said, "to outtalk or outshout Mr. Khrushchev. I want to outdo him—outproduce him."[32]

To Nixon's dismay Kennedy emerged as the more aggressive Cold War warrior:

I do not think the world can exist in the long run half slave and half free. The real issue before us is how we can prevent the balance of power from turning against us. . . . if we sleep too long in the sixties, Mr. Khrushchev will "bury" us yet. . . . The President must be commander in chief of the grand alliance for freedom.[33]

To counter this, Nixon increasingly resorted to descriptions of his own near assassination in Caracas, and his conspicuous success in Warsaw. Over and again he described the latter triumph. "A quarter of a million people lined the streets of Warsaw, many of them crying and others shouting, 'Long live Nixon—long live Eisenhower.' They knew what we know, that America stands for more than gross materialism. We stand for moral and spiritual ideals."

Kennedy respected the "new Nixon" image and did not go back, as he might well have done, to the more disreputable stories in the campaigns of Nixon's past. But Harry Truman, cynical about the transformation, embarrassed some of the younger Democrats by letting fly with barrages of abuse. "If Nixon had to stick to the truth he'd have very little to say. . . . You don't set a fox to watch the chickens just because he has had a lot of experience in the henhouse. . . . Nixon has never told the truth in his life. . . . He is against the small farmer. He is against small business, agriculture, public power. I don't know what the hell he's for, and that bird has the nerve to come to Texas and ask you to vote for him. If you do you ought to go to hell."[34]

In the resulting uproar, when Kennedy was urged to get Truman to apologize to the vice-president, he said with a grin:

I really do not think there is anything I can say to President Truman that is going to cause him, at the age of 76, to change his particular speaking manner. Perhaps Mrs. Truman can, but I do not think I can.

Nixon, replying to Truman, said Eisenhower "had restored

dignity and decency to the conduct of the government in Washington D.C. at the White House," and promised "never to indulge in anything that would make them ashamed of the man who is President of the United States, and I mean gutter language or anything of that sort."[35]

Nixon had predicted in advance that Kennedy would take Lyndon Johnson as his vice-presidential candidate, although many Democrats, including Robert Kennedy, met the decision with dismay.[36] It was a shrewder choice than Nixon's own. Nixon could have had Thruston Morton, a big genial senator from Kentucky who could have brought in many southern votes. As it was, he took a Brahmin from Massachusetts, Henry Cabot Lodge, who had been beaten by Kennedy in the senatorial campaign of 1952. Although Lodge had been for eight years United States ambassador to the United Nations and had made a record as an aggressive opponent of the Soviets, he could not shake the stigma of the former Kennedy defeat. Barry Goldwater called the choice "a disastrous blunder."[37]

An indifferent campaigner, Lodge was no match for the professionalism and canny opportunism of Lyndon Johnson, who won back for Kennedy the areas lost to Eisenhower in 1956— Texas and Louisiana—and ensured the Carolinas. Lodge was more liberal than Nixon, and early in the campaign suggested that there be a black in the cabinet. Although he did not name him, he had in mind the distinguished diplomat and Nobel Prize-winner, Ralph Bunche. But Nixon was embarrassed by the suggestion and forced Lodge to retreat into vacillation and confusion.

There is still some mystery why Nixon, against the pleas of his staff, agreed to meet Kennedy in a series of four television debates. The Republican Convention had seen Nixon forge ahead of Kennedy in the polls, 53 percent to 47 percent. His acceptance speech, according to TRB of the *New Republic,* had "sent millions into raptures," and was "one of the most impressively effective fifty minutes we ever witnessed. He rang every bell."[38] Nixon had shared a platform with Kennedy in West Virginia, and also at a Senate ceremony in March 1959. The latter in particular should have warned him about the Kennedy magic, but it had not. Both men had been asked to speak at the unveiling of portraits of five famous senators—Henry Clay, Daniel Webster, John C. Calhoun, Robert LaFollette, and Robert Taft. Nixon spoke briefly, in platitudes. But Kennedy livened the occasion by mischievously quoting the five dead senators against each other. He noted that Calhoun had said of Clay, "He is a bad man, an imposter, a creator of wicked schemes." Clay, he reported, had called Calhoun "a rigid fanatic, ambitious, selfishly partisan and sectional, a 'turncoat' with too much genius and too little sense." And John Quincy Adams had said Daniel Webster had "a gigantic intellect, envious temper, ravenous ambition, and rotten heart." The audience was convulsed.[39]

Nixon dismissed the Kennedy wit as pedantic, and counted on his own talents to demolish his opponent in the debates as he had Voorhis. Kennedy when speaking was inclined to rush, and to keep his voice too high. His only gesture was a monotonous poke with his forefinger. Nixon was a seasoned orator with a fine baritone voice. In addition to the debates, he promised to speak in all fifty states, and planned an exhausting schedule.

Six weeks before the first debate Nixon injured his knee, striking it against a car door in Greensboro, North Carolina. It developed a serious interior infection and he had to be hospitalized for two weeks. During this fortnight Kennedy's rating went up to 51 percent in the polls. Enraged at the interruption, Nixon left the hospital still feverish and insisted on a fifteen-thousand-mile tour covering twenty-five states before the first debate.

James Bassett and Leonard Hall were privately dismayed by what Bassett described as a kind of megalomania which made Nixon not only unmanageable but also unapproachable. He gave way to explosions of rage, generally to new and younger men like Robert Haldeman and John Ehrlichman who had moved into his inner circle and had not yet learned how to contain and defuse the fury. Haldeman, whose father had contributed to the Nixon slush fund in 1952,[40] "was by nature an excluder." This was the judgment of James Shepley, briefly on Nixon's staff in 1960, who said later, "When Nixon's needs met Haldeman's abilities, you had an almost perfect formula for disaster."[41] Haldeman's experience was entirely in advertising; he had no sense of politics. He did have a sense of Nixon's need for being comforted, listened to, and isolated from people who threatened him, but he never understood the indispensability of conviviality and gregariousness in a candidate.

Leonard Hall described the relationship between Haldeman and Nixon to David Halberstam as "darkness reaching for darkness." Haldeman learned, as Hall had before him, that Nixon was a chronic insomniac, that he frequently worked during the night and dictated memos to his staff in a tape recorder. These memos, Hall said, "were among the angriest and most paranoic documents around." He and Bassett had learned to ignore them; Haldeman "seemed to relish acting on them."[42]

Bassett remembered with pain one episode in the 1956 campaign when Nixon had exploded at his staff after a meeting with a group of young college editors at Cornell University who had thrown some tough questions at him. When he had climbed into the small private plane in which they were traveling, Nixon had flung himself upon Ted Rogers, yelling, "You son of a bitch, you put me on with those shitty-ass liberal sons of bitches, you tried to destroy me in front of thirty million people." An appalled Philip Potter of the *Baltimore Sun* had pulled him off. Bassett later had told Nixon his staff was on the point of mutiny.

"You didn't go into this campaign with a gun at your head," Bassett said. "You fought for it. What scares the hell out of me is that you would blow sky high over a thing as inconsequential as this. What in God damn would you do if you were president and got into a really bad situation?"

Nixon had replied, "I'll think about it." Then for six weeks, Bassett said, "he was the kindest boss we ever had."[43]

In the 1960 campaign Bassett as director of planning was kept in Washington. Leonard Hall was largely ignored, and the gentle Robert Finch, nominally in charge of the campaign, found it impossible to bend Nixon's inflexible will even on trifles. One result for Nixon was fatigue, exhaustion, and rage. It was during this period that the episode occurred where he kicked the seat of his military aide, Don Hughes, in an insensate fury.[44]

Nixon arrived for the first debate at Chicago, September 26, physically exhausted, twenty pounds underweight, his face wan, his collar hanging loosely about his neck. But he was keyed up mentally. Although James Bassett has said that he scorned studying the questions presented to him by James Shepley, Nixon insisted that he spent five hours cramming the answers to more than a hundred questions. "I felt that I was as thoroughly prepared for this appearance as I had ever been in my political life up to that time."[45]

Kennedy arrived in the studio some moments after Nixon, buoyant and confident, deeply tanned from recent campaigning in California. "I had never seen him looking so fit," Nixon said.

Nixon staffers had taken great pains to brief the TV crews about lighting: "Give our man lighting that will bring out the strong, mature lines in his face; we want to contrast him to the boyish Kennedy." And they urged the camera crews to avoid Nixon's unhappy left profile.[46] Ted Rogers, appalled at Nixon's appearance of illness, his failure even to purchase a new well-fitting shirt, urged him to use makeup. It is odd that with all his acting and television experience Nixon now rejected it outright, accepting only some "beard stick" powder to help cover the heavy shadow on his jowls, which served only to increase his pallor.

It was agreed in advance that the first debate should be on domestic issues, Nixon mistakenly believing that viewers would increase in numbers as the debates proceeded. It fell by lot to Kennedy to lead the debates, and he began with a brief but smashing attack on Khrushchev, trying to establish before seventy million viewers that he could be as tough or tougher than Nixon. He then went on to attack the Eisenhower administration as being stuck on dead-center, permitting increases in unemployment, racial discrimination, depression among farmers, and inadequate medical care for the aged. Nixon wrote later that he spoke "as effectively as I have ever heard him."

Instead of responding with an assault on his own, Nixon betrayed at once that he was shaken by Kennedy's skill. He admitted that there was much that Kennedy said with which he could agree. The nation cannot stand still, he said, "we are in deadly competition, a competition not only with the men in the Kremlin but the men in Peking." That he recognized he was himself to be *in deadly competition* thus surfaced in his very choice of words. Kennedy, he understood too late, was no Jerry Voorhis. "I realized," he wrote in *Six Crises,* "that I had heard a very shrewd, carefully calculated appeal, with subtle emotional overtones, that would have a great impact on a television audience."[47]

What little confidence remained in Nixon was shattered in the question period when Sander Vanocur of NBC repeated Eisenhower's gaffe made during his press conference of August 24, which Nixon had hoped would be forever buried. When a reporter asked what major ideas of Nixon's had been adopted by his administration, the president had said, "If you give me a week, I might think of one." Asked by Vanocur to comment, Nixon fumbled in obvious pain:

Well, I would suggest, Mr. Vanocur, that if you know the President, that that was probably a facetious remark. . . . I think it would be improper for the President of the United States to disclose the instances in which members of his official family had made recommendations, as I have made them through the years, to him, which he has accepted or rejected.[48]

Those who missed the television and heard Nixon and Kennedy only on radio thought Nixon had clearly bested his opponent. But many television viewers who saw the Nixon pallor, the trickle of sweat pouring down his chin, the struggle to overcome his discomfiture at the Vanocur question, remembered very little else. Nixon's running mate, Henry Cabot Lodge, watching the debate on TV in Texas, blurted out in Murray Fromsen's hearing when the debate was over, "That son-of-a-bitch just lost us the election!"[49]

Hannah Nixon called Rose Woods in dismay to ask if her son was ill, and a disturbed Pat Nixon immediately took a plane from Washington to Chicago.

When the word went out from the Nixon staff that the makeup had been to blame for their candidate's gaunt appearance, Kennedy quipped, "Regardless of whether the makeup is changed and the lighting is changed, Mr. Nixon's the same for fourteen years."[50]

In the second debate Nixon assumed the offensive. There was much argument about whether the United States should interfere in the shelling by Communist China of Quemoy and Matsu, islands close to the China coast still held by Chiang Kai-shek, with Nixon taking the hawkish stand. And he ridiculed Kennedy for suggesting that Eisenhower could have saved the Geneva conference by expressing regret to Khrushchev over the American-sponsored U-2 flight over his country. Reston in the *New York Times* said, "Nixon clearly made a comeback," and Joseph Alsop wrote, "The Nixon candidacy got a real lift." But the television audience had dropped by twenty million, and in the third and fourth debates remained about the same.[51]

The last two debates rehashed the earlier material. Reporters in the third debate tried to interject the religious issue with a question about the Ku Klux Klan leader endorsing Nixon. Both candidates refused to be drawn into the controversy. Kennedy insisted that Nixon had not the slightest sympathy for the Klan, and Nixon said, "I have ordered all of my people to have nothing to do with it."

In the fourth debate Nixon made an unfortunate slip of the tongue which caused much merriment among Democrats, but which could hardly have amused Pat Nixon, especially since he made it three times:

America cannot stand pat. We can't stand pat for the reason that we're in a race, as I have indicated. We can't stand pat because it is essential with the conflict that we have around the world, that we not just hold our own. . . .[52]

In the final debate Nixon attacked Kennedy for his aggressiveness in wanting to help the Cuban exiles, which, as we have seen, led him into lying in an effort to cover up the well-advanced CIA Cuban invasion plans he had sponsored. The debate revealed an increasing contrast between Kennedy's consciousness of a happy pact with destiny and Nixon's lack of faith in his own. In the last debate Nixon said:

In the years to come . . . what will determine whether Senator Kennedy or I, if I am elected, was a great President? It will not be our ambition . . . because greatness is not something that is written on a campaign poster. It will be determined to the extent that we represent the deepest ideals, the highest feelings and faith of the American people. In other words, the next President as he leads America in the free world can be only great as the American people are great.[53]

Nixon had been ahead in the polls before the debates; Kennedy pulled ahead after them. Both Republicans and Democrats reflected on Nixon's folly. Barry Goldwater said privately that the debates were "a disaster."[54] TRB wrote, "the debates ruined Nixon. At best he has been lucid and at worst didactic and pedestrian. . . . He stands as a man without a spiritual home, ready to twist any circumstances to his advantage, devoid of any genuine moral commitment to either liberalism or conservatism but trying to feel at home wherever the tides of circumstance happen to lodge him."[55] Max Ascoli, editor of *The Reporter,* who was not altogether happy about Kennedy, found a "nihilist quality" in Nixon. "He is not a true conservative," he wrote, not "a man with faith in the traditions they must strengthen," but a man given to "stunts and gimmicks," taking liberties with the truth.[56]

Theodore White, without meaning to insult the vice-president, wrote that "Kennedy exerts over Nixon the same charm a snake charmer exerts over a snake." He saw Nixon as no longer a cruel and vindictive opponent but as "a friendseeker, almost pathetic in his eagerness to be liked."[57]

Even Eisenhower's entering the campaign in the last fortnight, and his making genuinely enthusiastic speeches on Nixon's behalf, could not dispel the vice-president's melancholy. Still he fought on, stubbornly determined to fulfill his commitment to campaign in all fifty states, even though this meant traveling sixty-five thousand miles and making 180 major speeches. Four days before the vote he said in Rochester, New York:

I do not believe, apparently as my opponent does, that this is the time for greatness and I am the great man that America needs. I tell you I do know this: I do know that Cabot Lodge and I have been through the fire, the fire of decision. We have sat opposite Khrushchev and we have never been fooled by him and we never will.

Although he had called many times for "peace without surrender," he flubbed the line three days before the election, calling for "peace *and* surrender."[58]

The seesawing in the polls now became nightmarish for both candidates. Nixon, who he tells us had always believed that he would win, now had to face consciously the possibility that he might not. On the two most sensitive issues, Catholicism and race, he thought he had done well. Although he stood to benefit from an increasing anti-Catholic groundswell, he continued to denounce bigotry where he saw it and to insist that his followers leave the religious issue alone. He refused an endorsement from Billy Graham, who with the Southern Baptists had adopted a "No Catholic for President" resolution.[59]

He had made many statements in favor of rights for blacks, and was counted more liberal on the issue than Eisenhower, and at least as liberal as Kennedy, a newcomer to the issue. Nathaniel

George, a black friend from his Whittier College days who had talked and corresponded with Nixon about the problems of black youth, insisted Nixon was "definitely not bigoted."[60] In accepting the Republican nomination he promised blacks "the greatest progress in human rights" since the days of Lincoln. Nixon was not insensitive to mounting black resentment over the failure of desegregation, especially the continued denial of the right of blacks to eat in restaurants and lunchcounters. This had led to massive sit-ins, with many arrests and increasing fear of general violence. In his second debate Nixon said, "I have talked to Negro mothers . . . they tell their children how they can go into a store and buy a loaf of bread, but they can't sit at a counter and get a Coca-Cola." But instead of punitive government action he recommended "calling in the owners of the chain stores and getting them to take action."[61]

James Bassett, who had been convinced that Nixon was "consciously colorblind," was disturbed when he abruptly canceled a Sunday brunch with leading Chicago black clergymen and businessmen. Bob Haldeman called Bassett and said brusquely, "The boss says he ain't going to do that nigger thing in Chicago." Bassett protested in some heat, but Haldeman only repeated, "The boss says he ain't going to do that nigger thing."[62]

On October 19 word came to Nixon that the Rev. Martin Luther King, who had organized the Montgomery, Alabama, bus boycott of segregated busses that broke the back of the transportation segregation in the South, had been arrested with fifty-two other blacks in a sit-in at a restaurant in Rich's department store in Atlanta. All the other blacks were released save King, who was held in jail and then sentenced to four months at hard labor in the Georgia State Penitentiary. The excuse was a faulty driver's licence which technically made him subject to parole, which the judge said he had violated in the sit-in. King was whisked away, bound in handcuffs and leg irons, to Reidsville, the heart of rural Georgia, with no chance for appeal. Although King's radical gospel, like that of Gandhi, was based on nonviolence, his tactics had been so successful that they had led to much violence against blacks, and King lived daily with the threat of assassination. Many now feared he would be lynched in prison. His wife Coretta, six months pregnant, frantically called for help through friends to both Kennedy and Nixon.

Kennedy aide Harris Wofford first called Sargent Shriver, Kennedy's brother-in-law and the head of his Civil Rights section. He managed to find Kennedy at the O'Hare Inn in Chicago's International Airport and recommended action. Kennedy, without consulting anyone, immediately called Coretta King to express his sympathy. Robert Kennedy, at first alarmed by his brother's call, since three southern governors had warned Kennedy that to support King would lose him their states, was so angered when he heard the details of the arrest he called the Georgia judge to protest that King had a right to bail and an appeal. The black leader was shortly freed on $2000 bond.[63]

Nixon, pressed by his staff to take similar action, said coldly to Herbert Klein, "I think Dr. King is getting a bum rap. But despite my strong feelings in this respect, it would be completely improper for me or for any other lawyer to call the judge. And Robert Kennedy should have known better than to do so." Klein told the press Nixon had no comment.[64] Nixon had counted heavily on anti-Catholic sentiment among blacks, and knew that King's father had endorsed him. But Martin Luther King, Sr., insensed now at Nixon's silence, said of Kennedy, "Because this man was willing to wipe the tears from my daughter [in-law]'s eyes, I've got a suitcase of votes, and I'm going to take them to Mr. Kennedy and dump them in his lap."

The story, largely ignored in the white press, was headlined in the black media. Under Wofford's prodding a million pamphlets describing the freeing of King were printed and distributed among black churches. The Kennedy intervention, Theodore White wrote, "rang like a carillon" in the black parishes.[65] Later, in *Six Crises* Nixon said he urged Attorney-General William Rogers to take the matter up with the Justice Department but Rogers refused when he got no go-ahead signal from the White House.[66] But few believed that Eisenhower was really to blame.

Stevenson had won 60 percent of the black vote in 1956; estimates of the black vote for Kennedy after the election ranged from 68 to 85 percent. The vote was decisive in at least five states. Kennedy won New Jersey by 30,000 votes. The black Democratic vote in this state was 125,000. Michigan was won by 65,000; the black vote was 225,000. Missouri had 100,000 black Democratic votes; Kennedy won by 35,000. In South Carolina Kennedy won by 10,000; 40,000 blacks voted for him. In Illinois where Kennedy

carried the state by only 9000 votes, 250,000 blacks were said to
be in his column.[67]

The 1960 campaign tested Nixon's talents, experience, political acuity, and judgment. The Martin Luther King episode was a
decisive test of his compassion. Nixon's black driver in Washington, John Wardlaw, discussing the election with him later, did not
reproach him for his failure, but his message was unmistakable:

Mr. Vice President, I can't tell you how sick I am about the way my
people voted in the election. You know I had been talking to all my
friends. They were all for you. But when Mr. Robert Kennedy called the
judge to get Dr. King out of jail—well, they just all turned to him.[68]

By November 7 George Gallup refused to predict the outcome
of the election, saying it was too close to call. On election night
early returns put Kennedy well in the lead, but as the midwestern
and western states reported it became evident that Nixon might
just possibly do what Woodrow Wilson had done in 1916, go to
bed thinking he had lost and awaken the victor. California for a
time was declared a Kennedy state but Nixon forecast correctly
that absentee ballots would pull it back into his camp. He was thus
reluctant to make a concession speech, and Pat, for a while, was
adamant against it. Kennedy at the time said, "If I were in his
shoes I wouldn't concede either."

Demands for a statement and rumors that he was being a poor
sport were so insistent, however, that after midnight he agreed to
go to the auditorium of the Ambassador Hotel in Los Angeles and
make at least a partial concession.

Half the people in the auditorium were crying, Nixon said. "I
could see tears welling up in Pat's eyes, and before going on, I put
my arm around her."[69] He said briefly it looked as if the election
was lost, and thanked his aides, making a more formal concession
the following morning.

When writing *Six Crises* Nixon later recalled how he felt at the
moment of concession. "Now, it's really over. No more schedules,
no more crowds, no more handshakes, no more autographs, no
more speeches. Now, at last we can rest."[70] But he did not rest.
Although he had had only four hours sleep in forty-eight hours,
he prowled through the hotel corridors, Bassett said, like a restless lion. Wilma Bassett, going past the Nixon suite, recalled "a
long bony arm reaching out from an open door" and seizing hers.

It was Pat Nixon. She flung herself on the bed and cried like a child. As "Willie" Bassett stroked her back in a vain attempt at comfort, she said, "Now I'll never get to be First Lady."[71]

Final returns put Illinois and Minnesota in the Kennedy camp; he had 303 electoral votes to Nixon's 219. The first popular vote margin, however, was a scant 113,000 votes out of 68,800,000 cast. When they returned to Washington, Nixon wrote, the city was full of talk about vote frauds in Illinois, lost by 9000 votes, and Texas, lost by 49,000. Nixon reproached himself bitterly later for not asking the Justice Department to impound the Cook County votes the day after the election. He was certain Mayor Daley had organized his defeat. As evidence he cited vote frauds adding up to three or four thousand votes.

He quoted Kennedy in his first conversation with him after the election as saying, "Well, it's hard to tell who won the election at this point."[72] Why then did Nixon not contest it? In *Six Crises* and in his memoirs he said that his friends and associates, including Eisenhower, who had even offered to raise money to pay for the recount, urged it. But he had decided to "set a good example" and accede without a fight. Otherwise, he said, "there would be open-season for shooting at the validity of free elections throughout the world."[73] Nixon noted, moreover, that there were no facilities in Texas for a recount. But he did not inform his readers that when the vote was formally challenged in Illinois that the Illinois State Electoral Board, which was four to one Republican, voted unanimously to certify the Kennedy electorate.[74]

Eisenhower in his memoirs said nothing about urging Nixon to challenge the election returns. He wrote simply, "To waste time mourning the loss of any contest is never profitable."[75] Ralph de Toledano, Nixon biographer and journalist for *Newsweek,* said that it was Eisenhower and not Nixon who insisted that the election returns not be challenged. This, he maintained, Nixon told him at the time. And he was disturbed by what Nixon wrote in *Six Crises.* "This was the first time," he said, "I ever caught Nixon in a lie."[76]

In *Six Crises* Nixon listed sixteen circumstances which, had they been handled differently, might have won him the election, including his failure to call Mrs. Martin Luther King. He waited until 1976, however, when writing his memoirs, to tell the story of how he insisted that Eisenhower not campaign strenuously for him in the last fortnight in order to preserve his life.

After the inaugural ceremony on January 20, 1961, Nixon went to a farewell luncheon for Eisenhower hosted by Admiral and Mrs. Louis Strauss. "When I said goodbye to Eisenhower, he held my hand for a long time as he shook it. For a moment I thought he was going to become emotional, but he said simply, 'I want you and Pat to come up and visit us in Gettysburg very soon.' "[77]

That night Nixon asked his driver to come back for one more drive through the city. Hundreds of men and women in formal dress were on their way to the inaugural balls. "No one noticed us," he said.

He ordered Wardlaw to drive to the Capitol, where the car was parked in the space reserved for the vice-president. Nixon got out and walked up the broad stone stairs, past a surprised guard and into the Capitol building, down the long corridor to the Rotunda, then out onto the balcony that looks to the west. "The mall was covered with fresh snow," he said, "and the Washington Monument stood out stark and clear against a luminous gray sky, and in the distance I could see the Lincoln Memorial. I stood looking at the scene for at least five minutes. . . . As I turned to go inside, I suddenly stopped short, struck by the thought that this was not the end—that someday I would be back here. I walked as fast as I could back to the car."[78]

XXIX

A Problem with Donald

"THE HUGHES LOAN," a complicated financial intrigue involving Vice-President Nixon, his brother Donald, and Howard Hughes, became an issue in the last fortnight of the 1960 campaign and an even more embarrassing problem in Nixon's campaign against California governor Pat Brown in 1962. In both campaigns Nixon was accused of lying about the loan. He denied it then, and continued to deny it in his memoirs.

Donald Nixon in 1956 owned two restaurants and a grocery store in Whittier. He was ambitious to own a chain of restaurants, and tried unsuccessfully to raise $300,000 by a public stock subscription. There was a mild uproar when this stock was advertised in a Republican rally, and Donald apologized. He persuaded his mother to let him use a vacant lot she owned in Whittier as collateral for a bank loan. Even though the lot had an assessed value of only $13,000, the market value was between $40,000 and $50,000, and Donald, who planned to build a gas station on it, persuaded Union Oil Company to enter into a contract whereby they agreed to pay him a guaranteed income of $800 a month for fifteen years when the station was built.[1] A commercial lending firm would offer to lend him no more than $93,000 for the entire package. For Donald, whose restaurant business was in severe financial difficulties, this was not enough.

Both Richard and Donald Nixon knew Frank A. Waters, formerly from Whittier, now a Washington lobbyist. A few weeks after his election to the vice-presidency, Nixon called Waters about his brother's plight. Waters then called Noah Dietrich, executive vice-president of the Hughes Tool Company, one of the many branches of the immense Hughes empire.

"I've been talking to Nixon," Waters said. "His brother Donald is having financial difficulties with his restaurant in Whittier. The Vice President would like us to help him."

"Help him in what way?" Dietrich asked.

Waters replied that Donald Nixon needed a $205,000 loan. Dietrich said he whistled in astonishment. "Jesus, I've never transferred that much money to the political account. I can't do it on my own responsibility. You'd better talk to Howard."

The next day, Dietrich related, Howard Hughes called him and said, "I want the Nixons to have the money."[2]

Hughes, one of the nation's wealthiest men, and recipient of many national defense contracts, had long made a point of giving campaign gifts to both Republican and Democratic candidates. This money was different: it was not a campaign contribution but a virtually unsecured loan involving the vice-president's family. It would put Richard Nixon peculiarly in Howard Hughes's debt. Dietrich said later, "The whole thing had a bad smell to it. The more I heard about the transaction the less I liked it. I liked Richard Nixon. I had voted for him as United States Senator and twice as Vice-President. I didn't want to see anything happen to bring disrepute to Eisenhower or Nixon. . . . No one was to be held liable for the repayment of the loan if it went into default."

Dietrich tells us he was so disturbed he flew to Washington to warn Nixon. "If this loan becomes public information," he told him, "it could mean the end of your political career. And I don't believe that it can be kept quiet." Nixon replied, "Mr. Dietrich, I have to put my relatives ahead of my career."[3]

For billionaire Hughes the sum of $205,000 was trifling. But the loan could be potentially embarrassing for both the vice-president and for Hughes himself, especially if it could be proved that Nixon gave Hughes favors in return. As it turned out there was one government favor Howard Hughes very much wanted at the moment, notably an Internal Revenue Service ruling, hitherto denied, permitting his Howard Hughes Medical Institute to be classified as tax exempt. Whatever else was said in the conversation between Nixon and Dietrich the latter did not reveal. But after Dietrich was estranged from Hughes and he described the whole transaction in 1972, he pointed out that on March 1, 1957, three months after the loan was given to Donald Nixon, the Internal Revenue Service "had a change of heart toward the Howard Hughes Medical Institute." It informed Hughes "that it was reversing its original decision. The Howard Hughes Medical Institute would now be classified as a tax exempt charitable organization. At last Hughes was officially, legally, in a charity business worth tens of millions of dollars to him, both directly and indirectly."[4] That Nixon was responsible for the change in the IRS ruling has not been proved.

To protect everyone, extraordinary efforts were taken to keep the Hughes name hidden in the transaction. Dietrich transferred the money from the Hughes Tool Company's Canadian subsidiary and turned the money over to Frank Waters, whose name appeared on the loan rather than the Hughes Tool Company. The agreement was executed on December 10, 1956. The check for $205,000 was made out to Hannah Nixon. She then loaned $165,000 to Donald and used the remaining $40,000 to pay off a loan she had made jointly with him.

Noah Dietrich by now was predicting Donald's bankruptcy within ninety days. A Hughes management committee went to Whittier and recommended changes in his restaurant management. Donald was annoyed, and Vice-President Nixon communicated his displeasure to Dietrich. "My brother wants to run it his way," he said. The restaurant shortly closed and Donald Nixon went bankrupt in December 1957. Harry A. Schuyler of Whittier said, "Somebody told him he was a big shot, and he believed it and went broke. He extended himself too fast." Harold A. McCabe said, "that pretty well washed up what all the Nixons had. As far as what his mother had, that was pretty well washed out too."[5]

Meanwhile Waters, the "dummy owner" of the mortgage on Hannah Nixon's lot, turned it over to Philip Reiner, an accountant, who paid nothing for it. Reiner got the mortgage on September 13, 1957. Reiner shortly turned the mortgage over to Hughes Tool, the rightful owner, but continued to get $800 a month from the Union Oil Company. He paid taxes on the money and remained the registered owner.

In December 1958 the Nixons tried to wipe out the unpaid $205,000 loan by surrendering the Whittier lot to Reiner, and sent him the deed. Reiner gave the deed to Hughes's lawyer, James J. Arditto, but it was not recorded. In November 1960 Hannah Nixon was still listed as the owner of the lot by the Los Angeles County Recorder.[6]

As the story began to surface during the 1960 campaign, one man tried to sell it to Robert Kennedy for half a million dollars. Since the data were tenuous—Noah Dietrich had not yet confessed his role in the story—Kennedy remained unimpressed, although later as attorney-general he studied and discarded the possibility of prosecuting members of the Nixon family for criminal law violations that might have occurred.[7]

When Reiner learned of the attempt to sell the story, he decided to tell everything to the press. The *St. Louis Dispatch* and Drew Pearson both obtained copies of his story. Nixon now, in Arditto's words, "panicked and put out a cock-and-bull story," which his campaign manager, Robert Finch, and his old law partner, Thomas Bewley, released to Scripps-Howard columnist Peter Edson.

In his October 24, 1960, column titled "Vice President Bares Story of Kin's Deals," Edson said the $205,000 came from Frank Waters, whose wife had been a friend to Donald Nixon's wife. With Donald bankrupt, Hannah deeded the property to Waters, who in turn deeded it to Reiner, because he was "one of the creditors who had threatened foreclosure." Drew Pearson on October 26 published the correct version of the events, and asked why the vice-president, who had received his "clean as a hound's tooth" blessing from Eisenhower, had permitted his family to receive the big financial benefit from Hughes, one of the leading benefactors of American defense contracts. What, Pearson asked, had the vice-president done for Hughes?

Nixon meanwhile said repeatedly that he knew nothing of his brother's business transactions. He could not, however, deny that a key document had been notarized for his mother in the Senate Office Building in Washington, D.C.[8] Donald, however, finally admitted that the money had indeed come from Hughes. This was on October 31, just eight days before the election.[9]

How much the scandal damaged Nixon in 1960 is difficult to assess. He wrote that on election night his brother Donald "said with his voice breaking: 'I hope I haven't been responsible for your losing the election.' I reassured him: 'The only place the charge meant anything was here in California, and we are going to carry California anyway.' "[10] In *Six Crises* Nixon wrote deceptively about the loan. That his mother was deeply involved and knowledgeable concerning the whole transaction did not deter him.

During the last days of the campaign, the opposition had resurrected the financial troubles which had forced him [Donald] into bankruptcy two years before and had tried to connect me with a loan he had received from the Hughes Tool Company during that period. They had, of course, conveniently ignored the fact that my mother had satisfied the loan by transferring to the creditor a piece of property which represented over half her life savings and which had been appraised at an amount greater than the loan.[11]

In 1962, although Nixon threatened to "dump a load of political bricks" on anyone who raised the issue in his campaign against Brown, the Hughes loan surfaced again, and with greater impact. James Phelan's investigation detailing the intrigue to cover up the loan appeared in *The Reporter* in August and also in a Long Beach newspaper. On October 1, 1962, Tom Braden, editor and publisher of the *Oceanside Blade Tribune,* put the question to Nixon in the one press conference Nixon agreed to share with Pat Brown:

I wanted to ask you whether you as Vice President or as a candidate for governor, think it proper for a candidate for governor, morally or ethically, to permit his family to receive a secret loan from a major defense contractor in the United States?

Nixon replied at first civilly and with care. "I welcome the opportunity of answering it."

Six years ago, my brother was in deep financial trouble. He borrowed $205,000 from the Hughes Tool Company. My mother put up as security for that loan practically everything she had—a piece of property, which, to her, was fabulously wealthy, and which is now producing an income of $10,000 a year to the creditor.

He admitted his brother's subsequent bankruptcy, and denied ever doing anything for "the Hughes Tool Company," taking care not to say that he had never done anything for Howard Hughes. Then he made an impassioned speech, which he repeated in large part in his memoirs:

I had no part or interest in my brother's business. I had no part whatever in the negotiation of this loan. I was never asked to do anything by the Hughes Tool Company, and never did anything for them. And yet, despite President Kennedy's refusing to use this as an issue, Mr. Brown, privately, in talking to some of the newsmen here in this audience, and his hatchetmen have been constantly saying that I must have gotten some of the money—that I did something wrong.

Now it is time to have this out. . . . I have made mistakes but I am an honest man. And if the Governor of this state has any evidence pointing up that I did anything wrong in this case, that I did anything for the Hughes Tool Company, that I asked them for this loan, then instead of doing it privately, doing it slyly, the way he has—and he cannot deny it—because newsmen in this office have told me that he has said, "We are going to make a big issue out of the Hughes Tool Company loan."

Now he has a chance. All the people of California are listening. Governor Brown has a chance to stand up as a man and charge me with misconduct. Do it, sir![12]

Nixon trusted in the Hughes men to keep their mouths shut about his own involvement, and in fact the most important revelation from Noah Dietrich, that Nixon had initiated and urged the loan, was not made public until 1972.[13] The affable Pat Brown, who disliked confrontation, had not mastered the technicalities of the Hughes loan, and would not in any case have entered into an argument involving Nixon's mother, replied defensively. He said that his staff had not raised the matter, which was true. Nixon later said that Brown "cringed and went away like a whipped dog."[14] Brown himself felt that he had handled the matter badly, although the television response was good.[15]

Nixon handled the potentially explosive matter with aggressive bravado and denial. He still had to face persistent queries from reporters, and wrote in his memoirs that he was asked about the Hughes loan at least a hundred times.[16] Instead of answering, he said that he would talk about it only to Governor Brown directly. Discomfited reporters were at a loss how to proceed. Some felt Nixon should not in any case be held responsible for the financial imbecilities of his brother, forgetting that Howard Hughes was not likely to give a loan with so little security to a man of such notoriously bad business ability without good reason.

Jerome Waldie, however, Democratic caucus chairman, accused Nixon of "contempt of the press" and "fear of cross-examination at the hands of skilled reporters." "He will don the robes of a righteous avenging son, rushing to defend the honor and the good name of his mother. But her honor and good name are nowhere at stake and Nixon knows it."[17] When Brown finally challenged Nixon to debate the Hughes loan, Nixon's press secretary, Herbert Klein, said he had already answered it fully.[18] When questions persisted, Nixon replied testily and somewhat incoherently,

I have challenged Mr. Brown at any time to discuss the Hughes loan. I am not going to answer any questions by his hatchetmen. And I don't think that you as a member of the press should prostitute yourself to put questions by a hatchetman rather than to have Mr. Brown answer it.

Newsweek commented, "No politician improves his chances by charging a reporter with prostituting his profession."[19]

With Nixon's defeat in 1962 the Hughes loan was largely forgotten. It was not until Watergate, when at least a portion of the intricate financial transactions involving Hughes and Nixon became public, that journalists and historians, looking back to 1962, could see the erratically emerging pattern of entanglement. Tom Braden was one of many editors with a special interest in tracing the pattern. As punishment for his question about the Hughes loan in the press conference of October 1, 1962, he was audited by the Internal Revenue Service every year Nixon was in office as president.[20]

When Nixon was president, his brother Donald continued to be a serious embarrassment, and so too, to a lesser extent, his youngest brother Edward. Nixon at one point put Donald under electronic surveillance. Senate Watergate investigators explored allegations that Donald Nixon tried to fob off phony mining claims on the Hughes Tool Company. Bebe Rebozo, testifying about Donald, defended him as not dishonest but naïve.[21] Both Nixon brothers were linked to Robert Vesco, who fled to Costa Rica to escape prosecution for looting $224 million from an international investment fund. Donald Nixon's son, Donald, who had worked for Vesco, followed him out of the country, calling Vesco in 1971 his "mentor and best friend." Vesco aides testified that Edward Nixon had helped negotiate an unreported gift of $200,000 in cash to Richard Nixon's 1972 campaign fund. It was later returned. Vesco, it was said, used Donald Nixon to carry the threat that he would reveal the illegal gift if federal investigations into his affairs were not halted.[22] Senate investigators complained that Donald ignored crucial subpoenas. Both brothers escaped prosecution.

Nixon, who immortalized Donald on one presidential tape by calling him "my poor damn, dumb brother," in his memoirs wrote almost nothing of his difficulties with either brother. He did include an extract from his presidential diary of June 7, 1974:

I saw Don and Eddie after luncheon for (Prince) Fahd (of Saudi Arabia). Both brothers have stood up splendidly under tortuous conditions. Don has about forty thousand dollars in legal bills. Eddie has one of twenty thousand for legal fees.[23]

XXX

The Drubbing

Too many people are saying, "I don't like Nixon, but I don't know why."

— ARCH MONSON, REPUBLICAN FUNDRAISER, 1962[1]

RICHARD NIXON RESPONDED TO DEFEAT by going into isolation, retreating not only from politics but also from his family. After a vacation with Pat and Bebe Rebozo in the Bahamas, he flew alone to California, where he joined the law firm of Adams, Duque, and Hazeltine. Earl Adams, who had been one of the donors of the "Checkers fund," had given him the job. He lived alone for six months in a small bachelor apartment on Wilshire Boulevard.

I preferred to be alone. . . . the last thing I wanted to do was to talk to people about the election . . . virtually everything I did seemed unexciting and unimportant. . . . It was not an easy time.[2]

Chronically uninterested in food, he was content to heat up TV dinners and eat them alone while reading. "As time went on," he confessed in his memoirs, "I began to adjust to my new life and even to enjoy it." Although he said one of his reasons for moving to California was "to have more time with Pat and the girls,"[3] his family stayed on in Washington, the reason given that they did not want to interrupt their daughters' schooling, and it is evident that he sought solace in solitude rather than in the intimacy of his family. Although Pat made several trips to Los Angeles to find housing,[4] Nixon made no mention of this in his memoirs, and emphasized only his malaise and solitary life.

Like others who have tried to salve the wounds of failure he took refuge in the writing of a book. Nearly every man who reaches eminence in politics has some concern for the judgment of history, and most presidents have written memoirs as a last-ditch stand against the assaults they have been subjected to during their years in office. Buchanan, Grant, and Hoover, in particular, wrote books expressly to reconstitute a ravaged reputation. But three men who became president—Jefferson, Theodore Roosevelt, and Nixon—wrote a book in advance of election to the Oval Office and following great loss. Jefferson wrote his *Notes on the State of Virginia* after an inquiry into his failure as war governor of Virginia by his enemies in the Virginia Assembly. Written at the nadir of his career, the book became, in a subtle sense, "Notes on the State of Mind of Thomas Jefferson." What achieved renown as an eighteenth-century scientific, political, and intellectual landmark served also as an exercise in therapy.

Theodore Roosevelt, after the tragic deaths of his wife and his mother, which occurred on the same day, went west to the badlands of South Dakota, where he exorcised his grief in the arduous physical labor of the cowhand. There he wrote *Hunting Trips of a Ranchman,* in which there is a remarkable preoccupation with death and killing, but all very distant from his personal tragedy, which he never mentions. No woman appears in the book. It consists of a narrative of several trips, with infinitely detailed descriptions of his skill at killing wild fowl and deer.

Nixon's was the only book of the three that was openly introspective, and in which the therapeutic process is easy to follow.

In his introduction to *Six Crises* Nixon said, "the last thing I ever intended or expected to do after the 1960 election was to write a book." But publishers were pressing him for a memoir; Mamie Eisenhower urged it, and finally his aggressively devoted newspaper woman friend, Adela Rogers St. Johns—"the one who had the greatest influence in my decision"—arranged for Kenneth McCormick of Doubleday to fly out to Los Angeles with a contract. By that time Nixon was already sketching out a plan. Bob Haldeman, the only member of his political staff to stay around with an offer of aid after the defeat, promised to help with the research. This touched Nixon, for he had come to feel that friends in politics cared only for power and fled from a man in defeat as from one diseased. The gesture helped cement what was to be his closest political friendship in his years as president.

Nixon made no mention of aid from his wife in the writing, including only a graceless dedication, "TO PAT, she also ran," which discomfited everyone who knew her. Although he explained in the book that she had herself talked of writing a memoir and calling it *I Also Ran,* the joke was inept, and the explanation was buried in the text.

Nixon had mentioned to President Kennedy in April 1961 that he was thinking of writing a book, and Kennedy had replied somewhat wryly that "every public man should write a book at some time in his life, both for the mental discipline and because it tends to elevate him in popular esteem to the respected status of 'an intellectual.' "[5] Whether the young president intended it or not, the imputation was there that the former vice-president was not yet an intellectual, and this Nixon intended to erase. During the 1960 campaign he had said moodily to William Costello, "I'm an egghead but no one believes it."[6] Now he took as models for his book Walter Bedell Smith's *Eisenhower's Six Decisions* and Kennedy's own *Profiles in Courage.* Gradually the memoir evolved into a profile in the courage of Richard Milhous Nixon, with six selected crises as the ordeals through which he passed and which he met with varying degrees of fortitude. It became not only an exercise in therapy but also in self-definition.

To everyone who knew Nixon as cold, remote, and uptight, the book was most astonishing as revealing a veritable passion for self-analysis. *Six Crises* showed an introspective, troubled man, the epitome of moral virtue, but also a man subject to mortal fears of indecision and failure. Although a major theme was his delight in battle, he readily admitted an anxiety about whether to fight or run away. His fear of loss of control showed through at times as a kind of terror.

It was evident that even the limited therapy with Dr. Hutschnecker had galvanized his curiosity about himself, and had helped to relieve his shame about occasionally appearing naked before his enemies. Since he was in control of his own words, from the first dictation on tape to his assistant Alvin Moscow, to the final editing in page proof, he was in control, at least consciously, of the self-revelation, and the nakedness he chose to reveal was meant to stimulate empathy rather than disgust. But his special delight in parading the abuses to which he had been subjected unquestionably had roots in his childhood. There are many echoes of "the good dog letter" in *Six Crises,* the biting child, the abused child, and the weaknesses that made him—in Theodore

White's phrase of the moment—"one of life's losers." At one point we see the beginnings of the paranoia that became so obvious during Watergate, when he wrote that as a result of his facing down Hiss he was subjected to a vicious twelve-year smear campaign, including charges of bigamy, forgery, drunkenness, insanity, thievery, anti-Semitism, perjury, "the whole gamut of misconduct in public office, ranging from unethical to downright criminal activities."[7]

Still, the sympathetic reader would see Nixon largely as a mistreated hero, a courageous young statesman who had nearly been assassinated in the line of duty in Caracas, who had stood up to Khrushchev, who had behaved in the most exemplary fashion in Ike's illnesses, who had met "the exquisite agony" of each crisis with dignity and fortitude, and who was rewarded by having the 1960 election stolen from him.

Writing *Six Crises* helped restore Nixon's self-image and political identity. He told his readers he would have made a better president than Kennedy, that he would have supplied air cover to the Cuban guerrillas at the Bay of Pigs, and would if necessary have sent in American forces to destroy the infamous Castro. Over and again he underlined his preoccupation not only with becoming president but also with being a great man. In writing of a Washington reception for Congressional Medal of Honor winners, he described how one winner came up to him, and pointing to his new ribbon said, "You should be wearing this, not I. I could never have done what you did in Caracas." Nixon replied, "And I could never have done what you did during the Battle of the Bulge." He continued:

Perhaps we were both wrong. No one really knows what he is capable of until he is tested to the full by events over which he may have no control. That is why this book is an account not of great men but rather of great events—and how one man responded to them.[8]

The fund crisis was hardly a great event, nor was the kitchen debate, nor Ike's successive illnesses. What Nixon probably hoped was for his readers to make the essential reversal and read into his lines what he dared not write: "This book is not an account of great events but of a great man."

Eight years later, as president, in the euphoria of his first trip to China, when Mao said to him "Your book, *Six Crises*, is not a bad book," Nixon, obviously pleased, said lightly to Chou En-lai, "He reads too much."[9]

Long before he had finished the manuscript in November 1961, Nixon had secretly decided to run for governor of California, although he did not confide in his wife. James Bassett guessed it, and predicted it in the *Los Angeles Times* on April 23, but Nixon kept on publicly denying it. Meanwhile his book was further tailored into a campaign document. He had a natural flair for the dramatic, and in the long hours of dictating into a tape recorder and in the editing he learned a good deal about the art of autobiography. His editor, Kenneth McCormick, tells us that he wrote the last chapter on his own. "Why don't I try the chapter on defeat?" he said. "In the course of doing this I think I have learned to write."[10]

Six Crises was a bestseller; it made $250,000 for its author and reestablished him as a man of consequence in the Republican party. The reviews for the most part were respectful. Tom Wicker in the *New York Times* admired his occasional "incisive political judgment and general readability," but noted that the book "offers almost no answer at all to the question that has hung from the beginning over his head: what kind of a man is he?"[11] A few reviews were harsh. Richard Whelan wrote that "Nixon seems not to consider the possibility that the public distrusts a prig."[12] William Costello, whose tough little book *The Facts About Nixon*, serialized during the 1960 election in *The New Republic*, had established him as the most perceptive investigative reporter writing about Nixon, saw in *Six Crises* a "conflict between the outer and inner man, a contrast that like sheet lightning illumines not the events through which he moves so much as the man himself."[13]

Between the royalties for *Six Crises* and the $100,000 annual income from his law firm, Nixon for the first time in his life luxuriated in a big income. Moreover, the writing of ten articles for the Los Angeles Times-Mirror Syndicate—the burden of which he turned over largely to Stephen Hess[14]—brought an additional $40,000.[15] Nixon told Earl Mazo with satisfaction that in his first fourteen months in Los Angeles he had earned more than in his fourteen years of government service in Washington.[16]

The Nixons had sold their home at 4308 Forest Lane in Washington and had purchased a view lot at 410 Martin Lane in the fashionable Trousdale Estates high above the city of Beverly Hills. Pat and her daughters were loath to leave Washington. Reporters watching their departure reported all three were weeping. "We don't like to leave the house," Pat said.[17] Arriving in California in mid-June, they moved into a rented house at 901 North Bundy, in Westwood, which had a pool and a guest house, and lived there till the new house was finished. The "Trousdale house" was a conventionally elegant ranch-style home with the special California sybaritic emphasis on water, with four bedrooms, seven baths, and a 900-square-foot swimming pool. As Carey McWilliams pointed out dryly, "every night for a full week they can bathe in a different bathroom."[18] For Pat Nixon, who had lived for a time as a small child in a house with no indoor plumbing, the house became increasingly important. Eventually Nixon, too, according to Stephen Hess, "became inordinately proud of it."[19]

Vendors on Sunset Boulevard hawked maps to the movie-star homes in the area, and there were stars in the Trousdale development—Fred MacMurray and his wife June Haver, Joe E. Brown, Cesar Romero—even Groucho Marx, who gave the Nixons the touch of acid that was their inevitable lot, saying he wouldn't be dropping by:

I don't know my neighbors, and I don't expect to associate with them unless there's a bomb, and we all meet in the same hole in the ground. That's called the fusion ticket—or is it fission?[20]

The Los Angeles Times reported that Nixon was given a hefty "celebrity discount" for moving into the development. Journalists had discovered in the Los Angeles County Recorder's Office that James Hoffa, who had invested his Teamsters Retirement Fund heavily in the Trousdale development, owned a $42,000 mortgage on the Nixon lot, and that it had been sold to the former vice-president for only $35,000. Subcontractors working on the house, it was rumored, were asked to "donate" a certain amount of work free. Trousdale told reporters that the Nixons paid $125,000 for the house. David Halberstam reported the sum later as being $90,000.

Nixon was annoyed at the Los Angeles Times story and called the editor, Frank McCulloch, "in genuine bewilderment," asking, "What's wrong with what I did?"

McCulloch replied, "You're not entirely a private citizen, Dick. You've been Vice-President of the United States, and you may well have a political future."

"I don't see what's wrong," Nixon countered.[21]

When he announced his candidacy for governor in a press conference at the Statler-Hilton on September 27, 1961, one of the first questions asked was a demand for an explanation of how he got a Hoffa Teamsters Fund $42,000 lot for only $35,000. "Was it a gift?"

Nixon began his answer with civility, "I'm glad that it came up now," and stated that he had simply paid the asking price:

I might say, incidentally, that builders all over the state and county offered me lots free, which I did not take because I did not think that was appropriate.

He said his only real contact with Hoffa was a check to Bekins Van and Storage for $4300 for the cost of moving his household furnishings from Washington, of which $1000 would go to members of the Teamsters Union.

Then, as so often when faced with charges of impropriety, he became abusive:

Nobody is going to drive me out of this contest, and that, as far as this kind of smear is concerned, and that is exactly what it is. I intend no longer to take it lying down. . . . I so serve warning, here and now . . . that anybody that makes charges of this type will have to answer for them, and they will be in for the fight of their lives on the charges.[22]

He insisted over and again in the campaign that when he made the "Checkers" speech his only assets were an old car and a mortgage. Now, he said, his only assets were a newer car, a bigger mortgage, and two teenage daughters.

The Hoffa connection was forgotten until years later, when Nixon granted a pardon to the Teamsters president, who had been jailed for mail fraud and jury tampering. Even after Nixon's resignation one subcontractor who had admitted to friends he had donated some of his work free on the Nixon house refused to discuss the matter for publication "for fear of a lawsuit." We have here a foretaste of the early Nixon denials when researchers began exploring the expenditures on Nixon's estates in San Clemente and Key Biscayne. As president, he managed to get seventeen million dollars worth of improvements on his two properties, most of which, it is true, was spent for security and administrative purposes, but at least ninety-two thousand of which was spent for "the President's personal benefit" for such items as a new heating system, enlargement of windows, refurbishing of buildings, a shuffleboard court, and fences.[23]

In California, with the worst of his malaise behind him, Nixon discovered that to abandon politics, as his wife was hoping, was to sever his lifeline. To become president was as much an obsession as ever; once more he became absorbed with tactics and timing. To run for the House was an intolerable debasement; to run for the Senate was impossible; it would mean a rerouting of the popular Sen. Thomas Kuchel to the governorship. Kuchel, when sounded out by Republican National Chairman Thruston Morton on the matter, said dryly that he was "too old to play musical chairs, either politically or socially."[24] Nixon knew that if he ran for governor of California and won, this would give him a political base from which he could decide at leisure whether or not to challenge Kennedy in 1964. Since Kennedy seemed impregnable, Nixon's gut feeling at the moment was that he should not run in 1964 but wait until 1968, and let Goldwater or Rockefeller waste himself against the popular young president. Should Kennedy commit some major blunder, he could always come in from the wings as a last-minute candidate.

In any case, as he confessed in his memoirs, he "had no great desire to be Governor of California." As he wrote to Eisenhower, who was urging him to run, "our problems here are so complex and also we are, frankly, physically so far away from the centers of national and international news media that I simply do not believe it would be possible for me to continue to speak out at all constructively on national and international issues."[25] California problems—water, education, smog, freeways—were big. But Nixon, with his addiction to international politics, found it all boring. William Steif noted that in an interview with Nixon he spent 85 percent of his time telling him why he shouldn't run for governor.[26] He wanted to remain titular head of his party. He didn't have to run for office at all.

Pat Nixon for a time believed in his renewed promise that he had abandoned the political life she had come to loathe. As she told young Samuel Goldwyn, Jr., at a dinner when they were comparing careers in the movie business and in politics, "You think people in the movie business are competitive. They may be competitive but they are not mean. In politics they are the most vicious people in the world."[27]

She had quickly readapted to California, and was enamored with the work of decorating her new house. She had arranged for their daughters to start in the fashionable and conservative private Marlborough School in Beverly Hills in the autumn. She was back among old friends, with the privacy she cherished, but she was still treated like the wife of a vice-president. On her arrival, she and her husband had been feted with a welcome-home party by the Greater Los Angeles Press Club, with sixteen hundred guests. Her alma mater, the University of Southern California, had honored her with a doctor's degree[28]—a fact Nixon failed to note in his memoirs. The idea of a new uprooting should her husband become governor, the certainty of a calamitous drop in salary, plus a new move into the funky eighty-four-year-old Victorian mansion set aside for state governors in Sacramento, this in a hot interior valley in a city of little charm, filled Pat with dismay. Most of all she had hoped to spare her daughters the cruelty of a new campaign, remembering vividly what they had been subjected to in Washington, when Julie came home from school saying, "It hurts to be told your father stinks."[29]

Adela Rogers St. Johns, helping Nixon with *Six Crises* in the house on Bundy Avenue, overheard a rare and envenomed quarrel between Nixon and his wife over the prospect of his running for governor. "If you ever run for office again," Pat said, "I'll kill myself." Later, one day, when Adela returned in the late afternoon and found all the shades drawn and the door locked, she thought in a fleeting moment of horror that Pat had done just that.[30]

Although he repeatedly denied it at the time, we learn from his memoirs that Nixon never looked on the governorship of California save as a stepping-stone toward the presidency. Leonard Hall, who hoped to see him run against Kennedy in 1964, reinforced him, saying, "Who will remember Dick Nixon? You can only win in '64 if you run and win for the governor now."[31] And he warned him, as did others, about Nelson Rockefeller's emergence as the most popular leader in the party. The affable, moderate-to-liberal Republican governor of New York was certain to be reelected in 1962 and to run against Kennedy in 1964. Nixon had a special envy of Rockefeller, despite the fact that he had crushed easily his attempt to win the party's bid in 1960. Moderate Republicans had come to love Rockefeller almost as much as Democrats loved Kennedy. They forgave him his great wealth, admired his extensive philanthropies, and took him seriously as a presidential candidate—until, that is, they learned in 1962 that he had fallen in love with one of his campaign workers, Margaratta (Happy) Fitler, and was about to divorce his wife, the austere but respected Mary Todhunter Clark, to whom he had been married since 1930, and who was the mother of their five children. The divorce in 1962 was messy; "Happy" Fitler's husband forced her to give up custody of *their* children. Although Americans were increasingly forgiving of divorce, they were not ready for this one, and the change of wives proved costly for Rockefeller in 1964. But none of this Nixon could have predicted when he was wrestling with his own decisions in late 1961.

When Nixon continued to dally, and to tell the press he would not run for the governorship, right-wing Joseph Schell, a handsome, athletic young oilman supported by the John Birch Society, announced his candidacy. Then former California governor Goodwin Knight, a moderate Republican, entered the ring with considerable labor support. Knight disliked Nixon. In a party shakeup in 1958 Nixon had insisted that Knight run for senator so that William Knowland could run for governor. Both had lost, Knight to Democrat Clair Engle and Knowland to Pat Brown. Knight was shortly forced to drop out of the 1962 primary because of illness, but he never endorsed Nixon. Further rifts in the party appeared when former Republican Lt.-Gov. Harold J. Powers called Nixon "a discard from the rubble heap of national politics," when former Republican mayor of Los Angeles Norris Poulson came out for Brown, and when Earl Warren, Jr., switched parties and became Brown's assistant campaign manager.[32]

Although early polls showed Nixon had a twenty-point lead over Brown—57 percent to 37—two of his trusted former aides, Bob Finch and James Bassett, warned him against running. Bassett, who had soured on Nixon in 1960 and who had returned to the *Los Angeles Times* to replace the ailing Kyle Palmer in the post of political editor, talked privately of Nixon's meanness of spirit, dictatorial control over his own staff, and tendency to megalomania. He had, moreover, an accurate measure of the collective enmities Nixon had garnered among California Republican leaders. He shocked the former vice-president by telling him he could not win. Bob Finch, less harsh, told Nixon he thought he deserved a longer rest from politics for his own sake.[33] Even Robert Haldeman recommended against running, although he agreed later to manage the campaign.

Nixon was convinced, however, that he could never return to presidential politics without a strong party base at home. Although there had long been more Democrats than Republicans in the state, they were a volatile lot, undisciplined, without party bosses, who had switched allegiance by the thousands for Earl Warren. In the beginning of the campaign, certain of an easy victory, Nixon held Brown in contempt, and it was only later that he conceded "he was in the enviable political position of being a man whom no one particularly disliked."[34]

Brown was a rounding, affable, buoyant man, without guile or cunning, who so disliked offending people he was sometimes spoken of as "a tower of jelly." He had, however, taken a courageous and unpopular stand against capital punishment, and had been publicly jeered for staying the execution as long as was legally possible of the most famous man on California's death row, Caryl Chessman, who went to the gas chamber without ever having killed anyone. Nixon was strong for capital punishment, even advocating execution for "big-time dope peddlers on the second or third conviction."[35] Although Brown was dismissed by many as a bumbler, actually he had been an able administrator, and his four years had been scandal free. He had an infectious affection for his state and an intimate knowledge of its thirst for water. He had enlarged California's aqueduct and pumping system into the most elaborate irrigation system in the world. Bringing extra water to Los Angeles and San Diego counties had meant increased industry as well as agriculture—the state had 41 percent of the nation's new space industry—and California's population had rocketed. Believing devoutly that education was the state's best investment, he expanded the university system, keeping the tradition of free tuition, until it became a magnet for educational leaders the world over. His legislature was overwhelmingly Democratic, and cooperative.

Brown had, moreover, won the friendship of the powerful Chandler family, whose massive fortune had been built on local water rights and real estate. Nixon mistakenly thought he could count on the Chandlers to give him the same undeviating support as in the past, which meant a literal blotting out of most of the news coverage of his opponent. But Norman Chandler, with his wife's urging, had given over the reins of the *Los Angeles Times* to their son Otis, who was determined to transform the paper from a parochial conservative Republican sheet into a rival of the *New York Times*. He gave orders that Brown be given equal news coverage, although the editorial page generally favored Nixon. The new editor, Frank McCulloch, promised "to measure the length of Nixon and Brown stories" to ensure equality,[36] and hired two able new reporters, Richard Bergholz and Carl Greenberg, to cover the campaign.

Buff Chandler, who increasingly held Nixon in distaste, had preferred Rockefeller in 1960 and had cautioned Nixon then against running against Kennedy. She and her husband felt that Nixon had bungled the campaign. Nixon was dismayed now when Norman Chandler advised him against running, but did not pick up the signal. With the $40,000 contract from the Times-Mirror Syndicate for ten articles in his pocket, he had as yet no real understanding of the revolution at Times Mirror Square.

Franklin Roosevelt did not tell his wife of his decision to run for a third term, and she learned of it from others. Other politicians may have acted in the same fashion with their wives. Of his own decision in September 1961, Nixon wrote candidly in his memoirs, "I dreaded bringing up the subject with Pat and Tricia and Julie, so I left it until the last possible moment."[37] One friend said he broke the news at a small restaurant party after a football game, and that Pat went off to the restroom in tears. Journalist Maxine Cheshire said Pat was "visibly shaken" and that "details of the family argument have been widely circulated within the Republican party."[38] There are also unsubstantiated reports that the resulting private quarrel at home was searing and violent.

Nixon in his memoirs tells us nothing about the restaurant experience, writing rather that he made the announcement to his family on September 25, at home, the night before his promised decision to the press. It proved to be, he admitted, "a major new crisis for me and my family."[39] Still, as he described it, it was little more than a spirited family discussion.

"Pat, as I expected," he wrote, "took a strong stand against it. She said, 'If you run this time, I'm not going to be out campaigning with you as I have in the past.' " Julie, he said, seeing "such a strong difference of opinion," said "that she would approve whatever I decided." Only Tricia took "a positive line."

"I'm not sure whether you should run," she said, "but I kind of have the feeling that you should just show them you aren't finished because of the election that was stolen from us in 1960!"[40]

Julie, then fifteen, and Tricia, seventeen, it must be remembered, had been brought up with parents who were inordinately proud of the family tradition of self-control and who continually tailored the facade of family happiness. Pat Nixon told journalists, "We never have fights, we just move away from each other."[41] Of Julie's wretchedness we learn more from Earl Mazo than from her father. He was told that she said, "All I want is for everyone to love everyone and be happy. I can't study or do anything when one of us is not happy."[42]

Nixon wrote that as a result of the argument he decided not to run, and sat down at his desk to make some notes for the press. But he did not tell his wife. Instead he waited, and after half an hour she reappeared.

"I could tell from her voice that she was fighting not to show her tremendous disappointment." He let her speak first.

"I have thought about it some more," she said, "and am more convinced than ever that if you run it will be a terrible mistake. But if you weigh everything and still decide to run, I will support your decision. I'll be there campaigning with you just as I always have."

"I'm making some notes to announce I won't be running," he said.

But it was too late for Pat, and she did not press her victory. "No, you must do whatever you think is right."

"We sat for some time in silence," Nixon wrote. "Then she came over to me, put her hand on my shoulder, kissed me, and left the room. After she was gone, I tore off the top sheet of paper and threw it into the wastebasket. On a fresh page I began making notes for an announcement that I had decided to run."[43]

Pat did not, however, campaign as she had in the past. Richard Bergholz, following Nixon for the *Los Angeles Times,* said that save for an initial swing around the state he almost never saw her.[44] Nixon made a clumsy attempt to explain her absence, as Tom Wicker noted in the *New York Times:*

Our oldest daughter is sixteen and won't be home but two more years, so this year we decided Pat ought to stay with her and only go out with me on weekends.

Wicker said she was appearing "a bit more often than that," and was sympathetic with her more obvious problems. "She is told by gushing ladies with what must be maddening frequency how wonderful she would have been as First Lady."[45] When questioned about leaving her elegant new home and moving into the old governor's mansion, she replied valiantly, "It's not where you live but what you do. We've had everything you could want in a lifetime—all the status."[46]

By the end of the campaign Nixon, with his chronic affection for uncheckable statistics, was announcing that his wife had met thirty-six thousand five hundred women in twenty-two California cities, and had grasped forty-three thousand hands. He called her his "secret weapon."[47]

The campaign saw a reconciliation between Nixon and Murray Chotiner, who had been cast off as somewhat too foul-smelling in 1956. Nixon had refused in 1960 to support the irrepressible Chotiner's effort to replace Republican incumbent Alphonso Bell in Congress, but the 1962 campaign saw a burying of old animosities and Nixon's reembracing of the crafty old comrade. Chotiner, a more rabid anti-Communist than ever, was masterminding the primary campaign of an extreme right-wing Republican, Lloyd Wright, against Sen. Thomas Kuchel. Wright, former president of the American Bar Association, was on record favoring preventive war with the Soviet Union—"If we have to blow up Moscow that's too bad," he said[48]—and was close to the John Birch Society, then in the heyday of its influence. Its members had plastered billboards saying IMPEACH EARL WARREN! all over the West, and its leader, Robert Welch, was accusing Eisenhower of being "a dedicated conscious agent of the Communist conspiracy," and John Foster Dulles, "a Communist agent."[49]

Nixon scolded the John Birch Society for its attacks on Eisenhower and Dulles, but not on Earl Warren. And he tried to get the thirteen-thousand-member California Republican Assembly to expel the Birchers within its membership, at the same time maintaining good relations with what he called, even in his memoirs, his "close personal and political friends," House members John Rousselot and Edgar Hiestand, who were members of the Birch Society and who would not renounce Welch's wilder accusations. Chotiner, who was intent on keeping the right wing in Nixon's camp, blocked the expulsion of the Birchers from the California Republican Assembly, and succeeded instead in getting a simple resolution of condemnation for Bircher president Robert Welch. By this strategy he gained a foothold in Nixon's campaign, and in effect guaranteed the support of the volatile and paranoiac right wing in November.

Chotiner worked in the wings as an unpaid adviser under Robert Haldeman, encouraging a return to the old trickery of 1948 and 1950.[50] Haldeman, who had done his own share of redbaiting as a student at UCLA, where he had once purged the staff of the *Daily Bruin*,[51] fell easily into the accustomed ways of his two mentors. Bumper stickers appeared saying "Is Brown Pink?" A fake "Committee for the Preservation of the Democratic Party" sent out circulars, presumably from Democrats, warning that Pat Brown was being influenced by left-wing extremists. The committee violated California's new election laws, and an angry Brown took the matter to court and got a restraining order. Another mailing from a second phony committee, "Democrats from California," came too late in the campaign to be stopped by the courts. As Pat Brown recalled the episode,

Normally we wouldn't have pursued the matter after a victory, but we were so damn mad at the fraud we wanted a judgment and an admission of guilt from both Haldeman and Nixon. We got both. There was no fine, but they had to pay the court costs.[52]

What enraged Nixon was that the dirty tactics were exposed by the *Los Angeles Times* in the news columns, as they had never been in his earlier campaigns. Even Chotiner, with his perennial habit of denying guilt, insisting that they had never accused

Brown, a devout Catholic, of being a Communist sympathizer, admitted after the campaign that the court restraining order "clinched it in the mind of the public that there was dirty literature put out by the Nixon people."[53]

The *Los Angeles Times* exposed, too, the fact that GOP workers were selling a pamphlet "California Dynasty of Communism," by a former Communist who claimed to be an FBI agent, who wrote that Brown "over the years has established an unchallengeable record of collaborating with and appeasing Communists from top to bottom." The pamphlet showed a picture of Brown making what appeared to be a gesture of obeisance to Khrushchev, with the caption below, "Brown is a Red appeaser." The photograph was phony, cropped from one taken showing Brown greeting two small girls from Thailand, returning their "sambai" gesture, with hands palm-to-palm clasped beneath the chin. It had been combined with a photograph of the Soviet leader.[54]

Nixon called the cropped photograph "disgraceful,"[55] but continued in his speeches to imply that Brown was soft on Communism, saying he was "not capable of dealing with the Communist threat within our borders," and complaining that Brown had introduced no antisubversive legislation.[56] He advocated the continued enforcement of loyalty oaths, denounced colleges which invited speakers who had "taken the Fifth Amendment," including Nobel Prize-winner Linus Pauling as one who had no right to speak on state campuses. He called for "authoritative textbooks" on anti-Communism in all the public schools.[57]

This regression to out-of-date anti-Communist rhetoric demonstrated the staleness of his thinking and also, in Lou Cannon's phrase, his "misconception of what the campaign was all about."[58] It betrayed above all his basic boredom. When in one slip of the tongue he spoke of running for "Governor of the United States"—an error publicized by the *Los Angeles Times*—the voters sensed that Nixon's heart was in Washington not Sacramento. They resented it. One opinion poll showed four out of ten disbelieving Nixon's promise that he would stay in office all four years.[59] Brown meanwhile reiterated that "Nixon looks on Sacramento as a bush league stop on the way to Washington," and the Democrats accused him of "double parking in Sacramento on the way to the presidency."[60]

Nixon had no program for state improvement, calling instead

for a tax cut and decreased state expenditures, even in mental health. The state's mental hospitals, he said, were "winter resorts" for "derelicts."[61] He would "clean up the mess in Sacramento," he said, but when challenged by journalists to define the mess he answered only in generalities. Greenberg and Bergholz of the *Times* faithfully recorded his wilder utterances, taken down on the wire recorders he had come to detest, as they did the excesses of Pat Brown, who in one speech claimed he was "a better American than Richard Nixon." Even Nixon's embarrassing excuse for losing to Kennedy in 1960—"I was in the Navy in the South Pacific but I wasn't on a PT boat; that's why I'm here and not in Washington"—found its way into the *New York Times*.[62]

Nixon accused the Democrats of spending double that of the Republicans, and of having a slush fund of half a million to pay precinct workers, while Republican workers were all volunteer. Actually both parties admitted to spending about the same: the Republicans $1,421,553 and the Democrats $1,482,206.[63]

In the beginning of the campaign journalist William Steif found Nixon "hard, resourceful, resilient." By May of 1962 Tom Wicker was describing him as a man at bay, "if anything more reserved and inward, as difficult as ever to know, still driven by deep inner compulsions toward power and personal vindication, painfully conscious of slights and failure—a man who has imposed upon himself a self-control so rigid as to be all but visible."[64] "In 1960," one staffer told Tom Wicker, "Dick wouldn't listen. Now there's no one who dares say no." James Bassett, writing gently but ineffectually about Nixon in the *Los Angeles Times*, said privately of Nixon's staff, "After 1960 I didn't know a single 'No' man. Tough men, yes. Men who said 'Screw you!' to everyone else."[65] Kyle Palmer, dying of leukemia, periodically called the *Times* office demanding a more sympathetic treatment of Nixon.[66] It was not forthcoming, although in the end Otis Chandler, bowing to family pressure, had the newspapers formally endorse him.

During the campaign Kennedy came to California to urge a Brown victory. Through his secretary of the interior, Stewart Udall, he had given the governor an important plum in December 1961, a decision, reinforced by the courts, that the 160-acre limit for water from the new San Luis reservoir would apply only to the federal portion of the San Luis waters. This meant that owners of the big acreages in Southern California, like the Chandlers with their vast Tejon Ranch, would not have their water supply limited by federal fiat.[67]

Eisenhower, seeing Nixon slipping in the polls, came to San Francisco on October 8 and spoke glowingly of his vice-president at a special $100-a-plate dinner broadcast over closed-circuit TV to an audience of Republicans:

Everything he has done has increased my respect for him. . . . I can personally vouch for his ability, his sense of duty, his sharpness of mind, his wealth in wisdom. . . . never hesitant, never indecisive, never fearful, never brash, always firm, without arrogance, friendly without servility, courageous without truculence.

Nixon replied, "all the work I've done has been worth it just to hear these words from the greatest living American."[68] One Nixon aide grumbled privately, "If he'd only given that speech two years ago, Dick Nixon would be President."

The Eisenhower dinner was ruined for Nixon, however, when Arch Monson, Jr., San Francisco businessman, who was presiding, committed the supreme gaffe of the campaign, saying with genuine bewilderment over the TV circuit, "Too many people are saying, 'I don't like Nixon, but I don't know why.' "[69]

The polls showed Nixon had fallen to forty-seven, with Brown leading at forty-eight. The failure was peculiarly Nixon's. Pollster Samuel Lubell wrote on October 3 of the "almost unbelievable personal bitterness toward Nixon among many California voters."[70] Although the pollsters found the contest too close to call, Nixon by late October was certain he would lose. Publicly he insisted he would win "by one vote or more," but confided his despair to young Stephen Hess. When Hess began packing to return to the East Coast he asked Nixon, "You still think you are going to lose?"

Nixon replied, "Yes."

"You may be wrong."

"I'm not wrong."[71]

Brown in early October said, "If the election were held now," I would win by 500,000 votes. What it will be four weeks from now I don't know. I should beat his brains out, because I know California and he doesn't."[72] In Europe the *London Times* commented on the dirtiness of the campaign. *Le Figaro* predicted for

Nixon "a brilliant return to the center of the political stage."[73]

In the last week Nixon predicted wildly that the Democrats would put on a last-minute massive scare campaign, with "seven lies" and a whispering campaign "planned and executed by professional hatchetmen."[74] Whatever hope he may have had in a last-minute surge of voting enthusiasm was stifled by the Cuban missile crisis, bringing the possibility of nuclear war. Voters were riveted to their TV sets. Brown stopped campaigning and rushed back to Washington to act as vice-chairman of the Governors Conference on Civil Defense. His standing went up in the polls.

Nixon applauded Kennedy's rejection of Khrushchev's call for pulling U.S. missiles out of Turkey[75] and the U.S. naval blockade. He tried to quiet local hysteria, warning Californians not to hoard food and gasoline. Although Castro, he said, was a maniac, Khrushchev was not a madman like Hitler. He called for a program of fallout shelters to be built for schoolchildren, financed by school bonds. While supporting Kennedy in the crisis, privately he cursed the timing. "Now I knew," he wrote later, "how Stevenson must have felt when Suez and the Hungarian rebellion flared up in the last days before the election in 1956."[76]

Nixon lost to Brown by 297,000 votes out of six million cast. He watched the final desolating returns, worsened by contrast with Senator Kuchel's easy victory, in the presidential suite of the Beverly Hilton Hotel in Los Angeles. With him were Bob Finch, Murray Chotiner, Bob Haldeman, John Ehrlichman, Ronald Ziegler—all of whom he would take with him to Washington in 1968. Although it was apparent by midnight that he could not win, and Pat had slipped off to a separate room to weep quietly, Nixon refused to concede until early morning. Annoyed reporters kept urging his press secretary, Herbert Klein, to bring him down.

Klein made repeated trips, but Nixon, who according to Gladwyn Hill had been taking a combination of tranquilizers and alcohol,[77] continued to refuse. "Screw them!" he said. Finally Klein was persuaded to make the statement himself, and went below with some scribbled notes. "The boss won't be down," he said, his round, pudgy face betraying nothing of his agitation. "He plans to go home and be with his family."

Several journalists snickered. Upstairs, Haldeman watched the reaction on TV and was enraged. Thin-skinned, humorless, and hostile, as defensive as Nixon, and sensitive because he had managed the campaign badly, he proceeded to reinforce all of Nixon's worst instincts. He burst into a diatribe against "the liberal press," which was responsible, he said, for the new defeat, just as it had been responsible for the razor-thin loss to Kennedy. "They should be told just where the hell to get off."[78]

Shortly afterward surprised reporters saw the haggard, blue-jowled Nixon emerge from behind the curtains. He took the microphone abruptly from Klein, and as Jules Witcover put it, "literally spit out the words heard round the political world":

Good morning gentlemen. Now that Mr. Klein has made his statement, and now that all the members of the press are so delighted that I have lost, I'd like to make a statement of my own.

What followed—intemperate, vituperative, contradictory, and at times incoherent—revealed in fifteen minutes why Nixon in the past had been so intent on promising the electorate he would never lose his temper; it masked a deadly fear of what might happen if he did. Coming down the stairs Nixon had said to no one in particular that to lose to Brown after losing to Kennedy was like being bitten by a mosquito after being bitten by a rattlesnake.[79] But the mosquito had brought him down, and he could no longer contain his rage.

"I believe Governor Brown has a heart," he said acidly, "even though he believes I do not. I believe he is a good American, even though he feels I am not."

But it was against the press, finally, rather than Brown, that Nixon turned in earnest. As so often before an attack he began with a declaration of nonhostility: "I have no complaints about the press coverage." Then he proceeded to charge the press with bias, misrepresentation, and omission: "I would appreciate it if you would write what I say . . . *In the lead. In the lead!*" He exonerated an embarrassed Carl Greenberg, sitting in the front row, by saying, "he wrote every word that I said. He wrote it fairly. He wrote it objectively," although an examination of news releases in the campaign reveals that Dick Bergholz and other reporters had been as scrupulous as Greenberg in their dispatches.

The speech echoed again the whining, abused child, but this time it was laced with a vulgarity that shocked everyone who did not know how habitually the expressions sprang to his lips in private:

And as I leave the press, all I can say is this: for sixteen years, ever since the Hiss case, you've had a lot of fun—a lot of fun—that you've had an opportunity to attack me and I think I've given as good as I've taken. . . .

But as I leave I want you to know—just think how much you're going to be missing. You won't have Nixon to kick around anymore, because, gentlemen, this is my last press conference. . . .

I believe in reading what my opponents say, and I hope that what I have said today will at least make television, radio and the press first recognize the great responsibility they have to report all the news, and, second, recognize that they have a right and a responsibility, if they're against a candidate, to give him the shaft, but also recognize if they give him the shaft, put one lonely reporter on the campaign who will report what the candidate says now and then.

Turning to the ashen Klein, he said, "I know you don't agree. I gave it to them right in the ass. It had to be said, goddammit. It had to be said."[80]

Nixon had violated one of the most hallowed of American traditions, being a good loser in defeat. He admitted in his memoirs that many friends told him the valedictory was "a personal and political disaster"—with Maurice Stans warning him it would cost him $100,000 a year in new legal clients. But he also received, he said, "thousands of letters and wires from friends and supporters across the country who said they were glad someone finally had the guts to tell the press off."

"I have never regretted," he wrote, "what I said at the 'last press conference.' "[81]

XXXI

The Private Man

Recovery for invasion of privacy should not depend upon proof of actual malice. . . . injury to personality and feelings is as tangible as injury to body or reputation.

— RICHARD NIXON, ARGUING FOR THE RIGHT OF PRIVACY BEFORE THE SUPREME COURT, 1966[1]

NIXON AS PRESIDENT installed an elaborate taping system, invading the privacy of everyone who came into his three offices and authorized secret investigations of the sexual and drinking habits of his political rivals. When he ordered a twenty-four-hour surveillance over Edward Kennedy, he said to Haldeman, "Catch him in the sack with one of his babes."[2] Nevertheless, Nixon seemed inordinately jealous of his own privacy, and throughout his career fought against any kind of exposure. As president he punished editors who invaded it by having them audited by the IRS, and cancelling reporters' White House privileges.[3]

From 1962 to 1967, when he was not a candidate for public office, there was no major threat to the privacy of his family life. It was during these years, as a lawyer in New York, that he argued his only case before the Supreme Court, *Time v. Hill,* involving a Broadway play called *The Desperate Hours.* Here he defended the right of the James Hill family against what he declared was a privacy-damaging review of *The Desperate Hours* in *Life.* Something in this case touched Nixon, and he went to great trouble in it. When he lost, six to three, he taped a long analysis of his failure.

In 1952 the Hill family had been held prisoner by escaped convicts for nineteen hours. They had been treated courteously and released unharmed. The police, in apprehending the convicts, had killed two of them. The play fictionalized the original happening by having the convicts abuse the family by violence and verbal sexual assault. When *Life* reviewed the play, pictures were taken of the cast in the old Hill house. James H. Hill, who had moved and was seeking anonymity for his family, sued for invasion of privacy. A lower court had awarded $75,000 in damages, but Time, Inc. took the case to the Supreme Court with the argument that the First Amendment was at stake.

Nixon argued that the case involved—in Justice Louis Brandeis's famous phrase—"the constitutional right to be let alone."* Nixon claimed that the distortion of the facts for purposes of making the play more salable was fictionalization, and that the Hill family—injured in personality and feelings—did not have to prove actual malice to be awarded damages for libel. "Fictionalization is an appropriate constitutional test of liability," he said.

Justice William Brennan, writing the majority opinion, did not see *The Desperate Hours* as "reckless disregard of the truth," and he feared that the award of damages in the case would mean "a grave risk of serious impairment of the indispensable services of a free press." Justice Hugo Black said it would "frighten and punish the press." Fortas, Warren, and Clark dissented. Fortas urged the Hill family to seek out a new trial, and this Nixon urged, but Hill and Time reached a settlement out of court.[4]

The personal life of the president, like that of emperors and kings, has always been a matter of lively curiosity, not necessarily prurient. That feelings about wives, children, mistresses, and friends spill over into politics and war was taken for granted by Shakespeare, and has never been seriously questioned by historians, although they may flee from in-depth exploration of the matter. Since Nixon's own staff members have talked, as Safire did, about his "deep dark rage," and as Kissinger did, about his paranoia, depravity, and self-destructiveness, the modern biographer has an obligation to seek out the sources of the rage and paranoia if he can.

Nixon held that "a candidate's personal life and that of his family are not fair subjects for discussion unless they somehow bear directly on his qualifications for office."[5] Did his own vindictive treatment of his aides "bear directly on his qualifications for office"? And can the same question be asked about his difficulties with his wife? The failure of intimacy in the marriage of Franklin and Eleanor Roosevelt has been copiously documented. Roosevelt

*The Brandeis case involved wire-tappings.

continued to respect and to utilize the prodigious talents of his wife for the nation's good, and she permitted herself to be so used. Theirs was an extraordinary political partnership. It can be said, on the other hand, that neither the Trumans nor the Eisenhowers had a political partnership. But they did have viable marriages. With neither couple did the White House kitchen staff look on appalled as they did serving the two lonely Nixons, isolated in different wings, eating together only at dinner and then exchanging so few words that the waiters rushed the courses.

Rumors of a near break in the marriage in the early sixties, known to several California newsmen, were never printed when Nixon was in office. With his departure, the unspoken rule among newsmen, that the president's private life is his own, slackened. Woodward and Bernstein wrote in *The Final Days* that Pat "confided to one of her White House physicians" that "she and her husband had not really been close since the early 1960s." "She had wanted to divorce him after the 1962 defeat in the California gubernatorial campaign. She had tried, and failed, to win his promise not to seek office again. Her rejection of his advances since then had seemed to shut something off inside Nixon. But they stuck it out."[6]

Julie Nixon, in a passionate defense of her mother in response to *The Final Days,* did not deny or even mention the threat of divorce. She did deny the stories that in her last weeks in the White House her mother had been withdrawn and drinking heavily. Julie insisted that Pat was not "the perfect old-time political wife; tactful and self-effacing," but rather "the most independent and sufficient woman I know." And she added poignantly:

People who have labeled her "superhuman" or "Plastic Pat" underestimate her. She is a woman of tremendous self-control because all her life self-control has been necessary simply to survive.[7]*

*There is a persisting rumor that Nixon turned to a woman psychoanalyst for treatment after his defeat by Brown in 1962.

Jules Witcover wrote in *The Resurrection of Richard Nixon* (p. 34): "It has been suggested, in fact, that Nixon actually underwent professional psychoanalysis in those years [1962–1968]. The suggestion has been denied and no reliable testimony has been produced to support it." Robert Finch told me on March 1, 1977, that he had heard that Nixon had been treated by a woman psychiatrist in New York. Leo Katcher, a former Los Angeles reporter for the *New York Post,* told me on Oct. 22, 1975, that his brother, Herbert Katcher, a former lawyer for the New York Psychoanalytic Association, had told him that Nixon had some treatment "on the couch," but made him promise never to divulge the name of the doctor. When I asked if the psychoanalyst had been worried that Nixon might someday have great power, Katcher said, "I will say that she was deeply troubled."

Others believe that the woman psychoanalyst had been in Los Angeles, not New York,

Donnie Radcliffe of the *Washington Post* described a First Lady almost as gifted at denial as her husband. Pat insisted, she wrote, that she and her husband had never discussed quitting politics after 1962, and said also, in response to a question, that she had "never had any disappointing moments." "You can do anything you put your mind to," Mrs. Nixon said. "You can adjust to anything if you want to. . . . there was a part for me to play."[8]

Robert Pierpont, CBS White House correspondent, who remembered Pat's enthusiasm and vivacity in Whittier High School, described the change in her over the years. As wife of the vice-president, she seemed to him in interviews as "extremely uptight, difficult to talk to, very nervous, and not at all the happy outgoing personality I had remembered from high school days." And for the ten years preceding Nixon's resignation, Pierpont said, "I felt strongly that Nixon and his wife were trapped in a situation where the best she could do was not to hurt him. They tried to play the game of being the perfect husband and wife, but it came through as transparent. It looked so phony, so unrealistic."[9]

Richard Bergholz of the *Los Angeles Times* said, "he abused her perpetually but not physically. She was just a stick of furniture sitting on a stage. She was just someone who smiled and had that adoring look on her face when she'd heard the speech for the fiftieth time. We all suffered when she suffered."[10]

Kandy Stroud, on Pat Nixon's staff, told Lester David, "She gave so much and got so little of what was really meaningful to a woman—attention, companionship, consideration. Sometimes he was so brutally indifferent I wept for her."[11]

Jack Anderson, on the other hand, privy to much Washington gossip, described the Nixon marriage as a good one. He believed Nixon "loved his family very much."

At no time have I ever had a suspicion, save from irresponsible sources trying to make something out of nothing, that Nixon cheated on his wife or did not love her or in any way degraded her. He held his wife in

---

and that she treated Nixon in 1962 and 1963 before his move to New York. Prof. Foster Sherwood, former dean at UCLA, told me on Oct. 10, 1975, that a woman psychoanalyst sought out advice at UCLA for depositing her files on Nixon for safekeeping. The psychoanalyst in question denies the entire story, as does the psychiatrist who was said to have recommended the woman psychoanalyst to Nixon in the first place. Both Los Angeles physicians prefer to remain anonymous.

esteem and affection as far as I have been able to learn. She apparently had a healthy attitude about him . . . a little like my wife. Whenever I get to thinking that I'm important she always says just the right thing to pull me right back down to earth.

"Nixon's closeness to his wife," Anderson said, "was the only healthy thing about him."[12]

Old friends, when questioned in interviews about the Nixon marriage, took sides. Adela Rogers St. Johns said, "Pat was a desperately wrong wife for Nixon."[13] Ralph de Toledano spoke of Pat's "frostiness."[14] James Bassett described the Nixon behavior on the early campaign airplane trips, how "they would always sit across the aisle from each other, or still further apart; then as the plane circled for a landing they would 'put on their Dick and Pat smile,' and he would put his arm around her for the photographers." Bassett believed Nixon to be "asexual." Politics, he said, was Nixon's real passion.[15]

Traphes Bryant, among whose duties at the White House was to take care of the Nixon dogs, said in his memoir:

I always had the feeling that Mrs. Nixon was starved for affection, and just eager to grab something to hug. I felt sorry for her. She was so painfully thin. I never saw her grab the President and hug him, he seemed to need it too. She just grabbed Timahoe.[16]

As president, Nixon had his staff keep what was called "the daily diary," an astonishing record that chronicled what he did every moment of his life save for his trips to the bathroom. When this record was surrendered without protest to the Senate Watergate Committee, it was inevitable that staffers would look at how much time Nixon spent with his wife. At San Clemente, on July 6, 1972, for example, this president who had written with such emotion on the right to privacy seems not to have minded someone noting in a file that from 2:50 P.M. to 2:51 P.M. he spoke to his wife, that at 4:48 P.M. he met her at the pool area, that at 5:02 P.M. he returned to the compound residence. "Through the days and nights of his life," Jimmy Breslin noted, "his diaries showed he spent a half-hour, at the most up to an hour, a day with his wife."[17]

After the Nixon resignation Rebozo's role in the complexities of the Nixon marriage for the first time became a matter of public comment. *Time* reporters on August 19, 1974, wrote:

Looking from the outside, no one can say what any marriage is really like, but even during their private hours the Nixons were often apart. No one could overlook the many weekends he went off to Camp David or to the Bahamian Island of Robert Abplanalp with Charles G. "Bebe" Rebozo, leaving Pat alone. Her staff bristled at the way he ignored her in public appearances, and there were few of the usual affectionate gestures between husband and wife.

Whenever she was asked if she was happy, Pat usually said something like, "Yes, I am. I've got the greatest guy in the world." Once, when a reporter suggested that she had had a good life, Pat raised her eyebrows and retorted: "I just don't tell all."

Lester David, in *The Lonely Lady at San Clemente,* published what had long been known to newsmen, that when the Nixons went to the Florida White House, Pat and the girls slept in one house, Nixon in another, next to the house owned by Rebozo.[18] Woodward and Bernstein, in *The Final Days,* reported that Gen. Alexander Haig, Nixon's closest aide in the White House after the resignations of Haldeman and Ehrlichman, had said to Kissinger and his aides that the president "was an inherently weak man who lacked guts," and had "joked that Nixon and Bebe Rebozo had a homosexual relationship, imitating what he called the President's limp-wrist manner."[19]

The First Lady had long since given the lie to such sophomoric talk by accepting Rebozo as a warm friend. "Bebe is almost like a brother to me," she said, "and Julie and Tricia look upon him as an uncle."[20] Robert Finch, who was for a time a kind of surrogate son for Nixon and saw a good deal of the family, said, "Bebe had a fund of anecdotes. He was fun for Pat too. He genuinely liked her and the girls. And they were fond of him as an uncle." When Nixon was in a surly mood, Finch said, he was glad to have Rebozo around. "He invariably had the effect of blowing him up or diverting him . . . a kind of therapeutic thing . . . release of tension, just diverting." He was the only man, Finch recalled, who had access to the White House without being logged in save for Nixon's osteopath.[21]

During the Watergate crisis, when Helen Thomas of UPI asked Pat a pointed question, she "made almost a menacing gesture with her fists and said, 'You know I have great faith in my husband, I happen to love him.'"[22] She was sensitive, nevertheless, to the frequency of Rebozo's visits. Traphes Bryant reported that when Nixon and Rebozo were out on the presidential yacht *Sequoia,* relaxing, Pat would defend his absences, saying, in response to queries, "Oh, Dick can't come, he works eighteen hours a day."[23] She continued for the most part to live by the personal creed she had set for herself years before: "I keep everything in. I never scream. If I have a headache no one knows it, and if I were dying I wouldn't let anyone know." When she suffered a paralytic stroke in 1976, as a result, Nixon said, of reading *The Final Days,* she told no one. It was he who discovered the disability when he saw her struggling to make breakfast.[24]

The earliest evidence that Rebozo had become an important confidant, whom Nixon sought out in times of shame and failure as well as success, came in 1962. When Nixon told the press that they would not have "Dick Nixon to kick around anymore," he also said, "My plans are to go home. I'm going to get acquainted with my family again."[25] Instead, after two days he flew to Miami with Rebozo, who had been with him in "the last press conference," and it was with him that Nixon spent the next three weeks in the new Ocean Club on Paradise Island about one mile off Nassau. Pat and the daughters joined them for only three days at the end of November. And it was on this trip, consulting with Rebozo, and also Elmer Bobst and John S. Davies, that Nixon decided to abandon California for New York City.[26]

Nixon went to some pains to minimize the friendship. He dismissed Bebe in a conversation with his cousin Jessamyn West as "just a golfing partner."[27] Especially in his last year in the White House, Nixon saw to it that Rebozo was not logged in on his frequent visits, apparently lest unfriendly reporters make a counting. Haldeman noted that Nixon was always "edgy when Bebe's name was mentioned."[28]

Most observers looked on Rebozo as a substitute brother. Rebozo did his best to keep Donald from further humiliating the president when he became involved in what were said to be phony mining claims fobbed off on Howard Hughes, and may have encouraged Nixon's putting a wiretap on Donald. In his Senate Watergate testimony Rebozo said of Donald Nixon, "Many families have relatives they would like to keep in the closet for awhile now and then."[29] For a score of years Rebozo did seem to be the ideal brother, discreetly avoiding the press, self-effacing, supportive, and caring, a brother who did not waste family resources but instead parlayed them into a small fortune.

In his memoirs Nixon's references to Rebozo are infrequent and for the most part casual. He did describe him, however, as "one of the kindest and most generous men I've ever known . . . a man of great character and integrity." And in a rare glimpse into Rebozo's role in filling his own loneliness he included a diary entry made Christmas Day, 1972:

It is inevitable that not only the President but the First Lady become more and more lonely individuals. . . . It is a question not of too many friends but really too few. . . . As this Christmas Day ends I am thankful for Manolo and Fina, for the wonderful Filipinos and the staff, for Bebe, for Julie and Tricia, Pat, for all of those who basically are our family.[30]

Even an incomplete reconstruction of their meetings from published sources reveals that Rebozo, far from being a mere "golfing partner," was with Nixon in many of his most important hours of decision-making from 1954 to his resignation, a period covering twenty years. He was with Nixon in Florida shortly before the decision to attack Sen. Joe McCarthy in 1954. There are reports that he moved briefly to California, "at some financial sacrifice" friends said, to be with Nixon in 1962.[31] Rebozo was with Nixon in the Bahamas in 1962 when he decided to abandon California.

The decision to run in 1968, Nixon tells us, was made at a three-day meeting in Florida, where he was alone with Rebozo and Billy Graham.[32] The two advisers made an unlikely pair, Bebe the dark, unobtrusive, obsequious courtier, Graham the blond flamboyant meteor, soon to be the arranger of politico-spiritual rallies in which he and Nixon costarred. Four months earlier Billy Graham had delivered the sermon at the funeral of Nixon's mother. The ex-president's memory of the decision-making in 1968, as seen in his memoirs, was unusually acute. On the first night, he said, "we sat up late talking about theology and politics and sports. Billy read aloud the first and second chapters of Romans."* The next day Nixon and Rebozo on TV "watched the Green Bay Packers defeat the Dallas Cowboys 21–17 in subfreez-

---

*In his epistle to the Romans St. Paul rails against men of "wickedness, covetousness, maliciousness, envy, murder, debate, deceit, malignity, and haters of God." He blasts men and women guilty of "uncleanness through lusts," against men who, "leaving the natural use of women, burned in their lust one toward another."

ing weather in Green Bay." On the third day, when Nixon asked Billy Graham, "Well, what is your conclusion? What should I do?" Billy replied, "I think it is your destiny to be President."[33]

Rebozo was with Nixon in Florida when he wrote his inaugural address, and at Camp David when Nixon decided to invade Cambodia.[34] Pat Nixon was on the West Coast and Nixon and Rebozo were alone together at Key Biscayne when the president learned from Bob Haldeman of the Watergate break-in. His diary entry for that weekend, published in his memoirs, reflected pleasure in the relaxation and solitude:

The extra day, with good long swims in the morning and the afternoon, gave me, it seemed to me, a much bigger lift than I had realized was possible. I must make it a point to try to get three full days in the future.[35]

The lonely Christmas Day of 1972, which Nixon shared only with Pat and Rebozo, was the day he ordered the biggest air raid of the Vietnam War, the carpet-bombing of Hanoi on December 26.[36] Rebozo accompanied Nixon to the hospital when he had viral pneumonia in July 1973; a press photograph shows him saying to White House physician Dr. Tkach, "Take good care of him."[37] And Rebozo was alone with Nixon in Florida when he decided to fire Haldeman and Ehrlichman.[38]

In his Senate Watergate testimony Rebozo said he was in Washington more often than the president was in Florida.[39] As we have said, he was with the Nixon family on all the occasions of triumph and happiness, the inaugurals, the birthdays, and the weddings. He attended religious services at the White House. He was a frequent visitor at San Clemente, the purchase of which he had helped Nixon to finance, together with millionaire Robert Abplanalp. A rough chronology based on easily available data suggests that Rebozo was with Nixon about one day out of every ten when he was in the presidency.[40]

Much about this friendship remains obscure, but in one respect it was like a good marriage; they could be comfortably alone together for long hours without talking. Senator Smathers saw this early: "I've seen him and Bebe sit in a room for three hours, and neither ever say a word. Nixon's a little bit of a mystic. He gets all his information together, then he meditates and contemplates. And Bebe sits there." "Nixon wants to be alone," said another friend, "and with Bebe he is alone." Pat Hillings said Nixon didn't have many friends, "only Bebe Rebozo, because no one else will do what Bebe does. Bebe will sit in a room all alone with him for hours, saying nothing, while Nixon writes away on that long yellow pad he's always got. It would drive me nuts."[41]

Safire said Nixon "drew his coloration from the man he was with. . . . when he didn't want to be anybody but himself he sent for Rebozo."[42] The constant struggle either to impress a listener or to identify with him was inevitably exhausting. Rebozo, as Stephen Hess said, was like an old shoe. Although Kissinger believed that "Nixon would never want to appear weak before his old friend"—and it was true that Rebozo was with Nixon on two occasions of decision-making that saw enormous acceleration in the Vietnam War effort, the incursion into Cambodia and the resumption of the carpet-bombing of North Vietnam the day after Christmas 1972[43]—it would seem that Rebozo's chief function was to sit and listen to Nixon's long monologues about his plans, his future, and himself, without being bored or supercilious or skeptical. Pat Nixon said to Helen Smith, "Bebe is like a sponge; he soaks up whatever Dick says and never makes any comments. Dick loves that."[44] We know that Ehrlichman found these monologues unendurable, as did Ford. And it may well be that Pat, too, very early, had cut him off and that he had found in Rebozo the only friend who would not. Bob Finch said, "Pat never said the Pollyannish kind of thing, and I think in very intimate circles she would tease him and deflate and do the things that wives should do to men who hold great power."[45] At one Nixon party, a friend remembered, Pat interrupted one earnest discourse of her husband, saying lightly as she passed out Chiclets, "Here, take one of these, it's better than the baloney he puts out."

In 1968, when Karl Fleming asked Rebozo what he and Nixon talked about, he said, "We just talk about the things friends talk about. We like a lot of the same things—golf, boating, and the water."[46] Rebozo told Scott Armstrong, "He talks about what's on his mind. I just listen. Most of it is foreign policy stuff."[47] Safire, visiting Rebozo and Nixon in Florida in 1966, noted the genuine caring in the relationship:

Nixon announced he was going in the ocean for a dip. He did; Bebe figeted in his chair for a couple of minutes. Then he excused himself.

"He shouldn't be in by himself," he said, and he went out to the water's edge in case Nixon, a strong swimmer, should start to drown.[48]

Nixon seems to have been willing to risk the kind of gossip that frequently accompanies close friendship with a perennial bachelor, this despite his known public aversion to homosexuals, and his acute sensitivity to the damage that the label of homosexual on a friend could then bring to a public man. In 1964 when Lyndon Johnson's aide Walter Jenkins was arrested on a morals charge in a Washington, D.C., YMCA restroom, Nixon demanded that the president appear on television to explain "why the two men closest to him in the past ten years," Jenkins and Bobby Baker (the latter had been fired for financial peculations) "were both 'bad apples.' " Jenkins, Nixon said, "was ill. But people with this kind of illness cannot be in places of high trust."[49]

As late as 1969 in a meeting with the National Security Council staff Nixon began by commiserating with them for having to deal with "all those 'impossible fags' in the State Department."[50] And Nixon's aides, at their most destructive, were caught out in efforts to pin the label of homosexual not only on Democratic rivals Senators Jackson and Humphrey—among the "dirty tricks" of the 1972 campaign—but also on journalist Jack Anderson in 1971. Donald Young, Nixon's White House aide, according to W. Donald Stewart, said of the latter effort when Young tried to get him to frame Anderson, "It's the President's order."[51]

Rebozo's bachelorhood was less of an embarrassment to Nixon when he settled in 1969 into what *Newsweek* called a "somewhat antiseptic" relationship with the secretary of one of his business partners, Jane Anne Lucke, a handsome, high-spirited divorcée. "She says Rebozo visits her a couple of nights a week at her home. There she and her mother, who lives with her and her two sons, give Rebozo piano lessons, watch TV or play a card game called Spite and Malice."[52] Mrs. Lucke was invited twice to the White House, to the Johnny Cash dinner, where she sat on Nixon's right, and to Julie's twenty-first birthday party. On scores of other occasions Rebozo went to the White House alone. During the last terrible year of the Nixon presidency, although there were many hours Rebozo spent alone with Nixon at Camp David, going through pitchers of martinis it was said, he remained an important part of the decision-making of the whole family. He denied to the end the president's wrongdoing. "This is a great man," he said to Pat Buchanan, in the final days, when virtually the whole country had repudiated the president.[53]

Leonard Hall, who saw firsthand that "Rebozo had the run of the White House," was certain that his influence was nonpolitical, and was equally certain, up to 1974, that he had nothing to do with the raising of money. He was wrong on both counts. "Most presidents," Hall insisted, "want some kind of buffer. Bebe was Nixon's buffer."[54]

Many presidents have sought out a special confidant. Some, like Madison for Jefferson, Van Buren for Jackson, Mark Hanna for McKinley, Colonel House for Wilson, and Louis Howe for Franklin Roosevelt, were president makers. All of these men were intellectual catalysts, spawners of ideas, and two of them, Madison and Van Buren, followed their presidents into the White House. Some presidents have needed court jesters, like Harry Vaughan for Truman, or George E. Allen, who cracked jokes for FDR, Truman, and Eisenhower. Some, like William Howard Taft and John Kennedy, had supporting brothers. Harry Hopkins, who lived in the White House for a long period, was a kind of surrogate Roosevelt. He could travel, as Roosevelt could not. Churchill came to trust him as perfectly reflecting the ideas of the president, and joked that after the war he would see that Hopkins got a seat in the House of Lords with the title "Lord Root of the Matter."[55]

Rebozo—in Haldeman's phrase, "the swarthy Cuban"—was none of these. He stayed aloof from the palace guard, led by Haldeman and Ehrlichman, who cracked the whip for the clean-cut handsome young staffers—Herbert Porter, Bob Odle, Gordon Strachan, Jeb Magruder, Dwight Chapin, Stephen Bull, and John Dean—so alike, Traphes Bryant thought, "a man could hardly tell one from the other."[56] With these men, Charles Colson said, "machismo and toughness were equated with trust and loyalty; these were the keys to the cherished kingdom guaranteeing continued closeness to the throne." The unquestioning young lieutenants sought through *hubris,* "tough talk and derring-do to prove their political virility to Nixon and those of us around him."[57] With these men Nixon felt compelled to live up to the image of the macho president. "There was nothing," Kissinger said, "he feared more than to be thought weak."[58]

Although Rebozo was generally so quiet as to be invisible, he

did become known to the speechwriters. Safire said, "Rebozo was
a man's man and a kind of bachelor uncle to the girls; he wore
well as a friend, and, above all, he brooded well. . . . Bebe worshipped Nixon and hated Nixon's enemies."[59]

Except for John Mitchell, who knew Rebozo fairly well,[60] Bebe
seems to have shared nothing with the changing group of older
men whom Safire, in a chapter titled "The President Falls in
Love," called Nixon's "intellectual concubines." These men came
and went. The younger staff men, Safire said, would joke about
"The Boss in Love," and speculate on how long the infatuation
would last. Dan Rather, in his description of these men in *The
Palace Guard,* also conveyed the idea of "courtship." John Mitchell, Safire said, who lasted through mid-1970, would spend long
hours with Nixon, "plotting, relaxing, brooding, chuckling,
dreaming." There was Patrick Moynihan, "blooming in 1969's
spring." Connally came in like a comet, bedazzling and enthrall-
ing Nixon. Later came Colson, a Kennedy hater, in Dan Rather's
words, "a knee-to-the-groin man," who described himself as "a
flag-waving, kick-'em-in-the-nuts, anti-press, anti-liberal Nixon
fanatic."[61]

Finally there was Kissinger, the ultimate courtier, who had a
"tuning-wire" relationship with Nixon, and who lasted longest,
perhaps because he more than anyone recognized Nixon's desperate need to be shored up constantly against his darkest premonitions. Kissinger was the only man in Nixon's ever-changing
entourage of intellectuals who knew how to keep his intellect from
becoming threatening. He flattered; he effaced himself with wit
and drollery; he insinuated ideas and gave Nixon credit. He
admired Nixon's intellect and quickness at learning, but secretly
disliked him. After the resignation, he said "he'd never known
another man who combined such great gifts with such a capacity
for depravity and such a drive toward self-destruction."[62] And his
memoirs were peppered with anecdotes illuminating his basic
contempt.

Kissinger detested Rebozo and considered his influence on
Nixon mischievous. When Bebe appeared unexpectedly at a
Brussels hotel where Nixon was staying on his last trip to Europe
in 1974, Lloyd Shearer heard Kissinger mutter, "What's that son-
of-a-bitch doing here?"[63] When Rebozo was with Nixon at Camp
David, Kissinger said, it was "a conjunction that did not usually

make for the calmest reflection."[64] Kissinger permitted his aide, William Watts, to listen in on what became a notorious conversation between himself and Nixon just before the Cambodian invasion. The president, who was at Camp David with Rebozo, seemed drunk. He said to Kissinger, "Wait a minute—Bebe has something to say to you." Bebe came on the line and said, "The President wants you to know, if this doesn't work, Henry, it's your ass."

"Ain't that right, Bebe?" slurred Nixon.[65]

XXXII

The New York Years

When Nixon underlined what he himself believed was a definitive break with politics by moving to New York in 1963, he joined what Witcover called "a stodgy antique," the firm of Mudge, Stern, Baldwin and Todd, at a salary of $250,000 a year. His friends, who knew it was impossible for him to drop totally out of politics, did the scouting for him. As one member of the firm told Witcover later, "there just weren't too many places where he could get two hundred and fifty thousand dollars and all his time."[1] But the backwater firm soon became one of the fastest growing on Wall Street. Nixon in the beginning brought in the lucrative Pepsi-Cola account through his friend Donald M. Kendall, as well as the retainer for Robert Abplanalp's Precision Valve Corporation.[2] Later he forced a retraction from a newspaperman who had said he worked for the law firm only one day a week.[3]

The Nixons moved into a twelve-room apartment overlooking Central Park at 810 Fifth Avenue, in the same building as Nelson Rockefeller. They paid $135,000 for it, with an annual maintenance of between eight and ten thousand dollars. They put in $50,000 worth of improvements, and sold it in 1968 for $312,000. In the beginning he was described in the press as a "happy New Yorker." He joined the fashionable Metropolitan Club, which gave a reception in his honor. He joined also the Links and Recess Clubs, and country clubs in Westchester and New Jersey. His daughters went to the Chapin school; Tricia later went to Finch College and Julie to Smith. Both were featured in debutante balls in New York. The Nixons went often to the theater. "I like every play I've ever seen," Nixon told Robert Donovan, and added that *Aïda* was his favorite opera. He was driven to work by a chauffeur in a black Cadillac, so that he would have "an hour extra a day for reading."[4] It was all very orthodox behavior for the very rich. The days when Nixon felt too poor to install air conditioning in his vice-presidential home in Washington were gone. There was money for jewelry for his wife and Tricia and Julie. By 1974 the Nixon family jewelry, including that of his daughters, had a declared value (for insurance purposes) of almost two hundred thousand dollars.[5]

Although his office walls in New York were decorated by signed portraits of Queen Elizabeth, Prince Philip, Ayub Khan of Pakistan, King Baudoin of Belgium, King Bhumibhol of Thailand, and President Radhakrishnan of India, he was nevertheless avoided by ranking members of the Republican party in New York. Nelson Rockfeller never invited him to dinner. As Kissinger wrote, "he was shunned by people whose respect he might have expected as a former Vice President. . . . He was never invited by what he considered the 'best families.' This rankled and compounded his already strong tendency to see himself beset by enemies."[6]

He loathed the descent into anonymity. Once when an Associated Press photographer snapped his picture at a New York intersection and the picture appeared in the press the next day with the caption "The Forgotten Man," Nixon called the Associated Press, protesting that "everyone was looking the other way because they were waiting for a red light to change."[7] And although he told Robert Donovan in 1965, "New York is a very cold and very ruthless and very exciting and therefore an interesting place to live . . . a fast track,"[8] he admitted later in his memoirs that it was in this year that he told some of his friends, "if all I had was my legal work I would be mentally dead in two years and physically dead in four."[9]

He discovered in his first year in New York that to be received like a vice-president he must go abroad. When he went to Europe and Egypt with his family—accompanied on part of the trip by Rebozo—he called it "one of the happiest times of our lives." De Gaulle invited him to lunch and in a toast predicted his return to politics "in a very high capacity." Franco received him in Barcelona; Nixon found Franco "a subtle, pragmatic leader." In Rome he was received by the pope, and in Egypt Nasser entertained him at his home and arranged for a trip to the Aswan Dam. "Everywhere we went we were received as if I were still Vice President."[10]

One result was that Nixon became a frenetic traveler. Between

1962 and 1968 he went around the world six times, and had numerous shorter trips. And while on none of these was he received as cordially by the powerful as in 1963, he continued in this desperate search for a restoration of his political identity. He took elaborate notes, had them transcribed and cross indexed, building what became, as Tad Szulc noted, "his own personal archive on international affairs."[11]

There is contradictory evidence about Pat's reaction to New York, which one friend said for her was "like moving to another country." White House gossip had it that Pat was lonely in New York.[12] She told one friend New York was "a six-year vacation," "out of the rat race."[13]

Protecting her daughters had become crucial for her. It had stung the girls to see Kennedy buttons worn by their classmates in 1960. They felt the defeats of 1960 and 1962 as a personal affront. The privacy in New York, the healing anonymity of the vast city, salved the deep wounds. Whether the New York period brought a mere papering over of irreparable conflicts, or a conscious and agreed acquiescence in their going separate ways within the shell of the marriage, one can only speculate.

Pat told journalist Flora Schreiber in 1968, "When we first came to New York we were invited to many balls. We went. Later we decided to contribute and not go. We had so much of that kind of thing in Washington. Dick and I prefer to do more worthwhile things."[14] She supervised the fifty-thousand-dollar remodeling of their apartment with a gold and white decor—arranging the engraved views of Buckingham Palace, a gift from Queen Elizabeth, Nixon's two hundred curio elephants, two paintings by Eisenhower, a floral scroll from Madame Chiang Kai-shek. She herself made curtains for the bedrooms for her daughters. She took her husband's clients to New York museums. She went to his office as in the first campaign at Whittier, "to help out." "I've seen her there working her ass off," Earl Mazo told Lester David. "She'd come to the outer office early in the morning and sit at a desk near Rose Mary Woods and work like the devil, pecking away at a typewriter. And I'd say, 'Hey, what are you doing here?' And she'd say, jokingly, 'Can't afford another secretary.' "[15]

Nixon's flight from New York in travel became a kind of addiction, an ideal postponement, a flight from decision-making into fantasy. Although many of his trips from 1963 through 1967 included law firm business, he took every opportunity to relive his life as vice-president, visiting embassies, talking to foreign diplomats and leaders, keeping abreast of foreign affairs, utterly unable to shake off the daydream of one day returning to Washington as president. The shah of Iran welcomed him four times.[16]

On only two of his many trips abroad was he accompanied by his wife and daughters. Rebozo was with him on at least four.[17] Still faceless, unknown to newsmen, the silent Miami banker went unnoticed—he was not mentioned in the *New York Times* until 1968—and only later did it become apparent that he had been with Nixon in these years more than anyone realized.

Rebozo was with Nixon in London in 1966, and saw to it that they were entertained by the wealthy oilman John Paul Getty, who later, at Rebozo's solicitation, contributed funds through Nixon's lawyer Herbert Kalmbach.[18] Rebozo was with him on two trips to Hong Kong in 1966 and 1967. Nixon mentioned this in connection with his angry denial of a story that surfaced later in the scandal sheets concerning his alleged involvement with a pretty Chinese hostess in the Hong Kong Hilton bar.

Except for a later and even less believable account that Nixon had written twenty-two love letters to the wife of a Spanish diplomat, which surfaced briefly in the *London Standard* in June 1976, and which Nixon aides denounced as "a sordid hoax,"[19] no other rumor concerning Nixon's involvement with a woman other than his wife seems to have found its way into print.

In 1968, in an unusually candid interview, Nixon described something of what he meant by "having fun."

Some of my friends may be considered to be socially inferior to my associates and staffers, but I keep my friends apart from my business or political life. When I'm having fun, I don't want my work to intrude. Social affairs with intense talk of politics bore me to death. I hate staff parties. The business or political lunch is for the birds. I can eat in ten minutes. Why waste an hour or two eating?[20]

Rebozo, in a rare TV interview in 1974, told Walter Cronkite that Nixon was fond of practical jokes, and remembered an old story:

When the President moved into his new house in Key Biscayne (1968), Bob Abplanalp was coming over to visit us, we decided to play a trick on him. We had a couple of these ladies legs—it looks like real legs, they're skin-colored and all blown up, and we borrowed a wig and a wig-stand from a neighbor and put it in a bed with the wig hanging over the thing and the legs sticking out from under the sheet. I hid in the closet with a flash camera. Bob came in and he did not know whether to act like he did not see it, or what, but it was quite a riot.[21]

Abplanalp, who had first won Nixon's friendship in 1960 by telling him in a restaurant that he thought Kennedy had stolen the election, was the inventor of the aerosol bomb, and the millionaire owner of Precision Valve Corporation. A big, hearty, "inveterate convention-type man,"[22] full of jokes, he was totally unlike the shy and protective Rebozo, who feared that this new friend's raucous exchanges with the press would damage the president. He cringed when Abplanalp, in 1973, in reply to the question of what he planned to do with his property next to the president's San Clemente estate, replied, "I'm going to build a ten-story whorehouse on it."[23]

Haldeman in his memoir said Rebozo was jealous of Abplanalp, but there is no question but that this threesome, from 1960 forward, did have fun together, however sophomoric in nature, and usually without Pat Nixon. *Newsday* journalists reported in 1971 that when the president flew to Key Biscayne more than half the time he left Pat and his daughters behind in the compound and helicoptered with Rebozo over to Abplanalp's estate on the Bahamian island of Grand Cay.[24] Nixon and Rebozo were there with Haldeman when they first had news of the Watergate burglary.[25] The visits to Grand Cay dwindled, however, in the last year Nixon was in the White House; according to Scott Armstrong, there were no more than four or five.[26] In the months after the resignation Rebozo and Abplanalp seem to have been almost the only friends regularly permitted behind the gates at San Clemente. It was Rebozo, and not Abplanalp, however, to whom Nixon over the years turned in times of crisis.

Nixon did not permit the meshing of his finances with those of Rebozo until after his loss to Pat Brown. In 1962 he began to purchase stock in Fisher Island, a real estate venture in the Miami harbor area Rebozo and his partners were sponsoring. Rebozo, meanwhile, had become increasingly respectable in Miami. At the time of his first meeting with Nixon in 1950, he was president of two personal finance companies, the Mutual Finance Service and the Mutual Acceptance Corporation. As *Newsday* journalists reported, "The files of Dade County courts are filled with problems of people who borrowed from Rebozo's and other loan firms and then could not meet their payments." They told of one writ of attachment, executed on June 17, 1953, repossessing a two-wheel bicycle, a baby car seat, a tricycle, and a toy truck—this from a couple who had borrowed $150 and had signed a mortgage on their household goods.[27]

Rebozo sold both companies and in 1964 became a banker on Key Biscayne. He became a joiner, a philanthropist, and the president of the Miami Boys Clubs. Most of Rebozo's acquaintances were unaware of rumors of underworld connections, which surfaced later. The big shopping center, El Centro Comercial Cubano, designed for Cuban refugees and financed by Rebozo's bank, had been built by the Polizzi Construction Company of Coral Gables, a firm headed by Big Al Polizzi, who had been jailed in Ohio for violation of war price controls and tax evasion. Although he had seen his civil rights restored by the state of Florida in 1960, as late as 1964 he was described by the Federal Bureau of Narcotics as "one of the most influential members of the underworld in the United States."[28] One of the board members in Rebozo's Fisher Island Company was Walter Frederich, a millionaire former food retailer who had been convicted after World War II for providing sugar to potential bootleggers.[29] And Rebozo himself employed Franklin DeBoer, barred earlier by the Securities Exchange Commission of the right to be a stockbroker because of falsifying records and selling unregistered stock.[30] Rebozo took his own salary from his bank in cash, and paid his employees in cash.[31] He transacted business under the name Charles Gregory and also the name of his married sister Anita Reynolds and his bookkeeper Nicole Moncourt.[32]

In the early years of their friendship Rebozo was fiercely protective of Nixon's reputation in regard to money. In 1958 when the Sherman Adams scandal broke and Democrats were hoping that Nixon could be caught up in something similar, Rebozo told Miami newsmen:

They'll never find anything on that boy. He has paid his own way every time he has come down here, including his own plane fare. . . . He is a very selfless and dedicated man.[33]

Nixon's own investments in Florida, engineered by Rebozo, were circumspectly made. Nixon began buying stock in Fisher's Island in late 1962 at $1 per share. Eventually he owned 199,891 shares. These he had to sell when he became president. Rebozo persuaded the stockholders to buy back the Nixon stock at $2 a share, although it had not noticeably appreciated in value. The stockholders grumbled but agreed. It was a bonanza for Nixon of $200,000, and the act of the stockholders was deemed a gesture of affection and respect.[34]

George Smathers bowed out of his Bay Lane house, as did another neighbor, at modest prices, to permit the Nixons to create the Florida White House. Robert Abplanalp purchased the last of the five houses in the compound and leased it to the U.S. government. Rebozo was the only outsider to remain.

Like many others, Rebozo contributed to the widespread myth that Nixon was not interested in money. As late as 1974 he said to Watergate prosecutors, "He just does not concern himself at all with financial problems, never has." But Richard Danner, who had remained a friend to Rebozo and Nixon,* revealed in the same hearings that Nixon in 1967 had joined him and Rebozo in a meeting planning the accumulation of a special cash fund which would be kept secret from regular campaign contributions. They hoped to get money from J. Paul Getty and Howard Hughes in particular. Danner had joined the staff of Howard Hughes in Las Vegas, and together with Robert Maheu and Rebozo became one of several fundraisers for Nixon as president.

Eventually, according to government prosecutors, Rebozo had a special fund estimated by some at $790,000, most of it in cash.[36] The clandestine money raising, succeeding beyond anyone's wildest expectations, came to savor of medieval exactions of tribute for a king. The byzantine story of these machinations properly belongs in a volume on the presidential years, and has been summarized only briefly in a note at the end of this volume.[37] But there can be no question but that Rebozo contributed to Nixon's conviction that such largesse was his due, and that any failure to report the contributions, and a readiness to use them for illegal purposes, constituted a mere peccadillo.

---

*The nature of the continuing friendship between Danner and Rebozo can best be seen in the handful of letters they exchanged which were published in the Senate Watergate Hearings. Theirs is an oblique banter quite unlike the more formal letters between Rebozo and Nixon in the Vice-Presidential Archive.[35]

A Series of Accidents

You can't be interested in that. You can only be interested in who shot John.
— NIXON TO DAVID FROST, 1977[1]

EVERY PRESIDENT SINCE ANDREW JACKSON, the first to be threatened by a demented killer, has had to fight a dread of assassination. Lincoln suffered from premonitions that he would not live out his second term, and shortly before his death dreamed that he saw a coffin in the White House draped with a catafalque, and heard sounds of weeping. When he asked, "Who is dead?" he was told, "The president. He was killed by an assassin."[2]

John F. Kennedy, who received 870 death threats in the mail in his first year in office,[3] learned to joke about the threat. Once he played a charade, acting out his own assassination. As a friend took home movies he slumped to the floor while another friend poured catsup over him. It is said that everyone laughed.[4] During the Cuban missile crisis, when Khrushchev finally agreed to withdraw the missiles, the president said to his brother, "This is the night I should go to the theater." Robert answered, "If you go, I want to go with you."[5] Shortly before going to Dallas, John Kennedy observed seriously that no president could be protected against a high-powered rifle. After his brother's death, Robert Kennedy said, "I can't plan. Every day is like Russian roulette."

In March 1963 Nixon agreed to be the narrator of a film on the assassination of Leon Trotsky, to be called *The Great Prince Died*. Trotsky had been killed with an ax in 1940 in Mexico by a Stalinist agent who had pretended to be his friend, and who had infiltrated the staff of his fortress home.[6] Nixon answered the inquiry of the filmmaker by encouraging the production and expressing pleasure at the idea of being the narrator. The film, he said, will "focus public attention on the true dimensions of the sinister methods of the Communists, even in dealing with their own members who espouse slightly different ideas." He cited his own credentials as an anti-Communist, concluding, "It is a tough story, but in my opinion, carries a message the people of the Americas need to have."[7] The film was never made.

Several weeks after writing this letter, on April 20, 1963, Nixon made a savage attack on Kennedy's Cuban policy in a speech before the American Society of Newspaper Editors in Washington. The president, he said, had "goofed an invasion, paid tribute to Castro for the prisoners, then given the Soviets squatters' rights in our backyard." He called for a "command decision" to force the Russians from the Western Hemisphere.[8] The speech was headlined in the *Dallas Morning News*, NIXON CALLS FOR DECISION TO FORCE REDS OUT OF CUBA. Among the readers was Lee Harvey Oswald. Shortly after reading it, Marina Oswald related later, he retired to the bathroom, dressed, and came out with his snub-nosed, .38-caliber pistol strapped to his belt. "Nixon is coming," he said. "I want to go and have a look. I am going to go out and find out if there will be an appropriate opportunity, and if there is, I will use the pistol." When his wife remonstrated, Oswald said, "Perhaps I won't use my gun, but if there is a convenient opportunity, I will."[9]

Lee Harvey Oswald was intent on killing Gen. Edwin A. Walker not because he was blocking school integration but because he had taken up the cause of eliminating Fidel Castro. Fully expecting to be caught in the murder attempt, he left his wife a note in advance, telling her where to find him in the city jail, and ordering that she take all clippings of the incident to the Soviet embassy. Whatever happened, he wanted to be a hero in Moscow and Havana.[10]

Marina, faced with her husband's threat to kill Richard Nixon, realized for the first time that Lee was not intent simply on murdering Walker, but could kill anyone. Persuading him to follow her into the bathroom, she managed to slip outside and then with all her strength held the door shut, meanwhile begging him to give up the gun, threatening to tell the police, and warning that she could have a miscarriage. "I could lose the child because of you," she said. "You'll have killed your own child." Oswald finally surrendered the pistol, which she hid under their mattress. Later she returned it to him. Nixon did not come to Dallas for seven months, not until November 20, two days before the arrival of John F. Kennedy and his wife. He did not learn about Oswald's threat against his life until January 1964.

Nixon was in Dallas on November 20, 1963, for a meeting with the Pepsi-Cola bottlers. There was an ugly atmosphere in the city. When Adlai Stevenson had come to Dallas on October 24 to attend a United Nations Day luncheon and to make a speech before the Eleanor Roosevelt Foundation, he saw handbills with photographs of President Kennedy and underneath the caption WANTED FOR TREASON. Hatred of desegregation in the schools and restaurants had turned bigoted whites into a fury against the president, and had heightened their endemic xenophobia. To counter Stevenson's coming for United Nations Day, General Walker had organized a rival "United States Day." He sent his trained hecklers to spoil Stevenson's speeches, and as Stevenson left the hall one woman hit him on the head with a sign and two men spat in his face. Although he responded with indignation, "Are these people human beings or are these animals?" he nevertheless refused to let the police arrest the woman who had hit him, saying "I don't want to send her to jail; I want to send her to school."[11]

Nixon, interviewed by the press the day before Kennedy's coming, and told of planned demonstrations against the president, said to newsmen he hoped that both the president and vice-president would be treated with the respect they deserved. He also predicted that Kennedy might well dump Johnson for an opponent who would bring in more votes, "unless the race is a shoo-in." When asked if he would accept the GOP nomination in 1964, he replied, "I cannot conceive of circumstances under which that would happen."[12]

The day of the assassination Nixon was on his plane returning to New York.[13] At the airport he hailed a cab and asked to be driven to his office. When the cab stopped for a traffic light in Queens, a man ran up and asked, "Do you have a radio in your cab?"

"No," said the driver, "Why?"

"The President has just been shot in Dallas."

Nixon's first thought, he told Jules Witcover later, was "Oh my God, it must have been one of the nuts," a synonym with Nixon for a fanatic right-winger.[14]

When the cab driver, at Nixon's request, took him to his apartment rather than his office, they found the doorman at the entrance weeping. "Oh, Mr. Nixon, have you heard, sir?" he said. "It's just terrible. They've killed President Kennedy."

"I remembered," Nixon wrote in his memoirs, "how I felt when first Arthur and then Harold died."[15]

Shortly after he entered the apartment Stephen Hess arrived. He had been lunching with Nixon's editor from Doubleday, discussing plans for a new book Hess had agreed to help Nixon write on the 1964 election, something on the order of Theodore White's *The Making of the President*. Shocked and saddened, he had rushed to the Nixon apartment. The first thing Nixon did was to open up his attaché case and show Hess an article in a Dallas paper which reported his expression of contempt for the recent heckling of Adlai Stevenson. "Nixon said, in effect," Hess remembered, "I didn't fuel this thing."

He was enormously fearful, Hess said, lest the assassin be a right-winger. When finally Nixon succeeded in talking to J. Edgar Hoover, his first question was, "Was it one of the nuts?" "No," Hoover replied, "It was a Communist. He was known to the FBI as a member of the pro-Castro Fair Play for Cuba Committee."[16]

Nixon cancelled his engagement to play golf with Thomas Dewey and Roger Blough. He called Eisenhower, but when he learned he was asleep, did not have him wakened. Later Nixon and Hess were joined by Roger Keyes and Rose Woods. A television crew arrived and asked for Nixon's reaction to the assassination. He refused to take questions but made a brief statement:

President Kennedy yesterday wrote the last greatest chapter for his *Profiles in Courage*. Today millions of people throughout the world are trying to find words adequate to express grief and sympathy to his family. . . . The greatest tribute we can pay to his memory is in our own everyday lives to do everything we can to reduce the forces of hatred which drive men to do such terrible deeds.[17]

When Nixon conversed with his friends that afternoon about the effect of the assassination on the Democratic party, he talked of hatred, speculating, Hess said, that "there would be a severe blood bath between the new President, Johnson, and Attorney General Robert Kennedy." By the next day he had abandoned this idea, saying "Johnson would have it under control, and that the country would be united behind him."[18]

Meanwhile Leonard Hall and other politicians were arriving. As Witcover put it, while "the world's great streamed in and out of the White House to pay private respects to the dead President lying in state in a closed coffin, Richard Nixon held political court in his New York apartment. Old political associates came by to discuss with him the impact of the assassination on the Republican picture and what Nixon's posture should be."[19] A recent Harris poll had showed Nixon slightly ahead of Rockefeller, Romney, and Goldwater, but still losing to Kennedy by 55 percent to 45 percent. Eisenhower had repeatedly said Nixon would not run. But within forty-eight hours of the assassination, plans for writing the book on the 1964 election were shelved; Leonard Hall was off to visit Eisenhower and Nixon was back in politics as a serious potential presidential candidate.

He was by no means insensitive, however, to the massive trauma, the paralysis of shock and grief from which the nation was suffering. He called it "a terrible tragedy for the nation,"[20] and was himself far more shaken than his friends realized. Kennedy was killed at the height of his worldwide popularity. He had been hailed for his successful negotiation of the test-ban treaty on above-ground nuclear weapons and embraced as a new champion of blacks as he fought for the first major civil-rights legislation since Reconstruction. He had been loved by artists, whom he invited to the White House, and the intellectuals, whom he hired in droves. He was the only president, *Time* said later, who could "make poor folk hope and smart folk laugh and womenfolk faint."[21] In death, Tom Wicker wrote, he became "the symbol of all our incompleted selves and spoiled dreams and blasted hopes."[22]

In his letter of condolence to Jackie Kennedy, written the day after the assassination, Nixon stressed the personal friendship of his early months with Kennedy in the House of Representatives:

While the hand of fate made Jack and me political opponents I always cherished the fact that we were personal friends from the time we came to the Congress together in 1947. That friendship evidenced itself in many ways including the invitation to your wedding.

Nothing I could say now could add to the splendid tributes which have come from throughout the world to him. . . .

Jackie replied gently.[23] Neither, however, could have forgotten the blows of the 1960 campaign. Since his defeat Nixon had never been invited to the White House, a slight that galled him, as he made evident to David Frost in 1977.[24] Since the election, moreover, Nixon had seized every opportunity to snap at Kennedy's heels. In the steel crisis of April 1962, when the young president forced the steel barons to back down on an inflationary rise of six dollars a ton in steel prices, Nixon called it "the typical reaction of a bully."[25] He deplored Kennedy's handling of the Bay of Pigs, saying Eisenhower would never have failed to provide air cover. He objected to Kennedy's Laotian policy and he criticized him for not protesting more vigorously the building of the Berlin Wall. He opposed the sale of U.S. wheat to Russia. After an initial statement of approval he damned Kennedy's handling of the Cuban missile crisis.[26] In the *Saturday Evening Post* of October 12, 1963, Nixon made an impassioned denunciation of every aspect of Kennedy's foreign policy, deploring the president's policy of "accommodation," "disengagement," and "coexistence" with the Soviet Union, which he called "devices which add up to our approval of Soviet domination of Eastern Europe."

In the 1970s, revisionist historians, eagerly dismantling Camelot, would describe Kennedy as a steely cold warrior and condemn him for his truculence toward the Soviet Union. In 1963 Nixon saw only softness, acquiescence, and betrayal. He deplored Kennedy's military aid to Tito, called for pressure on the Soviet Union to take all its troops out of Cuba, and made an emotional but unspecific call for action:

Our goal must be a free Cuba, a free Eastern Europe, a free Russia, a free China. . . . The Communist goal is to impose slavery on the world. Our goal must be nothing less than to bring freedom to the Communist world.

He quoted a Hungarian student from Budapest, "The Russian bear is always most dangerous when its arms are outstretched in a gesture of seeming friendship. If you get too close, you will be crushed to death."[27]

Nixon had never spared Kennedy from attack in life, although as we have said he used few of the dirty tricks and the low blows of his earlier campaigns. After the Kennedy inaugural his attacks were generally those of a man trying to establish himself as a political pundit, a conservative Walter Lippmann for his party. Despite the intensity of these attacks it is evident that Nixon admired Kennedy. He also envied him. As Dan Rather put it, "Given the scope and intensity of the legend, better to be seen as Mordred than to have no role at all in Camelot."[28]

To Dick Schapp, Nixon said in 1968 that his resurrection in politics had been the result of "a series of accidents."[29] Surely among the crucial accidents were the failure of Lee Harvey Oswald to kill General Walker, and Oswald's decision to kill Kennedy rather than himself.

In his new preface to *Six Crises,* in 1968, he wrote that at his "last press conference" in 1962, "I was through." It was not by dint of his own calculations or efforts, he said, that he was back in politics—it was a matter of destiny:

No man, not if he combined the wisdom of Lincoln with the connivance of Machiavelli, could have maneuvered his way back into the arena. Sometimes a nation is ready for leadership and his is the right kind of leadership for the time. Only time will tell what course destiny will take in this watershed year of 1968.

When Nixon was pressed for his innermost feelings about the assassination he usually evaded his questioners. Although Stephen Hess said, "My strong impression was that he felt it could have been he who was killed," Nixon denied this in his memoirs. "I never felt the 'there but for the grace of God go I' reaction to Kennedy's death that many people seemed to imagine I would. After eight years as Vice President I had become fatalistic about the danger of assassination. . . . I did not think that if I had won in 1960 it would have been I rather than he riding through Dealey Plaza in Dallas at that time, on that day."[30]

In 1968 Nixon told Jules Witcover:

Even now women come up to me and say, "I cried all night the night you lost the election, but now I'm glad you weren't elected President because you wouldn't be here now." But I think it would not have happened to me. No two men are in the same place at the same time. . . . I've never had any sense of fear or trepidation, or superstition, none of that.

When Witcover asked him if he had suffered "a kind of personal guilt and stock-taking to which many others had confessed in the immediate aftermath," any kind of "self-analysis," Nixon replied,

"No, I'm something of a fatalist. I've always felt you keep churning away." He did, however, confess that he thought the Kennedy assassination had "a traumatic effect on the country greater than the death of Lincoln," adding, "It probably had a greater effect on me than on some closer to him."[31]

The "effect" on Nixon is to a considerable degree measurable, although there are subtleties extremely difficult to track. As we have said, the immediate consequence was that Nixon abandoned his plans to write a book, abandoned his projected role of political commentator, and went back into the Republican arena. As we shall see, too, once he became president he tried immediately to wrest control from Richard Helms, new director of the CIA, of all the still-secret documents on the Cuban invasion plans, and since almost everything of significance on the invasion had already been published save the assassination track record, it seems likely that this above all was what he wanted in his own possession, where he could be sure of its suppression.

We can trace also the beginning of what became a sporadic but nevertheless continuing denigration of Kennedy which sometimes assumed a character of great vindictiveness, particularly in his attempts to prove, first, that Kennedy had ordered the assassination of the Vietnamese leader Ngo Dinh Diem and his brother, and second, that it was the killing of these two brothers that started the Vietnam War. He would cover up or destroy all evidence of his own role in fueling the hatred between Castro and Kennedy. And he would expose Kennedy in sanctioning assassination.

There was a link binding General Walker, Richard Nixon, and John F. Kennedy in Oswald's murderous fantasies—the link was the attacks of all three men on Fidel Castro—but this link the Warren Commission played down. Most of the members did not know, or ignored, scattered evidence which would have suggested the intensity of Oswald's commitment to Castro. More important, all the data on the CIA plans to assassinate Castro were withheld from the commission by J. Edgar Hoover and three directors of the CIA, Allen Dulles (himself a member of the Warren Commission), John McCone,[32] and Richard Helms.

The Warren Commission did acknowledge from the beginning that there had been a kind of Cuban connection. In New Orleans, on August 9, 1963, Oswald had been involved in a small riot with Cuban refugees, who attacked him for distributing literature for the Fair Play for Cuba Committee. On August 17 he had told William Stucky of radio station WDSU that the Soviet Union had gone soft on Communism and that Cuba was the only truly revolutionary country in the world. Oswald subscribed to the Trotskyist *Militant* which had regularly given details of Castro's unceasing attacks on the United States, and had contained his accusations that Kennedy and the CIA were responsible for continuing acts of sabotage in Cuba.[33]

What none of the members of the Warren Commission and staff knew, save Allen Dulles, was that the CIA had indeed been instigating sabotage in Cuba since Eisenhower's time, and that this had not stopped under the Kennedys. Operation Mongoose, which meant accelerated sabotage, had been a pet project of Robert Kennedy's till its cancellation after the Cuban missile crisis. Although attempts to assassinate Castro through the CIA had officially been turned off by the Kennedys, some had continued, but whether this represented what the Church Committee called "a rogue elephant" mentality in the CIA or a reactivation in secret by the Kennedys may for a long time remain a subject of conflict among historians.[34]

Some members of the Warren Commission staff paid special attention to the fact that Castro in a sensational interview with Daniel Harker of the Associated Press, held in the Brazilian embassy in Havana, on September 7, 1960, had blasted the United States government for the continued attempts on his life. "Kennedy is the Batista of our time," he said, and warned against "terrorist plans to eliminate Cuban leaders." This interview was reported at length in the *New Orleans Times Picayune* on September 9, when Oswald was living in New Orleans. The *Picayune* article quoted Castro as saying, "We are prepared to fight them and answer in kind. United States leaders should think that if they are aiding terrorists' plans to eliminate Cuban leaders, they themselves will not be safe." Isaac Don Levine, who interviewed Marina Oswald extensively soon after the assassination, said Oswald had clipped this article, which was found among his papers. He immediately realized its significance. Others did not.[35]

Richard Nixon was closer to the truth than the Warren Commission when he wrote in the *Reader's Digest* of November 1964: "Castro was the indirect cause of the tragic snuffing out of John

Kennedy's life." Oswald, he said, was "a demented character" who had tried to kill General Walker and himself as well. "What brought him to this condition is still unknown. But certainly one of the major factors which warped his mind and drove him to this terrible deed was his contact with communism generally and with Castro's fanatical brand of communism in particular."[36] Afterward Nixon retreated from any further discussion of the dangerous subject.

If we look ahead briefly into the presidential years, we can see that Nixon made it a rule never to discuss directly the CIA attempts to assassinate Castro, always disguising his spoken and written inquiries by using the euphemism "Bay of Pigs." Second, he did his best to exaggerate the Kennedy involvement in the assassination of the brothers Diem. This involved extraordinary dueling with Richard Helms, who controlled the key documents. Many details have not been told, nor are they likely to be, since Helms and Nixon—in Sen. Howard Baker's words—"have so much on each other neither of them can breathe."[37]

One of Nixon's most striking omissions in his memoirs is his failure to indicate that he had ever heard of the CIA attempts to assassinate Castro, even though his book was written after the Church Committee hearings had received worldwide publicity. He failed even to mention his own unpublished disclaimer of involvement in the assassination attempts, which he had sent to the committee.

Haldeman tells us that immediately after Nixon became president, he called in Ehrlichman and told him "he wanted all the facts and documents the CIA had on the Bay of Pigs, a complete report on the whole project." Helms fought to keep the file. Six months later Ehrlichman told Haldeman:

Those bastards in Langley are holding back something. They just dig in their heels and say the President can't have it. Period. Imagine that! The Commander-in-Chief wants to see a document relating to a military operation, and the spooks say he can't have it. . . . from the way they're protecting it it must be pure dynamite.[38]

Ehrlichman's notes for September 18, 1971, written after a session with the president, reflect Nixon's continuing anxiety about the Castro assassination data:

Bay of Pigs—order to CIA [President] is to have the full file or else—
Nothing w/held[39]

When Helms again refused, Nixon summoned him personally. In a carefully written reference to this meeting in his memoirs, Nixon indicated he was interested only in "the role of the
Kennedy administration in the Diem assassination and the Bay of
Pigs." He asked Helms for key documents, promising he would
not use them "to hurt him, his predecessor, or the CIA." Helms
responded, "I have one President at a time. I only work for you."
Nevertheless, Nixon said, without telling us how he knew, the files
Helms delivered were "still incomplete."[40]

This significant meeting between Nixon and Helms neither
man has ever described in detail. It did succeed in bringing about
a temporary truce and a continuing burial of the problem of the
assassination track. What Nixon did with the documents Helms
brought to him he does not say. The dueling between the two
men ceased until the Watergate burglary. Then Nixon learned
with consternation that five of the men involved were former CIA
agents, and that four of them—E. Howard Hunt, Frank Sturgis,
Bernard Barker, and Eugenio Martinez[41]—had all been connected with the planning for the Cuban invasion when he was
vice-president. These men, some of whom, like Hunt and Sturgis,
knew about the Castro assassination attempts, could hardly, in
Haldeman's words, be "dropped like a stone." They knew too
much. Hunt in particular had an enormous potential for blackmail.[42]

Since the CIA and FBI had an agreement to stay out of each
other's territory, Nixon now sought to meet the Watergate crisis
by involving the CIA. He told John Dean to ask Haldeman to call
Gen. Vernon Walters and have him call the new FBI director,
Patrick Gray, and say, "Just stay the hell out of this—this is a business we don't want you to go any further on." To Haldeman,
Nixon said on June 23, 1972:

Just say (unintelligible) very bad to have this fellow Hunt, ah, he knows
too damned much, if he was involved—you happen to know that? If it
gets out that this is all involved, the Cuba thing it would be a fiasco. It
would make the CIA look bad, the whole Bay of Pigs thing which we
think would be very unfortunate—both for the CIA, and for the country, at this time, and for American foreign policy. Just tell him to lay
off.[43]

When Haldeman relayed Nixon's request to Helms, the CIA director coldly denied at first that there was any connection whatever between the Watergate break-in and the CIA. When Haldeman said, "The President asked me to tell you this entire affair may be connected to the Bay of Pigs, and if it opens up the Bay of Pigs may be blown," he was shocked by the violence of the reaction. The usually steely CIA chief gripped the arms of his chair and began shouting, "The Bay of Pigs had nothing to do with this! I have no concern about the Bay of Pigs!" But he shortly calmed down and said, "We'll be happy to be helpful." "Again I wondered," Haldeman wrote later, "*what was such dynamite in the Bay of Pigs story.*"[44]

Only much later Haldeman came to understand that "the Bay of Pigs" was really a code word for the assassination track. "In all of those Nixon references to the Bay of Pigs," he concluded, "he was actually referring to the Kennedy assassination . . . to the coverup of the CIA assassination attempts on the hero of the Bay of Pigs—Fidel Castro—a CIA operation that may have triggered the Kennedy tragedy and which Helms [and Nixon] desperately wanted to hide."[45]

The Diem story, also essential in illuminating the theme of fratricide in Nixon's life, we shall tell only briefly. In 1963 Nixon had encouraged Kennedy's support of the Catholic ruler of Vietnam. "The choice," he said in a speech on September 23, "is not between Diem and someone better but between Diem and someone worse." And he openly predicted that a coup would mean a Communist takeover.[46]

Diem, however, had made himself hated among the Buddhist majority in his state, letting his troops desecrate the sacred pagodas and arresting hundreds of Buddhist monks. Several suicidal immolations, where monks set fire to themselves to protest government indignities—belittled by Diem's sister-in-law, Madame Nhu, who spoke contemptuously of "putting mustard on the monks' barbecue"—caused worldwide horror.

Kennedy did secretly encourage a generals' revolt against Diem in August 1963, with CIA involvement in the planning. But the coup did not take place. Later, with rumors of a new coup, Kennedy sent Secretary of Defense MacNamara and Gen. Maxwell Taylor to Saigon. They urged pulling back from any support for the coup, and CIA Director McCone, in secret messages to his agents in South Vietnam, deplored all talk of assassination. Despite this retreat, a generals' coup did take place on November 2, 1963; Diem and his brother were both killed.

Although the Americans had had no role in the assassinations,[47] suspicion that the CIA had been involved was nevertheless worldwide. *Newsweek* in December 1963 reported that Prince Norodom Sihanouk, ruler of Cambodia, was obsessed with the idea that the CIA was trying to get rid of him "the same way it did with Diem." When Nixon visited Pakistan in 1964, President Ayub Khan said to him:

I cannot say—perhaps you should never have supported Diem in the first place. But you did support him for a long time and everyone in Asia knew it. . . . And then, suddenly, you didn't support him anymore—and Diem was dead. Diem's murder meant three things to many Asian leaders: that it is dangerous to be a friend of the United States; that it pays to be neutral; and that sometimes it helps to be an enemy![48]

After the publication of the *Pentagon Papers* in June 1971, Americans reading the hitherto secret summary of governmental American involvement in Vietnam learned for the first time that there had indeed been U.S. government and CIA involvement in the coup planned for August of 1963. There was no proof in the *Pentagon Papers,* however, of Kennedy's complicity in the assassination in November. This did not stop Nixon from instituting a search of State Department and Department of Defense cables, and of CIA files, in an effort to uncover incriminating data. He said publicly in his press conference of September 16, 1971: "I would remind all concerned that the way we got into Vietnam was through overthrowing Diem and the complicity in the murder of Diem."[49]

Two days later, Ehrlichman made the following notes after a meeting with the president:

A Kennedy target—Diehm [sic] incident the best ground—involved: Harriman (Muskie) Kennedy—
   . . . liberal press afraid of that affair—they wanted the killing—that murder triggered the whole war—Laotian Agreement (by Harriman) & the assassination & subsequent instability are the 2 basic events—LBJ can be with us on these—LBJ keeps saying JFK started the Vietnam war—he is right—How to get that story out?

... [president] wants the entire Diem file by next Friday because of press conference. ...

State's cables re Diem's coup. <u>all</u> from DOD and State.[50]

E. Howard Hunt was given authority by Charles Colson to see the State Department cable file. After considerable research he told Colson there was a "strong but inconclusive case" concerning Kennedy's complicity in the assassination of the brothers Diem, but that there was no "hard evidence" such as a cable. And he insisted that some cables were missing. When Colson asked him if he could "improve" on the cables he already had, Hunt proceeded to forge two cables, using scissors, paste, and a Xerox machine, to prove "that JFK had personally and specifically ordered the assassination of the deposed South Vietnamese President Ngo Dinh Diem and his brother, Ngo Dinh Nhu."[51]

Colson and Hunt, with what, according to Ehrlichman, seems to have been Nixon's cooperation, tried unsuccessfully to get a story based on the spurious cables published in *Life*. John Ehrlichman has written of this: "I was only aware of the forgery late, and can just deduce how all that happened. But I was aware of the Nixon-Colson-Hunt effort to produce the *Life* piece."[52] William Lambert, of *Life*, became suspicious when he was denied permission to see the original cables and copy them. He turned the story down.[53] Hunt did show the cables to Col. Lucian Conein, a former CIA agent in Saigon, who used them on a TV program extremely damaging to Kennedy.[54]

After the Watergate burglary, when John Dean examined the contents of E. Howard Hunt's safe, he found the faked cables and the notes exchanged between Colson and Hunt concerning possible publication in *Life*. Recognizing the devastating nature of the documents, he took them to Patrick Gray, acting head of the FBI, with the suggestion that he destroy them. Gray did.[55]

When the whole episode was examined in the Senate Watergate hearings, Hunt testified among other things that Nixon had been intent on proving that Kennedy "had authorized the assassination of another Catholic, and this would have some impact on the Catholic vote in the subsequent election, if there should be a Kennedy involved in the election."[56]

Nixon made only a scant but revealing reference to the matter in his memoirs, writing that Ehrlichman on the night of April 27, 1973, telephoned him at Camp David:

He told me that he thought I should recognize the reality of my own responsibility. He said that all the illegal acts ultimately derived from me, whether directly or indirectly. He implied that I was the inspiration behind them, and mentioned such things as the forged Diem cable. He also implied that I should resign.

Nixon went on to write that he then asked Ron Ziegler, his press secretary, to telephone Colson and "find out what happened on the Diem cable." Ziegler "came back a few minutes later and said that Colson had sworn that he himself had not known about the forgery. 'The President,' Colson had added, 'knew zero.' "[57] Thus Nixon exonerated himself, not by straightforward denial, not by writing that he knew absolutely nothing about the cable, but by saying, in effect, "Ziegler tells me that Colson says I knew nothing."

Ehrlichman later found in Nixon's frenetic involvement in trying to get the Cuban invasion and Diem files out of the hands of Richard Helms and into his own the central scenario for his novel *The Company*, which he wrote after his trial and conviction for participation in the Watergate coverup. In the novel, President Monckton (Richard Nixon) made it his chief object to destroy the image of his predecessor, Billy Curry, who is clearly John F. Kennedy:

He wants to end forever the Curry legend, raze the Curry temple brick by brick leaving nothing standing. He'll want to do it spectacularly on television, stamp it in the mind of every American. His line will be that Billy Curry murdered a priest in cold blood.[58]

As late as 1980, in *The Real War*, Nixon was still insinuating Kennedy's involvement:

On November 1, 1963, Diem was overthrown in a coup and assassinated. Charges that the U.S. government was directly involved may be untrue and unfair. However, the most charitable interpretation of the Kennedy administration's part in this affair is that it greased the skids for Diem's downfall and did nothing to prevent his murder. It was a sordid episode in American foreign policy.[59]

The Nixon Character

Once you get into this great stream of history you can't get out.
You can drown. Or you can be pulled ashore by the tide. But it
is awfully hard to get out when you are in the middle of the
stream—if it is intended that you stay there.

— NIXON TO EARL MAZO, 1959[1]

I HAVE LONG BELIEVED that the definitive judgment on a president is almost always written during his life or in the first obituaries. The patient work of historians and biographers may serve to rediscover it and underline it, but it has always already been said by a contemporary, and usually with distinction. Thus Walt Whitman could judge Lincoln even after his second year in office:

I think well of the President. He has a face like a Hoosier Michaelangelo, so awful ugly it becomes beautiful with its strange mouth, its deep cut, criss-cross lines, and its doughnut complexion. . . . Mr. Lincoln keeps fountain of first-class practical telling wisdom. I do not dwell on the supposed failure of his government; he has shown I think sometimes an almost supernatural talent in keeping the ship afloat at all, with head steady, not only not going down, and now certain not to, but with proud and resolute spirit, and flag flying in the sight of the world, menacing and high as ever. I say never yet captain, never ruler, had such a perplexing and dangerous task as his, the past two years. . . . a truly democratic genius.[2]

Many distinguished Americans have sat in judgment on Richard Nixon. There has never been anything like the unanimity, the searing eloquence, the sense of vital concern for the nation, in the negative judgments that echoed across the land in August 1974. My own statement here represents not a judgment but a summary of discoveries made in several years of research and writing about the shaping of Nixon's character. My indebtedness to the writings of others is evident in the text and in the notes. No source has been more fruitful than the writings of Nixon himself.

Plutarch wrote that character is fate. With Nixon, as we have seen, accident was also fate. But in the last years of his life when we see Nixon making choices that were essentially self-destructive, the Nixon character emerges as the decisive force in his life. Although it has been said by several writers that Nixon had "no sense of place," this is not true. His character began to be shaped in Quaker Whittier, a small walled town resisting the enemy with its bastions of decorum and constrictions of the spirit, providing for some inner peace but bringing to Nixon only a sense of strangulation. The fortress was earthquake-shaken by the discovery of oil in the twenties, with the erosion of even the stoutest Quaker virtues. It is no accident that Nixon as president, in scores of speeches, announced that America was and must remain "the richest and strongest nation on earth," with the word "richest" coming first.

There was a perpetual threat to the Whittier fortress in the surrounding Chicano society, with its taverns and dancehalls, its well-attended Catholic churches, with its more spontaneous gaiety. That Nixon was drawn to it is suggested by the fact that even before his marriage he thought of moving his law practice to Havana. The Caribbean became his favorite vacation place, especially after meeting the rich, generous, and nonjudgmental Rebozo.

The Whittier fortress was threatened too by the fantasy world of Hollywood, with its phantasmagoria of magic delights, and the mad, wild world of the stars, every detail of which was chronicled during Nixon's adolescence in the *Los Angeles Times*. As we have seen, this was part of his initial attraction to the stage, and to Pat Nixon, who had played Hollywood bit parts. On many occasions as president he joked, "I always like to see the celebrities." Thus he could say in one of the more bizarre of his exaggerations, in a ceremony honoring movie mogul Adolph Zukor, "I have traveled all over the world, and have met many people, kings, queens, princes, princesses, leaders. No one I have met in my travels is a greater man than Adolph Zukor."[3]

It can be seen that Nixon's "place" was an area of extraordinary volatility. Some Quakers successfully resisted the confusion in the soul. Nixon's cousin Jessamyn West is a notable example.

But she had parents of special quality, with a mother who was an angel of nurturing, who during Jessamyn's tubercular period lured her back from death. Hannah Nixon, a saint and not an angel, had a peculiar constriction of the spirit. Despite her countless benefactions to others she could not communicate a basic trust to any of her sons, a sense of being much loved. Her quietly enviscerating "little talks" had a lasting damaging effect. Taking Harold to Prescott when Richard was fifteen followed earlier abandonments, the first in his infancy and the second when she sent him away when he was twelve to live for six months with his aunt. And the shouting, belittling voice of the father, scapegoating his sons for his own failures, demanding instant obedience and proclaiming the message that fear rules in the world and not love, was preeminent in the development of Richard Nixon's character.

The sense of being unloved led to that of being essentially unlovable, to self-loathing. As a defense against this, the fantasy life took over. Nixon became intent on being a president, first of the Whittier High student body—and the failure to win this ever rankled in him—then president of the Whittier College student body, then president of the Duke University student law association, finally vice-president and president of the United States. Obtaining ever-greater glory and ever-increasing power became the most powerful motivating force in his life. Most men similarly crippled in childhood, who seek refuge in the grandiose fantasy, do not see fulfillment. Nixon did. But he could never be certain that the final fulfillment in 1968 was of his own making. Accident played too large a role for any assurance that he came to the presidency because the people wanted him.

Nixon in his speeches often spoke of character, citing his grandmother's, his mother's, and his wife's, and delivered many an earnest homily on the necessity for men of character in government. There was certainly an image here, which had some meaning for him, although again much of this may have been pious rhetoric. One must note that near the time of his resignation he referred several times to the cause of the Fall of Rome as being due to the loss of character in its leaders.

If Nixon had no emotional investment in truth, and only a slight investment in character, he certainly had an investment in applause. This was more essential to him than emotional communication, where he had manifest difficulties, more essential than achievement. The importance of applause for Nixon is underlined in a dream Nixon included in his memoirs. Sharing a dream is dangerous, as Nixon must certainly have recognized in therapy. But his self-revelations are often astonishing. The dream is illuminating, and the fact that he told it suggests that he wanted a wide audience to share in it.

He had recorded the dream first in his presidential diary during the 1972 campaign:

I had a rather curious dream of speaking at some sort of a rally and going a bit too long and Rockefeller standing up in the middle and taking over the microphone on an applause line. Of course, this is always something that worries a person when he is making speeches, as to whether he is going on too long. It is a subconscious reaction. It is interesting.[4]

Dreams are treacherous to speculate about in the absence of associations to them. The clinicians I have consulted about this dream agree that one of its most significant aspects is Nixon's loss of the microphone to Rockefeller "on the applause line." He was being deprived of that for which he desperately hungered. The nurturing which he wanted had never been forthcoming. Someone more handsome, more genuinely loved, had robbed him of it. Long before he reached the presidency political applause had become a substitute fulfilling the early hunger. The primitive certainty of being unloved and unlovable could never be silenced by applause, but it could be drowned out.[5]

In Nixon's earliest years neither of his parents was able to communicate a sense of basic trust or of his own worth. The clues were wrong. By the time of his first congressional campaign, there was a fundamental splitting between Nixon the man of virtue and Nixon the deceiver. Later, when he became president, the belief in himself as the man who would bring truth to government and peace to the world was not an act, yet the splitting continued. Over and again he would lead White House guests to the Lincoln Sitting Room, as he did his old Whittier patron, Tom Bewley, discoursing earnestly on how he would bring peace for a generation.

Self-deception was with Nixon always, as was his deceiving of others. As late as December 1978, speaking on television in Paris, Nixon could say, "I was not lying. I said things that later on seemed to be untrue."[6]

Hints of his paranoid style had begun early. In 1948 when

Nixon was campaigning for reelection to the House, he flew to Los Angeles, arriving in a bad storm. When he got to his speaking engagement in El Monte, he saw pickets outside. He began his speech with a description of the thunder and lightning as the plane descended, and spoke frankly of his own fear that he might not land alive. He said there were probably people in the present audience, and those outside picketing, who "wished that he would have died, and that his plane would have come down. But he had made it through, and was there."[7]

Watergate served to dramatize how feeble were Nixon's real defenses against the onset of paranoia in a major crisis where his massive denial of lying no longer served him. "Everybody thinks the people surrounding the President were drunk with power," Charles Colson said, "but it was not arrogance at all. It was insecurity. That insecurity began to breed a form of paranoia." This included Nixon most of all.[8]

During Watergate Nixon told Ehrlichman that he must be his conscience, a mantle Ehrlichman did not wear comfortably, and the very idea of which gives us some clue to the kind of conscience Nixon had come to value, although it should be noted to Ehrlichman's credit that he was the only one of the president's men who pressed him to "go the hangout road." The vulgarity of the phrase, with its exhibitionist flavor, surfacing as it did many times on the presidential tapes in the last year, is one of the countless evidences of the advance of impulse over defense in Nixon at this late date.

One issue has baffled many: whether Nixon had a conscience pricking at him when he lied. Nixon certainly knew right from wrong, or at least legal from illegal and truth from falsehood. *But he didn't care.* He had no emotional investment in the truth. He said to an early close associate, "You don't know how to lie. If you can't lie, you'll never go anywhere."[9] His denials of his lying, also very calculated in his early campaigns, became even more routine in the presidency.

The lack of his investment in truth or in what is right was expressed, for instance, when Nixon, adopting the facade of the moralizer, resorted only to the most primitive platitudes—"Two wrongs do not make a right"—or affirmed the opposite of what he surmised—"The truth always catches up with a lie." He had no real conception of social morality.

Nixon had a severely defective or almost nonexistent conscience, as we usually conceive of a conscience, that inner voice,
defining, directing, or simply pricking, mostly on an unconscious
level, when one is facing decisions involving a choice between
right and wrong. This does not mean that Nixon did not have a
powerful primitive inner voice, the unconscious memories of his
bellowing father, and his mother's soft-spoken barbs in their "little talks" telling him, in effect, "You are unloved; you are bad."
This inner voice, this unconscious self-hatred, was certainly a
powerful motivating force in Nixon's life. But it was not a conscience. It could be temporarily silenced by applause but it could
not be appeased by honesty or goodness of behavior. Indeed,
questions of lying and truthtelling were strangely irrelevant to it.
Let us remember that Nixon had the model of a saintly mother
who invented stories when it suited her, and a father who taught
him that to win is everything.

Delinquent children have an unerring instinct for seeking out
delinquent friends.[10] They reinforce each other. Nixon attracted
to him and selected many talented delinquents, most conspicuously Murray Chotiner, Spiro Agnew, and John Mitchell. He said
of Agnew, by way of explaining a vice-presidential choice that had
mystified the nation in 1968, "There is a mystique about a man.
You know he's got it." The real attraction may have been the smell
of delinquency. Agnew's protestations of his innocence of financial peculations as vice-president, in his book *Go Quietly, or Else,*
serve only to underline how much he had learned about the art
of denial of evil from Richard Nixon. He had also learned the
trick of converting lying into cash by publication. But he was
delinquent long before he moved into the vice-presidency.

Nixon corrupted many young men. It is troublesome to
remember that of the score of young lawyers involved in the
Watergate coverup, only one, Hugh Sloan, could not stomach the
massive deceit. Herbert Klein and Robert Finch were weak men,
but might have led less damaged lives had they never entered
Nixon's entourage.

Kissinger, Nixon's Talleyrand, survived, along with the innocuous and often fatuous Ronald Zeigler. Kissinger remained a
highly touted secretary of state under Gerald Ford because he
managed to keep clear of the Watergate coverup and because he
was aided by a prodigious intellect and inventive talent for inter-

national negotiation. His failure to persuade Nixon to end the
Vietnam War quickly—indeed, the degree to which he aided in
prolonging it and extending it into Cambodia—will remain a permanent blighting of his place in history.[11]

We have referred several times to Nixon's extraordinary interview with his former aide, Kenneth W. Clawson, in 1974 in San
Clemente. The former president, Clawson said, was sitting with
his phlebitic leg elevated, "filling the trouser leg like a thuringer
sausage in a frankfurter casing." Nixon described himself to
Clawson as "lean, mean and resourceful."[12] The meanness of
Nixon took many forms. Lou Cannon was shocked that a politician of so many years experience, with his own victory almost certain, should keep most of the $60,000,000 campaign funds in
1972 for his own election instead of distributing generously to
Republican congressmen and senators in need.[13] We have already
noted one of Nixon's aides telling Emmet Hughes, "When Nixon
is in trouble he believes the shortest distance between two points
is over four corpses." This meanness he may well have absorbed
from his father "the executioner," with his excessive work
demands, stinginess, and psychological abuse.

But blame for the more sinister theme of fratricide, running
like a lethal shadow through Nixon's life, should not rest with his
parents. It was a development unique to him, which even now
leaves me baffled and anguished. It surfaces too often to be accidental. Others have felt it. Theodore White, friendly to Nixon in
1972, castigated the liberal press for treating Nixon "as if the
brand of Cain were on him."[14] As we have seen, Nixon's first act
in Congress was not to attack the labor bosses, as he had promised, but to encourage the destruction of two brothers, Gerhart
and Hanns Eisler, one a Communist spy, and the other a Communist composer. The second was to attack Alger Hiss, a liar, and
also Hiss's brother Donald, who bore the name of Nixon's own
brother. He started and encouraged the CIA movement to
destroy Fidel Castro, and Raul Castro as well.

The assassinations of the two Kennedy brothers were of great
import in Nixon's life, especially the killing of John Kennedy by
Oswald, who had earlier talked of killing Nixon. In his youth
Nixon was haunted by the fear, communicated to his first biographer Richard Gardner as truth not fantasy, that Arthur had in

effect been murdered, dying as a result of his being hit on the head by a rock on the school playground. Afterward Richard watched the slow dying of his elder brother Harold, and knew of the implicit hint of suicide in Harold's failure to take care of himself. This must have produced enormous unconscious guilt, exacerbated when the money that had supported Harold's TB treatment was then used to send Richard to law school. These early trauma were reactivated with the Kennedy killings. Then the shooting and paralyzing of George Wallace by the demented Arthur Brenner, who had at first unsuccessfully stalked Nixon as the prime victim, and the political destruction of Edward Kennedy by the accidental drowning at Chappaquiddick, added to the fateful theme of death as an ally in Nixon's life. The pains to which Nixon went to try to prove that John Kennedy had connived in the assassination of the brothers Diem would seem to have been one more attempt to say, "Someone else is guilty, not I."*

Almost every one of Nixon's victories and political achievements save the elections to the vice-presidency had been won as a result of lying attack or the unexpected and fortuitous death of others. The deaths included not only the Kennedy brothers but also Martin Luther King—who it could be demonstrated had cost Nixon the 1960 election—whose death caused an outburst of violence which pointed voters toward the "law and order" candidate. What one does not know is whether or not Nixon suffered from an anxiety that the fate helping him was demonic and not divine.

Nixon talked about Fate occasionally, but almost never about God, although the bizarre episode shortly before his resignation where he asked Herry Kissinger to kneel down and pray with him would suggest that he was trying to extend his options, and wanted the world to know he could still pray. His belated call to Kissinger begging him not to relate the episode only increased the

---

*The suicides of two of Nixon's early biographers must be added to the list of untimely deaths that touched Nixon's life. Richard Gardner, the former Whittier College student and commercial artist who wrote the first Nixon biography, "Fighting Quaker," never published, killed himself and his wife and two daughters in 1952. His biography lay in manuscript on his desk, with a letter from Nixon, then vice-president, wishing him well with the publication. Gardner is not mentioned in the Nixon memoirs, and few outside the Whittier College staff know the story.[15]

Later, the friendly Hungarian refugee journalist Bela Kornitzer, who had spent some weeks with Nixon's mother gathering material for *The Real Nixon* (1960), also committed suicide.

certainty of the public's getting to know.[16] Whether he could not pray except in this public act with his secretary of state, smelling as it did of another staging, or whether he did find solace regularly in private prayer we do not know.

In his memoirs he often reproduced portions of his presidential diary, again suspect because he was writing for history and because of his penchant for rewriting, but which nevertheless convey an important sense of immediacy. One diary extract is worth scrutiny for its hint that he believed God was on his side. It was the eve of the election, 1972:

> We are not going to lose it, of course, lacking a miracle beyond which nothing has been seen up to this point. When I think of the ups and downs through the years someone must have been walking with us. The Peking trip, the Moscow trip, the May 8 decision and then the way we have handled the campaign—must deserve some grudging respect from even our own critics. The only sour note of the whole thing, of course, is Watergate and Segretti. This was really stupidity on the part of a number of people.

Nixon received 47,169,841 votes and McGovern only 29,172,767—60.7 percent to 37.5 percent. "This," he wrote, "was the second largest percentage of the popular vote in our history of two-party politics and the greatest ever given a Republican candidate." "Only Lyndon Johnson, running against Goldwater in the unique circumstances of 1964, had received fractionally more: 61.1 per cent.* I received the largest number of popular votes ever cast for a presidential candidate and the second largest number of electoral votes. No presidential candidate had ever won so many states."[17]

Still, he admitted that a few days later he also felt "a curious feeling, perhaps a foreboding, that muted my enjoyment of this triumphal moment. . . . I am at a loss to explain the melancholy that settled over me on that victorious night." He had had a painful tooth and did his best, writing in his presidential diary, to put the blame on the external cause.

> The tooth episode probably interfered to a considerable extent. Certainly by the time that I had to prepare for the office telecast I was not as upbeat as I should have been. The rest of the family seemed to think that they got enough of a thrill out of it. I think the very fact that the

---

*According to the Reader's Digest 1980 Almanac (p. 378), Franklin Delano Roosevelt received 60.8 percent in 1936.

victory was so overwhelming made up for any failure on my part to react more enthusiastically than I did.[18]

He went on to write in the memoirs perhaps the most chilling single line in the entire 1120 pages: "My first priority after the election was to end the war." He had made the same ordering in 1968. His solution was not continued negotiation, which was close to solution, but at a temporary stalement because of still-remaining differences between Hanoi and Saigon. Instead of coercing or writing off Thieu he loosed the most savagely destructive bombing of the entire Vietnam War, the Christmas carpet-bombing of North Vietnam. In his memoirs he records the negative press reaction, which he called "predictable":

The Washington Post editorialized that it caused millions of Americans "to cringe in shame and to wonder at their President's very sanity." Joseph Kraft called it an action "of senseless terror which stains the good name of America." James Reston called it "war by tantrum," and Anthony Lewis charged that I was acting "like a maddened tyrant."

He reported Republican Sen. William Saxbe of Ohio as saying he "appears to have left his senses," and Sen. Mike Mansfield as calling it "a stone-age tactic." But he was gratified to receive calls of support from Nelson Rockefeller, Ronald Reagan, and Sen. James Buckley. Sens. Howard Baker, Bob Taft, and Chuck Percy, he said, stood behind him, and John Connally "called daily to report some new and positive sampling of public opinion."[19]

He went on to quote from his presidential diary a paragraph that constitutes the most egocentric of all his attacks on the American media:

The record of the liberal left media on Vietnam is perhaps one of the most disgraceful in the whole history of communications in this country. I am not referring to the honest pacifists who have been against the war from the beginning, but to those in the media who simply cannot bear the thought of this administration under my leadership bringing off the peace on an honorable basis which they have so long predicted would be impossible.

The election was a terrible blow to them and this is their first opportunity to recover from the election and to strike back.[20]

He noted the support of Ronald Reagan, who had told him "that CBS under World War II circumstances would have been perhaps charged with treason."

The numbing character of these dozen pages continues. On

the day before Christmas he was at Key Biscayne. He had called
for a twenty-four-hour bombing halt for Christmas Day, and
there was intense and agonized pressure on him to continue the
moratorium. Plagued as always with insomnia, writing in his diary
at 4 A.M., he returned to the rare theme of his relation with God:

The main thought that occurred to me at this early hour of the morning
the day before Christmas, in addition to the overriding concern with
regard to bringing the war to an end, is that I must get away from the
thought of considering the office at any time a burden. I actually do not
consider it a burden, an agony, etc., as did Eisenhower and also to a
certain extent Johnson. As a matter of fact, I think the term glorious
burden is the best description.

On this day before Christmas it is God's great gift to me to have the
opportunity to exert leadership, not only for America but on the world
scene, because of the size of the mandate and also the strength of the
country. . . . A new group of Nixon loyalists, of course, is an urgent
necessity, but this really begins a period of always reminding myself of
the glorious burden of the presidency.[21]

Although admitting "considerable pressure" even from his
staff to continue the bombing halt, he wrote, "I disagreed completely. In fact, I personally ordered one of the biggest bombing
raids for December 26: 116 B-52 sorties were flown against tar-
gets in the Hanoi-Haiphong area. That afternoon the North Vietnamese sent the first signal that they had had enough."[22]

Again, death was his ally, this time still more massive killing
and mutilation. That he had come to delight in the slaughter and
had no quarrel with God concerning it was clear enough on the
presidential tape which showed his saying to his aides—para-
phrasing General Patton, his military hero—"Try and get the
weather, damn it, if any of you know of any prayers say them.
Let's get the weather cleared up. The bastards have never been
bombed like they're going to be bombed this time."[23]

We have seen in this volume abundant evidence of Nixon the
survivor, but very little of what became apparent in Watergate, an
impulse toward self-destruction. There remains a major question,
therefore, which is essential to any rounding out of the discussion
of the Nixon character: Why didn't he destroy the tapes? This
would have been easy to do at one point, and would have been
characteristic of Nixon the survivor. Leonard Garment, the most

sensitive and psychologically perceptive of all of Nixon's friends and staff, who it is to be hoped will one day abandon his vow of silence and contribute fully to the record of truth being compiled by others, assured me, in declining an interview, that one could trust Woodward and Bernstein's *The Final Days*. He apparently talked freely with these two courageous and tenacious journalists, whom history will record as having done a signal service to their country. In *The Final Days*, in discussing the decision not to destroy the tapes, they wrote that Garment told them, in effect, that Nixon wanted the world to see the ugliness of his mind. What Garment really said was that "Nixon wanted the world to see him go to the bathroom."[24] Along with the compulsive secrecy, the delight in coverup, the insatiate voyeurism, there was an unconscious urge to exhibit his own nakedness, his ineffable dirtiness.

Nixon in 1968 promised to bring us "truth in government." By not destroying the tapes he had brought us the worst of the truth about himself. The tapes meant his political destruction, the ruin of his reputation, the annihilation of the fantasy image of the good, decent, law-abiding president. It is important that he did not wait for the Supreme Court to force him to release the tapes. By voluntarily releasing the "White House Transcripts," mutilated and expurgated although they were, in advance of any Supreme Court action, he destroyed himself as president. That he cherished a conscious illusion that these transcripts would "vindicate" him before the American people was evidence of how far he had become dissociated from reality at that point.

When he came to explain in his memoirs why he had not destroyed the tapes, we see either that something of this stance was still with him, or that he had simply reverted to his habit of massive denial. Thus he could write:

If I had indeed been the knowing Watergate conspirator I was charged as being, I would have recognized in 1973 that the tapes contained conversations that would be fatally damaging. I would have seen that if I were to survive, they would have to be destroyed.

The tapes, he insisted, "indisputably disproved Dean's basic charge that I had conspired with him in an obstruction of justice over an eight month period." He was persuaded not to destroy them by Haig's reasoning "that the destruction of the tapes would create an indelible impression of guilt." "Finally," he said, "I

decided that the tapes were my best insurance against the unforeseeable future. I was prepared to believe that others, even people
close to me, would turn against me just as Dean has done, and in
that case the tapes would give me at least some protection."[25] In
effect, he needed them as a weapon against his own men.

Why had he installed the taping system in the first place? We
know that when he first entered the White House he immediately
had ordered the ripping out of the Lyndon Johnson taping system, which was voluntary and required activation. Sometime
before 1971, with Haldeman's encouragement, he developed the
idea of writing up his own presidential years, as Churchill had
done, and began to keep a diary as well as to install the automatic
taping system in three offices. He was fond of quoting Churchill's
advice that if you want your own history written properly you
must write it yourself. With the aid of the tapes, kept hidden from
the world, Nixon could establish himself if not as a great historian
at least as a president with total recall. Readers would be astonished at his encyclopedic memory, a memory in which he already
took considerable pride. He had hoped, he once indicated, after
his presidential years to teach at Oxford or Cambridge.

We know he would not have used the tapes honestly. In
expurgating the tapes for the White House Transcripts he not
only cut and mutilated, he also rewrote. Eighteen and one half
minutes of a crucial tape he destroyed totally. Prosecutor Leon
Jaworski was certain of this, but Nixon, in his memoirs, continued
to deny it, and said that the erasing might have been done accidentally by his lawyer.[26] Fred Buzhardt by now was dead and
unable to defend himself.

As Nixon went down, Pat nursed him as she had nursed her
mother and father in their dying. Through the years she had chosen to stay with her husband, putting up with the myriad of obligations, suffering his belittling and abandonment. He remained
her chosen shelter, her protection against the world. She could
not draw from within herself the necessary strength to stand up
to him, or to face life alone. She tranquilized herself, especially in
the early White House years, by spending endless hours writing
thank-you notes in longhand—she who could type speedily and
who had an ample staff—communicating with only faceless people. She had recourse, like her husband, in massive denial. Thus

she could say in Brussels in June 1974, when asked if she enjoyed being away from all the troubles at home, "I don't have any troubles; I know the truth."[27]

After the resignation Nixon invited his old football coach Chief Newman and his wife to San Clemente. When they were about to leave, Nixon gave them a photograph of himself and Pat beautifully dressed in evening clothes, both looking radiant. He signed it. When the Newmans went into the patio they met Pat, who talked a moment and then asked to see the photograph.

"I can sign that too," she said, and added to the photograph her tiny, rigid signature. As she handed it back, she said cryptically, "Tell Dick I did better than he did."[28] Which, thus spoken, may suggest that in her own struggle for survival the thought that she had done better than her husband was the most nourishing thought of all.

If Nixon ever loved anyone, it is often said, it was his daughter Julie. But this affection, too, had a kind of tortured quality. Julie Nixon has described how when she went to her father's office and told him she was going to marry David Eisenhower, he responded with a nod and went on working. She fled in tears to her mother. When she went to bed, she found a note, written by her father and left on her night table. It was gentle, affectionate, congratulatory. Nixon reproduced it in his memoirs:

November 22, 1967
Dear Julie.
I suppose no father believes any boy is good enough for his daughter. But I believe both David and you are lucky to have found each other—Fina often says—"Miss Julie always brings life into the home."
In the many years ahead you will have your ups and downs, but I know you will always "bring life into your home" wherever it is—

love
Daddy[29]

Nixon could not give way to spontaneous joy, or ambiguous joy mitigated by jealousy and a sense of loss, even with his favorite daughter. In this matter he could not even put on an act.

Pat Nixon told Jessamyn West that in the early years Julie and Tricia could make their father laugh, and "he could make them laugh." The fun, the laughter, what Pat described as "the good times," had long since disappeared in the relationship between

Nixon and his wife. But he did write her notes. Dianne Sawyer, secretary in the White House, who accompanied the Nixons to San Clemente in their retirement and remained there until the memoirs were finished, has said that Nixon wrote many notes to Pat, which she was privileged to read, although she would not indicate the number or divulge the nature of the contents. (She has taken "a private oath" not to write or to give interviews about her experience, at least while the Nixons are alive.)[30] Publication of these notes to Pat, or even a description of their feeling and content, may reveal a tenderness in Nixon which he has otherwise resolutely kept hidden. In any case the very recourse to notewriting tells us more of the warping of Nixon's capacity for love.

In his memoirs Nixon reproduced a diary entry written at San Clemente on July 27, 1974, the day he learned that the House Judiciary Committee had voted against him on the first article of impeachment:

I remember that Tricia said as we came back from the beach that her mother was really a wonderful woman. And I said, yes. She has always conducted herself with masterful poise and dignity. But, God, how she could have gone through what she does, I simply don't know.[31]

Oscar Wilde wrote that "each man kills the thing he loves," which for most men is not true. But Nixon, like Wilde, had this urge. He even damaged terribly Julie's love for him, permitting her to give 150 speeches on his behalf during Watergate, lying to her to the end. That there was some resentment on her part, and a desire to see her father punished, we see obliquely in a remarkable note she left on Nixon's pillow on August 6, 1974, begging him not to resign:

Dear Daddy:
    I love you. Whatever you do I will support. I am very proud of you. Please wait a week or ten days before you make this decision. Go through the fire a little bit longer. I love you. Julie
    Millions support you.[32]

When she turned to writing recently, it was to write a biography of her mother, not her father.

Of the eldest Nixon daughter, Tricia, little has been made public. Jessamyn West has said that Rose Woods once described Tricia as "hard as nails, like her mother."[33] We know that she was disliked by some White House journalists, and that she was the only one of the Nixon family to be mildly criticized by the White House photographer Ollie Atkins, in his gentle memoir, *Triumph and Tragedy: The White House Years.* Tricia was not without insight into her father. She kept a diary during the White House period, which Nixon persuaded her to let him mine for his book. Most of the extracts show Tricia as affectionate, loving, cheerful, and unseeing, saying, for example, "Daddy, of course, is always protective of everyone but himself."[34] But one extract he singled out for inclusion shook him a little. He wrote: "Tricia later showed me a note from her diary that reminded me that sometimes people around you understand things better than you understand them yourself":

Something Daddy said makes me feel absolutely hopeless about the outcome. He has since the Butterfield revelation repeatedly stated that the tapes can be taken either way. He has cautioned us that there is nothing damaging on the tapes; he has cautioned us that he might be impeached because of their content. Because he has said the latter, knowing Daddy, the latter is the way he really feels.[35]

If we look back to Adlai Stevenson's description of Nixon as "a man of many masks," and turn to the memoirs of Nixon's presidential aides, we will see that there was no real change wrought in this respect by his becoming president. He was the clean-spoken intellectual with men like Stephen Hess and Patrick Moynihan, and vulgar, abusive, and unbuttoned with Haldeman and Ehrlichman. Nixon's lawyer, Fred Buzhardt, said, "Nixon had to fabricate a personality."[36] Many noted Nixon's habit of referring to himself as "the President," as if the president had an identity quite independent of his own. His continuing dislike of his real self we see in his palpable fear of watching himself on television even when he had performed well.

Ehrlichman said he had no idea how many Nixons there were until he listened to the tapes.[37] When it came time to portray Nixon in his novel *The Company,* however, Ehrlichman singled out for description a president who was wholly evil. He called Nixon "President Monckton," after "the Mad Monk," which was his and Haldeman's private sobriquet for their president. Monckton is dour, colorless, sexless, vindictive, bitter, and morose, a man addicted to sleeping pills, contemptuous of food and friends, estranged from women including his wife, given to anal expletives and castration threats. He is insistently intent on proving that a noted columnist is a homosexual, as indeed Nixon had been concerning Jack Anderson.

Much has been made of Nixon's extraordinary capacity for survival. The survival through Watergate and into exile is the perpetuation of a life pattern. He survived to continue to deny his evil. Although he admitted to "mistakes" and to "screwing things up," there was never any real confession, which enraged Americans as much as anything else about his final years. The disintegration of his personality in 1974, with the hints of suicide, was halted by the punishment involved in the actual plummeting from the presidency in disgrace, by his partial admissions, of which the strongest came in his last tearful farewell to his White House staff, when he said to them, and also to a television audience of millions, "Always remember, others may hate you, but those who hate you don't win, unless you hate them, and then you destroy yourself."[38]

Death from phlebitis, which Nixon temporarily courted, especially by his refusal to follow his frantic doctor's orders in Egypt in 1974, was spared him by fate, by the excellence of his doctors, and by his own gut instinct for hanging on to life. His near death in San Clemente from an embolism related to the phlebitis was Nixon's last supreme ordeal after the resignation. He survived; it is possible that in his own eyes he may have felt that therefore he must not be guilty, or at least less guilty.[39] Thus he could return to the new life task, rebuilding his smashed reputation—and incidentally his personal fortune—by writing his memoirs, by conducting lucrative interviews with David Frost, by writing *The Real War.* Had he been impeached in the House, which he knew to be certain, and convicted in the Senate, which seemed likely, he would have lost his pension, his Secret Service protection, and all additional expense money. By resigning at the right moment he preserved them all.*

Henceforth he devoted his life to affirming that what he did was "normal" for the presidency, writing that other presidents had bugged and lied and covered up, perhaps even more than

---

*A General Services Administration study in 1980 estimated that Nixon in 1981 was expected to spend about $340,000 in addition to his $69,630 pension and the $150,000 allocated for staff salaries. In 1980 he had spent $1500 simply for duplicating and processing his photographs (*Los Angeles Times,* Nov. 24, 1980).

he. And he continued his life-long habit of placing the blame on others. John Kennedy and Lyndon Johnson, he insisted, were responsible for the Vietnam War. He said to David Frost when asked how as a Quaker he felt about Vietnam:

I hate all of it. I mean, I hate the war. I hated every minute of it. . . . believe me, it was a sore temptation not to just end it, and blame it on Kennedy and Johnson. They got us in. I didn't. They sent the men over there. I didn't.[40]

He could blame poor, damaged Martha Mitchell for Watergate and the venal press and media for abusing and distorting the truth about himself. He continued even in *The Real War* to imply that John F. Kennedy had been responsible for the assassination of the brothers Diem.

At San Clemente he chose his visitors with care, forbidding reporters access, protecting himself from unnecessary attack. Not long after his phlebitis ordeal, he invited his friend and defender, Gen. Vernon Walters, to visit him. He put a question to Walters knowing it would be answered gently. It was a question Nixon would never have dared to ask Judge John Sirica, Special Prosecutors Archibald Cox and Leon Jaworsky, or John Doar and the members of that extraordinary panel, the House Judiciary Committee, who wrote the resolutions for Nixon's impeachment, but it came to represent the Nixon litany in exile. The question he asked Walters was "What did I do wrong?"[41]

Notes

I. Man of Paradox

1. Arthur Miller, "The Limited Hang-Out," *Harper's*, September 1974; George V. Higgins, "The Friends of Richard Nixon, and How He Conned Them," *Atlantic*, November 1974; Jack McCurdy, "Scholars' Opinions Bode Ill for Nixon's Place in History," *Los Angeles Times*, Oct. 20, 1974. The McLaughlin comment was reported in the *Los Angeles Times*, Aug. 27, 1974, p. 13.
2. Osborne, *The Last Nixon Watch*, p. 5.
3. Woodward and Bernstein, *The Final Days*, pp. 214, 343.
4. For detailed answers to these basic Nixon defenses, see C. Vann Woodward, ed., *Responses of the Presidents to Charges of Misconduct*, especially Woodward's own introduction.
5. Jefferson to Moses Robinson, March 23, 1801, in *The Writings of Thomas Jefferson*, 20 vols., edited by Andrew A. Lipscomb and Albert E. Bergh (Washington, D.C., 1903), 10:237.
6. *Los Angeles Times*, Sept. 5, 1974, p. 16.
7. Newsom to FB, Aug. 14, 1975; Bewley to FB, June 15, 1976.
8. William Perdue to FB, Nov. 5, 1976; Frederick Albrink to FB, telephone interview, November 1976.
9. *Los Angeles Times*, March 11, 1980.
10. March Butz to FB, Aug. 15, 1974.
11. *RN*, p. 961.
12. Frady, *Billy Graham: Parable of American Righteousness*, p. 478.
13. *Public Papers of the Presidents of the United States*, (August 9) 1974, p. 630 (hereafter *Public Papers*); Kissinger, *The White House Years*, p. 62.
14. U.S. Congress, House, Committee on the Judiciary, tape transcript, March 18, 1973, *Transcripts of Eight Recorded Presidential Conversations*, 93rd Cong., 2d sess., May–June 1974, no. 34, p. 62.
15. For Nixon's plans for the yacht, see John Dean, *Blind Ambition* (New York: Simon & Schuster, 1976), p. 247.
16. Schaap, "Will Richard Nixon Trip over Himself on His Way to Victory?" p. 24ff.
17. Safire, *Before the Fall*, p. 364; Haldeman, *Ends of Power*, p. 74.
18. Haldeman, *Ends of Power*, pp. 74–75.
19. Gerald Shaw, California State University at Fullerton oral history interview, Oral History Project, no. 946, p. 3 (hereafter Cal. State archives).
20. Boris Goldenberg, *The Cuban Revolution and Latin America* (New York: Praeger, 1965), p. 187.
21. Reedy, *The Twilight of the Presidency*, p. 18.
22. Abrahamsen, *Nixon vs. Nixon*, p. 195, quoting an anonymous friend.
23. *RN*, p. 649.
24. Kenneth W. Clawson, "A Loyalist's Memoir," *Washington Post*, Aug. 9, 1979, p. D1.
25. Oscar Wilde, *Complete Works*, edited by Robert Ross (New York: Bigelow, Brown, 1921), 2:608, 620.
26. Aug. 1, 1959, reprinted as an Appendix to the paperback edition of Nixon's *Six Crises*, p. 478.
27. March 11, 1971, "Nixon's Meeting with Women of the White House Press Corps," unpublished manuscript, p. 15 (courtesy of Norma Mulligan). This did not appear in the presidential papers.
28. The speech was printed as an Appendix in the paperback edition of Nixon's *Six Crises*, Aug. 8, 1968.
29. Clawson, "A Loyalist's Memoir," p. D1.
30. Patricia Ryan Nixon as told to Joe Alex Morris, "I Say He's a Wonderful Guy," p. 93.
31. *Public Papers*, (April 7) 1974, p. 337. He had had three years of French-language study and one semester in French literature, his grades averaging a "B." He had never been able to speak or write French fluently (John E. Nichols, Whittier College registrar to FB, July 5, 1977; Paul Smith confirmed the lack of fluency).
32. Samuel Goldwyn, Jr., to FB.
33. Emmet Hughes, quoting a Nixon aide, *New York Times Magazine*, June 9, 1974, p. 70.

II. The Oil in the Lemon Grove

1. Richard Harris, "Reflections, Nixon and Lincoln," *New Yorker*, April 5, 1974, p. 110.
2. *Public Papers*, 1974, p. 631. Actually there were only three youths whom Hannah Nixon cared for in Arizona.
3. Alsop, *Nixon and Rockefeller, a Double Portrait*, p. 195.
4. *Public Papers*, 1974, p. 631.
5. George Kellog to FB, Aug. 26, 1974. See also Paul Smith interview, *The Young Nixon, an*

Oral Inquiry, edited by Reneé Schulte (California State University, Fullerton, 1978), p. 147.
6. March Butz to FB, Aug. 26, 1974.
7. Hannah Nixon as told to Flora Rheta Schrieber, "Richard Nixon, a Mother's Story," p. 212. "Oil was found in Olinda," Jessamyn West stated in a telephone interview on June 28, 1976, "but not in the flatter areas of Yorba Linda." See also Ralph de Toledano, *Nixon*, p. 20.
8. Richard Gardner, Nixon's first biographer, told the story correctly (see his manuscript, "Fighting Quaker," in the Whittier College library); Hoyt, *The Nixons: An American Family*, p. 186. Hoyt also wrote, "No oil was ever found there." Henry D. Spalding compounded Hannah Nixon's error, saying Frank lost his chance to be wealthy twice, once by selling the lemon grove to new owners "who struck oil on the land," the second time by failing to buy the Santa Fe Springs site (Spalding, *The Nixon Nobody Knows*, p. 36n). Earl Mazo told the story correctly in 1959, in *Richard Nixon, a Political and Personal Portrait*, p. 14n, as did David Barber in *The Presidential Character*, p. 399.
9. *Public Papers*, 1974, p. 100.

10. Kornitzer, *The Real Nixon*, p. 35; Spalding, *The Nixon Nobody Knows*, p. 39.
11. Mazo, *Richard Nixon*, p. 12; see also Pat Nixon, "I Say He's a Wonderful Guy," p. 18.
12. Butz, *Yorba Linda, Its History*, pp. 28, 40. Butz said Ralph Navarro was the "oldest living resident" of Yorba Linda, "born here in 1897," before Yorba Linda had a name.
13. *Los Angeles Times*, June 9, 1918, and April 19, 1930. For a complete record of the eclipses see Theodore Ritter von Oppolzer, *Canon of Eclipses* (New York, 1962), pp. 298–99. This volume charts 2000 eclipses.
14. Barber, *The Presidential Character*, p. 397.
15. Gardner, "Fighting Quaker," p. 18; see also Ella Eidson Furnas, Cal. State archives no. 856. Ella Eidson lived with the Truebloods. Robert Coughlan, in "Success Story of a Vice-President," p. 6, says each Nixon son paid a nickel.
16. Hutschnecker, *The Drive for Power*, pp. 301–2.
17. Woodward and Bernstein, *The Final Days*, p. 84. Woodward and Bernstein on "Face the Nation," April 18, 1976, said they had heard Buzhardt say this several times.
18. Presidential tape, March 23, 1971.

III. The Punishing Father

1. Television interview with David Frost, May 4, 1977.
2. *RN*, pp. 1, 4; Kornitzer, *The Real Nixon*, p. 79; Spalding, *The Nixon Nobody Knows*, p. 3.
3. *Richard Nixon, A Self-Portrait*, 1968 election film.
4. Shakespeare's father was also said to be a butcher. John Aubrey wrote, "His father was a butcher, and I have been told heretofore by some of the neighbours, that when he was a boy he exercised his father's trade, but when he killed a calfe he would do it in high style and make a speech" (Aubrey, *Brief Lives*, edited by Andrew Clark [1898], 2:225).
5. Lucile Parsons, daughter of Hannah's sister, Mattie Gibbons, Cal. State archives no. 607, p. 7; Bewley to FB, June 15, 1976.
6. Kornitzer, *The Real Nixon*, p. 25.
7. Hoyt, *The Nixons*, pp. 17, 29.
8. According to Oscar Marshburn, Nixon's uncle, who had become the stepson of Lutheria Wyman Nixon when she remarried in California after Samuel Brady Nixon's death (Abrahamsen, *Nixon vs. Nixon*, p. 6; Kornitzer, *The Real Nixon*, p. 71).
9. According to her sister, Olive Marshburn (Abrahamsen, *Nixon vs. Nixon*, p. 18).
10. Hoyt, *The Nixons*, pp. 171–72. Edith Milhous Timberlake, another sister, remembered Frank as "lonely" (Cal. State archives no. 969, p. 22).
11. Jessamyn West to FB, telephone interview, June 28, 1976; Alsop, *Nixon and Rockefeller*, p. 126; so Olive's son, Hadley Marshburn, reported (Cal. State archives no. 904, p. 5).
12. Jane Milhous Beeson, Cal. State archives no. 808, p. 6; Jessamyn West to FB, Sept. 29, 1976.
13. *Los Angeles Times*, July 12, 1952, p. 4.
14. *San Francisco Chronicle*, Jan. 3, 1969, quoted in Barber, *Presidential Character*, p. 408.
15. Lucile Parsons, Cal. State archives no. 607, p. 7. Several relatives tell of difficulties getting

Frank Nixon into a tuxedo when his son was inaugurated vice-president, although he had been, according to his brother Ernest, "a fancy dresser for a time" in his youth (Kornitzer, *The Real Nixon*, p. 71). For the two tuxedos story, see Alsop, *Nixon and Rockefeller*, p. 221; and Richard Spaulding, Cal. State archives no. 956, p. 6. The old one had been a gift.
16. Morgan, "Whittier '34," p. 35.
17. Pat Nixon, "I Say He's a Wonderful Guy," p. 18.
18. Thomas Bewley to FB, June 15, 1976; Hoyt, *The Nixons*, p. 183.
19. Abrahamsen, *Nixon vs. Nixon*, p. 32; Jessamyn West to FB, Sept. 29, 1976.
20. Jessamyn West to FB, and in *Whittier College Bulletin*, December 1954, p. 15; Merle West, Cal. State archives no. 981, p. 9; Jane Milhous Beeson, Cal. State archives no. 808.
21. Thomas Bewley to FB, June 15, 1976.
22. Kornitzer, *The Real Nixon*, p. 78.
23. Thomas Bewley to FB, June 15, 1976; Barber, *The Presidential Character*, p. 405.
24. Kornitzer, *The Real Nixon*, p. 79.
25. Hannah Nixon, "Richard Nixon, a Mother's Story," p. 208. For Jane Milhous Beeson's account of the story, see Cal. State archives no. 808.
26. Sigmund Freud, "A Child Is Being Beaten," *Complete Psychological Works*, 17:179–215.
27. Kornitzer, *The Real Nixon*, p. 65. See Samuel J. Sperling, "On the Psychodynamics of Teasing," *Journal of the American Psychoanalytic Association* 1, no. 3 (July 9, 1953).
28. Wills, *Nixon Agonistes*, p. 408.
29. Alsop, *Nixon and Rockefeller*, pp. 185–86.
30. *Public Papers*, (June 24) 1971, p. 771. A photograph of Richard Nixon with his cousin at the Grand Canyon, during his high school years, is noted by Michael Rogin and John Lattier, "Inner History of Richard Milhous Nixon," p. 20. Arthur J. Hughes, *Richard M.*

Nixon, p. 15, reported that Frank Nixon took his sons to Yosemite.
31. Lucile Parsons, Cal. State archives no. 924, pp. 4, 6.
32. *Richard Nixon, a Self-Portrait*, 1968 election film.
33. Herbert Hoover, *Memoirs* (New York, 1952), 1:6–7.
34. *Richard Nixon, a Self-Portrait*, 1968 election film, and speech in Centralia, Illinois, 1960, reported in Theodore White's *The Making of the President, 1960*, p. 341. How old Harold was when he made the demands for the pony Nixon did not make clear. Before his death at age twenty-three he had a car of his own, a little Ford that he cut down "like a bug," according to Ralph E. Palmer (Cal. State archivesno.927,p.16).
35. *The Senate Watergate Report* (New York: Dell, 1974), Final Report of the Ervin Committee, pp. 576, 579; U.S. Senate, Select Committee on Presidential Campaign Activities, *Hughes-Rebozo Investigation*, 93rd Cong., 2d sess., 26:12964.
36. Woodward and Bernstein, *The Final Days*, p. 238.
37. *Public Papers*, (Aug. 9) 1974, p. 631.
38. Mildred Jackson Johns to FB, Aug. 4, 1975; Mildred Sullivan Mendenhall to FB, July 13, 1976, and Cal. State archives no. 909; Wilma Funk, Cal. State archives no. 829; Kornitzer, *The Real Nixon*, p. 75.
39. Eisenhower, *At Ease: Stories I Tell to Friends*, p. 31.
40. Quoted in R. Rhodes, "Ike: An Artist in Iron," *Harper's*, July 1970, p. 71.
41. Hadley Marshburn, Cal. State archives no. 904, p. 4.
42. Nixon to David Frost, television interview, May 4, 1977. Earlier, in a conversation with Henry Kissinger concerning his trip to China in 1976, Nixon said, "There is an old quote which goes like this—from British history. A British Prime Minister's name, it was not Stonewall [Gladstone] said a major must for the Prime Minister was to have a good butcher." Kissinger replied, "You did what was necessary," and Nixon said, "A good butcher in terms of your own people." To which Kissinger replied, "I know." (Quoted in the *Wall Street Journal*, May 20, 1977, p. 14.)
43. See Chapter IV.
44. White, *The Making of a President, 1968*, p. 63; Safire, *Before the Fall*, p. 80; Price, *With Nixon*, p. 45.
45. Nixon to David Frost, March 23, 1977.
46. *Six Crises*, p. 124n.
47. Wallace Newman to FB, Aug. 14, 1975.
48. Nick Thimmesch, "What's Nixon Really Like,

Ask His Brothers," *Los Angeles Times*, Dec. 16, 1971.
49. Lucile Parsons, Cal. State archives no. 928, p. 4.
50. Kornitzer, "My Son: Two Exclusive and Candid Interviews with Mothers of the Presidential Candidates."
51. Mildred Sullivan Mendenhall, Cal. State archives no. 909.
52. Jessamyn West to FB, Sept. 29, 1976; Merle West to FB, July 6, 1976, and Cal. State archives no. 981, p. 8.
53. *Cardinal and White*, 1929, pp. 95–96.
54. Mary George Skidmore, Cal. State archives no. 952, p. 5.
55. Preface to *Six Crises* (paperback), p. xv.
56. Coughlan, "Success Story of a Vice President," p. 157.
57. *Public Papers*, 1969, p. 2. Raymond Price, collaborating on this speech, described Nixon's request to "keep this theme" of lowering the voice (Price, *With Nixon*, p. 48).
58. *Public Papers*, (Sept. 20) 1969, p. 734.
59. See *Public Papers*, 1972, pp. 919, 937, 978, 1056. William Safire tells us he found the phrase "silent center" in a speech by Sen. Paul Douglas and changed it to "silent majority." Nixon, he makes clear, cherished the phrase (Safire, *Before the Fall*, p. 50).
60. *Los Angeles Times*, July 30, 1960.
61. Kornitzer, "My Son: Two Exclusive and Candid Interviews . . ." p. 9; id., *The Real Nixon*, p. 72.
62. *Public Papers*, (Aug. 28) 1972, p. 825.
63. Edward Rubin to FB, April 23, 1975. Francis E. Townsend, a Long Beach, California, physician, authored the plan (*RN*, p. 7; Alsop, *Nixon and Rockefeller*, p. 187).
64. Barber, *Presidential Character*, p. 366; Safire, *Before the Fall*, p. 8.
65. Nathan Leites to FB; Mazlish, *In Search of Nixon*, pp. 27–28.
66. Jerry Dunphy, of CBS News, Los Angeles reported the slips. They were corrected in the *Public Papers*, (Nov. 19) 1971, pp. 1123–24.
67. *Los Angeles Times*, Dec. 22, 1953. The plane made an emergency landing in Phoenix.
68. *Ibid.*, Aug. 23, 1956.
69. *Ibid.*, Aug. 23, Sept. 3, 5, 1956; *ibid.*, Sept. 8, 1956. Eighteen years later, when Nixon was talking to Haldeman about Watergate he said on March 21, 1973, "But in the end we're going to be bled to death." He repeated this defending his innocence in his address to the nation on April 29, 1974 (*Public Papers*, 1974, p. 394).
70. Frank Holeman, quoted by Woodstone, *Nixon's Head*, pp. 42–43.

IV. The Saintly Mother

1. Marshall Clough, Jr., to FB, March 28, 1976.
2. Rev. Charles Ball, *Los Angeles Times*, Oct. 4, 1967.
3. *Public Papers*, (Aug. 9) 1974, p. 631.
4. Ibid., (June 25) 1971, p. 782. He repeated the story on Nov. 8, 1973, saying erroneously that it was the "last conversation" he had with his mother (*Public Papers*, 1973, pp. 927–28).
5. Nixon to Baruch Korff, in *The Personal Nixon: Staying on the Summit*, p. 46; see also *Public Papers*, 1971, p. 465; *RN*, pp. 13, 288.

6. Spalding, *The Nixon Nobody Knows*, p. 3.
7. Jessamyn West to FB, Sept. 29, 1976; Evlyn Dorn to FB, July 13, 1976; Kornitzer, *The Real Nixon*, p. 89; Alsop, *Nixon and Rockefeller*, p. 125.
8. Oscar Marshburn to FB, April 30, 1975; Adela Rogers St. Johns to FB, March 7, 1975; Helene Drown to FB, Feb. 8, 1979; Verna Hough to FB, March 26, 1976; anonymous informant to Dr. David Abrahamsen, *Nixon vs. Nixon*, p. 89.

9. *Los Angeles Times,* Feb. 25, 1960.
10. Hannah Nixon, "Richard Nixon, a Mother's Story," p. 216.
11. Rev. Charles Ball, Cal. State archives no. 802, p. 24; and *RN,* p. 117.
12. Abrahamsen, *Nixon vs. Nixon,* pp. 73, 25, 53.
13. Evlyn Dorn to FB, July 13, 1976.
14. Mazlish, *In Search of Nixon,* pp. 27–28.
15. *RN,* p. 4; Safire, *Before the Fall,* p. 555.
16. "Remarks at the Dedication of a Plaque Commemorating the Birthplace of the President's Mother, June 24, 1971," *Public Papers,* 1971, p. 773.
17. John Osborne, "White House Watch: Gabbing with Harlow," *New Republic,* May 13, 1978, p. 14.
18. *Public Papers,* (Sept. 25 and Sept. 26) 1969, pp. 745, 759.
19. Marshall Clough, Jr., to FB, telephone interview, March 28, 1976.
20. Edith Brannon, Cal. State archives no. 820, p. 16; William H. Barton, Cal. State archives no. 807; Olive Marshburn to FB, April 30, 1975; Ralph Shook, Cal. State archives no. 948, pp. 4, 15; Ola Welch Jobe to FB, Oct. 8, 1979.
21. Sheldon Beeson, Cal. State archives no. 809.
22. Hannah Nixon, "Richard Nixon, a Mother's Story," p. 212.
23. Ibid.; *Richard Nixon, a Self-Portrait,* 1968 election film; Abrahamsen, *Nixon vs. Nixon,* p. 52.
24. Rev. Stephen Ball, Cal. State archives no. 802; Evlyn Dorn to FB, July 13, 1976.
25. Mary George Skidmore, Cal. State archives no. 952, p. 1; Jackson, "The Young Nixon," p. 54A, and Hannah Nixon, "Richard Nixon, a Mother's Story," p. 207; James Grieves, Cal. State archives no. 868.
26. Alsop, "Nixon and the Square Majority," p. 41.

27. "Nixon's Meeting with Women of the White House Press Corps," March 11, 1971, unpublished manuscript (courtesy of Norma Mulligan).
28. This description was written by Garnett D. Horner of the *Washington Star,* and included in the *Public Papers,* 1970, p. 425. Raymond Price published the dictated recollections of that night in *With Nixon,* p. 174.
29. *Public Papers,* (May 28) 1970, p. 469.
30. Wills, *Nixon Agonistes,* p. 407.
31. *Los Angeles Times,* May 10, 1959; Hannah Nixon, "Richard Nixon, a Mother's Story," p. 216.
32. Virginia Shaw Critchfield, Cal. State archives no. 840, p. 6.
33. *Richard Nixon, a Self-Portrait,* 1968 election film; Kornitzer reproduced the school essay in *The Real Nixon,* p. 64.
34. Weymouth, "The Word from Mamma Buff," pp. 202–4.
35. Kornitzer, *The Real Nixon,* p. 326; id., "My Two Sons . . . Candid Interviews," pp. 28–29.
36. For the Hughes loan story, see Chapter XXIX. The party worker was Janet Goeske (Cal. State archives no. 867, p. 22).
37. *Public Papers,* (Jan. 31) 1974, p. 101; ibid., (Aug. 23) 1972, p. 794. See also *Six Crises,* p. 448.
38. *Nixon Speaks Out, Major Speeches . . . 1968,* Sept. 8, 1968, p. 256.
39. *Public Papers,* (Jan. 20) 1969, pp. 2–3; ibid., (Aug. 29) 1972, p. 837.
40. As reported by nurses in the Whittier rest home, who said that when Donald and Richard Nixon came together to the home, Don Nixon would remain in the car.
41. *RN,* pp. 287–88.
42. *New York Times,* Sept. 14, 1973, p. 41.

v. *The Unsmiling Child*

1. Kenneth W. Clawson, "A Loyalist's Memoir," *Washington Post,* Aug. 9, 1979, p. D1; The interview took place in 1974.
2. Mary George Skidmore, Cal. State archives no. 952, p. 1; Hannah Nixon, in Kornitzer, *The Real Nixon,* pp. 45–46; Allen Gaines, in Spalding, *The Nixon Nobody Knows,* p. 29; Behrens, in *The Young Nixon, an Oral Inquiry,* edited by Reneé Schulte (California State University, Fullerton), p. 224; Tom Dixon to FB, Nov. 28, 1975.
3. Jessamyn West to FB, Sept. 29, 1976; Jackson, "The Young Nixon," p. 54b.
4. Elizabeth Guptill Rez, letter to FB, Aug. 8, 1976.
5. *Richard Nixon, a Self-Portrait,* 1968 election film; Olive Marshburn to FB, April 30, 1975.
6. Published as an appendix in the paperback edition to Nixon's *Six Crises.*
7. Butz, *Yorba Linda,* pp. 20–30, 65.
8. Mary George Skidmore, Cal. State archives no. 952, p. 9; Blanche Burum, East Whittier grammar school teacher, Cal. State archives no. 828.
9. Edith Brannon, Cal. State archives no. 280; A. C. Newsom, Cal. State archives no. 919, p. 17; Herbert Warren, Cal. State archives no. 979, p. 2; Sheila Troupt to *Los Angeles Times,* Aug. 15, 1975, sect. 2, p. 6; Merle Wirt, Cal. State archives no. 981, p. 33.

10. Butz, *Yorba Linda,* p. 4.
11. *Los Angeles Times,* Jan. 5–13, 1913.
12. Elizabeth Eidson Furnas, Cal. State archives no. 856; and telephone interview with her daughter Phoebe Eidson Howard, Nov. 21, 1976.
13. Kornitzer, *The Real Nixon,* p. 34, and Spalding, *The Nixon Nobody Knows,* p. 29; Hoyt, *The Nixons,* pp. 178–79; Hannah Nixon, "Richard Nixon, a Mother's Story," p. 54.
14. Hannah Nixon, "Richard Nixon, a Mother's Story," p. 208.
15. Lucile Parsons, Hannah's niece, daughter of Elizabeth Milhous Harrison, Cal. State archives no. 928, p. 3.
16. Edith Milhous Timberlake, Cal. State archives no. 969, p. 40.
17. Ollie Burdg, Cal. State archives no. 835, p. 7.
18. Hannah Nixon, "Richard Nixon, a Mother's Story," p. 208; *Fullerton News Tribune,* Nov. 7, 1968, quoted in Abrahamsen, *Nixon vs. Nixon,* p. 38.
19. Mazo, *Richard Nixon,* p. 16.
20. Hoyt, *The Nixons,* pp. 184–85; Elizabeth Guptill Rez to FB, Aug. 8, 1976; Olive Marshburn to FB, April 30, 1975.
21. Mazo, *Richard Nixon,* p. 16; Kornitzer, *The Real Nixon,* p. 35. Spalding quotes the doctor, A. L. Roberts, as saying, "Had he reached the emergency room a few minutes later, Richard

would have been dead on arrival"; Spalding also said Quigley drove the Ford (Spalding, *The Nixon Nobody Knows*, p. 39).

22. Olive Marshburn to FB, April 30, 1975.

23. Elizabeth Eidson Evans to FB, Nov. 17, 1976. William H. Barton says he was taken to a hospital in Anaheim (Cal. State archives no. 807, p. 4). Hannah told a *Los Angeles Times* reporter what frightened her most was that Richard "hardly cried all the way to the hospital" (*Times*, July 24, 1960).

24. Edith Milhous Timberlake, Cal. State archives no. 969, p. 26; Jessamyn West to FB, July 6, 1976.

25. Ollie Burdg, Cal. State archives no. 835, p. 3.

26. Nixon, "Changing Rules of Liability in Automobile Accident Litigation," p. 489.

27. Korff, *The Personal Nixon, Staying on the Summit*, p. 49.

28. Bowers and Blair, "How to Pick a Congressman," p. 134.

29. Elizabeth Guptill Rez, Cal. State archives no. 936, pp. 10–11.

30. Kornitzer, *The Real Nixon*, p. 49; Mildred Jackson Johns to FB, Aug. 14, 1975. Mrs. Johns confirms other stories that Harold was the sickly child in the family.

31. Elizabeth Guptill Rez, Cal. State archives no. 936, p. 12, and letter to FB.

32. Kornitzer, *The Real Nixon*, p. 62.

33. Virginia Shaw Critchfield, Cal. State archives no. 840, pp. 2, 22.

34. Mary George Skidmore, Cal. State archives no. 952, p. 1; Mazo, *Richard Nixon*, p. 4.

35. Virginia Shaw Critchfield, Cal. State archives no. 840, p. 4.

36. Paul Ryan, Cal. State archives no. 941, p. 7.

37. Floyd Wildermuth, Cal. State archives no. 983, p. 1.

38. Gerald Shaw, Cal. State archives no. 946, p. 3.

39. Mazo, *Richard Nixon*, p. 21.

VI. *Splitting and Entitlement*

1. Kornitzer, *The Real Nixon*, p. 57 (the spelling is the original).

2. *Adams Family Correspondence*, edited by L. H. Butterfield (Series 2; Cambridge, Mass., 1963) 1:167, 3:11.

3. Barber, *Presidential Character*, p. 401.

4. Abrahamsen, *Nixon vs. Nixon*, p. 60.

5. Kornitzer, *The Real Nixon*, p. 59.

6. Jessamyn West to FB, Sept. 29, 1976. Elizabeth Guptill has described how Hannah would go home for a visit and then return, quite homesick, for her family.

7. Kornitzer, *The Real Nixon*, p. 57 (the spelling is the original).

8. Ibid., pp. 57, 59.

9. *Six Crises*, p. 295.

10. Hannah Nixon, "Richard Nixon, a Mother's Story," p. 208.

11. Jane Beeson, Cal. State archives no. 808, p. 18; Sheldon Beeson, Cal. State archives no. 809, p. 23; Dorothy Beeson, Cal. State archives no. 810, p. 21. Jane says it was Hannah who persuaded her to take Richard to Lindsay; Nixon said it was his aunt who persuaded his mother (Kornitzer, *The Real Nixon*, p. 64).

12. Jessamyn West, reporting the recollections of her brother Merle, to FB, Sept. 29, 1976.

13. Richard Gardner was the first to report the story, in "Fighting Quaker," unpublished manuscript, 1952, pp. 24–25. For the 1960 account see Hannah Nixon, "Richard Nixon, a Mother's Story," p. 208. For local publicity on the Teapot Dome, see *Whittier News*, Jan. 25, 1924.

14. Clemens, "Mark Twain and Richard Nixon," pp. 142–43.

15. Jackson, "The Young Nixon," pp. 57, 60.

16. *Public Papers*, (Sept. 22) 1972, p. 891.

17. Mildred Jackson Johns to FB, Aug. 14, 1975.

18. Stewart Alsop, "The Mystery of Richard Nixon," *Saturday Evening Post*, July 12, 1958, p. 57; Costello, *The Facts About Nixon*, p. 23.

19. Jackson, "The Young Nixon," p. 57.

20. Ibid., p. 58.

21. Hannah Nixon, "Richard Nixon, a Mother's Story," p. 207.

22. "Conversation with Howard K. Smith, ABC," March 22, 1971, *Public Papers*, 1971, p. 459; see also Lucile Parsons, who worked in the store, Cal. State archives no. 928, p. 6.

23. Lucile Parsons, Cal. State archives no. 928, p. 3.

24. Floyd Wildermuth, Cal. State archives no. 983, p. 25.

25. *Public Papers*, (Jan. 4) 1971, p. 8; see also ibid., (Dec. 13) 1970, p. 1124.

26. Jessamyn West to FB, telephone interview, June 28, 1976; Merle West to FB, July 6, 1976. Frank Nixon had one car, and an old car which had been made into a truck.

27. Lucile Parsons, Cal. State archives no. 607.

28. I. N. Kraushaar, Cal. State archives no. 994.

29. *Public Papers*, (Jan. 22) 1971, p. 51.

30. Kornitzer, *The Real Nixon*, p. 245.

31. *Six Crises*, pp. 249, 255.

32. Merle West to FB, July 6, 1976.

33. Kornitzer, *The Real Nixon*, p. 49; Wills, *Nixon Agonistes*, p. 171.

34. *Public Papers*, (April 17) 1969, p. 298; ibid., (April 18) 1974, p. 364.

35. Hugh Sidey, "Coming Home to Affluence," *Life*, March 10, 1972.

36. *Public Papers*, (Feb. 26) 1970, p. 214.

37. Ibid., (May 30) 1973, p. 240.

VII. *Death and Two Brothers*

1. *Six Crises*, p. 66.

2. Kornitzer, *The Real Nixon*, pp. 61–66.

3. Abrahamsen, *Nixon vs. Nixon*, p. 139.

4. Kornitzer, *The Real Nixon*, p. 62.

5. *Public Papers*, (Aug. 9) 1974, p. 631.

6. Gardner, "Fighting Quaker, the Story of

Richard Nixon," unpublished manuscript, p. 23.

7. Kornitzer, *The Real Nixon*, pp. 65–66.

8. Los Angeles County Hall of Records.

9. Kornitzer, *The Real Nixon*, p. 60; Edith Gibbons Nunes to FB, July 20, 1976; Olive

Marshburn to FB, April 30, 1975; Floyd Wildermuth, Cal. State archives no. 983, p. 18; Jessamyn West to FB, Sept. 20, 1976; Edith M. Brannon, Cal. State archives no. 818; Harry A. Schuyler, Cal. State archives no. 997; Virginia Shaw Critchfield, Cal. State archives no. 840, p. 13.

10. Kornitzer, *The Real Nixon*, pp. 65–66; *Richard Nixon, a Self-Portrait*, 1968 election film; *RN*, p. 10. I have seen no evidence to support Dr. David Abrahamsen's contention that Arthur had been ill for a long time, and that Richard had been sent to Lindsay to prevent infection. I am assured by a knowledgeable informant, who prefers to remain anonymous, that Nixon did not throw the rock.

11. Frank Gannon to FB, June 19, 1977.

12. In *RN* Nixon said, "Harold's long bout with tuberculosis began several years before Arthur died." This represents a change from his earlier statements, where he held that Harold contracted TB in 1928 or 1929. Compare *RN*, p. 11, and *Public Papers*, (Feb. 5) 1974, p. 127, for the latest of these statements.

13. *RN*, p. 10.

14. Hannah Nixon, "Richard Nixon, a Mother's Story," p. 212.

15. Dr. Rita Rogers, "Children's Reactions to Sibling Death." She tells a chilling story of a small boy whose sister died in a trash fire, who later took a job at Yosemite National Park, pushing burning embers over a cliff each night to delight the tourists with the famous "firefall."

16. See especially the episodes in Lima, Peru, and San Jose, California (*Six Crises*, p. 202; *RN*, pp. 492–93).

17. Edith Brannon, Cal. State archives no. 818; Kornitzer, *The Real Nixon*, p. 60.

18. Helen S. Letts, Cal. State archives no. 896; Harry A. Schuyler, Cal. State archives no. 997.

19. Jane Milhous Beeson describes Hannah's experience, Cal. State archives no. 808, p. 17.

20. *RN*, p. 14.

21. See Billy Graham's *Decision*, November 1962, as quoted by Mazlish, *In Search of Nixon*, p. 31. Ollie Burdg reported that Frank Nixon took his family into Los Angeles to hear evangelist Billy Sunday in the Yorba Linda days (Cal. State archives no. 925, p. 10).

22. Bruce Mazlish, who describes how Billy Graham had been beaten "hundreds of times" by his parents in his youth, believes that he rebelled against these parents in the beginning but nevertheless gave in *completely* to God the Father. Nixon, he holds, "neither rebelled nor, as a result, bowed so totally before authority" (Mazlish, *In Search of Nixon*, pp. 31, 34).

23. Coughlan, "Success Story of a Vice-President," p. 148.

24. Lucile Parsons, a cousin, said the Nixons "didn't like the kids Harold was running around with and he was sent away to school" (Cal. State archives no. 928, p. 5). Olive Marshburn hinted of Frank's troubles with the principal (Marshburn to FB, April 30, 1975). Coughlan ("Success Story of a Vice-President") learned, apparently in his interview with Nixon, that his mother wanted them both to stay at Whittier High. See also Abrahamsen, *Nixon vs. Nixon*, p. 87.

25. Evlyn Dorn to FB, July 13, 1976.

26. Spalding, *The Nixon Nobody Knows*, p. 39.

27. *Richard Nixon, a Self-Portrait*, 1968 election film.

28. *Public Papers*, (Feb. 5) 1974, p. 127; ibid., (Dec. 13) 1970, p. 1124.

29. Kornitzer, *The Real Nixon*, p. 59.

30. Budge Ruffner to FB, March 26, 1976.

31. Ibid., March 27, 1976.

32. Verna Hough to FB, March 26, 1976.

33. Jessie Lynch Brandt to FB, March 26, 1976.

34. The cabin, at 937 West Apache Drive, was later purchased and remodeled by Grace Bumpus, who was living there in 1976. The house had been purchased by the Arizona Historical Society, and had a plaque on it indicating that Richard Nixon lived there in 1928 and 1929.

35. Gardner, *Ends of Power*, p. 68.

36. Verna Hough to FB, March 26, 1976; Virginia Green Williams, telephone interview, April 23, 1976; Helen Rose Lynch Gay (Mrs. Ben Gay), telephone interview, March 29, 1976; Virginia Green Williams, telephone interview, April 23, 1976; Helen Rose Lynch Gay, telephone interview, March 29, 1976.

37. Marshall Clough, Jr., telephone interview, March 27, 1976.

38. Helen Rose Lynch Gay, telephone interview, March 29, 1976; Verna Hough to FB, March 26, 1976.

39. Gardner, "Fighting Quaker," p. 48.

40. Budge Ruffner to FB, March 26, 1976.

41. Spalding, *The Nixon Nobody Knows*, p. 73.

42. Clough said that he and his mother were in Los Angeles when Nixon passed his California bar exam. His mother took them both out to dinner to celebrate and bought champagne. It was, says Clough, "Nixon's first drink," another small Nixon untruth (telephone interview, March 27, 1976). See Chapter VIII.

43. Lyall Sutton, Cal. State archives no. 963, p. 12.

44. *Public Papers*, (May 30) 1973, p. 240.

45. Abrahamsen, *Nixon vs. Nixon*, p. 77.

46. "Nixon's Meeting with Women of the White House Press Corps," March 11, 1971, unpublished manuscript, p. 19. *Public Papers*, (Sept. 26) 1971, p. 998.

47. Edith Brannon, Cal. State archives no. 820, p. 4; Jackson, "The Young Nixon," p. 60. Edith Timberlake Paldanius, a cousin, visited the Nixon family in Prescott in 1932. She said Don was in bed, but Richard was selling tickets at Frontier Days (Cal. State archives no. 926, p. 37).

48. Marshall Clough, Jr., to FB, March 28, 1976; Jessamyn West to FB, Sept. 29, 1976; Richard Arena to FB, March 26, 1976; Abrahamsen, *Nixon vs. Nixon*, p. 89.

49. Floyd Wildermuth, Cal. State archives no. 983, p. 18; *RN*, p. 12.

50. The death certificate gives the time of death as 9 A.M., March 6, 1933. Nixon in his memoirs states mistakenly that he and his brother drove into Los Angeles on March 6.

51. Jessamyn West to FB, Sept. 29, 1976.

52. Kornitzer, *The Real Nixon*, p. 81.

53. Hannah Nixon, "Richard Nixon, a Mother's Story," p. 212.

54. Abrahamsen, *Nixon vs. Nixon*, p. 142.

55. Robert J. Lifton, "The Sense of Immortality, Death and the Continuity of Life," in *Explorations in Psychohistory*, edited by Lifton with Eric Olsen (New York, 1974), pp. 273–74. Lif-

ton writes that however the psychic numbing is expressed, there is a situation of meaningless and unfulfilled life, in which the defensive psychological structures built up to ward off death anxiety also ward off autonomy and self-understanding (ibid., pp. 283, 285).
56. Cain, *Survivors of Suicide*, pp. 3, 13.
57. Wills, *Nixon Agonistes*, p. 178.
58. Hannah Nixon said Donald went to the Guilford Preparatory School in Greensboro, and Kornitzer said he attended Guilford College. Actually a check reveals that he never attended either the preparatory school or the college, but did spend a semester in the Grimsley Senior High School, Greensboro, North Carolina, from Sept. 18, 1934 to Jan. 20, 1935.
59. Gardner, "Fighting Quaker," p. 16.

60. Witcover, *The Resurrection of Richard Nixon*, p. 64.
61. *Time*, Jan. 4, 1954, p. 11.
62. *Public Papers*, (Oct. 15) 1972, p. 984.
63. Golda Meir, *My Life* (New York: Putnam, 1975), p. 425.
64. *Public Papers*, (March 10) 1973, p. 181. This suicide was that of his cousin's son, who killed himself after experimenting with LSD; see Frances Timberlake, Cal. State archives no. 967, p. 6.
65. *Public Papers*, (March 20) 1974, p. 301.
66. Ibid., (July 2) 1974, p. 561. This memorial should not be confused with memorials for the Katyn Forest Massacre.
67. Ibid., (Aug. 24) 1972, p. 795; see also pp. 627, 632.

VIII. *Presidential Fever*

1. *Public Papers*, (June 16) 1969, p. 467.
2. Whittier College *Acropolis*, 1934, p. 37.
3. Safire, *Before the Fall*, p. 324.
4. Jackson, "The Young Nixon," pp. 58, 60.
5. Erikson, *Toys and Reasons*, p. 72.
6. *Six Crises*, p. xv.
7. Kenneth P. O'Donnell and David F. Powers, *Johnny We Hardly Knew Ye* (New York: Pocketbooks, 1973), p. 49.
8. Whittier College *Acropolis*, 1934, p. 81; Morgan, "Whittier '34," p. 34.
9. Kornitzer, *The Real Nixon*, p. 53; Mazo, *Richard Nixon*, p. 22; Whittier College *Acropolis*, 1932, p. 97; ibid., 1934, p. 81; William Flynn, *Kansas City Star*, Nov. 3, 1955, p. 10. For the calamitous trip in the junior year, see the reminiscences of Emmett Ingrum, Cal. State archives no. 883, p. 4; and Whittier College *Acropolis*, 1933, p. 80.
10. Weldon Taylor to FB, 1977.
11. Alsop, "Nixon on Nixon," p. 59.
12. William Hornaday, Cal. State archives no. 802, p. 16.
13. Kenneth Ball, Cal. State archives no. 804, p. 5.
14. Quoted in Abrahamsen, *Nixon vs. Nixon*, p. 111. Helen S. Larson disliked the "ruthless cocksureness" in Nixon, as noted by Kornitzer, *The Real Nixon*, p. 100.
15. Kornitzer, *The Real Nixon*, p. 108.
16. *RN*, p. 17.
17. Morgan, "Whittier '34," p. 34.
18. Barber, *Presidential Character*, p. 384.
19. Ola Welch Jobe to FB, Oct. 8, 1979.
20. Morgan, "Whittier '34," p. 34; and *Parade*, June 20, 1970.
21. *Six Crises*, p. 295.
22. Jessamyn West, *Whittier College Bulletin* 47 (December 1954): 17. Mrs. Robert Sullivan reported Harley Moore's prediction, and reminded Nixon of it when he was president (Cal. State archives no. 950, p. 14). Dr. Walter F. Dexter, Whittier College president, wrote in his letter of recommendation to Duke University, "I believe Richard Nixon will become one of America's important, if not great leaders" (Spalding, *The Nixon Nobody Knows*, p. 94).
23. *Six Crises*, p. 295.
24. Abrahamsen, *Nixon vs. Nixon*, p. 101.
25. *Public Papers*, (July 22) 1969, p. 539; Alsop, "Nixon and the Square Majority," p. 45.

26. Dean Twiggs, Cal. State archives no. 971, p. 63.
27. Jackson, "The Young Nixon," p. 60.
28. *RN*, p. 19.
29. Dean Twiggs, Cal. State archives no. 971, p. 61.
30. *Public Papers*, (July 30) 1971, p. 836.
31. *Six Crises*, p. 402.
32. Kornitzer, *The Real Nixon*, p. 111.
33. *Public Papers*, (July 30) 1971, p. 836.
34. Ibid., (Aug. 24) 1972, p. 806.
35. Alsop, *Nixon and Rockefeller*, p. 227.
36. Wood Glover, Cal. State archives no. 863, p. 5.
37. Joe Gaudio, Cal. State archives no. 860, p. 4. William Soeberg described how Nixon argued for two or three hours on their behalf (Cal. State archives no. 953, p. 14.
38. George Chisler, Cal. State archives no. 833, p. 9. Soeberg later admitted how he and Gaudio "painted up Whittier" after painting Occidental. "We thought we might as well . . . create a little bit of fire between the schools, and we did" (Cal. State archives no. 953, p. 14).
39. Sandy Triggs, Cal. State archives no. 972, p. 10.
40. Robert Halliday, Cal. State archives no. 872, pp. 15, 16; Wood Glover, Cal. State archives no. 863, pp. 4, 5.
41. Mazo, *Richard Nixon*, p. 24; Spalding, *The Nixon Nobody Knows*, p. 87; Alsop, *Nixon and Rockefeller*, p. 131.
42. Price, *With Nixon*, p. 122.
43. Morgan, "Whittier '34," p. 35.
44. Hoyt, *The Nixons*, p. 203.
45. Richard Gardner, in "Fighting Quaker" (unpublished manuscript, p. 54), said Nixon wrote the music as well as the words. Dean Twiggs said, "I don't know where he stole the tune, but I'm sure he didn't make that up. But at least he wrote the words" (Cal. State archives no. 971, p. 15). See also *RN*, p. 17.
46. Dean Twiggs, Cal. State archives no. 971, p. 16; Herman Fink, Cal. State archives no. 854, p. 2.
47. Joe Gaudio, Cal. State archives no. 860, p. 4. See also Wood Glover, Cal. State archives no. 863, p. 3. Nixon wrote in William Hornaday's yearbook, "Next year we are really going to do things around the initiation" (William Hornaday, Cal. State archives no. 802, p. 25).
48. Albert Upton to FB, telephone interview,

Sept. 19, 1976; William H. D. Hornaday, Cal.
State archives no. 802, p. 5. This skit is mistak-
enly described as *The Trysting Place* in many
Nixon biographies.

49. Mazo, *Richard Nixon*, p. 34.
50. Kornitzer, *The Real Nixon*, pp. 104, 106;
Spalding, *The Nixon Nobody Knows*, pp. 120,
121; Mazo, *Richard Nixon*, p. 23.
51. Erikson, *Toys and Reasons*, p. 69. See also Barber, *Presidential Character*, p. 361.
52. Weymouth, "The Word from Mamma Buff,"
p. 204.
53. Wills, *Nixon Agonistes*, p. 21.
54. Safire, *Before the Fall*, pp. 53, 55.
55. Poirier, "Horatio Alger in the White House,"
p. 100.
56. Frederick J. Teggart, *Theory and Processes of
History* (Berkeley, Calif., 1940), p. 313 (Teggart's *Processes of History* was published by Yale
University Press in 1918, and his *Theory of History* in 1925); *RN*, p. 16.
57. Coughlan, "Success Story of a Vice-President," p. 148.
58. *RN*, p. 15.
59. *Public Papers*, (Feb. 25) 1970, p. 203.
60. From a press conference, reprinted in the
Congressional Record, 105 (1959), pt. 5:6563.
61. Schlesinger, *The Imperial Presidency*, p. 266.
62. *Public Papers*, (Jan. 21) 1969, p. 5. The correc-
tion about its being Henry Wilson's desk
appeared in ibid., 1969, p. 909f.
63. *Six Crises*, p. 447; *Public Papers*, 1970, p. 526;
ibid., 1971, pp. 793, 1151. Sometimes Nixon
used the phrase "the whole human race"

rather than "all mankind" (see ibid., 1970, p.
15; ibid., 1971, pp. 562, 917). He variously
ascribed the date of the "Jefferson" quotation
as 1775, 1776, 1802. The Thomas Paine quotation may be found in his introduction to
Common Sense.
64. Kornitzer, *The Real Nixon*, pp. 40–41.
65. *Public Papers*, 1974, pp. 100–2; ibid., 1971, p.
898; ibid., 1974, pp. 156–57.
66. Wills, *Nixon Agonistes*, p. 17.
67. William Safire, *New York Times*, June 7, 1973,
quoted the original Theodore Roosevelt statement distributed to his supporters by Nixon
in 1960. For the Nixon paraphrase in his resignation speech see *Public Papers*, 1974, p.
629. Raymond Price described Nixon's specific request to include this in his resignation
speech (Price, *With Nixon*, p. 341).
68. Wills, *Nixon Agonistes*, p. 20.
69. Coughlan, "Success Story of a Vice-President," p. 148.
70. *Public Papers*, (Feb. 18) 1971, pp. 187–89.
71. Jules Witcover, *The Resurrection of Richard
Nixon*, pp. 52–53; Wills, *Nixon Agonistes*, pp.
20, 475, 480.
72. *Public Papers*, (Feb. 18) 1971, p. 189.
73. See Alexander and Juliette George, *Woodrow
Wilson and Colonel House: A Psychological Study*
(New York: Dover Paperbacks, 1956), for a
detailed treatment.
74. *Public Papers*, 1971, pp. 188, 1121; ibid., 1969,
p. 909.
75. Hannah Nixon, "Richard Nixon, a Mother's
Story," p. 216.

IX. The Monastic Years

1. *Parade*, June 20, 1970.
2. Jackson, "The Young Nixon," p. 61.
3. Ola Welch Jobe to FB, Oct. 8, 1979.
4. *Parade*, June 20, 1970.
5. Ola Welch Jobe to FB, Oct. 8, 1979; *Parade*,
June 20, 1970.
6. *RN*, p. 14.
7. *Parade*, June 20, 1970.
8. Mrs. Jobe said she and her husband agreed
with Dr. Abrahamsen's major thesis, that
Nixon was his own worst enemy (Ola Welch
Jobe to FB, Oct. 8, 1979).
9. Abrahamsen, *Nixon vs. Nixon*, pp. 107–8.
10. Ola Welch Jobe to FB, Oct. 8, 1979; Jackson,
"The Young Nixon," p. 61.
11. Morgan, "Whittier '34," p. 35.
12. "Coming of Age, The Young Nixon," a type-
script by Donald Jackson, quoted by Abrahamsen, *Nixon vs. Nixon*, p. 103; Ola Welch
Jobe to FB, Oct. 8, 1979.
13. Morgan, "Whittier '34," p. 35; Ola Welch Jobe
to FB, Oct. 8, 1979.
14. Edith Gibbons Nunes to FB, July 29, 1976.
15. Ola Welch Jobe to FB, Oct. 8, 1979.
16. Jewell Twiggs, Cal. State archives no. 971, p.
74; Charles Kendle, Cal. State archives no.
893, p. 10; Spalding, *The Nixon Nobody Knows*,
p. 62; Olive Marshburn to FB, April 20, 1975.
17. Ola Welch Jobe to FB, Oct. 8, 1979.
18. William Flynn, "Days at Duke in a Farmhouse," *Kansas City Star*, Nov. 4, 1955, p. 6.
19. *RN*, p. 20.
20. Hoyt, *The Nixons*, p. 214; *Public Papers*, (Oct.
12) 1972, p. 976.
21. William Perdue to FB, Nov. 5, 1976. See also

Alsop, "Nixon on Nixon," p. 59.
22. Ethel Farley Hunter Sheldon to FB, Jan. 8,
1978; Alsop, *Nixon and Rockefeller*, p. 231;
Kornitzer, *The Real Nixon*, p. 119.
23. William Perdue to FB, Nov. 5, 1976.
24. *Public Papers*, (Oct. 12) 1972, p. 976. He made
similar remarks in the 1960 campaign in
Atlanta (see White, *The Making of the President,
1960*, p. 306; *Public Papers*, [Nov. 18] 1973, p.
965). Nixon used the phrase "War Between
the States" at the National Prayer Breakfast,
Feb. 1, 1972, in connection with a reference
to Lincoln's Second Inaugural (*Public Papers*,
1972, p. 126).
25. Alsop, *Nixon and Rockefeller*, p. 233. Alsop
does not name Brownfield, but I am told by
Richard W. Kiefer that it was he who owned
the Packard (Kiefer to FB, Aug. 25, 1975).
26. Mazo, *Richard Nixon*, p. 25.
27. Alsop, *Nixon and Rockefeller*, pp. 230, 234,
237–39; Abrahamsen, *Nixon vs. Nixon*, p. 121.
28. Ethel Farley Hunter Sheldon to FB, Jan. 8,
1978.
29. *Public Papers*, (April 8) 1972, pp. 547–48. Graham B. Steenhaven had taken a U.S. team to
China in 1971, almost a year before Nixon
went to China.
30. Richard Kiefer to FB, Aug. 25, 1975; Spalding, *The Nixon Nobody Knows*, p. 100.
31. Kornitzer, *The Real Nixon*, p. 129; Hannah
Nixon, "Richard Nixon, a Mother's Story," p.
312.
32. Edward Rubin to FB, April 23, 1975.
33. Jackson, "Coming of Age in America," type-
script, quoted by Abrahamsen, *Nixon vs.*

Nixon, p. 116; Prof. David Cavers to FB, July 5, 1977.

34. *Duke University Law and Constitutional Problems* 3 (1936): 477–90 (see especially pp. 476, 478, 489). See Chapter IV.

35. *Duke Bar Association Journal* 4 (Spring 1936): 115–17.

36. Kornitzer, *The Real Nixon*, p. 117; *The Young Nixon, an Oral Inquiry*, edited by Reneé Schulte (California State University, Fullerton), p. 173.

37. Jack Anderson to FB, April 10, 1975.

38. Richard Kiefer to FB, Aug. 25, 1975; Kornitzer, *The Real Nixon*, p. 123.

39. Spalding, *The Nixon Nobody Knows*, p. 104; Alsop, *Nixon and Rockefeller*, p. 236.

40. Kornitzer, *The Real Nixon*, p. 123; Hoyt, *The*

Nixons, pp. 214, 215. Hoyt told David Abrahamsen, "Nixon himself had informed him that he had gained entrance to the office and found a key to the drawer and located the records" (Abrahamsen, *Nixon vs. Nixon*, p. 117).

41. Albrink to FB in a telephone interview, November 1976; Jackson, "The Young Nixon," p. 62; William Perdue to FB, Nov. 5, 1976.

42. Prof. David Cavers to FB, telephone interview, July 5, 1977.

43. Haldeman, *Ends of Power*, p. 170.

44. *Public Papers*, (Nov. 18) 1973, p. 965; White, *The Making of the President, 1960*, p. 306.

45. Jackson, "The Young Nixon," p. 62.

46. *Public Papers*, (May 28) 1969, p. 419.

x. *The First Law Case: Failure*

1. Kornitzer, *The Real Nixon*, p. 128.

2. Thomas Bewley to FB, June 15, 1976.

3. Spalding, *The Nixon Nobody Knows*, pp. 111, 112.

4. Evlyn Dorn to FB, July 13, 1976.

5. Thomas Bewley to FB, June 15, 1976.

6. Kornitzer, *The Real Nixon*, pp. 127, 128; Costello, *The Facts About Nixon*, p. 27.

7. Kornitzer, *The Real Nixon*, pp. 127, 131.

8. *Washington Watch*, Nov. 1, 1973. This consisted of a brief paragraph, based on Los Angeles lawyer Leonard Kaufman's recollections. Irving Wallace, who had talked with Kaufman, was cited as the source. I am indebted to Mr. Kaufman for permission to use three lawyers' briefs relevant to the case.

9. Thomas Bewley to FB, June 15, 1976.

10. EXTANT RECORDS
   1. Municipal Court, City of Los Angeles, No. 457600. Plaintiff Marie Schee, Defendants Otto A. and Jennieve Steuer, October 15 to July 27, 1940. A two-page summary, from the Municipal Court microfilm record. The original transcripts have been routinely destroyed.
   2. Superior Court of the State of California, County of Los Angeles, No. 436435. Complaint in Negligence. February 1939. Marie Schee and S. Émilie Force, Plaintiffs; Jeff. G. Wingert and Thomas W. Bewley, Defendants, 5 pp.
   3. Appellant's Opening Brief, District Court of Appeal, Second Appellate District, State of California, Division One, 2d Civil Suit, No. 13774. Marie Schee, Plaintiff and Appellant; Frank L. Holt, Marshall of the City of Los Angeles, Otto A. Steuer, Defendants and Respondent, August 1942, 55 pp. (Daniel Knapp, Lawyer for the Appellant.)
   4. Respondent's Brief, District Court of Appeal, Second Appellate District, State of California, 2d Civil Suit, No. 13774. Marie Schee, Plaintiff and Appellant; Frank L. Holt, Marshall of the City of Los Angeles, Otto A. Steuer and Jennieve Steuer, Defendants and Respondents. 29 pp. (David Schwartz, Lawyer for the Defendants.)
   5. Appellant's Reply Brief, District Court of Appeal, Second Appellate District, State of California, 2d Civil Suit, No. 13774. Marie Schee, Plaintiff and Appellant; Frank L. Holt, Marshall of the City of Los Angeles, Otto A.

Steuer and Jennieve Steuer, Defendants and Respondents. 30 pp. (Daniel Knapp, Lawyer for the Appellant.)
   6. "Schee vs. Holt," District Court of Appeals, 2d District, Division One, California, December 23, 1942, 56 Cal. App. 2d 364. Reprinted in 132 *Pacific Reporter*, 2nd Series. See pp. 544–45.

11. A two-page summary of the original case is on microfilm in the records of the Los Angeles Municipal Court, No. 457600, 1937–1940, Plaintiff Marie Schee, Defendants Otto A. and Jennieve Steuer, Oct. 15, 1937 to July 27, 1940. The original transcript was routinely destroyed after ten years, but extracts from it appeared in the other documents listed. From these it is possible to reconstruct the case in some detail. For a notice of the original judgment awarded to Marie Schee, the sum of $2160.75, see the two-page summary.

12. David Schwartz reported this conversation later to his nephew, Los Angeles lawyer Francis Schwartz (Francis Schwartz to FB, April 7, 1978).

13. Superior Court of the State of California, County of Los Angeles, No. 436435, Complaint in Negligence, February 1939, p. 3; Respondent's Brief, *Schee v. Holt* (California District Court of Appeal, Second District, 2d Civil Suit, No. 13774), p. 14.

14. Bewley freely admits to his own error, and to the payment of the $4800 out of court to satisfy their claims (Bewley to FB, June 15, 1976). Schee and Force, in the malpractice suit, argued that Bewley had promised them that even if the property were sold to a stranger their judgment claim "would still be preserved" (Superior Court of the State of California, County of Los Angeles, No. 436435, Complaint in Negligence, February 1939, p. 4). Bewley did write to Marie Schee on January 7, 1939: "Mr. Steuer still owes you $2,000 plus interest. That judgment was not affected in any way. . . . we will re-levy judgment on the property, just as soon as the sale is cleared up, and we can ascertain whether or not Steuer is claiming any interest in the property. If he has any interest whatsoever in the property then the judgment will attach" (Rep. Transcript, p. 58, 1.222 et seq., reprinted in Appellant's Opening Brief, *Schee v. Holt*, California District Court of Appeal,

Second District, 2d Civil Suit, No. 13774, p. 38).

Schee and Force alleged in the malpractice suit that they had never been advised that Nixon had used Schee's judgment to buy the Steuer property at the execution sale, and that afterward the defendants had failed to inform Schee of her "right, title, and interest" in the property. The firm of Bewley and Wingert was accused of acting "carelessly, negligently, incompetently, and unskillfully . . . in advising Schee and Force to bid at the trust foreclosure sale the amount of the sums owing under the second trust deed, and no more, thus allowing the property to be sold to a higher bidder, a person unknown to the plaintiffs" (Superior Court of the State of California, County of Los Angeles, No. 436435, Complaint in Negligence, February 1939).
15. Thomas Bewley to FB, June 15, 1976.
16. Appellant's Opening Brief, *Schee v. Holt*, California District Court of Appeal, Second District, 2d Civil Suit, No. 13774, pp. 8, 9, 41.
17. Ibid., pp. 19, 20, 23, reprinted from Transcript, p. 8, 1.17.
18. Irving Wallace, "Full Version with Documentation," unpublished paper cited in Tristram Coffin's *Washington Watch*, Nov. 1, 1973, and made available to FB.
19. *Washington Watch*, Nov. 1, 1973.
20. Wallace, "Full Version with Documentation."
21. Ibid.
22. Thomas Bewley to FB, June 15, 1976.
23. Alfred Paonessa to FB. Paonessa, now dead, said in a telephone interview in February 1975 that he had been questioned about the case at least thirty times.
24. Mazo, *Richard Nixon*, p. 35. Edwin Hoyt, in *The Nixons* (p. 230), wrote, "He made a trip to Havana and even considered setting up there." Evlyn Dorn, Bewley's secretary, remembers Nixon's talking about wanting to practice law in Latin America (Dorn to FB, July 13, 1976). Howard Kohn, in "The Hughes-Nixon-Lansky Connection," dates the trip as 1940, with Mazo as the source (*Rolling Stone*, May 20, 1976, p. 43).
25. Los Angeles Municipal Court, No. 457600.
26. *RN*, p. 25.
27. It is this case, where three briefs have been preserved, which gives us most of the details of the long litigation. The Appellate Court ruling may be seen in California District Court of Appeals, 2d District, Division One, *Schee v. Holt*, 56 Cal. App. 2d 364, December 1942, (reprinted in 132 *Pacific Reporter*, 2d ser., 544.)
28. The story first broke into the press in Tristram Coffin's *Washington Watch*, Nov. 1, 1973. This consisted of a brief account based on the recollections of Los Angeles lawyer Leonard Kaufman. Irving Wallace did considerable research on his own and was kind enough to supply me with the briefs which Leonard Kaufman had secured from Merton Schwartz. Without these the case could not have been reconstructed.
29. Thomas Bewley to FB, June 15, 1976.

XI. *A Problem with Touching*

1. Mary Gardiner, Cal. State archives no. 858, p. 15.
2. Coined respectively by Saul Pett and Mickie Ziffren.
3. Julie Nixon Eisenhower, "Mamie Eisenhower," *Ladies Home Journal*, June 1977, p. 110.
4. Steinem, "In Your Heart You Know He's Nixon," p. 35.
5. Alsop, *Nixon and Rockefeller*, p. 59.
6. Paul Smith to FB, July 6, 1976.
7. "Remarks at an Awards Dinner of the Nevada State Society of Washington, D.C.," *Public Papers*, (Nov. 8) 1973, p. 927.
8. "Nixon's Meeting with Women of the White House Press Corps," March 11, 1971, unpublished manuscript, not recorded in the *Public Papers*, and only partially reported in the *New York Times*, March 14, 1971, p. 1 (courtesy Norma Mulligan).
9. *RN*, p. 1023.
10. *Six Crises*, p. 134.
11. "Toasts of the President and Governor Love at a Dinner in Colorado Springs, Sept. 1, 1969," *Public Papers*, 1969, p. 693.
12. David, *Lonely Lady at San Clemente*, p. 180.
13. *Newsweek*, Feb. 22, 1960, p. 28.
14. *Los Angeles Times*, Feb. 21, 1969; Jessamyn West to FB, Sept. 29, 1976. See also her "The Real Pat Nixon," p. 61ff.
15. *Los Angeles Times*, Aug. 18, 1971.
16. John Brady, "Freelancer with No Time to Write: An interview with Gloria Steinem," *Writer's Digest*, Winter 1974, p. 17. Steinem's original interview was published in *New York* magazine, Oct. 28, 1968, p. 35.
17. "Nixon's Meeting with Women of the White House Press Corps," March 11, 1971.
18. David, *Lonely Lady of San Clemente*, p. 20.
19. Morris, *Uncertain Greatness*, p. 146.
20. Alsop, *Nixon and Rockefeller*, p. 59; *Time*, Feb. 29, 1960, p. 25.
21. "Remarks on Mrs. Nixon's Departure for Venezuela and Brazil," *Public Papers*, (March 11) 1974, p. 256.
22. Helen McCain Smith, "Ordeal! Pat Nixon's Final Days in the White House," as told to Elizabeth Pope Frank, pp. 133, 129; see also Woodward and Bernstein, *The Final Days*, p. 441.
23. "Remarks on Departure from the White House," *Public Papers*, (Aug. 9) 1974, p. 632. The extract came not from Roosevelt's diary, as Nixon said, but from a pamphlet he published for a few friends shortly after his wife's death.
24. Mary Gardiner, Cal. State archives no. 858, p. 15.
25. Woodward and Bernstein, *The Final Days*, p. 165.
26. Dixon to FB, Nov. 28, 1975.
27. Evlyn Dorn to FB, July 13, 1976.
28. Kornitzer, *The Real Nixon*, p. 136.
29. Mary Skidmore, Nixon's first-grade schoolteacher, in *Richard Nixon, an Oral Inquiry*, edited by Reneé Schulte (California State University, Fullerton), p. 87.
30. See the film documentary, *Milhous*.
31. *RN*, p. 89.
32. Helen McCain Smith, "Ordeal! Pat Nixon's Final Days in the White House," p. 129.
33. *RN*, pp. 188, 334, 753.

34. "Nixon's Meeting with Women of the White House Press Corps," March 11, 1971.
35. *Public Papers*, (Jan. 9) 1972, p. 26.
36. *RN*, p. 537.
37. Charles E. Young, who heard the statement, to FB.
38. Kornitzer, *The Real Nixon*, p. 134. Scott Meredith, in "Nixon the Actor," p. 92, noted that Nixon had already played in *First Lady*, a George S. Kaufman drama based on the life of Alice Roosevelt Longworth, in December 1937. Pat Nixon told Earl Mazo, "I met him there at the Little Theater" (Mazo, *Richard Nixon*, p. 31).
39. "Remarks Before the National Football Foundation and Hall of Fame Dinner, Dec. 9, 1969," *Public Papers*, 1969, pp. 1015–16.
40. *RN*, p. 23.
41. Mazo, *Richard Nixon*, p. 31. The friend, Elizabeth Cloes, who brought the two together, tells virtually the same story in her oral history interview (Cal. State archives no. 834, p. 2).
42. Alexander Woollcott, *The Dark Tower* (New York, 1934), pp. 24–25, 76. See also Meredith, "Richard the Actor," p. 52ff.
43. Evlyn Dorn to FB, July 13, 1976.
44. Mazo, *Richard Nixon*, p. 31.
45. Robert McCormick, Cal. State archives no. 908, p. 5. McCormick had once taken her on a date at Fullerton Junior College.
46. Mazo, *Richard Nixon*, p. 33.
47. Kornitzer, *The Real Nixon*, p. 133.
48. *RN*, p. 24.
49. Richard Kiefer to FB, Aug. 25, 1975; Merle West to FB, July 6, 1976.
50. Mazo, *Richard Nixon*, p. 33; *Life*, Oct. 11, 1965, p. 41.
51. Mazo, *Richard Nixon*, p. 31.
52. Pat Nixon as told to Joe Alex Morris, "I Say He's a Wonderful Guy," pp. 17–19, 92–96.
53. Erskine, "Dick and Pat Nixon: The Team on Ike's Team," p. 32.
54. Feldman, "The Quiet Courage of Pat Nixon," p. 116.
55. *New York Times*, Nov. 4, 1952, 20:7, 8.
56. Biographers Kornitzer and Spalding, and later William Safire, were told erroneously that Pat had been christened Thelma Catherine Patricia, and even Hannah Nixon was caught up in the web of misstatement and denial. Hoyt, Kornitzer, Costello, and Spalding gave the year of her birth as 1912. Mazo said it was 1913.
57. *RN*, p. 23. Robert Coughlan ("Story of a Vice-President," p. 157), stated that Pat was born on March 17. See Hoyt, *The Nixons*, p. 224; Kornitzer, *The Real Nixon*, p. 133; Costello,

The Facts About Nixon, p. 28; Spalding, *The Nixon Nobody Knows*, p. 123; Mazo, *Richard Nixon*, p. 31.
58. *Time*, Feb. 29, 1950, p. 25.
59. *Life*, Oct. 11, 1968, p. 42.
60. Mazo, *Richard Nixon*, pp. 31–32.
61. Myrtle Raine Borden, Cal. State archives no. 813, pp. 2, 3; Louise Raine Quinn, Cal. State archives no. 870, p. 9.
62. Marian Scheifele Conde, Cal. State archives no. 837, p. 4.
63. Myrtle Raine Borden, Cal. State archives no. 813, pp. 3, 9.
64. West, "The Real Pat Nixon," p. 127. Pat said her father died of silicosis, but the death certificate, signed by Dr. J. M. Furst, listed the cause as pulmonary tuberculosis (David, *Lonely Lady at San Clemente*, p. 32). See also Hoyt, *The Nixons*, pp. 223–24, and *Los Angeles Times*, Oct. 4, 1960.
65. John Brady, "Freelancer . . . an Interview with Gloria Steinem," *Writers Digest*, Feb. 1974, p. 17; Steinem, "In Your Heart You Know He's Nixon," p. 35.
66. Leona Stine Myler, Cal. State archives no. 915, p. 3. See the other descriptions of Thelma Catherine Ryan in the California State Fullerton collection. All call her Thelma or Buddy, and reflect affection.
67. West, "The Real Pat Nixon," p. 127.
68. *Time*, Feb. 29, 1960, p. 26.
69. West, "The Real Pat Nixon," p. 127.
70. Alsop, *Nixon and Rockefeller*, p. 195. This appeared earlier in his "Nixon on Nixon," p. 26ff. In the published version Nixon said he couldn't let his hair down with anyone. Mrs. Stewart Alsop informs me that her husband decided to leave out the original reference to Pat (Mrs. Stewart Alsop to FB).
71. Mazo, *Richard Nixon*, p. 34.
72. Thomas Bewley to FB, June 15, 1976; Evlyn Dorn to FB, July 13, 1976.
73. "Nixon's Meeting with Women of the White House Press Corps," March 11, 1971.
74. Dr. Harold Stone, Cal. State archives no. 959, pp. 1, 2 (Stone was Nixon's dentist).
75. Mazo, *Richard Nixon*, p. 34.
76. Evlyn Dorn to FB, July 13, 1976.
77. Edith Milhous Timberlake, Cal. State archives no. 969, p. 48. The aunt does not explain the absence of Nixon's brothers.
78. Edmondson and Cohen, *Women of Watergate*, p. 220.
79. Mazo, *Richard Nixon*, p. 34.
80. White, *Breach of Faith: The Fall of Richard Nixon*, p. 61.

XII. *Fighting Quaker*

1. *Whittier Daily News*, Nov. 3, 1945.
2. Costello, *The Facts About Nixon*, p. 52.
3. Bowers and Blair, "How to Pick a Congressman," p. 31ff.
4. Spalding, *The Nixon Nobody Knows*, p. 136.
5. Abrahamsen,*Nixonvs.Nixon,*p.144.
6. Rovere, *Senator Joe McCarthy* p. 95.
7. de Toledano, *Nixon*, p. 35.
8. *RN*, p. 28. As vice-president, when his car was stoned in Venezuela, he told Kornitzer, "I was never so close to physical danger as in Caracas" (Kornitzer, *The Real Nixon*, p. 289).
9. Quoted in de Toledano, *Nixon*, p. 35.
10. Jackson, "The Young Nixon," p. 66.
11. THE NAVY RECORD
   June 15, 1942 Appointed Lt. Junior Grade, U.S. Naval Reserve.
   August–October 1942 Naval Training School, Quonset Point, R.I.
   October 1942–May 1943 Aide to Executive Officer, Ottuma, Iowa, Naval Reserve Aviation Base.
   May 1943 Sailed on S.S. *President Monroe* to Espiritu Santo.
   June 1943 to January 1, 1944 Stationed on Guadalcanal, Vella Lavella, Bougainville,

Green Island. Supported consolidation of the northern Solomons (Bougainville) as officer in command of SCAT, South Pacific Combat Air Transport Command. August–December 1944 Fleet Air Wing Eight, Alameda, California. December 1944–March 1945 Bureau of Aeronautics, Navy Department, Washington, D.C. March 1945–March 10, 1946 Bureau of Aeronautics contracting officer for terminations, Office of the Bureau of Aeronautics. General Representative, Eastern District headquarters in New York. (Stationed in Middle River, Maryland.) Released March 10, 1946.

PROMOTIONS:
Promoted to Lieutenant, October 1, 1943.
Promoted to Lieutenant Commander, October 3, 1945.
Promoted to Commander (during the vice-presidency), May 21, 1969.

The official Nixon record, released May 21, 1969, by the Office of Naval Information, states: "In addition to the Commendation Ribbon, Commander Nixon has the American Campaign Medal; Asiatic-Pacific Campaign Medal; and the World War II Victory Medal. He is entitled to two engagement stars on the Asiatic-Pacific Campaign Medal for (1) supporting air action in Treasury-Bougainville operations (October 27–December 15, 1943) and (2) consolidation of the northern Solomons (Bougainville) December 15, 1943–July 22, 1944).

A letter of commendation, signed by Vice-Admiral J. H. Newton, after Nixon's discharge from the service, commends his "meritorious and efficient performance of duty as Officer-in-Charge of the South Pacific Combat Air Transport Command at Bougainville and later at Green Island from January 1 to June 16, 1944." Hannah Nixon permitted Bela Kornitzer to quote from this letter in *The Real Nixon*, p. 149.

12. Abrahamsen, *Nixon vs. Nixon*, p. 144, quotes Philip Mayer saying that Nixon was still at the naval base in Ottuma, Iowa, in January or February 1944, but James Udall told Kornitzer he was on the S.S. *President Monroe* with Nixon in April 1943 (Kornitzer, *The Real Nixon*, p. 144).
13. Kornitzer, *The Real Nixon*, p. 149.
14. Morison, *Breaking the Bismarcks Barrier, 22 July 1942–1 May 1944*, pp. 299, 365, 392–409. The Japanese base on New Britain was bypassed finally rather than captured, but it was made inoperable by air attack by April. See also U.S. Navy, *Communiques 301 to 600, March 6, 1943 to May 24, 1945*, p. 305.
15. Kornitzer, *The Real Nixon*, p. 149.
16. *RN*, pp. 28–29.
17. *New York Times*, July 25, 1959, p. 2.
18. Kornitzer, *The Real Nixon*, p. 148.
19. Wallace Black, Cal. State archives no. 812, p. 11; Stassen to FB, February 1977.
20. Mazo, *Richard Nixon*, pp. 158, 159.
21. Kornitzer, *The Real Nixon*, p. 148.
22. Morison, *Breaking the Bismarcks Barrier*, pp. 211–12.

23. *Public Papers*, (Belleville, Illinois, June 25) 1970, p. 519.
24. Lincoln, *Collected Works*, edited by Roy P. Basler, 1:510, July 27, 1848.
25. "Remarks at the Pentagon to Top Officials of the Department of Defense, January 31, 1969," *Public Papers*, 1969, p. 37.
26. Kissinger, *White House Years*, p. 1200.
27. *New York Times*, March 10, 1971.
28. Hoover, *Memoirs*, 2:12.
29. Nixon's comments at 4 A.M. at the Lincoln Memorial, as reported by Garnett D. Horner of the *Washington Star*, May 8, 1970, *Public Papers*, 1970, p. 424.
30. Jackson, "The Young Nixon," *Life*, Nov. 6, 1970; election film, *Richard Nixon, a Self-Portrait*, 1968.
31. de Toledano, *Nixon*, p. 34; Spalding, *The Nixon Nobody Knows*, p. 132.
32. Election film, *Richard Nixon, a Self-Portrait*, 1968.
33. Olive Marshburn to FB, April 30, 1975, and Cal. State archives no. 902, p. 8; "President's Press Conference, June 1, 1971," *Public Papers*, 1971, p. 689.
34. Thomas Emerson to FB, Oct. 10, 1977.
35. Kornitzer, *The Real Nixon*, pp. 139–40.
36. Emerson to FB, Oct. 10, 1977.
37. Kornitzer, *The Real Nixon*, p. 143; Mazo, *Richard Nixon*, p. 36.
38. Milton Viorst, "Nixon of the OPA," *New York Times Magazine*, Oct. 3, 1971.
39. Robert Semple, "Nixon's Presidency Is a Very Private Affair," *New York Times Magazine*, Nov. 2, 1969, p. 127.
40. "Remarks on Arrival at Quonset Point Naval Air Station, March 12, 1971," and "Exchange of Remarks with Reporters at Quonset Point Naval Air Station, March 12, 1971," and "Address at Graduation Exercises, Naval Officer Candidate School, March 12, 1971," *Public Papers*, 1971, pp. 425–26, 430.
41. Mazo, *Richard Nixon*, pp. 44–45.
42. Richard Heffner, Cal. State archives no. 875, p. 12.
43. "Nixon's Meeting with Women of the White House Press Corps," March 11, 1971.
44. Kornitzer, *The Real Nixon*, p. 146.
45. Spalding, *The Nixon Nobody Knows*, pp. 140, 116; Mazo, *Richard Nixon*, p. 37.
46. Wallace Black, Cal. State archives no. 812, p. 7; Philip Blew to FB, Dec. 16, 1974.
47. Kornitzer, *The Real Nixon*, p. 147.
48. Udall to Kornitzer, *The Real Nixon*, pp. 144–45, and to Jackson, "The Young Nixon," p. 66; Mazo, *Richard Nixon*, p. 37; de Toledano, *Nixon*, p. 36.
49. Kornitzer, *The Real Nixon*, p. 149; Spalding, *The Nixon Nobody Knows*, p. 142; Alsop, *Nixon and Rockefeller*, p. 144.
50. Evlyn Dorn to FB, July 13, 1976; Mazo, *Richard Nixon*, p. 38.
51. Jackson, "The Young Nixon," p. 66; Spalding, *The Nixon Nobody Knows*, p. 137.
52. Spalding, *The Nixon Nobody Knows*, pp. 137, 140.
53. Kornitzer, *The Real Nixon*, p. 149.
54. Nixon, as president, recalled the New Zealanders when toasting the prime minister of New Zealand on September 16, 1969 (*Public Papers*, 1969, p. 719).

XIII. *The Dragon Slayer*

1. Alsop, *Nixon and Rockefeller*, p. 187.
2. So Nixon told Alsop (*Nixon and Rockefeller*, p. 187). Frank Capra, director of the film, informed me that it was based on Lewis Foster's *Gentleman from Montana* (Capra to FB, Feb. 13, 1978).
3. Bullock, "Rabbits and Radicals, Richard Nixon's Campaign against Jerry Voorhis," p. 322, based on an interview with Day, Nov. 19, 1971. See also Bullock, *Jerry Voorhis, The Idealist as Politician* (New York, 1978), Chapter 13.
4. Nixon to Day, Dec. 4, 1945; Mazo, *Richard Nixon*, p. 44.
5. Kornitzer, *The Real Nixon*, pp. 160–61.
6. Bullock, *Jerry Voorhis*, p. 280.
7. Alsop, *Nixon and Rockefeller*, pp. 187–88.
8. Oral history interview with Jerry Voorhis, Claremont Graduate School, Oral History Project, p. 64.
9. Bullock, "Rabbits and Radicals," p. 322.
10. Voorhis, *The Strange Case of Richard Milhous Nixon*, p. 12.
11. Bullock, *Jerry Voorhis*, p. 123.
12. *Monrovia News Post*, Oct. 19, 1946, quoted in Bullock, "Rabbits and Radicals," p. 342.
13. Nixon campaign pamphlet, quoted in Voorhis, *The Strange Case of Richard Milhous Nixon*, p. 15; Bullock, "Rabbits and Radicals," p. 342.
14. Nixon, *RN*, p. 40; de Toledano, *Nixon*, p. 44.
15. Stassen, *Where I Stand*, p. 12.
16. Robert J. Donovan, *Conflict and Crisis, The Presidency of Harry S. Truman, 1945–1948* (New York, 1977), pp. 211, 235–36.
17. Bullock, *Jerry Voorhis*, p. 254.
18. de Toledano, *Nixon*, p. 39.
19. Donovan, *Conflict and Crisis*, pp. 231, 234.
20. Voorhis, *The Strange Case of Richard Milhous Nixon*, p. 9.
21. Wills, "The Hiss Connection Through Nixon's Life," p. 46.
22. Tom Dixon to FB, Nov. 28, 1975.
23. Mollenhoff, *Game Plan for Disaster*, pp. 110, 199.
24. Los Angeles Superior Court Judge Jerry Pacht, who jousted against Chotiner in one election, also insisted that Chotiner was only minimally involved with Nixon in 1946, and did not become the mastermind of his campaign until 1950 (Pacht to FB, Oct. 3, 1976).
25. Costello, *The Facts About Nixon*, p. 45.
26. Mollenhoff, *Game Plan for Disaster*, p. 25. Robert Kennedy, chief counsel for the Senate Permanent Investigating Subcommittee, hoped to discredit Nixon through Chotiner in the 1956 presidential campaign. Chairman McClellan, Arkansas Democrat, ordered that the probe be dropped. Nixon denied knowledge of the Reginelli case and said he had never authorized Chotiner to use his name to influence appointments. Chotiner filed a $1,250,000 suit against *Behind the Scene* for an article calling him "Nixon's secret link to the underworld" (*New York Times*, Jan. 12, 1956, 18:2).
27. Pacht to FB, Oct. 3, 1976.
28. Voorhis, *The Strange Case of Richard Milhous Nixon*, p. 12; Costello, *The Facts About Nixon*, pp. 44, 46; Hill, *Dancing Bear*, pp. 58–61.
29. Wills, *Nixon Agonistes*, pp. 75, 78.
30. Pat Nixon as told to Joe Alex Morris, "I Say He's a Wonderful Guy," pp. 17–19; Bowers and Blair, "How to Pick a Congressman," p. 132.

31. Bowers and Blair, "How to Pick a Congressman"; Wallace Black, Cal. State archives no. 814, p. 14.
32. Voorhis, *The Strange Case of Richard Milhous Nixon*, p. 20.
33. William Ackerman to FB, Jan. 2, 1979.
34. Spalding, *The Nixon Nobody Knows*, p. 176; Mazo, *Richard Nixon*, p. 38.
35. David, *Lonely Lady at San Clemente*, p. 67.
36. *RN*, p.36.
37. Georgia Sherwood to FB, Oct. 10, 1975; Tom Dixon to FB, Nov. 28, 1975.
38. Tom Dixon to FB, Nov. 28, 1975.
39. Costello, *The Facts About Nixon*, p. 58.
40. Bullock, *Jerry Voorhis*, pp. 256, 260–63.
41. *RN*, p. 38. He insisted, however, that there had been infiltration. Bullock reported that Nixon's staff had requested a copy of his 1973 article "Rabbits and Radicals" (Bullock to FB, March 28, 1979).
42. Bullock, "Rabbits and Radicals," p. 340; id., *Jerry Voorhis*, p. 271.
43. From the *Covina Argus-Citizen*, Oct. 18, 1946, quoted in Spalding, *The Nixon Nobody Knows*, p. 166.
44. Voorhis, *The Strange Case of Richard Milhous Nixon*, p. 16; and id., *Confessions of a Congressman*, p. 338.
45. Spalding, *The Nixon Nobody Knows*, p. 167; Bullock, "Rabbits and Radicals," p. 343.
46. The newspaper was the *Alhambra Post-Advocate*. See also Mazo, *Richard Nixon*, p. 48, and Spalding, *The Nixon Nobody Knows*, p. 166n.
47. Wallace Black, Cal. State archives no. 812, p. 16; Voorhis, in *The Confessions of a Congressman*, p. 331, says one large Los Angeles ad agency paid for many of the Nixon ads (see also p. 342); Costello, *The Facts About Nixon*, p. 55; Voorhis, Oral History interview, Claremont Graduate School, p. 45 (interviewed by Stephen Zetterberg, June 15, 1973).
48. Bullock, *Jerry Voorhis*, p. 275.
49. Mrs. Vita Remley learned the details from her niece, whom she encouraged to take the job to "find out what the Republicans are up to" (Vita Remley to FB, May 19, 1980); Bullock, *Jerry Voorhis*, p. 276. Lou Cannon was still expressing disbelief in the anonymous phone calls in 1974; see his article in the *Washington Post*, supplement, Aug. 9, 1974. For the Nixon denial see Mazo, *Richard Nixon*, p. 48n.
50. *Alhambra Post-Advocate*, Oct. 17, 1946; *Monrovia News-Post*, Oct. 18, 1946; *Whittier News*, Oct. 18, 1946; Bullock, "Rabbits and Radicals," p. 341. The bill authorized the transfer of the rabbit industry from the Department of the Interior to Agriculture.
51. Election film, *Richard Nixon, a Self-Portrait*, 1968.
52. Voorhis to FB, Feb. 22, 1978. The Voorhis letter to Nixon was published in Costello, *The Facts About Nixon*, pp. 58–59.
53. *Southern California Quarterly*, Fall 1973, pp. 319–59. The material later was included in Bullock's life of Voorhis in 1978.
54. Mazo, *Richard Nixon*, p. 39.
55. Herman Perry, Cal. State archives no. 929, p. 22; quoted by Lou Cannon, *Washington Post*, supplement, Aug. 9, 1974, p. 6.
56. Kornitzer, *The Real Nixon*, p. 163; Mazo, *Richard Nixon*, p. 49.
57. Costello, *The Facts About Nixon*, p. 59.

XIV. *The First Informer*

1. U.S. Congress, House, Committee on Un-American Activities, 80th Cong., 1st sess., Gerhart Eisler Hearings. Elfriede Eisler's testimony was reproduced in full in Erick Bentley's *Thirty Years of Treason, Excerpts from Hearings before the House Committee on Un-American Activities 1938–1968*, pp. 61–62. See also Stripling, *Red Plot Against America*, p. 62.
2. Costello, *The Facts About Nixon*, p. 179.
3. *Congressional Record*, 80th Cong., 1st sess., (Feb. 24) 1947, 93, pt. 1:1129–30.
4. Ibid.
5. Spalding, *The Nixon Nobody Knows*, pp. 177, 194.
6. *New York Times*, March 22, 1968, p. 47.
7. Carr, *The House Committee on Un-American Activities, 1945–1950*, p. 43.
8. Nixon's efforts led to a contempt citation for Josephson.
9. Helen Reid to Nixon, Sept. 28, 1948, Helen Reid Papers, Truman Library.
10. Costello, *The Facts About Nixon*, pp. 180–82; Weinstein, *Perjury*, pp. 7–8.
11. *RN*, p. 51.
12. Voorhis, *Confessions of a Congressman*, pp. 194, 346; *Congressional Record*, 80th Cong., 1st

sess., (April 16) 1947, 93, pt. 3:3545; Donovan, *Truman*, p. 299.
13. Truman pointed these out in speeches in 1960 attacking the Nixon record. See especially the Truman speeches in San Antonio, Texas, Oct. 10, 1960, and Waco, Texas, Oct. 11, 1960. Copies are in the Truman Library.
14. Carr, *The House Committee on Un-American Activities*, p. 223, from *Congressional Record*, July 18, 1945, p. 7737.
15. Feb. 10, 1948, HUAC hearings on proposed legislation to curb or control the Communist party. Nixon was in the chair (quoted in Bentley, *Thirty Years of Treason*, p. 256). See also *New York Times*, Dec. 23, 1948.
16. *Thirty Years of Treason*, pp. 248–72.
17. Alistair Cooke, *A Generation on Trial* (New York: Knopf, 1952), p. 65.
18. Carr, *The House Committee on Un-American Activities*, p. 454.
19. Costello, *The Facts About Nixon*, p. 189.
20. Donovan, *Truman*, p. 294.
21. Stephen Zetterberg, Oral History interview conducted by Enid Douglas, July 15, 1976, Claremont Graduate School Oral History Collection; see especially pp. 22–24.

XV. *The Impact of Whittaker Chambers*

1. Chambers, *Witness*, p. 456.
2. *Saturday Review*, May 24, 1952, pt. 1, p. 9.
3. Weinstein, *Perjury*, p. 584.
4. Zeligs, *Friendship and Fratricide*, p. 403.
5. Hiss, *In the Court of Public Opinion*, p. 384.
6. *Six Crises*, p. 1.
7. Ibid., p. 3.
8. Nixon, "Plea for an Anti-Communist Faith," *Saturday Review of Literature*, May 24, 1952, pp. 12–13.
9. Wright, "A Long Work of Fiction," p. 11. Both reviews were reproduced in the *New York Times*, Oct. 26, 1973, p. 43.
10. Presidential tapes. The latter was quoted in Wills, "The Hiss Connection Through Nixon's Life."
11. *Six Crises*, pp. 23–24.
12. For the Krivitsky story, see Chambers, *Witness*, p. 485, and Weinstein, *Perjury*, p. 331.
13. Weinstein, *Perjury*, p. 17.
14. *Six Crises*, pp. 70–71.
15. *RN*, pp. 72, 82. Ike had read de Toledano and Lasky on the case.
16. *Six Crises*, p. 4.
17. Weinstein, *Perjury*, pp. 7–8; Mazo, *Richard Nixon*, p. 51; Kornitzer, *The Real Nixon*, pp. 172–73.
18. *Six Crises*, p. 3.
19. Stripling, *Red Plot Against America*, p. 143.
20. Chambers, *Witness*, p. 793n; Hannah Nixon, "Richard Nixon, A Mother's Story," p. 214.
21. Weinstein, *Perjury*, pp. 64–66, 328–30. Berle's notes, later published, showed that Chambers had done more than hint at espionage, a fact Berle underplayed in his testimony before HUAC. It was not Berle but Isaac Don Levine who told of Berle's conversation with FDR about Hiss.
22. Chambers, *Witness*, p. 87. Chambers confessed to Luce that he had been a Communist, but did not tell him about his espionage.

23. Weinstein discovered the Gromyko proposal (see Weinstein, *Perjury*, p. 361). For evidence that Chambers had threatened to expose Hiss if he were made secretary-general of the U.N., see Abrahamsen, *Nixon vs. Nixon*, pp. 153–55, quoting a letter summarizing Father Cronin's report to Catholic bishops in 1945, which mentioned the threat.
24. Chambers, *Witness*, p. 793n.
25. Weinstein, *Perjury*, pp. 350, 356.
26. Ibid., pp. 358–59, 368. Weinstein notes that Elizabeth Bentley also implicated Hiss through statements of Charles Kramer and Harold Glasser (ibid., p. 356). Later evidence from Kim Philby, confessed British Communist spy, and Noel Field and his wife, also implicated Hiss (ibid., p. 360n). Hede Massing, first wife of Gerhart Eisler, testified at Hiss's second trial that she had known him as an underground agent (ibid., pp. 477–78).
27. Ibid., p. 84; Chambers, *Witness*, pp. 110, 122, 518.
28. Chambers, *Witness*, pp. 169, 171.
29. Trilling, "Whittaker Chambers and 'The Middle of the Journey,'" *New York Review of Books*, April 17, 1975, p. 20.
30. Weinstein, *Perjury*, p. 90.
31. Chambers, *Witness*, pp. 11, 25, 41, 193, 446, 701. Meyer Zeligs has noted that Chambers's baptism as an Episcopalian, September 26, 1940, was the anniversary of his dead brother's birth (Zeligs, *Friendship and Fratricide*, p. 328). See also Weinstein, *Perjury*, p. 332.
32. Chambers, *Witness*, pp. 413, 11, 9, 4, 491, 6.
33. Ibid., p. 232.
34. Chambers to William F. Buckley, Jr., May 9, 1957, in *Odyssey of a Friend, Whittaker Chambers' Letters to William F. Buckley, Jr., 1954–1961*, p. 175; Chambers, *Witness*, p. 359.
35. Weinstein, *Perjury*, pp. 117–19; Chambers,

Witness, pp. 563, 70; Weinstein, "Was Alger Hiss Framed?" *New York Review of Books*, April 1, 1976, p. 19.

36. Zeligs made much of the fact that Chambers, as a memento of his friendship with Hiss, had kept a piece of upholstery from an old wing chair that Hiss had given him. He had cleaned it and preserved it, Zeligs said, as a kind of "fetish" (Zeligs, *Friendship and Fratricide*, p. 234). Among the books Chambers translated was the two-volume *The Scorpion*, by Anna Elisabet Weirauch, the story of a young woman's involvement in the lesbian underworld in Berlin in the 1920s (published in 1932).

37. Weinstein, *Perjury*, pp. 379, 583.

38. *RN*, p. 238.

39. Chambers to William F. Buckley, Jr., March 16, 1960, in *Odyssey of a Friend*, pp. 284–85;

Chambers to Nixon, Feb. 2, 1961, Nixon Archive, Los Angeles Federal Archives and Records Center, Laguna Nigel, Calif., Series 320, Box 141.

40. Nixon to Esther Chambers, July 24, 1961, Nixon Archive, Laguna Nigel, Calif., Series 320, Box 141. After Whittaker Chambers's death, Esther was invited to the White House only once, to a Quaker gathering. Her son, John Chambers, covered the presidential campaign as a young reporter, but according to Allen Weinstein Nixon did not recognize him (Weinstein to FB, Dec. 30, 1978).

41. Tony Hiss, *Laughing Last*, p. 8. See also Barber, *Presidential Character*, p. 379.

42. Weinstein, *Perjury*, p. 557.

43. *Six Crises*, p. 57.

44. *RN*, pp. 902–3.

XVI. *The Destruction of Alger Hiss*

1. From the presidential tapes. Actually Hiss had been freed in 1950.

2. Chambers, *Witness*, p. 557.

3. *Six Crises*, p. 50.

4. Weinstein, "Nixon vs. Hiss," *Esquire*, November 1975, p. 74.

5. Haldeman, *Ends of Power*, book 4, "Who Ordered the Break-in?"

6. Mazo, *Richard Nixon*, pp. 56, 60.

7. *RN*, p. 54.

8. Tony Hiss, *Laughing Last*, pp. 165, 131, 128.

9. Chambers, *Witness*, p. 73; Weinstein, *Perjury*, pp. 263n, 264. Chambers also threatened Harry Dexter White, Julian Wadleigh, and others with exposure. Wadleigh, who left the party in 1940, confirmed Chambers's last visit to him for the *New York Post*, July 17, 1949 (Weinstein, *Perjury*, p. 263).

10. Weinstein said Hiss "sought almost total access at war's end to highly sensitive intelligence files that dealt with 'internal security' of America's major allies, including the Soviet Union" (Weinstein, *Perjury*, p. 362).

11. Tony Hiss, *Laughing Last*, p. 11; Hiss to Meyer Zeligs, in Zeligs, *Friendship and Fratricide*, p. 169.

12. Mary Hiss Emerson killed herself, some said, by drinking a bottle of Lysol. Tony Hiss said she ate lye (*Laughing Last*, p. 10). Mary had married a man seventeen years older than herself. Her husband at their wedding had been forty-two, the same age as her father at his suicide (Zeligs, *Friendship and Fratricide*, p. 176).

13. Weinstein, *Perjury*, pp. 79, 383–84, 401. During the pretrial period J. Edgar Hoover passed on a rumor that Hiss, "in answer to the question as to how Chambers happened to use the Hiss typewriter," was planning to use as a defense the accusation that Chambers, "an admitted pervert," was in the Hiss household having relations with Hiss's stepson, who in 1938 was only ten (ibid., p. 401). Actually Hiss was extremely solicitous of the reputation of his stepson, who later married and became the father of four children.

14. Tony Hiss, *Laughing Last*, pp. 8, 12, 34; Zeligs, *Friendship and Fratricide*, p. 143. Tony Hiss reported Hiss's cousin Elizabeth saying that "he was never unhappy; he cooperated with

his dominating mother" (*Laughing Last*, p. 18).

15. Weinstein, *Perjury*, p. 79.

16. Ibid., pp. 25n, 22, 24, 40, 236, 383n; Tony Hiss, *Laughing Last*, p. 2. Lee Pressman later admitted to having been a Communist party member (HUAC, pt. 2, p. 2848, August–September 1950). Perlo's wife informed on him (Weinstein, *Perjury*, p. 156). Julian Wadleigh confessed his participation in Communist party espionage in 1949 in a series of articles in the *New York Post*. He denied that he had given any of the documents to Chambers which came to be called, collectively, "the Pumpkin Papers."

Of all the friends who had known Hiss in the underground only one besides Chambers was persuaded to testify against him at his trial, Hede Massing, former wife of Gerhart Eisler (ibid., p. 477). Hiss continued to deny all these friendships, telling Allen Weinstein in 1977 that "the only person with whom I ever held a discussion of Communism while serving the government during the thirties was an AAA colleague, Abe Fortas" (ibid., p. 209).

17. The typing, according to experts hired by Hiss lawyers as well as by the government, exactly matched specimens of earlier letters, called "the Hiss standards," which Priscilla Hiss had written on the Woodstock typewriter. By themselves they were enough to clinch the case against Hiss, even without the typewriter.

Hiss's skill in selecting out and summarizing from the cables that which would be of greatest interest to the Soviet Union has been ably described by Weinstein, who read the original cables and was able to demonstrate that Hiss ignored material having to do with international economic affairs, relevant to Sayre's office, and concentrated on sensitive military and diplomatic matters. The four memos in Hiss's hand summarized State Department cables sent in March 1938, which included Chinese orders for French fighter-bomber pursuit planes, troop reinforcements and artillery in the Sino-Japanese War, and British plans for constructing new warships. The microfilm with State Department material concerned mostly German-American trade relations. It also contained three cables, dated January 1938, bearing Hiss's initials. Sayre was away from his office at the time these had been received. They dealt with aspects of the Sino-Japanese war of urgent interest to the Russians. One included an assessment of the war by Joseph Stillwell and a coded passage about Chinese Communist strategy. One described Japanese war supplies. The third, from Ambassador William Bullitt in Paris to Secretary of State Cordell Hull, marked "Strictly Confidential for the Secretary," included an assessment of Russian intentions toward the Sino-Japanese War. Sayre would say later that turning this cable over to the Soviets "was a crime of infinite gravity," since it would have permitted the breaking of the State Department code.

Most incriminating for Hiss were sixty-five typed sheets, sixty-four of which were typed on Priscilla Hiss's Woodstock N230099. They consisted of summaries of cables similar in form to the four memos in Hiss's hand, and were apparently typed copies of such memos. Some of the cables concerned military and diplomatic aspects of the Sino-Japanese war; others dealt with British arms purchases in the U.S., French hopes for reconciliation with the Germans, Czech fears of Hitler's expansion into Eastern Europe, and American diplomacy in Europe involving Hitler's pressure on Austria and her subsequent capitulation. Other subjects were Japanese economic plans for conquered Manchuria and responses of major European and Asiatic powers toward the Soviet Union. See Weinstein, *Perjury*, pp. 240–63, for a comprehensive summary.

18. Andrews and Andrews, *A Tragedy of History*, pp. 35, 39.
19. Weinstein, *Perjury*, p. 528.
20. John Chabot Smith, *Hiss*, p. 39.
21. Weinstein, *Perjury*, p. 208.
22. Tony Hiss, *Laughing Last*, p. 74.
23. Chambers, *Witness*, p. 363.
24. Weinstein, *Perjury*, p. 76.
25. *Six Crises*, p. 8.
26. Weinstein, *Perjury*, p. 385.
27. Nixon stated that after the hearing he called at once to check on the pseudonym (*Six Crises*, p. 8).
28. *Six Crises*, p. 11.
29. Ibid., p. 20; Andrews and Andrews, *A Tragedy of History*, p. 72.
30. Weinstein, *Perjury*, p. 368; *Six Crises*, p. 21.
31. Roth, editor of *Two Worlds*, would come forward later and offer to testify that Chambers had indeed used this name, as well as his real one. One of the poems "Tandaradei," he had printed in June 1926. It was later read into the record of Hiss's trial, in an effort to discredit Chambers.

Chambers would write in *Witness*, "At the time, nothing in the hearing at the Commodore Hotel appalled me like the moment when Hiss was asked to produce three witnesses who had known George Crosley, and realized that he could not do so, while across his face for an instant flitted an expression that meant that he felt he was trapped" (Chambers *Witness*, p. 615).
32. Weinstein, *Perjury*, p. 213.
33. Weinstein says no real connection between Smith's death and the Hiss case has ever been

established (*Perjury*, p. 42). Chambers called it a suicide, but said Justice Department officials said the reasons were purely personal. Bert and Peter Andrews, in saying he might have been "pushed to his death," reflected the conspiratorial rumors circulating at the time (*A Tragedy of History*, p. 113n).
34. *Six Crises*, pp. 23–24.
35. Chambers, *Witness*, p. 600.
36. de Toledano (*Nixon*, p. 69) reported the rumors about the cremation.
37. Hiss was certain that Nixon had advanced the date of the hearing because of White's death, hoping to distract public attention away from it with news of his confrontation with Chambers. Nixon denied that he knew of White's death before he changed the date of the hearing, but the 2 A.M. telephone call is suspicious.
38. *Six Crises*, p. 32; for the complete confrontation, see HUAC, pt. 1, pp. 975–1001.
39. Hiss, *In the Court of Public Opinion*, pp. 12, 85. Weinstein quotes Charles Dollard as saying to Hiss's lawyer, Edward McLean, that the various psychiatrists he had talked to about the case "all advocate the homosexual theory. They think that Alger's insistence upon Chambers' teeth was significant in this connection" (*Perjury*, p. 384).
40. *Six Crises*, p. 34; Chambers, *Witness*, p. 694.
41. Hiss, *In the Court of Public Opinion*, p. 90; Andrews and Andrews, *A Tragedy of History*, p. 80. Several witnesses later testified that they had no difficulty recognizing Chambers from the man they had known in the thirties.
42. Chambers, *Witness*, pp. 603, 615.
43. *Six Crises*, p. 36.
44. Ibid., p. 38.
45. Weinstein, *Perjury*, pp. 220–22, 481.
46. Ibid., p. 302. Drew Pearson, in the *Washington Post* of March 17, 1951, said W. Marvin Smith's death may have been related to the Hiss case along with the deaths of Harry Dexter White and Lawrence Duggan (Carr, *The House Committee on Un-American Activities*, p. 112). Hiss's lawyer, Edward McLean, wrote to his partner, William L. Marbury, on Dec. 28, 1948, that "Duggan may well have known some things that we don't know and that very possibly Welles knows them too" (Weinstein, *Perjury*, pp. 303–4; Chambers, *Witness*, pp. 777–80).
47. *Six Crises*, p. 37. After the Pumpkin Papers were released to the press, Nixon read into the *Congressional Record* the paper Harry Dexter White had given Chambers in 1938, and which he had kept hidden in Brooklyn. Thus Nixon tried to clear himself of the charge that HUAC had hounded an innocent man to his death.
48. Ibid., p. 38.
49. Bowers and Blair, "How to Pick a Congressman," p. 134.
50. Chambers, *Witness*, p. 749. Even John Chabot Smith, who continues to believe Hiss innocent, admitted that the documents persuaded William Marbury of Hiss's guilt (John Chabot Smith, *Alger Hiss, the True Story*, p. 247).
51. Weinstein, *Perjury*, p. 188.
52. Weinstein notes that Nixon never admitted the Vazzana leak. And it was Bert Andrews, not Nixon, who suggested that he subpoena the new Chambers evidence, Nixon not having thought of it himself, as he said in *Six Crises;* see Weinstein, *Perjury*, pp. 188–90.

53. Weinstein, "Nixon vs. Hiss," p. 147.
54. *Six Crises*, p. 49.
55. Weinstein, *Perjury*, p. 194. See also Levine, *Eyewitness to History*, p. 207, who was also told they reached four feet.
56. Weinstein, *Perjury*, p. 273; *Six Crises*, pp. 54–55.
57. Chambers, *Witness*, pp. 770–72.
58. *Six Crises*, p. 56.
59. Isaac Don Levine (*Eyewitness to History*, p. 180–81) points out that Nixon made no mention of his aid in *Six Crises*.
60. Weinstein found Nixon's lengthy questions and lists of contradictions in Hiss's testimony in the Justice Department files released in 1977 (*Perjury*, p. 469).

61. Ibid., pp. 477, 417.
62. Weinstein notes that the evidence of Hiss's guilt was established by the "Hiss standards" alone, and did not need the typewriter. Hiss did his best to keep the Woodstock from being "found" for five months. Donald Hiss kept his own knowledge of its whereabouts secret for two months. The typewriter was finally turned over to the government shortly before the FBI seemed certain to find it.
63. Weinstein, *Perjury*, pp. 546, 642; Tony Hiss, *Laughing Last*, pp. 137, 139.
64. *New York Times Book Review*, Feb. 20, 1977, p. 2.
65. Tony Hiss, *Laughing Last*, p. 71.

XVII. On Women and Power: Pat and the Pink Lady

1. de Toledano, *Nixon*, p. 94.
2. *RN*, p. 75.
3. Mazo, *Richard Nixon*, p. 79.
4. *RN*, p. 75.
5. Tom Dixon to FB, Nov. 28, 1975.
6. *New Republic*, May 5, 1958.
7. *RN*, pp. 78, 74.
8. Tom Dixon to FB, Nov. 28, 1975.
9. James Bassett to FB, March 27, 1975; Whelan, *Catch the Falling Flag*, p. 154.
10. Pat Nixon, "I Say He's a Wonderful Guy," p. 93; *Newsweek*, Feb. 22, 1960, p. 28; David, *Lonely Lady at San Clemente*, p. 87; *Los Angeles Times*, Oct. 17, 1962.
11. *Public Papers*, (April 16) 1969, p. 292.
12. Adela Rogers St. Johns to FB, March 7, 1974.
13. Kenneth Chotiner to FB, Feb. 18, 1978.
14. *Time*, Feb. 29, 1960, p. 25; *RN*, p. 240.
15. Dickerson, *Among Those Present: A Reporter's View of 25 Years in Washington*, pp. 193–94.
16. Marlene Cimons, "The Emergence of a New Pat Nixon," *Los Angeles Times*, Jan. 30, 1972; David, *Lonely Lady at San Clemente*, p. 84.
17. Tom Dixon to FB, Nov. 28, 1975.
18. James Bassett to FB, March 27, 1975.
19. Vita Remley to FB, May 19, 1980.
20. *Public Papers*, (April 16) 1969, p. 291.
21. Norma Mulligan to FB, April 16, 1975.
22. "Nixon's Meeting with Women of the White House Press Corps," March 11, 1971, manuscript (courtesy of Norma Mulligan).
23. *Los Angeles Times*, Dec. 1, 1957; *Newsweek*, Feb. 22, 1960, p. 28.
24. Republished in "Mrs. Pat—a British View," *The New Republic*, Dec. 22, 1958, p. 5.
25. Adela Rogers St. Johns to FB, March 7, 1974.
26. Kenneth Chotiner to FB, Feb. 18, 1978.
27. Douglas, "Why I Voted Arms for Europe," pp. 9, 10; *Los Angeles Times*, Nov. 30, 1950; Costello, *The Facts About Nixon*, p. 69.
28. Hill, *Dancing Bear*, p. 167.
29. As Nixon summarized it after the campaign for *U.S. News and World Report*, Nov. 17, 1950, p. 29.
30. Costello, *The Facts About Nixon*, p. 63; *Los Angeles Times*, Sept. 19, 1950.
31. *RN*, p. 70.
32. Costello, *The Facts About Nixon*, p. 70; *Los Angeles Times*, March 23, 1950.
33. *Los Angeles Times*, April 13, July 13, 1950.
34. Ibid., Aug. 30, 1950; see Costello's analysis in

The Facts About Nixon, pp. 64–67.
35. Costello, *The Facts About Nixon*, p. 67. Of the eighty-three contempt citations voted by Congress from March 1946 to November 1957, indictments were returned in seventy-three cases. Of these cases, juries voted forty-three times for acquittal; only thirty were convicted.
36. *Los Angeles Times*, Nov. 3, Nov. 2, Oct. 30, 1950; Costello, *The Facts About Nixon*, p. 69.
37. *Los Angeles Times*, Nov. 3, 1950; *RN*, p. 76; Costello, *The Facts About Nixon*, p. 73.
38. Rather and Gates, *The Palace Guard*, p. 4.
39. Costello, *The Facts About Nixon*, pp. 70–71; Spalding, *The Nixon Nobody Knows*, p. 276.
40. Stanley Coben, *A. Mitchell Palmer* (New York: Columbia University Press, 1963), p. 244; Harold Hyman, *To Try Men's Souls, Loyalty Tests in American History* (Berkeley, 1959), p. 297.
41. Castello, *The Facts About Nixon*, p. 73.
42. *RN*, p. 75.
43. Flannery, "Red Smear in California," p. 225.
44. Costello, *The Facts About Nixon*, p. 73.
45. Drew Pearson reported in his diary at the time, "Senator Fulbright has given to Hennings [Sen. Thomas C. Hennings] and to Senator Hayden [Carl Hayden] a copy of the Union Oil Company letter to Frank Wolckman of Sun Oil stating that Union had paid Nixon $52,000 in 1950." A footnote says that the Dec. 7, 1950, diary entry spells the name "Wolkmann." *Poor's Register of Directors* listed no Wolkmann, but did list a Franklyn Waltman of the Sun Oil Company (Pearson, *Diaries*, Nov. 30, Dec. 12, 1952, pp. 237, 239n). Costello (*The Facts About Nixon*, p. 114) indicates that the Senate investigation showed the letters to be forgeries.
46. Costello, *The Facts About Nixon*, p. 82; Pearson, *Diaries*, p. 239n; *Los Angeles Times*, Oct. 30, 1950.
47. *Los Angeles Times*, Aug. 30, 1950; *RN*, p. 76; Spalding, *The Nixon Nobody Knows*, p. 279.
48. The phrase was first used in the *Independent Review*, Sept. 29, 1950.
49. Joseph Alsop Papers, Library of Congress; see especially Nixon to Alsop, April 19, 1948.
50. Mrs. Stewart Alsop to FB, March 2, 1978.
51. David, *Lonely Lady at San Clemente*, pp. 80–81. Mrs. Douglas died on June 28, 1980.

XVIII. Nixon Among the Giants

1. *Public Papers*, 1969, p. 264–65.
2. Coughlan, "Success Story of a Vice-President," p. 6; *RN*, p. 80; *Six Crises*, p. 77.
3. *RN*, pp. 80, 492–93.
4. *Public Papers*, 1969, pp. 264–65.
5. *Los Angeles Times*, March 29, 1969, p. 1.
6. Chiang Kai-shek, in *RN*, p. 282; deGaulle, in Kissinger, *The White House Years*, p. 107; Hoover, in Roy Cohn, "Could He Walk on Water?" p. 254; Dirksen, in *Public Papers*, 1969, p. 707; Lewis, in ibid., p. 454.
7. Theodore White told Frank and Fritzie Manuel that Nixon told him he was fascinated by Newton's life.
8. Halberstam, *The Powers That Be*, p. 263.
9. Oct. 27, 1952, at Texarkana, Arkansas, and Oct. 18, 1952, at Utica, New York (clipping file, Harry Truman Library).
10. Merle Miller, *Plain Speaking*, pp. 135, 178.
11. *Public Papers*, (Dec. 26) 1972, p. 1159. For the awkward scene between Nixon and Truman at the presentation of the piano in the Truman Library, see ibid., (May 21) 1969, pp. 231–32, and *Los Angeles Times*, Dec. 27, 1972, p. 25.
12. *Congressional Record*, 82nd Cong., 1st sess., 97, (April 11) 1951, pt. 3: 3651–52.
13. Ibid., p. 3614; Manchester, *American Caesar*, p. 651. A copy of the Nixon resolution is in the Truman Library, PPF 200.
14. Philip Potter, "Political Pitchman, Richard M. Nixon," in Sevareid, *Candidates, 1960*, pp. 94–95.
15. *RN*, p. 81; *Six Crises*, p. 77.
16. *RN*, p. 82.
17. Pearson, *Diaries*, July 9, 1952, p. 219.
18. *RN*, pp. 81–82.
19. Eisenhower, *Mandate for Change*, pp. 46–47.

20. *RN*, p. 82.
21. Mazo, *Richard Nixon*, pp. 85–86.
22. *RN*, p. 84. Sen. Henry Cabot Lodge from Massachusetts also suggested the tieup in May (Parmet, *Eisenhower*, p. 92).
23. *RN*, pp. 84–85.
24. Ibid., p. 85.
25. Warren, *Memoirs*, pp. 250–52; Hill, *Dancing Bear*, p. 175.
26. Parmet, *Eisenhower*, notes that this was reduced to 60 percent.
27. *New York Times*, July 10, 11, 1952; Parmet, *Eisenhower*, pp. 78, 89; Mazo, *Richard Nixon*, p. 93.
28. *New York Times*, July 10, 1952.
29. Kornitzer, *The Real Nixon*, p. 211; Halberstam, *The Powers That Be*, p. 258.
30. *New York Times*, July 12, 1952, p. 5.
31. Ibid.; *RN*, p. 85.
32. *RN*, p. 86; Mazo, *Richard Nixon*, p. 95; David, *Lonely Lady at San Clemente*, p. 82.
33. Abigail Adams to Mary Cranch, *New Letters of Abigail Adams, 1788–1801*, edited by Stewart Mitchell (Boston, 1947), p. 49.
34. Patricia Ryan Nixon as told to Joe Alex Morris, "I Say He's a Wonderful Guy," p. 94; Spalding, *The Nixon Nobody Knows*, p. 300.
35. *New York Times*, July 12, 1952, p. 6; *RN*, pp. 86–87.
36. Mazo, *Richard Nixon*, pp. 96–97.
37. *New York Times*, July 12, 1952, p. 6.
38. *RN*, p. 89.
39. *New York Times*, July 12, 1952, p. 5.
40. Patricia Ryan Nixon, as told to Joe Alex Morris, "I Say He's a Wonderful Guy."
41. "Remarks at the Swearing in of New Members of the White House Staff," *Public Papers*, (Jan. 21) 1969, p. 8.

XIX. Checkers

1. *Six Crises*, p. 87; Erskine, "Dick and Pat Nixon," p. 33.
2. *RN*, p. 110.
3. Barber, *Presidential Character*, p. 417.
4. *Six Crises*, p. 93.
5. *Time*, Oct. 6, 1952, p. 21.
6. Costello, *The Facts About Nixon*, p. 96.
7. Robert J. Donovan, "Presidency and the Man: The People Must Take Him on Faith," *Los Angeles Times*, Nov. 10, 1968, p. G1; *New Republic* Sept. 8, 1952, p. 9.
8. Costello, *The Facts About Nixon*, p. 96.
9. Ibid. (the italics are the authors); Wilson, "Is Nixon Fit To Be President?"
10. Katcher to FB, Oct. 22, 1975.
11. *Six Crises*, p. 79; *RN*, p. 92.
12. Alsop, *Nixon and Rockefeller*, p. 60.
13. *U.S. News and World Report*, Oct. 3, 1952, p. 21.
14. Quoted in Wilson, "Is Nixon Fit To Be President?" pp. 33–42. The *Los Angeles Times* labeled this the "original letter setting up the fund need." It was not the original letter, but one circulated ten months later (Costello, *The Facts About Nixon*, p. 106).
15. Mazo, *Richard Nixon*, p. 123. A pamphlet prepared by a "Whittier Citizens Committee" insisted that the fund was really $29,000, and that there may have been two funds. A copy is

in the Truman Library. Leo Katcher, in interviewing Dana Smith, saw a document labeled "Fund No. 2" on his desk (Katcher to FB, Oct. 22, 1975).
16. *San Francisco Chronicle*, Sept. 19, 1952, repeated with slight variations in *The New Republic*, Oct. 13, 1952, p. 2, and Costello, *The Facts About Nixon*, pp. 99–100.
17. Leo Katcher to FB, Oct. 22, 1975.
18. Costello, *The Facts About Nixon*, pp. 100–1; Halberstam, *The Powers That Be*, p. 261.
19. Costello, *The Facts About Nixon*, p. 97; Mazo, *Richard Nixon*, pp. 119–20.
20. *Six Crises*, p. 89.
21. Anderson, *Confessions of a Muckraker*, p. 26.
22. Mazo, *Richard Nixon*, p. 101.
23. Their pamphlet, published in 1952, also raised the possibility of a second fund. A copy is in the Truman Library. It is titled "The Nixon We Know."
24. Costello, *The Facts About Nixon*, p. 112; *Washington Star*, Sept. 24, 1952; Anderson, *Confessions of a Muckraker*, p. 326; Costello, *The Facts About Nixon*, p. 112.
25. Pearson, *Diaries*, Oct. 28, 1952, pp. 227–28; *RN*, p. 108; Wilson, "Is Nixon Fit To Be President?" p. 41.
26. *RN*, pp. 93–94.
27. Sherman Adams, *First-hand Report* (New

York: Harper, 1951), p. 37; Parmet, *Eisenhower*, p. 135.

28. *RN*, p. 96; Parmet, *Eisenhower*, p. 135.
29. *RN*, pp. 96–97, 99.
30. Mazo, *Richard Nixon*, p. 120.
31. *Six Crises*, p. 87.
32. *U.S. News and World Report*, Oct. 3, 1952, pp. 61–62.
33. Alsop, *Nixon and Rockefeller*, p. 146. Nixon had claimed a deduction of $1294.05 on his 1951 income tax for "unreimbursed" business expenses, entertainment in Washington—official business and expenses on trips. The income tax returns were published in *Look*, Feb. 24, 1953, p. 35.
34. Costello, *The Facts About Nixon*, p. 111.
35. *U.S. News and World Report*, Oct. 3, 1952, pp. 61–62; Mazo, *Richard Nixon*, pp. 110n, 113.
36. Mazo, *Richard Nixon*, pp. 117–18.
37. *RN*, p. 98. For a bowdlerized version, "fish or cut bait," and a somewhat different account of the conversation, see Nixon's earlier *Six Crises*, p. 100.
38. Stevenson, like many state governors, was the funnel through which campaign funds were channeled to party members for campaign purposes. Unfortunately he was not careful in his accounts, and expenses for some purposes that were clearly personal found their way into his worksheets. When Nixon demanded an accounting, Stevenson aides, working under pressure, found a total of $84,026.56, of which $18,150 had been spent to augment the salaries of his aides. For Sherwood Dixon's campaign he had given $45,037.19, and $17,410 had been dispensed to the campaigns of other candidates. Of the remaining $13,429.37, approximately $3000 had been given for the political campaigns of Scott Lucas, George Kells, Kick Daley, and four candidates of the Illinois Supreme Court. Stevenson on September 25, 1952, wrote out a check for $10,542.59 to the "Stevenson-for-Governor Committee," which had long been disbanded. This his biographer Martin believes was an effort to repay money which had been spent "on a mixture of his political and personal affairs." The dating of the check looked bad in the Stevenson record, but it is clear that he repaid for many political items unnecessarily in an effort to clear his record. The IRS never demanded additional money after auditing his books.
   The Nixon memoirs distort biographer Martin's description of the accounting, failing to explain how much of the Stevenson fund went into campaigns of Democratic party colleagues. See *RN*, pp. 99–100, and Martin, *Adlai Stevenson of Illinois*, pp. 695–98.
39. *RN*, p. 103; *Six Crises*, p. 110; Mazo, *Richard Nixon*, pp. 127–28.
40. Erskine, "Dick and Pat Nixon," p. 33; *RN*, p. 103.
41. Kornitzer, *The Real Nixon*, p. 79.
42. Nixon's father had broken his arm driving a tractor on his Pennsylvania farm and had moved to Florida and then back to California. *Look* (Feb. 24, 1953, p. 41) reported the farm as rented, also the Florida house.
43. The idea of using "Checkers" was suggested by Hearst reporter Adela Rogers St. Johns,

who urged him to remember how FDR had made political capital out of Republican abuse of his dog Falla (St. Johns to FB, March 7, 1975).

44. Pat put the record straight on September 6 in her article in the *Saturday Evening Post*, "I Say He's a Wonderful Guy," saying that Pat was her nickname (p. 93). He had been accused of falsifying her name and birthdate to win the Irish Catholic vote.
45. For the complete text see Kornitzer, *The Real Nixon*, pp. 194–205, and *U.S. News and World Report*, Oct. 3, 1952, pp. 61–62.
46. *Newsweek*, Oct. 6, 1952, pt. 2, p. 25; *Los Angeles Times*, Sept. 25, 1952.
47. O'Brien, "The Night Nixon Spoke, a Study in Political Effectiveness," pp. 31, 43, 48, 51.
48. *RN*, p. 100; Rowse, *Slanted News, A Case Study of the Nixon and Stevenson Fund Stories*, pp. 43, 123; *Life*, Oct. 6, 1952, pp. 25–31.
49. *Time*, Oct. 6, 1952, p. 19; Halberstam, *The Powers That Be*, p. 193; *Commonweal*, Oct. 10, 1952, p. 3.
50. Ike was angered, too, by Nixon's demand that Stevenson and Sparkman publish their financial holdings. He was perforce required to publish his own. This meant that the public learned that he had been permitted by the Internal Revenue Service to publish his *Crusade in Europe* with a special tax advantage. Instead of paying regular income tax on his earnings, at a rate of 75.6 percent, he had been permitted tax status as an "amateur" writer, and had paid a capital gains tax instead at a 25 percent rate spread over three years. He therefore profited from his book by $562,000 rather than $187,000. Ike's total income over ten years had been $888,303.09, including $635,000 from his book. His tax payment had been less than 25 percent. Stevenson, whose ten-year income had been $500,046, had paid 42 percent in taxes, leaving a net of $211,980 (*Newsweek*, Oct. 6, 1952, pt. 2, p. 26; Parmet, *Eisenhower*, pp. 138–39; *U.S. News and World Report*, Oct. 3, 1952, p. 33; Alsop, *Nixon and Rockefeller*, p. 65).
51. *RN*, p. 105.
52. *Six Crises*, p. 121; Mazo, *Richard Nixon*, p. 133.
53. *Six Crises*, pp. 121–22. In his memoirs Nixon tells less of the nastiness of the dueling with Ike. Mazo, *Richard Nixon*, pp. 133–34.
54. *Six Crises*, p. 123; Mazo, *Richard Nixon*, p. 135.
55. *Six Crises*, p. 123; *RN*, pp 106–7.
56. *RN*, p. 107; Kornitzer, *The Real Nixon*, p. 107.
57. *Six Crises*, p. 126; Mazo, *Richard Nixon*, pp. 125–26; *RN*, p. 108.
58. Erskine, "Dick and Pat Nixon," p. 33; Mazo, *Richard Nixon*, p. 136.
59. Halberstam, *The Powers That Be*, p. 331.
60. Woodstone, *Nixon's Head*, p. 30; Alsop, *Nixon and Rockefeller*, p. 193.
61. John Dean, *Blind Ambition* (New York: Simon & Schuster, 1976), p. 40; U.S. Congress, Senate, Committee on Watergate and Related Activities, *The Hughes-Rebozo Investigation*, 93rd Cong., 2d sess. 21:9833, 9829; 22:10385.
62. U.S. Congress, House, Committee on the Judiciary, Hearings, *Transcripts of Eight Recorded Presidential Conversations*, 93rd Cong., 2d sess., May–June 1974, p. 183.

xx. McCarthy

1. "Quizzing Nixon," *U.S. News and World Report,* Aug. 29, 1952, p. 38.
2. Roy Cohn to FB, April 26, 1979.
3. Rovere, *Senator Joe McCarthy,* p. 49. Nixon in his memoirs said Acheson later became his friend (*RN,* p. 110). But Acheson in his own memoir, *Present at the Creation, My Years in the State Department* (New York: W. W. Norton, 1969), does not once mention Nixon, an omission that could hardly have been accidental.
4. Roy Cohn to FB, April 26, 1979. Recent publication of Eisenhower tapes, transcribed in the presidential library at Abilene, Kansas, shows Eisenhower warning Nixon that he wanted "no implication" of support for McCarthy's slanderous description of Democratic party history as "20 years of treason" (*Los Angeles Times,* Oct. 29, 1979, p. 15).
5. Rovere, *McCarthy,* p. 7.
6. "The politics of civility" is Edward Shils's phrase. Robert Griffith wrote an excellent biography of McCarthy, *The Politics of Fear, Joseph R. McCarthy and the Senate.*
7. Bryce Harlow to John Osborne, *New Republic,* May 13, 1978, p. 13.
8. Eisenhower, *Mandate for Change,* p. 330.
9. *RN,* pp. 141, 158–59.
10. Mazo, *Richard Nixon,* p. 151; *RN,* p. 149.
11. Griffith, *The Politics of Fear,* p. 48. McCarthy had already attacked his opponents in Wisconsin as Communist-supported (Anderson and May, *McCarthy: The Man, the Senator, the "Ism",* pp. 108–10).
12. *RN,* p. 146.
13. Speech in *Augusta* (Maine) *Reporter,* Sept. 30, 1952, p. 1.
14. What he really held in his hand was a letter from Secretary of State Byrnes to Rep. Adolf Sabbath of Illinois. It had no list of Communists in it. It was an old letter, July 26, 1946, recommending against permanent employment of 285 individuals on charges ranging from incompetence and drunkenness to a suspicion of disloyalty. Eighty had resigned or been fired, leaving 205. By the time he spoke in Wheeling, 46 had been cleared after full field investigations and were working (Anderson and May, *McCarthy,* pp. 188, 204; Rovere, *Arrivals and Departures,* p. 97; Rovere, *McCarthy,* p. 129).
15. *New York Times,* June 2, 1950; Griffith, *The Politics of Fear,* pp. 103–4; Mazo, *Richard Nixon,* p. 142. The replacement was made in January 1951, and caused a flurry of criticism. Sen. Charles E. Potter, in *Days of Shame,* describes McCarthy's harassment of Mrs. Smith.
16. Anderson, *Confessions of a Muckraker,* pp. 209, 247–48.
17. *RN,* pp. 138–39; Mazo, *Richard Nixon,* pp. 141–42; Anderson, *Confessions of a Muckraker,* p. 213; de Toledano, *Nixon,* p. 168n. Pearson sued McCarthy for assault, but dropped the suit after the Senate condemnation (Pearson, *Diaries,* p. 215n).
18. Hughes, *Ordeal of Power,* p. 92.
19. *RN,* p. 140.
20. Rovere, *McCarthy,* pp. 194, 201.
21. Cohn, *McCarthy,* pp. 74, 76, 81; Rovere, *McCarthy,* pp. 201–2.
22. *U.S. News and World Report,* pt. 1, Sept. 11, 1953, p. 28ff.
23. The *New York Times,* March 12, 1954, published the entire thirty-four-page army report, with the forty-four requests for preferential treatment.
24. Murrey Marder of the *Washington Post,* in one of the first serious newspaper exposés of McCarthy's sloppy research, demonstrated that "for all the smoke and blathering McCarthy had not found a single Communist" at Fort Monmouth (Halberstam, *The Powers That Be,* p. 200).
25. Roy Cohn to FB, April 26, 1969; Sherman Adams, *First-hand Report* (New York: Harper, 1951), pp. 143–45; Straight, *Trial by Television,* p. 120; Cook, *The Nightmare Decade: The Life and Times of Senator Joe McCarthy,* p. 480; Anderson, *Confessions of a Muckraker,* p. 265. Anderson said the decision was made in January 1954.
26. *New York Times,* Feb. 27, 1954; Griffith, *The Politics of Fear,* p. 247; Parmet, *Eisenhower,* p. 347.
27. Griffith, *The Politics of Fear,* p. 247; Parmet, *Eisenhower.* Nixon did not attend the luncheon, but was told what happened by Senator Mundt.
28. Parmet, *Eisenhower,* p. 267.
29. Potter, *Days of Shame,* p. 17. See also Harold Stassen, Oral history interview, Dulles Archives, Princeton University, pp. 31–32.
30. Stevenson, *Papers,* 4:327–33, March 5, 1954.
31. Bassett Diary, March 8, 1954, pp. 39–40, and March 12, 1954, p. 48.
32. Shils, *The Torment of Secrecy: The Background and Consequences of American Security Policies,* p. 193.
33. The *New York Times,* March 14, printed the entire text, p. 44.
34. Nixon's falsification of numbers received very little exposure. Eisenhower's own Civil Service Commission chairman, Philip Young, testified late in 1954 that "he knew of no single government employee who had been fired by the Eisenhower administration for being a Communist or fellow traveler." Young later revealed that an analysis of 3746 employees who were dismissed or who resigned showed that 41.2 percent had been hired by the Eisenhower administration itself. Still later, a Senate investigation committee reported that 53 percent of those ousted as security risks had been hired by Reupblicans (see Costello, *The Facts About Nixon,* p. 127).

    On Nov. 1, 1954, in Denver, Nixon raised the number separated from government jobs to 6926, and said 96 percent of the "Communists, fellow travelers, sex perverts, people with criminal records, dope addicts, drunks, and other security risks removed under the Eisenhower security program" were hired by the Truman administration.

    Eisenhower's own figures were somewhat different. In *Mandate for Change* (p. 315) he said, "During 1953–54, 8008 cases of security risks were identified by properly appointed boards. As a result, 3002 were dismissed as security risks, and 5006 resigned before their cases were acted upon."
35. *RN,* pp. 146–47.
36. *Time,* March 22, 1954.
37. Roy Cohn to FB, April 26, 1979; Griffith, *The Politics of Fear,* p. 249n; *Army-McCarthy Hear-*

ings, pp. 394–96; Potter, *Days of Shame*, pp. 31–32.

37. William S. White, in "Nixon: What Kind of President" (*Harper's*, January 1958, p. 27), wrote that Nixon *did* assist in the destruction of McCarthy, but that he did not "risk any final or open rupture with McCarthyites."

38. Senator Symington to FB.

39. Drew Pearson, June 12, 1954, quoted in Griffith, *The Politics of Fear*, p. 257.

40. *New York Times*, March 13, 1954, p. 1; Potter, *Days of Shame*, p. 42; *RN*, p. 147.

41. See U.S. Congress, Senate, Committee on Government Operations, Permanent Subcommittee on Investigations, *Charges and Countercharges Involving Secretary of the Army Robert T. Stevens . . . Senator Joe McCarthy, etc.*, 83rd Cong., 2d sess., 1954.

42. *RN*, pp. 147–48; Bassett Diary, May 10, 1954, p. 135; ibid., April 28, 1954, p. 107.

43. Flanders to Paul Hoffman, in Griffith, *The Politics of Fear*, p. 272.

44. Edward Bennett Williams, *One Man's Freedom* (New York, 1962), pp. 60–63. Williams, later

Nixon's enemy, was counsel for Watkins. He had refused to be McCarthy's lawyer because of his special demands.

45. Griffith, *The Politics of Fear*, p. 308; Watkins, *Enough Rope*, p. 129.

46. *RN*, p. 148.

47. U.S. Congress, Senate, Select Committee to Study Censure Charges, *Hearings on S. Res. 301*, Report No. 2508, 83rd Cong., 2d sess.

48. Cohn, *McCarthy*, pp. 252, 254.

49. Cohn to Abrahamsen, in *Nixon vs. Nixon*, p. 165.

50. Bassett Diary, May 5, 1954, p. 119. Bassett reported Senator Dirksen's telling him how McCarthy "at a recent hearing" was drinking tumblers full of straight bourbon whiskey hidden in his briefcase (ibid., March 30, 1954, p. 69; Cohn, *McCarthy*, p. 224).

51. Chambers, *Odyssey of a Friend*, Aug. 2, 1955, p. 100.

52. Anderson, *Confessions of a Muckraker*, p. 271.

53. Cohn, *McCarthy*, p. 256.

XXI. *Stevenson and Nixon*

1. Aug. 17, 1956, quoted in *RN*, p. 178.

2. Martin, *Adlai Stevenson of Illinois*, p. 746.

3. Stevenson, *Papers*, 4:146, Oct. 8, 1952.

4. Ibid., 4:29, from "The Perfectionist and the Press," in *As We Knew Adlai*, p. 170.

5. Sevareid to Carl McGowan, Oct. 2, 1952; Stevenson, *Papers*, 4:134.

6. Martin, *Adlai Stevenson and the World*, pp. 206, 126.

7. Brower, "Inside the Humless Machine, a Longing for Poetry," pp. 36–39.

8. *RN*, p. 111.

9. Martin, *Adlai Stevenson of Illinois*, p. 693.

10. *Newsweek*, Sept. 15, 1952, p. 32; *RN*, p. 112.

11. Hughes, *Ordeal of Power*, p. 196.

12. *RN*, p. 111.

13. Stevenson, *Papers*, 4:105, 115–16, Sept. 26, 1952. For the text of Eisenhower's speech, see *New York Times*, Sept. 23, 1952.

14. Sevareid to Carl McGowan, Oct. 2, 1952; Stevenson, *Papers*, 4:133–34.

15. Martin, *Adlai Stevenson of Illinois*, p. 741.

16. In an Oct. 23, 1952, television speech. Weinstein, in *Perjury*, quotes from this speech and discusses Stevenson's reply. He notes that Stevenson buckled a little under attack, and trimmed and qualified his "unqualified 1949 endorsement of Hiss's reputation" (pp. 511–12). See also Costello, *The Facts About Nixon*, p. 116.

17. Stevenson, *Papers*, 4:168–70, Oct. 23, 1952. See Matthew 16:26.

18. Costello, *The Facts About Nixon*, p. 118; Harry Truman Library clipping file; *Los Angeles Times*, Oct. 31, 1952.

19. Weinstein, *Perjury*, p. 511; and id., "Nixon vs. Hiss," *Esquire*, November 1975, p. 152;

Anderson, *Confessions of a Muckraker*, p. 120.

20. Martin, *Adlai Stevenson and the World*, p. 181.

21. Martin, *Adlai Stevenson of Illinois*, pp. 44–45. When his own son, John Fell Stevenson, at eighteen, suffered an automobile accident in which two friends were killed—John had been driving over a hill when a truck passing another truck on a hill hit him head-on—Stevenson wrote to Agnes Meyer, "Who knows what the death of his dearest friends beside him in the front seat will mean and do inwardly" (Martin, *Adlai Stevenson and the World*, p. 240).

22. Martin, *Adlai Stevenson of Illinois*, pp. 87, 307.

23. Stevenson, *Papers*, 4:193, Nov. 6, 1952; Martin, *Adlai Stevenson and the World*, p. 181.

24. Quoted in Bassett Diary.

25. *New York Times*, Oct. 21, 1954, p. 22; Costello, *The Facts About Nixon*, p. 126.

26. *Washington Post*, Nov. 5, 1954; Costello, *The Facts About Nixon*, p. 127.

27. Spot announcements over radio stations for the GOP (Costello, *The Facts About Nixon*, p. 130).

28. Ibid., pp. 128–29. Nixon himself later admitted that the Soviet economy was expanding more than that of the U.S. (*New York Times*, Oct. 24, 1954, sec. 4, p. 1).

29. *New York Times*, Oct. 29, 1954, p. 2.

30. *RN*, p. 162; *New York Times*, Oct. 29, 1954; Stevenson, *Papers*, 4:409, Oct. 16, 1954; *New York Times*, Oct. 21, 1954, p. 22; Costello, *The Facts About Nixon*, p. 131.

31. *RN*, p. 163; Costello, *The Facts About Nixon*, p. 132.

32. *RN*, p. 163.

XXII. *Prelude to Vietnam*

1. Coffin, "The Private Life of Pat Nixon," pp. 23–29.

2. Thomas Powers, *The Man Who Kept the Secrets, Richard Helms and the CIA* (New York, 1979), p. 85.

3. *RN*, p. 133.

4. Costello, *The Facts About Nixon*, p. 150.

5. *RN*, p. 134.

6. *Time*, Jan. 4, 1954, p. 11.

7. *Public Papers*, 1973, p. 674.

8. Ford, *A Time to Heal*, p. 205.

9. *U.S. News and World Report*, Jan. 1, 1954, pp.

66–69; Bassett Diary.
10. *New York Times*, Dec. 15, 1953.
11. *RN*, p. 134.
12. Ibid., p. 157.
13. Ibid., from Nixon's diary of the day.
14. Ibid., p. 205.
15. Mosley, *Dulles: A Biography of Eleanor, Allen, and John Foster Dulles*, p. 342.
16. *RN*, pp. 204–5; Nixon on Dulles, Oral History Archive, Dulles Collection, Princeton University Library, dated Feb. 21, 1966.
17. *RN*, p. 204.
18. Schlesinger, *A Thousand Days*, p. 280.
19. Hughes, *Ordeal of Power*, p. 105.
20. Eisenhower, *Mandate for Change*, pp. 178–81; Hoopes, *The Devil and John Foster Dulles*, p. 185; Brodie, *War and Politics*, p. 105.
21. *Congressional Record*, 83rd Cong., 2d sess., 1954, 100, pt. 16:A1286–87; *New York Times*, March 15, 1954.
22. Schlesinger, *A Thousand Days*, p. 288.
23. E. J. Kahn, Jr., "Communists' Capitalist," *The New Yorker*, Oct. 17, 1977, p. 84; see also Brodie, *War and Politics*, p. 121.
24. Hoopes, *The Devil and John Foster Dulles*, p. 200.
25. For a discussion of the difficulties inherent in the domino theory, see Brodie, *War and Politics*, pp. 144–53.
26. Parmet, *Eisenhower*, p. 364; Hoopes, *The Devil and John Foster Dulles*, pp. 210–11; Brodie, *War and Politics*, p. 179.
27. *RN*, p. 154. The idea had been discussed in a National Security Council planning board meeting.
28. Hoopes, *The Devil and John Foster Dulles*, p. 197.
29. Dr. Eugene Pumpian-Mindlin to FB, March 1, 1975.
30. Bassett Diary, pp. 120–136.
31. Hoopes, *The Devil and John Foster Dulles*, p. 211.
32. *Congressional Record*, 83rd Cong., 2d sess., 1954, 100, pt. 4:4672–81; Parmet, *Eisenhower*, p. 367; Schlesinger, *A Thousand Days*, p. 301.
33. Hoopes, *The Devil and John Foster Dulles*, pp. 217, 219; Parmet, *Eisenhower*, p. 369.
34. There are slight variations in reported versions of this statement. One of the most complete appeared in the *Christian Science Monitor*, April 19, in an article by Richard Strout. Jim Bassett's diary has a brief summary of the speech and Nixon's replies to questions, including one concerning the loyalty of Oppenheimer. He said he believed him loyal, but to obtain a security clearance he must disassociate himself "from his equivocal past" (April 16, 1954, pp. 84–85). See also *RN*, pp. 152–53, and Eisenhower, *Mandate for Change*, p. 353n.
35. This continued throughout the election in the fall of 1954. See especially Nixon's speech of

Oct. 31, 1954.
36. *Christian Science Monitor*, April 19, 1954. This was consistent with his old stance as congressman, when he urged sending MacArthur back to Korea and the bombing of supply bases in China. In the Senate, April 22, 1951, he had deplored the fact that the U.S. could not win in Korea "because we are restricted in the use of both strategic bombing and naval power."
37. *RN*, p. 153.
38. Bassett Diary, p. 117.
39. *New York Times*, May 7, 1954; Hoopes, *The Devil and John Foster Dulles*, p. 227.
40. Reprinted in *Congressional Record*, 83rd Cong., 2d sess., 1954, 100, pt. 21:A6116. James Hagerty, Ike's press secretary, told Herbert Parmet later it was "almost inconceivable" that he would have so spoken without the knowledge of the White House (April 11, 1969, interview, Parmet, *Eisenhower*, p. 368).
41. Hoopes, *The Devil and John Foster Dulles*, p. 222.
42. Ibid., p. 239. Dulles did set up a new military pact—the Southeast Asia Treaty Organization (SEATO), including Thailand, Pakistan, the Philippines, the U.S., Britain, France, Australia, and New Zealand. Dulles, who hoped to see Laos "a bulwark against communism," proceeded to pour three hundred million dollars into the country, most of which went to outfit the Royal Laotian Army with conventional American military weapons and transport, although the nation had no all-weather roads. The army was taught conventional maneuvers, rather than counterguerrilla warfare (Schlesinger, *A Thousand Days*, pp. 302–4).
43. Brodie, *Strategy in the Missile Age*, p. 154.
44. Brown, *Conscience in Politics*, pp. 202, 218.
45. Stevenson, *Papers*, 6:110–21, Speech before the American Society of Newspaper Editors, April 21, 1956; Stevenson, "Why I Raised the H-Bomb Question," *Look*, Feb. 5, 1957, reprinted in Stevenson, *Papers*, 6:439–46.
46. *New York Times*, Oct. 17, 1956.
47. Costello, *The Facts About Nixon*, p. 163; Stevenson, *Papers*, 6:442.
48. Stevenson, *Papers*, 6:248–50, 283–88, 324, 439–46. Soviet Premier Bulganin on Oct. 21, 1954, had written to Eisenhower saying the Soviet government was "prepared to conclude an agreement with the United States of America immediately for discontinuing atomic tests" (Brown, *Conscience in Politics*, p. 207). Ike denounced the letter as interference in the American election.
49. Stevenson to Chakravarti Rajagopalachari, *Papers*, 6:344.
50. Brown, *Conscience in Politics*, pp. 189–222; Stevenson, *Papers*, 6:424n.

XXIII. Hidden Problems: The Early Surfacing

1. Hutschnecker, *The Drive for Power*, p. 10.
2. James Bassett to FB, March 27, 1975.
3. *Durham* (N.C.) *Sun*, April 6, 1954; *Newsweek*, April 19, 1954, p. 43.
4. *Los Angeles Times*, June 14, 1954. The speech was published in the *Congressional Record*, 83rd Cong., 2d sess., 1954, 100, pt. 21:A6116.

5. Hannah Nixon, "Richard Nixon, a Mother's Story," p. 216.
6. *Six Crises*, p. 70.
7. Halberstam, *The Powers That Be*, p. 5. In *RN*, Nixon wrote that Rayburn mistakenly believed that he had called him a traitor (p. 432).

8. Bassett Diary, July 15, 1954, p. 237.
9. Mazo, *Richard Nixon*, p. 152; *RN*, p. 163.
10. Halberstam, *The Powers That Be*, p. 604.
11. Hutschnecker, *The Drive for Power*, p. 4.
12. Erskine, "Dick and Pat Nixon," p. 35.
13. Hutschnecker, *The Drive for Power*, p. 5.
14. Ibid., pp. 83–84.
15. Ibid., p. 54.
16. Ibid., pp. 19–24. He appeared before the Senate Committee on Rules and Administration on Nov. 7, 1973.
17. Ibid., p. 318. Hutschnecker reproduced several of his *New York Times* articles, one on the testing of children and one on the Department of Peace, as appendices in his *The Drive for Power*.
18. Hutschnecker, "The Mental Health of Our Leaders," pp. 51–54.
19. Hutschnecker, *The Drive for Power*, pp. 83–84.
20. Ibid., pp. 83–84, 16, 132, 198, 296, 266, 36, 84, 48, 55, 35, 301–2.
21. Jean M. White, *Los Angeles Times*, Nov. 25, 1973.
22. Dr. Hutschnecker to FB.
23. Leonard Hall to FB, Aug. 29, 1975.
24. Kissinger, *The White House Years*, p. 26.
25. Leonard Hall to FB, Aug. 29, 1975.
26. Erskine, "Dick and Pat Nixon," pp. 32–37.
27. Mazo, *Richard Nixon*, pp. 4, 5.
28. Mrs. Stewart Alsop to FB, March 2, 1978.
29. W. T. Jones and Molly Mason Jones to FB, Dec. 11, 13, 1979. Jones was professor of philosophy at Claremont College at the time and Mrs. Jones was professor of psychology at Scripps. They date the party as 1948 or 1949. Pat was not with her husband.
30. Earl Chapman, Cal. State archives, Aug. 5, 1970, p. 10. Chapman knew Nixon at Whittier High, and was a teacher there when Pat taught at the high school.
31. Kornitzer, *The Real Nixon*, p. 273.
32. Erskine, "Dick and Pat Nixon," pp. 32–37.
33. Bassett Diary, March 13, 1954, p. 53.
34. Bassett to FB, March 27, 1975.
35. *The New Republic*, Oct. 25, 1954.
36. Erskine, "Dick and Pat Nixon," p. 33.
37. Jessamyn West to FB, Sept. 29, 1976.
38. Leonard Hall to FB, Aug. 29, 1975.
39. Robert L. King, *New York Times*, Sept. 7, 1973.
40. Bassett to FB, March 27, 1975.
41. Safire, *Before the Fall*, pp. 92–93.

42. George Reedy to FB, March 25, 1977.
43. U.S. Congress, Senate Watergate Hearings, *Hughes-Rebozo Investigation*, 21:11461, 11513.
44. Nixon to Rebozo, Nov. 28, 1952, Nixon Archive, Vice-Presidential Papers, Los Angeles Federal Achives and Records Center, Laguna Nigel, Calif.; *Miami News* clipping, Marro file.
45. Nixon to Rebozo, Jan. 13, 1956, Nixon Archive, Vice-Presidential Papers, Laguna Nigel, Calif.
46. Nixon to Rebozo, Sept. 8, 1956, Jan. 22, 1958, Nixon Archive, Vice-Presidential Papers, Laguna Nigel, Calif.
47. Rebozo to Nixon, Nov. 5, 1957, Nixon Archive, Vice-Presidential Papers, Laguna Nigel, Calif.
48. Senate Watergate Hearings, *Hughes-Rebozo Investigation*, 24:11505–6.
49. Dan Rather to FB, Aug. 30, 1975.
50. Marshall Clough, Jr., to FB, March 28, 1976, telephone interview.
51. Leinster, "Nixon's Friend Bebe," p. 21.
52. Clay Blair, Jr., "Bebe's Search for Machismo," *Boston Globe*, Oct. 4, 1970.
53. Witcover, *The Resurrection of Richard Nixon*, p. 38.
54. "Rebozo and a U.S. Loan: Capitalizing on Friends," *Newsday*, Special Report, part 2, Oct. 6–13, 1971.
55. Robert Greene to FB, March 20, 1977. Nixon was so outraged by the *Newsday* articles on Rebozo that he ordered John Dean to have the IRS institute an audit of Greene's finances, which was done. Dean testified to this in the Senate Watergate Hearings. Members of the *Newsday* staff were blacklisted from White House reporter privileges. See Senate Watergate Hearings, 22:10375.
56. See Martin Waldron, "Nixon's Close Friend Who Is Able to Keep a Secret," *New York Times*, Dec. 23, 1968, p. 34, and the searching and detailed story of Rebozo's rise in "The Story of Bebe Rebozo: The Making of a Millionaire," by six reporters of *Newsday*, part 1 of a six-part series, published as a special report in *Newsday*, Oct. 6–13, 1971. An early article on Rebozo appeared in the *Miami Herald*, Jan. 22, 1955.
57. Witcover, *The Resurrection of Richard Nixon*, p. 212.

XXIV. *Death Wishes*

1. *Public Papers*, (Feb. 4) 1971, p. 110.
2. Adlai Stevenson to Geoffrey Crowther, Jan. 23, 1957, Stevenson, *Papers*, 6:430.
3. *Six Crises*, pp. 131, 142.
4. Phyllis B. Papkins, "Princess Alice," *Los Angeles Times*, Dec. 14, 1975, pt. 5, p. 20.
5. Kearns, *Lyndon Johnson and the American Dream*, p. 164.
6. *RN*, pp. 87–88; *Six Crises*, p. 142.
7. Erskine, "Dick and Pat Nixon," p. 35.
8. John Osborne, "White House Watch: Gabbing with Harlow," *New Republic*, May 13, 1978, p. 13.
9. Mazo, *Richard Nixon*, p. 157.
10. Osborne, "White House Watch: Gabbing with Harlow," p. 14.
11. *RN*, p. 164; *Six Crises*, pp. 132–33.
12. Dr. Walter Tkach, *New York Times*, Sept. 14, 1973, p. 41.

13. *Six Crises*, p. 135.
14. *RN*, p. 166.
15. *Six Crises*, pp. 141, 145.
16. Bassett Diary, Feb. 24, 1954, p. 12.
17. *Six Crises*, pp. 149, 143–44.
18. Hughes, *Ordeal of Power*, pp. 317, 176.
19. *Six Crises*, p. 162.
20. Ibid., p. 152.
21. Osborne, "White House Watch, Gabbing with Harlow," p. 14.
22. *Six Crises*, p. 159.
23. Halberstam, *The Powers That Be*, p. 334; Leonard Hall to FB, Aug. 29, 1975.
24. Hughes, *Ordeal of Power*, p. 173. He denied that he had said Nixon wasn't "presidential timber," but conceded he may have said he was not ready for the presidency (*Los Angeles Times*, Dec. 2, 1962).
25. Costello, *The Facts About Nixon*, p. 230.

26. Mazo, quoting an anonymous Nixon friend, *Richard Nixon*, p. 164.
27. Hughes, *Ordeal of Power*, p. 250; Parmet, *Eisenhower*, pp. 171, 418, 526–27.
28. *Six Crises*, pp. 160–61.
29. *RN*, p. 170; Parmet, *Eisenhower*, p. 430.
30. Herbert Mitgang to FB.
31. Rogin and Lottier, "The Inner History of Richard Milhous Nixon," p. 25.
32. Costello, *The Facts About Nixon*, p. 152.
33. Hughes, *Ordeal of Power*, p. 232.
34. Quoted in the *Fresno* (California) *Bee*, Feb. 22, 1956, Truman Library clipping file.
35. *Six Crises*, p. 165; Costello, *The Facts About Nixon*, p. 146; Mazo, *Richard Nixon*, p. 165.
36. Costello, *The Facts About Nixon*, p. 148.
37. *RN*, p. 171.
38. Parmet, *Eisenhower*, p. 452.
39. Few knew that an embarrassment of great potential damage to Nixon had become acute that same week. Murray Chotiner, Nixon's lawyer and campaign manager, had been accused by a Senate subcommittee of influence peddling in military procurement, and there were charges that he had defended an unsavory criminal accused of being involved in the white-slave traffic. He was issued a subpoena for April 25, but risked a citation for contempt by failing to appear. Thus he discreetly kept himself out of the newspapers until Nixon was safely in Eisenhower's good graces as the candidate for 1956. Nixon publicly severed connections with Chotiner during this period, but privately kept in touch, and when he became president he brought him back to the White House as a consultant. See Costello, *The Facts About Nixon*, p. 148; Mazo, *Richard Nixon*, p. 168.
40. *RN*, p. 167.
41. Ibid., p. 173.
42. Hughes, *Ordeal of Power*, p. 250.
43. *Six Crises*, p. 168.
44. Parmet, *Eisenhower*, p. 432.
45. Costello, *The Facts About Nixon*, p. 151.
46. *RN*, p. 176.
47. Bassett to FB, March 27, 1975.
48. *New York Times*, Aug. 24, 1956, pp. 10–11.
49. *RN*, p. 178.
50. Stevenson, *Papers*, 6:316, 306, Nov. 5, 1956, Oct. 27, 1956.
51. *RN*, p. 178.
52. Speech in St. Louis, *Los Angeles Times*, Nov. 3, 1956, p. 2.
53. *RN*, p. 179.
54. Stevenson, *Papers*, 6:324, Nov. 5, 1956.
55. *RN*, p. 180.
56. *Six Crises*, p. 171.
57. Ibid., pp. 175–77.
58. Barry Goldwater, *With No Apologies* (New York, 1979), p. 216.
59. *Six Crises*, p. 321; Osborne, "White House Watch: Gabbing With Harlow," p. 14.
60. Halberstam, *The Powers That Be*, p. 336.
61. *RN*, p. 222.
62. Eisenhower, *Waging Peace*, pp. 602, 652 (italics added).
63. Julie Nixon, "Mamie Eisenhower," *Ladies Home Journal*, June 1977, p. 107.

xxv. *On the Throwing of Rocks*

1. *Andean Air Mail and Peruvian Times*, Lima, May 9, 1958, p. 2.
2. Mazo, *Richard Nixon*, p. 241.
3. *Newsweek*, May 26, 1958, p. 24.
4. *Los Angeles Times*, May 10, 1958, sect. 3, p. 4.
5. M. Rivera-Torres, "Latin American Exile on Nixon's Tour," *New Republic*, June 9, 1958, p. 19; *Six Crises*, pp. 208–9.
6. *Time*, March 26, 1958, pp. 36–37. Eugen Weber estimated that U.S. aid before the Marshall Plan amounted to $17 billion in Europe, and $11 billion after (Weber, *A Modern History of Europe* [New York: W. W. Norton, 1971], p. 1092n).
7. *New York Times*, May 9, 1958, p. 1.
8. *Six Crises*, p. 188.
9. *U.S. News and World Report*, May 9, 1958, p. 44.
10. *Six Crises*, p. 190; "Nixon's Own Story of His Trip," *U.S. News and World Report*, May 30, 1958, p. 8.
11. *Andean Air Mail and Peruvian Times*, Lima, May 16, 1958, p. 2.
12. *Six Crises*, pp. 197–99; Vernon A. Walters, *Silent Missions* (Garden City, N.Y.: Doubleday, 1978), p. 320.
13. Now the Museo San Marcos.
14. Walters, *Silent Missions*, p. 323; Nixon, *Six Crises*, p. 202. Enrique Zeleri, editor of Peru's *Caretas*, informed me in Lima in 1980 that there had been Trotskyites among the student leadership but that the college was relatively conservative. Nixon, he said, was "a natural target" because of his right-wing sympathies. Charles Lummis, of Lima, holds today that the confrontation was Nixon's doing, and was unnecessary.
15. *New York Times*, May 9, 1958, p. 1.
16. For a dramatic picture of Nixon here, see *Life*, May 19, 1958, pp. 20–25.
17. *RN*, p. 188; *Six Crises*, p. 202; Szulc to FB, Sept. 17, 1979.
18. Walters, *Silent Missions*, p. 324; *Six Crises*, pp. 202–3, and *New York Times*, May 9, 1950, p. 1. I am indebted to Szulc and Hartmann for clarifications (Szulc to FB, Sept. 17, 1979; Hartmann to FB, Sept. 28, 1979). Lima newspapers did not describe the event in detail.
19. *Six Crises*, p. 204; *RN*, p. 188.
20. *Andean Air Mail and Peruvian Times*, May 9, 1958, p. 2.
21. *Six Crises*, pp. 204, 209; *Los Angeles Times*, May 19, 1958, p. 12.
22. *Six Crises*, pp. 207, 199.
23. Ibid., p. 213.
24. *Los Angeles Times*, May 10, 1958, sect. 3, p. 4.
25. Walters, *Silent Missions*, pp. 328–29; *Six Crises*, pp. 214–15; *Los Angeles Times*, May 14, 1958, p. 13.
26. Walters, *Silent Missions*, pp. 331–32; *Six Crises*, p. 219; *RN*, p. 190.
27. *Six Crises*, p. 220; Walters, *Silent Missions*, p. 333; *Los Angeles Times*, May 14, 1958, p. 1.
28. *Time*, May 26, 1958, pp. 16–17; *New York Times*, May 14, 15, 1958.
29. *New York Times*, May 15, 1958, p. 28; "Judgments and Prophecies," *Time*, May 26, p. 18; Mazo, *Richard Nixon*, p. 252.
30. Garry Wills, "Hurray for Politicians," *Harper's*, September 1975, p. 49. Wills misdates the

occasion, saying it took place in 1953 instead of 1958.
31. *Time*, May 26, 1958, pp. 16–17.
32. Quoted in *Time*, May 26, 1958, p. 18.
33. *New York Times*, May 18, 1958, sect 4., p. 12B.
34. *The New Republic*, May 26, 1958, p. 10.
35. *Los Angeles Times*, May 15, 1958, p. 1; Eisenhower, *Waging Peace*, p. 519.
36. For Sherman Adams's own defense, see his *First-hand Report* (New York: Harper, 1951).

37. Clark Galloway, "I Saw Nixon Mobbed," *U.S. News and World Report*, May 23, 1958, p. 48; *New York Times*, May 15, 1958, p. 11.
38. *Six Crises*, p. 232–33.
39. Ibid., p. 234.
40. Osborne, *Second Year of the Nixon Watch*, pp. 163–64; Schell, *The Time of Illusion*, p. 128.
41. *RN*, pp. 492–93.
42. Schell, *The Time of Illusion*, p. 130.
43. Ibid., p. 179.

XXVI. *Khrushchev*

1. *Six Crises*, p. 239; *Public Papers*, 1974, p. 630.
2. Bassett to FB, March 27, 1975; and Halberstam, *The Powers That Be*, p. 333.
3. Leonard Hall to FB, Aug. 29, 1975.
4. *Six Crises*, p. 264.
5. Ibid., p. 244.
6. Martin, *Adlai Stevenson and the World*, p. 435.
7. Nikita S. Khrushchev, *Khrushchev Remembers*, edited by Strobe Talbott (New York: Bantam, 1970), p. 398.
8. Humphrey, *Education of a Public Man*, pp. 301–3.
9. Hughes, *Ordeal of Power*, p. 281.
10. Hoopes, *The Devil and John Foster Dulles*, p. 493.
11. In *Six Crises* Nixon went to some effort to conceal this, still another presidential slight, writing that Ike "on the eve of my departure" had told him "he had decided to invite Khrushchev to visit the United States and he authorized me to discuss the trip privately with the Soviet Premier" (pp. 242–43).
12. Parmet, *Eisenhower*, p. 427.
13. *Six Crises*, p. 242.
14. Harold Macmillan, *Riding the Storm, 1956–59* (New York, 1971), p. 608.
15. *Six Crises*, p. 239.
16. Ibid., p. 248.
17. Ibid., p. 250.
18. *RN*, p. 203.
19. *Six Crises*, pp. 236, 258, 265.
20. Ibid., p. 236.
21. *RN*, pp. 207–8.
22. Interview with Henry Trofimenko, then a journalist for a Moscow newspaper, who was present. See also *Six Crises*, p. 254; *Newsweek*, Aug. 13, 1959, p. 15.
23. *Six Crises*, p. 254.
24. Safire, *After the Fall*, pp. 3–4.

25. *Newsweek*, Aug. 3, 1959, p. 15.
26. *New York Times*, July 20, 1959, p. 2; ibid., July 27, 1959, p. 10; *Time*, Aug. 10, 1959, p. 9.
27. *Newsweek*, Aug. 3, 1959, p. 15.
28. Stevenson to William Baggs, Stevenson, *Papers*, 7:360.
29. *Six Crises*, p. 438. The butcher in the market had been persuaded to send a letter to the newspapers describing the incident, and both *Pravda* and *Izvestia* said Nixon had "degraded" a Soviet citizen.
30. *Six Crises*, pp. 262–63.
31. Konrad Kellen, *Khrushchev, a Political Portrait* (New York, 1961), pp. 3, 255. Kellen points out that Khrushchev told only half the story; Pinya was badly beaten by the guards posted outside and was taken back to prison, where he died. The story was written by a Ukrainian author, Volodymyr Vynnychenko, at the turn of the century.
32. Nikita S. Khrushchev, *Khrushchev in America* (New York: Crosscurrents Press, 1960), p. 107.
33. *Six Crises*, p. 287.
34. Speech of Khrushchev in Moscow on his return, Sept. 28, 1959, *Khrushchev in America*, p. 220.
35. Eisenhower, *Waging Peace*, p. 447.
36. *Khrushchev in America*, p. 41.
37. *Six Crises*, p. 282.
38. Ibid., pp. 272–73.
39. Safire (*Before the Fall*, p. 6) says Nixon went there as a lawyer for "John Shaheen's oil companies."
40. Safire, *Before the Fall*, p. 6.
41. *Khrushchev Remembers*, p. 458. Henry Trofimenko has informed me that Khrushchev was actually living outside Moscow at the time.

XXVII. *The Assassination Track*

1. U.S. Senate, Select Committee to Study Governmental Operations with Respect to Intelligence Activities, *Alleged Assassination Plots Involving Foreign Leaders, An Interim Report*, Hearings, 94th Cong., 1st sess. p. 316 (referred to hereafter as the Church Committee Report).
2. Richard Nixon, "Cuba, Castro and John F. Kennedy," p. 298.
3. One of my students confessed that he was consumed with remorse because by accident he had accompanied a friend who took his gun to the home of Siran Sirhan and sold it to him. The gun was shortly used to assassinate Robert Kennedy. Had the student somehow

blocked the sale, he thought, he would have had a decisive impact for good on history. By not blocking it, he had inadvertently had an evil impact. He had been questioned by the FBI, and had been so shaken by his involvement he could not bring himself to put the story to paper.
4. Church Committee Report, p. 71n.
5. Church Committee, Final Report, 4:157–58. This was in a statement sent from San Clemente.
6. Thomas Powers, *The Man Who Kept the Secrets: Richard Helms and the CIA* (New York: Knopf, 1979), Church Committee Report, p. 92.
7. As reported in *Newsweek*, Oct. 2, 1978, p. 62.

8. Dulles, *The Craft of Intelligence*, p. 189 (italics Dulles's).
9. Powers, *The Man Who Kept the Secrets*, pp. 103–9, 111–13, 147, 330; Peter Wyden, *Bay of Pigs, the Untold Story* (New York, 1979), pp. 23–25, 40–41, 109–10, 114–19; Bissell to FB, telephone interview.
10. *Six Crises*, p. 352; Mario Lazo, *Dagger in the Heart* (New York: Funk & Wagnalls, 1968), p. 160. Pawley met with Rubottom, William Wieland, Douglas Dillon, and others in the State Department as well as Allen Dulles. He said to Wieland, reminding him that Castro had taken part in the Communist bid for power in Bogota in 1948, "If you permit Castro to come to power, you are going to have more trouble than you have ever seen in your life" (Lazo, *Dagger in the Heart*, p. 160, quoting from the Report of the Senate Subcommittee on the Judiciary, "The Case of William Wieland," 1962, p. 109).
11. Eisenhower, *Waging Peace*, pp. 520, 521.
12. Nikita S. Khrushchev, *Khrushchev Remembers*, edited by Strobe Talbott (New York: Bantam, 1970), pp. 489–90.
13. *RN*, p. 201.
14. Nixon, "Cuba, Castro and John F. Kennedy," p. 283. Thomas Powers states that General Walters, the linguist who had accompanied Nixon to Latin America, was present, but conceded that Walters does not mention this in his own memoir, *Secret Missions* (Powers, *The Man Who Kept the Secrets*, p. 259).
15. Thomas, *Cuba, the Pursuit of Freedom*, p. 1211n. For Nixon's praise of Batista, see Bonsal, *Cuba, Castro, and the United States*, pp. 13, 171. JFK reminded audiences of this in October 1960.
16. Wyden, *Bay of Pigs*, p. 28.
17. Thomas, *Cuba, the Pursuit of Freedom*, p. 1210.
18. *RN*, p. 202.
19. Wyden, *Bay of Pigs*, p. 27.
20. Nixon, "Cuba, Castro and John F. Kennedy," p. 294.
21. Wyden, *Bay of Pigs*, p. 26.
22. Nixon, "Cuba, Castro and John F. Kennedy," p. 286.
23. Kissinger, *The White House Years*, p. 641.
24. Wyden, *Bay of Pigs*, p. 29.
25. Nelson, *Cuba, the Measure of a Revolution*, p. 31; Bonsal, *Cuba, Castro, and the U.S.*, p. 76. Eisenhower himself broke off diplomatic relations with Trujillo and urged a partial economic blockade (Eisenhower, *Waging Peace*, p. 538). The CIA began shipping arms to Trujillo's enemies, but seems not to have been involved in his assassination (Church Committee Report, pp. 191–214).
26. Boris Goldenberg, *The Cuban Revolution and Latin America* (New York: Praeger, 1965), p. 187; Lynn Darrel Bender, *The Politics of Hostility: Castro's Revolution and U.S. Policy* (Hato Rey, Puerto Rico: Inter-American Universities Press, 1975), p. 6.
27. Nelson, *Cuba, the Measure of a Revolution*, p. 26; Bonsal, *Cuba, Castro, and the U.S.*, pp. 104–8.
28. *Look*, Sept. 23, 1959, pp. 92–98.
29. Szulc, "As Castro Speaks: 'The Wall! The Wall!' " p. 11; Goldenberg, *The Cuban Revolution*, p. 209; Bender, *The Politics of Hostility*, p. 117. By 1979 there were 540,000 Cubans in Miami and 35,000 in Puerto Rico.
30. Szulc, "As Castro Speaks," p. 82; Bonsal,

Cuba, Castro, and the U.S., pp. 129–32.
31. Church Committee Report, p. 92.
32. Nixon, "Cuba, Castro and John F. Kennedy," p. 288; Wyden, *Bay of Pigs*, pp. 19–21.
33. Ike had learned from his trip to Latin America in February 1960 that he could not get cooperation in economic sanctions against Cuba unless he took some action first against the hated Trujillo (Eisenhower, *Waging Peace*, p. 538). See Eisenhower's statement of Jan. 26, 1960, "The U.S. government adheres strictly to the policy of non-intervention in the domestic affairs of other countries . . ." (Bonsal, *Cuba, Castro, and the U.S.*, p. 122).
34. Reprinted in *Six Crises*, Appendix, p. 439.
35. National Security Meeting, March 10, 1960. See Wyden, *Bay of Pigs*, p. 24.
36. *RN*, p. 203; *Six Crises*, p. 352.
37. Church Committee Report, p. 93 (from the minutes of the meeting). The Eisenhower reference to the "black hole of Calcutta" was to an episode in India in 1756, when Siraj-ud-Daula captured the English settlement in Calcutta and imprisoned between sixty-five and one hundred fifty English prisoners in a "hole" eighteen feet by fourteen feet ten inches. After twenty-four hours only twenty-one emerged alive.
38. Church Committee Report, p. 93 (italics were added by the committee).
39. Ibid., p. 318.
40. As Thomas Powers wrote, "the Dulles brothers did not want to overthrow Sukarno exactly, just force him to suppress the PKI, send the Russians packing and get on the American team" (Powers, *The Man Who Kept the Secrets*, p. 89). Although one CIA pilot, Allen Laurence Pope, had been shot down in a B-26 after accidentally bombing a church and killing most of the people in it, Eisenhower successfully denied any CIA involvement, and the press, notoriously flaccid in the Eisenhower years, did not explore the fiasco. This may have been one of the reasons Nixon felt as president that he could gull reporters concerning the secret bombing of Cambodia.
41. Schlesinger, *Robert F. Kennedy*, p. 454.
42. At least not until 1979, with the murder of Hafizullah Amin in Afghanistan.
43. McMillan, *Marina and Lee*, p. 286.
44. Wyden, *Bay of Pigs*, p. 23.
45. Church Committee Report, p. 92 (italics are provided by the committee).
46. Ibid., p. 57. American Ambassador Arthur Gardner had suggested to Batista, when Castro was still in the Sierra Maestra, that someone in the CIA be used to assassinate him. Batista had replied, "No. No. We couldn't do that. We're Cubans." Gardner, astonishingly, related this to Hugh Thomas (see *Cuba, the Pursuit of Freedom*, p. 947). Bonsal described with distaste Gardner's "unnecessarily florid and spectacular cordiality" to Batista (Bonsal, *Cuba, Castro, and the U.S.*, p. 131).
47. Gen. Robert E. Cushman to FB, March 1, 1978.
48. Nixon, "Cuba, Castro and John F. Kennedy," p. 289. For Nixon's and Dulles's combined efforts to persuade Eisenhower to proceed with the anti-Castro operations, see *Waging Peace*.
49. Dulles, in *The Craft of Intelligence*, writes disapprovingly of the Russian KGB, which, he said, was guilty of planned assassination (pp.

88, 169, 197–98).
50. Haldeman, *Ends of Power*, pp. 38–39.
51. Bissell to FB, telephone interview.
52. Wyden, *Bay of Pigs*, pp. 23–24; Church Committee Report, p. 91.
53. Hunt, *Give Us This Day*, p. 38; Bissell to FB.
54. Church Committee Report, p. 16. CIA planning in the assassination of Trujillo, Diem, and later when Nixon was president, Allende, are described at length in the Church Committee hearings. Whether Nixon, who often attended NSC meetings, was present at the meeting of Aug. 18, 1960, has not been made public. According to Dr. Jack B. Pfieffer, CIA historian of the Bay of Pigs, Nixon attended two dozen meetings, including several NSC meetings, concerned with the evolution of the U.S. government's anti-Castro effort culminating in the Bay of Pigs (Pfieffer to FB, Feb. 27, 1978).
55. Church Committee Report, p. 263; Schlesinger, *Robert F. Kennedy*, p. 486.
56. Church Committee Final Report, 4:157–58.
57. Church Committee Report, pp. 150, 277; Wyden, *Bay of Pigs*, p. 24.
58. Church Committee Report, p. 316.
59. See Powers's excellent biography, *The Man Who Kept the Secrets*.
60. As quoted in *Newsweek*, Oct. 2, 1979, p. 62.
61. Cushman to Wyden, as reported in Wyden, *Bay of Pigs*, p. 29; Bissell to FB; Cushman to FB.
62. Bissell to FB; Powers, *The Man Who Kept the Secrets*, p. 103. The plan Eisenhower had okayed in the National Security Council meeting of March 10, 1960, was much more modest; it envisaged the training by CIA agents of twenty-five Cuban exiles, who would then train other exiles to plan for Castro's overthrow.
63. Powers, *The Man Who Kept the Secrets*, pp. 86–87.
64. Ibid., p. 88; Goldenberg, *The Cuban Revolution*, p. 347.
65. Powers, *The Man Who Kept the Secrets*, p. 106.
66. See the October 1960 issue. *The Nation*, on November 19, drawing on this material, raised the question for a larger audience, and this stimulated the *New York Times* to send a reporter to Guatemala and break the story on Jan. 10, 1961. Dulles had managed to stop publication of a story in the *Miami Herald* in August 1960 describing how Cuban exiles were being trained in the Miami area, this in direct violation of the Neutrality Act (see Wyden, *Bay of Pigs*, pp. 45–46).
67. Wyden, *Bay of Pigs*, pp. 29–32; Bissell to FB.
68. Wyden, *Bay of Pigs*, p. 68.
69. Ibid., pp. 29–30; Cushman to FB.
70. Dr. Jack Pfeiffer, CIA historian, to FB, Feb. 27, 1978.
71. Wyden, *Bay of Pigs*, p. 68.
72. Earlier in the year Ernest Hemingway had said, "I just hope to Christ the United States doesn't cut the sugar quota. That would really tear it. It will make Cuba a gift to the Russians" (Bonsal, *Cuba, Castro, and the U.S.*, p. 151).
73. Suarez, *Cuba, Castro and Communism*, p. 111; W. Hyland and R. W. Shryock, *The Fall of Khruschev* (New York: Funk & Wagnalls), p. 27; Keith Wheeler, "Communism's Takeover in Castro's Cuba," *Life*, July 18, 1960, pp. 16–18.

74. Goldenberg, *The Cuban Revolution*, p. 195; Theodore Draper, *Castroism, Theory and Practice* (New York, 1969), p. 85; Bender, *The Politics of Hostility*, p. 101.
75. Wheeler, "Communism's Takeover in Castro's Cuba," pp. 16–18.
76. *Life*, Oct. 13, 1960, pp. 28–29.
77. Eisenhower, *Waging Peace*, pp. 444, 438, 447.
78. *Life*, Oct. 13, 1960, pp. 28–29; *Time*, Oct. 10, 1960.
79. A decent reluctance in the CIA to go that route resulted first in somewhat juvenile nonlethal plans to destroy "the Castro image." The CIA's Technical Services worked with a disorienting chemical, kin to LSD, which was to be sprayed in Castro's broadcasting studio; cigars were impregnated with a similar substance. A strong depilatory, which it was hoped would make Castro's famous beard fall out, was prepared, to be put on his shoes some night when he left them outside a hotel door for shining. By August, however, Technical Services had become truly murderous, preparing cigars contaminated with botulinium toxin "so potent a person would die after putting one in his mouth." The poisoned cigars for Castro, finally ready in October, were not delivered until Feb. 13, 1961; after that nothing more was heard of them (Church Committee Report, pp. 13–29, 4).
80. Prouty went public with the story after a bitter attack by Richard Helms on CBS correspondent Daniel Schorr (see Schorr, *Clearing the Air*, p. 148).
81. Paul Maskil, "CIA Sent Bedmate to Kill Castro in 1960," *New York Daily News*, Jan. 13, 1976. As Arthur Schlesinger, Jr., who researched this story with care, reported, Sturgis first supported the girl's account. Later "they fell out" (Schlesinger, *Robert F. Kennedy*, pp. 482, 974).
82. Church Committee Report, pp. 74, 75n; Schlesinger, *Robert F. Kennedy*, p. 482. Castro had closed the casinos in January 1959; they were temporarily open to foreign tourists in February, but closed again in September 1961 (Church Committee Report, p. 74n).
83. In 1959 Maheu was an obscure but imaginative ex-FBI agent who had set up his own investigative agency in Washington. At the height of his influence he told one friend, "you could have access to everyone, including the Pope" (Senate Watergate Hearings, 24:11576). At this point he had done some useful work for the CIA, and was known for his willingness to take on jobs too dirty or too sensitive for the agency (Church Committee Report, p. 77).
84. Church Committee Report, p. 367; Wyden, *Bay of Pigs*, p. 41; Church Committee Report, p. 85n. There has since been speculation that Castro wanted him freed, so that his drugs might continue to flow through Cuba to the United States, thereby earning foreign exchange, and that Trafficante acted as a double agent in the assassination plans. Which might explain, as Schlesinger has suggested in his ironic discussion of the subject, why "Castro survived so comfortably the ministrations of the CIA" (Schlesinger, *Robert F. Kennedy*, p. 484).
85. Church Committee Report, p. 81.
86. Ibid., p. 79, quoting a memo from Hoover to the DCI, Oct. 18, 1960; ibid., p. 82.

87. Wyden, *Bay of Pigs*, p. 110; Schorr, *Clearing the Air*, p. 154. A bizarre accompaniment to this story involved Judith Campbell (Exner), a friend of both Giancana and Rosselli, who was introduced to John F. Kennedy by Frank Sinatra and for a time claimed to be his special friend. White House logs showed seventy telephone calls from her to the young president before J. Edgar Hoover moved in to stop the friendship in February 1962 (Schlesinger, *Robert F. Kennedy*, pp. 494–95; Wyden, *Bay of Pigs*, p. 44).

88. Nixon, *Speeches*, 1960, p. 74.

89. *Six Crises*, pp. 353–54; Wyden, *Bay of Pigs*, p. 67n; *New York Times*, July 24, 1960.

90. *The Nation* picked up Ronald Hilton's October account in the *Hispanic-American Review* [13, no. 10 (October 1960): 693], and asked in an editorial, "Are We Training Cuban Guerillas?" which prompted the *Times* to send Paul P. Kennedy into the area. His story was published over Allen Dulles's protests on Jan. 10, 1961. Bonsal said Castro knew about the Cuban exiles in Guatemala within days of their arrival (*Cuba, Castro, and the U.S.*, p. 135).

91. *Speeches of Senator John Kennedy*, p. 1168, quoted in Bonsal, *Cuba, Castro, and the U.S.*, p. 171.

92. American Legion Convention at Miami, in *Six Crises*, p. 353.

93. After *Six Crises* appeared, with Nixon's charge that Kennedy had betrayed Eisenhower's confidence, Kennedy issued a denial, March 20, 1962, saying Dulles had confided in him only "operations relating to Cuba," and not the invasion plans (*Six Crises*, p. 354n). Dulles backed up Kennedy, according to Wyden, and said there had been an "honest misunderstanding" by Nixon (Wyden, *Bay of Pigs*, p. 67n). Wyden also relates that after the incident blew over, Kennedy said to Goodwin, "If I win this election, I won it. If I lose, you lost it." Later, just before the Bay of Pigs, Kennedy said to Goodwin, "Well, Dick, we're about to put your Cuban policy into action" (Wyden, *Bay of Pigs*, p. 66n). Nixon continued to insist that Kennedy had indeed been briefed; it had been confirmed, he said, by a telegram from Fred Seaton (*Six Crises*, pp. 354–55).

94. *Six Crises*, pp. 354–55.

95. *RN*, p. 221.

96. *Six Crises*, pp. 356–57; *RN*, p. 221.

97. Nixon, "Cuba, Castro and John F. Kennedy," p. 286.

98. Ibid., p. 291.

99. Castro, two weeks before the invasion, imprisoned two hundred thousand Cubans he suspected of being disloyal. This effectively eliminated the Cuban opposition, who might have come to the aid of the exiles in the invasion force.

XXVIII. *Nixon and Kennedy*

1. Kennedy to John Galbraith, quoted in David Halberstam, "Press and Prejudice," *Esquire*, 86, 1974, p. 114.

2. White, *The Making of the President, 1960*, p. 324.

3. See especially *Life*, Oct. 30, 1960, p. 36.

4. Alsop, *Nixon and Rockefeller*, p. 179.

5. White, *The Making of the President, 1960*, p. 127. TRB wrote, "The wonder is not that a Catholic was elected by a close vote, but that he was elected at all" (*New Republic*, Nov. 21, 1960).

6. *RN*, p. 253.

7. U.S. Senate, *Speeches, Remarks, Press Conferences and Study Papers of Vice President Richard M. Nixon, August 1 through November 7, 1960*, 87th Cong., 1st sess., Senate Report no. 994, pt. 2: 830, 839, 949.

8. Speech accepting the nomination, July 28, 1960, in *Six Crises*, p. 442; White, *The Making of the President, 1960*, p. 367.

9. Schlesinger, *Robert F. Kennedy and His Times*, p. 219.

10. Walter Cronkite, in a TV interview with Nixon on Sept. 12, 1960, reminded Nixon of this, and gave the statement national publicity.

11. Kornitzer, "My Sons, Two . . . Candid Interviews," pp. 28–29.

12. As reported by Edward Nixon to Floyd Wildermuth, a cousin, Cal. State archives no. 983, p. 22.

13. Barry Goldwater said he sent evidence of vote fraud in West Virginia to Attorney-General William Rogers but the Republican administration never pursued it (Goldwater, *With No Apologies* [New York: Berkley, 1980], p. 106).

14. Barber, *Presidential Character*, p. 302.

15. See Whalen, *The Founding Father*.

16. Kennedy, *Speeches*, Sept. 29, 1960, p. 109; Whalen, *The Founding Father*, p. 395.

17. Diana Trilling, "The Jaguar and the Panther," *London Times Literary Supplement*, Nov. 22, 1977, p. 1.

18. Nixon, *Speeches*, 1960, Reno airport, Aug. 2, 1960, p. 1126.

19. Bruce Lee, *John F. Kennedy: Boyhood to White House* (Philadelphia: Saunders, 1964), p. 104.

20. *Newsweek*, Feb. 22, 1960, p. 28.

21. Ibid., Oct. 17, 1960, p. 32.

22. *New York Times*, Nov. 18, 1969, p. 5.

23. *Time*, Feb. 29, 1960.

24. William Costello, "Nixon on the Eve, a Candidate in Search of an Identity," *New Republic*, Nov. 7, 1960, p. 17; *Newsweek*, Oct. 10, 1960, p. 24; Richard L. Strout, *TRB: Views and Perspectives on the Presidency* (New York: Macmillan, 1979), p. 342.

25. *Los Angeles Times*, Sept. 29, 1960.

26. Ibid., June 22, 1960.

27. Mary McGrory, "The Perfectionist and the Press," in *As We Knew Adlai*, p. 177.

28. *U.S. News and World Report*, May 16, 1960, pp. 98–106.

29. *The Reporter*, Sept. 29, 1960, p. 18.

30. CBS retrospective, Nov. 4, 1960, in Kennedy, *Speeches, 1960*, p. 358.

31. Joseph Alsop to Paul Miller, Oct. 6, 1960, Alsop Papers, Library of Congress; Joseph Alsop to David Barrett, Nov. 8, 1960, Alsop Papers, Library of Congress.

32. Kennedy, *Speeches*, Alexandria, Va., Aug. 24, 1960, p. 45; *Time*, Oct. 3, 1960, p. 17.

33. Kennedy, *Speeches*, Oct. 29, 1960, Philadelphia.

34. Speeches in Missouri, Tennessee, and Texas,

Clipping file, Truman Library.
35. Nixon, *Speeches, 1960,* Long Beach, California, October 12, p. 544.
36. Schlesinger, *Robert F. Kennedy,* pp. 206–11.
37. Goldwater, *With No Apologies,* p. 119.
38. TRB, *The New Republic,* Aug. 8, 1960, p. 2; ibid., Nov. 7, 1960, p. 2.
39. *Congressional Record,* 86th Cong., 1st sess., 105, 1959, pt. 3: 3976.
40. White, *Breach of Faith,* p. 92.
41. Halberstam, *The Powers That Be,* p. 335; Rather and Gates, *The Palace Guard,* p. 125.
42. Halberstam, *The Powers That Be,* p. 335.
43. Ibid., p. 332; Bassett to FB.
44. Haldeman, *Ends of Power,* p. 75.
45. *Six Crises,* p. 337.
46. *New Republic,* Oct. 10, 1960, p. 2.
47. *Six Crises,* p. 338.
48. Nixon, *Speeches, 1960,* Sept. 26, 1960, p. 75.
49. Fromsen to FB, 1979.
50. Kennedy, *Speeches,* Sharon, Pennsylvania, Oct. 15, 1960, p. 596.
51. *Six Crises,* pp. 63, 346.
52. Nixon, *Speeches,* p. 277.
53. Ibid., p. 278.
54. Goldwater, *With No Apologies,* p. 125.
55. *New Republic,* Nov. 7, 1960.
56. *The Reporter,* Oct. 27, 1960, p. 18.
57. White, *The Making of the President, 1960,* p. 339.
58. Nixon, *Speeches,* Rochester, New York, Nov. 1, 1960, p. 945; White, *The Making of the President, 1960,* p. 342.
59. TRB, *New Republic,* May 30, 1960.
60. Nathaniel George, Cal. State archives no. 862; *Six Crises,* p. 443.

61. Nixon, *Speeches,* second debate, p. 150.
62. Bassett to FB, March 27, 1975.
63. White, *The Making of the President, 1960,* pp. 362–64; William Robert Miller, *Martin Luther King, Jr.* (New York: Avon, 1969), pp. 111–13.
64. *Six Crises,* pp. 362–63.
65. White, *The Making of the President, 1960,* p. 363.
66. *Six Crises,* pp. 390–91.
67. Richard M. Scammon, "How the Negroes Voted," *New Republic,* Nov. 21, 1960; White, *The Making of the President, 1960,* p. 363; Harry Golden, *Mr. Kennedy and the Negroes* (New York: World, 1964), p. 70. Later in 1968, when Martin Luther King was murdered and Nixon was persuaded by his staff to attend the funeral, he complained that his attendance was "a serious mistake that almost cost us the South" (Whalen, *Catch the Falling Flag,* p. 149).
68. *Six Crises,* p. 403.
69. Ibid., p. 389.
70. Ibid., p. 390.
71. James Bassett to FB; Wilma Bassett to FB, March 27, 1975.
72. *Six Crises,* p. 407.
73. Ibid., p. 413.
74. Don McLeod, "Did the Democrats Steal It in 1960?" *New York Post,* July 12, 1973, quoted in Schlesinger, *Robert F. Kennedy,* p. 220.
75. Eisenhower, *Waging Peace,* p. 602.
76. de Toledano to FB.
77. *RN,* p. 227.
78. Ibid., pp. 227–28.

XXIX. *A Problem with Donald*

1. James R. Phelan, "The Nixon Family and the Hughes Loan," *The Reporter,* Aug. 16, 1962, p. 20ff.
2. Dietrich and Thomas, *Howard, the Amazing Mr. Hughes,* pp. 282–83; Anderson, *Confessions of a Muckraker,* p. 331n.
3. Dietrich and Thomas, *Howard,* pp. 283–84.
4. Ibid., p. 286.
5. Harry A. Schuyler, Cal. State archives no. 997, p. 15; Harold A. McCabe, Cal. State archives no. 962, p. 18.
6. Phelan, "The Nixon Family and the Hughes Loan," p. 24; Anderson, *Confessions of a Muckraker,* p. 332.
7. *New York Times,* Jan. 24, 1972, 24:1.
8. Hill, *Dancing Bear,* p. 175.
9. Phelan, "The Nixon Family and the Hughes Loan," p. 20ff.
10. *Six Crises,* p. 398.
11. Ibid.

12. *Los Angeles Times,* Oct. 2, 1962; *RN,* pp. 242–43.
13. Dietrich talked to Drew Pearson and Jack Anderson in 1972. His published account appeared in *Howard,* pp. 283–86, in 1976.
14. *Los Angeles Times,* Nov. 6, 1962.
15. Pat Brown to FB, July 9, 1980.
16. *RN,* p. 243.
17. *Los Angeles Times,* Aug. 27, 1962.
18. Ibid., Oct. 6, 1962.
19. *Newsweek,* Oct. 29, 1962, p. 19.
20. Tom Braden to FB, March 2, 1978.
21. Senate Watergate Hearings, 21:10070.
22. Ibid., 20:9599, 9601; 21:9700–2; 10119, 10120; 24:11627–29, 11643, 11648, 11676. For Donald Nixon's testimony see ibid., 22:10665–732. See also *Newsweek,* Aug. 4, 1980.
23. *RN,* p. 1003.

XXX. *The Drubbing*

1. "Will It Be Brown or Nixon," *Newsweek,* Oct. 29, 1962.
2. *RN,* pp. 231–32.
3. Ibid., p. 236.
4. Earl Mazo, "A Family's Comeback. The Nixons Now," *Good Housekeeping,* March 1962, p. 71.
5. *Six Crises,* p. xi.
6. William Costello, "Nixon on the Eve, Candidate in Search of an Identity," *New Republic,*

7, 1960, p. 17.
7. *Six Crises,* p. 70.
8. Ibid., p. xiv.
9. *RN,* p. 564.
10. John Corry, "Editor Without Panache," *New York Times,* Oct. 16, 1975, p. 37.
11. Wicker, *New York Times Book Review,* April 1, 1962.
12. *National Review,* May 22, 1962, p. 372.
13. *New Republic,* April 9, 1962, p. 23.

14. Stephen Hess to FB, March 1, 1978.
15. Spalding, *The Nixon Nobody Knows*, p. 420.
16. Mazo, "A Family's Comeback. The Nixons Now," p. 71.
17. *Los Angeles Times*, June 16, 1961.
18. Carey McWilliams, "Has Success Spoiled Dick Nixon?" *The Nation*, June 2, 1962, p. 493.
19. Hess to FB, March 1, 1978.
20. David, *Lonely Lady at San Clemente*, p. 122.
21. Halberstam, *The Powers That Be*, p. 344. Carey McWilliams in *The Nation* (June 2, 1962, p. 493) said Trousdale had quoted the figure of $125,000. His estimate that the house was actually worth $300,000 was too high. The Nixons sold it in July 1963 for $183,000. Nancy Manella, who researched the story for "60 Minutes," reported that the internal revenue stamps on the deed indicated a purchase price of $35,000. Willard J. Lewis, the real estate dealer, refused to quote a figure for the sale, she said (Manella to FB, June 26, 1979).
22. *Los Angeles Times*, Sept. 28, 1961, p. 8.
23. U.S. Congress, House, Committee on the Judiciary, *Final Report on Impeachment* (New York: New York Times, Bantam Books, 1973), pp. 316–17.
24. *Los Angeles Times*, Jan. 7, 1961.
25. *RN*, p. 237.
26. William Steif, "Richard Nixon on the Knife's Edge," *New Republic*, Aug. 7, 1961, p. 10.
27. Samuel Goldwyn, Jr., to FB, July 1, 1975.
28. *Los Angeles Times*, Feb. 21, 1961.
29. David, *Lonely Lady at San Clemente*.
30. Adela Rogers St. Johns to FB, March 7, 1974.
31. *RN*, p. 239.
32. Carl Greenberg, "Chotiner Looks at Nixon's Future," *Los Angeles Times*, November 25, 1962, p. G1; *Los Angeles Times*, Oct. 2, 1962.
33. Finch to FB, March 1, 1977; Bassett to FB, March 27, 1975.
34. *RN*, p. 239.
35. *Los Angeles Times*, Sept. 20, 1962.
36. Halberstam, *The Powers That Be*, p. 346.
37. *RN*, p. 239.
38. *Los Angeles Times*, Feb. 11, 1968; Edmondson and Cohen, *Women of Watergate*, p. 221.
39. *RN*, p. 237.
40. Ibid., p. 240.
41. *Los Angeles Times*, Feb. 21, 1969.
42. Mazo, "A Family's Comeback. The Nixons Now," p. 71ff.
43. *RN*, p. 240.
44. Bergholz to FB, July 1, 1980.
45. Wicker, "Nixon Starts Over—Alone," p. 106.
46. *Los Angeles Times*, Oct. 17, 1962.
47. Ibid.
48. *Newsweek*, Jan. 29, 1962, p. 19.
49. *RN*, p. 241.
50. Chotiner moved into an office in the White House after Nixon became president. His services were largely secret. Their nature can be suggested by one story: Robert Vesco, accused of massive fraud by the Securities and Exchange Commission, told Walter Cronkite

that when he offered Nixon a campaign contribution of $250,000, Chotiner specified that it be paid in cash (*Newsweek*, April 15, 1974, pp. 33–35). John Ehrlichman referred to "secret Chotiner fund" in his scribbled note of April 27, 1973 (reproduced in House Judiciary Committee Hearings, 93rd Cong., 2d sess., *Statement of Information*, Appendix III, May-June 1974, p. 247). Chotiner died in 1974 as a result of an automobile accident near his home. His car was run into by a maintenance man driving a CIA truck. Chotiner's son, Kenneth, was satisfied after extensive investigation that there was no foul play involved (Kenneth Chotiner to FB, Feb. 18, 1978).
51. Rather and Gates, *The Palace Guard*, p. 118.
52. Brown to FB, July 9, 1980.
53. Greenberg, "Chotiner Looks at Nixon's Future," p. G1.
54. *Los Angeles Times*, Oct. 15, 1962; Brown to FB, July 9, 1980.
55. *Los Angeles Times*, Oct. 8, 1962.
56. Hill, *Dancing Bear*, pp. 174–75.
57. *Los Angeles Times*, Sept. 16, Oct. 19, 1962.
58. Lou Cannon to FB, April 28, 1980.
59. Hill, *Dancing Bear*, p. 173.
60. *Los Angeles Times*, Oct. 1, 1962; Stephen Hess to FB, March 1, 1978.
61. *Los Angeles Times*, Oct. 19, 1962.
62. Wicker, "Nixon Starts Over—Alone," p. 106.
63. *Los Angeles Times*, Dec. 7, 1962.
64. Steif, "Nixon on the Knife's Edge," pp. 10–11; Wicker, "Nixon Starts Over—Alone," p. 106.
65. Bassett to FB, March 27, 1975.
66. Halberstam, *The Powers That Be*, p. 346.
67. William Steif, "Nixon's Uphill Campaign," *New Republic*, Feb. 26, 1962, p. 20.
68. *Los Angeles Times*, Oct. 9, 1962.
69. "Will It Be Brown or Nixon?" *Newsweek*, Oct. 29, 1962.
70. *Los Angeles Times*, Oct. 3, 1962.
71. Witcover, *The Resurrection of Richard Nixon*, p. 31.
72. *Newsweek*, Oct. 29, 1962, p. 23.
73. *Los Angeles Times*, Nov. 6, 1962.
74. Ibid., Nov. 1, 1962.
75. Ibid., Oct. 25, 1962. It was not known until the publication of Robert Kennedy's *Thirteen Days* that Kennedy's brother had made an implicit promise indirectly to Khrushchev that the missiles, long considered obsolete in any case, would indeed be pulled out of Turkey. Kennedy had ordered it before the crisis, but it had not been implemented.
76. *RN*, p. 244; *Los Angeles Times*, Oct. 28, 1960.
77. Hill, *Dancing Bear*, p. 164.
78. Rather and Gates, *The Palace Guard*, p. 129.
79. *Los Angeles Times*, Nov. 8, 1962.
80. Ibid.; Hill, *Dancing Bear*, pp. 274–79; Witcover, *The Resurrection of Richard Nixon*, pp. 21–22. David, in *Lonely Lady at San Clemente*, uses the word "ass" rather than "behind."
81. *RN*, p. 246.

XXXI. *The Private Man*

1. U.S. Supreme Court, *Reports*, 17:1063, *Time v. Hill* 385 U.S. 374 (1966).
2. Haldeman, *Ends of Power*, p. 60.
3. Senate Watergate Hearings, 22:10368–475; Robert Greene to FB, March 30, 1977.
4. Nixon did not mention the case in his mem-

oirs. See *Time v. Hill* (385 U.S. 374), U.S. Supreme Court *Reports*, 17:1063, 468–74; Witcover, *The Resurrection of Richard Nixon*, p. 127ff; Philip B. Kurland, "The Private I: Some Reflections on Privacy and the Constitution," *University of Chicago Magazine*,

Autumn 1976, p. 7ff. Brandeis had argued for the right to be let alone in a 1928 dissent when the majority of the Court held that wiretapping was legal. Brandeis came down vigorously against it, and later his view was adopted by the Court.

5. *Six Crises*, p. 455.
6. Woodward and Bernstein, *The Final Days*, pp. 165–66.
7. *Newsweek*, May 24, 1976, p. 13.
8. *Washington Post*, "The Fall of the President," Aug. 9, 1974, p. 101.
9. David, *Lonely Lady at San Clemente*, pp. 89, 186.
10. Richard Bergholz to FB, July 1, 1980.
11. David, *Lonely Lady at San Clemente*, p. 191.
12. Jack Anderson to FB, April 19, 1975.
13. Adela Rogers St. Johns to FB, March 7, 1975.
14. Ralph de Toledano to FB, Aug. 28, 1975.
15. James Bassett to FB, March 27, 1975.
16. Bryant, *Dog Days at the White House*, p. 267.
17. Breslin, *How the Good Guys Finally Won: Notes from an Impeachment Summer*, pp. 114–15.
18. David, *Lonely Lady at San Clemente*, pp. 193–94.
19. Woodward and Bernstein, *The Final Days*, p. 197.
20. Spalding, *The Nixon Nobody Knows*, p. 446.
21. Robert Finch to FB, March 1, 1977. Rebozo testified in the Senate Watergate Hearings that he was not logged in (*Hughes-Rebozo Investigation*, 21:10064).
22. Helen McCain Smith, "Ordeal! Pat Nixon's Final Days in the White House," p. 127.
23. Bryant, *Dog Days at the White House*, p. 249.
24. Christine Kirk and Steve Dunleavy, "Angry Nixons Blame the Woodward and Bernstein Book for Pat's Stroke," *The Star*, Aug. 3, 1976, p. 9. Julie said, "That book did contribute to the stroke, I'm sure" (quoted in Anna Quindlen, "Julie Eisenhower's Soft Selling of Her Book—and Herself," *New York Times*, June 19, 1977, p. 44).
25. Witcover, *The Resurrection of Richard Nixon*, p. 19.
26. *RN*, p. 347; Witcover, *The Resurrection of Richard Nixon*, p. 39; *The Breaking of a President*, p. 509.
27. Jessamyn West to FB, Sept. 29, 1976.
28. Haldeman, *Ends of Power*, p. 265. Watergate investigators requested ten conversations they believed to be recorded on the White House taping system. Some had not been recorded. Apparently some care had been taken to see that it was not working. These may have included conversations with Rebozo (Paul R. Michel, Watergate Special Prosecution Force Memorandum, Oct. 16, 1975, National Archives, Record Group 460).
29. Rebozo testimony, Senate Watergate Hearings, *Hughes-Rebozo Investigation*, 21:10070. Rebozo said, "I wouldn't be logged in if I just went over for dinner." Scott Armstrong who saw the White House logs informs me this was true only in the last year Nixon was in office.
30. *RN*, pp. 739–41. Manolo and Fina Sanchez were Cuban refugees who had been with the Nixons since 1961 as butler and maid.
31. *The Breaking of a President*, p. 512.
32. *RN*, pp. 292–93.
33. Ibid., p. 293.
34. Price, *With Nixon*, p. 48; William Shawcross, *Sideshow: Kissinger, Nixon, and the Destruction of Cambodia* (New York: Simon & Schuster, 1979), p. 142; Morris, *Uncertain Greatness*, p. 147.

35. *RN*, p. 627.
36. Ibid., p. 740.
37. *The Breaking of a President*, p. 510.
38. *RN*, p. 836.
39. Senate Watergate Hearings, *Hughes-Rebozo Investigation*, 21:10062.
40. *Newsday* researchers found that by October 1971 Nixon had spent seventy-one days at the Florida White House. About half of the time, they discovered, Nixon was on Abplanalp's island, Grand Cay, to which he helicoptered with Rebozo. "But rarely, perhaps only once or twice, has he been joined on Grand Cay by his wife or daughters" ("The Florida of Richard Nixon," Part 6, *Newsday*, Oct. 13, 1971, p. 37R).
41. Witcover, *The Resurrection of Richard Nixon*, p. 38; Leinster, "Nixon's Friend Bebe," p. 20; Hillings to Nancy Dickerson, *Among Those Present*, p. 231.
42. Safire, *Before the Fall*, p. 604.
43. Shawcross, *Sideshow*, p. 142; *RN*, p. 740.
44. Helen McCain Smith, "Ordeal! Pat's Final Days in the White House," p. 128.
45. Finch to FB, March 1, 1977.
46. Fleming, *Los Angeles Times West*, Dec. 8, 1968, p. 66.
47. Armstrong to FB, April 15, 1980.
48. Safire, *Before the Fall*, p. 614.
49. Mellenhoff, *Despoilers of Democracy*, p. 349.
50. Morris, *Uncertain Greatness*, p. 156.
51. Bob Woodward, "Ex-Official Says He Was Told to 'Prove' Jack Anderson Had a Homosexual Affair," *Washington Post*, and *Los Angeles Times*, Oct. 13, 1975. Stewart, an investigator for the Pentagon, refused to take part in the charade.
52. *Newsweek*, April 24, 1974, p. 34. There is some evidence that Rebozo gave Mrs. Lucke $7000 in stocks (Michel, Watergate Memorandum, p. 37).
53. Woodward and Bernstein, *The Final Days*, p. 350.
54. Leonard Hall to FB, Aug. 29, 1975.
55. Robert E. Sherwood, *Roosevelt and Hopkins* (New York: Harper & Row, 1950), p. 5.
56. Bryant, *Dog Days in the White House*, p. 254.
57. Charles Colson, *Born Again* (Lincoln, Va.: Chosen Books, 1976), p. 72.
58. Kissinger, *White House Years*, p. 247.
59. Safire, *Before the Fall*, pp. 613–14.
60. Martha Mitchell told Winzola McLendon that when she was unable to reach Nixon she got to him through Rebozo, using the White House line, through which he could always be reached. She described overhearing him and her husband plotting "some of the tactics they were going to use to silence or at least discredit the national press," this when Mitchell was under fire for his part in the Watergate burglary (Winzola McLendon, *Martha* [New York: Random House, 1979], p. 12).
61. Rather and Gates, *The Palace Guard*, p. 287; Safire, *Before the Fall*, pp. 496–508.
62. John Osborne, *New Republic*, March 20, 1976, p. 7.
63. Lloyd Shearer to FB.
64. Kissinger, *White House Years*, p. 1155.
65. Quoted in Shawcross, *Sideshow*, p. 142. Roger Morris in *Uncertain Greatness* (p. 147) tells a slightly different version.

XXXII. *The New York Years*

1. Witcover, *The Resurrection of Richard Nixon*, p. 42.
2. Abplanalp wrote to Nixon on Jan. 13, 1961, asking that he "accept a retainer from our company" no matter what law firm he joined (Vice-Presidential Archives, Los Angeles Federal Archives and Records Center, Laguna Nigel, Calif.).
3. *New York Times*, April 25, 1965, 6:14.
4. Ibid.
5. Julie Eisenhower—$44,000; Tricia Cox—$49,000; Patricia Nixon—$70,000 to $80,000 (Paul R. Michel, Watergate Special Prosecution Force Memorandum, Oct. 16, 1975, National Archives, Record Group 460).
6. Kissinger, *White House Years*, p. 20.
7. Witcover, *The Resurrection of Richard Nixon*, p. 51.
8. *New York Times*, April 25, 1965, 6:14.
9. *RN*, p. 265.
10. Ibid., pp. 248–50.
11. Szulc, *The Illusion of Peace*, p. 16.
12. Bryant, *Dog Days at the White House*, p. 241.
13. David, *Lonely Lady at San Clemente*, p. 124.
14. Flora Schreiber, *Good Housekeeping*, July 1968, p. 187.
15. David, *Lonely Lady at San Clemente*, p. 126.
16. Nixon, *The Real War*, p. 272.
17. Rebozo was with him on the trip to Europe in 1963, two trips to Hong Kong in 1966–1967, and to Latin America in 1967.
18. Michel, Watergate Memorandum, p. 216.
19. *Los Angeles Times*, June 5, 1976.
20. To Flora Schreiber, *Good Housekeeping*, July 1968, p. 188.
21. This appeared the last week in December 1973. The occasion was described in part in *Newsweek*, April 22, 1974, p. 33.
22. Scott Armstrong's phrase.
23. *Time*, Oct. 29, 1973, p. 87.
24. *Newsday*, Oct. 13, 1971, p. 37R.
25. Haldeman, *Ends of Power*, p. 4.
26. Scott Armstrong to FB, April 14, 1980.
27. *Newsday*, Oct. 6, 1971, p. 6R.
28. Ibid., Oct. 7, 1971, p. 14R.
29. Ibid., Oct. 13, 1971, p. 42R.
30. Lukas, *Nightmare*, p. 363. DeBoer was indicted in September 1974 for securities fraud dating back to the early 1960s (Michel, Watergate Memorandum, p. 245).
31. So Rebozo testified (Senate Watergate Hearings 21:10070).
32. Michel, Watergate Memorandum, p. 31, Senate Watergate Hearings, 22:10489.
33. *Miami Herald*, June 15, 1958, Vice-Presidential Archives, Laguna Nigel, Calif., in Rebozo correspondence.
34. I am indebted to Anthony Marro of the *New York Times*, who shared his excellent file on Rebozo's finances which analyzed how they were meshed with those of Nixon.
35. Danner wrote to Rebozo on Feb. 24, 1971: ". . . old Father Time has finally got you in his clutches. Or, (and I hate to think this) those certain psychological changes I detected in you a couple of years ago, such as constant invitations for me to stay at your house, have finally changed the direction of your interests." To which Rebozo replied on March 1, 1971, "Only a third degree depraved mind could have given birth to thoughts such as those expressed therein. . . . Frankly you are not my type. But have no fear . . . now that I am acquainted with your warped thinking, I'll make arrangements upon your next visit to stay at the Y.M.C.A."
Later Bebe urged Danner to visit him, "Come on down. . . . I'll afford you the 'queen for a day room.' " Danner replied, "One of these days I will try to sneak off and come down and spend a quiet visit with you and submit myself to the indignities and penuriousness one associates with you when you are on your best behavior" (Senate Watergate Hearings, 21:10160–61, 24:11524–25, April 12, 19, 1973).
36. John M. Crewsdon, "Nixon's Taped Remarks on Apparent Slush Fund Called Key Evidence in Rebozo Inquiry," *New York Times*, Dec. 9, 1974. Haldeman said Rebozo "in effect, maintained a private fund for Nixon to use as he wished" (*Ends of Power*, p. 22).
37. Some of the Rebozo-collected money went to pay for the Florida White House pool. Another five thousand dollars from the sum was laundered to buy diamond earrings for Pat (Senate Watergate Hearings, 26:12692–94; Michel, Watergate Memorandum, p. 6). How much of it went to meet the bribery demands of E. Howard Hunt and the other Watergate burglars as payment for their silence is still uncertain. Nixon said on the presidential tape of March 21, 1973, talking with John Dean concerning E. Howard Hunt's exactions, "We could get a million dollars. We could get it in cash. I know where it could be gotten . . . the question is who the hell would handle it."
The most widely publicized gifts of cash, first published by Jack Anderson on Aug. 5, 1971 (*The Anderson Papers*, pp. 28–30), consisted of two bags of $50,000 each, delivered to Rebozo by Richard Danner from Howard Hughes in 1970. They had come to Danner from Hughes through Robert Maheu. Although Rebozo had a reputation for getting interest on money even if he had it for only a few days, he testified that he kept the money in his safety-deposit box for three years and then returned it untouched to Hughes through an intermediary, William E. Griffin, lawyer for Abplanalp.
Herbert Kalmbach, Nixon's lawyer, testified, however, that Rebozo told him the IRS was "pressing him to prove it was not undeclared income," and said he had given portions of it to Nixon's brothers and to the presidential secretary, Rose Woods. Donald and Edward Nixon denied it, as did Rose Woods (Michel, Watergate Memorandum, pp. 8, 188–89, 136). There is some evidence supporting Kalmbach's charge on the presidential tape for April 25, 1973:
PRESIDENT: Remember I told you later that I could get $100,000?
HALDEMAN: That makes—that rings a bell 'cause you talked about Rose having some money or—something. I remember that. [Michel, Watergate Memorandum, Exhibit 5A, p. 31]
When Kalmbach urged Rebozo to get a good lawyer, Rebozo replied, "This touches the President's family, and I just can't do anything to add to his problems at this time,

Herb." Nine months later, Kalmbach testified, Rebozo denied his earlier story. "Undoubtedly I have not told you," he said, "that after you and I talked last spring regarding the Hughes money, I found that I had not in fact disbursed the safety deposit box. I found that the wrappers around that cash had not been disturbed, and so it was clear that no part of this money had been used during the several years it was in my box" (Senate Watergate Hearings, 21:10189–91.)

Rebozo testified that one of his first acts was to call in an old FBI friend, Ken Whitaker, and ask him "if, through their crime lab, they could ascertain that the money—by smell, feel, touch, deterioration, or something—had been locked up, in fact, that long" (Senate Watergate Hearings, 21:9970, 22:10453). When the money was finally taken out of the safety-deposit box, it was discovered that the original wrappings had been replaced by rubber bands, the packets of $50,000 each had been shuffled, and thirty-five of the bills were of a later date than when Richard Danner originally delivered them in July 3, 1970. Records of access to this safety-deposit box were not kept, as was normal with other boxes (Michel, Watergate Memorandum, pp. 139, 21, 31, 136).

In his press conference of Oct. 26, 1973, when asked about the $100,000 Rebozo had put in his safety-deposit box, Nixon said, "Let me say that he showed, I think, very good judgment in doing what he did. He received a contribution, he was prepared to turn it over to the finance chairman when the finance chairman was appointed. In that interlude . . . the Hughes company, as you all know, had a fight of massive proportions, and he felt that such a contribution to the campaign might be embarrassing" (*Public Papers*, 1973, p. 903). (For Rose Woods's denial that she had received money from this fund, see Senate Watergate Hearings, 22:10227.)

Evidence surfacing in the Watergate hearings revealed that Robert Abplanalp had briefly loaned Rebozo $225,000 in April 1972, which theoretically would have made it possible for him to replenish the $100,000 in the safety-deposit box, but the connection was never established (Senate Watergate Hearing, 22:10470–71). In 1977 Rebozo agreed to pay $52,454 in back taxes to the IRS for 1970 and 1971 (*Los Angeles Times*, Jan. 7, 1977, p. 8).

There is some evidence that Robert Maheu gave $50,000 to Nixon in the Bahamas in December 1968, although Maheu denied it. Nixon's deposition concerning all these matters has not been released to the public (Michel, Watergate Memorandum, pp. 153, 157). Among other possibly relevant items emerging in the hearings was that from 1968 through 1970 Rebozo had a safety-deposit box in the Manufacturers Hanover Trust Bank in New York, to which Rose Woods was a cosigner. She denied ever using it (Michel, Watergate Memorandum, p. 59).

Government prosecutors throughout the investigation of Rebozo had great difficulty getting data from him. He never gave over information concerning businesses he owned other than his bank. His earnings and ownership under his alias, Charles Gregory, were never examined. By the time Rebozo returned from Europe in 1974, the Senate Watergate investigations were over and the momentum of reform was spent. Rebozo was finally informed that there was not enough evidence for an indictment (Michel, Watergate Memorandum, p. 269; Carmine Bellino summary, Senate Watergate Hearings, 26:12957; Samuel Dash, *Chief Counsel: Inside the Ervin Committee, the Untold Story of Watergate* (New York: Random House, 1976), pp. 243–45).

During the Nixon presidency Rebozo's wealth accelerated, by his own account, sevenfold, from $653,000 to $4.5 million.

XXXIII. *A Series of Accidents*

1. *Los Angeles Times*, Sept. 18, 1977, sect. 5, p. 5.
2. Carl Sandburg, *Abraham Lincoln: The War Years*, 4 vols. (New York: Harcourt Brace Jovanovich, 1974), 4:244–45.
3. *Newsweek*, Dec. 2, 1963.
4. *Merriman Smith's Book of Presidents*, pp. 229–30.
5. Robert F. Kennedy, *Thirteen Days*, p. 110.
6. See Isaac Don Levine, *The Mind of the Assassin* (New York: Farrar Straus, 1959; reprinted in 1979 by Greenwood Press, Westport, Conn.).
7. Nixon's letter was offered for sale and advertised in the *Scriptorium*, Catalogue No. 3, 1974, where the letter was reproduced.
8. *Los Angeles Times*, April 21, 1963.
9. President's Committee on the Assassination of John F. Kennedy Report (hereafter the Warren Commission Report), 5:392. Priscilla McMillan believes Oswald was merely testing his wife, but it seems more likely that Oswald read the account of the Nixon speech hastily and thought him to be in Texas rather than in Washington. The Warren Commission missed the importance of the appearance of this attack in the Dallas paper on April 21, 1963. It concluded that Oswald was not actually planning to shoot Nixon at that time, and noted that no edition of a Dallas paper from Jan. 1 to May 15, 1963, mentioned any proposed visit by Mr. Nixon to Dallas.
10. McMillan, *Marina and Lee*, p. 283.
11. Martin, *Adlai Stevenson and the World*, p. 774.
12. *Dallas Morning News*, Nov. 22, sect. 4, p. 1.
13. The best books on the Kennedy assassination, aside from the Warren Commission Report, are McMillan, *Marina and Lee*; Charles Roberts, *The Truth About the Assassination* (New York: Grosset & Dunlap, 1967); and Belin, *November 22, 1963: You Are the Jury*. Daniel Schorr's chapter on the assassination in *Clearing the Air* helps explain the relation between Oswald and Castro and clarifies mysteries about Oswald's motivation. Schorr also illuminates the story of what the Warren Commission was not told about the CIA involvement in the Castro assassination attempts. See also Isaac Don Levine's chapter on the assassination in *Eyewitness to History*.
14. Witcover, *The Resurrection of Richard Nixon*, p. 60.
15. *RN*, pp. 252–53.
16. Nixon, "Cuba, Castro, and John F. Kennedy,"

p. 298; Witcover, *The Resurrection of Richard Nixon*, p. 60; and Stephen Hess to FB, March 1, 1978.

17. *New York Times*, Nov. 24, 1960.
18. Witcover, *The Resurrection of Richard Nixon*, p. 62. Later, in 1968, on the day Robert Kennedy announced his candidacy against Lyndon Johnson, Nixon twice mentioned Johnson's poor health and said, "Bobby may kill him" (Whalen, *Catch the Falling Flag*, p. 97).
19. Witcover, *The Resurrection of Richard Nixon*, pp. 62–63.
20. *Los Angeles Times*, Nov. 24, 1960.
21. *Time*, Nov. 19, 1973, the tenth anniversary of the assassination.
22. Tom Wicker, "Kennedy Without End, Amen," *Esquire*, June 1977, p. 69.
23. RN, p. 253. Nixon reproduced Jackie's letter of reply in her own hand, on pages 254–55 of his memoirs.
24. Frost, *I Gave Them a Sword*, p. 285.
25. *Los Angeles Times*, Oct. 2, 1962.
26. Ibid., April 21, 24, Aug. 21, Oct. 11, 1960.
27. Nixon, "Khrushchev's Hidden Weakness," *Saturday Evening Post*, Oct. 12, 1963, pp. 25–27.
28. Rather and Gates, *The Palace Guard*, p. 81.
29. Schaap, "Will Richard Nixon Trip Over Himself on the Way to Victory?" *New York*, June 10, 1968, p. 26.
30. *RN*, p. 253.
31. Witcover, *The Resurrection of Richard Nixon*, pp. 60, 61, 64.
32. That McCone knew at least about the pre-Bay of Pigs assassination planning was revealed in the Church Committee Report, p. 269n.
33. The House Assassinations Committee of 1978, which went through all the old and new evidence, agreed with the original Warren Commission Report that neither the Cuban nor Soviet governments was responsible. Castro, interviewed by members of the House committee on April 3, 1978, said it would have been for him "a tremendous insanity," and "the perfect pretext" for the U.S. to invade his country (*Newsweek*, Oct. 2, 1978, p. 62).
34. See Schlesinger, *Robert F. Kennedy*, p. 547; Wise, *The Politics of Lying*.
35. Levine, *Eyewitness to History*, p. 248. It was general knowledge that Oswald had gone to Mexico City in an attempt to get a visa to join Castro's forces in Cuba. He had shown the Cuban embassy papers demonstrating his Communist sympathies. When he was told that he must first get a visa to the Soviet Union he had become abusive. What the American public was not told was that on his second visit to the Cuban embassy he had said, "Someone ought to shoot that President Kennedy. Maybe I'll try it." Daniel Schorr, who put this jigsaw puzzle together with skill, said the FBI learned about this threat from secret sources in 1964 but J. Edgar Hoover suppressed it (Schorr, *Clearing the Air*, pp. 176–77). Castro himself was told of the threat at the time, and related the story later to British journalist Comer Clark in July 1967. When Clark asked Castro why he had not warned Kennedy, Castro replied that first there were no diplomatic relations between the two countries, second that the plot might

have been used as an excuse for an invasion, and third that he felt Oswald was "a wild man" not to be taken seriously ("Castro Says He Knew of Oswald Threat to Kill JFK," *National Enquirer*, Oct. 15, 1967, quoted in Schorr, *Clearing the Air*, p. 177).

In any case, J. Edgar Hoover did not tell the Warren Commission. And Allen Dulles, Richard Helms, Robert F. Kennedy, and Richard Nixon did not inform the commission about the long history of CIA-inspired sabotage in Cuba and the attempted assassinations. Even Castro's interview in the Brazilian embassy, where he threatened to retaliate for attempts on his life, was not mentioned in the Warren Commission Report. Staff member Wesley J. Liebeler wrote a memo urging that attention be paid to it, but General Counsel J. Lee Rankin ruled against its inclusion on the ground that there was no evidence Oswald had seen a report of it (Schorr, *Clearing the Air*, p. 174). Thus "the Cuban connection" was kept muted.

Arthur Schlesinger has speculated that one reason Allen Dulles withheld what he knew from the Warren Commission was that he feared Robert Kennedy "might hold the CIA responsible for his brother's death." But Robert Kennedy surely had his own problems with the "Oswald-Castro connection." His brother had stopped the assassination attempts, or thought he had—some continued after his inaugural—but Robert Kennedy had vigorously urged continued harassment and sabotage. In 1965, when Robert Kennedy was "pressed by a group of Peruvian intellectuals—one person insisting, 'Castro! Castro! What have you done about Castro?' he said to his interpreter, 'Tell them that I saved his life.'" Later, when Jack Anderson in 1967 was breaking the story about the CIA and gangster attempt to kill Castro, he wrote that "Bobby, eager to avenge the Bay of Pigs fiasco, played a key role in the planning." When Robert Kennedy read this, he said in anger to his assistants Peter Edelman and Adam Walinsky, "I didn't start it. I stopped it. . . . I found out that some people were going to try an attempt on Castro's life and I turned it off" (Schlesinger, *Robert F. Kennedy*, p. 498). But none of this did Robert Kennedy tell to the Warren Commission (ibid., p. 494). To admit to such evil on the part of the American government and the CIA would not have proved a direct connection between Castro and Oswald—that he acted alone all seem to have believed—but it would have helped explain Oswald's motivation. It would also have poured gasoline on the conspiratorial fires already raging in the country. Whether this was the major reason for the silence one cannot know; how much private agony and guilt contributed to the silence will also never be known.

36. Nixon, "Cuba, Castro and John F. Kennedy," p. 298.
37. Haldeman, *Ends of Power*, pp. 26–27.
38. Ibid., p. 26.
39. U.S. Congress, House, Committee on the Judiciary, Hearings, *Statement of Information*, Appendix III, 93rd Cong., 2d sess., May–June 1974, p. 197.
40. *RN*, p. 515.

41. Martinez was still getting a retainer of $100 a month from the CIA (Haldeman, *Ends of Power*, p. 34).
42. There is no evidence that Nixon had met Hunt back in 1959 and 1960, although he knew of Hunt's activities concerning the Cuban invasion planning through his liaison aide, General Cushman, who was now deputy director of the CIA. Nixon admitted in his memoirs only that he knew Charles Colson had brought Hunt into the White House "to research the origins of the Vietnam War" (*RN*, p. 633). General Cushman, however, testified that Charles Colson had briefed Nixon about Hunt's intelligence background in regard to Cuba (Senate Watergate Hearings, 8:3303).
43. This was one of the so-called smoking gun transcripts which, as Haldeman noted, helped "seal Nixon's doom" (*Ends of Power*, p. 32).
44. Haldeman, *Ends of Power*, p. 38 (italics Haldeman's).
45. Ibid., p. 40. See also Daniel Schorr's *Clearing the Air*, whose chapter on the assassination problem, Haldeman admits, greatly clarified his own understanding of the matter.
46. *Los Angeles Times*, Sept. 24, 1963.
47. The most comprehensive research into the matter of Kennedy's complicity in the coup and assassination of Diem and his brother was done by the Church Committee in 1976, and by historian Arthur Schlesinger, Jr., for his *Thousand Days* and his *Robert F. Kennedy and His Times*. These studies exonerate Kennedy from any complicity in the assassination of Ngo Dinh Diem and Ngo Dinh Nhu, but also make it clear why the rumors persisted. When the dissenting generals in August secretly planned a coup to overthrow Diem and his brother, Kennedy authorized a cable to the new U.S. ambassador in Vietnam, Henry Cabot Lodge, written by Roger Hilsman and Averell Harriman, saying the U.S. "would find it impossible to continue support . . . militarily and economically" unless the Nhus were removed from the scene. If Diem remains obdurate "then we are prepared to tell all military commanders we will give them direct support in any interim period of breakdown central government mechanism" (Church Committee Report, p. 219).

Five days later Kennedy informed Lodge he reserved the right to change his mind in the matter (Church Committee Report, p. 219). But Lodge, who had been Nixon's vice-presidential candidate in 1960, was a super-hawk intent on Diem's overthrow. Secretary of State Dean Rusk asked Roger Hilsman to prepare a memorandum listing "all possibilities." Joseph A. Mendenhall of the State Department wrote the memo, and possibility number 10 was later pulled out of context and used against Kennedy when the memo was leaked by Lyndon Johnson in 1968. It stated that in the event of a last-ditch stand in the palace the U.S. should encourage the coup group to fight the battle to the end, and destroy the palace if necessary to gain victory. "If the family is taken alive, the Nhus should be banished to France or any other European country willing to receive them. . . . Diem should be treated as the generals wish" (Morton Kondrake and Thomas B. Ross first pub-

lished this in the *Chicago Sun Times* of June 23, 1971; see Wise, *The Politics of Lying*, pp. 172–73).

The August coup was never carried out. Diem, however, became increasingly unpopular in South Vietnam, and Kennedy became ever more eager to withdraw from the quagmire. Angered at Lodge's intransigeance, increasingly hawkish and unwillingness to take orders, Kennedy told his brother Robert he would recall him in November and find an excuse to fire him (Schlesinger, *Robert F. Kennedy*, p. 715).

When the dissenting generals in Vietnam planned a new coup in October, CIA chief John McCone sent strong cables to his people in South Vietnam against the idea of assassination but continued to favor "covert" contact with the generals. On Oct. 2, 1963, Secretary of Defense MacNamara and Gen. Maxwell Taylor after a trip to Saigon recommended against supporting the new coup, and Kennedy approved the report but suggested that "alternative leadership should be identified and cultivated" (Neil Sheehan and E. W. Kenworthy, *The Pentagon Papers* [New York: Quadrangle Books, 1971], pp. 215–16; Church Committee Report, p. 220). McCone recommended hands-off should there be a new coup, and said Kennedy agreed (Church Committee Report, p. 221). On October 5 and 6, Lodge received cables forbidding "active encouragement to the coup" but okaying "covert" contacts with alternative leadership (Sheehan and Kenworthy, *The Pentagon Papers*, p. 257). Lodge, who ardently wanted Diem out, did not exert himself to save Diem when the coup came. After a brief siege at the palace, Diem and his brother fled through a tunnel but were captured in a Catholic church in Cholon, taken in an armored truck, and murdered.

When Kennedy heard the news, General Taylor said, "he rushed from the room with a look of shock and dismay on his face which I had never seen before." Schlesinger, then an adviser in the White House, said he had not seen Kennedy so depressed since the Bay of Pigs. Diem had fought for his country for twenty years, Kennedy said, and it should not have ended like this (Schlesinger, *Robert F. Kennedy*, p. 721; id., *Thousand Days*, pp. 997–98; Maxwell D. Taylor, *Swords and Plowshares* [New York: W. W. Norton, 1972], p. 301).

Lodge, however, was triumphant. To the CIA's William Colby he praised CIA behavior during the coup, and "made it clear it was under his full direction" (William Colby and Peter Forbath, *Honorable Men* [New York: Simon & Schuster, 1978], p. 217). And in a cable to Kennedy on November 6 Lodge said, "I believe prospects of victory are much improved. . . . The coup was Vietnamese and a popular affair, which we could neither manage nor stop after it got started and which we could only have influenced with great difficulty. But it is equally certain that the ground in which the coup seed grew into a robust plant was prepared by us and that the coup would not have happened (as) it did without our preparation" (Schlesinger, *Robert F. Kennedy*, p. 721).
48. *RN*, pp. 256–57.

49. *Public Papers*, 1971, p. 953.
50. U.S. Congress, House, Committee on the Judiciary, *Statement of Information*, Appendix III, 93rd Cong., 2d sess., May-June 1974, pp. 197–98.
51. Szulc, *Compulsive Spy*, p. 133.
52. John Ehrlichman to FB, Oct. 11, 1980.
53. Lambert said Colson's law partner, Charles Morin, told him on April 28, 1973, that the cables were spurious. But when he met with Colson and his attorney the next day, Colson denied ever seeing the spurious cables and

refused to confirm that they were forgeries (Senate Watergate Report, 1:204–6).
54. Senate Watergate Report, 1:206.
55. Gray testimony, Senate Watergate Hearings, 9:3468; John Dean, *Blind Ambition* (New York: Simon & Schuster, 1976), pp. 114–15.
56. Senate Watergate Report, 1:206. For Hunt's testimony, see Senate Watergate Hearings, Campaign Activities, 9:3666–813.
57. *RN*, p. 846.
58. Ehrlichman, *The Company*, p. 159.
59. Nixon, *The Real War*, p. 103.

XXXIV. *The Nixon Character*

1. Mazo, *Richard Nixon*, p. 157.
2. Roy P. Basler, *The Lincoln Legend* (reprint of 1935 ed.; New York: Octagon, 1969), p. 95.
3. This was in the period Nixon was out of office (Harold Horowitz, who heard the statement, to FB, Nov. 6, 1980).
4. *RN*, p. 686.
5. Conversations with Dr. Bruce Brodie and Dr. Maimon Leavitt.
6. *Los Angeles Times*, Dec. 4, 1978, sect. 2, p. 7.
7. Eva Crittendon, who was there, described the speech to Steve Zetterberg, Nixon's opponent in 1948. See the Zetterberg oral history interview, conducted by Enid Douglass, July 15, 1976, Claremont Graduate School Oral History Project.
8. Colson, quoted in "The Nixon Years," *Washington Post*, Aug. 9, 1974, p. 4.
9. Abrahamsen, *Nixon vs. Nixon*, p. 194.
10. See Redl and Wineman, *Children Who Hate*.
11. See especially William Shawcross's *Sideshow: Kissinger, Nixon and the Destruction of Cambodia* (New York: Simon & Schuster, 1979).
12. Clawson, "A Loyalist's Memoir," *Washington Post*, Aug. 9, 1979, p. D1.
13. Lou Cannon to FB.
14. *New York Times Magazine*, June 9, 1974, p. 70; White, *The Making of the President, 1972*, p. 488.
15. I am indebted to Dr. Paul Smith for data on Gardner's death.
16. Woodward and Bernstein, *The Final Days*, pp. 423–24. Kissinger never denied the episode.
17. *RN*, p. 716.

18. Ibid., p. 717.
19. Ibid., p. 738.
20. Ibid.
21. Ibid., pp. 739–40.
22. Ibid., p. 741.
23. *Los Angeles Times*, June 29, 1974, p. 18. Nixon's fondness for the movie *Patton*, and for the Ladislas Farago biography on which it was based, are well known. He showed the film several times in the White House.
24. Bob Woodward to FB.
25. *RN*, pp. 902–3.
26. Ibid., p. 952. See John J. Sirica, *To Set the Record Straight* (New York: W. W. Norton, 1979), p. 199.
27. CBS News.
28. Chief Newman and Mrs. Newman to FB.
29. *RN*, p. 359.
30. West, "The Real Pat Nixon," p. 128; Dianne Sawyer to FB.
31. *RN*, p. 1053.
32. Ibid., p. 1070.
33. Jessamyn West to FB.
34. *RN*, p. 1060.
35. Ibid., p. 976.
36. Bob Woodward to FB.
37. Helen Dudar, "John Ehrlichman's Latest Chapter," *Chicago Tribune Magazine*, May 6, 1979, p. 66.
38. *Public Papers*, (Oct. 9) 1974, p. 632.
39. Nathan Leites to FB.
40. Frost tape, March 25, 1977.
41. Walters, *Silent Missions*, p. 609.

Bibliography

The Writings of Richard Nixon

"Application of the Inherent Danger Doctrine to Servants of Negligent Independent Contractors." *Duke Bar Association Journal* 4 (Spring 1936).

"Asia After Vietnam." *Foreign Affairs* 46, no. 1 (October 1967).

"Changing Rules of Liability in Automobile Accident Litigation." *Duke University Law and Constitutional Problems* 3 (1936).

"Commencement Charge to Whittier College Class of 1959." *Whittier College Bulletin* 53 (May 1960).

"The Crisis in Asia." *Whittier College Bulletin*, 47 (December 1954).

"Cuba, Castro and John F. Kennedy." *Reader's Digest*, November 1964.

"Four Great Americans, Tributes Delivered by President Richard Nixon." *Reader's Digest*, 1972.

"The Greater Menace," *Educational Record* 39, no. 1 (January 1958).

Joint Appearances of Senator John F. Kennedy and Vice President Richard M. Nixon and Other 1960 Campaign Presentations, Senate Report 994, part 3. 87th Cong., 1st sess., Washington, D.C., 1961.

Nixon Speaks Out. Major Speeches and Statements. . . . in the Presidential Campaign of 1968. New York, 1968.

Oral history interview on John Foster Dulles. Interview conducted by Richard D. Challenes, Feb. 2, 1966. Dulles Oral History Collection, Princeton University.

"Plea for an Anti-Communist Faith." *Saturday Review of Literature*, March 24, 1952, pp. 12–13.

Public Papers of the Presidents, 1969–1974, 5 vols., Washington, D.C., 1971–1975.

RN, the Memoirs of Richard Nixon. New York, 1978.

"Rule of Law," Address, April 13, 1959, before U.S. Academy of Political Science, New York. Whittier College Pamphlet, 1959.

"The Whittier Address of Vice President Richard M. Nixon, on the occasion of his celebrating his nomination for President of the United States." Whittier College, Aug. 2, 1960.

A New Road for America, President Richard M. Nixon, Major Policy Statements, March 1970 to October 1971. New York, 1972.

Speeches, Remarks, Press Conferences and Study Papers of Vice President Richard M. Nixon, August 1 through November 7, 1960. 87th Cong., 1st sess., Senate Report no. 994, pt. 2. Washington, D.C., 1961.

The Presidential Transcripts, The Complete Transcripts of the Nixon tapes, . . . with Commentary by the Staff of the Washington Post. *Washington Post*, 1974.

Six Crises. Garden City, N.Y., 1968.

The Real War. New York, 1980.

Selected Books and Articles

Abrahamsen, David. *Nixon vs. Nixon—A Psychological Inquest.* New York: Farrar, Straus & Giroux, 1976.

Alsop, Stewart. *Nixon and Rockefeller, a Double Portrait.* Garden City, N.Y.: Doubleday, 1960.

———. "Nixon and the Square Majority, Is the Fox a Lion?" *Atlantic*, February 1972.

———. "Nixon on Nixon." *Saturday Evening Post*, July 12, 1958, p. 26ff.

Anderson, Jack, with George Clifford. *The Anderson Papers.* New York: Random House, 1972.

———, with James Boyd. *Confessions of a Muckraker, the Inside Story of Life in Washington During the Truman, Eisenhower, Kennedy and Johnson Years.* New York: Random House, 1979.

——— and May, Ronald. *McCarthy: The Man, the Senator, the "Ism."* Boston: Beacon Press, 1952.

Andrews, Bert, and Andrews, Peter. *A Tragedy of History: A Journalist's Confidential Role in the Hiss-Chambers Case.* Washington, D.C.: R. B. Luce, 1962.

Arendt, Hannah. *Between Past and Future: Eight Exercises in Political Thought.* New York: Viking Press, 1968.

As We Knew Adlai, the Stevenson Story, by Twenty-two Friends. Edited by Edward P. Doyle. New York: Harper, 1966.

Atkins, Ollie. *Triumph and Tragedy: The White House Years, by Ollie Atkins, Personal Photographer to President Richard M. Nixon.* New York: Playboy Press, 1977.

Barber, James David. *The Presidential Character: Predicting Performance in the White House.* Englewood Cliffs, N.J.: Prentice-Hall, 1972.

Barlett, Donald L., and Steele, James B. *Empire: The Life, Legend, and Madness of Howard Hughes.* New York: W. W. Norton, 1979.

Bassett, James. Diary. Manuscript, courtesy of Mrs. James Bassett.

Belin, David. *November 22, 1963: You Are the Jury.* New York: Quadrangle Books, 1973.

Block, Herbert. *Herblock Special Report: Words and Pictures on Nixon's Career from Freshman Congressman to "Full, Free, and Absolute Pardon."* New York: W. W. Norton, 1976.

———. *Herblock's State of the Union.* New York: Viking Press, 1974.

Bonsal, Philip W. *Cuba, Castro, and the United States.* Pittsburgh, Penna.: University of Pittsburgh Press, 1971.

Bowers, Lynn, and Blair, Dorothy. "How to Pick a Congressman." *Saturday Evening Post,* March 19, 1949, p. 31ff.

Brady, John. "Freelancer with No Time to Write," an interview with Gloria Steinem. *Writers Digest,* February 1974, p. 12ff.

The Breaking of a President. Vol. I, *A PhotoHistory of President Nixon's Blunders.* Compiled by Marvin Miller. Industry, Calif., 1974.

Breslin, Jimmy. *How the Good Guys Finally Won: Notes from an Impeachment Summer.* New York: Ballantine Books, 1976.

Brodie, Bernard. *Strategy in the Missile Age.* Princeton, N.J.: Princeton University Press, 1959.

———. *War and Politics.* New York: Macmillan, 1973.

Brower, Brock. "Inside the Humless Machine, a Longing for Poetry." *Life,* October 1968, pp. 37–38.

Brown, Stuart Gerry. *Conscience in Politics, Adlai E. Stevenson in the 1950s.* Syracuse, N.Y.: Syracuse University Press, 1961.

Bryant, Traphes, with Frances Spatz Leighton. *Dog Days at the White House: From Truman to Nixon.* New York: Macmillan, 1976.

Bullock, Paul. "Rabbits and Radicals, Richard Nixon's 1946 Campaign Against Jerry Voorhis." *Southern California Quarterly,* Fall 1973, pp. 319–59.

Butz, March D. *Yorba Linda, Its History.* Santa Ana, Calif., 1970.

Cain, Albert C. *Survivors of Suicide.* Springfield, Ill.: Charles C Thomas, 1972.

Carr, Robert K. *The House Committee on Un-American Activities, 1945–1950.* Ithaca, N.Y.: Cornell University Press, 1952.

Chambers, Whittaker. *Odyssey of a Friend, Whittaker Chambers' Letters to William F. Buckley, Jr., 1954–1961.* Edited with Notes by William F. Buckley. New York: Putnam, 1970.

———. *Witness.* New York: Random House, 1952.

Chesen, Eli S. *President Nixon's Psychiatric Profile.* New York: Wyden Books, 1973.

Clemens, Cyril. "Mark Twain and Richard M. Nixon." *Hobbies,* November 1970, pp. 142–43.

Coffin, Patricia. "Private Life of Pat Nixon," *Look,* July 27, 1954, pp. 23–29.

Cohn, Roy. "Could He Walk on Water?" *Esquire,* November 1972, p. 117ff.

———. *McCarthy.* New York: New American Library, 1968.

Cook, Fred J. *The Nightmare Decade: The Life and Times of Senator Joe McCarthy.* New York: Random House, 1971.

Costello, William. *The Facts About Nixon.* New York: Viking Press, 1960.

Coughlan, Robert. "Success Story of a Vice-President." *Life,* Dec. 14, 1953.

David, Lester. *The Lonely Lady at San Clemente, the Story of Pat Nixon.* New York: Thomas Y. Crowell, 1978.

Demaris, Ovid. "The Private Life of J. Edgar Hoover." *Esquire,* September 1974, pp. 71–77.

de Toledano, Ralph. *Nixon.* New York: Henry Holt, 1956.

———, and Lasky, Victor. *Seeds of Treason: The True Story of the Hiss-Chambers Tragedy.* New York: Funk, 1950.

Deutsch, Helene. "The Impostor." *Psychoanalytic Quarterly* 24 (1955): 502–5.

Dickerson, Nancy. *Among Those Present: A Reporter's View of 25 years in Washington.* New York: Random House, 1976.

Dietrich, Noah, and Thomas, Bob. *Howard, the Amazing Mr. Hughes.* Greenwich, Conn.: Fawcett, 1977.

Donovan, Robert J. *Eisenhower: The Inside Story.* New York: Harper, 1956.

Douglas, Helen G. "Helen Gahagan Douglas Speaks Out." *Parent's Magazine,* July 1972, pp. 52–53.

———. "Why I Voted Arms for Europe." *New Republic,* Aug. 29, 1949, pp. 9–10.

Dudar, Helen. "John Ehrlichman's Latest Chapter." *Chicago Tribune Magazine,* May 6, 1979, pp. 20–21, 65–66.

Dulles, Allen. *The Craft of Intelligence.* New York: Harper & Row, 1963.

Edmondson, Madeleine, and Cohen, Alden Duer. *The Women of Watergate.* New York: Pocket Books, 1975.

Ehrlichman, John. *The Company: A Novel.* New York: Simon & Schuster, 1976.
Eisenhower, Dwight D. *At Ease: Stories I tell to Friends.* Garden City, N.Y.: Doubleday, 1967.
——. *Mandate for Change: The White House Years, 1953–1956.* New York: Doubleday, 1963.
——. *Waging Peace: The White House Years, a Personal Account, 1956–1961.* New York: Doubleday, 1965.
Erikson, Erik H. *Toys and Reasons.* New York: W. W. Norton, 1977.
Erskine, Helen W. "Dick and Pat Nixon: The Team on Ike's Team." *Colliers,* July 9, 1954, pp. 32–37.
Etheredge, Lloyd. "Hardball Politics, a Model." *Political Psychology,* Spring 1979, pp. 3–26.
Feldman, Trude B. "The Quiet Courage of Pat Nixon." *McCall's,* May 1975, p. 74ff.
Fingarette, Herbert. *Self-Deception.* Atlantic Highlands, N.J.: Humanities Press, 1969.
Flannery, Harry W. "Red Smear in California." *Commonweal,* Dec. 8, 1950, p. 225.
Fleming, Karl. "Will the Real Richard Nixon Please?" *Los Angeles Times West,* Dec. 8, 1968, p. 65ff.
Flynn, William. "Richard Nixon's Life Story." *Kansas City Star,* Oct. 30 to Nov. 6, 1955. (Reprinted from the *Boston Globe.*)
Ford, Gerald R. *A Time to Heal: The Autobiography of Gerald R. Ford.* New York: Harper & Row, 1979.
Frady, Marshall. *Billy Graham: A Parable of American Righteousness.* Boston: Little, Brown, 1979.
Freud, Sigmund. *Complete Psychological Works,* standard edition, 24 vols. New York: Macmillan, 1964. See "On Narcissism," 4:73ff; "Mourning and Melancholia," 14:243–58; and "A Case of Paranoia," 14:263ff.
Frost, David. *I Gave Them a Sword: Behind the Scenes of the Nixon Interviews.* New York: Morrow, 1978.
——. "Interviews with the Candidates." *New York,* June 10, 1968, p. 42ff.
Gardner, Richard. "Richard Nixon, the Story of a Fighting Quaker," Manuscript, Whittier College Library.
George, Alexander L. "Assessing Presidential Character." *World Politics* 26 (January 1974): 234–82.
Goytisolo, Juan. "Twenty years of Castro's Revolution." *New York Review of Books,* March 22, 1979, pp. 17–24.
Greenacre, Phyllis. "The Impostor." *Psychoanalytic Quarterly* 27 (1958): 359–80.
Greenberg, Carl. "Chotiner Looks at Nixon's Future." *Los Angeles Times,* Nov. 25, 1962, p. G1.
Griffith, Robert. *The Politics of Fear: Joseph R. McCarthy and the Senate.* Lexington, Ky.: University Press of Kentucky, 1970.
Halberstam, David. *The Powers That Be.* New York: Knopf, 1979.
Haldeman, H. Robert, with Joseph DiMona. *The Ends of Power.* New York: Quadrangle Books, 1978.
Healy, Paul F. "Busiest Vice President We Ever Had!" *Saturday Evening Post,* Sept. 19, 1953, pp. 22–23.
Hellman, Lillian. *Scoundrel Time.* With an introduction by Garry Wills. Boston: Little, Brown, 1976.
Higgins, George V. *The Friends of Richard Nixon.* Boston: Little, Brown, 1975.
——. "The Friends of Richard Nixon, and How He Conned Them." *Atlantic,* November 1974, pp. 41–52.
Hill, Gladwyn. *Dancing Bear: An Inside Look at California Politics.* New York: World, 1968.
Hispanic-American Review 13, no. 10 (October 1960): 681ff.
Hiss, Alger. *In the Court of Public Opinion.* New York: Knopf, 1957.
Hiss, Tony. *Laughing Last.* Boston: Houghton Mifflin, 1976.
Hoopes, Townsend. *The Devil and John Foster Dulles: The Diplomacy of the Eisenhower Era.* Boston: Little, Brown, 1973.
Hoyt, Edwin P. *The Nixons: An American Family.* New York: Random House, 1972.
Hughes, Arthur J. *Richard M. Nixon.* New York: Dodd, Mead, 1972.
Hughes, Emmet John. "A White House Taped." *New York Times Magazine,* June 9, 1974.
——. *The Ordeal of Power: A Political Memoir of the Eisenhower Years.* New York: Atheneum, 1963.
Humphrey, Hubert H. *The Education of a Public Man, My Life and Politics.* Garden City, N.Y.: Doubleday, 1976.
Hunt, Howard. *Give Us This Day: The CIA and the Bay of Pigs.* New Rochelle, N.Y.: Arlington House, 1973.
Hutschnecker, Arnold A. *The Drive for Power.* New York: M. Evans, 1974.
——. "The Mental Health of Our Leaders." *Look,* July 16, 1969, pp. 51–54.
——. *The Will to Live.* New York: T. Y. Crowell, 1951.
Jackson, Donald. "The Young Nixon." *Life,* Nov. 6, 1970, p. 54ff.
Johnson, Haynes. *The Bay of Pigs.* New York: W. W. Norton, 1964.
Kearns, Doris. *Lyndon Johnson and the American Dream.* New York: Harper & Row, 1976.
Kennedy, John F. *Profiles in Courage,* memorial edition, with a special foreword by Robert F. Kennedy. New York: Harper & Row, 1964.
——. *Speeches, Remarks, Press Conferences and Statements of Senator John F. Kennedy, August 1 through November 7, 1960.* U.S. Senate, 87th Cong., 1st sess., 994, pt. 1. Washington, D.C., 1961.
Kennedy, Robert F. *Thirteen Days: A Memoir of the Cuban Missile Crisis.* New York: W. W. Norton, 1969.
Kernberg, Otto. *Borderline Conditions and Pathological Narcissism.* New York: Aronson, 1975.
Kirk, Christina, and Dunleavy, Steve. "Angry Nixons Blame the Woodward and Bernstein Book for Pat's Stroke." *The Star,* Aug. 3, 1976, p. 9.
Korff, Baruch. *The Personal Nixon: Staying on the Summit.* Washington, D.C., 1974.

Kornitzer, Bela. "My Son: Two Exclusive and Candid Interviews with Mothers of the Presidential Can-
    didates." *Los Angeles Times, This Week,* Sept. 18, 1960, p. 9f.
————. *The Real Nixon: An Intimate Biography.* Chicago: Rand McNally, 1960.
Lattimore, Owen, *Ordeal by Slander.* Boston: Little, Brown, 1950.
Leinster, Colin. "Nixon's Friend Bebe." *Life,* July 31, 1970.
Levine, Isaac Don. *Eyewitness to History.* New York: Hawthorn, 1973.
Lifton, Robert Jay, and Olson, Eric, eds., with essays by Erik Erikson and Kenneth Keniston. *Explora-
    tions in Psychohistory.* New York: Simon & Schuster, 1975.
Lodge, Henry Cabot. *The Storm Has Many Eyes.* New York: W. W. Norton, 1973.
Lopez-Fresquet, Rufo. *My 14 Months with Castro.* New York: World, 1966.
Lukas, J. Anthony. *Nightmare: The Underside of the Nixon Years.* New York: Viking Press, 1976.
Mailer, Norman. *Miami and the Siege of Chicago.* New York: Signet, 1968.
Manchester, William. *America Caesar: Douglas MacArthur.* Boston: Little, Brown, 1978.
Mankiewicz, Frank. *Perfectly Clear: Nixon from Whittier to Watergate.* New York: Popular Library, 1974.
————. *The Final Crisis of Richard M. Nixon.* New York: Quadrangle Books, 1974.
Martin, John Bartlow. *Adlai Stevenson and the World.* Garden City, N.Y.: Doubleday, 1977.
————. *Adlai Stevenson of Illinois.* Garden City, N.Y.: Doubleday, 1976.
Mathison, Richard R. "Richard M. Nixon, The American Dream, Whittier High to the White House."
    Los Angeles Times West, Jan. 12, 1969, pp. 7–10.
Matthews, Herbert L. *Fidel Castro.* New York: Clarion, Simon & Schuster, 1969.
Mazlish, Bruce. *In Search of Nixon: A Psychohistorical Inquiry.* New York: Basic Books, 1972.
Mazo, Earl. *Richard Nixon: A Political and Personal Portrait.* New York: Harper, 1959.
————, and Hess, Stephen. *Nixon, a Political Portrait.* New York: Harper & Row, 1968.
McCarthy, Joseph. *Major Speeches and Debates of Senator Joe McCarthy, 1950–51.* Reprinted from the
    Congressional Record. Washington, D.C., 1952.
McCarthy, Mary. *The Mask of State: Watergate Portraits.* New York: Harcourt Brace Jovanovich, 1974.
McGinniss, Joe. *The Selling of the President 1968.* New York: Trident, 1969.
McMillan, Priscilla Johnson. *Marina and Lee.* New York: Harper & Row, 1977.
Meredith, Scott. "Richard the Actor." *Ladies Home Journal,* September 1975, p. 52ff.
Michel, Paul R. Hughes-Rebozo Memorandum. Records of the Watergate Special Prosecution Force,
    National Archives, Record Group 460.
Miller, Arthur. "The Limited Hang-Out." *Harper's,* September 1974, pp. 13–20.
Miller, Merle. *Plain Speaking: An Oral Biography of Harry S Truman.* New York: Putnam, 1974.
Mollenhoff, Clark R. *Despoilers of Democracy.* Garden City, N.Y.: Doubleday, 1965.
————. *Game Plan for Disaster: An Ombudsman's Report on the Nixon Years.* New York: W. W. Norton,
    1976.
Morgan, Lael. "Whittier '34, Most Likely to Succeed." *Los Angeles Times West,* May 10, 1970, pp. 34–38.
Morison, Samuel Eliot. *History of United States Naval Operations in World War II,* vol. 6, *Breaking the Bis-
    marcks Barrier, 22 July 1942–1 May 1944.* Boston: Little, Brown, 1950.
Morris, Roger. *Uncertain Greatness: Henry Kissinger and American Foreign Policy.* New York: Harper &
    Row, 1977.
Mosley, Leonard. *Dulles: A Biography of Eleanor, Allen, and John Foster Dulles and Their Family Network.*
    New York: Dial Press, 1978.
Nelson, Lowry. *Cuba, the Measure of a Revolution.* Ann Arbor, Mich.: University of Michigan Press, 1972.
Nixon, Hannah, as told to Flora Rheta Schreiber. "Richard Nixon, a Mother's Story." *Good Housekeeping,*
    June 1960, p. 54ff.
Nixon, Patricia Ryan, as told to Joe Alex Morris. "I Say He's a Wonderful Guy." *Saturday Evening Post,*
    Sept. 6, 1952, p. 17ff.
O'Brien, Robert W. "The Night Nixon Spoke: A Study in Political Effectiveness." Whittier College
    dissertation, 1969.
"On Liars and Lying." *Salmagundi,* no. 29 (Spring 1975).
Oppolzer, Theodore, ritter von. *Canon of Eclipses.* New York: Dover, 1962.
Osborne, John. *The Nixon Watch.* New York: Liveright, W. W. Norton, 1970.
————. *The Second Year of the Nixon Watch.* New York: Liveright, W. W. Norton, 1971.
————. *The Third Year of the Nixon Watch.* New York: Liveright, W. W. Norton, 1972.
————. *The Fourth Year of the Nixon Watch.* New York: Liveright, W. W. Norton, 1973.
————. *The Last Nixon Watch.* New York: New Republic, 1975.
————. "Was Nixon Sick of Mind?" *New York,* April 21, 1975, p. 37ff.
Parmet, Herbert S. *Eisenhower and the American Crusades.* New York: Macmillan, 1972.
Pearson, Drew. *Drew Pearson's Diaries, 1949–1959.* Edited by Tyler Abell. New York: Holt, Rinehart &
    Winston, 1974.
Phelan, James R. "The Nixon Family and the Hughes Loan." *The Reporter,* Aug. 16, 1962.
Phillips, Cabell. *The Truman Presidency: The History of a Triumphant Succession.* New York: Macmillan,
    1966.
Poirier, Richard. "Horatio Alger in the White House." *Harper's,* September 1972.
Potter, Charles E. *Days of Shame.* New York: Coward-McCann, 1965.

Price, Raymond. *With Nixon.* New York: Viking Press, 1977.
Rangell, Leo. "Lessons from Watergate." *Psychoanalytic Quarterly* 45, no. 1 (1976).
———. *The Mind of Watergate: A Study in the Compromise of Integrity.* New York: W. W. Norton, 1980.
Rather, Dan, and Gates, Gary Paul. *The Palace Guard.* New York: Harper & Row, 1974.
Redl, Fritz, and Wineman, David. *Children Who Hate.* New York: Collier, 1962.
Reedy, George E. *The Twilight of the Presidency.* New York: New American Library, 1970.
Rogers, Rita. "Children's Reactions to Sibling Death," Excerpta Medica International Congress Series, No. 134. *Psychosomatic Medicine* (Proceedings of the First International Congress of Psychosomatic Medicine), Spain, September 1966.
Rogin, Michael, and Lottier, John. "The Inner History of Richard Milhous Nixon." *Transaction,* November–December 1971, pp. 19–28.
Rogin, Michael Paul. *The Intellectuals and McCarthy: The Radical Spectre.* Boston: MIT Press, 1969.
Rovere, Richard H. *Arrivals and Departures.* New York: Macmillan, 1976.
———. "Eisenhower Revisited—a Political Genius? a Brilliant Man?" *New York Times Magazine,* Feb. 7, 1971.
———. *Senator Joe McCarthy.* New York: Harcourt Brace, 1959.
Rowse, Arthur Edward. *Slanted News: A Case Study of the Nixon and Stevenson Fund Stories.* Boston: Beacon Press, 1957.
Safire, William. *Before the Fall: An Inside View of the Pre-Watergate White House.* Garden City, N.Y.: Doubleday, 1975.
Schaap, Dick. "Will Richard Nixon Trip Over Himself on His Way to Victory?" *New York,* June 10, 1968, p. 24ff.
Schell, Jonathan. *The Time of Illusion.* New York: Random House, 1976.
Schlesinger, Arthur M., Jr. *A Thousand Days: John F. Kennedy in the White House.* Boston: Houghton Mifflin, 1965.
———. *The Imperial Presidency.* Boston: Houghton Mifflin, 1973.
Schorr, Daniel. *Clearing the Air.* Boston: Houghton Mifflin, 1977.
Senate Select Committee on Presidential Campaign Activities. *The Watergate Hearings, Break-in and Cover-up,* as edited by the staff of the *New York Times.* New York: Times Books, 1973.
Sevareid, Eric, ed. *Candidates 1960: Behind the Headlines in the Presidential Race.* New York: Basic Books, 1960.
Shils, Edward A. *The Torment of Secrecy, the Background and Consequences of American Security Policies.* Glencoe, Ill.: The Free Press, 1956.
Smith, Helen McCain. "Ordeal! Pat Nixon's Final Days in the White House, by Helen McCain Smith as told to Elizabeth Pope Frank." *Good Housekeeping,* July 1976, pp. 127–30.
Smith, John Chabot. *Alger Hiss: The True Story.* New York: Holt, Rinehart & Winston, 1976.
Smith, Merriman. *Merriman Smith's Book of Presidents, A White House Memoir.* Edited by his son, Timothy G. Smith. New York: W. W. Norton, 1972.
Sorensen, Theodore C. *Kennedy.* New York: Harper & Row, 1965.
Spalding, Henry D. *The Nixon Nobody Knows.* Middle Village, N.Y.: Jonathan David, 1972.
Stassen, Harold. *Where I Stand.* Garden City, N.Y.: Doubleday, 1947.
Steinem, Gloria. "In You Heart Your Know He's Nixon." *New York,* Oct. 28, 1968, p. 20ff.
Stevenson, Adlai E. *Papers,* vols. 4–7. Boston: Little, Brown, 1977.
Straight, Michael. *Trial By Television.* Boston: Beacon Press, 1954.
Stripling, Robert E. *Red Plot Against America.* Drexel Hill, Penna.: Bell, 1949.
Suarez, Andres. *Cuba, Castro and Communism, 1959–1966.* Cambridge, Mass.: MIT Press, 1967.
Szulc, Tad. "As Castro Speaks: 'The Wall! The Wall!' " *New York Times Magazine,* Dec. 13, 1959.
———. *Compulsive Spy.* New York: Viking Press, 1974.
Theoharis, Athan. *Seeds of Repression: Harry S. Truman and the Origins of McCarthyism.* Chicago: Quadrangle, 1971.
Thirty Years of Treason: Excerpts from Hearings before the House Committee on Un-American Activities 1938–1968. Edited by Eric Bentley. New York: Viking Press, 1971.
Thomas, Hugh. *Cuba, the Pursuit of Freedom.* New York: Harper & Row, 1971.
Truman, Harry S. *Memoirs by Harry S. Truman,* vol. 1, *Years of Decisions;* vol. 2, *Years of Trial and Hope, 1946–1952.* Garden City, N.Y.: Doubleday, 1956.
U.S. Congress. House. Committee on the Judiciary. *Transcripts of Eight Recorded Presidential Conversations.* Hearings before the Committee on the Judiciary, House of Representatives, 93rd Cong., 2d sess., pursuant to H. Res. 803, a resolution authorizing and directing the Committee on the Judiciary to investigate whether sufficient grounds exist for the House of Representatives to exercise its constitutional power to impeach Richard M. Nixon, President of the United States of America. Serial No. 34, May–June 1974. Washington, D.C., 1974.
U.S. Congress. House. Committee on Un-American Activities. *Excerpts from Hearings Regarding Investigation of Communist Activities in Connection with the Atomic Bomb.* Hearings before the Committee on Un-American Activities, House of Representatives, 80th Cong., 2d sess., Sept. 9, 24, and 26, 1948. Washington, D.C., 1948.
———. *Hearings on Gerhart Eisler. Investigation of un-American Propaganda Activities in the United States.*

Hearings before the Committee on Un-American Activities, House of Representatives, 80th Cong., 1st sess., Feb. 6, 1947. Washington, D.C., 1947.

———. *Hearings on Proposed Legislation to Curb or Control the Communist Party of the United States.* Hearings before the Subcommittee on Legislation of the Committee on Un-American Activities, House of Representatives, 80th Cong., 2d sess., on H.R. 4422 and H.R. 4581, Feb. 5, 6, 9–11, 19, and 20, 1948. Washington, D.C., 1948.

———. *Hearings Regarding Communism in Labor Unions in the United States.* Hearings before the Committee on Un-American Activities, House of Representatives, 80th Congress, 1st sess., Feb. 27, July 23–25, 1947.

———. *Hearings Regarding Communist Espionage in the United States Government.* Hearings before the Committee on Un-American Activities, House of Representatives, 80th Cong., 2d sess., Part 1: July 31, Aug. 3–5, 7, 9–13, 16–18, 20, 24–27, 30, Sept. 8, 9, 1948; Part 2: Dec. 10, 14, 1948. Washington, D.C., 1948.

———. *Hearings Regarding the Communist Infiltration of the Motion Picture Industry.* Hearings before the Committee on Un-American Activities, House of Representatives, 80th Cong., 1st sess., Oct. 20–24, 27–30, 1947. Washington, D.C., 1947.

———. *Investigation of un-American Propaganda Activities in the United States.* Hearings before the Committee on Un-American Activities, House of Representatives, 80th Cong., 1st sess., on H.R. 1884 and H.R. 2122, bills to curb or outlaw the Communist party of the United States. Washington, D.C., 1947.

U.S. Congress. Senate. Select Committee on Presidential Campaign Activities. *The Senate Watergate Report.* The final report of the Senate Select Committee on Presidential Campaign Activities (the Ervin Committee). New York, 1974.

U.S. Navy. Office of Public Information. *Navy Department Communiques 301–600 and Pacific Fleet Communiques, March 6, 1943–May 24, 1945.* Washington, D.C., 1945.

Voorhis, Jerry. *Confessions of a Congressman.* Garden City, N.Y.: Doubleday, 1948.

———. Oral History Interview, Claremont College Graduate School Oral History Project, interviewed by Stephen Zetterberg, June 15, 1973.

———. *The Strange Case of Richard Milhous Nixon.* Middlebury, Vt.: Paul S. Eriksson, 1972.

Warren, Earl. *The Memoirs of Earl Warren, Chief Justice.* Garden City, N.Y.: Doubleday, 1977.

Washington Post, staff of. *The Fall of a President.* Washington, D.C., 1974.

Watkins, Arthur V. *Enough Rope, the Inside Story of the Censure of Joe McCarthy.* Salt Lake City: University of Utah Press, 1969.

Weaver, John D. *Warren: The Man, the Court, the Era.* Boston: Little, Brown, 1968.

Weinstein, Allen. *Perjury: The Hiss-Chambers Case.* New York: Knopf, 1978.

West, Jessamyn. "The Real Pat Nixon." *Good Housekeeping,* February 1971, pp. 66–71ff.

Weymouth, Lally. "The Word from Mamma Buff." *Esquire,* November 1977, pp. 154–57, 200–212.

Whalen, Richard J. *Catch the Falling Flag: A Republican's Challenge to His Party.* Boston: Houghton Mifflin, 1972.

———. *The Founding Father: The Story of Joseph P. Kennedy.* New York: New American Library, 1964.

White, Theodore H. *Breach of Faith: The Fall of Richard Nixon.* New York: Atheneum, 1975.

———. *The Making of the President, 1960.* New York: Atheneum, 1961.

———. *The Making of the President, 1964.* New York: Atheneum, 1965.

———. *The Making of the President, 1968.* New York: Atheneum, 1969.

———. *The Making of the President, 1972.* New York: Atheneum, 1973.

Wicker, Tom. "Nixon Starts Over—Alone." *New York Times Magazine,* May 16, 1962, p. 17ff.

Wills, Garry. *Nixon Agonistes.* Boston: Houghton Mifflin, 1970.

———. "The Hiss Connection Through Nixon's Life." *New York Times Magazine,* Aug. 25, 1974.

Wilson, Richard. "Is Nixon Fit to Be President?" *Look,* Feb. 24, 1953.

Wise, David. *The Politics of Lying: Government Deception, Secrecy, and Power.* New York: Random House, 1973.

Witcover, Jules. *The Resurrection of Richard Nixon.* New York: Putnam, 1970.

Woodstone, Arthur. *Nixon's Head.* New York: St. Martin's Press, 1973.

Woodward, Bob, and Bernstein, Carl. *All the President's Men.* New York: Simon & Schuster, 1974.

———. *The Final Days.* New York: Simon & Schuster, 1976.

Woodward, C. Vann, ed. *Responses of the Presidents to Charges of Misconduct: White House Under Fire.* New York: Delacorte Press, 1974.

Wright, Charles Alan. "A Long Work of Fiction." *Saturday Review of Literature,* March 24, 1952, p. 11.

Zeligs, Meyer A. *Friendship and Fratricide: An Analysis of Whittaker Chambers and Alger Hiss.* New York: Viking Press, 1967.

Zetterberg, Stephen. Oral History Interview, Claremont Graduate School Oral History Project, interviewed by Enid Douglass, July 15, 1976.

Interviews

Dr. David Abrahamsen
William F. Ackerman
Frederick Albrink
Patricia Alsop
Jack Anderson
Richard Arena
Scott Armstrong
Jeff Banchero
James and Wilma Bassett
Richard Bergholz
Thomas Bewley
James D. P. Bishop, Jr.
Richard Bissell
Tom Braden
Kathleen Brown
Pat Brown
Paul Bullock
March Butz
Lou Cannon
David F. Cavers
Kenneth Chotiner
Nancy Chotiner
Marshall Clough, Jr.
Judge James Cobey
Rev. T. Eugene Coffin
Roy Cohn
Ellen Cochran
Jess Cook
Alwn Cranston
Whit Cromwell
Gen. Robert E. Cushman
John Dean
Mary De Orio
Ralph de Toledano
Tom Dixon

John Doar
Evlyn Dorn
Enid Douglass
Helene Drown
Chris Duran
Esther Eisley
Mel Elfin
Daniel Ellsberg
Elizabeth Eidson Evans
Ladislas Farago
Simmons Fentress
Robert Finch
Murray Framsen
Ellen McClure Eidson Furnas
Robert Greene
Leonard Hall
Diane Henry
Stzphen Hess
Gladwyn Hill
Harold Horowitz
Phoebe Howard
Dr. Arnold A. Hutschnecker
Richard Jacobs
Ola Welch Jobe
Mildred Jackson Johns
Mr. and Mrs. William T. Jones
Leo Katcher
George Kellog
Leonard Kaufman
Richard Kiefer
Thomas Kiernan
Herbert Klein
Isaac Don Levine
Anthony Lewis
John Lindsay

Dr. John E. Mack
Rod MacLeish
Nancy Manella
Olive Marshburn
Oscar Marshburn
Anthony Marro
Richard Mathison
Earl Mazo
Mildred Sullivan Mendenhall
Herbert Mitgang
Norma Mulligan
Mark Neuman
Wallace J. Newman
Roy Newsom
John E. Nichols
Edith Nunes
Frances H. Obetz
Judge Jerry Pacht
Judge A. J. Paonessa
William Perdue
Jack B. Pfeiffer
Dr. Eugene Pumpian-Mindlin
Dan Rather
George Reedy
Vita Remley

James Reston, Jr.
Mary Guptill Rez
Edward Rubin
Thomas R. Ryan
Adela Rogers St. Johns
Francis Schwartz
Lloyd Shearer
Ethel Hunter Sheldon
Foster Sherwood
Georgia Sherwood
Paul S. Smith
Richard Solomon
Helmut Sonnenfeldt
Weldon Taylor
Henry Trofimenko
Albert Upton
Jerry Voorhis
Jessamyn West
Dr. Joelyn West
Merle West
Floyd Wildermuth
Virginia Green Williams
Robert G. Wolstoncroft
Enrique Zeleri
Paul and Mickey Ziffren

Index